THE EFFECTIVE NURSE
Leader and Manager

THE EFFECTIVE NURSE
Leader and Manager

LAURA MAE DOUGLASS
RN, BA, MS, PhD

Consultant, Nursing Leadership and Management;
Former Chairman, Department of Nursing,
Point Loma College, San Diego, California;
Former President, California Board
   of Registered Nursing;
Former Nursing Education Instructor
   and founder and director of RN refresher programs,
Good Samaritan Hospital, San Jose, California

FIFTH EDITION
with 92 illustrations

 Mosby

St. Louis Baltimore Boston Carlsbad Chicago Naples New York Philadelphia Portland
London Madrid Mexico City Singapore Sydney Tokyo Toronto Wiesbaden

Mosby
Dedicated to Publishing Excellence

A Times Mirror
Company

Publisher: Nancy L. Coon
Editor: N. Darlene Como
Developmental Editor: Dana L. Knighten
Project Manager: Deborah L. Vogel
Production Editor: Jodi Willard
Manufacturing Supervisor: Theresa Fuchs
Designer: Pati Pye

Fifth Edition

Copyright© 1996 by Mosby–Year Book, Inc.

Previous editions copyrighted 1980, 1984, 1988, 1992

Printed in the United States of America
Composition by Top Graphics
Printing/binding by RR Donnelley & Sons Company

Mosby-Year Book, Inc.
11830 Westline Industrial Drive
St. Louis, Missouri 63146

Library of Congress Cataloging in Publication Data
Douglass, Laura Mae.
   The effective nurse: leader and manager / Laura Mae Douglass.—5th ed.
      p. cm.
   Includes bibliographical references and index.
   ISBN 0-8151-2779-0 (pbk.)
   1. Nursing services—Administration. 2. Leadership. I. Title.
   [DNLM: 1. Nursing, Supervisory. 2. Nurse Administrators.
3. Leadership. WY 105 D737e 1996]
RT89.D667 1996
362.1'73'068—dc20
DNLM/DLC   95-19342
for Library of Congress   CIP
95 96 97 98 99 / 9 8 7 6 5 4 3 2 1

To
My daughter **Linda** for her unconditional
love, encouragement, and help

My son **Wade** for his utmost confidence
in my ability and for the many things he has taught me

PREFACE

This book approaches nursing personnel and their roles as leaders and managers in light of the massive changes that are occurring in the healthcare delivery system today. The healthcare system is presently undergoing unprecedented change. How nurses react to these changes will affect them for years to come, either positively or negatively. Coupled with these changes is the significant advance in technology. The combination of computer science, information science, and nursing science has taken nursing practice to new heights. Added to these factors is the matter of cultural diversity. Dynamic social change has also profoundly affected how nurses lead and manage. The intent of this book is to reflect the latest in leadership and management thinking and practice in all types of healthcare settings, while considering the impact of change.

Survival as a leader and manager depends on the nurse's ability to adapt personal resources to the job situation as quickly and as effectively as possible. It is vitally important that nurses receive preparation for the leadership/management position *before* their appointment. Nurses should be introduced to the concept of leadership and management as one of challenge and excitement, with the opportunity to see what needs to be done in the interest of the consumer. Nurses need to know how to spark a group of workers into getting the job done while understanding the theory underlying the action.

The effective nurse is portrayed as able to lead and to manage. Leadership and management are presented as a learned process that can become habitual with practice. To be successful, a leader must have followers. The nurse leader earns the right to direct others within formal or informal situations. Managers, on the other hand, are appointed to their positions and may or may not possess leadership qualities. Effective nurses acquire skill as leaders and managers and are able to function in the healthcare delivery system with assurance, knowing they are well equipped for their roles.

The book is designed to provide a practical, purposeful means of instruction. Each chapter contains (1) behavioral objectives for the major concepts included, (2) presentation of key concepts and theories, (3) a summary of major ideas at the end of each chapter, (4) questions for study and discussion, (5) references, (6) suggested readings that may be used for further study, and (7) sample questions to test the reader's knowledge that are constructed like those on the NCLEX examination. An added feature is the inclusion of a workbook section, entitled "Critical Thinking Activities," at the end of the text to assist the student in study. The glossary provides a ready reference to terms used throughout the book.

The instructor may program student activities in the classroom or learning laboratory, or students may control their own learning experiences by moving at their own pace and evaluating their own progress. A further advantage to this book is that the student may complete the course of instruction even at a time when his or her clinical assignment is not in a setting that lends itself to application of the concepts of leadership and management. This manual allows the practitioner to reinforce learning through a systematic review of important concepts. It also provides ready reference for leaders and managers who need resource material for their practice.

ORGANIZATION OF THE BOOK

Chapter 1 introduces the concepts of leadership and management at first, middle, and top levels, indicating similarities and differences in the roles and emphasizing the need for an effective nurse to be both a leader *and* a manager. The many and diverse forces that affect the nurse leader and manager and the need for adequate preparation are discussed. A behavioral science approach is continued as an effective method for increasing the nurse manager's ability to provide quality care to patients and clients.

Chapter 2 reviews the styles of leadership and management used by people in authority positions. A flexible approach is taken whereby effective nurses lead and manage according to their individual style of leadership, followers' characteristics, and expectations and conditions present in the work situation. Male and female leadership styles are compared.

Chapter 3 considers healthcare reform and its impact on organizational systems. An overview of organizational structure in healthcare agencies is presented, with focus on the decentralized approach. Discussion of magnet hospitals and community health and home healthcare nursing is also included. The bureaucratic and human relations approaches to management are compared, and rationales are offered for selection of an appropriate organizational structure for a health agency.

Chapter 4 examines nursing personnel and the impact of healthcare reform on their various roles. A discussion of role theory follows. The functional roles of nurse managers are examined. A survey of nurse populations, nursing educational programs, and nurse licensure practices in the United States is given. Contemporary and expanding roles for nurses are presented, including the emerging role of the nurse case manager.

Chapter 5 focuses on positive and negative aspects of the current job market and on the nursing staffing process and factors that influence nurse staffing delivery systems. Staff projection, data collection, and patient classification are presented with examples of how to compute staffing needs, including use of the computer for patient classification. Systems used for the delivery of patient care are reviewed.

Also included are recruitment, selection, and placement of nursing personnel and criteria important to the staffing process. Circumstances that affect job satisfaction are discussed. Total care, functional, team, primary, modular and nurse case management delivery systems are presented along with the advantages and disadvantages of each. Cross-functional, multidisciplinary teams are included.

Chapter 6 discusses the planning and decision making processes and their importance for nursing managers at the top, middle, and lower or first levels. Nursing process and patient care planning with standard care plans are emphasized. Included is material concerning assessment of the work situation, need identification and priority setting, management by objectives, implementation of the plan, and evaluation or control. The scientific, pragmatic, and intuitive approaches to decision making are introduced along with a discussion of group decision making.

Chapter 7 concentrates on the direction-giving process used by the nurse manager at the lower or first level. The significance of the delegation process and barriers to effective delegation are considered. Numbers of nursing personnel necessary for provision of care and mix of the work group are discussed with reference to criteria and responsibilities for assurance of quality care. Detailed guides are presented for preparing assignments and worksheets and for supervising ongoing nursing activities.

Chapter 8 studies the communication process and differentiates between interpersonal and organizational communication. Guidelines for effective communication are given. A health communication model is introduced, and an effective communication model for the nurse manager is set forth. Barriers to the communication process are identified. The informal or "grapevine" channel of communication is reviewed, and positive and negative features of the system are identified. Cross-cultural communication and the gender factor in nursing is considered. Content regarding information systems and the use of computer technology has also been added.

Chapter 9 recognizes the existence of conflict in all organizational settings and the importance of nurse managers developing skill in conflict resolution. The chapter considers change; stress; attitudes toward conflict; types of conflict; consequences of conflict; the process of conflict resolution; and passive, aggressive, and assertive behaviors. Conflict in a multicultural environment and conflict as the result of sexual harassment are included.

Chapter 10 considers the nature, purpose, and types of control. Financial control is approached with recognition of the tremendous pressure the healthcare industry is under to control costs and improve productivity. Patient care redesign is discussed, including managed care and case management. Financial control systems are explored under decentralization, with examples of how to prepare and administer a budget.

The discussion of control of nursing services provides the steps necessary for task analysis and for quality control of nursing care. A section is included on performance review and controlling the problem employee.

Chapter 11 considers the emergence and implication of healthcare reform on staff training and development. It develops the logic of staff development for first-level leadership and management, including management skills needed by staff nurses, how these skills are acquired; and the nurse population in need of training and development, specifically the new employee, the new graduate, and staff nurses who need preparation for the preceptor role. Knowledge important to the success of all training and development programs, such as role clarification, the adult learner, the teaching-learning process, and the theory of group dynamics (with application to the small work group) is reviewed. Three staff development programs are presented: orientation of the new employee, new graduate internship, and the preceptor training program. A section is included on self-learning programs, and it discusses methods that both small and large agencies can use to improve and upgrade employee performance.

Chapter 12 contains two significant topics: legal and ethical issues. Legal terms important to nursing are defined, the nurse practice act is explored, and diversionary programs are explained.

The value of malpractice insurance carried by both the employer and the individual and the protective measures the nurse can take to prevent personal lawsuit are emphasized. The role of the nurse as a witness in court is outlined, along with directions as to how best to defend oneself if sued. Ethical issues are presented, including the meaning of transcultural nursing and a comparison of ethnocentric and ethnorelative attitudes. The nurse's responsibility for implementing the Patient Self-Determination Act is included. The importance and purposes of an ethics committee are emphasized, with case studies for consideration.

I am especially grateful to my colleagues and the many students who have enrolled in my nursing leadership and management classes. Their probing questions, comments, and suggestions have helped me maintain interest and currency in the field of leadership and management.

I wish also to thank the nursing personnel in the clinical settings where I have taught and practiced for their generous sharing of knowledge and expertise and for being models of what an effective nurse leader and manager should be. Appreciation is extended to Dr. Lorraine Hultquist for her assistance with Chapter 12.

I want to extend a sincere thank you to Dana Knighten and to Darlene Como for their excellent editorial assistance throughout the preparation of this manuscript.

Laura Mae Douglass

CONTENTS

4 Nursing Personnel and Their Roles 71

5 Staffing Process and Nursing Care Delivery Systems 95

9 Change, Stress and Conflict Resolution   217

10 Control   245

11 Staff Training and Development   279

12 Legal and Ethical Issues   311

NURSING LEADERSHIP and MANAGEMENT

BEHAVIORAL OBJECTIVES

On completion of this chapter, the student will be prepared to:

- Define the leadership process and differentiate between formal and informal leadership.

- Explain the significance of managerial influence and identify methods of application.

- Identify the relationship among authority, power, and ability and relate it to leadership and management.

- Differentiate between the terms leadership and management.

- Define the nurse management process.

- Apply the behavioral science approach to nursing management.

- Indicate how nurses learn to lead and manage.

Most of the readers of this book will spend much of their lives working in healthcare organizations, at all levels from staff nurse to the highest positions of responsibility. Whatever the role, all nurses lead and manage to some degree. In the business world employees must first learn to be successful subordinates. Before they are promoted to the role of leaders/managers, they must first prove that they can take direction. But the very nature of the role of nurse requires leadership/management from the first day of employment. Nursing is a **decision-making** process in which the nurse helps the **patient/client** reach a state of optimal health. In this process the nurse assesses a need or problem, formulates plans for a nursing action, implements the plans, and evaluates the procedure. Furthermore, nurses accomplish goals for nursing care through the help of others, in agencies of every size and type, and by using whatever system for delivery of quality nursing care is in effect.

Many and diverse forces that require decision-making skills and abilities according to the level of nursing practice impact the nurse leader and manager. Figure 1-1 is a sample of the

FIGURE 1-1. Sample of forces that impinge on the nurse leader/manager.

types of issues the nurse manager currently faces. The serious economic crunch in the United States greatly affects delivery of health-care services, which creates a need for the nurse manager to seek ways to deliver high quality healthcare while striving for cost-effectiveness. In the process, the nurse manager is confronted with such major issues as downsizing, mergers, staffing and labor problems (see Chapter 4), substitution of nurse technicians for nurse professionals (see Chapters 4 and 5), increased complexity of care (see Chapter 5), standards and guidelines for nursing practice (see Chapter 10), governmental policies (see Chapters 3 and 10), and social and cultural issues (see Chapters 8, 9, and 12).

Understanding of individual strengths, weaknesses, and potential	+	Knowledge of basic ingredients for leadership and management	+	Learning from other people and experiences	+	Systematic use of self to get the right things done at the right time	=	Effective leadership and management

Ultimately, leadership development is self-development. This book is based on the belief that an understanding of the leadership and management process will help nurses value themselves as leaders and managers and acquire the knowledge and skills necessary to be responsible **leaders** and **managers** in all nursing settings.

EFFECTIVE NURSE LEADERS AND MANAGERS

To compete in the 1990s, organizations of all types are focusing on improving productivity, quality, and service. In each of these areas it is important to tap the talents of the available human resources in the organization. Effective leaders and managers experiment and take risks. Because risk taking involves mistakes and failure, leaders and managers learn to accept the inevitable disappointments.

Leadership and **management** can be an exciting experience. It is a *learned* process. To be successful, potential nurse leaders/managers prepare for the role with the expectation that they are capable of becoming effective leaders/managers.

The nurse must identify his or her individual strengths, weaknesses, and potential (or capacities); acquire knowledge of the theory and practice of leadership and management; learn from other people and experiences; and use self systematically to get the right things done at the right time (see formula above).

This chapter introduces the concepts of leadership and management, differentiates between them, and applies merging concepts to nursing practice in any setting.

LEADERSHIP

The word *leadership* is an intriguing one and conjures up images of all kinds of people. Certain names come to mind—Confucius, Plato, Abraham Lincoln, John F. Kennedy, Martin Luther King, and more recently, Margaret Thatcher, General Norman Schwarzkopf, Hilary Clinton, and Janet Reno. One may think of a relative or teacher who had a noticeable effect on one's life. In nursing, who would not name Florence Nightingale if asked for a single example of a leader in the profession?

Leadership is present in any group of people, regardless of age or setting, in normal times or in times of crisis. Watch children play; a leader soon emerges. The same pattern occurs in all life situations—in games, clubs, committees, political parties, religious bodies, and all social and work groups. Some people rise to the position of leader, whereas others want to follow their direction.

Leadership Process

Leadership is "the use of one's skills to influence others to perform to the best of their ability toward goal achievement."[1, p. 134] Leadership, or the exercise of power and influence, involves one individual trying to change the behavior of other individuals. It is the art of getting others to want to do what one deems important.

To be a leader, *one must have followers.* Leadership requires that one or more persons be willing to be led. A leader is the person who communicates ideas to others and influences their behavior to achieve an **objective.** A leader is able to command the trust, commitment, and loyalty of followers. The leader's behavior is crucial, because the degree to which group objectives are understood and accepted strongly affects the quality and quantity of work performance.

Most work is done by ordinary people. Many of these people become leaders who take responsibility for reaching group goals. Keith Davis, noted management expert, comments that "leadership transforms the potential of machines and people into reality of organization."[2, p. 12] Therefore, an effective leader has the ability and the power to guide one or more persons toward achieving single or multiple **goals.**

Leadership is not a fixed position; it is a process. The dynamics of leadership include the leader's and employees' goals, leader/manager behaviors, the achievement of organizational goals by the leader and followers, and the situation (Figure 1-2).

Formal and Informal Leadership

There are two types of leaders, formal and informal. The *formal* or appointed leader is chosen by administration and given official or legitimate authority to act. Formal power has its greatest impact when the followers accept the leader, and the members work positively toward goal accomplishment. An *informal* leader does not have official sanction to direct the activities of others. Informal leaders can play a valuable role in organizations if their behavior and influence are congruent with the goals of the organization. If the informal leader influences the other workers to perform their work more efficiently and effectively, then that person is acting in support of the organization's purposes. An informal leader is chosen by the group itself, as in a social group, church organization, political party, or work group. Leaders of informal groups usually become leaders because of age, seniority, special competencies, or an inviting personality. Informal leaders can extend their influence over several groups, or they

may be looked to for guidance on matters pertaining to only one specific competency. Some informal leaders are recognized for their ability to communicate with and counsel others.

There are positive and negative ramifications of informal leadership in work situations. In hospitals, for example, a nursing group may go through the motions of accepting the leadership of the formally appointed team leader but look for sanction to act from another, thus creating conflict and confusion. This same group may also accept orders from the team leader and have these orders reinforced by a team member who is highly supportive of the team leader. The ideal situation is for the person who has been appointed formal leader to function in such a way that all members of the work group want to be influenced by that person.

Nursing leadership most commonly occurs in formal, organized settings such as hospitals, public health departments, and clinics where the nurse is officially sanctioned to practice.

INFLUENCE

Influence is the ability to affect the perceptions, attitudes, or behaviors of others. Influence can reside in individuals, groups, or entire organizations. In some ways an organization can be thought of as a system of influence. Researchers have identified specific kinds of influence. Eight different influence actions have been delineated.[3]

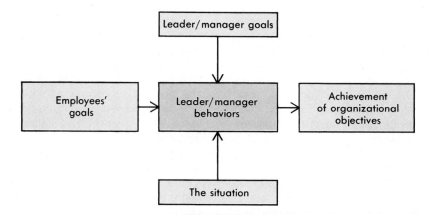

FIGURE 1-2. The dynamics of leadership.

1. *Assertiveness.* Sending direct messages to others; standing up for oneself and one's rights without violating the rights of others
2. *Ingratiation.* Making an individual feel important or good before making a request; acting humble or friendly before making a request
3. *Rationality.* Trying to convince someone by relying on a detailed plan, supporting information, reasoning, or logic
4. *Sanctions.* Giving or preventing pay increases or promotions; promising extra benefits
5. *Exchange.* Offering an exchange of favors; reminding a worker of a past favor; offering to make a personal sacrifice
6. *Upward appeal.* Obtaining formal or informal support of a higher-up; sending someone to see the next person in authority
7. *Blocking.* Backing up a request with a threat to damage an individual's opportunity for advancement; threatening to stop working with someone; ignoring or not being friendly with a person until he or she gives in to a request
8. *Coalitions.* Getting co-workers to back up a request; having someone attend a conference at which a request is made

Researchers have found that there is no difference between the tactics used by male and female employees. Influence tactics vary according to different leadership styles. Employees wishing to influence authoritarian managers generally rely on ingratiation, upward appeal, and blocking. Rationality is used most often to sway participative managers.

Managerial Influence

The term **managerial influence** implies a host of managerial actions such as motivation, power, leadership, and behavior modification. Although the results may be the same, each of these various influence processes works in a different way. Consider the actions of Teresa, a newly appointed nurse manager who was given the administrative position with the expectation that she "turn things around." The nursing unit had recently been operating haphazardly, with people coming and going pretty much as they desired. As a result, more of the nurses' auxiliary staff than usual were required to provide even minimal care.

EXAMPLE: Teresa made a concerted effort to become acquainted with every staff member, indicating that she was interested in each as an individual. She met with all members in small groups, letting them know that she was the new manager and as such expected certain consistencies and behaviors (including showing deference to the manager, reporting for work on time, taking breaks according to schedule, and working for the provision of quality care). She explained the importance of compliance (to achieve efficiency and effectiveness), indicating that positive results would lead to job satisfaction and possible advancement, whereas failure to comply would lead to disciplinary action, even dismissal.

In terms of the eight influence tactics just discussed, nurse manager Teresa relied on ingratiation (showing concern for workers), assertiveness (outlining expectations), rationality (explaining the importance of changes), and sanctions (describing the results of choices). In all probability, most of the influence tactics will come into play, to some degree, before a nursing unit runs smoothly. Because influence is such a fundamental part of effective management, leaders and managers need as many techniques as possible at their command. In nurse manager Teresa's case, she must continue the process of influencing for some time before optimum functioning of the unit is achieved.

AUTHORITY AND POWER

Leadership and management in an organization inevitably require **authority** and **power** to influence the thoughts and actions of other people. Authority is the legitimate right to give commands and to act in the interest of an organization. Authority is an officially sanctioned responsibility. Power is the **ability** to obtain, retain, and motivate people and to organize informational and material resources to accomplish a task. Power is central to the leadership process in the development of a manager's self-confidence and willingness to support staff members.[4] The desire for power is universal. From this vantage point, power should be accepted as a natural part of any individual or organization. Power is not evenly distributed among individuals or groups, but every individual has some degree of power.

Competence and intelligence are prerequisites for handling power in a healthy manner. Nurse managers have a responsibility to recognize and develop their own power to coordinate and uphold the work of staff members. Motivation for power, or a need to have an impact on others, is highly desirable for people with management responsibilities. Nurse managers who understand power, its bases, and its responsibilities have an advantage for getting things done through others. In exerting power, nurses never need to separate their own ethical values and morals from a situation.[5]

Power affects organizations in the following ways:

It influences decisions.

EXAMPLE: A primary nurse decides to sign up to care for more critical patients after hearing her nurse manager's suggestion that she extend herself.

It influences behavior.

EXAMPLE: An LPN achieves a month of perfect attendance after receiving from his nurse manger verbal and written warnings about absenteeism.

It changes situations.

EXAMPLE: The productivity of a nursing station increases dramatically following the installation of computerized work stations.

Note the word *ability* in the definition of power. Authority is the right to direct the activities of others. Authority, although an officially sanctioned privilege, may or may not get results. Power, on the other hand, is the demonstrated ability to get results. As illustrated in Box 1-1, a nurse may at one time possess authority but have no power, or possess both authority and power. The first situation, having authority but no power, occurred in one hospital where staff nurses refused to follow the nurse manager's example in caring for patients with acquired immunodeficiency syndrome (AIDS). Power without authority can occur, for example, when a staff member responds to the wishes of a visitor to bring in pets, a practice not condoned by the agency. Finally, a nurse manager who gets his or her staff to work diligently on a special research project has both authority and power.

Basis of Power

It is important for the nurse manager to understand that the power to influence can originate from a variety of sources. One of the most widely used descriptions of organizational power was proposed by French and Raven,[6] who list five forms of power a leader/manager may possess:

1. **Legitimate power** is given to the manager by the organization because of the manager's position in the hierarchy. The organization usually sanctions this form of power by titles such as director of nurses, supervisor, clinical coordinator, nurse manger, or team leader.
2. **Reward power** is based on the ability of the manager to control and administer rewards to others (such as promotions and praise) for compliance with the leader's orders or requests.
3. **Coercive power** is founded on fear, depending on the manager's ability to use punishment of others (such as reprimands, isolation,

---

Box 1-1.   Relationships among authority, power, and ability

AUTHORITY BUT NO POWER	AUTHORITY PLUS POWER	POWER BUT NO AUTHORITY
The nurse has the right but not the ability to get the job done.	The nurse has the right and the ability to get the job done.	The nurse has the ability but not the right to get the job done.

harassment, and blaming) for noncompliance with the manager's orders.

4. **Expert power** is derived from some special ability, skill, or knowledge demonstrated by the individual. For example, the only nurse who knows how to operate the kidney dialysis machine may use that expertise to influence the schedules of others.

5. **Referent power** can be shown in at least two forms in an organization. First, it can be based on a certain attractiveness or appeal of one person to another. *Charisma* is a term frequently used in conjunction with referent power. For example, the nurse who is consistently supportive, helpful, and empathetic of others may be able to easily influence others to agree with his or her views. Referent power may also be based on a person's connection or relationship with another powerful individual. For example, the assistant to the director of nurses may be seen by an aspiring nurse to have much influence with the director, and therefore the assistant's referent position has great power over that nurse.

Legitimate, reward, and coercive power are given to the manager by the organization and are based on the control of important organizational resources. Expert and, to some extent, referent power are based on the characteristics of the individual and may or may not be given by the organization. The ability to influence others is founded on the strength of the leader's or manager's power base. A manager who functions with all five power factors is in the best position to influence workers. However, such a situation may be more ideal than real. Most leaders find themselves in managerial situations in which they must influence with a limited power base.

EXAMPLE: Primary nurse Peter has become quite expert in oncology care. For 3 years he has worked part-time while attending the local university to earn a degree in his field of interest. He applies what he has learned to caregiving. Returning patients often ask for him to be assigned to them again. Because he is recognized as an expert, his requests for special supplies and equipment and for modification of patient care are rewarded, and his suggestions and proposals are put into effect.

 MANAGEMENT

Similarities and Differences Between Leaders and Managers

Although leadership and management are closely related, they are not identical. A leader may or may not have official appointment or power to lead, whereas a manager has been appointed to a particular position in the organizational structure and therefore has the power to guide and direct the work of others according to predetermined policies.

Leaders and managers may differ in the concept of their roles. Managers develop through the work of others, whereas leaders depend on inner qualities for personal growth. Managers are interested in maintaining routine and order in a controlled and rational structure, whereas leaders are often interested in risk taking and in exploring new avenues or ways of doing things. Managers tend to treat workers according to their role in the work place (e.g., assistant, **licensed practical nurse/licensed vocational nurse [LPN/LVN],** nurse manager), whereas leaders interact with others as people, considering feelings empathetically. Box 1-2 presents a summary of the similarities and differences between leaders and managers.

Definitions of Management

No single definition of management has been universally accepted. Some popular definitions include the following:

- "Management is the process of working with and through others to achieve organizational objectives in a changing environment"[7, p. 9]
- "Management is the process of obtaining and organizing resources and of achieving objectives through other people. Management is dynamic rather than static"[8, p. 27]
- "Management is planning, directing, coordinating and controlling, including leadership, giving direction, developing staff, monitoring operations, giving rewards fairly and representing both staff members and administration as needed"[9, pp. 99-100]

Box 1-2.   Similarities and differences between leaders and managers*

LEADERS	MANAGERS
May or may not have official appointment to the position	Are appointed officially to the position
Have power and authority to enforce decisions only as long as followers are willing to be led	Have power and authority to enforce decisions
Influence others toward goal setting, either formally or informally by modeling the way	Carry out predetermined policies, rules, and regulations
Are interested in risk taking and exporing new ideas	Maintain an orderly, controlled, rational, and equitable structure
Relate to people personally in an intuitive and empathetic manner	Relate to people according to their roles by enabling others to act
Feel rewarded by personal achievements	Feel rewarded when fulfilling organizational mission or goals by fostering collaboration
May or may not be successful as managers	Are managers as long as the appointment holds

*The effective nurse blends the roles.

- "Management is the process of getting work done through others. Nursing management is the process of working through nursing staff members to provide care, cure and comfort to patients."[10, p. 1]

Management Process

The following definition will be used as a basis for discussion of the **management process:** *The management process consists of working with human and physical resources and organizational and psychologic processes within a creative and innovative climate for the realization of goals.*

The management process can be applied to nursing management as shown in Figure 1-3. Nursing management can be viewed as a relationship of inputs and outputs in which the human and physical resources and organizational and psychologic processes are merged to achieve the organizational goals for delivery of quality nursing care.

Organizational Structure and Management Functions

When nurses become leaders of formal work groups, they are primarily concerned with car-

rying forth objectives for the nursing care of a prescribed number of patients/clients. However, all activities are accomplished in an organized structure that provides necessary control. **Organizational structure** is a mechanism through which work is arranged and distributed among the members of the organization so that the goals of the organization can logically be achieved. For example, most hospitals function in a highly organized, bureaucratic structure in which control comes from the top and the lines of authority are spelled out in detail (e.g., board of directors to director of nursing services to supervisors to nurse managers, to case managers to primary care nurses to team leaders to staff nurses). The most common means of informing nursing personnel of structure is through meetings, formal and informal messages, and policies and procedures manuals. An example of structure in nursing is the system used to provide nursing care such as team nursing, functional nursing, primary care nursing, and case management.

Levels and Types of Managers

Different levels and types of managers are typically found in health organizations. Nurse managers are usually classified by their level in an agency and by their responsibilities. Table 1-1

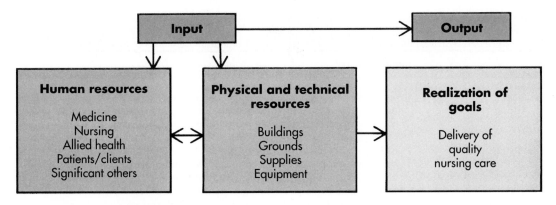

FIGURE 1-3. Planning, organizing, directing, and controlling through human and physical resources for goal realization.

shows the basic level of nurse managers. This book is primarily for **first-line managers;** therefore **middle** and **top managers** are discussed only as their roles affect the first-line manager.

Nurse Management Process

Successful management involves active participation by managers in the four basic managerial functions: planning, organizing, directing/leading, and controlling. These functions are interrelated, and most nurse managers use the components simultaneously to achieve organizational goals.

As Figure 1-4 indicates, the **nursing management process** is carried out within the organizational structure on a cyclic or continuous basis. First, managers **plan** or focus on deciding what to do. The planning process provides the framework for performance. For example, at this stage the team leader of a group of nursing personnel would be concerned with the number and kinds of patients to be cared for, the qualifications of the nursing staff to provide that care, the geographic location of the patients, and the physical resources available to do the job.

Second, the nurse manager must decide how to do the job; in other words the nurse manager must **organize** to establish order and to systematically achieve the goals for provision of care. At this stage the team leader establishes authority to act by exercising responsibility and establish-

ing accountability relationships and informing each person of his or her assignment.

Third, the nurse manager **directs** performance. In essence the manager focuses on leading nursing staff in the most effective manner possible. At this point in the management process, the team leader concentrates on how the assignments are being accomplished—on members' skills, knowledge of what they are doing, motivation, and **interpersonal relationships**. The team leader examines his or her own leadership style as it relates to goal achievement.

Fourth, managers **control** or evaluate performance against established standards of performance. This function involves evaluating individual and group performance; examining indicators of effectiveness and efficiency through patients/clients and services rendered; and investigating problems that may have developed in communication, resource allocation, and interpersonal relationships.

Finally, attention is given to what needs to be **changed.** All activities of the management process—planning, organizing, directing/leading, and controlling—are examined to determine what factors or activities may or may not need correction or change so that goals can be achieved. The change component generally occurs in each of the four management functions and therefore is not considered as a separate entity. Nurse manager activities are presented in more detail throughout the remainder of the book.

Table 1-1.	Nurse managers and their responsibilities
LEVEL	**RESPONSIBILITY**
Top managers	Responsible for the overall operations of nursing services; establish objectives, policies, and strategies; represent the organization in community affairs, business arrangements, and negotiations; typical titles: director of nursing services, chairman, executive vice president
Middle managers	Usually coordinate the nursing activities of several units; receive broad, overall strategies and policies from top managers and translate them into specific objectives and programs; typical titles: supervisor, coordinator; clinical nurse managers and case managers are included at this level as they use collaborative management to move patients/clients through the system
First-line managers	Directly responsible for the actual production of nursing services; act as links between higher level managers and nonmanagers; typical titles: nurse manager, team leader, primary care nurse

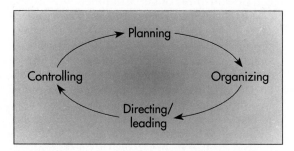

FIGURE 1-4. The nursing management process.

BEHAVIORAL SCIENCE APPLIED TO NURSING MANAGEMENT

The Behavioral Science Approach

In the **behavioral science approach,** individuals are given first consideration. Individuals are viewed as unique, each with his or her own culture, set of values, needs, personal skills, and expertise. When individuals join an organization, they become part of a group that works together in a climate that encourages caring, trust, open two-way communication, innovation, risk taking, and problem solving. Figure 1-5 presents a model of management, with consideration given to the behavioral science approach.[11]

Human and Physical Resources

In the behavioral science model, individuals are of great significance. This, however, does not negate the need for consideration of human and physical resources. In light of universal healthcare reform, mounting pressures for greater efficiency increase the need for managers and leaders to be keenly aware of the physical plant and available resources and how to use them efficiently.

Organizational and Behavioral Processes

Structure

All organizations require **structure.** Structure consists of the framework of jobs, relationships among jobs, and operational systems and processes that an organization uses to carry out its strategy. Chapter 3 provides examples of organizational structure.

The management process

The management processes of planning, organizing, directing/leading, and controlling are used to achieve organizational goals (see Chapters 6, 7, and 10).

Education and training

Education and training is an integral part of the management process. Chapter 11 provides

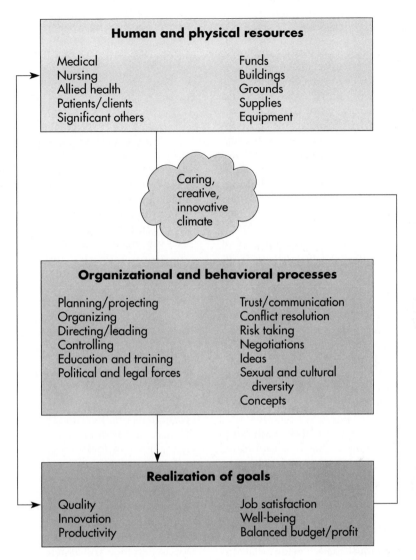

FIGURE 1-5. The behavioral science approach to nursing leadership and management.

theories for and examples of developmental programs.

Political and legal forces

Political and legal forces directly influence the way organizations operate. Changes in political forces that impinge on the healthcare delivery system have been especially significant in recent years. Examples include Medicare, Medi-cal, pre-payment systems, and health maintenance organizations (see Chapter 3). Changes will continue to impact healthcare organizations, such as the present consideration of a healthcare plan for all people. The political system operating on a healthcare agency can extend far beyond government institutions. It includes the entire complex of individuals, groups, and institutions that possess the power to influence an organization's survival and growth.

Climate, culture, and caring within the organization

One of the softer aspects of a formal organization is the emotional **climate**. In an organizational context, climate concerns behavior, attitudes, and feelings of personnel. Managers and leaders strive to create a climate that promotes job satisfaction. **Culture** refers to more deep-rooted assumptions, beliefs, and values. It comprises socially inherited characteristics that are handed down from one generation to the next, often on a preconscious level. Culture is the sum of many factors, including beliefs, practices, habits, likes, dislikes, norms, customs, and rituals.

Developing long before theories about **caring** even evolved, caring has been a central part of the rich heritage of nursing. Caring leadership motivates and inspires individuals to contribute their unique talents to a common goal. Caring leaders are not soft, simpering individuals who allow others to bend them in any direction but instead expect dedication and commitment to excellence. However, caring leaders recognize that people are human and thus can make mistakes. There is a need to provide caring for the caregiver, which can be in the form of emotional support, physical safeguards, recognition, dignity, and respect.

Brandt[12] studied theories of both leadership and care. She is convinced that by combining concepts from both disciplines, nursing leaders can develop a work environment that fosters a caring, creative, and innovative climate.

Realization of goals

Healthcare agencies must make certain that the output and all functions of the organization satisfy predetermined goals. **Quality control** standards are of vital importance. It is the nurse manager's responsibility to know what these standards are (see Chapter 10) and to monitor them as they apply to the manager's area and scope of practice. *Productivity* includes most efficient use of facilities, space and equipment, employees, and the services rendered. An agency that operates without careful regard to cost is in trouble. All nurse managers are held accountable for a balanced **budget,** making adjustments as necessary. *Job satisfaction* and a *sense of well-*

being are also factors that concern nurse managers. Application of the behavioral science approach can lead to a satisfying and productive organization.

INTERDEPENDENT RELATIONSHIPS IN THE MANAGEMENT ROLE

As discussed, management is considered a process, with consideration given to the many factors that may influence the process. Figure 1-6 illustrates the interdependent relationships that exist and summarizes forces presented in this chapter that impinge on the manager. The organizational structure, authority and power, management process, available resources, and behavioral components have a bearing on one another. The effectiveness of the leader/manager depends on the individual's knowledge and ability to function within this framework.

LEARNING TO LEAD AND TO MANAGE

How does one become the best leader possible? Kouzes and Posner[13] concluded that leaders and managers can make a difference and have a significant impact on people and organizations when they take advantage of opportunities to lead. Their analysis of all responses suggests three major categories of opportunities for learning to lead and to manage. In order of importance, these categories are (1) trial and error through job experience and assignments, (2) relationships with other people with whom they have come in contact, and (3) formal training and education.

Trial and Error Through Job Experience and Assignments

There is just no suitable surrogate for learning by doing. Whether hooking up an IV, preparing medications, manipulating a patient lift, managing a four-patient assignment within a given time period, or giving directions to a nursing team, the more chances one has to serve in leadership roles, the more likely it is that one will develop

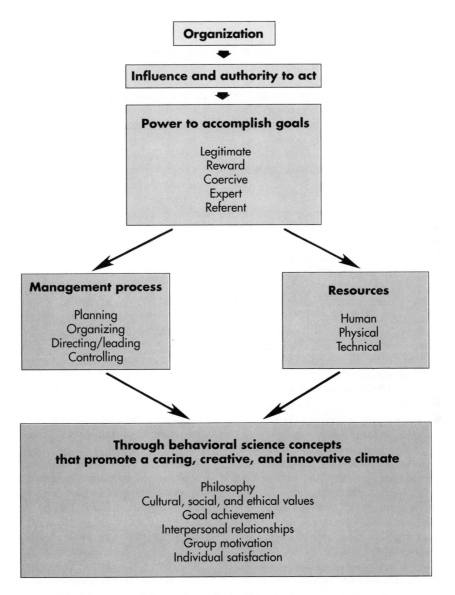

FIGURE 1-6. Interdependent relationships in the management role.

the skills to lead. Important leadership lessons come only from challenges and the resulting failures and successes of action.

Students of leadership and management seek new and tougher assignments that are beneficial to their development. This is why student nurses are rotated from one setting to another and given increased responsibility and challenges throughout their program. Learning from leadership experiences is much like watching game films after an athletic event. These documentations show how the plan was carried out, what was done well, and where improvement is needed. Athletic teams make extensive use of postgame reviews; similarly, nurse leaders and managers can use inductive learning experiences such as these to prepare them for their roles.

Relationships With People

Contact with others in similar circumstances has always been an essential source of guidance. One can recall the parent looked to for advice and support, the special teacher who generated curiosity for a favorite subject, the neighbor who allowed one to watch or even participate in a project, the counselor who gave valuable feedback about behavior and its impact, or the first employer who taught the rudiments of the job and how to survive and get ahead.

Of all the potential relationships at work, the three most important are top managers, mentors, and peers. **Top managers** are obviously important because they can help one to advance or can slow one's progress. They serve as extremely important sources of performance feedback and modeling. The best managers are those who challenge, show **trust,** spend time with employees, and show consistency in their behavior. Bad managers may not be pleasant to work with, but they can be good examples of what not to do. **Mentors** are persons such as instructors, team leaders, or co-workers. They are particularly valuable as informal or formal sponsors and coaches. They teach one how to navigate the system and introduce one to the rudiments and the fine points of the job. **Peers,** or those in similar positions, provide a sounding board for and support to the novice leader, which is often needed in any work situation.

Formal and Informal Education and Training

Education and training in leadership and management was not recognized as an important part of the nursing curriculum until the 1970s, when it became apparent that nurses sadly lacked the ability to effect changes in the healthcare system and to influence others in which directions to go. Gradually all nursing curricula have come to include theory and experience in leadership and management, with most states requiring leadership and management content to be an integral part of all registered nursing programs.

All large healthcare agencies, and many smaller ones, have an internal education and training department. See Chapter 11 for a description of a program that prepares team leaders. Courses in leadership and management are offered at all levels in most colleges and universities and are attended by many nurses.

SUMMARY

1. The serious economic crunch in the country affects all aspects of healthcare delivery.
2. All nurses lead and manage to some degree.
3. Leadership and management is a learned process.
4. To perform well as a leader and manager, the nurse must identify individual strengths, weaknesses, and potential; acquire knowledge of leadership and management; learn from other people and experiences; and use self systematically to get the right things done at the right time.
5. Leadership is the art of getting others to want to do what one deems important.
6. The dynamics of leadership include the leader and manager roles, employee and organizational goals, leader and manager behaviors, and the situation.
7. A formal leader is appointed by administration and given authority to act; an informal leader influences others to act without official sanction.
8. Influence is the ability to affect the perceptions, attitudes, or behaviors of others. Influence can reside in individuals, groups, or organizations.

9. Managerial influence includes motivation, power, leadership, and behavior modification.
10. Authority and power are necessary to achieve organizational goals. Authority is the legitimate right to give commands. Power is the ability to obtain, retain, and influence people and informational and material resources to accomplish a task.
11. There are five different forms of power: legitimate (given by right of position), reward (ability of manager to control and administer rewards), coercive (based on fear, depending on the manager's ability to use punishment), expert (derived from manager's ability and skill), and referent (individual charisma or connection or relationship with another powerful person).
12. The management process is the process of working with human and physical resources and organizational and psychologic processes within a caring, creative, and innovative climate for the realization of goals. The effective nurse manager uses planning, organizing, directing/leading, and controlling to achieve individual and organizational goals.
13. Nursing management depends on the interrelationships among organizational structure, tasks to be accomplished, and workers and resources to do the job.
14. Three levels and types of managers are typically found in a health agency: top managers (responsible for overall operations), middle managers (coordinate the nursing activities of several units), and first-line managers (directly responsible for the actual production of nursing services).
15. Applying the behavioral science approach to nursing management increases the nurse manager's effectiveness as a leader. In the behavioral science mode, individuals are considered unique, each with his or her own culture, set of values, needs, and personal skills and expertise, all of which are considered important in the management of an organization. When individuals join an organization, they become part of a group that works together in a climate that encourages trust, open two-way communication, risk taking, and problem solving.
16. The behavioral science approach to nursing leadership and management occurs when the human and physical resources and organizational and behavioral processes of an organization are used and function within a caring, creative, and innovative climate to promote the realization of organizational goals.
17. Interdependent relationships in the management role include the organizational structure, influence and authority to act, power to accomplish goals, management process in effect, available resources, and use of behavioral science concepts.
18. Nurses become effective leaders and managers through trial and error in job experience and assignments, relationships with other people with whom they have come in contact, and formal and informal training and education.

? Questions for Study and Discussion

1. Which concepts of leadership and management should be most heavily weighted for managerial success and effectiveness?
2. Explain the difference between formal and informal leadership.
3. Consider the following situation: You are a newly hired primary care **registered nurse** (RN). As part of your orientation, your department manager remarks that she wants to help you learn as much as possible about the nursing unit. Your assignment for this day is to provide care to four patients who require considerable attention. However, the department manager frequently interrupts your services with requests such as, "Come see the way we do this procedure," "Take this specimen to the lab—you need to know where it is," and "Help Doris with her patient; it will be a good opportunity for you to observe a more experienced nurse." Because of the fre-

quent interruptions, you fall far behind in your work, causing you to work overtime, for which you are reprimanded by the department manager. Referring to this situation, describe a behavior that reflects one of the different influence actions (assertiveness, ingratiation, rationality, sanction, exchange, upward appeal, blocking, and coalition). Not all influence actions are included in this situation.

4. What do the terms *authority* and *power* mean to you? How would you differentiate between the two?

5. Considering the five bases of power (legitimate, reward, coercive, expert, and referent), which tactics do you usually use to influence your parents, instructors, or supervisor? Would it be better to rely on other tactics? Explain.

6. On which base(s) of power do you suppose the first-line department manager of a nursing unit relies most? Explain.

7. Prepare three columns. Write your own definition of management for you as a (a) student, (b) staff nurse, and (c) department manager. How are they the same? How do they differ?

8. Define the behavioral science approach. How does this method apply to nursing management? Give examples.

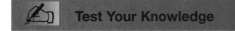

Test Your Knowledge

BEHAVIORAL OBJECTIVE

Define the leadership process and differentiate between formal and informal leadership.

Jessica has recently passed the **National Council Licensure Examination (NCLEX)** RN examination and is applying for a team leader position at a local hospital. Although she has studied leadership and management, she is concerned about telling people who are more experienced than she what to do.

_____ 1. During orientation to the nursing team, Jessica's first priority is to:
   a. Determine the daily routine.
   b. Recall the principles of leadership and management so that she can apply them properly.
   c. Understand the individual strengths, weaknesses, and potential of team members.
   d. Watch closely every movement her mentor makes.

_____ 2. Upon completion of the orientation period, Jessica will be leading the team without close supervision. She has a right to assume that the team members will:
   a. View her as a capable leader.
   b. Recognize that learning to lead is a process.
   c. Accept the premise that Jessica was appointed to the position; therefore she can lead.
   d. Assume Jessica is skilled, knowledgeable, and efficient.

BEHAVIORAL OBJECTIVE

Explain the significance of managerial influence and identify methods of application.

Influence is any attempt by a person to change the behavior of others. Jessica praises the nurse manager's ability to get things done quickly and well and then asks to leave work 2 hours early.

_____ 3. Which type of influence is Jessica applying?
   a. Ingratiation
   b. Sanction
   c. Exchange
   d. Assertiveness

Trouble is brewing among the home healthcare staff. Because of the need for expansion, upper management has decided to install the latest in computerized equipment, which will connect the main office to home healthcare activities. Old-timers are reacting negatively to having to become proficient with equipment that they believe will only increase their workload. Two or three valued members indicate that they will never learn to master the new machines and feel threatened by the constant monitoring.

_____ 4. The nurse manager speaks to the negative staff and lets them know that their job is in jeopardy unless they comply. Which influence tactic is in effect?
a. Upward appeal
b. Coalition
c. Blocking
d. Rationality

BEHAVIORAL OBJECTIVE
Identify the relationship among authority, power, and ability and relate it to leadership and management.

As a staff nurse in pediatrics, you observe that your nurse manager appears unable to bring about a change in visiting hours. She wants to allow parents to be with their children night and day. However, despite her talk about the desirability of such a plan, nothing happens.

_____ 5. Which key element in organization do you think is missing?
a. Authority but not power
b. Power but not authority
c. Influence but not ability
d. Ability but not influence

_____ 6. You note that the nurse manager is not giving up on her plan. She attends a management meeting and turns on her charm in an attempt to have her plan accepted. Which method of power is she employing?
a. Referent power
b. Expert power
c. Legitimate power
d. Reward power

BEHAVIORAL OBJECTIVE
Differentiate between the terms leadership and management.

Tim has accepted a position as manager of a public health department. He wishes to demonstrate competence and ability to lead and manage.

_____ 7. What signifies Tim's right to hold this position?
a. He brings with him a good record.
b. He has been officially appointed.
c. He can guide and direct the work of others.
d. He understands community health nursing.

BEHAVIORAL OBJECTIVE
Define the nurse management process.

Jan is a first-line manager responsible for the care of 12 patients. She is concerned because for 3 weeks medications have been delivered to the nursing unit as much as 2 hours late. She has called the pharmacy, but the situation has not improved.

_____ 8. Jan's first action should be to:
a. Write the pharmacy a memo.
b. Contact the nursing supervisor.
c. Notify the doctors of the patients.
d. Consult her nurse manager.

_____ 9. As a first-line manager, Jan acts as a link between:
a. Top managers and middle managers.
b. Supervisors and coordinators.
c. Higher level managers and non-managers.
d. The vice president and the nurse manager.

BEHAVIORAL OBJECTIVE
Apply the behavioral science approach to nursing management.

Alesandra is employed as nurse manager of a busy outpatient surgi-center. One of her goals is to spend more time applying the behavioral science approach to nursing leadership and management.

BEHAVIORAL OBJECTIVE

Apply the behavioral science approach to nursing management.

_____ 10. Alesandra strives to create a climate that promotes job satisfaction. To her, climate has to do with:
   a. Deep rooted assumptions, beliefs, and values.
   b. Behavior, attitudes, and feelings.
   c. A rich heritage in nursing.
   d. Socially inherited characteristics.

_____ 11. Alesandra is admonished by her supervisor to spend less time nurturing staff and more time on increased production and cost control. Alesandra's response to this dictum is to:
   a. Present her view that a satisfied staff is more productive than a dissatisfied staff.
   b. Resign because this plan is untenable.
   c. Agree to comply because this is her required role.
   d. Send a production report to the president of the company, highlighting her accomplishments.

BEHAVIORAL OBJECTIVE

Indicate how nurses learn to lead and manage.

Lamar is experienced in psychiatric nursing. He is interested in becoming a nurse manager of an acquired immunodeficiency syndrome (AIDS) center, but he does not meet all the qualifications for the job. He is unsure how to acquire the necessary knowledge, understanding, and skills.

_____ 12. In addition to receiving education about human immunodeficiency virus (HIV) and AIDS and communicating with nurses practicing in the field, Lamar's next step is to:
   a. Reduce his fear of contact with HIV/AIDS patients.
   b. Convince the employer that he is the one for the job.
   c. Obtain hands-on experience in the workplace.
   d. Offer suggestions for improving group therapy sessions.

REFERENCES

1. Rothwell J: *In mixed company: small group communication,* Fort Worth, 1992, Harcourt Brace Javanovich.
2. Davis K: *Human behavior at work: organizational behavior,* ed 5, New York, 1977, McGraw-Hill.
3. Barney J, Griffin R: *The management of organizations,* Boston, 1992, Houghton Mifflin.
4. Kipnis D, Schmidt S, Wilkinson I: Intraorganizational influence tactics: explorations in getting one's way, *J Appl Psychol* 58(4):440-452, 1990.
5. Menke K, Ogborn S: Politics and the nurse manager, *Nurs Manage* 24(12):35-37, 1993.
6. French J, Raven B: The basis of social power. In Cartwright D, Zander A, editors: *Group dynamics, research and theory,* ed 3, New York, 1968, Harper & Row.
7. Kreitner R: *Management,* ed 4, Boston, 1992, Houghton Mifflin.
8. Hellriegel D, Slocum J: *Management,* ed 5, New York, 1989, Addison-Wesley.
9. Tappen R: *Nursing leadership and management: concepts and practice,* ed 2, Philadelphia, 1989, FA Davis.
10. Gillies D: *Nursing management: a systems approach,* ed 2, Philadelphia, 1989, WB Saunders.
11. Henry J, Walker D: *Managing innovation,* London, 1991, Sage Publications.
12. Brandt M: Caring leadership: secret and path to success, *Nurs Manage* 25(8):68-72, 1994.
13. Kouzes J, Posner B: *The leadership challenge,* San Francisco, 1987, Jossey-Bass.

SUGGESTED READINGS

Adams C: Innovative behavior in nurse executives, *Nurs Manage* 25(5):44-47, 1994.

Anderson C: From the editor: Power: an elusive franchise, *Nurs Outlook* 42(5):205-206, 1994.

Begamy T: Your image is brighter than ever, *RN* 57(10):28-34, 1994.

Beyers M: Is there a future for management? *Nurs Manage* 26(1):24-25, 1995.

Brandt M: Caring leadership: secret and path to success, *Nurs Manage* 25(8):68-72, 1994.

Catalano J: A survey of educators' activities to empower nurses for practice, *Nurs Outlook* 42(4):182-187, 1994.

Curtin L: Leadership in tough times, *Nurs Manage* 25(1):7-8, 1994.

Curtis R, Yen J: Administrative exemplars, *Nurs Manage* 25(6):85, 1994.

Grinde T: Implementing a nursing administration local area network, *Nurs Manage* 25(7):36-37, 1994.

Johnson J and others: Succession management: a model developing nursing leaders, *Nurs Manage* 25(6):50-55, 1994.

Kippenbrak T, May F: Turnover at the top: CNOs and hospital characteristics, *Nurs Manage* 25(9):54-57, 1994.

Koerner J: Encouragement versus empowerment? A nurse executive responds, *J Nurs Adm* 24(4):12-15, 1994.

Mancuso L, Toye S: A new managerial style: "partners in excellence." 25(8):83, 1994.

Neubauer J: The learning network: leadership development for the next millennium, *J Nurs Adm* 25(2):23-32, 1995.

Reimer J and others: Power orientation: a study of female nurses and non-nurse managers, *Nurs Manage* 25(5):55-58, 1994.

Sharp N: The nurses' agenda: priorities for 1995, *Nurs Manage* 26(2):21-22, 1995.

Smith P and others: The new nurse executive: an emerging role, *Nurs Manage* 24(11):56-62, 1994.

Wolfe S: What is the Supreme court doing to nursing? *RN* 57(12):59-60, 1994.

STYLES of LEADERSHIP and MANAGEMENT

BEHAVIORAL OBJECTIVES
On completion of this chapter, the student will be prepared to:

- Determine what impact personal characteristics and traits have on leadership and management.

- Compare and contrast the conclusions of the Ohio State Leadership Studies, the Managerial Grid, the Fiedler Contingency Model, and the Path-Goal Theory.

- Differentiate among authoritarian, democratic, and permissive styles of leadership and determine the style of leadership that best supports a successful managerial role.

- Interpret the process of management by situation.

In Chapter 1 it was determined that (1) leadership is the ability to inspire and influence others to achieve goals through formal and informal procedures, and (2) management requires authority and power to implement the organizational goals of planning, organizing, directing, and controlling human and physical resources and technology. In addition, it was noted that effective managers use behavioral science concepts to achieve their purposes.

Another important issue is the wise and systematic *use of self* to get the right things done at the right times. This chapter discusses leadership style, or the *way* in which a leader/manager uses personal influence to achieve the objectives of the organization.

Leaders interact with individuals and work groups in many ways. The interactions of individuals and groups represent the most critical relationship in an organization. No matter how large or small the enterprise, each person involved is a leader and/or follower and is part of the work situation. Leadership involves other people, and by their willingness to follow the group leader, group members help to make the leadership/management process possible. How leaders work with followers and how both work with the job situation determine the success of the individual manager and of the organization. Every nurse leader/manager develops a characteristic style of seeking, wielding, and reacting to power. Studying individual characteristics and the ways in which styles of behavior and nurse leaders/managers affect the healthcare delivery system allows nurses to interact more productively and more harmoniously to achieve personal and organizational goals.

HISTORICAL CONCEPTS OF LEADERSHIP

The phenomenon of leadership in organizations has been extensively studied for years. Three major historical approaches center on leadership traits, leadership styles, and behavioral styles.

Leadership Traits

During most of recorded history, the prevailing assumption has been that leaders are born and not made. During the first several decades of this century, hundreds of studies were conducted to identify important leadership traits. **Traits** are personal, psychologic, and physical **characteristics** that are identified in an individual.

According to today's media, a leader must possess qualities such as intelligence, charisma, decisiveness, enthusiasm, strength, bravery, integrity, and self-confidence. Thus one might conclude that to be a leader, a person must be a superwoman or superman (e.g., Winston Churchill, Margaret Thatcher, Susan B. Anthony, John F. Kennedy, Martin Luther King, Jr., Mother Theresa, Mahatma Ghandi, Golda Maier, and Cesar Chavez). Everyone may agree that these individuals meet the definition of a leader, but they also represent human beings with utterly different characteristics.

Warren Bennis, noted management consultant, is convinced that successful leaders share some common traits.[1] He interviewed 90 highly successful leaders, including both male and female corporate and public-sector executives. Four common traits or competencies were identified: management of attention, management of meaning, management of trust, and management of self (Box 2-1).

Numerous other studies have been conducted on trait identification. Six traits have been identified as being consistently associated with leadership:[2]

- Drive and ambition
- Desire to lead and influence others
- Honesty and integrity
- Self-confidence
- Intelligence
- In-depth technical knowledge related to the area of responsibility

The premise of trait studies was that *if behaviors could be defined, potential leaders could be identified.* For the most part, the results of the studies were disappointing. For every set of leaders who possessed a common trait, a long list of exceptions was also found, and the list of suggested traits has grown so long that the leadership trait theory has little practical value.

Leadership Styles

Style is an important factor in the leadership/management process. A style is the way in which something is said or done; it is a particular form of behavior directly associated with an individual. **Leadership style** is how a leader uses interpersonal influences to accomplish goals. Individual behavior is influenced by formative years and by all the input in a person's life thereafter. Thus the style or approach taken by a nurse manager toward patients/clients, nursing staff members, and other associates strongly reflects prior experiences.

Behavioral Styles

During World War II, the study of leadership took a significant turn. Spurred on by their lack of success in identifying useful leadership traits, researchers next began to investigate other variables, especially the behaviors or actions of leaders, or behavioral styles. The proposed hypothesis was that the behaviors of effective leaders was somehow different from the behaviors of less effective leaders. Thus the goal was to develop a fuller understanding of leadership behavior. As Figure 2-1 illustrates, rather than focusing on what the leader *is like*, researchers observed how the leader *actually behaves*.

A number of studies looked at behavioral styles in leaders. Four of the most popular theories are the Ohio State leadership studies, the University of Michigan Managerial Grid, the Fiedler Contingency Model, and House's Path-Goal theory.

Box 2-1.   Common traits of successful leaders as identified by Bennis

1. Management of attention

The leader demonstrates a mix of vision or intelligent foresight and strong personal commitment.

EXAMPLE: Rene, community health nurse, has a mental image of spearheading the establishment of a center for pregnant women in a downtown neighborhood. Her strong personal dedication attracts others and inspires them to join in the fulfillment of her dream.

2. Management of meaning

The leader possesses unusual communication skills.

EXAMPLE: Rene surveys the environment and proposes a site for the center, determining what is needed to start the program; she describes enthusiastically and succinctly what is needed and why. Her persuasive ability to communicate the need aligns others with the cause.

3. Management of trust

The leader remains constant and secure and builds trust by making others aware of his or her steadiness of purpose.

EXAMPLE: Rene is persistent, even dogmatic, about her intent to initiate a program for pregnant women. She befriends several single mothers while making her survey. In so doing, she lets others know where she stands.

4. Management of self

Successful leaders develop their strengths and learn from their mistakes. They generally reject the idea of failure.

EXAMPLE: Rene determines that she is best at discussing needs and organizing forces. She believes herself to be weak in generating funds. She compensates for this weakness by using her strong communication skills to enlist the support of others talented in fundraising.

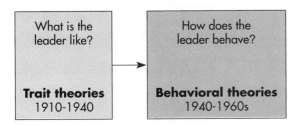

FIGURE 2-1. Shift of researchers' attention in the study of the leadership role.

The Ohio State leadership series

The Ohio State studies in the 1940s attempted to describe what successful leaders do.[3] Researchers identified the following key dimensions of leadership behavior:

1. **Initiating structure,** or the extent to which a leader is likely to define and structure his or her role in the search for goal attainment (e.g., planning, organizing, controlling, directing). The leader characterized as high in initiating structure may assign group members to particular tasks, expect workers to maintain definite standards of performance, and emphasize the achievement of goals.

2. **Consideration** is described as the extent to which a person is likely to have job relationships characterized by mutual trust, respect for co-workers' comfort, well-being, status, and satisfaction. A leader high in consideration could be described as one who is friendly and approachable, helps staff with personal problems, and treats people as equals.

The theory proposed by the Ohio State study was that a combination of *high structure* and *high consideration* (high-high) leads to greater leadership effectiveness (Box 2-2).

The managerial grid

Blake and Mouton studied the relationship between leadership style and productivity. Using leadership dimensions similar to the Ohio State studies, Blake and Mouton developed the Managerial Grid, a trademarked and widely recognized classification of leadership styles that uses a two-dimensional grid to classify them.[4] The assumption behind the theory is that people are basically good and trustworthy. Therefore managers can delegate tasks, allow staff to structure their own work, and feel little need for close supervision. Blake and Mouton remain convinced that there is one best style of leadership, that of *high concern for people* as well as *high concern for production*. As Box 2-3 indicates, concern for people involves promoting friendship; maintaining morale; helping co-workers get the job done; and attending to things that matter to people such as promotions, pay, working conditions, and benefits. Concern for production involves a desire to achieve greater output (e.g., handle greater patient-care loads) and cost effectiveness (e.g., use a minimum of staff and supplies while maintaining optimum care). Blake and Mouton stress that the most successful leaders/managers must not only be versatile enough to select the course of action appropriate to a given situation but must also exercise high concern for people and production. A nursing team is an excellent example of high concern for people with high concern for production.

Although studies seemed to demonstrate a positive relationship between high initiating structure and high consideration (approximately 80%), this premise could not be proved conclusively because other combinations such as low initiating structure and high consideration sometimes resulted in higher performance and productivity. It became clear that the work situation also had a profound influence in determining the relationship between leadership behavior and performance.

The Fiedler Contingency Model

Among the various leadership theories thus far, Fiedler's Contingency Model is the most thoroughly tested.[3] It is the product of more than 30 years of research by Fiedler and Chemers from the University of Washington. Fiedler and Chemers believed that a leader's characteristics or traits are fixed and cannot be changed. Consequently, they were largely concerned with the leadership situation. They refined the idea of a

---

Box 2-2.   Sample behaviors of a manager with high initiating structure and high consideration

HIGH INITIATING STRUCTURE	HIGH CONSIDERATION
1. Organizes and defines group activities and makes clear the manager's relation to the group	1. Promotes mutual trust, respect, and rapport
2. Defines the role expected of each member	2. Shows concern for group members' needs
3. Assigns tasks, plans ahead, explains how tasks are to be done	3. Allows participation in decision making
4. Pushes for achievement of organizational goals	4. Encourages two-way communication

---

Box 2-3.   Sample behaviors of a manager with high concern for both people and production

HIGH CONCERN FOR PEOPLE	HIGH CONCERN FOR PRODUCTION
1. Maintains comfortable work tempo and conditions	1. Task oriented; promotes work accomplishment
2. Promotes satisfying interpersonal relationships	2. Interdependent in achieving a common goal
3. Works for equitable pay, promotions, and benefits for workers	3. Quality and quantity oriented

situational approach to leadership by attempting to define the particular style of leadership that is appropriate for a given situation and then creating a match between the style and the situation.

Fiedler and Chemers isolated three situational criteria that they believe can be manipulated to create the proper match with the behaviors of the leader: (1) task structure, (2) leader-member relations, and (3) position power. The outcome variable of effectiveness follows (Figure 2-2).

Task structure. The first situational factor is concerned with the nature of the worker's task and measures the degree to which the task is routine or complex. For example, a staff nurse in a labor and delivery unit may work in a fairly structured area with specific tasks, whereas the nurse manager may work with less structured tasks such as planning for overall functions of the labor and delivery, nursery, and neonatal units. The following example illustrates Fiedler and Chemers' theory that it is better to fit a leader's characteristics to the situation than to try to alter the leader's characteristics.

EXAMPLE: Nancy was assigned to be a department manager in an oncology unit where the pace was slow and there was heavy emphasis on emotional and spiritual matters. Nancy believed her primary competencies to be in triage and technical skills and felt inadequate to the task required of her new assignment. She requested a transfer to either Intensive Care or the Emergency Room. Fiedler and Chemers would have supported this request rather than encourage her to change her ways, believing that Nancy would be far more efficient if moved to a situation more suitable for her personality.

Leader/member relationships. The leader/member relationships factor measures the relationships between the leader and the co-worker. The degree of confidence, trust, and respect that members have in their leader are measured along a continuum of good to poor. The idea is that the better the relationship between leader and co-worker, the easier it will be for the leader to exercise influence.

Leader position power. The final situational factor of leader position power concerns the extent of the leader's power base, or the ability of the leader to influence the behavior of co-workers through legitimate, reward, or coercive behavior. According to Fiedler, position power can vary from strong, such as that exercised by the vice president of nursing services, to weak, such as that exhibited by a nursing assistant.

Effectiveness. The major outcome variable in the Fiedler Contingency Model is effective-

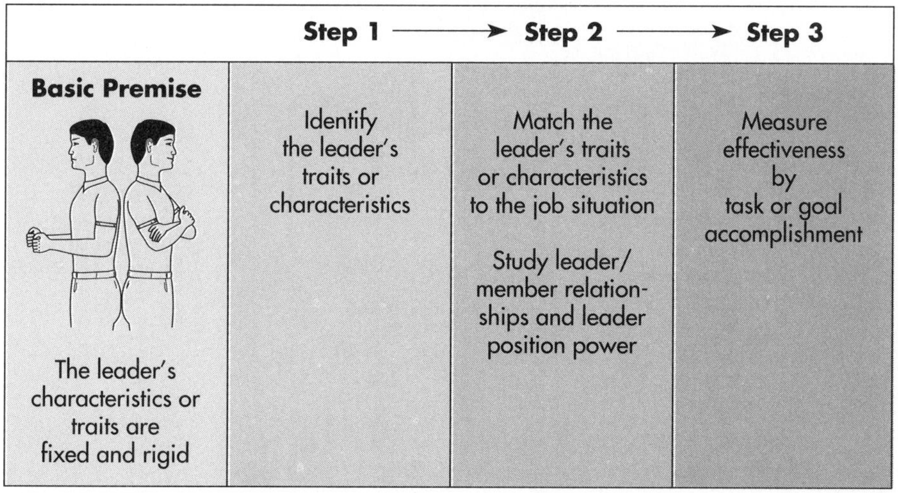

	Step 1 ⟶	Step 2 ⟶	Step 3
Basic Premise	Identify the leader's traits or characteristics	Match the leader's traits or characteristics to the job situation Study leader/member relationships and leader position power	Measure effectiveness by task or goal accomplishment
The leader's characteristics or traits are fixed and rigid			

FIGURE 2-2. The Fiedler Contingency Model.

ness, which is measured by the degree of task or goal accomplishment. Fiedler and Chemers assume that an individual's leadership style is a fixed and rigid quality; the leader is either relationship or task oriented and will not change. Because the leader's style is rigid, to achieve the highest level of effectiveness one must diagnose the situation and then select a manager whose style best fits that situation.

Fiedler and Chemers' model has been the subject of a growing body of research. Questions arise as to whether managerial style is indeed fixed and why more attention was not given to the interactions between leadership style and the situation. Even with these concerns, Fiedler and Chemers' model has proven to be a significant addition to the study of leadership in organizations.

Path-goal model

The Path-Goal Theory, developed by House and associates, states that the role of the leader in eliciting work-goal–directed behavior consists of increasing personal rewards to workers for goal attainment.[3] Barriers to reaching goals are reduced, making the payoffs easier. The leader uses directive, supportive, participative, and achievement-oriented styles, depending on the situation. Unlike Fiedler and Chemers, House and associates believe that the leader can adapt his or her leadership style to the situation. For example, the leader can give positive reinforcement immediately following a desired behavior:

"Phil, you handled that difficult situation very well. I liked the way you first diffused Mrs. Lowe's anger and then set about resolving the problem. Very well done! Would you consider role playing this incident at our next staff meeting?"

Phil receives immediate positive reinforcement and is offered the opportunity to demonstrate his ability in a teaching situation. Figure 2-3 shows that, according to the Path-Goal-Theory, different leader behaviors can affect group members' motivation to perform.

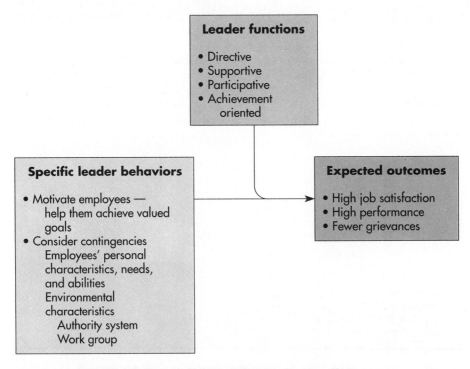

FIGURE 2-3. House's Path-Goal Theory of leader effectiveness.

Learned Behavior

Researchers have begun to recognize that, unlike characteristics, behaviors can be learned. Therefore it is assumed that individuals who are trained in the appropriate style can lead and manage more effectively. The fact that a manager's personality or past experience helps form his or her leadership style does not mean that the style is unchangeable. Managers learn that some styles work better for them than others; if a style proves unsatisfactory for a particular situation, the manager can alter it. However, managers who attempt to adopt a style that is greatly inconsistent with their basic personality are unlikely to use that style effectively.[4]

AUTHORITARIAN, PERMISSIVE, AND DEMOCRATIC STYLES OF LEADERSHIP AND MANAGEMENT

Research indicates that the styles of leadership used by leaders/managers vary with organizations and are tailored to fit their needs. There are simply too many kinds of leaders, personnel, tasks, organizations, and environments for one leadership/management style to apply to all cases. Furthermore, numerous ways of classifying styles of leadership/management are used. Although some theorists label styles differently from others and offer a variety of ranges of behavior representative of a specific style, all describe the authoritarian, democratic, and permissive styles as basic approaches to management.[5]

Authoritarian Style of Leadership/Management

Classic research conducted by Lewin, Lippit, and White[6] in 1939 shows that an **authoritarian** style of leadership ranges from very rigid to benevolent practices. In the strictest sense, authoritarianism functions with high concern for task accomplishment but low concern for the people who perform those tasks. Likert[7] characterizes the authoritarian style of leadership as exploitive, or using the workers' efforts to the best possible advantage of the employer without regard to the workers' interests. In the extreme use

of authoritarian leadership, communications and activities occur in a closed system, as illustrated in Figure 2-4. Managers make all work-related decisions and order workers to carry them out. Managers also rigidly set standards and methods of performance. The authoritarian leader frequently exercises power, sometimes with coercion. Failure to meet the manager's goals may result in threats or punishment.

The authoritarian personality is firm, insistent, self-assured, and dominating with or without intent, and it keeps at the center of attention. This kind of manager has little trust or confidence in workers, and workers in turn fear the manager and believe they have little in common with him or her. McGregor[8] has produced perhaps the most famous description of attitudes assumed by authoritarian leaders. He maintains that they view individuals as naturally lazy, self-centered, not very bright, lacking in ambition, disliking responsibility, preferring to be led, indifferent to organizational needs, resistant to change, and lacking creative potential (see also Chapter 3).

Many managerial leaders take issue with those who believe authoritarian leadership to be a "put-down" of persons. Proponents of a more conservative or benevolent approach to authoritarian leadership value workers and their capabilities but believe there is a need for strong structure and order. In the benevolent authoritarian approach, managers still issue orders, but workers have some freedom to com-

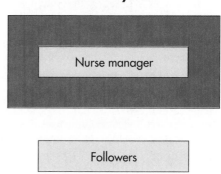

Closed System

Nurse manager

Followers

FIGURE 2-4. Authoritarian style of leadership. Dark area represents predominant control.

ment on those orders.[8] Workers are given flexibility to carry out their tasks within carefully prescribed limits and procedures. A benevolent authoritarian may give orders, use praise, demand loyalty, or make followers think they are actually participating in decisions even though they are doing what the leader wants. In general, these managers have a condescending attitude toward those they lead, and the followers are cautious when dealing with their managers.

Some form of authoritarian leadership has been used in nursing for many years. It reflects a very directive type of leadership that stresses giving orders by the nurse manager and taking orders by other members of the nursing staff. Authoritarian leadership is particularly suitable in situations of crisis when clear directions are of the highest priority. It is often referred to today as a *directive* or *controlling* style of leadership.

Certain followers are most productive with authoritarian leadership and derive a sense of security and satisfaction under this style of management. In turn, this type of management provides strong motivation and psychologic rewards to the leader. Authoritarianism allows for the possibility that the manager is likely to think and act faster and more effectively than others. Leaders with authoritarian styles are known for their ability to excel in times of crisis, to get tough jobs done, and to bring order out of chaos when those around them falter.[1]

> EXAMPLE: Nurse manager Fay wants her nursing unit to win the annual hospital award for optimum attendance. She issues a bulletin itemizing her expectations: everyone will report to work on time; there will be no unexcused lateness or absence; and penalties will be assigned for failure to comply.
>
> Fay is making policy without input from her staff. As a result they feel defensive, fearful, and exploited.

> EXAMPLE: Ron enters a room and notes that a patient is having severe respiratory difficulty. He punches the call-light and demands immediate help; when help arrives, he gives appropriate orders.
>
> In this instance, Ron correctly assigns people to clearly defined tasks; there is no thought of exercising participatory decision making. The staff experiences security in the procedure.

Permissive, Ultraliberal, or Laissez-faire Style of Leadership/ Management

The **permissive** (or ultraliberal or laissez-faire) style of leadership/management is at the opposite end of the continuum from the authoritarian style. Some would say that calling the permissive style "leadership" is a contradiction in terms and that leadership is absent under this system. Under this style of leadership, the general climate is one of lack of central direction or control. The permissive manager wants everyone to feel good, including the manager. This leader avoids responsibility by relinquishing power to followers, and he or she permits followers to engage in managerial activities such as decision making, planning, setting goals, and structuring and controlling the organization.

It has been estimated that fewer than 25% of all employees can operate responsibly with the permissive style and that only 10% of all managers accept and use this style. According to Lewin, Lippitt, and White, permissive leaders believe it is the responsibility of the organization to supply money, materials, equipment, and workers and that managers have the responsibility to direct their own efforts toward achievement of organizational goals. Permissive leaders assume that workers are ambitious, responsible, accepting of organizational goals, dynamic, flexible, intelligent, and creative.[9] Figure 2-5 illustrates how the leader assumes a small role and relinquishes the bulk of the management process to followers. This style can be effective in highly motivated professional groups such as in research projects in which independent thinking is rewarded. The very liberal style of leadership is oriented to higher social, ego fulfillment, and self-actualization needs. However, this style is not generally useful in the highly structured healthcare delivery system in which organization and control form the baseline of most operations.

> EXAMPLE: Carol, a supervisor, informed the five department managers under her supervision that they were to assume full responsibility for staffing their stations. Four managers were delighted with the responsibility and followed through well, keeping within agency staff guidelines. The fifth manager staffed her station from day to day according

Permissive System

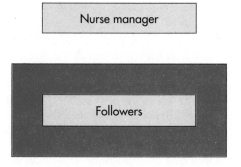

FIGURE 2-5. Permissive, ultraliberal, or laissez-faire style of leadership. Dark area represents predominant control.

Open System

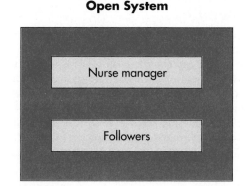

FIGURE 2-6. Democratic, participative, or consultive style of leadership. Dark area represents shared control.

to her desires and with no regard to guidelines. She allowed her staff to arrive late and leave early for personal reasons. She called in extra help when staff members complained, without investigating the causes of their difficulties or the resulting cost. Because there was little control, the staff took more and more liberties, which created inefficiency and chaos. The matter came to a climax when an emergency occurred and the staff was inadequate to handle the crisis. The supervisor had abdicated her responsibility, which allowed the group to drift into an untenable situation.

Democratic, Participative, or Consultive Style of Leadership/Management

In the **democratic** (or **participative** or consultive) approach, the manager is "people oriented" and focuses attention on human aspects and on building effective work groups. Interaction between manager and personnel is open, friendly, and trusting. A collaborative spirit or joint effort exists, which allows for governance through group participation in decision making. Figure 2-6 demonstrates the open system of communication that prevails; the democratic manager consults with group members, solves problems with them, and assumes that others want to be considered in the process. There is a mutual responsiveness to meeting group goals, and work-related decisions are made by the group. The democratic manager at-

tempts to develop the group's sense of responsibility for the good of the whole and for individual accomplishments. Thus the goals set by the work group may not always be the ones personally favored. The democratic manager tries to give workers feelings of self-worth and importance. Performance standards exist to provide guidelines and permit appraisal of workers rather than to provide managers with a tool to control workers.

Some decisions do not permit the nurse manager to exercise total democracy, but use of the democratic process whenever possible permits each member to identify with the work setting by establishing challenging goals, providing opportunities to change or improve work methods, pursuing professional and personal growth, recognizing achievement, and helping personnel learn from their mistakes. Likert's research studies[7] revealed that a democratic style of leadership leads to high productivity and is the most desirable form of management in a wide variety of work situations.

EXAMPLE: Martha, a department manager, delegates authority to the primary care nurses for care of 26 patients. She depends on them to use an interdisciplinary approach to plan and implement appropriate care. Martha retains ultimate responsibility for all outcomes. Thus she maintains an active two-way flow of upward and downward communication, ensuring accountability and at the same time providing for flexibility and creativity among the nursing staff.

Comparison of Styles of Leadership

There are many similarities and differences in behavior, attitudes, and conditions present in the various leadership styles (Box 2-4). As mentioned previously, not all of the behaviors are evident at any one time; however, each of the three styles of leadership is usually consistent within its category. A nurse manager uses all the styles separately or together, depending on his or her flexibility and the circumstances inherent in each situation.

LEADERSHIP AND MANAGEMENT BY SITUATION

A comparative study of leadership styles seems to suggest that a democratic style of leadership is the style of choice in most situations. However, there are too many factors to consider to make so broad an application. Researchers have turned their attention from classifying behaviors that label managers as authoritarian, democratic, or permissive to considering **management by situation.**

Manager's Choice of Leadership Style

All situational-leadership theorists share one fundamental assumption: successful leadership occurs when the leader's style matches the situation. The premise is that styles of leadership should not be stereotyped as either forceful, participative, or permissive. Management should instead be viewed as a process composed of a range of possible options in which the manager chooses a leadership style complementary to the need.

In 1958, Tannenbaum and Schmidt[10] were among the first theorists to identify forces they believed should influence a manager's choice of leadership style. Those identified were (1) forces in the manager, (2) forces in the subordinates, and (3) forces in the situation. Although Tannenbaum and Schmidt personally favored the democratic style, they found that managers need to consider certain practicalities before deciding

Box 2-4. Comparative summary of democratic, authoritarian, and permissive styles of leadership

DEMOCRATIC	AUTHORITARIAN	PERMISSIVE
Participative	Conservative	Ultraliberal
Group goals	Organizational goals	Individual goals
Open	Defensive	Open
Facilitating	Restrictive	Permissive
Freeing	Coercive, pressuring	Abdicating
Encouraging	Discouraging	Frustration, conflict
Accepting	Rejecting	Accepting and rejecting
Variety	Sameness	Differences
Equality	Inequality	Equality
Trusting	Fearing	Indifferent
Available supervision	Constant surveillance	Supervision as requested
Encouragement, assistance	Force	Self-direction
Freedom of choice	Obedience	Freedom of choice
Cooperation, group loyalty	Competition	Limited group alliance
Opportunity	Exploitation	Uncontrolled
Challenge	Threat	Permissive
Recognition	Praise	Acceptance
Self-discipline	Punishment	Self-gratification
Satisfaction	Reward	Acceptance

which style of leadership to use. Fiedler and Chemers' Contingency Theory[11] is more explicit in its description of factors to consider when determining a style of leadership. According to this theory, the manager is asked to review (1) the work situation, (2) the manager's leadership style and expectations, and (3) the follower's characteristics and expectations.[11] Fiedler and Chemers believe that when these three forces are considered and adaptations are made, the situation is likely to be harmonious, with a willingness on the part of all those involved to cooperate in accomplishing goals.

The challenge, according to Fiedler and Chemers, is to analyze a leader's basic motivation and then match him or her with a suitable situation to form a productive combination. They believe it is more efficient to move leaders to suitable situations than to tamper with their personalities (e.g., trying to get a task-motivated person to become relationship motivated or vice versa).[11]

The Health Care Advisory Board maintains that poor management causes more nursing turnover than most administrators realize.[12] DeCrosta[13] says that use of *situational leadership,* first developed in 1988 by Hersey and Blanchard,[14] can help nurse managers to retain nurses on their staffs. Situational leadership is a management system based on the following equation:

The situation at hand
+ The professional readiness of the staff member

The nurse manager assesses each nurse's needs and determines which leadership behaviors will help that nurse get the job done with the fewest problems. The nurse manager first considers the nurse's ability (knowledge, experience, skill) and then determines his or her willingness (confidence, commitment, motivation, and energy) to complete a given task.

The next step in Hersey and Blanchard's situational leadership method is to match one of four managerial styles of leadership to the follower's readiness. Specifically, the nurse manager matches task behaviors to the nurse's ability. These task behaviors are telling, selling, participating, and delegating (Box 2-5).

Situational leadership allows the nurse manager to move from one style to another as each situation presents itself. The manager must make transitions carefully, such as moving from a telling to a delegation style through supporting and coaching steps. Easy to learn and effective when applied, situational leadership helps the nurse manager improve staff competency and relationships by applying the appropriate style of leadership to each particular situation.

Manager's Style of Leadership and Expectations

How a manager leads is influenced by his or her background, knowledge, values, and experiences (forces in the manager) and the relationships or interdependency between the manager and the other personnel. The manager is likely to choose a style that complements his or her personality. The greater the manager's need to control the situation, the more likely it is that he or she will select an authoritarian or conservative leadership style. The greater the belief in followers' competency and in the ability of members to work responsibly, the more likely it is that he or she will take a democratic or participative approach. The greater the belief that workers have the ability to achieve with minimal structure and direction, the more likely it is that he or she will follow a permissive or democratic style of leadership.

Followers' Characteristics and Expectations

The characteristics and expectations of followers must also be considered before managers can choose an appropriate leadership style. Followers differ in their response to leadership, and ultimately the response of followers to the manager's leadership determines how effective the manager will be.

Knowledge, competency, and *level of the workers* are important characteristics to consider. For example, capable persons usually require much less supervision than new or inexperienced workers; less prepared personnel require carefully planned, detailed guidance. The nurse manager's task is to know the qualifications of each member assigned to the nursing team and provide them with the right amount of supervision and guidance.

Box 2-5.   Hersey and Blanchard's situational leadership

The nurse manager uses high amounts of task behavior when the subordinate nurse has little or no ability for the task, and low amounts of task behavior when the subordinate nurse is able to perform the task, as illustrated by the following examples:

1. Telling

EXAMPLE: Cora was new to use of the crash cart. During orientation, she was shown its contents and procedure. When a code was called, Cora assisted the leader and was told what to do each step of the way. After the code, the procedure was reviewed thoroughly.

The leader knew Cora did not have the skill to manage a code but did have the ability to learn. Through gradual initiation Cora gained competence and moved into a participating style.

2. Selling

EXAMPLE: Lena is resistant to floating to other nursing units when asked to do so and makes life miserable for the nurse manager because of her complaining. The nurse manager explains that there are many benefits to be gained from different environments such as learning new skills, making new friends, and the possibility of becoming more visible to the agency, which would be an asset in the event that an opportunity for advancement arises.

The nurse manager could have insisted that Lena take her turn but chose instead to sell the benefits of floating to Lena, knowing that willingness in a worker contributes to high productivity and satisfaction.

3. Participating

EXAMPLE: Sydney, a new employee, was hesitant to administer IV medications to oncology patients because he was afraid of causing skin erosion as a result of his lack of experience. He continued to ask for supervision even though the nurse manager believed him to be competent.

A participating nurse manager would compliment Sydney on his competence in giving oncology medications, then suggest that he proceed on his own and ask for help if he believed he needed it. Sydney followed the plan and gradually weaned himself away from a dependent position.

4. Delegating

EXAMPLE: Nursing Assistant Theresa was assigned to a surgical nurse unit unfamiliar to her. She was frightened of all the suction equipment, of the IVs, and of touching patients. The nurse manager assigned Theresa to work with an experienced nursing assistant for one week, asking that she teach Theresa the art of caring for surgical patients.

Both performance and attitude changed once the new assistant understood the situation and her role, and she was able to move quickly to a participatory role.

Attitudes and *needs of followers* are also influential factors in selecting a leadership style. Some workers are extremely dependent and prefer a highly structured environment in which they make very few decisions about work activities. This kind of worker is most comfortable with an authoritarian manager. Persons fitting into this category may be a great asset to the organization. They may be very reliable and willing workers who gladly perform the most difficult and distasteful assignments on request. New workers are likely to need a period of close supervision dur-

ing orientation, and the worker's preference for this structured situation may be temporary.

At the opposite end of the continuum is the follower who has a strong need for minimal structure and prefers to chart his or her own activities and decide what will be done. This person is less likely to relate closely with a group or team endeavor. This independent personality is usually driven to achieve and to master every situation and desires a manager who respects individual drives and ambitions and allows free rein. If the job situation is wrong for such a follower, he or she can be harmful to the organization.

Followers who perform best in a moderately structured environment are those who want to have a limited part in the decision-making process but who also allow others to make major decisions. They are usually competent workers who do not want constant overseeing but prefer democratic leadership that provides reassurance that they are performing correctly and well. In contrast to the follower who wants everything clearly spelled out, the follower who enjoys a participative relationship wants to know the goals but also wants to have a voice in how they will be achieved.

Flexibility of Managers to Use Various Leadership Styles

Ideally a manager will be able to (1) adequately assess the followers' characteristics and expectations; (2) identify the interpersonal relationships among the leader and followers, the tasks to be accomplished, and the degree of power to do the job; and (3) choose a leadership style that best fits the situation. If a manager's leadership style is relatively inflexible, he or she will function well only in certain situations. Such a limitation hampers an individual's career, for to use a manager who has only one leadership style an organization must adapt the job to the manager rather than the manager to the job.

Fiedler and Chemers[5] believe that leadership styles are inflexible and discourage reeducating managers to use different styles. Others, however, believe strongly that most managers can be extremely flexible in responding to influences in the work setting and that their behavior can be changed. For example, behavioral scientists Hersey, Blanchard, and Landy[15,16] believe that managers can develop the ability to select and use different leadership styles—from making decisions solely on their own to various degrees of group participation—in accordance with their analysis of the needs of the leader, followers, and work situation.

This book is based on the assumption that nurses who believe they have the potential to be flexible in their leadership style can learn to be effective as leaders in the different situations a nurse manager encounters.

Men's and Women's Leadership Styles

Differences in male and female leadership style were studied recently by Eagly, Makhijani, and Klonsky.[17] They found that women often use a different leadership style than men and that different styles can be a plus in the dynamic organizational world of the 1990s. Women tend to adopt a more democratic, participative style. They encourage consultation and exchange of ideas, share power and information, and seek to enhance group members' self-worth. Women tend to rely on their charisma, abilities, and networking and interpersonal skills to influence others toward goal achievement.

Conversely, the researchers found that men are more apt to be direct and to use a command and control style of leadership. They rely on the organization's formal authority structure and their assigned position for their base of influence. The researchers stated that today's organizational goals of flexibility, teamwork, trust, and information sharing are replacing the rigid structures of competitive individualism, control, and secrecy. The most effective managers listen, motivate, and support their teams; the researchers concluded that many women seem to do these things better than men. Thus the leadership styles that women typically use can afford them greater success at their jobs.

This chapter has introduced a number of leadership theories. A problem arises concerning how to make these theories relevant to an organization's need for effective leaders and managers. Clearly, the models and findings cannot provide with certainty the best answers about how to lead and to manage. However, theorists *can* offer the nurse leader and manager a basis on which to make sound decisions.

SUMMARY _____

1. Traits are the personal, psychologic, and physical characteristics identified in an individual.

2. According to Bennis, four common traits are common in successful leaders: management of attention, management of meaning, management of trust, and management of self.

3. Style is a particular form of behavior directly associated with an individual; leadership style is the way in which a leader uses interpersonal influences to accomplish goals.

4. Between 1910 and 1940, leaders were identified according to their traits. Since 1940, leaders have been assessed according to their behaviors.

5. The Ohio State studies in the 1940s described what successful leaders do. Researchers identified consideration for people and initiating structure as key dimensions of leadership behavior.

6. The Managerial Grid studied the relationship between leadership style and productivity. Researchers found that the employee-oriented manager has more productive workers than the task-oriented manager.

7. Fiedler and Chemers were largely concerned with the leadership situation. They believed that a leader's characteristics or traits are fixed and cannot be changed; therefore a specific kind of leader should be matched with a specific kind of environment.

8. The Path-Goal Theory states that the role of leader in eliciting work-goal–directed behavior consists of increasing personal rewards to workers for goal attainment and making the path to these payoffs easier by reducing barriers to goal achievement. The leader uses directive, supportive, participative, and achievement-oriented styles according to the situation. Unlike Fiedler and Chemers, House and associates believe that the leader can adapt his or her leadership style to the situation.

9. An authoritarian style of leadership/management varies from very rigid (highly structured, power ridden, leader oriented, and task centered) to benevolent (strong structure, with some consideration for workers and their preferences). The authoritarian style is most effective in crises when highly specialized skills are required and options for activities are limited.

10. A permissive, ultraliberal, or laissez-faire style of leadership/management functions with minimal structure in a free-rein environment, and leadership is relinquished by the leader to the followers. This style is most effective when independent activity is desired.

11. A democratic, participative, or consultive style of leadership/management is moderately structured and allows for group governance through collaboration or joint effort. This style is most useful in situations in which openness and trust prevail, all group members are capable of decision making, and there is time to function by majority rule.

12. Styles of leadership/management may appear separate and distinct, but in practice they are not. A manager functions in one style most of the time, but depending on individual flexibility and the circumstances, the leader may use combinations of all styles at one time.

13. One goal of an organization is for its managers to use a style of leadership that promotes a high level of work performance in a wide variety of circumstances as efficiently as possible and with the least amount of disruption. Effective nurse managers assess their individual styles and then work toward the adoption of those leadership styles that best complement the structural environment, tasks to be accomplished, and personnel involved. Management by situation is a process in which a leader chooses a behavioral approach that best fits his or her leadership style and expectations, the followers' characteristics and expectations, and the work situation.

14. The task of an effective manager is to work toward bringing as close together as possible all forces that influence the situation.

15. To accomplish the management process, the leader must know self, followers, and the character of the work situation and be flexible enough to make necessary adaptations or changes.

16. Three researchers found that women tend to adopt a more democratic, participative style of leadership than men and that the leadership styles women typically use afford them greater success at their jobs.

---

1. Think of the best leader you have ever known personally. In terms of traits, characteristics, style, and situational factors, why was that person a good leader?
2. Do you agree with the situational leadership theorists' claim that there is no one best style of leadership? Why or why not?
3. Summarize what the Ohio State Model, the Managerial Grid, Fiedler's Contingency Model, and the Path-Goal Theory have taught managers about leadership.
4. Assume that you are the department manager of a pediatric unit. You have observed that Cynthia, one of your staff RNs, becomes impatient and sometimes angry with noncompliant children. You walk into the room just as the RN shouts at a 4-year-old to "sit down and be quiet or you will be sorry!" State what your approach would be if you were (1) an authoritarian manager, (2) a permissive manager, or (3) a participative manager.
5. Do you ever feel that you have power? Over what situations? Where does the source of your power originate?

BEHAVIORAL OBJECTIVE
Determine what impact personal characteristics and traits have on leadership and management.

Rachel studied historical and contemporary concepts of leadership and management. She concluded that there are very few absolutes but that there are some facts and principles that may be applied to practice.

_____ 1. Rachel made the following assumptions about characteristics:
   a. There is a high correlation between verbosity and the ability to get the job done.
   b. One characteristic of a manager is the ability to organize the workload well.
   c. Assessment of personal characteristics is a reliable tool for determining a leader/manager's potential.
   d. There is good evidence that certain personal qualities favor success in the nursing managerial role.

_____ 2. As the nurse manager of an oncology unit, Rachel finds that her strongest areas of management lie in communications skills and her weakest in budgeting. She compensates for this weakness by enlisting the help of the agency controller. Which kind of management is Rachel using?
   a. Management of attention
   b. Management of meaning
   c. Management of trust
   d. Management of self

BEHAVIORAL OBJECTIVE
Compare and contrast the conclusions of the Ohio State Leadership Studies, the Managerial Grid, the Fiedler Contigency Model, and the Path-Goal Theory.

Grady was appointed to start up a live-in chemical dependency unit in the hospital. He was given freedom to use whichever behavioral style he thought best fit the situation.

_____ 3. Grady went into this project believing that people are basically good and trustworthy and can structure and carry out their own work satisfactorily with very little supervision. His philosophy best matches which style of leadership?
   a. The Fiedler Contingency Model
   b. The Managerial Grid
   c. The Ohio State Leadership Studies
   d. The Path-Goal Theory

_____ 4. Grady is still pondering over the best behavioral style for his chemical dependency unit. While he is deciding, he posts a bulletin for all staff to see, which recognizes staff achievements. Which behavioral style is Grady suggesting?
   a. The Ohio State Leadership Studies
   b. The Managerial Grid
   c. The Path-Goal Theory
   d. The Fiedler Contingency Model

BEHAVIORAL OBJECTIVE

Differentiate among authoritarian, democratic, and permissive styles of leadership and determine the style of leadership that best supports a successful managerial role.

Leslie manages a skilled nursing home that is staffed predominantly with nursing assistants.

_____ 5. Each of the RNs is assigned 20 patients with 3 experienced ancillary staff members. Which management style best suits the situation?
   a. Authoritarian
   b. Permissive
   c. Participative
   d. Closed

_____ 6. Leslie is making rounds one evening when a patient begins choking on his dinner. She cannot position him by herself to do the Heimlich maneuver. Which leadership style is most appropriate here?
   a. Authoritarian
   b. Permissive
   c. Participative
   d. Democratic

BEHAVIORAL OBJECTIVE

Interpret the process of management by situation.

Denise manages an orthopedic unit. Her staff members have diverse characteristics and abilities. She embraces situational leadership as appropriate for her unit and recognizes that it will take time, effort, and knowledge for her to move from one style to another.

_____ 7. Denise has decided that Carl has had sufficient training for the nurse manager role. Despite his hesitancy to work alone, she assigns him to serve as nurse manager on the next weekend. Which behavioral style is in effect?
   a. Telling
   b. Selling
   c. Participative
   d. Delegating

_____ 8. Nursing assistant Dan is new to orthopedic nursing and is unfamiliar with the use of a circular bed. After having him read the instructions, Denise demonstrates how to operate the bed. She follows up this procedure by having Dan operate the bed under her supervision. Which type of situational leadership did Denise use?
   a. Telling
   b. Selling
   c. Participating
   d. Delegating

REFERENCES

1. Kreitner R: *Management,* ed 5, Dallas, 1992, Houghton Mifflin.
2. Robbins S: *Essentials of organizational behavior,* ed 4, Englewood Cliffs, NJ, 1994, Prentice Hall.
3. Barney J, Griffin R: *The management of organizations,* Dallas, 1992, Houghton Mifflin.
4. Adler N: *International dimensions of organizational behavior,* ed 2, Belmont, Calif, 1991, Wadsworth Publishing.
5. Galbraith J and others: *Organizing for the future: the new logic for managing complex organizations,* San Francisco, 1993, Jossey-Bass.
6. Lewin K, Lippitt R, White R: Patterns of aggressive behavior in experimentally created social climates, *J Sociol Psychol* 10(2):271-299, 1939 (historical).
7. Likert R: *The human organization,* New York, 1967, McGraw-Hill.
8. McGregor D: Leadership motivation: essays of Douglas McGregor, Cambridge, Mass, 1968, MIT Press. (Edited by Warren Bennis and Edgar Schein with the collaboration of Carolyn McGregor.) (historical)
9. House R, Oakley J: Personality and charismatic leadership, *Leadership Q* pp. 224-229, Summer 1992.
10. Tannenbaum R, Schmidt W: How to choose a leadership pattern, *Harv Bus Rev* 55(5):162-164, 1973.
11. Fiedler F, Chemers M: *Leadership and effective management,* Glenview Ill, 1974, Scott, Foresman & Co.
12. Health Care Advisory Board: *Nurse recruitment and retention,* Washington, DC, 1987, The Board.
13. DeCrosta A: Meeting the nurse retention challenge: an interview with Connie Curran, *Nursing 89* 19(5):170-171, 1989.
14. Hersey P, Blanchard K: *Management of organizational behavior: utilizing human resources,* ed 5, Englewood Cliffs, NJ, 1988, Prentice Hall.
15. Hersey P, Blanchard K: *Management of organizational behavior: utilizing human resources,* ed 5, Englewood Cliffs, NJ, 1988, Prentice Hall.
16. Mathis L, Jackson J: *Human resource management,* ed 7, Minneapolis/St Paul, 1994, West Publishing.
17. Eagly A, Makhijani M, Klonsky B: Gender and evaluation of leaders: a meta-analysis, *Psychol Bull* 1(1):3-22, 1992.

SUGGESTED READINGS

Adams C: The impact of problem-solving styles of NE-CRO pairs on nurse executive effectiveness, *J Nurs Adm* 24(11):17-21, 1994.
Bates S, Fosbinder D: Using an interview guide to identify effective nurse managers, *J Nurs Adm* 24(45):33-38, 1994.
Brandt M: Caring leadership: secret and path to success, *Nurs Manage* 25(8):68-72, 1994.
Curtin L: Leadership in tough times, *Nurs Manage* 25(11):7-8, 1994.
Gregory C: Creating a vision for a nursing unit, *Nurs Manage* 26(1):38-41, 1995.
Hrezo R, Witte R: Leadership: moving into the twenty-first century, *OR Ambu Surg* 24(5):196Q-197Q, 1993.
Johnson J and others: Succession management: a model for developing nursing leaders, *Nurs Manage* 25(6):50-55, 1994.
Klakovich M: Connective leadership for the 21st century: a historical perspective and future directions, *Adv Nurs Sci* 16(4):42-54, 1994.
Loraine K: Leadership from the child within, *Nurs Manage* 26(2):57-58, 1995.
Puetz B, Thomas D: Bridging a gap between administrators and staff, *RN* 58(1):19, 1995.
Tyrrell R: Visioning: an important management tool, *Nurs Econ* 12(2):92-95, 1994.
Wheeler K, Barrett E: Review and synthesis of selected nursing studies on teaching empathy and implications for nursing research and education, *Nurs Outlook* 42(5):230-236, 1994.

ORGANIZATIONAL STRUCTURE and MANAGEMENT SYSTEMS

BEHAVIORAL OBJECTIVES

On completion of this chapter, the student will be prepared to:

- Give reasons for organizational structure and its composition. Identify significant factors that influence organizational relationships.

- Compare the advantages and disadvantages of the bureaucratic and human relations approaches to organization and management.

- Explain the rationale for selecting an organizational structure and management system.

- Differentiate between retrospective and prospective systems and give examples of each.

- Compare and contrast current provisions for healthcare and evaluate reform proposals.

- Cite the degree to which healthcare costs have risen in the past three decades.

- State the purpose of most healthcare institutions.

- Differentiate between government-owned, voluntary, and proprietary hospitals.

- Describe a typical urban or rural magnet hospital.

- Describe a hospital merger and its implications for the nurse manager.

- Define public health services and explain the role of the community health nurse.

- Define home health agencies and the role of visiting nurses.

- Describe a hospital that meets the standards of the Joint Commission on Accreditation of Health Care Organizations (JCAHO).

Professional people will spend most of their professional lives working in organizations, either as staff members, managers, or both. This chapter is about organizations—why they are formed and how they are managed, the impact of healthcare reform on organizations, and how nurse managers can best help organizations respond to these reforms and set and achieve their goals.

Nurses practice in many different types of organizations, most of which focus primarily on the provision of healthcare services, such as hospitals, clinics, **health maintenance organizations (HMOs),** public health agencies, nursing homes, skilled nursing facilities, community mental health centers, and neighborhood health centers. Other organizations with different primary purposes may use nurses as one part of their system. For example, nurses are employed in prisons, schools, day-care centers, and businesses and industries. Nursing services vary widely from highly specialized care to preventive treatment. Regardless of the services rendered, nurses function within the existing organizational structure, both formal and informal. Because most nurses are employed in hospitals, this chapter focuses primarily on nursing management in hospitals. Other healthcare settings are discussed where appropriate.

ORGANIZATIONS AND ORGANIZATIONAL STRUCTURE

Common Characteristics of an Organization

An **organization** signifies an institution or functional group such as a business, government agency, or hospital or other healthcare agency with a formal intentional structure of roles or positions. The term *organization* also refers to the process of organizing, or the way in which work is arranged and allocated among the members of an institution so that the goals of the enterprise can be efficiently achieved. Organizations share four characteristics: (1) a common goal or purpose, (2) coordination of effort, (3) division of labor, and (4) an established delegation of authority.[1]

The strength of an organization lies in its ability to marshal resources to attain a goal while remaining flexible enough to allow for creativity and growth. The purpose and goals of an organization determine the way it is organized. For example, hospitals and other such agencies are created to provide healthcare. They accomplish these goals by first dividing the work among groups and individuals and then linking the subparts together. Providing healthcare services requires the combined knowledge, coordination, and control of enormous numbers of people and resources, which enables goals to be met that would otherwise be difficult or even impossible to reach (Box 3-1).

Formal and Informal Structure

Each organization has both a formal and an informal structure that determines work and interpersonal relationships. The formal structure is usually highly planned and publicized, whereas the informal structure is unplanned and likely to be concealed. This chapter focuses on the formal structure. Informal or covert structure is discussed in Chapter 8.

Organizational structure refers to the process or way a group is formed and its channels of authority, span of control, and lines of communication.[1] It is the basic framework of positions, groups of positions, reporting relationships, and interaction patterns that an organization adopts to carry out its strategy. As Figure 3-1 shows, there are five elements of organizational structure: (1) designing jobs, (2) forming departments and work units, (3) creating a hierarchy, (4) forming a span of control, (5) and coordinating and integrating activities.

Job design

The first element of organizational structure is the design of jobs so that both employer and employee understand what is expected and what degree of authority each has. For example, the vice president of nursing services or a director in an executive role needs to have responsibility for and control over the entire continuum of nursing services—acute, chronic, wellness, prevention, and long-term—as they apply to the agency. If part of the responsibility is withheld, the position is weakened. Likewise, the functions and authority of each job in the entire institution must be clearly delineated.

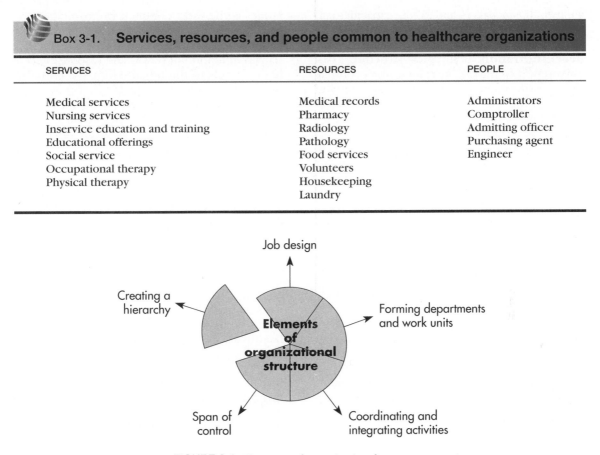

Box 3-1.   Services, resources, and people common to healthcare organizations

SERVICES	RESOURCES	PEOPLE
Medical services	Medical records	Administrators
Nursing services	Pharmacy	Comptroller
Inservice education and training	Radiology	Admitting officer
Educational offerings	Pathology	Purchasing agent
Social service	Food services	Engineer
Occupational therapy	Volunteers	
Physical therapy	Housekeeping	
	Laundry	

FIGURE 3-1. Elements of organizational structure.

Departments and units

After an organization has determined how to structure various jobs, it must decide how to arrange them into logical departments or units. Nursing, for example, is usually divided according to specialty areas (e.g., medical, surgical, intensive care, coronary care). Other departments are labeled according to their services (e.g., laboratory, radiology).

Hierarchy

Once an organization determines its job design and arrangement of departments, it develops a network of reporting relationships. This involves the creation of a **hierarchy,** which is a pattern of reporting relationships throughout an organization. An organization's hierarchy serves two

purposes: (1) to specify which positions are responsible for which areas of operations, and (2) to specify the authority of different positions relative to one another. Those with the greatest decision-making authority are at the top, and those with the least authority are at the bottom.

Span of control

Span of control can be defined as the number of persons who report directly to the manager. Considerations that enter into the question of how many managers are needed for a specific number of workers include: (1) the level in the organization in which the work takes place, (2) the geographic location, (3) the nature of the work being performed, (4) the abilities and availability of the managers, and (5) the capacities and self-direction of the followers. For nurses the span of control is usually well delineated through **decentralization.** In a typical structure, assistants report to nursing directors, area coordinators or supervisors report to the assistants, and on down the line in the chain of command, including nurse managers, nurse case managers, team leaders, primary care nurses, and other staff nurses. The ratio of nurse managers to followers varies with rank or level. The higher the rank or level, the greater the number of employees for which the manager is responsible (e.g., vice president or director of nursing services). The lower the rank or level (e.g., team leader), the fewer the number of persons assigned to the manager's span of control.

The span of control is controlled to allow improved communication, efficiency, and coordination. Too wide a span may mean that the managers are overextending themselves and that the workers or followers are receiving too little guidance or control. The managers may feel harassed and frustrated in trying to deal as best they can with all their responsibilities. Too narrow a span of control may mean that managers are underused and that workers or followers are overcontrolled, which results in a waste of human resources.

Coordinating and integrating activities

Creating a hierarchy and distributing authority involves establishing vertical relationships up and down the organizational structure. In addition, attention must be focused on horizontal relationships across the organizational structure. The degree of coordination and integration that an organization needs is determined by the extent to which its people and groups are interdependent or how much they must rely on one another to get their work done. Nursing activities are highly coordinated and integrated, with one individual or group depending on another for cooperation.

Centralization and Decentralization

The two major forms of organizational structure are (1) *centralized control* and (2) a *decentralized* or *participatory* approach. The centralized

model is the most common in hospitals; however, decentralized organizational structures are gaining popularity.[2] **Centralization** is the systematic retention of power and responsibility at higher levels of the organization. Decentralization is the systematic delegation of power and responsibility to middle and lower levels of the organization. Few organizations are fully centralized or decentralized; some are made up more of one form than the other.

Impact of computer-based information

The traditional definition of centralization and decentralization assumes that decentralization of management requires upper-level managers to relinquish control. This is no longer true with the development of a sophisticated computer-based information system. Decisions can be decentralized yet be closely monitored by top management through the monitoring capability of its computer system. There are very few healthcare settings not equipped with a computer system for instant retrieval of relevant information and a fax machine for immediate delivery of and replies to documents and messages. With these devices, management can become less formal and more decentralized without giving up control.[3]

Advantages and disadvantages of a centralized organization

The advantages of the centralized form are twofold. First, it can be highly cost-effective, because the special services are grouped together, which eliminates duplication of effort. Second, it makes management easier, because managers need to be experts in only a concentrated range of skills.

The disadvantage of the centralized structure is that as the organization becomes larger and more complex, the hierarchical arrangement can prove to be cumbersome. For example, a hospital may have a single department of nursing, yet within the department there may be specialties such as open-heart surgery, oncology, burn center, trauma, and neonatal intensive care. This much responsibility in the hands of a single department head dilutes the attention that is given to each department. Another drawback is that this arrangement does not readily adapt to change. Obtaining quick decisions or actions on specific problems may require more time because such decisions must be made by higher level managers.[2]

Advantages and disadvantages of a decentralized organization

The decentralized or participatory approach is a behavioral system in which the large structures are broken down into smaller units and authority is delegated to those closer to the majority of workers. Each under the control of its supervisor and director of nursing services, traditional nursing specialties (e.g., medical, surgical, pediatrics, labor and delivery) are made into departments on a par with other hospital departments such as laboratory, dietary, and social services (Figure 3-2). Top management still retains ultimate responsibility for the operations of the various hospital departments, but planning and implementation for each department is carried out by the department head, who functions autonomously and with authority to administer that department 24 hours a day. The types of decisions to be decentralized are important and include who controls the budget; who has power over hiring and firing; who handles disciplinary measures, promotions, and transfers; and who handles disputes between staff and management.

The advantages of decentralization can be very positive. As middle managers, the department heads can (1) reflect their interests and have a voice in decision making, (2) improve quality of care through 24-hour continuity, (3) increase communication between and within departments, (4) have better interpersonal relationships, and (5) problem solve with greater imagination and creativity because the members know what improves patient care in their areas.

One disadvantage of decentralization could be the initial cost in developing managers and training staff; however, turnover rate under decentralization has been found to be low, and the time, effort, and skill needed to make the system work has proved advantageous. The most serious problem that can occur is a communication breakdown.

Organizational Charts

An **organizational chart** is meaningful only to the extent that the system represented on paper is a reality. Its precision sometimes masks what is actually occurring in an institution. Hierarchies are far more complex than the average description would indicate. Most observers agree that the dynamic levels throughout the hospital organization are those that occur through informal day-to-day interactions, not through periodic maneuvering of structural arrangements. Important considerations include to what degree the formal organization is consistent with what actually occurs and to what degree the hierarchy obstructs or serves the organizational purpose.[2]

One's understanding of a given organizational structure can be tested by using the form provided in Figure 3-3. Assume that you are a team leader. List those persons with whom you have professional contact in a given day or time, and identify the nature of your relationship with them within the organizational structure of the agency. This relationship or experience may consist of the following exchanges:

Team leader and dietitian	Discussion of need for change in diet for a patient who is not tolerating present food
Team leader and nursing assistant	Discussion about assistant's failure to ambulate a patient
Team leader and physician	Telephone conversation about patient's progress
Team leader and director of nursing service	Discussion about general work conditions
Team leader and nurse manager	Discussion about need for more nursing personnel on healthcare team

If, after completing the exercise, you are hazy about some lines of authority and uncertain about which of the responses is appropriate, then the organizational structure provided is inoperative and needs further clarification.

The use of such an exercise can dramatize the wide variety of relationships that exist in an organization. Such an exercise may also clearly indicate that a large part of one's time is oriented at the same level or downward rather than upward, where authority is thought to be. Analysis also suggests that authority does not always reside at

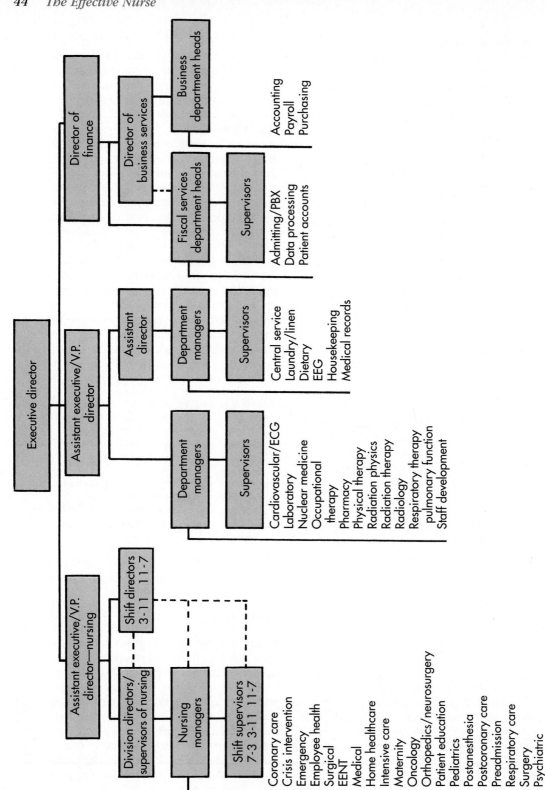

FIGURE 3-2. Organizational structure under a decentralized or participatory approach.

1	2	3	4	5
Name of person with whom you had contact	His or her role in the organization	Who made the initial contact?	Reason for the communication	Relationship within the organizational structure*
Joan Atkins	Pharmacist	Pharmacist	Drug requested not available	b, c

*Place the letter(s) of your response in column 5.

a. Above me in chain of command, but I do not report directly to him/her.

b. Above me in chain of command, and I report directly to him/her.

c. An associate, on the same level with me.

d. He/she is under my direct control.

e. I guide this person's activities, but he/she reports to another person.

f. This person is a part of the organization, but I have no formal control over him/her or he/she over me.

g. A patient, client, or representative.

FIGURE 3-3. Analysis of contracts with hospital personnel in relation to organizational structure. (Modified from Brown D: Looking into nursing leadership. In *The professional nurse looks at authority and hierarchy.* Washington, DC, 1966, Leadership Resources.)

the top of the organization, as the typical organizational structure would indicate; instead it may be found at all levels. There is immense power throughout any organizational structure. The nurse manager needs to be aware of the system and its significance in relation to activities inherent in the role.

Organizational Designs
Bureaucratic approach to management

Sociologist Max Weber[4] and management writers Frederick Taylor[5] and Henri Fayol were major contributors to the so-called scientific or classical approach of **bureaucracy,** a centralized, hierarchical structure based on legalized, formal authority. Most hospitals are structured according to this mechanical design because modern managers believe that the bureaucratic format offers a model for placing large numbers of people with diversified skills and abilities into an easily identifiable and programmed structure. Members of a bureaucratic organization are guided in their actions by (1) rules and regulations, (2) specialization of tasks and division of labor, (3) appointment by merit, and (4) an impersonal climate. Weber praised bureaucracy for its rationality, its clear chain of command, and its impartiality. He also admired the clear specification of authority and responsibility, which he believed made it easier for the organization to evaluate performance and distribute rewards fairly.

Rules and regulations. Weber saw the need for a consistent system of rules and regulations that pertained to the rights and duties of personnel in different positions. All bureaucracies have rules and regulations for each office, which ensures accountability and promotes impersonality. The system usually takes the form of policies, bylaws, procedures, and committees. Ideally, each office has representation in the formulation of the rules and regulations, which provides uniformity and coordination. The basic rationale for rules and regulations is that the manager can use them to promote efficiency, which is the overpowering and central goal of bureaucracy, and to eliminate uncertainty in task performance resulting from individual differences. When em-

ployees know who is to do what, and when and how they are to do it, they feel more secure.

The bureaucratic organizational design is still evident today in many healthcare institutions. Policy and procedure manuals are common in hospitals. Various formats are used, but each supplies information on policy and on each major job, outlining its requirements, limitations, and relationships to other jobs in the enterprise. Such manuals are particularly important in nursing because of the vast differences in preparation, titles, and licensing. Among the personnel are assistants, licensed practical or vocational nurses, and registered nurses. Although there is much overlap in nursing functions, there is also a need to establish guidelines to ensure that nurses function at their capacity on the basis of educational preparation and within legal limits. The bureaucratic manager needs to know the precise limits of his or her sphere of responsibility and competency to avoid infringing on that of others. For example, the nurse manager can exercise leadership with assurance when it is known where his or her responsibility begins and ends.

Specialization and division of labor. One goal of specialization and division of labor is to produce more and better work with the same effort, in the belief that it is natural for personnel to become expert in and responsible for the performance of their specific duties.[5] Technical ability qualifies a person for a given office and protects him or her against arbitrary dismissal. The need for division of labor is probably the primary reason for establishing organizational structure. When there is more to be accomplished than any one person can do, the usual procedure is to assess the activities necessary for accomplishment of overall objectives, divide them, and assign them to departments that perform the specialized functions. This is called *departmentalization* or **decentralization** and is demonstrated in the typical organizational structure shown in Figure 3-2. As with span of control, decentralization should be considered according to (1) purpose, (2) functions, (3) persons and things, and (4) territory or geographic location.[6] However, in healthcare facilities decentralization is almost always made on a functional or task-oriented basis and incorporates the benefits of specialization, such as operating room, radiologic, medical, surgical, and nursing services. A disadvantage of decentralization is that sometimes little kingdoms are established and create conflicts when vested interests take precedence over attainment of institutional goals. Problems of coordination also become more complex as changes occur and departments multiply.

Appointment by merit. Employment and promotions within a bureaucracy are made on the basis of seniority and achievement. Employees who accept the objectives of the organization and produce the quality and quantity of services desired receive higher financial rewards, benefits, and status.

Impersonality. Weber believed that a manager should be formal in attitudes and without affection or enthusiasm. He thought that emotional attachments would interfere with rational decisions. Weber's ideas of relationships with people neglect the human aspects of organization members; they are assumed to be motivated only by basic economic incentives. As the educational levels, affluence, and work expectations of organization members have risen over time, this criticism of Weber's ideas has become more severe.

Human relations or participatory approach to management

The **human relations** (or participatory) movement was a pointed effort to make managers more sensitive to their employees' needs. It developed as a result of two very different historic influences—unionization and studies of human relations.

Unionization. From the late 1800s to the 1920s, U.S. industry increased rapidly in an attempt to meet the many demands of a burgeoning population. Cheap labor was readily available, and there was a seller's market for finished goods. However, the Great Depression of the 1930s left millions unemployed. Many people considered business the culprit, which caused sympathy to turn from management to labor. Congress passed the Wagner Act in 1935, which legalized union-management collective bargaining. Management began to seek ways to quell the

pressure for all-out unionization. Unionization began to filter into nursing, although at a much slower rate than in industry.[7]

Studies of human relations. Early behavioral and human relations researchers attempted to deal with what they viewed as the major inadequacy of the classic bureaucratic model—the neglect of the human element in the organization. They argued that an industrial organization has two objectives: economic effectiveness *and* employee satisfaction.[3] The basic principle of the human relations approach is that when things go well for the worker, the organization profits. Two factors are distinguishable in the human relations approach. First, certain leadership characteristics are associated with productivity and good management. Second, emphasis is placed on the worker, particularly as a member of a work group.

Study of the human relations approach began in the late nineteenth century and focused on democratic structure, multidirectional communications, and promotion of general satisfaction of the worker. Self-development, individualization, initiative, and creativity were identified as attributes to be promoted and encouraged. Several researchers have made significant contributions to the humanistic approach.

Mayo-Hawthorne studies. From 1927 to 1932, Mayo and his Harvard associates[8] conducted the famous **Mayo-Hawthorne studies** of human behavior in work situations in a Western Electric plant. They discovered that productivity is likely to increase when special attention is given to workers by management, regardless of changes in the working conditions; this phenomenon is called the Hawthorne effect. They also found that informal work groups and an informal social environment among employees, which allow for group decision making, greatly influence productivity. For Mayo and his associates, the concept of the social man wanting on-the-job relationships had to replace Weber's concept of the rational man who is motivated by personal economic needs. They did not argue against the bureaucratic structure but proposed that improvements be made by making the structure less formal and by permitting more employee participation in decision making. The

Hawthorne effect can occur in a variety of areas. For example, the Clinton administration and several congressional leaders attribute the decline in healthcare price inflation from 7.4% to 5.4% to it. They assign the lowered costs to scrutiny, which stimulated a desired change in behavior.[9]

Follett studies. With a background in law, political science, and philosophy, Follett[10] served as a management consultant until her death in 1933. She had a strong conviction that managers should know that each employee is a complex collection of emotions, beliefs, attitudes, and habits. She believed that to get employees to work harder, managers must recognize the motivating desires of the individual. Follett urged managers to motivate performance rather than simply demand it (Figure 3-4). Historians credit Follett with being decades ahead of her time.[11]

McGregor studies. As mentioned in Chapter 2, McGregor[12] believes that the vertical division of labor that characterizes bureaucratic organizations is partly based on a set of negative assumptions that many managers have about workers. He refers to these assumptions as Theory X, in which managers believe that workers have little ambition, desire security above everything else, and avoid work unless coerced. Therefore a rigid, formal hierarchy is designed to control employees. McGregor suggests that organizations can meet their goals much more effectively if they attend to the human needs of organization members and use their potential. He developed Theory Y, a set of assumptions about the worker that is compatible with the human relations approach. According to Theory Y, workers can enjoy work, and, if conditions are favorable, they will exercise self-control over their performance. Individuals are motivated by opportunities to interact with their superiors rather than by financial rewards alone. According to McGregor, personal goals can be achieved through formal organizational structure, policies, and goals.

Argyris's structure. Argyris[13] states that in most formal organizations, managers have almost complete responsibility for planning, organizing, directing, and evaluating the work of their employees. For example, bureaucratic managers often have complete authority to set work schedules and reward, discipline, or dismiss employees. Argyris contends that such domination causes workers to lose heart and become passive and dependent. He maintains that when the human needs of self-reliance, self-expression, and self-fulfillment are not met, workers become dissatisfied and frustrated and cause trouble or leave, which increases costs. Argyris suggests an organizational design that allows workers a much greater degree of independence and decision-making power and creates a more informal and flexible organizational climate. He also favors the formation of teams for special projects. This type of structure is known as the matrix organizational structure.

Maslow's theory. Dr. Abraham Maslow,[14] a noted psychologist and the father of motivation theory, determined that people can best be understood by studying human needs and their influence on behavior. His theory has probably received more attention and application to organizational environments than any other because his classifications have direct implications for managing human behavior in an organization. Maslow says that a human is an ever-wanting creature; as one need is satisfied, another appears to take its place. The individual is then motivated to satisfy the new need. Maslow developed a hierarchy of needs on the basis of his clinical experiences. Figure 3-5 provides an example of these needs and suggestions regarding how they relate to a member of an organization.

FIGURE 3-4. Follett's concept of motivation and management.

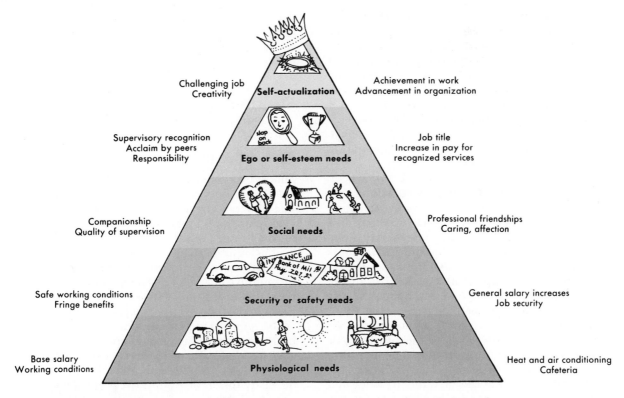

Challenging job
Creativity

Achievement in work
Advancement in organization

Self-actualization

Supervisory recognition
Acclaim by peers
Responsibility

Job title
Increase in pay for
recognized services

Ego or self-esteem needs

Companionship
Quality of supervision

Professional friendships
Caring, affection

Social needs

Safe working conditions
Fringe benefits

General salary increases
Job security

Security or safety needs

Base salary
Working conditions

Heat and air conditioning
Cafeteria

Physiological needs

FIGURE 3-5. Maslow's Hierarchy of Needs applied to members of an organization.

Note that the hierarchy is arranged in a triangle that illustrates the needs of each person: (1) physiologic needs, (2) security or safety needs, (3) social needs, (4) ego or self-esteem needs, and (5) self-actualization or self-fulfillment needs. The hierarchy of needs theory indicates that an individual must first satisfy the lower level needs before realizing higher level needs. It is possible to move in and out of the levels according to an individual's current needs. The strength and priority of these needs will vary with each person. Furthermore, what motivates a person at one time may have no motivation for that same person at another time. Another way to look at the pyramid is to vary the thickness of the layers according to different attitudes, values, and perceptions of life.

Likert's studies. Likert[15, 16] shares the views of McGregor, Argyris, and Maslow. In his research on effective group performance, he found that traditional authoritarian manages are less able to

motivate their staff to high standards of achievement than are managers who promote their staff's feelings of worth and importance. Likert created an organizational model that includes bureaucratic methods in which organizations and managers are held accountable for their group's performance. This model also provides for a system in which (1) supportive relationships are encouraged, (2) group decision making occurs when appropriate, and (3) high performance goals are set. The principle of supportive relationships suggests that attending to one another's needs should add to a sense of personal worth and importance among individual members. Through the use of group decision making and high performance goals, managers can help group members feel that they are responsible for decisions affecting them and are an integral part of the organization. The setting and attainment of high performance goals enables organization members to develop a sense of pride and accomplishment.

Advantages of the human relations approach to management. The human relations approach makes it clear that people are the key to productivity. According to the advocates of this approach, technology, work rules, and standards do not guarantee good job performance. Success depends on motivated and skilled individuals who are committed to organizational objectives. Only a manager's sensitivity to individual concerns can foster the cooperation necessary for high productivity.[3]

Limitations of the human relations approach to management. A common limitation of the human relations approach is that most managers function within a bureaucratic environment in which one organizational design is adopted and employee individualism is not encouraged. Also, opponents believe that a truly democratic approach is time consuming and that work goals may not be met, particularly when the objectives of lower-level employees are not consistent with the goals at the top level or power base of the organization. Furthermore, some individual differences are overlooked because not everyone can or wants to work in a moderately structured environment. Some persons prefer the security of strong control and clearly defined activities and limits.

Adoption of an Appropriate Organizational Structure and Management System

Selection of an organizational structure and mangement system is crucial to the efficiency and effectiveness of the organization. The structure and system selected must match the purposes and goals of the organization and be compatible with the needs of those charged with their achievement. The consequences of an inappropriate structure and management system include inefficiency, high cost, unrest, dissatisfaction, or even outright failure of the organization. Rarely is one structure or system used exclusively; after selection of a system there can be many changes, because an organization is a dynamic process with a continuous need for appraisal and adaptation. In Box 3-2, the bureaucratic and human relations approaches are represented in the extreme. One

can readily see that parts of each system are present in any organized structure and management system.

HEALTHCARE REFORM AND ITS IMPACT ON ORGANIZATIONAL STRUCTURE

State of Affairs

Almost everyone in America is concerned about healthcare because it impacts everyone's life. The federal government, state government, healthcare providers, most nursing organizations, and some of the general public are alert to healthcare reform and its implications. In 1994, the battles over healthcare reform resulted in a resounding defeat of President Clinton's proposal that healthcare be made available to all regardless of ability to pay and that most employers be required to provide their employees with health insurance. The recent Republican gains in state and federal governments ensure that any future efforts for healthcare reform will need to be vastly different from those previously proposed. Congressional factions are likely to mount strong opposition to any suggestion of dismantling the for-profit insurance industry or of legislating employer mandates for healthcare coverage.

Predictions

Healthcare reform through managed competition will likely gain more advocates and prevail over future efforts to introduce a single-payer system or a national health insurance plan. Although some initial steps will be taken to achieve wider access to healthcare, universal coverage probably will remain an unrealized long-term goal. The **American Nurses Association** (ANA) probably will continue to advocate universal healthcare coverage while working with the new congressional majority to achieve some extension of access to care.[17]

Nurses' Responsibility

Registered nurses must become adept at understanding and negotiating the **healthcare sys-**

> **Box 3-2. Comparison of characteristics of bureaucratic and human relations approaches to organizational structure and management systems**

BUREAUCRATIC APPROACH (CONSERVATIVE, TECHNICAL, SCIENTIFIC)	HUMAN RELATIONS APPROACH (DEMOCRATIC, PARTICIPATIVE, LIBERAL)
Control is organizational.	Control is democratic or participatory.
Leaders are appointed by head(s) or hierarchy.	Leaders are approved by followers.
Directions are one-way; nonquestioning obedience is demanded.	Communication system is open, multidirectional.
Organization manipulates employer needs and serves its goals; loyalty is to organizational goals.	Goals are consistent with individual goals; otherwise workers' first loyalty is to profession; second to organization.
Workers at each level are viewed as objects to be used interchangeably to complete the work.	Workers are matched carefully with work assignment; value is given to individualism, self-control, initiative, and creativity.
Manager is a controller.	Manager is a facilitator.
Personnel are manipulated; management defines objectives.	Natural work groups define own objectives.
Class and class status structure lead to job satisfaction.	Acceptance as part of a stable group leads to satisfaction.
Physiologic factors (e.g., strength, speed, skill) produce fluctuations in production.	Social conditions (e.g., acceptance, common interests) determine level of production.
Workers relate to the organization individually.	Members of small groups relate to one another and then to the organization.
Job fragmentation and specialization occur.	Individual behavior is subject to the group.
Economic factors are the primary motivation; emphasis is on quantity of output in least amount of time.	Social forces and quality of service are more important than economic factors.

tems and in seeking ways to overcome barriers to needed care, both for the patients' sake and for the nurses' protection. Hospital restructuring and managed competition plans often place the nurse in a compromising position. For example, some nurse managers are expected to place more emphasis on dismissing patients from a healthcare setting than on providing what is best for the patients.

Nurses must be alert to what is happening around them and maintain close contact with their legal representatives. The ANA is working with the National Labor Relations Act and collective bargaining agencies to ensure that nurses' interests are considered and protected. Nurse leaders should face healthcare restructuring optimistically and view this period in nursing's history as an opportunity for nurses to participate in reshaping the healthcare system.[18]

HEALTHCARE REIMBURSEMENT SYSTEMS

It would be difficult to overstate the extent of change that has affected healthcare delivery systems during the last decade. In the early 1980s, hospitals and community health agencies experienced a revenue squeeze imposed by **third-party payers**. Hospitals struggled with rapidly increasing labor and technology costs and declining inpatient revenues. Added to this struggle has been competition from groups such as health maintenance organizations (HMOs) and private-sector delivery systems (e.g., surgicenters, urgent care units, diagnostic facilities, outpatient clinics).

Retrospective Payment Systems

Retrospective payment for health services is reimbursement made to healthcare providers *af-*

ter the services have been given. Some government services and private insurance companies have used this system. An example of retrospective payment is the Johnson administration's "Great Society" program, which resulted in Public Law No. 89-97—the Social Security Amendments of 1965—that established Titles XVIII (Medicare) and XIX (Medicaid) of the Social Security Act.[19] Private-sector organizations, including health insurance agencies such as Blue Cross and Blue Shield, HMOs, and **preferred provider organizations** (PPOs), also received retroactive payments. Under the retrospective payment plan, hospitals were encouraged to promote extended hospital stays, because the longer patients were hospitalized, the higher the revenue and the greater the profits. Physicians also reaped benefits from extended stays through greater reimbursement for services.[20]

I have attended meetings sponsored by government officials and addressed to physicians and hospital administrators, admonishing them to curtail the length of hospital stay (LOS) of their patients and to seek ways to reduce costs during hospitalization. Physicians and hospital administrators were warned that unless they found ways to resolve the problem, the government would find a solution. Hospitals, however, have been slow to respond.

Prospective Payment System and Diagnosis-Related Groups

In 1983 Public Law 98-21, a Social Security Amendment, was passed, providing hospital reimbursement under Part A of the Medicare program. This bill revolutionized the healthcare system. It provided for **prospective payment** for hospital services given to Medicare patients rather than the previous method of retrospective reimbursement by which most healthcare bills were covered. The prospective payment system (PPS) was gradually phased into hospitals beginning in 1983 and set payment levels on services *before* they were provided. Four hundred sixty-seven different **diagnosis-related groups** (DRGs) were identified. The Health Care Financing Administration (HCFA) used Medicare data from previous years to determine a fixed payment for each DRG. Under this system, a hospital is paid a flat fee for the treatment of a patient

with a given diagnosis. As a result, hospitals now have an incentive to control costs, because if their costs are below the prospective payment reimbursement, they may keep the difference; if the costs are higher, hospitals must absorb the difference and face a break-even or lose situation.[6] The PPS firmly moved the delivery of healthcare into the business world, where the ability to compete is essential to survival. The implications for nursing services are grave.[21] Nurse managers are challenged to seek ways to provide quality care within a stringent budget (see Chapter 10).

Managed Care and Managed Competition

The traditional approach to providing employees with healthcare benefits has been through health insurance purchased from insurance carriers such as Mutual of Omaha, State Farm, Blue Cross, and Blue Shield. According to the United States Chamber of Commerce, the average employee receives $3600 for health-related benefits. All healthcare plans depend on the principles of **managed care** and **managed competition.** By definition, managed care represents an integration of healthcare financing with the provision of care. It replaces the unregulated structure of care delivery in which financing and care provision were separate. Managed competition is an economic strategy to reform the healthcare system by stimulating price competition and quality improvement.

In both public and private sectors, managed care systems are currently considered by the majority to be the most logical approach to cost containment. Price competition provides strong incentives to hospitals and other healthcare agencies to constantly seek ways to minimize the costs of their products and services so that they can be priced competitively and sold in the marketplace. To keep production at a minimum, agencies must be innovative in their use of capital and labor and find the least costly number and combination of resources to produce their products.[22] However, some hospitals and other healthcare providers and many physicians strongly oppose price competition because of the threat it would pose to those whose costs are high or those who are not providing a high-level quality of care. Instead, many physicians and hospitals favor a regulatory approach to govern the economic activity of healthcare, which is an approach they have controlled and used to monopolize the provider market. This has permitted them to raise prices and compete only on the basis of amenities and other less risky and nonprice mechanisms.

Faced with spiraling costs for healthcare benefits, employers are using a variety of managed care strategies to contain costs. Examples are copayment, self-funding, utilization review, HMOs, and PPOs. Other cost-management efforts include providing preventive health and physical wellness programs and encouraging employees and their families to have more healthy lifestyles. All of these measures have a significant impact on healthcare organizations, because as the bulk of healthcare gradually moves away from hospitals into satellite or outlying facilities or into home endeavors, the hospital structure is affected and must face the issues squarely or go under.[22]

Health maintenance organizations

A health maintenance organization is a major force in the health industry. It is a managed care system in which healthcare services are provided on the basis of fixed monthly charges for each enrollee. The HMO can be either nonprofit or for-profit, and prevention as well as correction is emphasized. Secure Horizons is an example of an HMO. With this type of HMO, the senior citizen continues to pay Part B of Medicare and signs the fee over to Secure Horizons. By contractual agreement with the government, they in return assume responsibility for a full range of healthcare services with few limitations.[23]

Preferred provider organizations

Preferred provider organizations (PPOs) are another cost containment strategy of a managed care system. They are modified HMOs that provide healthcare for a lower cost when the enrollee uses participating providers, who are paid on the basis of negotiated or discount rates. A healthcare provider contracts with an employer or an employer group to provide healthcare services to employees at a competitive rate. Hospital-based PPOs and groups of physicians who

sign with a PPO have the assurance of a continuing source of options, even though employees have the freedom to go to other providers if they want to pay the difference in costs.[23]

The Omnibus Budget Reconciliation Act

Since 1966 healthcare policy has been left to the whim of the congressional budget process, culminating in the 1980s with annual budget reconciliation acts. The **Omnibus Budget Reconciliation Act** (OBRA) of 1989 affects most areas of healthcare policy.[24] The purpose of the budget reconciliation process is to bring spending that is not controlled through the regular congressional appropriations process into conformity with the annual budget resolution. Since the passage of the Social Security Amendments of 1983—the act that established the PPS—the Secretary of Health and Human Services, in consultation with the Prospective Payment Assessment Commission, is required to make annual adjustments to the rates paid to hospitals covered by the Social Security Act. Although an annual increase was promised, no such increase has ever been approved by Congress or set by the Secretary.[25] This situation adds to the financial stress on hospitals.

Adaptations to Reimbursement Systems

Even with the current focus on healthcare reform, there is a trend to recruit, retain, and reward physicians to gain access to their patients. Therefore hospitals offer improved facilities, increased power, and financial incentives. Both proprietary and nonprofit hospitals have banded together into chains and alliances with varying degrees of centralized control. Financial managers have assumed more important roles with the advent of computerized data systems that are designed to maximize revenues through the PPS and PPOs. Expansion of utilization review and the case manager role has emerged as a direct outgrowth of the need to relate the PPS and PPOs to provision of care (see Chapters 5 and 7). The businesslike attitudes and strategies now embraced by nonprofit hospitals have created in some circles the perception that the distinctions between nonprofit and for-profit hospitals are disappearing.

Rises in Healthcare Costs

In spite of the efforts to curtail expenditures, the cost of healthcare in the United States has risen dramatically in the past three decades. In 1960 approximately $26 billion was spent on healthcare, which represents 5.4% of the nation's gross domestic product (GDP). By 1994, healthcare costs rose to $1 trillion, or approximately 16% of the GDP. Left unchallenged at the present rate, healthcare will consume 32% of the GDP by the year 2030.[23,26]

HEALTHCARE INSTITUTIONS AND THE HOSPITAL

A large number of healthcare organizations in the United States today are acute care hospitals. Healthcare institutions usually possess a common basis for existence: to serve the health needs of the public. Until recent years the hospital has been a place for care of the sick and the dependent. Today the hospital is becoming a center of technical services for the sick *and* the well, with emphasis on preventive services and health promotion for the general population. Goals are reached in accordance with the type of health setting. Inherent in meeting health needs are (1) administering patient care, (2) educating health agency personnel and the public, (3) engaging in research, and (4) protecting the health of the public. The emphasis given to these different functions varies from hospital to hospital, depending on the basic philosophy and goals of the particular hospital.

The history of hospitals can be traced to the healing temples of ancient Egypt. The evolution of the modern hospital is usually associated with the development of the Christian ethics of faith, humanitarianism, and charity. The American hospital is based essentially on the British prototype, yet it has a uniqueness of its own.[6]

The **American Hospital Association** (AHA) defines a hospital as an institution with the primary function of providing diagnostic and therapeutic patient services for a variety of surgical and nonsurgical medical conditions. A number of guidelines to protect the interests of the consumer are provided by the AHA at the federal and state levels. These guidelines are concerned with items such as (1) an adequate number of beds (no fewer than six); (2) a safe and sanitary environment; (3) an identifiable governing body that is legally and morally responsible for the conduct of the hospital; (4) a chief executive who is responsible for the operation of the hospital in accordance with established policy; (5) a medical staff that is accountable for maintaining proper standards; (6) continuous registered nurse supervision of nursing services; and (7) pharmacy, food, x-ray, laboratory, and operating room services.[27] Nursing is the largest department in any hospital.

Healthcare Agencies

Healthcare agencies are of three types: (1) **government owned** at the federal, state, or local levels; (2) **voluntary**, or nonprofit; and (3) **proprietary**, or for-profit.

Government-owned healthcare agencies

Government-owned healthcare agencies are official bodies that provide health services to selected groups of people under the support and direction of the local, state, or federal government. Their services are often provided without cost to the client or are offered at a reduced rate to the medically indigent. These organizations answer directly to the sponsoring governing agency or boards and indirectly to elected officials and taxpayers (Box 3-3). People cared for at the federal level include veterans, military personnel, and their families. These services are usually housed in very large facilities where the bed capacity ranges from hundreds to thousands. There are also those who need protective services that are available through the U.S. Department of Public Health, such as Indian services and Marine hospitals. The healthcare needs of federal prisoners are also provided by the federal government.

Voluntary healthcare agencies (nonprofit)

Voluntary healthcare agencies are nonprofit, tax exempt organizations designed to meet the

---

Box 3-3.   Examples of government-owned hospitals operating under support and direction of the voting public

FEDERAL	STATE	LOCAL
Army	Psychiatric	City
Navy	Chronic diseases	County
Veterans Administration	State university	City/county
Public Health Service	Medical school	
Indian service	Hospitals	
Marine hospitals	Prisons	
Department of Justice		
Prisons		

---

healthcare needs of the general public. Operation without profit does not mean that voluntary agencies do not need to be concerned with their financial well-being. Although they have no stockholders interested in profit, they still must plan to have sufficient money to expand, to be prepared for inflation or depression, and to be able to meet all financial obligations. Consequently, most nonprofit agencies have receipts in excess of expenditures, which are held until they are needed. These monies differ from profits in that the funds are redirected into the agency for its maintenance and growth rather than routed into the hands of stockholders. Box 3-4 lists the major types of owners. Basic support for an important part of a voluntary agency's capital budget depends on client fees, which are determined on an individual basis, and gifts. Orientation is toward service for religious, ethnic, economic, or special interest groups.

Generally speaking, services established by large corporations are fairly secure in their finances, but healthcare agencies established by local governmental agencies for those who cannot pay for their own care have always been severely underfinanced and understaffed. This causes frustration for healthcare providers because they see the need for their services but are hampered by lack of funds.[6]

Proprietary healthcare agencies (for-profit)

Proprietary healthcare agencies operate for profit. They serve people who can pay for their

services directly or indirectly. These privately owned corporations function under the direction of stockholders such as physicians, a corporation, or a board of trustees. Box 3-5 gives examples of owners of private healthcare agencies. Personnel practices, client services, growth, and emphasis on quality or quantity of care vary among agencies. Many proprietary agencies receive supplementary private and public funding for provision of healthcare, research, and special services and are in a position to provide some financial assistance to eligible clients who can afford ordinary care but cannot handle catastrophic illness. Hemodialysis and transplantation of human organs are examples of services that are financially out of reach for the average citizen but can be made available by special arrangement.[28]

Differences between proprietary and voluntary agencies

Anders[28] conducted a 2-year study on a for-profit (proprietary), a nonprofit (voluntary) hospital, and a skilled nursing facility to determine the differences between the two styles of management. He found no significant differences among the facilities in terms of length of stay, but there was a marked difference in cost. Cost problems in the voluntary hospital, and to a lesser degree in the proprietary hospital, were related to major delay problems in processing patients (particularly for discharge), unavailable outside resources, discharge planning, and physician involvement. Room rates were discovered to be higher in for-

Box 3-4.   Examples of voluntary healthcare organizations operating under the support of nonprofit organizations

CHURCH AFFILIATED	COMMUNITY	INDUSTRIAL	SPECIAL INTEREST GROUPS
Salvation Army	Any community	Railroad, lumber	Shriners
Roman Catholic		Union	Cancer, muscular dystrophy
Presbyterian		Kaiser-Permanente	Mental retardation
Baptist			Others
Lutheran			
Methodist			
Seventh Day Adventist			
Others			

Box 3-5.   Examples of proprietary health agencies operating as profit-making organizations

Individual owner
Partnership
Corporation
Multisystem
Single
Chain

profit organizations, probably because of their need to pay taxes and to compensate for Medicare/Medicaid patients. The more controlled structure in the for-profit hospital contributed to cost containment, whereas in the voluntary hospital, critical pathways for monitoring patient progress were in place but not monitored as closely. The study suggests that for-profit hospitals are more efficient in operative procedures and that voluntary hospitals would benefit from studying their organizational policies and structure.[28]

Magnet Hospitals
Urban magnet hospitals

Urban magnet hospitals are medium-to-large community hospitals or medical centers that have a reputation for higher rates of retention of nurses and for excellence in nursing prac-

tice.[29,30] The ANA-sponsored studies of 741 hospitals across the United States reveals that the nursing staffs of urban magnet hospitals are composed of a high median percentage of RNs (81%) and typically have few middle managers concerned with clinical decision making. The nursing units generally operate autonomously, are self-governing, and participate in nurse-physician collaboration in department-wide issues that relate to them. Because the nursing staffs are educated, experienced, and clinically competent, they assume responsibility for patient care with the help of clinical nurse specialists (see Chapter 4). As a result, a nurse manager's span of control can increase. For example, there are now fewer nursing directors in areas such as medical-surgical nursing and parent-child nursing. The nurse managers appointed are specialists in budget and financial planning, strategic and operational planning, and education and research. Evening and night supervisors are no longer needed to supervise responsible, autonomous staff nurses. In one of the 16 magnet hospitals surveyed, nurse managers are on beeper call for consultation on any nursing problem the staff cannot handle. In all but three of the magnet hospitals studied, scheduling and staff replacements are decentralized to the nursing unit for the RN staff to manage. The nursing care delivery system is flexible and ever changing and dictated primarily by patient needs. Eight-hour total patient care and case management are the dominant delivery systems.

Rural magnet hospitals

Almost half of the hospitals in the United States are rural and small, with bed capacities ranging from 37 to 96. Occupancy rates range from 25% to 62%, compared with the 84% rate recorded in the ANA Magnet Hospitals Studies of urban hospitals. All **rural magnet hospitals** offer medical-surgical care of adults and children. Great emphasis is placed on caring for the elderly, and a number of hospitals have added extended care facilities. Almost every hospital has identified a specialty in which it has invested resources such as a dialysis unit, radiation center, or computerized pharmacy information. Emergency medical services and helicopter pads are provided by many rural magnet hospitals, which enables rapid response to special local emergencies and access to hospital affiliations and networks for special care. Community health education is often offered by these hospitals.

Fuszard and associates[29, 30] used the procedure from the three Magnet Hospitals Studies to examine 10 rural hospitals of excellence in Georgia. All rural hospitals studied were public hospitals, some receiving partial funding from county governments. The researchers found that there were nearly 50% fewer registered nurse positions in rural magnet hospitals than in urban magnet hospitals and that licensed practical nurses (LPNs) are the backbone of their staffs. In contrast to the total patient care and case management methods of patient care delivery used by urban hospitals, rural hospitals use functional nursing, team nursing, and primary nursing; only one rural hospital is introducing case management. Another difference between rural and urban magnet hospitals is in the style of nursing management. Urban hospitals tend to decentralize leadership, whereas rural hospitals operate under a traditional hierarchy of directors, supervisors, and nurse managers. Levels of education for nurse administrators and nursing staff members differ, with urban hospitals having the greatest number of nursing personnel with baccalaureate nursing degrees and advanced preparation. However, some rural hospitals are developing incentives and are offering full tuition support for those who pursue advanced education. Figure 3-6 provides an overview of rural magnet hospitals.

Mergers and Acquisitions Among Healthcare Organizations

Most healthcare organizations begin as simple businesses that want to maintain their independent status. However, current trends make it almost impossible to compete in the present market without entering into some kind of alliance with a similar institution. A common practice is for healthcare organizations to enter into a merger or an acquisition. A **merger** occurs when one organization purchases another organization of approximately the same size; an **acquisition** occurs when one organization is considerably larger than the other. Organizations use mergers and acquisitions to acquire complementary products or complementary services, which are linked by common technologies and common clients.[1] Box 3-6 describes four types of mergers.

The objective of most mergers and acquisitions is to increase organizational power so that the organization can gain leverage. This is accomplished by eliminating redundancy and increasing purchasing power. Some hospitals are developing alliances that result in reduction of management overhead, such as pooling assets and restructuring governance. Financially strong corporations can purchase in large quantities and eliminate duplication in services. An example is the merging of two large Boston hospitals in 1994, Massachusetts General and Brigham and Women's. The merger is expected to save more than $160 million in annual operating costs and duplicate services, but the process will require tough, aggressive measures to prepare all who are involved. Also in 1994, Medica, Minnesota's second largest HMO, merged with HealthSpan, Minnesota's largest health system. The new organization, Allina Health Systems, will have tremendous market clout. These types of organizations hope to quickly achieve the high level of integration that took Kaiser-Permanente years to develop.[31]

Because much of the rationale for combinations is financial, of primary concern is the elimination of employees with responsibilities that overlap in both entities. Naturally employees will be anxious about their future. Who will be eliminated? What operations will be closed? Who will be required to relocate or lose employment? Stress follows anxiety because the climate and

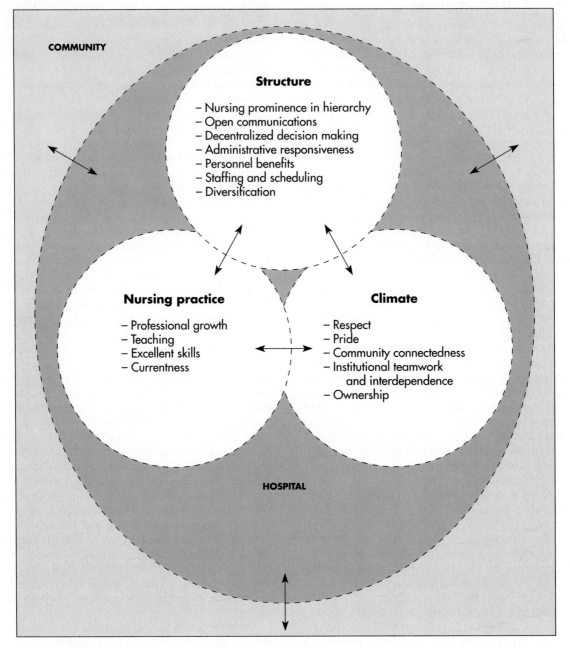

FIGURE 3-6. Rural magnet hospitals of excellence. (From Fuszard B and others: Rural magnet hospitals of excellence, Part 2, *JONA* 24[2]:40, 1994.)

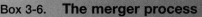

Box 3-6.   The merger process

Pritchett[32] proposes four ways to merge organizations:

1. The rescue posture   The agency in trouble welcomes help from a purchaser.
2. The collaborative posture   This is the most common merger procedure. It occurs in an environment in which each party desires to merge and there is a feeling of mutual respect and interest in working together.
3. The contested merger   Only one agency or party has a strong desire to merge, but both parties see some gain to be had from the merger.
4. The raid posture   One organization takes over another by surprise, thus producing shock and antagonism.

culture of the organization are strained. Human resource experts can help employees with these adjustments. See Chapter 9 for a discussion of helping people cope with change.[6]

Mergers and Acquisitions and the Nurse Manager

Mergers and acquisitions affect all nurses; staff members begin to worry about their place in the new structure. Unless plans for the merger or acquisition are clarified quickly and nurses understand how the change will affect them, staff members will gradually resist and withdraw from their original commitment to the workplace. The role of nurse managers is to help their staff overcome negative influences. Before this goal can be accomplished, nurse managers must resolve any negative feelings they themselves might be experiencing. Gathering information and establishing a power base within the enlarged system becomes vital.

Managers can best accomplish staff adjustment to a merger or acquisition through persuasion and by helping their staff see that the change is inevitable and can have positive outcomes. The key to an effective merger is horizontal and vertical communication in areas of productivity, momentum, teamwork, power distribution, self-preservation activities, commitment levels, and staff attrition.

Neither a fast-paced nor a slow-paced rate of change is desirable in a merger. Fast-paced changes add stress, and slow-paced changes drag out the trauma. Overall, a moderate rate of change seems advisable—fast enough to reduce

anxiety and slow enough to provide thorough communication during the process.[3] The appropriate rate of change is in effect when all parties concerned understand the process and are moving forward with plans for integration.

Compatibility of merging organizations needs to be determined. Each organization involved in the merger is at a different level of development; therefore, attention must be directed toward finding a common ground (see Chapter 9).

PUBLIC HEALTH/COMMUNITY HEALTH SERVICES

Winslow is known for his classic definition of **public health:** "Public health is the science and art of (1) preventing disease, (2) prolonging life, (3) promoting health and efficiency through organized community effort."[9,p.6] The key phrase in this definition is *through organized effort.* The term *public health* connotes efforts made through public channels, including government agenices such as health departments that serve the people in accordance with tax-supported legislation. The newer term *community health* extends the scope of public health to include efforts organized on a community basis for the public good through both government and private agencies, including private agencies supported by private funds. Examples of such efforts are the American Heart Association and the American Diabetic Association.[9]

Community health nursing uses a synthesized body of knowledge from the public health sciences and professional nursing theories to im-

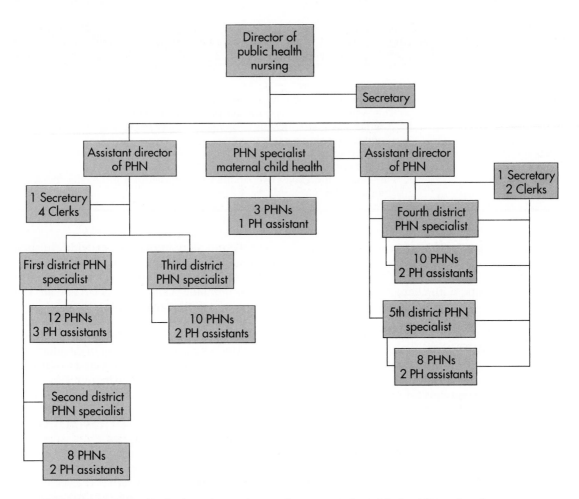

FIGURE 3-7. Example of a typical organizational structure of a public health nursing department.

prove the health of the entire community. Community health nurses are responsible to the population for the promotion of health and prevention of disease, from individual health problems to those that affect the entire community.[9]

Public Health/Community Health Organizational Structure

The structure of a public/community healthcare system includes the resources (e.g., money, people, physical plant, technology) and the organizational configurations necessary to transform these resources into health services.[33] Ideally

there would be a single, coherent organization with all public health groups in alignment. In reality, public health is practiced in a complex set of organizational and jurisdictional relationships (Figure 3-7). In the United States, each state has ultimate responsibility for the health of its residents; however, public health activities are usually delegated to local health departments. About half of the states have combined health and social service agencies. In some states there is a super- or umbrella-agency structure, which causes public health services to become predominantly a welfare program and the broad vision of public health to be overshadowed.

The city or county is divided into districts. The Director of Public Health Nursing is responsible for all functions, which are delegated through assistant directors. For each district there is a Public Health Nurse Specialist who directs and supervises the Public Health Nurses (PHNs) and is available for sharing his or her expertise with all the staff. Secretaries and clerks are available to PHNs for administrative services. One specialty area (maternal-child health) is singled out in this sample chart; however, there may be more specialties or none if the director elects to incorporate all services into the daily activities of the districts.

Healthcare Reform and Public Health

The American Public Health Association is committed, in principle, to (1) providing universal access to comprehensive healthcare funded through a single payer (although this is not a present-day option), (2) defending the public health goal to improve the health of the nation and creating substantial initiatives for disease prevention and health promotion, and (3) maintaining the rightful place of public health in monitoring the country's state of health and the accountability of system management. Public health leaders grant that meeting their commitment will require a larger work force and appropriate training, which means a significant increase in funding. These proposals are reported to have been rejected by the Office of Management and Budget, and the Department of Health and Human Services is said to have precluded any funding for academic preparation and preventive medicine from the 1995 fiscal year budget. Nevertheless, the public health movement plans to continue to debate the issues, enumerating what is necessary to advance the health as well as the care of the people of the United States.[33]

HOME HEALTHCARE/VISITING NURSE SERVICES

Origin

Home healthcare in the United States began with the visiting nurse service approximately 100 years ago.[8] Visiting nurse societies were originally managed by nonnurses, but by 1900 the organizations had hired nurses to supervise the nursing staff. The societies were financed by charities, public boards, churches, and voluntary boards; fees for services were charged if the client could pay. By 1920 a large number of health insurance carriers covered client charges. In 1966, when Title XVIII of the Social Security Act was implemented, Medicare began funding home healthcare for the aged and disabled. Provision for home healthcare shifted from private and charitable sectors to third-party payment modes, with Medicare as the primary source of reimbursement. In 1983 the introduction of the PPS by Public Law 98-21 of the Social Security Amendments gave hospitals a fixed amount of money to care for Medicare patients. These changes motivated hospitals to refine and improve their efforts to better control length of stay. More and more patients were discharged with the need for continuing, intermittent home health services.

Services Provided

In the past, services provided by home healthcare agencies included skilled nursing, home health aide service, physical therapy, occupational therapy, speech pathology, and medical social services. In recent years more comprehensive services have been instituted, including respiratory therapy; parenteral nutrition; intravenous therapy; chemotherapy; home ventilator management; apnea therapy; cardiac monitoring; high-risk pediatric home care; and treatments for those with physical disabilities, mental illnesses, and AIDS.

Home healthcare agencies are either voluntary, proprietary, or hospital-based. The services provided follow a physician-approved plan of treatment. Another component of home healthcare is hospice services, which specialize in care of the terminally ill. Hospices are commonly associated with visiting nurse services and agencies under the auspices of religious organizations.

Accreditation and monitoring of home healthcare agencies varies greatly according to state regulation. There are more than 12,000 home healthcare agencies in the United States, and over half have Medicare certification. The JCAHO, the National Institutes of Health (NIH), and the American Public Health Association also accredit home healthcare agencies.

Organization

According to Medicare regulations, the director of nursing of a home healthcare agency (who may also be the administrator, executive director, or president in some agencies) must be a registered nurse. The ANA standard for a home healthcare nursing director requires a professional nurse with a master's degree. The administrator is responsible for the administration and direction of all client care activities and is charged with fostering the professional growth of the clinical staff. As the home healthcare industry has begun to mature, it is not uncommon to see home healthcare agencies being managed by administrators with business, public administration, health care, or hospital administration degrees, or experience, or both (Figure 3-8).

ACCREDITATION OF HEALTHCARE INSTITUTIONS

Control of healthcare institutions first occurs at municipal (city and county) and state levels. Each facility that provides healthcare services is required to meet minimal standards established by authoritative bodies, usually through city, county, and state public health commissions or departments. Beyond this basic precautionary assurance of safety to the public, a hospital that desires to be accredited at the national level usually seeks sanction from the JCAHO, which is the primary body for evaluation of healthcare institutions at the national level. This group provides essential guidelines for facilities, services, and organizations. It is subscribed to by the AHA, the American Medical Association (AMA), the American College of Physicians (ACP), American Association of Homes for the Aging (AAHA), and the American Nursing Home Association (ANHA). Additional criteria, through means of other voluntary **accreditation** bodies, are required by some groups or agencies before they will fund or use routine or special healthcare services. Federal funds are major sources of income and are provided through such avenues as Medicare, construction grants, and education appropriations for medical residencies and internships and nursing education and practice.

The quality of nursing service care is influenced by and closely associated with the quality of hospital and medical care. Although nursing

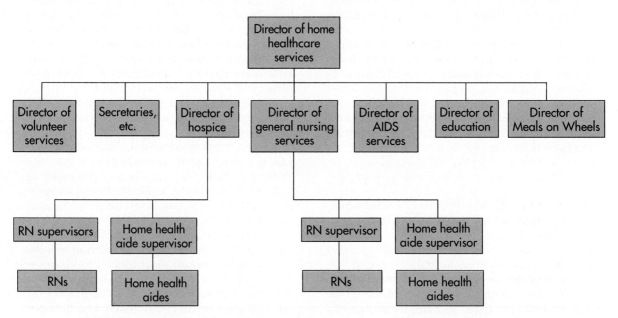

FIGURE 3-8. Example of the organizational structure of a typical home healthcare agency.

services are reviewed in accordance with specific criteria established by the JCAHO, the ANA has not been successful in gaining professional representation on the commission.

SUMMARY

1. Organization involves generating a mechanism to coordinate the work of members into a unified, orderly, and harmonious whole.
2. Organizations share four characteristics: common goal, coordination of effort, division of labor, and established delegation of authority.
3. Each health organization has both a formal structure (highly planned and publicized) and an informal structure (unplanned and concealed).
4. Developing an organization includes designing jobs, forming departments and work units, creating a hierarchy, developing a span of control, and coordinating and integrating activities.
5. There are two major forms of organizational structure: centralized control and the decentralized or participatory approach.
6. An organizational chart illustrates the formal organizational structure typically used by hospitals and other healthcare organizations.
7. There are basically two approaches to organization and management: bureaucratic and human relations.
8. Bureaucracy is the classic approach and is based on a hierarchical structure with legalized, formal authority. Common characteristics are (a) rules and regulations, (b) specialization of tasks and division of labor, (c) appointment by merit, and (d) an impersonal climate. Most hospitals have a bureaucratic structure.
9. There are four basic criticisms of the classic bureaucratic form of organization and management: (a) it neglects the human aspects of organization members, who are assumed to be motivated only by economic incentives; (b) it does not consider rapidly changing and uncertain environments; (c) as the organization grows, top managers become progressively out of touch with realities at the lower levels of the organization; and (d) there may be a breakdown in communications between managers and followers which permits counterproductive personal insecurities to flourish.
10. Advantages of the human relations approach to management include a key emphasis on people, which results in a staff of motivated individuals who are committed to organizational objectives.
11. There are four basic criticisms of the human relations approach to organization and management: (a) most persons function better in a bureaucratic environment, which makes it difficult to apply a participatory approach to management; (b) it is time-consuming; (c) organizational goals may not be met; and (d) not everyone likes to work in a moderately structured environment.
12. In selecting an organizational structure and management system, one must consider what is best for an agency's efficiency and effectiveness in relation to its purposes, overall goals, and congruency of the workers.
13. In the latter part of the twentieth century, healthcare reform will work through managed competition and pit one agency against another to provide quality healthcare at the lowest cost possible.
14. Registered nurses must be adept at gatekeeping and in seeking ways to overcome barriers for those needing care.
15. Retrospective payment for health services is reimbursement after the services have been provided.
16. Prospective payment involves setting payment levels for services before they are provided.
17. DRGs form the basis of a PPS for hospital services given to Medicare patients.
18. Established in 1983, the PPS sets fixed fees for services given to Medicare inpatients and is based strictly on diagnosis, not on treatment choices or the actual cost of an individual's care. Under this system, hospitals fare better financially by providing fewer services to more patients.

19. A PPO is a health financing and delivery arrangement in which a group of health-care providers (e.g., physicians, hospitals) offer their services to healthcare providers on a predetermined financial basis.

20. OBRA (1989) was designed to bring spending for Medicare and Medicaid, which are not controlled through the regular congressional appropriations process, into conformity with the annual budget.

21. Healthcare agencies are adapting to new reimbursement systems by rewarding physicians with incentives, making alliances with other healthcare agencies, and using stricter financial controls.

22. Costs for healthcare have risen dramatically from $26 billion in 1960 to $1 trillion in 1994 and from 5.4% to 16% of the nation's GDP.

23. Managed care represents the integration of healthcare financing with provision of care.

24. Managed competition is an economic strategy to reform the healthcare system by stimulating price competition and quality improvement.

25. The majority of healthcare providers consider manged care to be the most logical approach to cost containment. Many physicians, some hospitals, and other healthcare providers strongly oppose price competition; they favor the regulatory approach, which they have used to control the market.

26. Price competition provides strong incentives for healthcare providers to seek ways to minimize costs and be competitive.

27. As the bulk of healthcare gradually moves from hospitals to satellite facilities and into home care endeavors, hospital structure is affected and must either face the issue or go under.

28. The purpose of most health institutions is to serve four primary needs of the public: (a) patient care, (b) education, (c) research, and (d) protection of public health.

29. The AHA defines a hospital as an institution whose major purpose is to provide patient services. Guidelines are provided at national and state levels to protect the interest of the consumer.

30. There are three types of healthcare organizations: (a) government owned, (b) voluntary or nonprofit, and (c) proprietary or for-profit.

31. Voluntary health agencies are nonprofit, tax-exempt organizations designed to meet the health needs of the general public.

32. Proprietary health agencies operate for profit.

33. Costs for delivery of healthcare services are generally higher in voluntary hospitals than in proprietary hospitals because for-profit hospitals are more efficient in operative procedures.

34. Magnet hospitals are medium-to-large-size urban or rural community hospitals or medical centers that have a reputation for high retention of nurses and excellence of nursing practice. The units in these hospitals are often autonomous and self-governed. The nurse manager's role is typically broad in scope.

35. Community hospital mergers consist of incorporating groups of hospitals under one umbrella. The major goal is to increase the power of hospital systems in highly competitive marketplaces. There are four types of mergers: (a) rescue, (b) collaborative, (c) contested, and (d) raid.

36. Public health services are those conducted on a community basis for the public good. The mission of public health is to ensure conditions in which people can live healthy lives.

37. The American Public Health Association is committed to (a) universal access to comprehensive healthcare that is funded through a single payer, (b) initiatives for disease prevention and promotion of health, and (c) maintenance of the place of public health in monitoring the country's state of health and the accountability and management of systems.

38. Community health nursing focuses on the health of the whole community. The community health nurse works with other disciplines in the nursing process of as-

sessment to identify problems, develops plans for intervention, implements plans, and evaluates their impact on the health status of those served.

39. Public health organizational structure includes resources (money, people, physical plant, technology) and the organizational configuration necessary to transform these resources into health services.

40. The Director of Public Health Nursing is responsible for all functions, which are delegated through assistant directors.

41. Home healthcare services/visiting nurse associations include traditional services such as skilled nursing, home health aide services, varied therapists, and medical so-

cial services. In recent years, more comprehensive services have been included, such as respiratory therapy, parenteral nutrition, intravenous therapy, and chemotherapy. There is an increased need for continual, intermittent home health services.

42. Home healthcare agencies are either voluntary, proprietary, or hospital based. The services follow a physician-approved plan of treatment.

43. JCAHO is the primary body at the national level for evaluation of healthcare institutions. It has support from most health professional organizations. The ANA does not yet have representation.

? Questions for Study and Discussion

1. What is meant by "span of control?" What is your span of control as a student? If you were a staff nurse, what would be your span of control? To whom would you be responsible?

2. Select a past or present place of employment. Diagram to whom you would go with a problem and to whom that person would go with a problem, and so on to the top. Are there any gaps you cannot complete? If applicable, why do you think you did not know the lines of authority from the lowest level to the top?

3. Would you rather work in a centralized or decentralized organization? For what reasons?

4. What are the characteristics of a bureaucracy? In your opinion, how applicable are these characteristics to most healthcare delivery systems today? What is your rationale?

5. What do unionization and the human relations approach to management have in common?

6. Select one human relations expert and explain his or her philosophy of management. Do you agree with this person? Explain why or why not.

7. Give the rationale for the merging of healthcare agencies. What are the advantages and disadvantages of merging?

8. Explain the differences between retrospective and prospective payment systems. Which system is currently the most popular? Why?

9. What is a PPO? Who belongs to PPOs? Why do health agencies vie for healthcare-providing purchasers' business?

10. List several ways healthcare agencies can adapt to reimbursement systems. Are you disturbed by any of the means suggsted? Explain.

11. Bring to class examples of healthcare reform systems. What implication do these plans have for the staff nurse?

12. How is the college/university you attend owned and organized? Can your educational institution be compared with one kind of healthcare structure? Which one? In what way?

13. Compare the similarities and differences among government owned, nonprofit, and proprietary healthcare delivery systems.

14. Upon graduation from your nursing program, would you consider applying for a staff position at a magnet hospital? What are your reasons for applying? For not applying?

15. Define the terms *public health services* and *community health nursing*. What are the differences in scope of practice?

16. Explain the differences between the roles of a public health nurse and a home healthcare nurse.

✎ **Test Your Knowledge**

BEHAVIORAL OBJECTIVE

Give reasons for organizational structure and its composition. Identify significant factors that influence organizational relationships.

As Executive Vice President of a large hospital, Marilyn understands that organizational structure and its composition is important to goal achievement. She reviews some basic concepts.

_____ 1. Healthcare organizations are formed for specific purposes. Which of the following is the most accurate response?
  a. To care for the sick and to promote health
  b. To provide a place for specialists to bring their clients
  c. To engage in research
  d. To coordinate and control people and resources

_____ 2. A hierarchy refers to a body of persons or things organized so that the power structure:
  a. Is shared among those at the same level.
  b. Begins at the bottom and moves upward.
  c. Begins at the top and moves downward.
  d. Moves according to situation.

_____ 3. Controlling the number of persons who report directly to the manager is best described as:
  a. A hierarchy.
  b. Span of management.
  c. Authority.
  d. Recordkeeping.

BEHAVIORAL OBJECTIVE

Compare the advantages and disadvantages of the bureaucratic and human relations approaches to organization and management.

As a student, Margaret was assigned to several healthcare facilities. Part of her assignment was to observe the organizational structure of each.

_____ 4. While at the children's hospital, Margaret noticed an environment that had much laughter, and she felt a warm and caring spirit among the staff. She identified the style of organization as:
  a. Participative.
  b. Bureaucratic.
  c. Centralized.
  d. Organized.

_____ 5. While assigned to Labor and Delivery, Margaret was told by the nurse manager that staff members are given no recognition for a job well done because they are simply meeting expectations. In reviewing the theories of management, Margaret correlated the manager's philosophy with that of Weber, who believed that:
  a. Emotional attachments interfere with rational decisions.
  b. Impersonality costs the company time.
  c. Impersonality cost more money.
  d. Impersonality does not require as many rules.

BEHAVIORAL OBJECTIVE

Explain the rationale for selecting an organizational structure and management system.

At the end of the term, Margaret was to cite which criteria she would use to determine an organizational structure.

_____ 6. Margaret selected an organizational structure on the following premise:
  a. It should be unchangeable.
  b. It should be used exclusively.
  c. It should match the purposes and goals of the agency.
  d. It should have fixed purposes.

BEHAVIORAL OBJECTIVE

Differentiate between retrospective and prospective payment systems and give examples of each.

Mrs. Lowry, a 96-year-old, lived during the time of President Johnson's "Great Society" program. She fell and fractured her femur and needs hospitalization.

_____ 7. Mrs. Lowry could expect the cost of her care to be covered by:
   a. Personal savings.
   b. A prospective payment system.
   c. A retrospective payment system.
   d. A government fund for the disabled.

The health agency comptroller is struggling to comprehend a system that is concerned with DRGs.

_____ 8. The comptroller understands that under this system, the clients are:
   a. Indigent.
   b. On Medicare.
   c. On welfare.
   d. Covered by private insurance.

BEHAVIORAL OBJECTIVE

Compare and contrast provisions for current healthcare and evaluate reform proposals.

Carl and Lucille are retired and are selecting a managed healthcare plan. They want one that will cover as many of their needs as possible.

_____ 9. Carl and Lucille are reviewing what HMOs have to offer. Which of the following features do *not* define an HMO?
   a. It is a managed care system.
   b. Services are provided on the basis of a fixed monthly charge per enrolee.
   c. The organizations can be either nonprofit or for-profit.
   d. The client may select his or her own physician.

_____ 10. Carl and Lucille investigate the meaning of "managed care" and discover that the primary feature of this system is:
   a. Fixation of healthcare costs.
   b. Separation of financing and healthcare.
   c. Stimulation of price competition and quality care.
   d. Integration of government and healthcare providers.

_____ 11. Carl and Lucille's attention is drawn to proposed healthcare reforms. They conclude that there are three major differences in the suggested plans:
   a. Insurance, malpractice, and paperwork requirements.
   b. Security, coverage for funeral expenses, and no out-of-pocket expenses.
   c. Continuous health coverage, a health plan for all, and a move toward all nonprofit agencies.
   d. Control, freedom of choice, and the degree of power vested in the government versus the people.

BEHAVIORAL OBJECTIVE

Cite the degree to which healthcare costs have risen in the past three decades.

_____ 12. While reviewing the current status of healthcare Carl and Lucille learn that, left unchallenged, healthcare will consume approximately how much of the GNP by the year 2030?
   a. 12%
   b. 22%
   c. 32%
   d. 42%

BEHAVIORAL OBJECTIVE

State the purpose of most healthcare institutions.

Ramonah is working toward a master's degree in healthcare administration. She has a class in top-level management.

_____ 13. Ramonah learns that the overall purpose and goals of a healthcare facility is to:
   a. Care for the sick.
   b. Provide preventive services.
   c. Serve the health needs of the public.
   d. Seek out those who need special care.

_____ 14. The emphasis given to the functions of a hospital ultimately depends on:
   a. The hospital's basic philosophy and goals.
   b. The allotted budget.
   c. Requests of consumers for services.
   d. Available equipment.

BEHAVIORAL OBJECTIVE

Differentiate between government-owned, voluntary, and proprietary hospitals.

_____ 15. Another term for a voluntary health agency is:
   a. Nonprofit.
   b. For-profit.
   c. Proprietary.
   d. Government owned.

BEHAVIORAL OBJECTIVE

Describe a typical urban or rural magnet hospital.

Heather, a clinical specialist in neurology, accepts a position in a magnet hospital because of its uniqueness.

_____ 16. Which of the following does *not* describe a magnet hospital?
   a. The nurse manager's span of control is less than in a more traditional hospital.
   b. The majority of the RN staff are RNs.
   c. The retention rate of RNs is higher than in a more traditional hospital.
   d. Total patient care and case management are the predominant delivery systems.

BEHAVIORAL OBJECTIVE

Describe a hospital merger and its implications for the nurse manager.

John has been informed that the small community hospital in which he is employed is to be merged with a similar one in the vicinity. He is experiencing fears until he attends seminars to explain the process.

_____ 17. John learns that the primary goal of merging healthcare agencies is to:
   a. Become larger.
   b. Serve the needs of more people.
   c. Increase power in the marketplace.
   d. Become better known.

_____ 18. John has learned that the rate of change in a merger or acquisition is important. The optimal pace is to:
   a. Merge quickly so everyone can fit into their roles easily.
   b. Merge slowly so that people have time to adjust.
   c. Merge at a moderate rate so people are not traumatized.
   d. Merge when all possible outcomes are figured out.

BEHAVIORAL OBJECTIVE

Define public health services and explain the role of the community health nurse.

David is a public/community health nurse assigned to an urban district that includes a neighboring school. He finds that there is a high incidence of gastrointestinal upsets among the school children, which is causing many absences.

_____ 19. David's *first* action is to:
   a. Determine the cause of the upsets.
   b. Distribute medication to stop the symptoms.
   c. Call a doctor to the school.
   d. Shut down the cafeteria.

BEHAVIORAL OBJECTIVE

Define home health agencies and the role of the visiting nurse.

Sylvia decided to join the RN staff of the local Visiting Nurse Association (VNA). She made this decision knowing there are significant differences between the role of the community health nurse and the visiting nurse.

_____ 20. One major difference between the two departments is that the VNA nurse:
- a. Conducts demographic studies.
- b. Is concerned primarily with children.
- c. Is responsible for collecting fees for services.
- d. Administers skilled care.

BEHAVIORAL OBJECTIVE

Describe a hospital that meets JCAHO standards.

As Vice President of Nursing Services and as a member of the executive committee, Marilyn adheres to the JCAHO standards. This responsibility requires understanding the guidelines.

_____ 21. Which of the following statements is *not* reflective of the JCAHO standards?
- a. The guidelines of the agency are developed in the community in which the hospital exists.
- b. The governing body must have legal sanction to act in the interest of the hospital.
- c. The names of members of the governing body are privileged information.
- d. The medical staff supervises nursing services.

REFERENCES

1. Barney J, Griffin R: *The management of organizations,* Dallas, 1992, Houghton Mifflin.
2. Kreitner R: *Management,* ed 5, Dallas, 1992, Houghton Mifflin.
3. Robbins S: *Essentials of organizational behavior,* Englewood Cliffs, NJ, 1994, Prentice Hall.
4. Weber M: *Economy and society,* New York, 1968, Bedminster Press (historical).
5. Taylor F: *Scientific organization,* New York, 1947, Harper & Brothers (historical).
6. Longest B: *Management practices for the health professional,* ed 4, Norwalk, Conn, 1990, Appleton & Lange.
7. Wilson N, Hamilton C, Murphy E: Union dynamics in nursing, *JONA* 20(2):35-39, 1990.
8. Mayo E: *The human problems of an industrialized civilization,* New York, 1953, Macmillan (historical).
9. Swanson J, Albrecht M: *Community health nursing,* Philadelphia, 1993, WB Saunders.
10. Parker L: Control in organizational life: the constitution of Mary Parker Follett, *Acad Manage Rev* 9(19):736-745, 1984 (historical).
11. Bluedorn A: The classics of management, *Acad Manage Rev* 11(4):451-454, 1986 (historical).
12. McGregor D: *The human side of enterprise,* New York, 1960, McGraw-Hill (historical).
13. Argyris C: *Integrating the individual and the organization,* New York, 1964, John Wiley & Sons (historical).
14. Maslow A: *Motivation and personality,* ed 2, New York, 1970, Harper & Row (historical).
15. Likert R: *New patterns of management,* New York, 1961, McGraw-Hill (historical).
16. Likert R: *The human organization,* New York, 1967, McGraw-Hill (historical).
17. Mahlmuster L: *What's ahead for health care, professional practice?* NURSEweek 8(1):1;26-27, 1995.
18. Mahlmuster L: *Healthcare law will proliferate in 1995,* NURSEweek 8(1):26, 1995.
19. The Health Insurance for the Aged Act, *The Social Security Amendments of 1965,* Dow Jones-Irwin (historical).
20. Sullivan T, Moore V: A critical look at recent developments in tax exempt hospitals, *J Health Hosp Law* 23(30):65-80, 1990.
21. Mathis R, Jackson J: *Human resource management,* ed 7, Minneapolis, 1994, West Publishing.
22. Buerhaus P: Economics of managed competition and consequences to nurses, Part I, *Nurs Econ* 12(1):10-17, 1994.
23. Harrington C, Estes C: *Health policy and nursing: crisis and reform in the US health care delivery system,* Boston, 1994, Jones and Bartlett.

24. The Omnibus Budget Reconciliation Act of 1989, Conference Report No. 101-386, first session, PL 101-239, 1989 (historical).

25. Epstein J: An examination of the Omnibus Budget Reconciliation Act of 1989: the evolution of national health policy, *J Health Hosp Law* 23(2):53-59, 1989.

26. Solovy A: Taming the tiger, *Hosp Health Network* 68(5):26-34, 1994.

27. American Hospital Association: Hospital terminology, Chicago, 1988, The Association (historical).

28. Anders R: Administrative delays: is there a difference between for-profit and nonprofit hospitals? *JONA* 23(11):42-50, 1993.

29. Fuszard B and others: Rural magnet hospitals of excellence, Part I, *JONA* 24(2):35-41, 1994.

30. Fuszard B and others: Rural magnet hospitals of excellence, Part II, *JONA* 24(2):21-26, 1994.

31. Beckman D: Looking beyond the mergers, *Hosp Manage Rev* 13(2):3, 1994.

32. Pritchett P: *After the merger: managing the shock-waves,* New York, 1985, Dow Jones-Irwin.

33. Susser M: Health care reform and public health: weighing the proposals, *Am J Public Health* 84(2):173-174, 1994.

SUGGESTED READINGS

Blancett S and others: Anniversary update: the progress of nursing administration, *J Nurs Adm* 25(1):5-8, 1995.

Boston C: Cultural transformation, *J Nurs Adm* 25(1):19-20, 1995.

Buerhaus P: Economics of managed competition and consequences to nurses, Part I, *Nurs Econ* 12(1):10-17, 1994.

Curtin L: Healthcare reform: innovations at the state level, *Nurs Manage* 25(4):30-35; 38-40; 42, 1994.

Dirschel K: Decentralization or centralization: striking a balance, *Nurs Manage* 25(9):49-51, 1994.

Grimaldi P: New PPS rules take effect, *Nurs Manage* 25(11):39-40, 1994.

Jacobs S, Pelfrey S: Applying just-in-time philosophy to healthcare, *J Nurs Adm* 25(1):47-51, 1995.

Knollmueller K: Thinking about tomorrow for nursing: changes and challenges, *J Contin Educ Nurs* 25(5):196-201, 1994.

Special report: Urge to merge, *Hosp Health Network* 68(5):37-40, 1994.

Tumulty G, Jernigan I, Kobut G: Reconceptualizing organizational commitment, *J Nurs Adm* 25(1):61-65, 1995.

NURSING PERSONNEL and THEIR ROLES

BEHAVIORAL OBJECTIVES

On completion of this chapter, the student will be prepared to:

- Define the meaning of role analysis and identify factors that affect roles in nursing practice.

- List and explain the functional roles of nurse managers.

- Explain the impact of changes in the healthcare system on nursing roles.

- Define the advanced practice nurse and list the barriers that prevent such nurses from practicing at their full potential.

- Explain the different programs in nursing education.

- Identify the major categories of nursing personnel and the preparation, education, and role required for each position.

The preceding chapters have discussed the process and styles of leadership/management, organizational structure, and management systems. The nurse leader/manager also needs to know about types of nursing personnel and their roles. This chapter discusses the impact of healthcare reform on nursing roles, role theory and role expectation in the typical organizational structure, nurse population, nurse education, nurse registration, and the expanded role of the nurse. Armed with knowledge about these topics, the nurse leader/manager can better fulfill the responsibilities of the position.

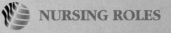 **NURSING ROLES**

A **role** is a group of related activities carried out by an individual. The concept of role is drawn from the behavioral sciences and is defined as a prescribed way of behaving or as a social prescription for a person with a specific position in a group. In a healthy organization, everyone knows his or her role, and the roles mesh in a way that encourages cooperation and reduces dysfunctional conflict. Therefore **role analysis,** which is *the systematic clarification of interdependent tasks and job behavior,* is of vital importance.

Role Characteristics

Certain features characterize a role: (1) it requires a person to behave in a certain way; (2) it implies transaction with others as social interaction occurs; (3) it involves expectations and perceptions by both the role enactor and those with whom he or she relates; (4) it depends on social norms regarding values, judgments, and feelings; (5) it leads to conformity because boundaries for practice are usually established; and (6) it may create conflict by placing demands on an individual that he or she cannot fulfill or that are incompatible with his or her personal preferences.[1]

The Nurse's Role

The nurse's perceived role is determined in part by *sources of roles* and *multiple roles.* Sources that form a nurse's role are institutional requirements (e.g., rules and regulations, job descriptions), patient/client expectations (e.g., patients' rights), peer expectations (group norms), and the nurse's conception of what behaviors the role implies (Box 4-1). A second key characteristic of a nurse's role are the multiple roles to perform during a typical day. For example, in **nurse case management,** the nurse is a manager (planner, organizer, director, controller), coordinator, collaborator, expert clinician, and communicator with patients, families, and all others who influence care.

Each member of a role set (e.g., nursing group or team) is influenced by his or her own performance and the actions of others. Members may be rewarded or punished because of one person's behavior and may require certain actions,

called role expectations, from that person to perform his or her own tasks. The sources of role expectation and the varied nursing roles can lead to role problems if there are unclear, ambiguous messages. Role conflict also arises if the nurse receives different directions from different sources (e.g., physician, supervisor, patient, interdisciplinary personnel) who all expect compliance (Figure 4-1). Another problem occurs if a nurse is undergoing a power struggle or is unwilling or unable to accept the norms associated with his or her role. Unless the problem is identified and resolved, stress and job dissatisfaction occur.

The Nurse Executive's Role
Professional organization

The American Organization of Nurse Executives (AONE) is the 26-year-old national organization of nurse executives and nurse managers. Leaders within the AONE are committed to a "bold, extensive transformation of AONE to position the nation's association of nursing leaders to remain a strong, responsive organization for the future."[2, p.18] The organization declares its roles to be those of providing leadership, professional development, and advocacy; promoting research to advance nursing practice and patient care; promoting nursing leadership excellence; and helping to shape healthcare public policy. Two guiding principles of the AONE are that its membership and leadership reflect the growing diversity of nursing leadership roles and employment settings and that there be representation and participation of all members across the United States.[2]

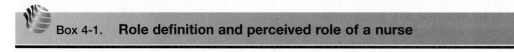

Box 4-1.   Role definition and perceived role of a nurse

Role definition

Organized set of expected behaviors of a nurse in any given position

Nurse's role as perceived by various sources

Meets institutional requirements (rules, regulations, job descriptions)
Meets patient/client needs (patient's rights)
Maintains professional values and attitudes
Works within group norms
Establishes effective communication strategies and social interaction

Problem areas

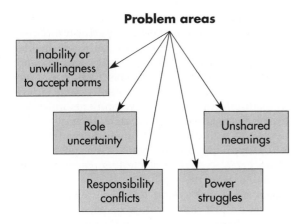

FIGURE 4-1. Situations that lead to role conflict.

Stability

From 1988 to 1992, Kippenbrock and May[3] studied a national sample of 102 hospitals to determine the rate of turnover for chief nurse executives and the hospital characteristics that affect turnover. They found the average turnover rate to be 21.6%, which they considered extremely high. Only two characteristics were significant for the turnovers and were identified only for 1992: (1) a decline in the number of rural hospitals, and (2) lower occupancy rates. Further studies confirm that the turnover rate for nurse executives is increasing. It has been suggested that graduate programs offer curricula that emphasize communication, problem-solving, team building, and conflict resolution.

The Nurse Manager Role

As Box 4-2 indicates, the core of functional roles in nursing management remains essentially the same in many different systems of care, but in an increasing number of agencies management must become more sophisticated. Because patient care is no longer seen as unit based, the nurse manager must think of the entire spectrum of healthcare, from a patient's entry into the system to resolution of the problem. Interdisciplinary relationships must also be developed and maintained. Nurse managers have traditionally been comfortable with managing their own departments or units and meeting occasionally with their peers and supervisors. Now, as with

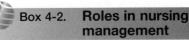

Box 4-2. Roles in nursing management

Sherman[4,5] identified seven functional roles in nursing management that were further identified in a research study of 48 nurse managers and 20 nursing supervisors at six hospitals in Wisconsin.[7]

1. *Planning,* including for self, for the nursing unit(s), and for emergencies
2. *Organizing,* ranging from arranging one's own and others' workloads to participating in analysis of wages, working conditions, and procedures for handling supplies, drugs, and equipment
3. *Staffing,* including interviewing and orienting new staff, as well as being involved in inservice programs
4. *Leading,* including being familiar with the agency's mission, philosophy, and goals; coordinating activities of nursing personnel; and providing advice on nursing practice as needed
5. *Communicating,* including listening to all personnel, maintaining effective horizontal and vertical relationships, and publicizing staff's achievements to higher management
6. *Decision making,* including problem solving and selling major change ideas to supervisors
7. *Controlling,* including safety and quality assurance activities

case management and outcomes management, the concept of autonomous leadership becomes outmoded, and the nurse manager must become very involved with every department or unit that provides care to a patient.[6]

Patz, Biordi, and Holm[7] conducted a survey of nurse managers employed in 103 health centers across the United States. They questioned the nurse managers about the characteristics or roles they considered to be the most important in management. As Box 4-3 indicates, human management skills were considered the most important; general nursing skills were considered least important. The researchers suggest that nurse managers are often more immersed in administrative activities and assume that clinical skills are basic to their understanding. Giving top priority to human management skills has much significance to the beginning practitioner, because he or she must learn how to relate well with others, whatever the setting. Early acquisition and de-

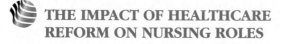

Box 4-3.   Roles considered to be the most important in nursing management[7]

1. Human management skills
2. Flexibility/negotiation/compromise
3. Support of the chief officer
4. General management knowledge
5. Total organizational view
6. Good sense about organizational issues
7. Fiscal management skills
8. Medical staff relations
9. General nursing skills

velopment of human management skills will help the nurse in career development.

THE IMPACT OF HEALTHCARE REFORM ON NURSING ROLES

The changes in the healthcare delivery system that have occurred and continue to occur will deeply affect nursing roles. Some of these changes have already been felt in the downsizing of nursing staff and in fewer employment opportunities for new graduates. It is predicted that only two out of every three hospitals will emerge from competition intact. Some hospitals will close, and others will be converted to ambulatory facilities, clinics, or rehabilitation centers. Rural hospitals will be at the highest risk. A shift from the present illness healthcare system to a wellness system will require more focus on primary care and health promotion. Because of an increase in the aging population, demands for chronic care will increase. Patients who require intensive care will be found in nursing homes, restorative care facilities, and home settings.[8]

Change can work for or against nursing; it will occur with or without input from nurses. As one nurse leader says, "Burying our heads in the sand, digging our heels in, stiffening our backs, sealing our lips, and gritting our teeth will not stop change."[9, p. 74] Changes in nursing can bring the profession together or can cause conflict and divisiveness. How nurse leaders respond to change sets the tone for their followers.

It is clear that if nurses want to define their new roles in a managed competition environment and thereby take greater control of their future, they must take the initiative and become more involved in the central discussions and policy debates surrounding the issues. Nurses must remain informed about developments in healthcare reform and communicate with and support local, state, and national nursing organizations that represent the interests of the profession. They can also contact elected representatives, influential academics, and others who are closely involved in reforming the healthcare system. This is not the time for quarrels regarding supervision of practice, levels of education, advanced education, titles, restrictive regulations, geographic restrictions, or dependent prescriptive authority. All nurses want accessible healthcare in the United States and therefore must work to do their best within the scope of their competency and educational preparation.[10]

The healthcare reform literature does not adequately discuss the role that nurses could play under a managed competition system. For example, the designers of managed competition proposals have neglected the possibility that nurses in advanced-practice positions could assume new clinical, economic, and managerial roles that would strengthen the development of price competition, raise quality, and increase access to healthcare. **Advanced practice nurses** (APNs) are those RNs who are prepared by certification or by advanced degree(s) to deliver competent, quality care to those who require specialized services. Pearson, editor-in-chief of *Nurse Practitioner: American Journal of Primary Health Care,* states that APNs are fully qualified to help patients reach a higher level of wellness at a lower cost. However, she admonishes that their full potential cannot be realized until unnecessary restrictions on the APN's scope of practice are eliminated. This journal conducted a state-by-state legislative review of the legal and prescriptive authority and reimbursement status for APNs. Serious barriers to APN practice remain in many states in three areas: (1) prescriptive authority, (2) direct reimbursement, and (3) autonomous practice.[11] APNs must now be fully poised to participate in a newly modeled American healthcare system.[12] Each state should make the necessary changes in nurse practice acts so that APNs will be ready to act according to the new rules.

American Medical Association's Reaction

Physicians at the American Medical Association (AMA) meeting in December of 1993 strongly reacted to the ANA's estimate that APNs could deliver 60% to 80% of the public's primary care needs at a reduced rate and without a loss in quality. The AMA report condemns expanded roles for RNs, attacks nurses' educational qualifications, and criticizes the "variable" requirements for certification. The report states that "it's irrational to jeopardize patient safety by allowing unsupervised APN practice." The physicians deny that using APNs would save money; instead they assert that costs would increase by necessitating a separate level of providers who would refer complex cases to physicians.[13,p.73]

Following these heated exchanges the AMA and ANA met and agreed to put their energies into healthcare reform. AMA executive vice president Todd and ANA president Betts concluded that physicians "have largely abandoned primary care, yet…continue to object to anyone else picking up the pieces." The ANA and AMA have agreed to form a working group that addresses "problems of mutual concern" while at the same time they continue to pursue their own, very different agendas.[14,p.76]

Public Reaction

In 1994, researchers at the Robert Wood Johnson Foundation conducted a study for the Harvard School of Public Health. They randomly polled 2000 Americans and found that two thirds of them support the idea of a nurse providing primary care. More men (76%) than women (58%) reacted favorably; only 26% of the women polled strongly backed the proposal, and 40% were strongly opposed. The willingness to accept a trained RN as a primary provider increased with income level. In addition, only 48% of blacks liked the idea of expanded roles in comparison to 67% of whites and 58% of Hispanics. The least receptive age groups were those over 65 and those under 30; support increased to over 70% in other age brackets.[15]

Number of Advanced Practice Nurses and Nurse Practitioners

Of the 2.2 million RNs in the United States, approximately 100,000 are considered APNs. About one half of these APNs deliver primary care. Twenty-five thousand nurse practitioners are mostly engaged in primary care as members of a multidisciplinary team.[16]

Education

In the past, nurse practitioner (NP) education has varied in length from 3 months to 2 years; the current trend is 2 academic years. This trend is associated with the sharp increase in the number of NP programs that offer master's degrees rather than certificates. Most nursing programs seek NLN accreditation; NLN standards for clinical training vary. The National Directory of Nurse Practitioner Programs polled 103 institutions. They list 208 specialty programs, 194 of which offer master's degrees. The average number of clinical practice hours is 486, and the average number of didactic hours is 406.[17]

Cost

Through the Division of Nursing, Bureau of Health Professions, and Human Resources and Services Administration, the federal government is conducting a study to ascertain the cost of educating NPs.[18] The available data estimate the cost to be $11,500 per student enrolled in a 1½- to 2-year program; there are approximately 3000 to 3500 graduates. The 1993 funding level for all nursing programs was $15.6 million. Although most healthcare reform packages recommend doubling the number of NPs, it is predicted that the level of support for NP programs will remain the same or increase only slightly during the next few years.

Certification

Certification is a credential that is issued by a professional body and helps protect the consumer by affirming a person's excellence in a particular area. In nursing, being certified in a specialty area attests to the nurse's knowledge and indicates commitment to excellence and professional achievement.

Twice a year, the American Nurses Credentialing Center (ANCC), a subsidiary of the ANA, offers multiple-choice certification examinations in nurse generalist, NP, clinical specialist, and nursing administration. Qualifications for these examinations vary. A baccalaureate in nursing is currently required for all new generalist certification examinations. However, in 1998 a baccalaureate degree in nursing will be required for all generalist examinations. Once a nurse is certified in a specific field of practice, he or she must continue to earn the right to practice by being recertified periodically. ANCC certification is granted for 5 years, with a specific number of continuing education units required within the specific time.[19]

 **NURSE LICENSURE**

Purpose

A license is a legal document that permits a person to legally offer his or her skills and knowledge to the public in a particular jurisdiction.

The purpose of nursing licensure is to protect society from unskilled and incompetent persons who would practice or offer to practice nursing. All professional nurses who practice for hire are required to have a license. A 1993 data analysis bank reported there to be 2.2 million registered nurses in the United States.[20]

To accomplish licensure, it is necessary to define the scope of practice in the appropriate field coming under control. Each state has the responsibility to develop its own nurse practice act and to establish regulatory measures for implementation. Students or nurses should obtain a copy of the nurse practice act of their state and study it for professional guidelines and implications.

Testing

Nursing is leading the way to a new era of testing that takes advantage of today's technology and measurement theory. The National Council of State Boards of Nursing, Inc. (NCSBN) contracts for the development of an examination that tests the knowledge, skills, and abilities that are essential to the safe and effective practice of entry-level nursing. The use of a national examination facilitates licensure by endorsement from one state or territory to another. **Computer adaptive testing** (CAT) calculates the candidate's present level of competence, scans a bank of multiple-choice items for those most closely keyed to that level, and repeats the process until he or she has correctly answered enough questions to meet the passing standard. The total time for test taking will vary with the number of questions CAT finds necessary to measure the candidate's ability. RN candidates will answer at least 75 but no more than 265 questions. This new method is seen as both more precise and more efficient.[21]

Foreign Nurse Licensure

With backing from the American Nurses Association (ANA) and the National League for Nursing (NLN), the Commission on Graduates of Foreign Nursing Schools (CGFNS) was created in 1978 to administer a biannual test of nursing and English language competencies. Currently, 43 of the 53 state-registered nurse boards (including Guam, Puerto Rico, and the Virgin Islands) insist on CGFNS certification. Until 1995 the Immigration and Naturalization Service (INS) and the Department of Labor also required certification for an H-1 visa. These were issued after a sponsoring employer submitted proof to the INS that the "alien" was a duly licensed professional registered nurse. Approximately 10,000 foreign nurses have entered the United States each year with temporary H-1 visas. A large number of foreign nurses have come from the Philippines.

 **NURSING EDUCATION**

Nursing education for RNs in the United States began in New York in the latter half of the nineteenth century. The schools followed the English ideals of nursing, were run by nurses, and were affiliated with the hospital. Service training was an integral part of the education. Education generally involved 1 year of training, followed by 1 to 3 years of employment at the hospital. Lectures were given by physicians, and bedside training was provided by nurses.[22]

The number of such nursing schools grew rapidly in the late nineteenth century as more hospitals opened and demanded the free labor provided by student nurses. The exploitation of students led nurses to join forces to upgrade their status, and they formed organizations that were the precursors to the NLN and the ANA. This mobilization led to improvements in nursing education through registration and accreditation of schools. Nursing licensure was accomplished in every state by 1923.[23]

Today registered nursing education programs operate with specific goals and guidelines to enable graduates to meet the licensure requirements of their respective states, which are usually comparable with other states with the aid of endorsement or reciprocity. Table 4-1 provides a description of nursing education programs in the United States.

Basic RN Nursing Schools

As of 1994, there were approximately 1400 nursing schools in the United States; within these schools were 135,102 **associate degree,** 111,841

baccalaureate, and 22,934 **diploma** students (Figure 4-2). The total number of students (269,877) is a 4.6% increase over 1992.[24] The NLN found fall enrollments rising by 9.5% in baccalaureate Bachelor of Science in Nursing (BSN) programs and by 1.9% in Associate Degree in Nursing (ADN) programs. Enrollment in diploma nursing schools was down by 1.4%. Schools continue to say that they receive nearly three applications for each student who is admitted.

Men in Nursing Schools

The proportion of men in all nursing programs has increased from 4.4% in 1986 to 11.1% in 1992 (Figure 4-3).[26] This may be a result of the appeal of the healthcare reform proposals, which has opened the door to a much broader range of nursing possibilities than ever before. The increased number of men in nursing may also be a result of increased parental approval. In 1979, only one third of the women and one fifth of the men questioned said it would be acceptable for their son to become a nurse. However, according to a current RN survey, more than 40% of mothers

Table 4-1. Nursing education programs in the United States

CATEGORY	PROGRAM BASE	LENGTH OF PROGRAM	STATE LICENSURE REQUIREMENTS	RECOGNITION
Assistants, orderlies, attendants	Hospital, adult education, community colleges, private schools	3-6 months	No	Certification optional—required in most states
Practical nurse or vocational nurse	Hospital or hospital/community college	1-1½ years	Yes (LPN/LVN)	Certification
Diploma programs	Hospital or hospital/community college	3 years	Yes (RN)	Certification
Associate degree programs	Hospital/community college	2 years	Yes (RN)	Associate in arts degree (AA)
Baccalaureate degree programs	College or university	4-5 years	Yes (RN)	Bachelor of science degree in nursing (BSN, BS)
Master's degree in clinical nursing or nursing education programs	University	1½-2 years	Varies with individual state	Master's degree in nursing in specialty area (MSN, MS)
Doctoral programs in nursing	University	3-4 years	Varies with individual state	Doctoral degree in nursing in specialty area (PhD, EdD)

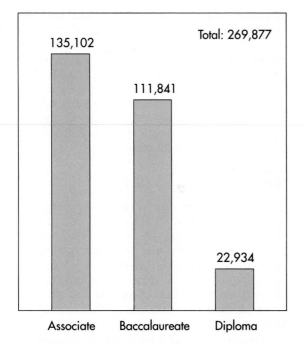

FIGURE 4-2. Fall enrollment for basic RN nursing programs. (Modified from National League for Nursing data review, Publication No 19-2642, New York, 1994, The League.)

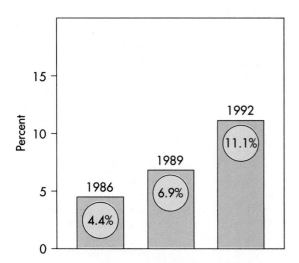

FIGURE 4-3. Percentage of men enrolled in baccalaureate, associate degree, and diploma programs. (Modified from National League for Nursing: *Men in nursing: how the ranks are growing,* Nursing Datasource, Publication No 19-2526, New York, 1993, The League.)

and fathers approve of nursing as a career choice for their sons. Public opinion has also changed from a clear majority preferring a female nurse to a slight majority indicating no preference.[27]

RNs Returning to Nursing Schools

The smallest enrollment increase, slightly over 2%, is found for registered nurses returning to school. The slim increase is thought to be a result of government cutbacks in tuition reimbursement and the limited use of incentive programs by employing agencies.[25]

Baccalaureate Programs
Traditional path

The RN who wishes to earn a BSN should matriculate with an NLN-accredited college or university, because this will be an important requirement when seeking to obtain certification, become a nurse practitioner, or acquire a master of science or doctoral degree. Most RNs who enroll in a traditional BSN program have other responsibilities such as part- or full-time employment, family, and other personal situations that require time and energy situations. Two professors in a school of nursing, Dick and Anderson,[28] studied RN-to-BSN students for their level of job burnout as a result of attending school. They found that students experienced some burnout, but their moderate level of burnout was not higher than that reported among other nurses in clinical practice. This could be attributed to the overall support given by employers (e.g., adjusting schedules), colleagues, and family. Other students may be looking toward possible advancement to other positions. In addition, an educational program has a buffering effect on burnout because students are increasing their knowledge of nursing and how to function within complex organizations.

Alternate paths

In the near future RNs with BSNs or more advanced degrees will most likely be in the greatest demand. The nurse who has earned a diploma or an associate degree and desires to earn a BSN but is unable to follow a traditional path may wish to explore alternate paths. The Regents College of the State University of New York offers one such program and is NLN accredited.

In such alternate programs, a student can sign up with one of the five regional performance assessment centers in the United States. Credits are granted for completion of traditional programs, and recognition is given for experience. The applicant must successfully complete 2½ hours of testing, which consists of four performance examinations. Costs of these alternate programs are considerably lower than those offered at other institutions, and students can complete most of the program requirements in their own home. Many nurses see this flexibility as the only feasible way they can return to school.[29]

A second innovative program, called **Mind Extension University** (ME/U), began in the fall of 1994. It is a cable network that specializes in long-distance education in partnership with California State University, and it is accredited by the NLN and the Western Association of Schools and Colleges. The program is designed for self-directed, working professionals and is available via cable television, satellite, and videotape; the program has no on-campus requirements. Requirements do include a current RN license, a minimum of 56 transferable college credits, and a grade point average of 2.0 or higher. A special admissions policy is available for diploma graduates.[30]

Changes Needed in the Nursing Educational System

The nursing profession is attempting to be a primary contributor to healthcare reform. The AONE has critically analyzed the entire education system and has suggested that core issues need to be considered, options scrutinized, and a plan adopted in a timely fashion. Six pressing immediate issues include, but are not limited to, the following:

- Differentiating nursing practice roles to match the needs of consumers and the competencies of providers
- Including primary care processes and skills in all curricula
- Integrating structures and systems-thinking (the interaction with larger social, political-legal, and economic systems)
- Including an economic framework as part of all delivery decisions
- Initiating and advancing interdisciplinary collaboration
- Designing an appropriate curriculum that

will support the nonphysician providers used in all healthcare settings

The Tri Council for Nursing, the national nursing coalition of the American Association of Colleges of Nursing (AACN), the ANA, the NLN, and the AONE are committed to spearheading the process of curriculum revision. The AONE believes that "not only must the educational system for tomorrow's students be reformed, but also the degree-completion programs for the thousands of currently employed registered nurses working in acute care hospitals."[31,p.33]

SCOPE OF NURSING PRACTICE

In the early 1950s, nurses recognized the need to accept greater responsibility and provide reasonably priced healthcare services to more people. The explosion of medical technology and the intense focus on the managed care mode of healthcare delivery has expanded the RN's preparation and skills, allowing the nurse to move into the distinctive activities of primary healthcare. The following paragraphs provide representative examples of the current variety of nursing roles.

Staff Nurse

RNs working at the staff level provide the bulk of primary nursing practice. Licensed graduates from diploma, AD, and BSN programs are eligible to function as beginning practitioners in acute, intermediate, long-term, and ambulatory healthcare facilities and, depending on preparation for certification, in home healthcare and community health agencies. All RNs should be able to apply the nursing process of assessment, planning, implementation, and evaluation. Placement of new RN graduates depends on interest, aptitude, and availability of position. Depending on experience, education, and training, RNs may advance to many diverse avenues of practice.

Critical Care Nurse

Critical care has progressed from a "do the best you can" approach into an enormous specialty based on a solid body of scientific knowledge and intricate skills. The **critical care nurse** (CCN) uses the primary nursing delivery system, which allows a certain degree of independence, and also serves as a full-fledged team member in patient management.[32] CCNs monitor complicated systems such as balloon angioplasty, pacemakers, hemodynamics, intraaortic balloon pumping, bedside hemodialysis, and advanced neurologic and surgical procedures; they often teach physicians, primarily interns, and residents in teaching hospitals about caring for critically ill patients. CCNs have input into the design and purchase of equipment, including bedside computers; they also help design products and techniques for practice. Some CCNs have become politically involved with right-to-die and living-will legislation and the right of nurses to pronounce death in the absence of a physician. CCNs are quickly moving toward using a **case-management** approach with critically ill patients. Many agree that when a CCN is in constant attendance, he or she is best able to manage the patient's total care in union with all disciplines involved. The American Association of Critical Care Nurses (AACCN) is the CCN's official organization.

Critical care nurses preferably have a BSN and advanced preparation in critical care nursing. Many nursing schools and colleges offer 4- to 12-month programs in critical care nursing in conjunction with hands-on experience in critical care units. Before enrolling in such a program, a nurse should have 2 to 3 years of clinical practice. Master's-level programs in critical care are also available and provide a thorough grounding in the basic sciences, in-depth preparation in gerontology, interpersonal focus, and preparation to work collaboratively with **professional nurse case managers,** physicians, and other interdisciplinary personnel. Graduates from these advanced-degree programs are prime candidates for managerial roles.

Clinical Nurse Specialist/Nurse Clinician

The role of **clinical nurse specialist** (CNS) evolved in response to a need. As hospitals developed specialty care units such as critical care, trauma care, diabetic treatment centers, and oncology, nurses became experts in providing care for those with particular needs. The Nurse Train-

ing Act of 1964 helped many schools establish expanded programs and master's degree programs, and clinical specialization became the primary focus of new curricula. Bullough and Bullough[33] define the CNS as a specialist in nursing who has a master's degree, whereas a **nurse clinician** (NC) is a specialist who may or may not have a master's degree. The AACCN is one of the many accrediting agencies that certifies nurses in specialty areas. A CNS certification is available through this organization after proof of experience and successful completion of a written examination.

EXAMPLE: Sara, a clinical nurse specialist, is assigned to an oncology unit. She is called to see Mary, a 32-year-old with a diagnosis of leg sarcoma who is experiencing intense stress and is threatening to give up all treatment. Sara spends time talking with Mary and her husband and performs an initial assessment and determines what approach to follow. She arranges for a visit with the hospital psychiatrist, and together they learn that Mary believes there is no hope for her; she prefers to spend the rest of her life with her husband and two children rather than in the hospital. After speaking with the physician, Sara explains to Mary that she has an excellent chance of recovery if she follows the prescribed therapy. Sara helps Mary to understand the treatment and resolve her anxieties, and she administers Mary's next few chemotherapy treatments. Sara follows Mary's course of treatment until dismissal, and offers support to Mary and guidance to the nursing staff.

The role of the CNS is evolving rapidly in two directions: (1) toward an almost total blending with that of the nurse practitioner, and (2) toward the role of the professional nurse case manager. Curtin, editor of *Nursing Management,* believes the CNS's role will most likely be combined with those of the NP and nurse case manager by the end of the decade.[34]

Acute Care Nurse Practitioner

An **acute care nurse practitioner** functions in settings where critically ill patients reside. This type of nurse provides special expertise not otherwise available. The first ANA credentialing examination for acute care nurse practitioners was given in early 1995. The certification includes physiology, advanced assessment, advanced pathophysiology, pharmacology, diagnostic reasoning, clinical decision making, and advanced therapeutics.[35]

Operating Room Nurse/Perioperative RN

When patients are admitted before and/or after surgery, the **operating room nurse** (ORN) monitors patient progress from the time he or she enters the operating room until he or she is dismissed to the attending staff nurse. In outpatient settings, the ORN performs a preoperative patient assessment, prepares the patient for surgery, sets up for surgery, assists the surgeon during the procedure, manages patient recovery, and follows up with patients in their homes and workplaces by telephone or a home visit.

With surgical procedures becoming more complex and more procedures being performed in outpatient settings, the ORN needs more advanced skills. Most ORN staffs consist of nurses with diplomas and ADs; some have BSN degrees. The American Association of Operating Room Nurses (AAORN) supports the ANA's position that baccalaureate nursing education should be the entry-level preparation for ORNs. The AAORN helped support the Joint Commission on Accreditation of Health Care Organizations (JCAHO) standards for nursing in operating rooms and specifically states that supervisors, nurse managers, and circulating nurses in surgical and obstetric services must be qualified RNs.

Community Health Nurse/Public Health Nurse

A community consists of a group of people who live in the same locality, under the same government and/or with shared interests and needs. A community provides safety, security, mutual protection and support, a means for socialization, and avenues for finding assistance for specific needs. A **community health nurse/public health nurse** (PHN) functions within this communal framework. The PHN serves the health needs of his or her assigned portion of the public.[36] He or she delivers care to the community as a whole, to populations within the community, to families, and to individuals.[35] The goal of the community health nurse is to improve community health by identifying people who are at high risk for illness, disability, or death. Clients are selected from epidemiologic studies and referrals by physicians and other health-related personnel. Community health nurses work closely with the interdisciplinary health team, including physicians, sanitarians, nutritionists, and health educators. They provide little hands-on care to clients but instead focus on other areas, including prenatal care, substance abuse, and communicable diseases such as acquired immunodeficiency syndrome (AIDS).

The PHN usually works out of a state, city, or county public health department and carries a "caseload" of families or individuals, depending on assignment. Public health nursing includes independent roles and responsibilities described as *primary* (prevention of illness before it has a chance to occur), *secondary* (early detection of actual or potential health hazards), and *tertiary* (prevention of further deterioration of an existing problem). The PHN maintains records of patient's progress and healthcare needs, makes assessments, provides healthcare education, and makes referrals for other necessary health-related services. PHNs have a BSN degree that has a basic component of community health nursing. A PHN certificate is issued by the state after completion of the program and several years of hospital nursing experience. Master's and doctoral programs in community health nursing are available at many major universities.

Nursing leadership in community health nursing

Nursing leadership in the community is important and requires an understanding of its basic power structure, its action process, and its strategies for influencing the flow of power and decision making.[35]

Expansion of community health services

Community health nursing has traditionally focused on preventive healthcare. Although prevention remains the first priority, additional roles are being added for the community health nurse. Early discharge of patients began to be encouraged in 1983, when the Health Care Financing Administration implemented the prospective payment system (PPS) for medicare and when health maintenance organizations (HMOs) and other managed-care options developed. Community health care nursing was affected across the country, and nurses expanded and increased their efforts to meet the challenges. Community health nursing has been complicated further by the increased age of patients, increased patient acuity levels, shortened hospital stays, larger geographic distances between family members, and inadequacy of funds.[36]

In addition to the traditional community health nursing role, other community-focused nursing roles have evolved. Examples of such roles are the home healthcare nurse, occupational health nurse, hospice nurse, nurse practitioner, nurse midwife, and school nurse, all of whom require special skills and abilities.

Home healthcare nurse/visiting nurse.

Although community/public health nursing is based on a wellness model, home healthcare has evolved as a medical model. The term *home healthcare* describes a system in which healthcare and social services are provided to homebound or disabled people in their homes rather than in medical facilities. Providers plan, coordinate, and make available the appropriate home care services through the use of employed staff, contractual arrangements, or a combination of both.[36] Home health is the largest employer of nurses within community-based nursing roles. The most common types of home health agencies are official (public), nonprofit, proprietary (for-profit), chains, and hospital-based agencies. The majority of **home health nurses** work in an official Visiting Nurse agency. An executive director of a major Visiting Nurse Association in Texas says that "home healthcare is the field of the future." With the changes in managed care and reimbursement, patients are being admitted to an acute care facility only if they have an acute condition. Patients are rapidly discharged to their homes under the direction of a home healthcare nurse.[37,p.626]

Goals.

One home healthcare agency in New England has developed a set of goals that expresses its philosophy.[38] Its overall goal is to provide and coordinate the services necessary to maintain the patient at home as long as possible. It also has four specific goals: (1) to reduce the fragmentation of care and promote the efficient and cost-effective use of resources; (2) to delay or limit the effects of chronic illness through skilled observation, anticipatory guidance, and health promotion; (3) to help patients and their families make informed decisions about their healthcare and to increase access to services through teaching, counseling, and long-term planning; and (4) to improve patient outcomes by mutually identifying problems between the patient/family and the care provider.

A core of services is generally provided by any home healthcare agency following a physician-approved plan of treatment. Home health nurses are currently pressing for the right to practice independently. The home healthcare nurse visits a designated number of clients each day, assesses their needs, provides hands-on care such as a bed bath or change of dressing/tubes, provides emotional and psychologic support, determines patient progress, and maintains records.

Preparation.

Preparation of home health nurses must be commensurate with their goals and expectations. The ANA has established standards for the practice of home health nursing. These standards are differentiated into two levels of practice: (1) the generalist home health nurse, who is prepared at the baccalaureate level; and (2) the specialist nurse, who is prepared at the graduate level. To become credentialed by the ANCC, the home health nurse must have an RN license in the United States or its territories and have at least a BSN. He or she must also have practiced as a licensed RN for at least 2 years, practiced as a licensed RN in home health nursing for a minimum of 2000 hours within 48 months of the application, and currently practice home health nursing a minimum of 8 hours each week.[31]

Occupational health nurse.

Occupational health nursing, a branch of public health nursing, is defined by the American Association of Occupational Health Nurses (AAOHN) as:

"...the application of nursing principles in conserving the health of workers in all occupations. It emphasizes prevention, recognition, and treatment of illnesses and injuries, and requires special skills and knowledge in the fields of health education and counseling, environmental health, rehabilitation, and human relations." (American Association of Occupational Health Nurses, 1976).[36,p.598]

As workplaces have continued to change dramatically, the role of the **occupational health nurse** (OHN) has become even more diversified and complex. Often working as the only on-site health professional, the occupational health nurse can develop surveillance programs, counsel employees, coordinate health promotion activities, set up comprehensive referral networks, treat individuals for emergency and primary healthcare problems, consult with business partners, and manage the overall occupational health service.

Approximately 30,000 nurses are in occupational health nursing, and approximately one half of them work alone. Most OHNs have a diploma and have been practicing occupational health nursing for a minimum of 12 years. However, the educational level of the group is escalating and moving toward the baccalaureate degree. More than 2000 AAOHN members have AAOHN certification, which represents education earned in degree or continuing education programs. Formal and organized specialty training is available in only a few universities.

Hospice nurse. The role of the **hospice nurse** is to provide support and instruction to the terminally ill and to keep them at home as long as possible. In March of 1994, the first ANA certification examination was offered to hospice nurses.[35] Candidates must be licensed RNs with 2 years of full-time or equivalent experience in hospice practice. Hospice nurse certification covers end-stage disease process, palliative therapy, interdisciplinary collaborative practice, education and advocacy, and issues.

Nurse practitioner. Nurse practitioners (NPs) are currently recognized as a critical component of healthcare reform. The competence, quality of care, and cost effectiveness of NPs has been clearly established. NPs meet many of the healthcare access needs and are necessary to the success of any proposed healthcare reform. As discussed previously, the immediate question is how to promote effective advanced nursing practice and alleviate statutory (legal) barriers to autonomous practice, the right to prescribe medications, and direct reimbursement to the NP. NPs currently have the legal right to practice in all states and have some degree of prescriptive authority in 43 states, including the District of Columbia. Truly independent NP practice, which is defined as having maximum independence in practice without physician supervision or collaboration, is permitted in Alaska and New Mexico.[10]

The NP is responsible for providing comprehensive care to both healthy and ill patients. He or she educates patients and/or their families to promote wellness, prevent health problems, maintain current health, and intervene in acute or chronic illness. All functions are completed within standardized guidelines, and orders are developed and sanctioned by the employing agency's governing body. If the NP is practicing independently, he or she follows the statutory rules of the state. Typical roles include (1) conducting comprehensive or episodic health assessments, (2) making medical diagnoses, (3) writing orders for diagnostic studies and therapeutic procedures, (4) prescribing and regulating medications in conjunction with a physician, (5) maintaining records and documents, and (6) using effective communication skills in teaching and counseling.

An NP may establish an independent practice or work in collaboration with other nurses and/or physicians. He or she may also choose to work in an HMO, a physician's office, an outpatient department, a clinic, a geriatric facility, a public health agency, a business or industry, a university, or a voluntary agency.

The ANCC offers certification examinations for adult nurse practitioners, family nurse practitioners, gerontologic nurse practitioners, school nurse practitioners, and pediatric nurse practitioners. Most pediatric nurse practitioners are certified by a separate organization, the National Association of Pediatric Nurse Associates and Practitioners. Obstetric-gynecologic nurse practitioners are certified only by the Nurses' Association of the American College of Obstetricians and Gynecologists. Each of these certifying bodies requires RN licensure, graduation from a recognized NP program, and successful completion of a certifying examination. Most employers recommend that NPs have several years of clinical hospital practice before enrolling in NP programs.

Nurse midwife. A **nurse midwife** follows the birthing process from inception through delivery. The nurse midwife gives prenatal care, attends labor and delivery, and cares for mothers and infants in the postpartum period. Midwives have a deep interest in preventive health measures and enlist client participation in care. Midwives generally function within the community in birthing centers, HMOs, and in hard-to-reach areas; they may also practice among high-risk groups. Studies by such groups as the ANA and the Institute of Medicine report that the neonatal mortality rate has dropped significantly as a result of attendance by nurse midwives.[33] However, nurse midwives have experienced great difficulty in achieving acceptance, particularly by physicians who may believe that their practices are threatened. Resistance remains high in some states, including California. There are 32 educational programs accredited by the College of Nurse-Midwifery. Of this group, 15 are certificate programs, 16 are at the master's level, and 1 awards a doctor of nursing science degree.[39]

> EXAMPLE: Fern, a nurse midwife, works out of a neighborhood family practice center. There she encounters Sandra, a 14-year-old girl who is 6 months pregnant. Fern establishes rapport with Sandra and her family and conducts a physical assessment. She determines that Sandra is anemic and undernourished and has many cavities. Fern asks a social worker in the agency about Sandra's home conditions, and together they develop a plan for dietary supplements and dental care. Fern carefully follows Sandra's progress and makes plans for the desired home delivery. Sandra and her family choose to put the baby up for adoption, and arrangements are made with a local agency. Fern delivers a healthy 6 lb 2 oz boy without difficulty and has access to a nearby hospital and physician if necessary. Fern follows through with completing the birth certificate and placing the infant with an adoption agency. Fern attends Sandra throughout her postpartal period and refers her to Planned Parenthood classes.

School nurse. The goal of school nursing is to support the educational process by helping students keep healthy and by teaching students and teachers preventive practices. The **school nurse** may be responsible for one or more schools. Responsibilities may include first aid, screening, follow-up, control of communicable diseases, immunizations, teaching health classes, transmitting knowledge that supports healthful behavior, conducting health-related studies, and responding to calls from other schools. School nurses may also act as student advocates and consultants. Preparation for the school nurse includes a BSN plus a school health credential,

which is awarded by the state after successful completion of a designated number of prescribed courses beyond the baccalaureate level. A small number of school nurses have become school nurse practitioners and perform physical examinations and follow ill children in the home, especially in schools where there is no contact with physicians.

Professional Nurse Case Manager

By definition, managed care represents the integration of healthcare financing and the provision of care; it replaces the unregulated structure of care delivery in which financing and care provision are separate. A fundamental principle of managed care is that all healthcare-related choices have a price. From a patient's entry into the system through discharge, the nurse case manager assesses the patient and develops care according to expected outcomes in terms of cost and quality.[40] In some respects a nurse case manager is a combination of manager, primary care nurse, clinical specialist, nurse practitioner, and community health nurse. The professional nurse case manager (PNCM) moves beyond the traditional discipline boundaries of time or shift and geographic or nursing-unit orientation. The case management model attempts to integrate nursing and all other interdisciplinary services for a patient's total illness episode, both in the hospital and in the community.[41]

A nurse case manager's effectiveness relies on his or her knowledge, judgment, attention, and skill to deliver the greatest improvements in care. See Chapter 5 for a description of the nurse case management delivery systems. The ANA publication, *Nursing Case Management,* recommends a BSN as the minimal level of educational preparation for a PNCM and strongly recommends preparation at the graduate level.

Rehabilitation Nurse

Rehabilitation nurses have many roles, the most important of which is education.[42,43] The nurse teaches the client to perform self-assessment, make decisions about beginning or continuing various self-care measures, perform everyday activities, and evaluate his or her progress and recovery. These clinical nurse specialists serve on the rehabilitation team as educators, consultants, and liaisons within their organizations and communities. They conduct research and help apply the findings.

Inpatient units are the most common setting for rehabilitation nursing. Three fourths of rehabilitation clients have problems related to stroke, musculoskeletal or orthopedic disorders, traumatic brain injury, or spinal cord injury. Other clients have burns, cardiac or pulmonary disease, cancer, or AIDS. Fifty-nine percent of the clients are elderly.

Formal training is available through the Association of Rehabilitation Nurses (ARN), some private education providers such as companies, and some rehabilitation hospitals. Several universities now offer master's degrees in rehabilitation nursing. Once a rehabilitation nurse possesses the necessary skills and knowledge and has at least 2 years of experience in the field, he or she is eligible for the Certified Rehabilitation Registered Nurse (CRRN). The examination is offered annually by the ARN. More than 8000 nurses have earned the CRRN since 1986. By the year 2000, a BSN degree will be required to take the examination.

Nurse Informaticist

Nursing informatics is defined as a combination of computer science, information science, and nursing science for the management and processing of nursing data, information, and knowledge to support the practice of nursing and the delivery of nursing care.[44,45] The **nurse informaticist** (also referred to as a *nurse informatician, nursing information specialist, system specialist,* and *designer of nursing information systems*) can be found in clinical practice, education, administration, and research. The nurse informaticist can be found at the bedside, teaching in colleges and universities, employed by vendors, managing the information systems of healthcare agencies, and developing software.

Approximately 5000 nurses have identified themselves as nursing informaticists. There are both national and international membership organizations that include networking and regular meetings. The ANA and the NLN support such organizations because they recognize that this field is crucial to progress. The ANA will soon be granting certification in informatics as a nursing specialty.

Nurse Entrepreneur

An **entrepreneur** is an individual who organizes, operates, and assumes the risk for business ventures. The number of **nurse entrepreneurs** increased in the 1980s as many creative and energetic nurses, believing that bureaucracy was stifling their innovative ideas, left hospitals and organizations to establish businesses of their own.[46] Examples of such businesses include independent nursing practices, consultant services, product-developing companies, and case management companies.

Kathleen Joseph, a clinical educator in a large hospital, created a board game for teaching entitled "Code Blue Game," which is currently being marketed nationwide. Another nurse secured funding for a pilot study that led to a system for recycling 80% of waste products from the operating room. Jo Manion, an independent nursing consultant, coined the term **nurse intrapreneur**, which describes nurses who have developed innovative ideas for improving patient care, education, and other nursing services or hospital operations. She suggests that intrapreneurship offers nurses a new opportunity to harness their creativity and reap its rewards without needing to start a business and give up the financial security of employment.

Travel Nurse

Traveling nurses are recruited for assignments that involve at least 13 40-hour weeks; after that, the nurse has the opportunity to join the organization as a permanent employee.[47,48]

The **travel nurse** must have an adaptable personality, be competent in his or her nursing skills and abilities, and not be afraid of challenge. The criteria for employment as a travel nurse includes the following:

- At least 1 year of experience in the appropriate clinical area
- Documentation of work history and above-average references
- Successful completion of skills evaluation, including a pharmacology examination
- Current CPR certification
- Physician documentation of good health, including state and hospital-specified inoculations
- Licensure in the state and acceptance into the assigned country

- Knowledge of fire, safety, infection control, and the standards of the Occupational Safety and Health Administration (OSHA)

Compensation usually matches the salaries of permanent employees. In addition to the salary, there is travel reimbursement, housing subsidies, and bonuses. Steven Francis, president of American Mobile Nurses (AMNs) in San Diego, states that flexibility and opportunity are the biggest draws for RNs. Taking a job in another country is a wonderful chance to experience a variety of learning experiences, see the country, acclimate to new cultures, or investigate possible places for relocation.

Licensed Practical Nurses/ Licensed Vocational Nurses

As late as the 1920s, most RNs were private duty nurses working in homes. In hospitals with nursing schools, student nurses provided the labor; hospitals without schools employed untrained or "practical" nurses. By 1940 healthcare delivery had shifted from the home to the hospital, and both RNs and practical nurses became the major source of labor. The resulting competition between these two groups increased pressure by the ANA and other interested groups for licensure of practical nurses. After a considerable struggle, stratification of nursing was first formalized in 1938 with the passage of a nursing licensure act in New York. This act required licensing of all hired nurses; established two levels of nursing, registered (RN) and practical (PN); and restricted nursing functions to members of these two groups. All states subsequently passed similar acts. By 1955 all states had licensing boards of licensed practical nurses (LPNs).[49]

Ever since World War II when the number of LPNs increased astronomically (from eight schools before the war to over a thousand after), LPNs have gradually widened their scope of practice. Initially LPNs were not allowed to administer medications in acute-care hospitals; later, they could give oral medications but not intramuscular injections. Gradually they advanced to regulating the flow of IVs but not adding medications to the IV. This is the current situation. LPNs and licensed vocational nurses (LVNs) seek to expand their role; this effort creates conflict between LPNs/LVNs and RNs. LPNs/LVNs feel demeaned when they believe that a narrow,

illogical differentiation strategy is being used to restrict their functions, whereas RNs fear that their roles may be taken over by nurses who are not as well equipped to perform them.

The Kaiser-Permanente Medical Care Program in Northern California services 68,000 members. In 1994 this organization used Permanente Nursing Research funds to determine whether LVNs working with RN supervision could safely and effectively provide selected patient instructions to adult medical patients by telephone.[50] Using 84 different protocols, LVNs learned to screen calls and give selected instructions to patients. The protocols were designed to prevent independent decision making by LVNs, which is prohibited by California state law. Initially RNs regretted the loss of their role in the advice system, and a variety of disenchanted feelings surfaced before the staff accepted the new system. The ANA does warn RNs not to be too quick to relinquish pieces of their practice without careful consideration.

Unlicensed Assistive Personnel

All across the United States, RNs are being replaced by unlicensed **assistive nursing personnel,** or **ancillary nursing personnel.** These employees are designated as nursing assistants, orderlies, or attendants, depending on the facility that employs them and the type of services they perform. Short programs offered in preemployment training and/or orientation, as well as adult education courses, community colleges, and private schools provide the necessary preparation for these occupations.

Standardization and regulation of course content or employment requirements depends on each state and the hiring practices of each facility. Many states require that unlicensed nursing personnel be certified to practice and fulfill certain requirements, such as completion of an approved program and employment as a nursing assistant for at least 2 years.

In hospitals and other agencies, the range of practice and job responsibilities for ancillary staff must be clearly defined. To help ensure adequate supervision and quality care by nursing assistants, the Tri Council, comprising the AACN, AONE, ANA, and NLN, believes that the nursing profession should determine the educational preparation necessary for nursing assistants and define their specific responsibilities. The Tri

Council also believes that assistive nursing personnel should be regulated by licensure; this belief is yet to be realized.

Nurses and other members of the healthcare team are being asked to share the responsibility of doing everything possible to contain costs. A question is being raised in the nursing profession regarding the safety of hiring more nursing assistants when nursing currently demands a greater level of expertise than ever before. A nurse's first priority is for patient welfare. Therefore the idea of replacing RNs and LPNs/LVNs with lesser-educated assistive personnel is causing concern. Nurses are just as anxious about these lesser educated healthcare workers delivering nursing care as physicians are about nurses delivering medical care.[51]

Historically, healthcare organizations have used substitution of labor to meet patient care needs. This results in part from the nurses' failure to define or capitalize on their special contribution to patient outcomes. Nurses claim that it is better for patients to receive basic care from professionals, but they have not been able to show that such care improves patient satisfaction or quality of care. As hospital-based case management gradually moves into a dominant mode for delivery of care (see Chapter 5), an increased use of different levels of direct-care providers will be realized. Nurses have the responsibility to prove their worth and to prevent erosions in the quality of healthcare.[52]

SUMMARY

1. A role is an organized set of expected behaviors in any given position. A nurse performs multiple roles in a typical day.
2. Role characteristics include behaving in a prescribed way; social interaction; mutual expectations; perceptions by the role enactor and those with whom he or she relates; social norms regarding values, judgments, and feelings; and conformity.
3. Sources that define a nurse's role are institutional requirements, patient/client expectations, peer pressure, and the nurse's conception of what the role implies.
4. Functional roles in nursing management include planning, organizing, staffing, leading, communicating, decision making, and controlling.

5. Situations that lead to role conflict include an inability or unwillingness of an individual to accept norms, role uncertainty, responsibility conflict, power struggles, and unshared meanings.
6. The AONE is an organization of nurse executives and nurse managers. The organization provides leadership, professional development, advocacy, and research in nursing practice and patient care; promotes nursing leadership excellence; and helps shape healthcare public policy.
7. The rate of nurse executive turnover is high in the United States and is increasing as a result of lower occupancy rates and a decline in the number of rural hospitals.
8. The nurse manager role continues to be one of planning, organizing, staffing, leading, communicating, decision making and controlling. However, because of a higher level of sophistication, the nurse is challenged to consider the entire spectrum of healthcare, from entry into the system to problem resolution.
9. Serious barriers to APNs include prescriptive authority, direct reimbursement, and autonomous practice.
10. Opinions differ among physicians and nurses regarding APNs. There appears to be solid public support for receiving most routine care from a "well-trained" nurse.
11. There are approximately 100,000 APNs in the United States.
12. Certification is a credential issued by a professional body that affirms excellence in a particular area and helps protect the consumer from harm. The ANA certifies specialists at the RN generalist level and clinical specialty areas at the master's level. Several independent specialty organizations certify qualified nurses who work in the community.
13. A license is a legal document that permits a person to offer his or her skills and knowledge to the public in a particular jurisdiction. The purpose of licensure is to protect society from unskilled and incompetent persons who would practice or who would offer to practice nursing.

14. The CGFNS administers a biannual test of nursing and English language competencies. Most of the state Registered Nurse Boards require CGFNS certification. Each year approximately 10,000 foreign nurses enter the United States with temporary visas (H-1). About 20,000 foreign nurses take the RN licensure examination each year.

15. The United States has approximately 1400 nursing schools; there are approximately 135,000 AD students, 112,000 BSN students, and 23,000 diploma students.

16. In 1992, 11.1% of those enrolled in nursing programs were men, an almost 7% increase in 6 years.

17. The number of RNs returning to school is decreasing and is thought to be a result of government cutbacks in tuition reimbursement and limited incentive programs by employing agencies.

18. The Regents College of the State University of New York offers an NLN-accredited alternate path to a BSN.

19. The AONE has suggested improvements in nursing education that include (1) differentiating nursing roles to match patient needs, (2) including primary care processes and skills, (3) integrating structures and systems-thinking, (4) including an economic framework, (5) considering interdisciplinary collaboration, and (6) designing a curriculum to support nonphysician providers in all healthcare settings.

20. Staff nurses provide the major share of primary nursing practice. They function in acute, intermediate, long-term, and ambulatory healthcare facilities. All staff nurses should be able to apply the nursing process to practice.

21. The CCN is a hospital-based RN with advanced preparation and experience in critical care. The CCN may or may not be certified.

22. The CNS is a certified RN who provides expert care for patients with particular needs. The CNS expands the scope of inpatient care by providing direct patient care with greater comprehensiveness, continuity, and coordination of all patient services.

23. The ORN functions in both inpatient and outpatient settings. The ORN's skills include expertise in assessment, preparation, assisting, and patient recovery. ORNs sometimes follow up on patients in their homes and workplaces and oversee services in recovery care centers.

24. The PHN works within a framework of community. The purpose of a community is to provide safety, security, mutual protection and support, a means for socialization, and avenues for finding assistance for specific healthcare needs. The PHN performs independent roles while providing primary, secondary, and tertiary care.

25. The home healthcare nurse/visiting nurse provides a core of home health services to patients following a physician-approved plan of treatment.

26. The term home healthcare describes a system in which healthcare and social services are provided to homebound or disabled people in their homes rather than in medical facilities. Home health is the largest employer of nurses within community-based roles. The most common types of home health agencies are official, nonprofit, proprietary, chains, and hospital based. The majority of home health nurses work in an official Visiting Nurse agency.

27. Occupational health nurses emphasize prevention, recognition, and treatment of illnesses and injuries. Occupational health nursing requires special skills and knowledge in the fields of health, rehabilitation and human relations.

28. NPs are registered nurses who provide primary patient care and have special training beyond the requirements for nursing licensure in medical history taking, physical assessment skills, and patient management. All functions are completed within standardized guidelines and orders that are developed and sanctioned by an appropriate governing body. Common classifications are family, pediatric, obstetric-gynecologic, and psychiatric–mental health nurse practitioners.

29. A nurse midwife follows the birthing process from inception through delivery.

Nurse midwives generally function in the community in birthing centers, in HMOs, in hard-to-reach areas, and/or they practice among high-risk groups.

30. OHNs, also called industrial nurses, provide consultation services, assess environmental hazards, complete preemployment histories and physical examinations, provide health education, and are employed as full- or part-time nurses.

31. A school nurse supports the educational process by helping students maintain health and by teaching students and teachers preventive practices.

32. The concept of PNCM emerged in the mid-1980s and is rapidly gathering momentum. The PNCM assesses the patient and develops care around expected outcomes, both in terms of cost and quality, from a patient's entry into the system through discharge.

33. The rehabilitation nurse teaches the patient to make self-assessments, make decisions about undertaking or continuing various self-care measures, perform everyday activities, and evaluate his or her own progress and recovery. Three fourths of rehabilitation clients have problems related to stroke, musculoskeletal or orthopedic disorders, traumatic brain injury, or spinal cord injury.

34. The nurse informaticist's practice is fairly new and is defined as a combination of computer science, information science, and nursing science. The practice is designed to help manage and process nursing data, information, and knowledge to support the practice of nursing and the delivery of nursing care.

35. A nurse entrepreneur organizes, operates, and assumes the risk for business ventures. In 1980 nurses began to branch out on their own and capitalize on their innovative ideas for the improvement of nursing care.

36. The term *intrapreneur* has been coined to describe the nurse who designs products or systems under the framework of the employer, who provides an avenue for testing and marketing of the product and at the same time provides the nurse with the security of steady employment.

37. Traveling nurses are recruited for assignment in the United States and foreign countries for at least 13 40-hour weeks; they have the opportunity to join the employing agency as a permanent employee after that. Traveling nurses must meet specific criteria.

38. LPNs and LVNs are prepared in vocational schools that stress clinical experiences in various healthcare settings and focus on the nursing process, caregiving, and health teaching. Because nursing is becoming more complex, the number of LPN/LVN schools is gradually declining.

39. Assistive nursing personnel (nursing assistants, orderlies, and attendants) perform designated nursing and support services that do not require RN/LPN licensure. Nursing assistants are being used more often in health agencies, both in and out of hospitals, as a result of pressure to conserve costs.

❓ Questions for Study and Discussion

1. If you accept the role of staff nurse, what personal characteristics would be expected of you? Do you think you would have a problem meeting any of these expectations? Please explain.

2. Describe the roles of nurse manager. In which of these roles do you believe yourself to have the most potential? Do any of the roles have negative connotations for you? Please explain.

3. What is the purpose of RN licensure? Do you think each state should have the right to develop its own criteria for nursing practice, rather than the national government developing criteria for all states?

4. What, if anything, do you think should be done to increase the very low percentage of ethnic and minority RNs? If you are Caucasian, would you be willing to give up your

space in a nursing program for an equally qualified student from an ethnic or minority background? Why?

5. As a staff nurse, you are concerned that the RN/nursing assistant ratio is decreasing. How would you go about proving that it is better for patients to receive professional nursing care?

6. Explain the purpose of nurse certification. Who is the primary certifying association?

7. Select the nursing role you would like to practice in the future. Explain the preparation required for the role and its scope of practice. What sparks your interest in this field?

8. Does the role of professional nurse case manager appeal to you? In what ways? If not, why is the role not inviting?

9. As a nurse practitioner, you are defending before the state legislature your right to maintain an independent primary care nursing practice. You want to be able to write prescriptions for selected medications and receive direct reimbursement for your services. What would you say?

Test Your Knowledge

BEHAVIORAL OBJECTIVE

Define the meaning of role analysis and identify factors that affect roles in nursing practice.

Greg is to manage a nursing unit for quadraplegic patients. He is unsure of the agency's expectations and how to perceive himself in this situation.

_____ 1. Greg engaged in a process called "Role analysis," which meant that he:
   a. Systematically clarified interdependent tasks and job behavior.
   b. Learned the names and job titles of all personnel.
   c. Studied cost and production on the nursing unit that he will manage.
   d. Assembled a personal profile of each employee assigned to the unit.

_____ 2. Greg found that the term *role* encompasses all of the following definitions except:
   a. An expected behavior.
   b. A specific position.
   c. An independent activity.
   d. A social pattern.

_____ 3. As manager of the quadraplegic unit, Greg will be responsible for implementing primary nursing. Expectations for role fulfillment will include all of the following except:
   a. Adhering strictly to a specific job description.
   b. Maintaining professional attitudes.
   c. Working within the organizational structure.
   d. Planning nursing care independently of others.

BEHAVIORAL OBJECTIVE

List and explain the functional roles of nurse managers.

_____ 4. Greg wants to be prepared for the nurse manager role. The most important characteristic he needs to have to succeed is:
   a. General nursing skills with quadraplegics.
   b. Human management skills.
   c. Fiscal management skills.
   d. Good relations with the medical staff.

BEHAVIORAL OBJECTIVE

Explain the impact of changes in the healthcare system on nursing roles.

Laura has just completed all requirements for the RN status and is looking forward to providing healthcare. She discovers that she does not have the option to choose where she will practice or what she will do.

_____ 5. Laura discovers that some hospitals are closing and that the following group is at the highest risk:
   a. Urban hospitals
   b. Rural hospitals
   c. Emergency centers
   d. Restorative care facilities

BEHAVIORAL OBJECTIVE

Define the advanced practice nurse and list the barriers that prevent such nurses from practicing at their full potential.

Janice has decided to enter into advanced nursing practice. She realizes that she needs to follow certain steps to reach her goal.

_____ 6. Janice must define the role. She investigates and concludes that the differentiating feature of advanced practice nurses (APNs) is that they:
   a. Have practiced nursing for a number of years.
   b. Are skilled in a particular area.
   c. Are certified or have an advanced degree.
   d. Have the ability to lead/manage.

BEHAVIORAL OBJECTIVE

Explain the different programs in nursing education.

Cindy wants to enroll in an RN program. She investigates the similarities and differences among the various programs.

_____ 7. Cindy learns that the following nursing program has the highest enrollment:
   a. Schools for advanced preparation
   b. Diploma
   c. Associate
   d. Baccalaureate

BEHAVIORAL OBJECTIVE

Identify the major categories of nursing personnel and the preparation, education, and role required for each position.

_____ 8. Cindy learns most nurse practitioner programs generally last:
   a. 2 years.
   b. 6 months.
   c. 1 year.
   d. 3 years.

Cindy decides that as long as she is comparing specific nursing roles, she should examine other possibilities. She learns the following:

_____ 9. RN, staff-level nurses have the following in common with nurse practitioners except:
   a. RN staff-level nurses are eligible to function as beginning practitioners.
   b. RN staff-level nurses apply the nursing process.
   c. RN staff-level nurses are certified by the ANCC.
   d. RN staff-level nurses have official sanction to practice.

_____ 10. Hospice nurse certification covers:
   a. Rehabilitation.
   b. Palliative therapeutics.
   c. Transplant responsibilities.
   d. Rescucitation.

_____ 11. A professional nurse case manager engages in each of the following roles with the exception of:
   a. Integrating healthcare financing and provision of care.
   b. Developing care around expected outcomes.
   c. Combining managing with primary care, specialist roles, nurse practitioners, and community health nurses.
   d. Concentrating on a patient's successful entry into the system.

REFERENCES

1. Kreitner R: *Management,* ed 5, Dallas, 1992, Houghton Mifflin.
2. Anderson R: The new AONE, *JONA* 24(4):18-24, 1994.
3. Kippenbrock T, May F: Turnover at the top: CNO's and hospital characteristics, *Nurs Manage* 25(9):54-57, 1994.
4. Sherman V: Nursing's management crisis, *Supervisor Nurs* 11(10):31-33, 1989.
5. O'Neil K, Gajdostik K: The head nurse's managerial role, *Nurs Manage* 20(6):39-41, 1989.
6. Kerfoot K, Luquire R: Today's care unit manager, *Nurs Econ* 11(5):321-323, 1993.
7. Patz J, Biordi D, Holm K: Middle nurse manager effectiveness, *JONA* 21(1):15-24, 1991.
8. Vitello J: Time to choose your own critical path, *Crit Care Nurse* 14(1):142, 1994.
9. LaBeur M: Forecasters of change, *Nurs Manage* 24(6):74, 1994.
10. Birkholz G, Walker D: Strategies for state statutory language changes granting fully independent nurse practitioner role, *Nurse Pract* 19(1):54-58, 1994.
11. Pearson L: Annual update of how each state stands in legislative issues affecting advanced nurse practice, *Nurse Pract* 19(1):11-13;17, 1994.
12. Chow M: Nurses as primary care providers: an old idea whose time has come, *Calif Hosp* 8(4):10;12-14, 1994.
13. AJNNEWSLINE: AMA assails broader role for RNs: ANA sees "inaccuracy and innuendo," *Am J Nurs* 94(2):76;81, 1994.
14. AJNNEWSLINE: ANA, AMA declare a truce in health care reform war, *Am J Nurs* 94(3):76, 1994.
15. NEWSLINE: Majority OK RNs for primary care, says Harvard study, *Am J Nurs* 94(2):77, 1994.
16. Sharp N: Recognizing APNs: it's now or never! *Nurs Manage* 25(2):14, 1994.
17. Morgan W, Trolinger J: The clinical education of primary nurse practitioner students, *Nurse Pract* 19(4):62-66, 1994.
18. Letters to the Editor: Federal government focus regarding health care, *Nurse Pract* 19(1):74, 1994.
19. American Nurse Credentialing Center: Why become certified? *Nurs 94* 24(3):88a-88l, 1994.
20. Division of Nursing: *Data compiled by the data analysis branch,* Rockville, Md, 1993, Division of Nursing.
21. AJNNEWSLINE: Licensure goes high-tech with new computerized exam, *Am J Nurs* 94(3):77-80, 1994.
22. Watson J: The evolution of nursing education in the US: 100 years of a profession for women, *J Nurs Educ* 16(7):31-37.
23. McCloskey J, Grace H: *Current issues in nursing,* ed 3, St Louis, 1990, Mosby.
24. National League for Nursing: *Trends in contemporary nursing education,* vol 1, Pub No 19-2642, New York, 1994, The League.
25. AJNNEWSLINE: Students still flock to schools though jobs are harder to find, *Am J Nurs* 94(2):77-80, 1994.
26. National League for Nursing: *Nursing datasource,* Pub No 19-2526, New York, 1993, The League.
27. Begany T: Your image is brighter than ever, *RN* 57(10):28-34, 1994.
28. Dick M, Anderson S: Job burnout in RN-to-BSN students: relationships to life stress, time commitments, and support for returning to school, *J Contin Educ Nurs* 24(3):105-109, 1993.
29. Dailey M: Taking an alternative path to your BSN, *Nurs 94* 94(3):84-86, 1994.
30. RN NEWSWATCH: BSN program without campus, *RN* 57(10):17, 1994.
31. American Organization of Nurse Executives: A call for reform of our nursing education system, *Nurs Manage* 24(1):33, 1993.
32. Wilson V: From sentinels to specialists, *Am J Nurs* 90(10):32-43, 1990.
33. Bullough B, Bullough V: Nursing in the community, St Louis, 1990, Mosby.
34. Tappen R: *Nursing leadership and management: concepts and practice,* ed 2, Philadelphia, 1989, FA Davis.
35. RN NEWSWATCH: Acute care NPs, hospice nurses jump on the certification bandwagon, *RN* 57(10):15-16, 1994.
36. Swanson J, Albrecht M: Community health nursing: promoting the health of aggregates, Philadelphia, 1993, WB Saunders.
37. Gonzales B, Harris M: Home health care: field of the future, *Nurs 94* 25(3):92, 1994.
38. Michaels D: Home health nursing: toward a professional practice model, *Nurs Manage* 25(4):68-72, 1994.
39. American Colleges of Nurse-Midwives: Education programs accredited by the division of accreditation, *J Nurse Midwife* 29(2):173, 1984.
40. Packard N: The price of choice: managed care in America, *Nurs Adm Q* 17(3):8-15, 1993.
41. Kerfoot K, Luquire R: Today's patient care unit manager, *Nurs Econ* 11(5):321-323, 1993.
42. Preston K: Rehabilitation nursing: a client-centered philosophy, *Am J Nurs* 94(2):66-70, 1994.
43. Stevens K: Portrait of a rehabilitation nurse, *Nurs 93* 24(11):73m-73k, 1993.
44. Simpson R: Shifting perceptions: defining nursing informatics as a clinical specialty, *Nurs Manage* 24(12):20-21, 1993.

45. Carty B: The protean nature of the nurse informaticist, *Nurs Health Care* 15(4):174-177, 1994.
46. Manion J: The nurse intrapreneur: how to innovate from within, *Am J Nurs* 94(1):38-42, 1994.
47. AbuGharbieh P: Culture shock: culture norms influencing nursing in Jordan, *Nurs Health Care,* 14(2):245-247, 1993.
48. Dardenne P: See the world, *Am J Nurs* 94(2):345-347, 1994.
49. National League for Nursing: *State-approved schools of nursing LPN/LVN 1994,* ed 36, Pub No 19-2623, 1994, The League.

50. Buccini R, Ridings L: Using licensed vocational nurses to provide telephone patient instructions in a health maintenance organization, *JONA* 24(1):27-33, 1994.
51. Chavigny K: AMA's policy and nursing's role in emerging systems, *Nurs Manage* 24(12):30-34, 1993.
52. McCloskey J and others: Nursing management innovations: a need for systematic evaluation, *Nurs Econ* 12(1):35-42, 1994.

SUGGESTED READINGS

American Association of Neuroscience Nurses: Scope of practice statement, *J Neurosci Nurs* 26(1):47, 1994.

Anderson C: Restructured organizations: traversing hills and valleys, *Nurs Outlook* 41(5):198-199, 1993.

Anderson C: Advanced practice: quality control, *Nurs Outlook,* 42(2):54-55, 1994.

Archibald P, Bainbridge D: Capacity and competence: nurse credentialing and privileging, *Nurs Manage* 25(4):49-50;54-56, 1994.

Cerne F: HMOs and reform, *Hospitals Health Network* 67(24):20-21, 1993.

Crawley W: Case management: managing the nurse case manager, *Health Care Superv* 12(4):84-89, 1994.

Dijkhuizen S: Meeting the basic and educational needs of foreign nurses, *J Contin Educ Nurs* 26(1):15-19, 1995.

Duffield C: Nursing unit managers: defining a role, *Nurs Manage* 25(4):63-67, 1994.

Fiesta J: Managed care: whose liability? *Nurs Manage* 26(2):31-32, 1995.

Garcia M, Niemeyer D, Robbins J: Collaborative practice: a shared success, *Nurs Manage* 24(5):72-75, 1993.

Guerrero J, Hansen M: Career ladder program, *J Contin Educ Nurs* 24(1):32-36, 1993.

Hurley M: Where will you work tomorrow? *Nurs Manage* 57(8):31-35, 1994.

Kirschling J and others: "Success" in family nursing: experts describe phenomena, *Nurs Health Care* 15(4):186-189, 1994.

Letvaks S: Doctor's office, may I help you? *RN* 57(6):80, 1994.

Michaels D: Home health nursing: towards a professional practice model, *Nurs Manage* 25(4):68-72, 1994.

News In Mental Health Nursing: *J Psych Nurs* 32(4):44, 1994.

NURSING NEWS: Hard-to-fill specialties, *Nurs 94* 24(1):10, 1994.

Pearson L: Annual update of how each state stands on legislative issues affecting advanced nursing practice, *Nurse Pract* 19(1):11-13;17-19, 1994.

Perra B: The clock is running on RNs who won't change, *RN* 58(2):20-24, 1995.

Presley A: Perspectives on public health nursing: an interview, *J Nurs Adm* 24(1):7-8, 1994.

RN NEWSWATCH: Nursing lacks ethnic and racial diversity, *RN* 57(7):12, 1994.

Robinson S, Barberis-Ryan C: Advanced practice nursing: playing a vital role, *Nurs Manage* 24(2):45-47, 1995.

STAFFING PROCESS and NURSING CARE DELIVERY SYSTEMS

BEHAVIORAL OBJECTIVES

On completion of this chapter, the student will be prepared to:

- Analyze the job market and trends in the 1990s and state the implications for the jobseeker.

- Explain the staffing process of recruitment, selection, and placement of personnel.

- List the criteria that are important to the staffing process and identify major components of each.

- Define the systems used to deliver nursing care such as total, primary, functional, team, modular, and nurse case management, and determine the advantages and disadvantages of each.

- Identify the meaning of cross-functional, multidisciplinary teams and the patient-focused model and determine the advantages and disadvantages of each.

An organizational structure may be designed on paper, but to come to life it must be staffed with people. Such efforts are referred to as **staffing,** a separate and fundamental function of management. Staffing is the use of recruitment, selection, and development of personnel to assign competent people to the roles designed for the organizational structure. This chapter discusses the job market, employment procedures, criteria important to the staffing process, and nursing care delivery systems, which are all vital to the staffing process and nursing care delivery systems.

THE JOB MARKET

Cost reduction, downsizing, and restructuring of delivery systems are affecting job security and staffing patterns from coast to coast. Not all healthcare agencies are laying off nurses, but many are failing to replace nurses who leave. As a result, nurses may be "juggling more responsibilities while trying to deal with a changing staff mix."[1,p.57]

Job Choices

Both new graduates and experienced nurses are asking, "Where have all the jobs gone?" Reduced hours and layoffs in all disciplines are common across the country. Vogel,[2] a registered nurse and president of the National Association for Health Care Recruitment, warns that nurses may no longer find a job waiting for them in the area of nursing in which they would most like to practice. New graduates may now need to take their second or third choices or move to a location or state that has more openings. Vogel states that "the national economy, concerns about health care reform, hospital mergers, and closing of smaller hospitals have all been implicated in the tighter job market."[2,p.5]

Even though jobs are currently harder to find, the demands on employed nurses have increased. Nurses are caring for more critically ill patients on general units, intensive care units (ICUs) have higher acuity, and outpatient services are becoming more complex. Vogel states that recruiters across the country report an applicant/position ratio of approximately 10:1. She suggests that the jobseeker remain focused, ask pertinent questions, and, most important, remain professional in all endeavors.

National Trends

A number of national changes in the job market have been cited recently in the literature and include the following:

- Washington state's Group Health Cooperative has agreed with a coalition of 11 unions to cut 200 to 350 jobs, but it will provide severance pay for those who volunteer to quit and will pay for job counseling, retraining, and extended healthcare benefits.[3]
- Chicago's University of Illinois Hospital wants to eliminate 156 registered nurse (RN) full-time equivalents (FTEs) and replace them with assistive personnel.[3]
- Of the more than 1000 hospitals polled, 27% are making cuts, mostly between 5% and 14% (see Figure 5-1).[3]
- In 1990, administrative costs accounted for 24.8% of hospital spending in the United States. As the number of patients in hospitals declines, there is the dangerous poten-

tial for cost cutting in administration, particularly in managed care.[3]
- Many nurses today who work in private community hospitals and are not covered by a written contract or union agreement are working as an "at-will" employee; this means that he or she can be terminated at any time, usually to cut costs. However, it is illegal to terminate a nurse on the basis of sex, race, age, pregnancy or disability.[4]
- Joel states that "responding to pressure to cut operational costs, hospitals have been quick to downsize their work force and substitute less expensive personnel."[5,p.7]
- The redesign of all personnel and the use of licensed practical nurses (LPNs) and nursing assistants (NAs) at one Iowa facility have reduced its RN staff from 63% to 46%.[6]
- According to the 1993 National Association for Health Care Recruitment Survey (conducted by *Nursing 93,* Springhouse Corporation), the average vacancy rate for RNs is at a 14-year low of 5%.[7]

A Note of Optimism

A contrasting view is presented by the American Hospital Association (AHA). They report that 77% of all hospitals are experiencing a nursing shortage as a result of an increased aging population, rapid expansion of long-term care, advances in technology, increased acuity of care, and the need for more primary care. The secretary's commission on nursing for the U.S. Department of Health and Human Services states that "hospitals must be more efficient by making more appropriate use of the special expertise of nurses." The commission believes that nursing care delivery systems must be structured to use the current pool of RNs to their maximum potential.[8,pp.78;80]

 **EMPLOYMENT PROCEDURES**

Recruitment

To **recruit** nurses, one can fill vacancies from within the facility, hire graduates from schools and colleges, place advertisements and announcements, and use professional and private nurse employment agencies, both national and international. Less formal means of recruitment are recommendations by employees and friends. Some applicants initiate their own contacts. Geographic location is an important factor in choosing where to work. Magnet hospitals such as large municipal hospitals associated with educational institutions are very appealing to nurses, particularly new graduates; these large health facilities offer a wide range of opportunities and convenient access to the attractions of urban life.

Experienced Nurses

Nurses who have practiced for a number of years and have become experts in their fields carry more clout with recruiters. Such nurses can negotiate salaries, work schedules, and other important benefits. If the nurse's spouse has health insurance, some employers will trade health insurance for child care. If relocation is necessary, the employer may offer a mortgage subsidy program or arrange for a lower interest rate in the purchase of a home, and it may pay moving expenses. Recruiters assess the nurse's potential value to the agency and then devise a plan they hope will attract that nurse.[9]

In today's world, nurses must learn to become entrepreneurs, catalog their achievements, shop around for the best wage and benefit package in the desired environment, sell themselves to recruiters, and negotiate the best possible offer.

Supplemental Staffing

Supplemental staffing involves the use of nurses who are available and on-call at their homes or who are employed by nurse registries, private agencies that hire nurses to provide a pool of nursing staff to consumers.

Proponents of supplemental staffing

Those who use supplemental staffing argue that it provides healthcare agencies with much-needed labor while providing supplemental nurses with greater flexibility and control over their practice. Health agencies can maintain minimal nursing staffs commensurate with their average daily patient census; when the census increases, agencies can augment their staff with independent or registry nurses. Such a plan helps

healthcare agencies prevent overstaffing during times of low census. Another advantage, and a significant issue, is that the healthcare agency is not responsible for payment of benefits of the supplemental staff.

Opponents of supplemental staffing

Opponents claim that the use of supplemental staffing disrupts the consistency and continuity of patient care. The independent or registry nurses may also need continual orientation. There may be a negative impact on the morale of permanent employees, who often receive lower hourly wages than the supplemental staff. Nurses may not understand that the independent or registry nurse must pay for a benefit package out of his or her wages. Although some maintain that supplemental nurses are given heavier, more difficult assignments than regularly employed nurses, others argue that they receive lighter or easier assignments.

Comparison of supplemental staff to hospital nurses

Hughes and Marcantonio[10] surveyed 6720 nurses; half were registry nurses and half were regularly employed in hospitals. All nurses had worked approximately 14 years. They attempted to determine if the two groups differ in terms of sociodemographic characteristics, work schedules, and clinical practice.

Sociodemographic characteristics. Hughes and Marcantonio discovered that registries contained more male nurses and more minority groups. The education of the two groups was fairly equal, although more registry nurses had master's degrees.

Work schedules. Registry nurses were less likely to work day shifts and more likely to work evenings and nights. They were also slightly more likely to work weekend shifts and fewer hours per week.

Clinical practice. Hospital nurses reported taking more health histories and using computers more often to document care. In some healthcare facilities, registry nurses were not allowed to document care into the computer; this task was assigned to a staff nurse to avoid data-entry error. Nevertheless, registry nurses reported better opportunities to use their skills in contrast to hospital nurses, who felt limited in their opportunities. This is most likely because hospital nurses have less time to devote to clinical activities. Hospital staff nurses must serve on committees, supervise ancillary personnel, and collaborate with other departments; they therefore devote more time to indirect patient care activities.

Supplemental personnel should be screened as carefully as other hospital nurses. A critical need for nurses does not justify failure to exercise reasonable care when screening registry nurses or hiring temporary nurses. If the nurse manager knows that the registry nurse is incompetent but fails to act upon that knowledge, the user of the RN services may be liable. The nurse manager also has a legal duty to communicate any pertinent information about a registry nurse's performance to the appropriate registry.[11]

Nurse registries are a part of the healthcare system because the marketplace demands them. Establishment of guidelines such as those mentioned in Box 5-1 can help offset serious problems that jeopardize patient care.

Selection of Nursing Personnel

Responsibility for staffing an organization with nursing personnel rests with every manager at every level. Figure 5-1 illustrates the typical staffing procedure. Staffing requires coordination between the personnel department and nursing services. The personnel department ordinarily provides staff in accordance with department requests. Usually the personnel department screens applicants for information such as valid licensure, education, experience, preferences, and health status. The nursing service personnel are then responsible for selecting an applicant and placing him or her in a specific job. Top-, middle-, and lower- or first-level managers collaborate to select the best person for each position.

During the interview, the personnel department should inform the prospective employee about the salary and wage plan, fringe benefits, working conditions, expectations, working hours

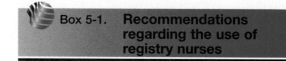

Box 5-1.   Recommendations regarding the use of registry nurses

The Harvard Risk Management Foundation has provided a number of excellent recommendations for hospitals and other health agencies to consider when using registry nurses.[11]

1. Contract with a select group of carefully screened agencies. Ascertain that each agency has a thorough evaluation program for its nurse employees.
2. Develop a written contract with the registry that addresses the issue of liability.
3. Require the registry and/or the nurses to carry sufficient malpractice insurance (minimum individual limits of $1,000,000).
4. Establish an orientation program for all registry nurses who work in the health facility and include an evaluation of competence levels.
5. Inform patients that they are receiving care from registry nurses.
6. Minimize the use of registry personnel as much as possible and try to assign them to low-risk settings.
7. Make it clear to registry nurses that they are to identify any portion of their assignments that is beyond their abilities.
8. Independently verify the registry nurse's licensure status, references, and disciplinary and malpractice history.

and time off, the possibility of having individual requests considered, orientation to the job, evaluation procedures, promotion policies, and opportunities for inservice and continuing education. The standards of nursing care adopted by the health facility should be reviewed and clarified, and the methods used for delivery of patient/client care should be explained. The prospective employee should feel comfortable enough in the interview to discuss any matter pertaining to employment. Supplying the prospective employee with as much information as possible regarding the agency and the job reduces the probability of dissatisfaction and short-term employment and thereby contributes to increased quality of care and cost-effectiveness.

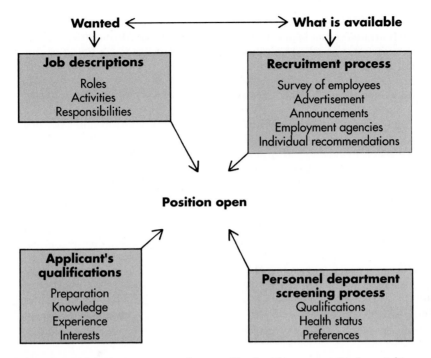

FIGURE 5-1. Typical employment procedure used by healthcare agencies in matching applicants with job openings.

Induction and Orientation

Induction consists of those formal procedures an employee follows immediately after being hired. Such procedures include (1) getting on the payroll, (2) arranging for deductions (e.g., income tax, health insurance), and (3) completing routine records.

Orientation is the formal process of familiarizing the new employee with the organization and his or her place in it. The new worker becomes aware of his or her role in meeting the goals of the organization. The amount of time and emphasis devoted to orientation varies with the size of the agency and the scope of services offered. Orientation also depends on the agency's provision for training in the form of (1) teaching personnel, (2) equipment and other teaching resources, (3) space availability for classes and practice, (4) new employee needs, and (5) urgency for the new employee to begin working. A successful orientation helps speed the transition process by building the nurse's identification with the agency, helping the nurse become acquainted with fellow personnel, and providing the nurse with important information about the organization.

THE STAFFING PROCESS

In any healthcare agency, the staffing process is one of the most important and difficult tasks of a nurse manager. Attempting to fill schedules with available personnel while also considering their varied and diverse competencies and numerous special requests can challenge the ability of any manager.

Effects of Absenteeism

Studies of absenteeism in the workplace have been conducted over the past three decades and have shown that individual needs, relationships with co-workers and supervisors, working conditions, work policies, and compensation affect the extent to which an individual is gratified or fulfilled in his or her work. A satisfied employee tends to be absent less often than a dissatisfied employee.[12] A dissatisfied employee may often be absent and may experience stress that disrupts co-workers. Such a situation can pose serious staffing problems for the nurse manager. When an employee does not report for work, a substitute must be hired to do the job, and the quantity and quality of work is likely to suffer (Figure 5-2). The key concern of organizations is to minimize feigned absenteeism and reduce legitimate absences as much as possible.[13]

Staff Burnout
Characteristics

Burnout has been associated with three composite factors: (1) emotional exhaustion, or feeling overextended and worn out from work, (2) depersonalization, or a lack of appropriate responses to the nurse's efforts, and (3) a diminished sense of personal accomplishment.[14] Recent studies show that burnout among nurses is also associated with work-related factors such as workload, hours worked each week, team size, and amount of patient contact.[15]

Burnout is characterized by apathy, alienation, job dissatisfaction, and a depersonalization of patients (Figure 5-3). Picture a nurse going off duty, driving home, and collapsing on the couch:

> "Wow! What a terrible day—just like all the others. I feel like a hamster running the treadmill, running hard but getting nowhere. I'm bombarded with more than I can do and no one appreciates me. I don't think I can go on. What's it all about anyway? Who cares about what happens to me?"

Buffers

Researchers have begun to investigate variables that reduce or buffer burnout. Tarolli-Jager,[16] a nurse researcher, has identified one such buffer,

"I'm ill and won't be at work today."

"My car broke down, my grandmother died, I have jury duty...."

FIGURE 5-2. Absence for any reason seriously affects the staffing process and quality of care.

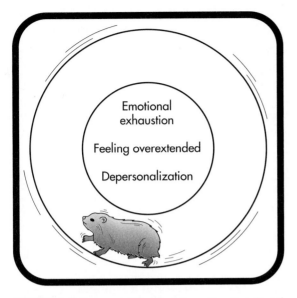

FIGURE 5-3. Burnout. (Modified from Corrigan P and others: Staff burnout in a psychiatric hospital: a cross-legged panel design, *J Org Beh* 15[1]:65-74, 1994.)

called *personal hardiness.* She found that the higher a nurse's level of personal hardiness, the more job satisfaction he or she experienced; he or she was also less likely to experience burnout. The converse proved true as well; the weaker the nurse in personal hardiness, the greater the likelihood of burnout. Three personality characteristics determine hardiness: (1) commitment, (2) control, and (3) challenge (Figure 5-4).

Commitment. Commitment involves a strong sense of dedication to self and others. In nursing, commitment is entrusting the professional self to an agency for honorable service. The nurse might ask, "Have I decided to give this job all I have in the interest of providing quality care, or am I constantly looking over my shoulder to see if I can do better elsewhere?"

LACK OF COMMITMENT: "You can be a sucker if you want and never take a sick day to go to the beach. As for me, I'm going to take all I can get—this lousy organization owes it to me!"

COMMITMENT: "I like my job. Our patients come first, and we know what is expected of us. Our nurse manager asks our opinion about things and really listens to what we say. I don't mind having to change my schedule once in a while because I feel appreciated."

Control. Having control means that a nurse can influence the course of events in his or her life. When a nurse has no or very limited control over events, he or she experiences high stress.

NO CONTROL: You come on duty expecting to work on the orthopedic unit where you feel competent and comfortable. However, the census is low; therefore you are sent to ICU for the day and are assigned to care for a patient who has a severe head injury and is on life support. You feel inadequate to cope with the situation but are reassured by the ICU staff, who say, "We'll look in on you; you'll be all right." You feel trapped because you need the job and fear dismissal if you refuse the assignment.

IN CONTROL: You have been sent to ICU from the orthopedic unit and have been assigned to a patient whose needs exceed your capabilities. You explain to the ICU nurse manager that you cannot cope with this situation and request reassignment. You are advised to stay and accept the assignment. However, you excuse yourself and report back to the nurse manager of orthopedics, who must take responsibility from there.

Challenge. A challenging career offers opportunities to use one's abilities, energies, and resources or provides an opportunity to attempt what one believes he or she can accomplish. Work without challenge leads to mistakes and boredom, but a challenging career can be exciting and productive. Most people also want security in the workplace. They like to be free of worry about their jobs and to feel satisfied that if they function well, their job will be secure.

CHALLENGE: Diane was asked by her nurse manager if she would like to move from her position of team leader to that of case manager. She was assured that she would receive education and training for the position. Diane was excited because she considered the proposal an opportunity to broaden her sites and learn a more sophisticated role.

THREAT: Sara was asked by her nurse manager if she would like to consider the position of case manager. Sara's mind whirled with concern. Was the nurse manager trying to get rid of her? What if she

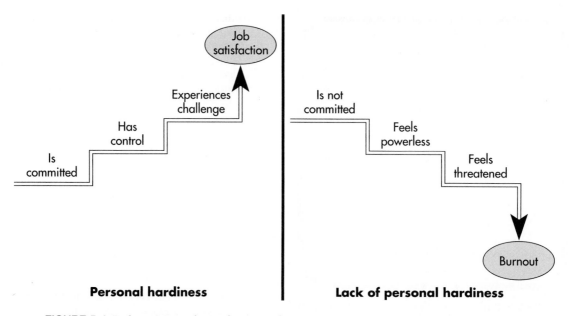

FIGURE 5-4. Pathway[s] to job satisfaction or burnout. (Modified from Tarolli-Jager K: Personal hardiness: your buffer against burnout, *Am J Nurs* 94(2):71-72, 1994.)

accepted and then failed? She refused the proposal and tried to work harder and better at her present job to prove her worth.

Important Criteria

Each organization has unique staffing criteria; however, all healthcare facilities have certain basic criteria.

Nurse staffing carries forward the structure and goals of the organization. The organizational chart, in conjunction with job specifications, indicates the numbers and types of workers needed to fill the various nursing positions. For example, however desirable it may be, it is not possible to hire an additional nurse to provide specialized care to ileostomy patients unless that position is incorporated into the total organizational plan through proper channels. Nurse staffing depends on the existing standards of an organization. If an agency adopts professional nursing standards as prescribed by the American Nurses Association (ANA), it must require individualized nursing care; effective communication among nurses, physicians, staff, patients/clients, families, and community; participation in decisions that in-

fluence their role in nursing care; and provisions for continuing education. Staffing must include an adequate number of qualified professional and nonprofessional personnel to meet these standards.

Job specifications are clear and in writing. For practical purposes, staffing an organization begins with identifying roles and creating a written record of the minimal requirements necessary to perform the job. **Job descriptions,** or performance responsibilities, spell out precise roles, including duties, activities, responsibilities, and expected results. Job descriptions cannot possibly list all duties and responsibilities; such a list would be cumbersome and impractical. Job descriptions simply spell out the minimal requirements for job fulfillment. Furthermore, the job description is always subject to interpretation; with time, the typical nurse modifies the role to some degree as a natural result of individuality and change.

Implementation

Today's nurse manager is faced with many challenges in negotiating the healthcare environment. What is appropriate for one healthcare agency may not work well for another. Guidelines and models are available to the nurse managers to use and modify individual agency requirements and conditions. Implementing the staffing process involves data collection, patient classification, and staff mixing and scheduling.

Data collection

The initial step in implementation of a staffing system is to develop a means for data collection. Ideally, the nurse who is responsible for seeing that care is delivered to a unit (usually the nurse manager) is the best source of information. The objectives for assigning nursing staff to patients/clients are: (1) to match patient care needs with available resources, (2) to ensure cost-effectiveness, (3) to provide a basis for budgetary justification of needed positions, (4) to measure efficiency of care delivery, (5) to assess quality and quantity of care delivered, and (6) to ensure equitable patient care assignments.[17]

In hospitals, patient census figures; average length of stay in the hospital; and patient discharges and admissions as they relate to seasons, months of the year, and days of the week are studied first. An analysis of these data will reveal definite patterns. In some units, such as a surgical unit, more patients may be admitted at the beginning of the week, whereas in a geriatric unit there may be more admissions at the end of the week or before holidays. The census in most agencies generally drops significantly around Christmas, picks up after the first of the year, and decreases again during the summer. Other factors influencing hospital census are physicians' vacations or conventions, demographic information such as age of population, and the economic status of the community.

Patient classification systems

A **patient classification system** is a method of grouping patients according to the amount and complexity of their nursing care requirements. In most classifications, patients are grouped according to the time and ability required to provide care. Lewis and Carini[18] cite three types of patient classification systems: (1) descriptive, which is a narrative description of the various degrees of care required by a particular patient, (2)

checklist, which simply lists patient problems according to patient acuity, and (3) time-based, which lists patient needs according to level of acuity (e.g., minimal, partial, acute, complex) and ascribes the amount of nurse time needed to fulfill these needs. The delivery system in effect (e.g., modular, team, total care, primary nursing) and the mix of nursing personnel (e.g., RNs, LPNs, licensed vocational nurses [LVNs], nursing assistants) influence staff allocation. Some projectors of needed staff use a point system (e.g., 1 to 9 points for minimal care, 10 to 20 points for partial care, and 21 to 30 points for total care) or ascribe hours of needed care (e.g., 1 to 2 hours for minimal care, 3 to 4 hours for partial care, and 5 to 7 hours for total care). The 24-hour figures are then computed and prorated according to shifts, depending on when the bulk of nursing care is given. Table 5-1 offers a sample of one form that may be used for staff projection after the necessary data have been gathered. Other data unique to a specific unit may be added as desired. If, for example, there are 22 patients on the day shift, either read on the chart or compute as follows:

Three require minimal care:	$3 \times 0.17 = 0.51$
Fourteen require partial care:	$14 \times 0.27 = 3.78$
Five require total care:	$5 \times 0.36 = \underline{1.80}$
Total number of nursing personnel needed to staff the day shift:	6.09

Compute the number of nursing personnel needed to staff the evening and night shifts using Table 5-1 and the following information:

1. There are 24 patients on the evening shift, classified as follows:

Five require minimal care:	$\times$	$=$
Sixteen require partial care:	$\times$	$=$
Three require total care:	$\times$	$=$
Total number of nursing personnel needed to staff the evening shift:		

2. There are 26 patients on the night shift, classified as follows:

Seven require minimal care:	$\times$	$=$
Fourteen require partial care:	$\times$	$=$
Five require total care:	$\times$	$=$
Total number of nursing personnel needed to staff the night shift:		

Unless the classification of care of patient population remains fairly stable, the projector

Table 5-1. Numbers of nursing personnel needed to staff a unit*

NUMBER OF PATIENTS	CLASSIFICATION OF PATIENTS								
	MINIMAL			PARTIAL			TOTAL		
	DAY	PM	NIGHT	DAY	PM	NIGHT	DAY	PM	NIGHT
1	0.17	0.14	0.10	0.27	0.15	0.07	0.36	0.30	0.20
2	0.34	0.28	0.20	0.54	0.30	0.14	0.72	0.60	0.40
3	0.51	0.42	0.30	0.81	0.45	0.21	1.08	0.90	0.60
21	3.57	2.94	2.10	5.67	3.15	1.47	7.56	6.30	4.20
22	3.74	3.08	2.20	5.94	3.30	1.54	7.92	6.60	4.40
23	3.91	3.22	2.30	6.21	3.45	1.61	8.28	6.90	4.60
24	4.08	3.36	2.40	6.48	4.00	1.68	8.64	7.20	4.80

*Formula: for the number of staff needed, the number of nursing personnel required to care for one patient (according to classification) is multiplied by the number of patients in that classification.

will need to classify patients each day before determining the numbers of staff needed. Of course, estimates need to be projected for at least 2 weeks when developing the staff schedule. Necessary adjustments will be made from day to day, depending on the differences between projection and actuality.

Classification by computer. Computers can greatly simplify patient classification. The classification system can be programmed and brought up onto the screen for instant viewing and alteration.

Disadvantages of classification systems. Staff shortages can complicate the use of a patient classification system. Because of shortages, staffing in nursing homes is often determined on the basis of the patients' needs, not the care they get. The problem is perpetuated if future staffing is based on previous allotments.[17]

Little information exists about what actually happens when there is a shortage of staff. Reports indicate that some tasks are dropped and others curtailed. Blurring of nursing roles can also occur in classification systems. For example, nursing homes often lump together RNs, LPNs, and NAs. Disregarding the type or level of personnel may have serious implications for funding.

Staff mix

Another step in implementation is determining the ratio or mix of nursing personnel who will provide the care. Again, this decision depends on the philosophy of the institution and the kind of delivery of care (functional, modular, team, total, primary). For example, in acute care facilities, it is generally agreed that staff should mainly consist of registered nurses, followed by LPNs/LVNs and, finally, assistants.

Staff scheduling

Schedules for work and time off should meet organizational goals with fairness and equity among personnel. Basically, a schedule for a nursing staff pattern adheres to the following criteria:

1. Policies, standards, and practices of the employing agency on the use of professional and paraprofessional nursing personnel
2. Appropriate ratio or balance between professional and paraprofessional or supportive staff
3. Continuity of services (For the promotion of quality care, nurses must care for the same patients/clients over time and work with the same nursing personnel.)
4. Approved master staffing budget with effective and economical assignment of per-

sonnel through avoidance of maldistribution and overstaffing

5. Satisfaction of staff members in their work
6. Consideration of vacations and other scheduled time off, which needs to be planned well in advance to provide for year-round distribution
7. Allowance for adjustments in case of illness, emergencies, or changes in care needs
8. Staff members informed of their work schedules at least 2 weeks in advance of implementation (longer if possible)
9. Protection of the rights of individuals against discriminatory action because of sex, ethnic differences, or religious beliefs

Centralized versus decentralized staffing systems. Work schedules can be developed on centralized systems, decentralized systems, or both. A **centralized staffing** system is impersonal and is completed by the director of nursing services or a designate, who develops a master plan for nursing personnel in the health facility. *Decentralized* staffing is a more personal approach; the middle and lower or first levels of management determine staffing. There are advantages and disadvantages to each system (Table 5-2). Most systems have some components of both centralization and decentralization; for example, a centralized organization may have decentralized staffing.[19]

Traditionally, nurse managers or their counterparts at the lower or first level of management develop a schedule for their units, and the supervisor (middle level) fills any vacant spots from his or her greater number of shifts. The staffing person in the director of nursing services office (top level) allocates any additional necessary personnel by drawing on nurses from other units, the float list (if one exists), part-time nurses who will work on call, or outside agencies. Regardless of the staffing system in effect, a master plan for the entire facility is maintained for overall control.

Scheduling in advance. Schedules provide workers with advance notice. Like other members of the work force, nurses appreciate knowing their work schedules well in advance. The nurse population is predominantly female, with a median age of 37.7 years; 70% of the nurses are married, and there is a high proportion of young nurses. Therefore problems related to spouses' schedules, child care, and social activities may

Table 5-2. Comparison of the advantages and disadvantages of the centralized and decentralized staffing systems

STAFFING SYSTEM	ADVANTAGES	DISADVANTAGES
Centralized	Conserves time Scheduler is familiar with overall situation Easier to handle need for help with qualified personnel in times of illness, absence, or emergency Less frequent requests for special privileges Compatible with computerization	Denies nurse manager the right to make staffing decisions Minimal opportunity for personal contact with staff Limited knowledge of workers' abilities, interest, and needs Limited knowledge of nursing care needs in the separate departments and units of nursing
Decentralized	Nurse manager is accountable for staffing decisions Scheduling is based on knowledge of personnel and patient/client needs Greater control of activities; can rearrange schedule quickly as needed Fresh ideas generated for improvement of system	May be time consuming Sometimes results in insufficient numbers of qualified personnel necessary to meet unforeseen needs Increased number of requests for special privileges

weigh heavily on nurses' minds. They must know their schedules in advance to maintain harmony in their homes and to meet individual needs.

An erratic or poorly planned schedule creates confusion and anger among the staff. Chronic problems such as a posting of the work schedule immediately before it goes into effect, last-minute changes in days off, overtime, long stretches without relief, split days off, few weekends free, and preferential treatment of some workers can cause interpersonal relationships to suffer. Dissatisfaction leads to dissension, reduced work performance, lateness, increased absences, lethargy, and dropouts. These undesirable circumstances can be avoided by developing carefully planned work schedules well in advance of implementation and by considering all criteria necessary for good scheduling.

The traditional way to schedule nursing personnel is to arrange coverage for each department for 7 days a week, with a 5-day work week for round-the-clock service—a mammoth task. One expert has approached the problems of RN assignment with computation. However, with full-time employment and the usual holidays and vacations, there are either too few or too many nurses to cover staffing positions, regardless of the mix. The traditional staffing pattern tends to underuse nursing resources on weekdays and overuse them on weekends and holidays. The typical 2-week work schedule shown above for nursing personnel is an illustration of the traditional system. This schedule was made with a given directive that there must be at least two RNs assigned to each day. Note that RNs A and B have a weekend off, while RN C has none. (A schedule for a longer time would allow rotation.) Monday was selected as the overstaffed day, as this day is generally most demanding of nursing services in hospitals. Analyze the schedule for problems; then plan an alternative schedule to see if problems can be minimized. This hypothetic schedule does not consider other important scheduling criteria such as the needs of individual patients/clients, workers, and the environment. An example illustrates this point. In past years, common practice has been for nurses to work two weekends out of every three. Many hospitals now have nurses work only every other weekend. A quick perusal of the sample work schedule reveals that more RN personnel are needed to supply this one concession.

DAY	RN TEAM LEADER		
	A	B	C
S	x	Off	x
M	x	x	x
T	Off	x	x
W	x	Off	x
Th	x	x	Off
F	x	x	Off
Sa	Off	x	x
S	Off	x	x
M	x	x	x
T	x	x	Off
W	x	x	Off
Th	Off	x	x
F	x	Off	x
Sa	x	Off	x

Cyclic staffing system. A better way to designate work time is to develop a **cyclic** plan, in which workdays and time off are regularly repeated for 4-, 6-, 7-, or 12-week periods. To be successful, the system requires centralization; sufficient numbers of full-time, qualified staff; and other groups of nursing personnel who are willing to work part-time, float, and be on call for emergencies. In this system the staff is treated fairly and equally. Everyone has the same number of weekend days off, and the problems of overstaffing or understaffing are solved. This preprogrammed system also works well on the computer. The disadvantages of centralized staffing as outlined in Table 5-3 also apply to cyclic staffing. Figure 5-5 presents a master time schedule for a 4-week cycle.

Other staffing patterns being tried by nurse managers are the 40-hour, 4-day work week and a 7 days on, 7 days off plan. These and other options will continue to be studied in the hope of simplifying and improving the assignment of nursing personnel. Table 5-3 presents a description of four methods of staffing patterns and the advantages and disadvantages of each.

A computer program can be developed to create staffing schedules that take into account such factors as shift variations, staff/patient ratios, and staff requests. Whereas nurse managers previously spent as long as 8 hours devising the work schedule for a single unit, a computer can develop a completed schedule in less than an hour.

Self-scheduling. In all scheduling systems, staff members often make special requests, which can disrupt any schedule and push the

Table 5-3. Four methods of staffing patterns

METHOD	DESCRIPTION	ADVANTAGES	DISADVANTAGES
Conventional	Centralized-decentralized combination is the oldest and most common; nurse manager makes up staffing pattern for particular unit; it is then incorporated and centralized in master plan in nursing office.	Pattern can be altered at central office to best meet needs; nurse manager can use the "float concept" to his or her advantage; the precise measurement of nursing hours needed per patient population is measurable with this pattern	If there is too much decentralization, cohesiveness and order will be lost
Cyclic	The staffing pattern repeats itself every 4-6, 7-12 weeks.	Pattern provides for float personnel to fortify staff when need arises; good and bad hours are distributed fairly among all staff and no favoritism is shown; each person knows his or her pattern and can plan ahead; once a cyclic pattern is established, laypersons can work with it	A constant, sufficient number of the appropriate mix of personnel is required
Forty hours; 4 days	Forty hours a week is worked in 4 days, followed by a block of off-duty time.	The large time block off may offset the possibility of fatigue; staff may have more weekends off; overlapping may provide for better coverage at meal time	Fatigue is possible, resulting in poorer quality of care; studies in other disciplines have shown an increase in accidents and a lack of overall productivity
Seven days off; 7 on	A 10-hour day is worked for 7 days, followed by 7 days off.	Nurses are paid for 8 hours with no vacation or holidays allowed; they are given 70 hours of sick leave; better continuity of care is achieved because the same staff may cover almost an entire hospitalization of a patient; there is better communication with physicians and other staff; inservice program is strengthened	Pattern may be too hard on personnel physically; staff may desire holidays and vacation time

nurse manager's patience to the limit. When requests are not granted, nurses feel stressed and dissatisfied, especially if they believe favoritism has been exhibited.[20] Today nurses want more autonomy and more control over their lives; self-scheduling may be one way to fulfill this need.

Members of a critical care unit at Edward Hospital in Naperville, Illinois developed an innovative approach for scheduling that they believe leads to increased team spirit and collaboration, more cooperation among staff and with management, increased professionalism, and decreased staff turnover and absenteeism.[21] With **self-scheduling,** nurses select their own work schedules within daily staff requirements and usually for 1-month periods. Nurses plan their work periods on the basis of predetermined goals and guidelines. This democratic process fosters increased cohesiveness and teamwork. The self-scheduling method allows the nurse

Category	Name	WEEK 1							WEEK 2							WEEK 3							WEEK 4						
		S	M	T	W	Th	F	S	S	M	T	W	Th	F	S	S	M	T	W	Th	F	S	S	M	T	W	Th	F	S
RN Full Time		Ch		X	X		X	Ch	Ch	X	X		X	X			X	X	X	X	X			X	X	X	X		Ch
RN Full Time		X	X	X	X	X				X	X	X	X	X	Ch	Ch		X	X	X	X			X	X	X		X	X
RN Full Time		X	X	X		X	X			X	X	X		X		X		X	X	X	X			X	X	X	X	X	X
RN Full Time			X	X	X	X	X			X	X	X		X	X	X	X	X	X	X			Ch	Ch	X	X	X	X	
RN 16 hrs.		X					X	X					X	X					X	X						X	X		X
RN 16 hrs.				X			X	X					X	X	X				X					X				X	
RN 16 hrs.			X				X	X		X					X			X	X	X									
Nurse Asst. FT			X	X	X		X	X	X	X	X		X	X			X	X	X		X	X	X	X	X	X		X	
Nurse Asst. FT		X	X	X		X	X	X	X	X	X			X	X	X	X	X	X			X	X	X	X			X
Nurse Manager			X	X	X	X	X			X	X	X	X	X			X	X	X	X	X			X	X	X	X	X	
Total RNs on duty		4	5	5	5	4	4	4	4	4	5	5	4	4	5	4	5	5	5	4	4	4	4	5	5	5	4	4	4

Key: Ch = Charge nurse
X = Work day
Blank space = Day off

FIGURE 5-5. Example of cyclic scheduling.

manager to become the facilitator rather than the controller.[20]

 NURSING CARE DELIVERY SYSTEMS

A **nursing care delivery** system delivers nursing care effectively and efficiently to patient populations. Each method has certain advantages and disadvantages. The choice of delivery system must be made on the basis of clearly defined standards of care and measured against what is best for the patient. No one component of a system stands alone. It is dangerous to redesign the work of nurses without careful reassessment of all those systems with which nursing interfaces.

Nursing care delivery systems have often not kept pace with the rapid and complex changes in healthcare. Historically, four basic delivery services have been used: (1) **total care** (previously referred to as *case nursing*), (2) **primary nurs-**ing, (3) **functional nursing,** and (4) **team nursing.** More recent innovations include **modular nursing** and **cross-functional, multidisciplinary nursing** such as case management and the patient-focused–care model.

Total Care Nursing

Total care, or case method, nursing is the oldest of the care systems. One nurse is assigned to one patient/client for the delivery of total care. The nurse functions within the system of nursing care that is used by all staff (Figure 5-6). The one-to-one pattern is common assignment for student nurses, private duty nurses, and community health nurses, for special circumstances in which single care is needed (e.g., isolation, intensive care units). In total care nursing it is possible for one nurse to be assigned to more than one patient/client if that nurse can meet the objectives of the assignment. Note the broken and unbroken lines in Figure 5-6. For the student nurse

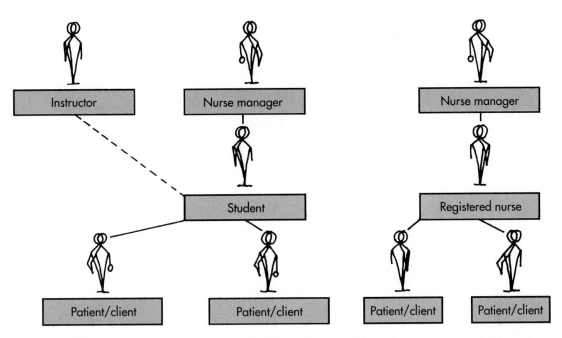

FIGURE 5-6. Lines of authority in a typical healthcare facility with total care or case method nursing.

there is a dual allegiance between instructor and nurse manager. Whereas the student meets individual learning needs through the instructor's guidance, the nurse manager has the ultimate responsibility for patient/client care. Because nursing assistants cannot give medications or administer many treatments, and because in many instances their assessment skills are inadequate for the delivery of total care, individual nursing is no longer possible in most hospitals as a major pattern of care.

Primary Nursing

Primary nursing is both a philosophy of nursing care and a model of organizing that care to achieve high-quality outcomes. Its goals are to achieve patient-centered, individualized care that is coordinated, comprehensive in scope, and continuous from admission to discharge. Staffing for primary nursing usually requires that one RN primary nurse be assigned four to six patients (depending on patient acuity); two or more of these patients are the nurse's primary patients. Primary nurses have accountability, authority, and autonomy for the care of their primary patients and for attention to the patients' families from admission

to discharge.[17] Primary nurses are accountable for the outcomes of the nursing care, not just for the care itself.

The primary nurse may provide nursing care services to the patient/client individually or through coordination of care with associates. Coordination is accomplished through direct communication (on the job or by telephone), nursing care plans, notes, and other records. The primary nurse, physician, and nurse manager control the quality of patient/client care by maintaining an effective communication system. Effective communication is accomplished through regular meetings to discuss the rationale for care, to plan comprehensive care, to solve problems, and to evaluate and coordinate patient/client care. Figure 5-7 illustrates the peer or colleague relationship among the nurse, physician, nurse manager, and all others. It also demonstrates that the patient/client is the center of focus of all functions.

The quality of care given depends on the ongoing nursing care plans, clarity of directions, and the ability of the primary care nurse. Selection of nurses who are qualified to function in the primary pattern of care is important. For best results, the primary nurse should be a registered

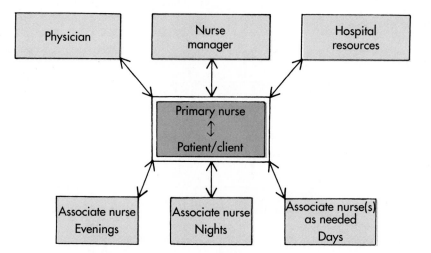

FIGURE 5-7. Lines of authority in a typical healthcare facility with primary nursing.

professional nurse who is prepared for the role. Primary nurses are expected to be clinically competent, take nursing histories, do all initial assessments, develop care plans, effectively problem solve, and accept a new role of independence for planning and providing comprehensive care.

Primary nursing has the advantage of being focused on the needs of patients/clients and on increasing care and effectiveness. The patients/clients are more satisfied because they can identify with one nurse whom they believe has a vested interest in their welfare. The communication system is improved because there are fewer channels to go through to get things done. Nurses have the opportunity to function autonomously as professionals and to use their capacities, which may lead to greater satisfaction with hospital nursing and result in less employee turnover.

One disadvantage of primary nursing is the overall reduction in administrative efficiency because each nurse's leadership is restricted to a small group of patients/clients. The nurses' preparation for and interest in primary nursing also must be considered. Role confusion can occur when LPNs/LVNs are assigned patient care. They are not assigned primary patients but are used as associate nurses under the supervision of the RNs, and their roles overlap frequently. Communication problems may arise between the primary nurse and other nursing staff.

Functional Nursing

Functional nursing is a system of care that is borrowed from industry and concentrates on duties or activities. This pattern of care involves an assembly-line approach in which the nurse manager delegates major tasks to individual members of the work group. One member may be assigned to work at the desk, another to pass medications, another to administer all treatments and/or monitor IVs, and another to give hygienic care. Members of the working group are highly dependent on each other for completion of the group's total assignments (Figure 5-8). Nursing care plans provide an important link between the workers and quality of care, because there is limited opportunity for members of the nursing group to meet and coordinate their efforts. Established protocol and procedure are followed closely.

The advantages and disadvantages of the functional system are controversial among nurses and hospital administrators. Many hospital administrators consider the functional system the most economical way to deliver nursing services. This may be true if primary consideration is given to production and secondary consideration is given to quality. Another advantage named is that the nurse manager maintains greater control over work activities. In this autocratic system the manager bears responsibility for all activities of those providing care and for the quality of care given. However, as chief of all activities, the nurse manager is barraged with input from all sides—physi-

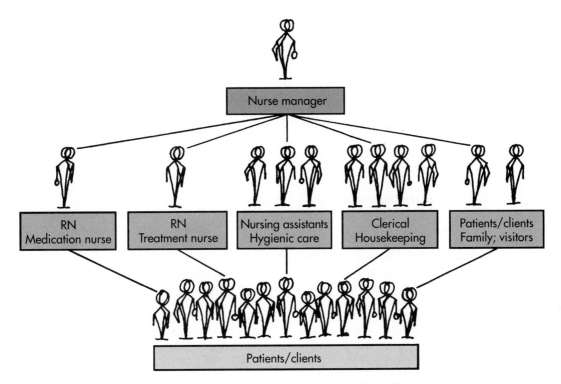

FIGURE 5-8. Lines of authority in a typical healthcare facility with functional nursing.

cians, nursing staff, students, patients/clients, visitors, and the public. In addition, the nurse manager must complete administrative functions. This dichotomy of roles often becomes overwhelming and leads to inadequate fulfillment of job expectations.

Some workers are more secure in the dependent roles required in functional care. The manager may enjoy telling people what to do, and some workers are comfortable following orders and performing repetitive tasks. However, the more significant issue is that of patient/client care. The functional design is aimed at conservation of workers and cost. The psychologic and sociologic needs of the patients/clients are often overlooked, thus defeating the very purpose of care systems.

Team Nursing

In team nursing a professional nurse leads a group of healthcare personnel in providing for the health needs of an individual or group of people through collaborative and cooperative effort. Team nursing was developed in the 1950s as a result of social and technologic changes. World War II drew many nurses away from hospitals, which left gaps. Services, procedures, and equipment became more extensive and complicated and required more specialization. Team nursing was one attempt to meet the increased demands for nursing services, better use of the knowledge and skills of professional nurses, and increased patient/client and worker satisfaction.[22]

With the aid of a Kellogg grant, Lambertsen[23] studied the system of team nursing in a large New York City hospital in the 1950s. She concluded that team nursing, if properly used, could serve as one good way to effectively use nursing personnel with diversified backgrounds and skills. Newcomb[24] focused on helping nurse managers see the value of team nursing, and she later expanded her writing to include the entire team. Others, such as Kron[25] and Douglass,[26] have contributed to the knowledge of team nursing.

Team nursing is based on a philosophy of certain beliefs and values: (1) the worth of every individual, (2) the need for a qualified person to be the overall coordinator and interpreter of plans for care, (3) emphasis on co-equal status with minimal hierarchical lines of demarcation between leaders and followers, and (4) sensitivity and responsiveness to the need for adaptability and change.

Team nursing can be identified by specific characteristics. A nursing team (1) is always led by a nurse licensed to practice; (2) functions wherever there are health needs that focus on the patient's total needs; (3) includes the patient in the development and implementation of care plans whenever possible; (4) is changeable and adaptable; and (5) recognizes and appropriately uses each individual's talents, abilities, and interests to the fullest.

A clear line of organizational structure is needed for the nursing team to provide a mechanism for horizontal and vertical communication. When team nursing is used, the nurse manager or designated person delegates leadership responsibility to a nurse leader for a specific group of patients/clients (Figure 5-9). Team members relate to the team leader, who in turn relates directly to the nurse manager. The nurse manager's role changes from that of an organizer and manager of tasks to a coordinator, consultant, and evaluator.

Team nursing is one form of decentralization. The intent is to bring decision-making authority, responsibility, and accountability to an operational level. This is accomplished by reducing the degree of vertical control at the top level and developing increased horizontal communications at lower levels. In this system the team leader can use any or all patterns of nursing care according to the needs of the patients/clients and the capabilities and desires of the caregivers.

Determining the staff mix and the number needed to ensure provision of quality care depends on the patient group and its nursing needs. In general units, a nursing team cares for 10 to 20 patients, with three to five nursing staff members assigned to their care.

A nurse's task is more complex with team nursing than with the functional approach because more managerial skills are required. The team leader is challenged to include all team members in the problem-solving approach according to their abilities. Inherent in the philosophy of team nursing is a belief that all members have the right to be entrusted with responsibility, given authority to act, and held accountable for their actions. At the heart of team nursing is the communication system, which is important for providing direction, giving reports of assignments in progress and those completed, focusing on patient/client care, acquiring information, and assessing team relationships.

An advantage of team nursing is that all team members are involved in planning, executing, and evaluating. When all parts are working satisfactorily, this involvement provides job enrichment and job expansion to all workers, especially at lower levels on the team.

The disadvantages of team nursing are viewed from different perspectives. Some believe this method of assignment to be more costly, because the overall efficiency of the nursing unit is reduced by fragmented distribution of personnel. Others point to the increased amount of time needed for several team leaders to perform similar managerial tasks of assessment, delegation, and controlling of work groups. The element of error is another factor to consider. There are risks with decentralization of responsibility; confusion may occur when several people are receiving orders (e.g., from nurse manager to team leader to nursing staff members). Also, some nurses may prefer a more independent or dependent system and not wish to take on the responsibility of leading a group.

Modular Nursing

Modular nursing is a modification of team and primary nursing.[6,27] It is a geographic assignment of patients that encourages continuity of care by organizing a group of staff to work with a group of patients in the same locale. For example, a module might consist of five or six rooms side by side along one hall, or a group of rooms or cubicles that surround a nursing station. The fixed geographic area typically represents 10 to 12 patients per module. This nursing care delivery system is sometimes used when there are not enough registered nurses to practice primary

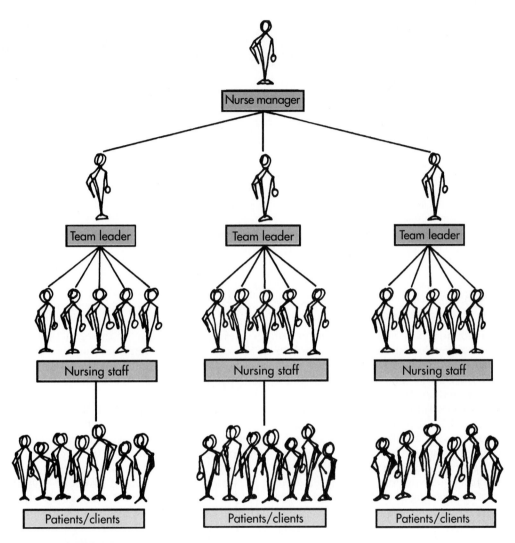

FIGURE 5-9. Lines of authority in a typical healthcare facility with team nursing.

nursing. With financial constraints and census fluctuations plaguing hospitals, ways are being sought to provide a more efficient delivery system that ensures quality patient care and promotes professional nursing. In team nursing the RN *directs* care given by team members; however, in modular nursing each RN *delivers* direct care to a group of patients and is assisted by paraprofessionals. In addition to caregiving, the RN plans care for all patients in the module and directs paraprofessionals in the more technical aspects of care.

For 12 years the Medical Center of Delaware delivered nursing care according to a primary nursing model. With the shortened lengths of stay and increased patient acuity, RNs had little time to supervise LPNs and nursing assistants. A task force of key nurse management and staff members convened to assess the situation and develop a modular system. Although the number of RNs and LPNs decreased and the number of nursing assistants increased, RNs and paraprofessionals were better satisfied because unit efficiency was improved (Box 5-2).

Box 5-2.   **Advantages and disadvantages of three care delivery modes**

	MODULAR	PRIMARY	TEAM
Continuity of care	Yes	Yes	No
Close nurse/patient relationship	Yes	Yes	No
Patient knows nurse	Yes	Yes	No
Increased coordination time	Yes	No	Yes
Combines nurse's skills	Yes	No	No
Reduces time for RN in indirect activities	Yes	No	No
Lunch/break coverage	Yes	No	Yes
RN performs RN/Rx	Yes	Yes	No
Decreased time looking for assistance	Yes	No	No

From Bennett M, Hylton J: Modular nursing: partners in professional practice, *Nurs Manage* 20(2):24, 1990.

Cross-functional, Multidisciplinary Teams

All over the country, new models for delivery of care are being developed and refined, such as case management and the patient-focused–care model in which nurse managers are used at a more sophisticated level. Traditionally nurse managers were successful if they managed patient care in their units; this is no longer enough. To ensure cost-effective and high-quality care, the nurse manager is required to integrate with other units and other people, which means frequent communication, networking, planning creative patient care, and seeing in and beyond the care unit to achieve goals.

Case management

With the concept of "managed care" becoming the cornerstone of healthcare reform, considerable attention is being given to the practice of case management. Health administrators and providers are being challenged to control spiraling health costs while maintaining quality within the healthcare system. In the past 10 years, healthcare services have been moving out of hospitals and into ambulatory and community settings, which is creating the need for a managed care system that provides continuous quality monitoring.

The concept of case management is not new. Public health nurses and social workers have used the case method since the turn of the century. The term *case manager* began to appear in nursing literature in the mid-1980s, and the scope of coordinated services has gradually expanded so that it now suggests a well-defined approach to delivery of healthcare services.[27]

Case management versus managed care. To avoid confusion, it is important to differentiate between the terms *case management* and *managed care*. In a managed care system such as health maintenance organizations (HMOs) and preferred provider organizations (PPOs) (see Chapter 3) "an agency or corporation contracts with a group of providers to deliver specific services for a limited cost per enrollee."[28, p.16] Case management, on the other hand, refers to "a service carried out by a professionally trained individual who provides and/or coordinates health or social services."[28, p.16] Both managed care delivery systems and managed care provider models are important to the smooth functioning of the healthcare system.

Nursing case management. The ANA describes nursing case management as "a healthcare delivery process whose goals are to provide quality healthcare, decrease fragmentation, enhance the clients' quality of life, and contain costs."[29, p.30] The professional nurse case manager (PNCM) "is responsible for assessment of patient and family, establishment of the nursing diagnosis, development of the nursing care plan, delegation of nursing care to associates, activation of interventions, coordination and collaboration with the interdisciplinary team, and evaluation of outcomes."[30,p.29] In institutions these activities occur before admission until at least 2 weeks after discharge. In communities these activities occur in any setting—the home, clinic, extended care facilities, or hospital—for as long as necessary. The best-known examples of those who use nurse case managers are prepaid healthcare plans, HMOs, and PPOs. This consumer trend of choosing managed care systems reflects support for services that are cost-effective yet maintain quality outcomes.[31]

In an acute care setting, a PNCM may carry an active caseload of approximately 40 patients; 10 in the acute care setting and 30 follow-up patients in the community. The case manager may have another 40 to 50 patients who have stabilized and require only a monthly telephone call for ongoing outcome evaluation (Figure 5-10).[19]

Initially the PNCM spends time with the patient and family to establish an open, working relationship and to gather information about previous health; reasons for hospitalization; previous and current levels of physical, psychologic, and spiritual functioning and coping abilities; and availability of resources and social supports. With these data, the PNCM, patient, family, primary nurse, and physician identify potential and cur-

rent problems, prescribe a course of nursing treatment during the in-hospital stay, and formulate a discharge plan.[32]

The PNCM is also responsible for collaborating with the multidisciplinary healthcare team and with community agencies to facilitate the achievement of agreed-on health outcomes. Within home and community settings, the PNCM continues to assess patient and family healthcare needs and suggests or arranges for interventions as appropriate. The PNCM teaches, counsels, and collaborates with other healthcare professionals.[19] See Box 5-3 for a summary of case management models.

The growing complexity of the community healthcare delivery system has created some negative consequences, such as clients becoming lost in the system or receiving duplication of services, primarily because of lack of coordination of services. Case managers are now being employed in a variety of healthcare settings. They help clients navigate the maze of healthcare providers as they move from one level of care to another. Private insurance companies such as Blue Cross/Blue Shield and HMOs have found that in addition to providing better service, case managers can save companies money. Case managers are becoming important in the field of mental health as they work with the mentally ill population to secure the care and funds needed for survival.[33]

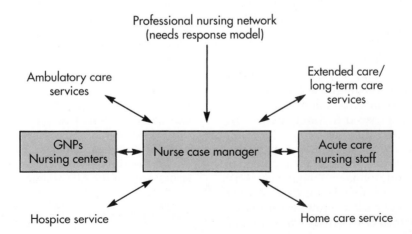

FIGURE 5-10. Organizational structure of a delivery system in an acute care agency that uses the nurse case manager. (Reprinted with permission from Ethridge P, Lamb G: Professional nurse case management improves quality, access, and costs, *Nurs Manage* 20[3]:30, 1989.)

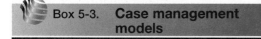

Box 5-3. Case management models

Curtin describes four models of case management usually practiced in a hospital setting:[33]

1. *The North Eastern model* (unit-based primary caregiver) is an extension of primary nursing. The primary nurse initiates the relationship before admission whenever possible, actively engages in discharge planning, coordinates all inpatient activities, and follows the patient for at least 2 weeks after discharge.
2. *The Arizona model* (nurse case manager) establishes criteria for the selection of high-risk patients in each clinical area. These patients are referred to a case manager, who has at least a baccalaureate and is already in a management position (nurse manager or supervisor). The case manager monitors and coordinates the patient's care with the primary nurse, physician, and other appropriate healthcare providers. The case manager participates in discharge planning and follows patients through discharge and the nursing home, home health agency, physician's office, and/or clinic for an indefinite but extended period of time.
3. *The HMO model* (monitoring system) coordinates care with hospital personnel in an attempt to control expenditures while delivering quality care. High-risk patients are followed over time in an effort to control use of resources.
4. *The insurance-based and state-based (medical) model* (monitoring system) is designed to cut costs. Here the case manager reviews records and progress, identifies problem areas, and follows them over time.

Nurse case manager in an integrated system. An innovative program that has the potential to develop a comrehensive approach for HIV-positive persons is the Integrated Case Management Model that has been in development in Atlanta, Georgia since 1986.[35] An agency called AID Atlanta was established and funded by the Robert Wood Johnson Foundation AIDS Demonstration Project agencies. Case management sites include local county health departments, hospital infectious disease clinics, a freestanding clinic, and the AID Atlanta midtown site. This approach seeks to integrate community-focused case managers into the medical clinics,

therefore bridging the gap between the need for medical care and the need for social services within the community. The interdisciplinary approach uses the expertise of social workers, nurses, pastoral counselors, and therapists to develop client-centered plans of care across the continuum of need. Figure 5-11 shows a four-phase system that seeks to provide case management services on the basis of need and to coordinate and limit duplication of services. The system allows a client to enter the system at any point and to interact and develop a relationship with the case manager over a period of time without feeling pressured into a formal system.

Clients who are not in crisis but wish to enter the system to take advantage of specific programs or volunteer services are assigned to low-need case management, which could last for years. These clients may become volunteers themselves and therefore learn the system very well, which will be useful when they need additional care. High-need case management focuses on intensive case management of clients who present a crisis or who are at high risk for developing emotional, physical, or financial problems. With these clients, case managers have a more intensive role and carry out their responsibilities of comprehensive assessment intervention, support, and ongoing reassessment of needs.

The AID Atlanta case management staff broadly defines case management in their system as "a partnership between the case manager and client."[34, p.57] Standards have been developed on the basis of structure (policies, procedures, personnel), process (method of proceeding), and outcome models (expected results). The challenge for case managers has been obtaining a balance between standards that are specific enough to be meaningful yet general enough to be adapted to the operations of the various case management sites. Client input has been solicited through satisfaction surveys and a client advisory council. Professional nurses have strongly influenced the development, management, and restructuring of the AID Atlanta model.

Patient-focused–care model

The Kaiser-Permanente Health System is designing four "gateway hospitals" with cross-functional teams to provide care across the continuum of

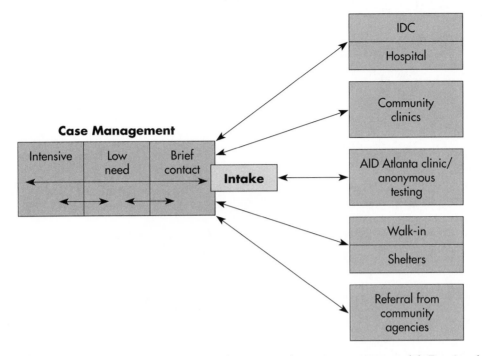

FIGURE 5-11. Schematic representation of the integrated case management model. (Reprinted with permission from Sowell R, Meadows T: An integrated case management model: developing standards, evaluation and outcome criteria, *Nurs Adm Q* 18[2]:55, 1994.)

health and illness. The hospital is no longer the center of care; it is a part of the whole integrated health system.[35] Whether the setting is a clinic, outpatient treatment center, nursing home, or inpatient unit, successful nurse managers in such an integrated system become conversant with the network of resources beyond the nursing unit walls. They integrate with other units and other people to ensure cost-effective, high-quality care.

Successful nurse managers also consider the total costs of healthcare, not just those that pertain to direct nursing care in the hospital unit. The nurse manager recognizes that different cultures often exist in different units, such as in the operating room, intensive care unit, labor and delivery unit, clinics, and acute care floors. This is true also for various cultures in pharmacy, laboratory, and dietary. The goal is for all to function as one large high-performing team that has many smaller cross-functional and cross-facility teams supporting the patient care objectives. In an integrated system, it is dysfunctional for every unit

to have its own culture, and it is not conducive to proper growth. According to the Kaiser-Permanente philosophy, as the cross-functional team becomes more sophisticated, nurse managers will not be working primarily with other nurses, but instead will be managing the work of many other personnel in different kinds of cross-functional teams and structures.

The patient-focused–care model is an example of such a strategy of care delivery and was first implemented in 1989 in Florida, where several hospitals joined a consortium to conduct pilot studies of patient-focused care.[36] In 1992 Hawaii's Castle Medical Center was the first facility to complete a hospital-wide reorganization to patient-focused care. The central idea in the patient-focused concept is that cross-trained caregivers from various backgrounds form a self-governed team and provide 90% of patient services, such as nursing, admitting and discharge, respiratory, physical therapy, ECGs, x-rays, laboratory tests, and in-house transportation (Figure 5-12). Primary services are close to

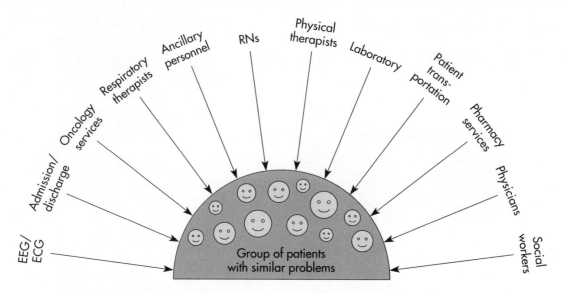

FIGURE 5-12. Example of a patient-focused unit under the direction of a nurse manager. Access to each service is in close proximity to the patient. (Modified from Clouten K, Weber R: Patient-focused care . . . playing to win, *Nurs Manage* 25[2]:34-36, 1994.)

the patient, similiar patient populations are grouped together, ancillary personnel are provided to each unit, care partners are established, documenting is the exception, and "servers" containing patient care items are at the bedside along with a computer for recording patient progress and communicating within and outside of the unit.

The patient-focused delivery system has brought financial benefits. Patient, staff, and physician satisfaction has also increased primarily because of their ability to relate to a consistent and available staff team. The patient-focused–care model requires major changes, not only for structure and for the team of caregivers, but also for the nurse manager. There is a question of who is the leader of the multidisciplinary team. If it is the nurse manager, does he or she understand the other departments well enough to manage them, and are they willing to accept the nurse's leadership? Team conflict, problem resolution, standards of care, and selection and evaluation of team members are other issues to be considered. The patient-focused–care delivery system is fairly new; therefore many problems have yet to be solved. Time and further study will determine if patient-focused care is a viable alternative for healthcare delivery.

SUMMARY

1. The downsizing, restructuring, and reduced cost of delivery systems are affecting job security and staffing patterns from coast to coast.
2. The demands on employed nurses are greater; they are juggling more responsibilities while trying to cope with a changing staff mix.
3. Examples of national trends are job cutting, eliminating RN FTE positions and replacing them with assistive personnel, and employing "at-will" nurses who can be terminated at any time. The average RN vacancy rate in 1993 was 5%.
4. The AHA reports a contrasting view and claims a 77% nursing shortage in hospitals as a result of an increased aging population, rapid expansion of long-term care, advances in technology, increased acuity of care, and the need for more primary care.
5. Supplemental staffing is the use of nurses who make themselves available on an on-call basis from their homes or through nurse registries, which provide a pool of nurses for hire.
6. Those in favor of supplemental staffing say much-needed labor is supplied to the agen-

cies and that nurses have greater flexibility and control over their practice. Healthcare agencies can employ only the help that is needed for a given situation, and they do not have to pay nurse benefits.

7. Opponents to supplemental staffing claim that patient care is disrupted because of inconsistency, lack of continuity of patient care, and the need for constant orientation. Pay discrepancies between regular nursing staff and agency personnel may also be an issue.

8. Registry staff should be carefully screened and oriented to the employing agency to avoid disruptions in service and maintain provision of quality care.

9. A satisfied employee tends to be absent less often than a dissatisifed employee. Absenteeism causes the quantity and quality of patient care to suffer.

10. Burnout may be described as emotional exhaustion, or feeling overextended and worn out from work; depersonalization, or lack of appropriate responses to the nurse's efforts; and a diminished sense of personal accomplishment.

11. Staffing follows the structure, goals, and standards of the organization.

12. Job specifications must be clear and in writing.

13. A description of performance responsibilities should spell out the job content for each of the roles in the agency.

14. Staff members are to be matched to their jobs as well as possible, with attention to abilities, aptitude, interest, and need.

15. The nurse employee is responsible for making personal requests for placement to the proper authorities.

16. The numbers of RNs and paraprofessionals should be correlated according to the philosophy of the agency, patient/client needs, methods of nursing care, availability of qualified nursing personnel, and any problems unique to the agency.

17. Work schedules are developed through a centralized system, a decentralized system, or a combination of both.

18. Centralized work schedules are developed by the top level of management for the entire work force. The advantages are conservation of time, knowledge of the overall situation, ability to handle unforeseen circumstances more easily, easy computerization, and less frequent requests for special privileges. Disadvantages include minimal opportunities for personal attention and the limited knowledge that top-level management has regarding workers and the specific nursing care needed by individual patients/clients.

19. Decentralized scheduling is accomplished at the middle and lower levels of management. The advantages are knowledge of personnel and patients/clients served and greater control of on-the-job activities, which allows the schedule to be altered more quickly. Disadvantages include length of time needed for scheduling, lack of sufficient qualified personnel necessary to meet all nursing situations, and an increased number of requests for special privileges.

20. The staffing system most commonly employed is a combination of centralized and decentralized planning, with cooperative efforts among schedulers.

21. Schedules provide workers with advance notice. They are planned for either 2-, 4-, 7-, or 12-week periods.

22. Traditional scheduling is based on the 5-day work week with round-the-clock coverage. Whatever the mix, with full-time employment there will either be overstaffing or understaffing. Problems can be minimized by using part-time help and sharing personnel among departments and units.

23. The cylic staffing system is recommended. In this system, days and time off are repeated on a 4-, 6-, 7-, or 12-week basis. Sufficient numbers of qualified staff are needed to ensure the success of the system.

24. Self-scheduling is a system in which nurses are given responsibility for selecting their own work schedules within the daily staff requirements. Nurses plan their work periods on the basis of predetermined goals and guidelines.

25. Total care nursing is the assignment of one nurse to one patient/client for the

provision of total care. Student nurses and private duty nurses are examples of total care nurses.

26. Primary nursing is a continuous and co-ordinated nursing process in which an RN provides the initial patient/care assessment and assumes accountability for planning comprehensive 24-hour care for the length of hospitalization or for the duration of care needed.

27. Functional nursing is a task-oriented system of care with an assembly-line approach; it functions under an autocratic system, with concentration on conservation of workers and cost. Great responsibility rests with the nurse manager for coordinating and supervising all activities. The patient/client does not get much individual attention.

28. Team nursing is a plan of care in which a group of nursing personnel are led by a qualified nurse to plan, direct, and evaluate the delivery of care to a group of patients/clients. The system focuses on total patient/client care, includes the patient/client in the planning process, is adaptable, and recognizes and uses individual members' talents, abilities, and interests to the fullest extent.

29. Modular nursing is a modification of team and primary nursing. It is a geographic assignment of patients that encourages continuity of care by organizing a group of staff (RNs and paraprofessionals) to work with a group of patients.

30. In a managed care system, an agency or corporation contracts with a group of providers to deliver specific services for a limited cost per enrollee. Examples are HMOs and PPOs.

31. Case management refers to a service carried out by a professionally trained individual who provides and/or coordinates health or social services.

32. The professional case manager is responsible for the assessment of patient and family, establishment of the nursing diagnosis, development of the nursing care plan, delegation of nursing care to associates, activation of interventions, coordination and collaboration with the inter-disciplinary team, and evaluation of outcomes before admission and until at least 2 weeks after dismissal.

33. Curtin describes four models of case management usually practiced in a hospital setting: (1) the North Eastern model (unit-based primary caregivers), (2) The Arizona model (baccalaureate-prepared nursing case managers working with patients, nursing associates, and interdisciplinary personnel from before admission to after discharge), (3) the HMO model (a monitoring system by the case manager), and (4) the insurance-based and state-based medical model in which the case manager reviews records and progress in an effort to reduce costs.

34. To be positive, relationships must be nurtured among the case manager, physicians, primary nurses, public health nurses, and other interdisciplinary staff.

35. There are varying standards for preparation as a nurse case manager. The ANA recommends a BSN as minimal level of education.

36. The Integrated Case Management Model for HIV-positive clients in Atlanta, Georgia seeks to integrate community-focused case managers into the medical clinics, which bridges the gap between the need for medical care and social service within the community. Services are based on level of need, which allows the client to enter the system at any point and establish a relationship with the case manager over a period of time.

37. The Kaiser-Permanente case management/outcomes management HMO system that uses cross-functional teams to provide care across the continuum of health and illness. Four "gateway hospitals" are provided, which offer clinics, an outpatient treatment center, a nursing home, and inpatient services. The nurse integrates with other units and other people throughout the system to ensure cost-effective, high-quality care.

38. The patient-focused–care model is a multidisciplinary method of delivery in Florida, where several hospitals joined a consortium to conduct pilot studies. The

central idea is that cross-trained caregivers from various backgrounds form a self-governed team and provide 90% of patient services. The primary services are close to the patients. Patients with similar problems are grouped together, and ancillary and professional people provide care. The RN may or may not be the case manager.

? Questions for Study and Discussion

1. Explore your feelings concerning the job market now and as projected for the 1990s. Where do you fit in? Will there be a need for you to alter your plans regarding choice of jobs?
2. What are your priorities in selecting a job as an RN? How do they compare with those of other graduating seniors in the class?
3. What plans would you make to find employment as an RN?
4. Assume that as department manager of a post-surgical nursing department, you are to staff the unit with nursing personnel. What are the basic guidelines you will use to decide on the numbers and kinds of staff?
5. Have you worked with supplemental RNs? If so, what have been your reactions to their work? Have you noticed any changes in the patient care delivery system? What about quantity and quality of patient care?
6. Define a patient classification system. Explain one system commonly used.
7. What is a nursing care delivery system? Choose one system to define, and describe the RN's role in that system.

✍ Test Your Knowledge

BEHAVIORAL OBJECTIVE
Analyze the job market and trends in the 1990s and state the implications for the jobseeker.

Michelle is having a difficult time finding a job as a staff nurse. She considers herself well prepared but inexperienced. She cannot find anyone who will meet her needs.

_____ 1. Michelle has come to realize that there are three major factors affecting the job market. Which is the exception?
   a. Her lack of experience
   b. Emphasis on cost reduction
   c. Restructuring of nursing care delivery systems
   d. Closure of hospitals

BEHAVIORAL OBJECTIVE
Explain the staffing process of recruitment, selection, and placement of personnel.

Michelle moved to an urban area and found employment in a large metropolitan hospital. She needed to assimilate several facts and concepts.

_____ 2. She learned that one of the following items is incompatible with the staffing process. Which one is it?
   a. Matches jobs with people
   b. Considers gender of staff
   c. Is involved with education
   d. Evaluation

_____ 3. Another item of interest to Michelle is the major factors that contribute to the need for RNs. Which is the exception?
   a. Increased intensity of medical practice
   b. Nurse professional goals
   c. Prolonged hospitalization for many patients
   d. Changes in patient characteristics

_____ 4. Michelle must know certain things before employment. Which is the exception?
   a. Fringe benefits
   b. Salary
   c. Working conditions
   d. Problems that concern peers

BEHAVIORAL OBJECTIVE

List the criteria that are important to the staffing process and identify major components of each.

Lonnie is responsible for staffing four nursing units. He learns all that he can to ensure optimal staffing. The following facts guide him in the staffing process:

_____ 5. Which of the following statements is true?
   a. An organizational chart can provide guidelines for staffing.
   b. The staffing procedure is the same for all health agencies.
   c. Job specifications need not be in writing as long as personnel know what is expected of them.
   d. The assessment of general ability, aptitude, skills, and experience is too time-consuming.

_____ 6. Which of the following statements is false?
   a. The mix of RNs, LPNs/LVNs, and nursing assistants influences the staffing pattern.
   b. A patient classification system describes the system for delivery of nursing care (e.g., team nursing or primary nursing).
   c. Ideally the nurse who is responsible for seeing that 24-hour care is delivered is the best one to compute staff hours.
   d. A cyclic staffing system means that the work schedule is regularly repeated for a specific number of weeks.

BEHAVIORAL OBJECTIVE

Define the systems used to deliver nursing care such as total, primary, functional, team, modular, and nurse case management, and determine advantages and disadvantages of each.

Jennifer has been given the responsibility for selecting a nursing care delivery system that complements the mission and goals of the hospital. She needs to acquire knowledge of the various systems. She reviews the following items and selects the best answers.

_____ 7. Delivery system of nursing care is defined as:
   a. A job description.
   b. A procedures manual.
   c. A method.
   d. Rules and regulations.

_____ 8. Another name for total care nursing is:
   a. One-to-one.
   b. Student nursing.
   c. Emergency care.
   d. Community health nursing.

_____ 9. Modular nursing:
   a. Is a modification of team and primary nursing.
   b. Means that all nursing care is given by RNs.
   c. Provides modules of nursing care plans via computer.
   d. Increases coordination time.

_____ 10. Nursing case management:
   a. Is another form of total care nursing.
   b. Arranges care on a continuum from before hospitalization until discharge.
   c. Is practiced primarily in the home.
   d. Includes arranging the work schedule of staff nurses.

_____ 11. Three of the following statements are considered by many hospital administrators to be advantages of the functional system of nursing. Which is the exception?
a. Economical system for the delivery of nursing care
b. Greater control of work activities
c. Staff may feel secure in a dependent role
d. Psychologic and sociologic needs are emphasized

BEHAVIORAL OBJECTIVE

Identify the meaning of cross-functional, multidisciplinary teams and the patient-focused model and determine the advantages and disadvantages of each.

For years Carrie has managed a single nursing unit. She sees evidence of the need to extend her sights beyond nursing unit walls. To do this, she needs to increase her understanding.

_____ 12. Carrie began the process by recognizing that cross-functional nursing means:
a. Delivery of care to all people.
b. Integration with other units and other people.
c. Mixing ethnic backgrounds of nurses and patients.
d. Using functional nursing in several units.

_____ 13. Carrie learns the meaning of managed care, which is to:
a. Manage the care of one or more patients in a nursing unit.
b. Deliver services by contractual agreement for a limited cost per enrollee.
c. Provide and/or coordinate health or social services by professionally trained individuals.
d. Manage the delivery of quality care.

REFERENCES

1. Meissner J: How's your job security? *Nurs 94* 24(3):57, 1994.
2. Vogel D: Changing Times, *Am J Nurs* 94(2):5, 1994.
3. AJN Newsline: Headlines, *Am J Nurs* 94(2):77-78, 1994.
4. Advice, P.R.N., *Nurs 94* 24(2):12, 1994.
5. Joel L: Restructuring: under what conditions? *Am J Nurs* 94(3):7, 1994.
6. Abts D, Hofer M, Leafgreen P: Redefining care delivery: a modular system, *Nurs Manage* 25(2): 42; 45, 1994.
7. Nursing News: Recruitment trends: hard-to-fill specialties, *Nurs 94* 24(1):10, 1994.
8. Davis B: Effective utilization of scarce resources: RNs, *Nurs Manage* 25(2):78; 80, 1994.
9. Barigar D, Sheafor M: Recruiting staff nurses: a marketing approach, *Nurs Manage* 21(1):27-29, 1990.
10. Hughes K, Marcantonio R: The clinical practice of supplemental nursing personnel, *Nurs Admin Q* 17(3):83-87, 1993.
11. Fiesta J: Law for the nurse manager: agency nurses—whose liability? *Nurs Manage* 20(3):16, 1989.
12. Kohler S, Mathieu J: Individual characteristics, work perceptions, and affective reactions influences on differential absence criteria, *J Org Behav* 14(6):515-530, 1993.
13. Barney J, Griffin R: *The management of organizations:* Boston, 1992, Houghton Mifflin.
14. Corrigan P and others: Staff burnout in a psychiatric hospital: a cross-legged panel design, *J Org Behav* 15(1):65-74, 1994.
15. Schaufeli W, Janezur B: Burnout among nurses, *J Cultural Psych* 25(1):95-113, 1994.
16. Tarolli-Jager K: Personal hardiness: your buffer against burnout, *Am J Nurs* 94(2):71-72, 1994.
17. Gillies D: *Nursing management: a systems approach,* ed 2, Philadelphia, 1989, WB Saunders.
18. Lewis E, Carini P: *Nurse staffing and patient classification,* Rockville, Md, 1984, Aspen Systems.
19. Willington M: Decentralization: how it affects nurses, *Nurs Outlook* 34(1):37, 1986.
20. Tully K: Self-scheduling: a strategy for recruitment and retention, *Focus Crit Care* 19(1):169-173, 1992.
21. Beltzhoover M: Self-scheduling: an innovative approach, *Nurs Manage* 25(4):81-82, 1994.
22. Marriner-Tomey A: *Guide to nursing management,* ed 3, St Louis, 1988, Mosby.
23. Lambertsen E: *Nursing team: organizational and*

functional, New York, 1953, Columbia University Press.

24. Newcomb D: *The team plan,* New York, 1953, GP Putnam's Sons.

25. Kron T: *The management of patient care: putting leadership skills to work,* ed 6, Philadelphia, 1987, WB Saunders.

26. Douglass L: *The effective nurse: leader and manager,* ed 4, St Louis, 1992, Mosby.

27. Bennett M, Hylton J: Modular nursing: partners in professional practice, *Nurs Manage* 20(2):24, 1990.

28. Marschke P, Nolan M: Research related to case management, *Nurs Adm Q* 17(3):16-21, 1993, Aspen.

29. Ethridge P, Lamb G: Professional nursing care management improves quality, access and costs, *Nurs Manage* 23(3):30, 1989.

30. Zander K: Managed care within acute care settings: design and implementations via nursing case management, *Health Care Superv* 2:27-43, 1988.

31. Zander K: Nursing case management: strategic management of cost and quality outcomes, *J Nurs Adm* 18(5):23-30, 1988.

32. McKenzie C, Torkelson, Holt M: Care and cost: nursing case management improves both, *Nurs Manage* 20(10):30-34, 1989.

33. Curtin L: Editorial opinion: the news from the front, *Nurs Manage* 20(30):7-8, 1989.

34. Smith G: Using the public agenda to shape PHN practice, *Nurs Outlook* 37(2):57-62; 79, 1989.

35. Kerfoot K: Today's patient care unit manager, *Nurs Econ* 12(1):54-55, 1994.

36. Clouten K, Weber R: Patient-focused care ... playing to win, *Nurs Manage* 25(2):34-36, 1994.

SUGGESTED READINGS

Abts D, Hofer M, Leafgreen P: Redefining care delivery: a modular system, *Nurs Manage* 25(1):40-46, 1994.

Beltzhoover M: Self-scheduling: an innovative approach, *Nurs Manage* 25(4):81-82, 1994.

Croft A: A psychiatric patient classification system that works! *Nurs Manage* 24(1):66-72, 1993.

Crutchfreed J, Allgier P, Gaston-Johansson F: Job satisfaction and the 12-hour shift, *Nurs Manage* 26(2):54-57, 1995.

Curran C: An interview with Mary Beth Pais (Patient care managers), *Nurs Manage* 12(1):5-9, 1994.

Fiesta J: Staffing implications: a legal update, *Nurs Manage* 25(6):34-35, 1994.

Gibbons K and others: Self-staffing: improving care and staff satisfaction, *Nurs Manage* 25(10):74;76;80, 1994.

Godfrey C: Downsizing: coping with personal pain, *Nurs Manage* 25(10):90-93, 1994.

Guild S and others: Development of an innovative nursing care delivery system, *J Nurs Adm* 24(3):23-28, 1994.

Huber D, Blegen M, McCloskey J: Use of nursing assistants: staff nurse opinions, *Nurs Manage* 25(5):64-66, 1994.

Joel L: Restructuring: under what conditions? *Am J Nurs* 94(3):7, 1994.

Kostvich C and others: The clinical technician as a member of the patient-focused healthcare delivery team, *Nurs Manage* 24(12):32-38, 1994.

Kovner C and others: Changing the delivery of nursing care, *J Nurs Adm* 23(1):24-33, 1993.

Madden M, Ponte P: Advanced practice roles in the managed care environment, *J Nurs Adm* 24(1):56-62, 1994.

Marschke P, Nolan M: Research related to case management, *Nurs Adm Q* 17(3):16-21, 1993.

McCaffery M: Home health-care update 94, *Nurs Manage* 24(6):62-64, 1994.

Murphy R and others: Work redesign: a return to the basics, *Nurs Manage* 25(2):37-39, 1994.

NEWSLINE: Major job losses foreseen in shift to managed care, *Am J Nurs* 95(1):73-75, 1995.

Parkman C, Loveridge C: From nursing service to professional practice, *Nurs Manage* 25(3):63-67, 1994.

Russ A: Downsizing: a survival kit for employees, *Nurs Manage* 25(8):66-67, 1994.

Sierk T: Implementation of a salary model for staff nurses, *Nurs Manage* 25(1):36-37, 1994.

Smith G: Hospital cost management for psychiatric diagnosis: focusing on quality and cost outcomes, *J Psychosoc Nurs Ment Health Serv* 32(2):3-4, 1994.

Stearley H: Stat nursing: alive and well, *Nurs Econ* 12(2):96-99;101;105, 1994.

Townsend M: Twenty-four hour care teams, *Nurs Manage* 25(6):62-64, 1994.

Wimpsett J: Nursing case management: outcomes in a rural environment, *Nurs Manage* 25(1):41-43, 1994.

PLANNING and DECISION MAKING
Fundamental Processes

BEHAVIORAL OBJECTIVES

On completion of this chapter, the student will be prepared to:

- Define the overall planning process and apply it to organizational planning.

- Compare and contrast the scope of planning for top-, middle-, and lower- or first-level managers.

- Discuss the scientific, intuitive, and emotional approaches to decision making.

- Demonstrate how the nursing process can be used in decision making.

- State the functions of group decision making, compare the advantages with the disadvantages, and discuss the power of group decision makers.

- Explain the purpose and procedure of management by objectives.

- Indicate how plans are implemented to achieve objectives.

- Explain the evaluation or controlling process as part of the planning process.

Planning is simply deciding in advance what will and will not be done in the next minutes, hours, days, months, or years. Deciding not to plan is a plan in itself. It has been said that, "If you don't care where you are going, any road will take you there." Planning bridges the gap between where one is and where one wants to go. It answers in advance the who, what, when, where, why, and how of future actions. Plans affect how people will work and for how long. They determine the rate, effectiveness, and quality of a program. Planning considers the seen and unseen and recognizes that all factors influence each other.

Planning is having a specific aim or purpose and mapping out a program or method beforehand. There is a difference between planning and purpose. Purpose is making a resolution or intending to accomplish something. As with New Year's resolutions, unless specific steps are taken to achieve the resolution or purpose, nothing happens. Planning is making a commitment and establishing tools that can measure the outcome.

As the population of the world grows and the means of communication become more sophisticated, the opportunity for working together increases. The number of interactions; possibilities for overlap and duplication in plans; and the possibility for confusion among different people, structures, and organizations multiply at a fantastic rate. If one's goals and means to reach them are not clear, one will continually collide with other people's plans. By announcing goals and clearly indicating the steps needed to achieve them, one establishes points of communication with others who are also making new plans and working with old ones.

This chapter should help nurses who want to influence their environment and make things happen. It is designed for the nurse who is seeking more effective ways to improve current and future performance. It offers principles of planning and decision making and guides to using these principles in nursing practice. It deals with those aspects of planning and decision making that directly affect the nurse manager on a personal and organizational level. The chapter focuses on key elements of the processes, presenting them in a way that illustrates the interdependence of planning and decision making in the total activity of managing.

THE PLANNING PROCESS

In general, planning is an intellectual process that is based on facts and information, not on emotions or wishes. Plans are means, not ends. Planning is a continuous process of assessing, establishing goals and objectives, and implementing and evaluating or controlling them; the process is subject to change as new facts are known. If plans are fixed and unchangeable, then most likely they will fail. In the planning process the necessary steps are mapped out and point toward the goal, but as each major step is taken, a reevaluation or feedback occurs that requires examination of progress against set standards of performance. As conditions change, plans are revised and updated.[1]

In organizations, the primary function of management is to plan for results. **Organizational planning** uses the continuous process of assessing, establishing goals, and implementing and evaluating them to ensure that decisions regarding the use of people, resources, and environment help achieve current and future agency goals (Figure 6-1; Box 6-1).

SCOPE AND LEVEL OF PLANNING

Scope is defined as the breadth of or opportunity to function. In management, scope of planning means how far the manager can go in developing plans for self and others. As Figure 6-2 illustrates, successive levels of plans are made by top-level management that include overall strategic goals and plans for a period of years. Middle-level management develops intermediate goals and plans for from 6 months to 2 years. Lower-level management outlines goals and their implementation for a period of 1 day to 1 year. The first consideration in developing plans is to decide whether the process should be top-down, bottom-up, or interactive.[1] Not surprisingly, interactive planning tends to be more successful than top-down or bottom-up planning. Generally people like to be informed of proceedings that affect them and included in all phases of planning. Figure 6-3 shows that each management person has responsibilities specific to each role but that the responsibilities are interrelated and ongoing.

FIGURE 6-1. The continuous planning process applied to management.

Box 6-1.   Reasons for planning

For both conceptual and practical reasons, the necessity of planning has been emphasized by many people in many ways. Gehrman, manager of the Exxon Company USA, gives the following reasons for planning, which aptly apply to nursing administration[2]:

1. *Planning increases the chances of success by focusing on results, not activities.* Most studies on planning have been done in the business sector and have shown that although planning does not guarantee success, planners consistently outperform nonplanners. Planning helps focus on objectives, and employees can see the results of their labor. Knowing the objectives of the enterprise helps employees relate what they are doing to meaningful outcomes. This principle can be applied to hospitals and other healthcare agencies. Although most are nonprofit systems, this does not mean they are not concerned with making a profit. The delivery of care is a big industry and has the problem of providing many intangible or difficult-to-measure services. These facilities could experience greatly improved results if they followed effective planning procedures.

2. *Planning forces analytic thinking and evaluation of alternatives, therefore improving decisions.* Through the reasoning process the manager seeks to minimize risk and maximize opportunity.

3. *Planning establishes a framework for decision making that is consistent with top management's objectives.* The overall planning process in any organization is a top-to-bottom proposition. Top managers set broader objectives with longer time horizons than do lower-level managers. This downward flow of objectives creates a mean-end chain.

4. *Planning orients people to action instead of reaction.* For any given period, the best use is made of available resources. Guesswork is eliminated, and the manager can successfully direct his or her activities with foresight, influence, and action.

5. *Planning includes day-to-day and future-focused managing.* Determining how specific tasks can best be accomplished on time and with available resources is important and must be addressed, but the manager must look beyond the immediate focus to the future and plan how to pursue the organization's long-term goals.

6. *Planning helps avoid crisis management and provides decision-making flexibility.* When plans anticipate emergencies, they allow the worker to function more calmly and efficiently when an actual crisis occurs. For example, tragedy may be averted when staff members can respond to a fire with proper reporting procedures, protection of enviroment, and the use of emergency equipment. When personnel know signs and symptoms of conditions for hypoxia or alkalosis versus acidosis, they may be able to prevent irreparable damage or even save a life.

7. *Planning provides a basis for measuring organizational and individual performance.* Managers can evaluate the environment, resources, and employees' effectiveness when they know what is expected. The entire planning process leads to a continuous inspection of assessment, goal and objective setting, and implementation of plans.

8. *Planning increases employee involvement and improves communications.* Although time-consuming, employee involvement in how things are to be done and by whom creates a feeling of ownership and therefore a strong commitment to goal achievement.

9. *Planning helps one discover the need for change.* Planning can point out opportunities for new or different services. It guides management thinking to future desirable activities, indicates how best to make change, and directs attainment of goals. Change is occurring in all sectors and certainly in the health field, which has become one of the biggest industries in the United States. As the industry grows, the amount of lead time for planning becomes longer.

10. *Planning is cost-effective.* Costs of health services are accelerating at a rapid rate. Although many fiscal matters are beyond the manager's control, particularly at the lower levels of management, some costs can be contained by planning for efficient operation. For example, projecting the number of nurses needed to care for a group of patients or ordering enough surgical supplies for one nursing unit to provide an even flow of work without excess is important in the total scheme of agency operation.

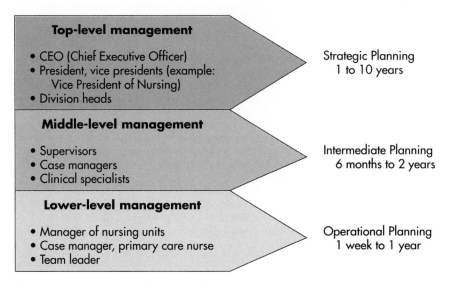

FIGURE 6-2. Three levels of planning in nursing.

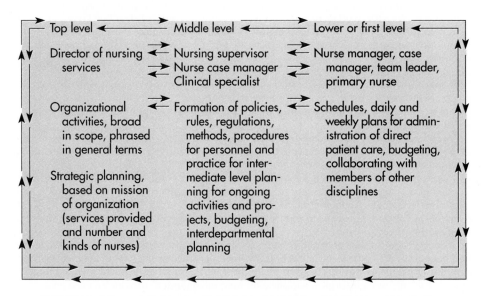

FIGURE 6-3. Scope of planning for nurse managers in a healthcare organization.

Top-Level Managers

Top-level managers comprise a small group of executives who form the highest classification of managers. Top managers are typically titled Chief Executive Officer (CEO). Top-level nurse executives are commonly named vice president, associate administrator, or director of nursing services. Top management's scope of responsibility is the overall management of the organization.

Strategic planning

Top-level managers engage in **strategic planning,** which is a systematic process of determining how to pursue the organization's long-term goals with the available resources. It has been said that "any organization that doesn't have a plan for its future isn't likely to have one." Strategic goals directly support the organization's mission statement, or its purpose for being. A mission statement reflects the individuality of each particular organization in terms of its tangible resources, its market, the services it provides, and the areas that the organization plans to pursue.

Trends versus fads

Curtin,[2] editor of *Nursing Management,* cautions strategic planners to distinguish between trends and fads. A *fad* is something that enjoys brief popularity, such as providing jacuzzis and recreational rooms for maternity patients, which may be abandoned when it proves no longer useful or is fiscally unsound. A *trend,* on the other hand, is a movement or idea that has a sound foundation of demographic, scientific, financial, and sometimes political roots. For example, **outlier facilities,** which provide services outside the hospital, are developing at a rapid rate; these surgi-centers, skilled nursing care facilities, high-intensity home care services, and rehabilitation units are probably here to stay and must be considered in planning for the future.

Environmental factors

To understand implications for the future, it is important for strategic planners to engage in environmental assessment. For example, healthcare agencies want to know what the future holds for them. Western society is moving toward universal access to care. Reimbursements per case will decrease, but volume will increase. Institutions that provide traditional healthcare must move out of their comfortable niches and become part of an integrated network that incorporates diverse outpatient facilities, alternate and nontraditional therapies, and the use of advanced technology.

Implications of environmental factors for nurses

Nursing's future is in a state of flux. Nurses are feeling uneasy and are asking themselves where they fit into the picture. New graduates are wondering if they will have a job or whether the healthcare reform will include only those nurses who can engage in advanced managed care or even in managed competition, which is gaining greater strongholds.

Curtin conducted an environmental study of implications for nursing's future, using Health One's environmental tool.[3] She concluded that hospitals will need to make strategic plans for the future by having (1) small (compared to their customer base), flexible, highly productive work forces, (2) control of outlier physicians and outlier patients (patients who are receiving services outside the hospital), and (3) satisfied customers who pay for and receive the services. Curtin is convinced that these goals can be achieved by focusing on patient care and by having excellent, innovative nursing services. She believes this is an opportune time to implement differentiated nursing practice (Figures 6-4 and 6-5).

Middle-Level Managers

Middle-level managers can encompass many levels in an organization, depending on the size and philosophy of the institution. Middle managers direct the activities of other managers, usually of units or departments, both inside and outside of the hospital. Common titles for middle managers in nursing include supervisor, coordinator, case manager, and clinical specialist. As in all industries in the 1990s, middle-manager positions are receiving close scrutiny to see if they can be eliminated or if several jobs can be merged. The answer is frequently "yes," and the affected nurse managers must learn new and more demanding roles and often receive the same salary, or they

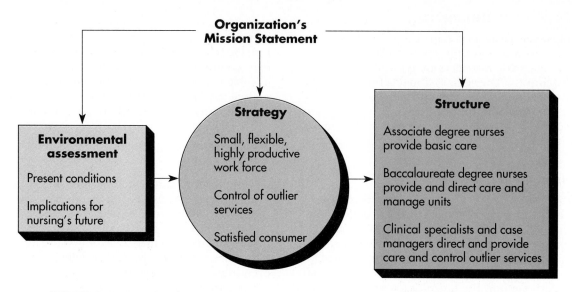

FIGURE 6-4. Example of overall strategic planning for nursing's future by top-level management. (Modified from Curtin L: Learning from the future, *Nurs Manage* 25[1]:7-9, 1994.)

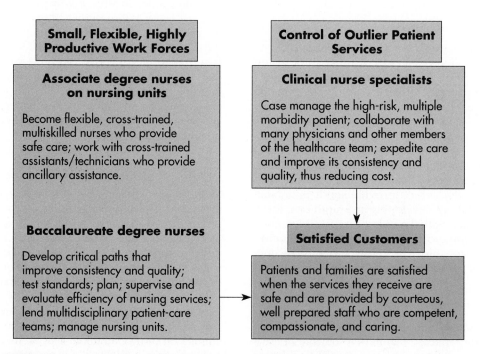

FIGURE 6-5. Example of specific strategic planning for differentiated nursing practice by top-level management. (Modified from Curtin L: Learning from the future, *Nurs Manage* 25[1]:7-9, 1994.)

are demoted to a position with less responsibility and fewer financial rewards. Middle managers report to the vice president of nursing services or the appropriate counterpart.

One of the primary responsibilities of middle managers is to direct the activities that actually implement the broad operating policies of the organization (see Figure 6-3). In interactive planning, the supervisors participate in the formation of such policies at the top level, which makes it much easier to implement them. The case manager coordinates and oversees the work of nurses and other interdisciplinary personnel for a selected group of patients, both inside and outside of the health agency. The clinical specialist may function independently or as a case manager and care for patients who require special treatment.

Lower- or First-Level Managers

Lower- or first-level managers constitute the lowest level at which individuals are responsible for the work of others; they often participate in the work itself. Examples of lower- or first-level managers include the clerical supervisor in an office and the foreman in a manufacturing plant. Examples in nursing include the department or unit manager, case manager, team leader, or primary nurse. Lower-level managers accomplish the objectives designed by strategic planners, and they may or may not have participated in the planning process. Lower- or first-level nurses are responsible for the management of all nursing care on the nursing unit or for administering direct nursing care to one or more patients/clients (see Figure 6-3). Departmental managers in healthcare settings are involved in tactical planning and develop annual budgets for their departments, determine staffing needs and patterns of nursing care, and engage in an ongoing evaluation process so that decisions may be made for the improvement of current operations. Case managers, who plan care for patients from admission through discharge, may function within a unit or department base and interface with other people and departments as necessary. Team leaders plan, direct, and participate in providing care to a group of patients. Primary nurses plan for the care of the patients for whom they are responsible.

 DECISION-MAKING PROCESS

Decision making is the process of developing a commitment to a particular course of action. Decision making pervades all of the basic management functions: planning, organizing, directing, and controlling. Iacocca[4] has stated that if he had to sum up in one word the qualities of a good manager, he would say that it all comes down to decisions.

Variables in Decision Making

In view of the present need to provide quality care to all people at the least cost possible, nursing leaders are making decisions that benefit both the patients/clients and the healthcare organizations. Therefore it is imperative that nurse managers become skilled and even sophisticated in the decision-making process. Today's decision makers face three difficult variables: (1) comlexity, (2) uncertainty, and (3) the need to use different information-processing styles.

The following situation will be used in discussing the variables present in decision making:

> The nurse manager is faced with the dilemma of whether or not to introduce overlapping shift patterns. The manager has decided that an overlap in staff at crucial times on all shifts would benefit the patients served, as well as improve the managerial process. Now the manager must sell the idea to nursing staff and administrators.

Complexity

For managers, complexity is a self-perpetuating cycle that consists of multiple criteria, intangibles, risk and uncertainty, long-term implications, interdisciplinary input, and value judgments (Figure 6-6).[5]

Multiple criteria. Typically, a decision must satisfy a number of criteria that represent different interests. For example, to change to an overlap in shifts, agreement must first come from nursing staff who would be involved in the change, nursing administrators who have the power to sanction change, and the financial officer who controls the purse strings. Hospital standards of patient care must be ensured continu-

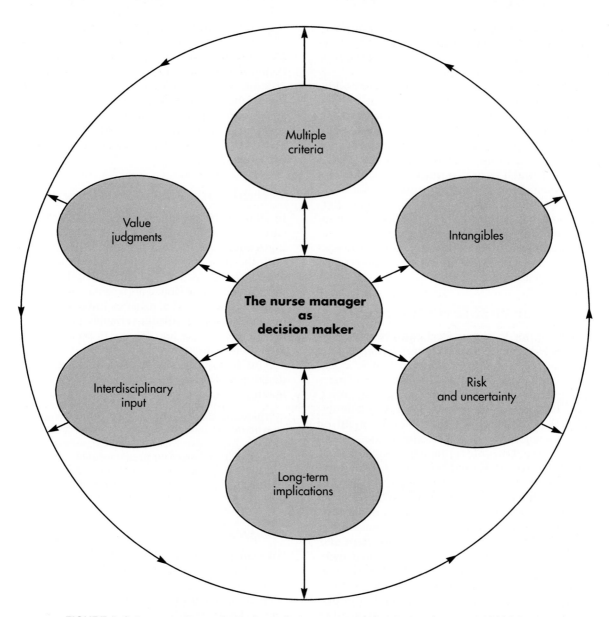

FIGURE 6-6. Sources of complexity for today's managerial decision makers. (Modified from Kreitner R: *Management,* ed 5, Boston, 1992, Houghton Mifflin.)

ously. Balancing conflicting interests is a major challenge for the nurse manager.

Intangibles. Although they are difficult to measure, factors such as employee morale and bureaucracy often determine decision alterna-

tives. For example, some staff nurses may believe that they have less opportunity for promotion if their skills and competencies are not evaluated by a single manager. Others may believe they are losing close touch with their peers by working with two sets of staff only at peak times.

Risk. Unfortunately, the outcome of a situation cannot always be known in advance. A nurse manager is functioning in a risk situation if there is some possibility of physical or psychologic loss, harm, or danger to either property or person. He or she can calculate reasonably accurate probabilities on the basis of historical data and past experiences. The decision maker is advised to consider each situation, list its risks against its values or possible good outcomes for self and others, and choose the alternative that has the fewest negative variables among its outcomes. Box 6-2 offers an example of a decision-making strategy. In this case the nurse manager studies the situation, considers the variables, and chooses to go along with the addition of overlap staffing, for he or she decides that the risks are manageable. Preplanning sessions with nursing staff and concerned administrative personnel can resolve most of the possible risks of this shift change. Ongoing evaluation of the new staffing pattern will help identify problem areas so that

they may be solved before they become major issues. If the nurse manager had concluded that the risks outweighed the advantages, he or she would have either given up the idea or worked to revise it.

Uncertainty. Everyone is aware of varying degrees of uncertainty in daily personal lives. One attaches high degrees of certainty and confidence to the prospect that the sun will rise tomorrow, that family members will show love, and that friends will be there when needed. But confidence wanes when circumstances become more uncertain. Events such as a loved one's death or a friend's moving away fill one with uncertainty.

Societies respond to uncertainty in different ways. Some socialize their members into accepting uncertainty with equanimity; people in such societies, including the United States, are somewhat comfortable with uncertainty. The individualistic ethic is one of the most frequently used

---

Box 6-2.   A strategy for decision making under risk and uncertainty

Situation: Addition of overlapping nursing shifts to cover high-intensity time periods.

RISK OF SITUATION	VALUE OF SITUATION
1. Nurses may resent having to come to work at odd hours and may refuse to cooperate.	1. Nursing loads will lighten, which will result in fewer errors and improved patient care.
2. Nurses may feel fragmented when they cannot finish all the tasks they began.	2. Nurses will be more satisfied with the overall outcomes of their jobs.
3. Nurses will need to rearrange their home and child-care schedules, which may not always work out to their satisfaction.	3. Some nurses may begin to like the flexibility and learn to be creative in their time management.
4. Nurses may feel they are losing close relationships by having their time split between two shifts at peak hours.	4. Nurses will have the opportunity to expand the boundaries of their relationships and choose which ones to nurture.
5. It may become difficult to share ownership of assignments.	5. Nurses will learn to collaborate and will get off duty on time.
6. Nurses may be in conflict with their peers because of differing opinions regarding patient care.	6. Nurses will develop stronger interpersonal and interdependent skills and relationships.
7. Quality of care may decrease.	7. The level of skills and knowledge will increase as nurses learn from one another.
8. The budget may not continue to provide for a sufficient number of nurses.	8. Adjustments can be built into the system.

stereotypes to describe Americans. A representative and democratic type of government promotes adaptation to uncertain situations.[6]

The proposed massive changes of a reformed healthcare system have created much uncertainty in the nursing profession. Many graduates are having difficulty finding desired positions. The registered nurse vacancy rate in hospitals is lower than in recent years. Nurses are moving into new territory by expanding their roles within institutions and within outlier facilities. They are actively participating in legislative matters that concern the future of nursing. Such activities create uncertainty but also satisfaction that nurses are asserting themselves in a positive way.

Long-term implications. Managers are becoming increasingly aware that their decisions have not only an intended short-term impact but also an unintended long-term impact. They must consider both the immediate and the future outcomes. For example, overlap coverage for all shifts will alleviate pressure on the nursing staff that is caused by the high intensity of patient care during specific time periods. However, if patient census changes and less coverage is needed, nurses may resent having to rearrange their schedules, since they have already planned child care and family life around the former schedule and may experience difficulties with change.

Interdisciplinary input. Rarely is one manager completely responsible for an entire package of decisions. A single decision is usually a link in a chain that has passed from one person to another. For example, in the proposal for shift overlap, the nurse manager would meet with nursing staff and administrators because what affects one nursing unit affects all units. Nurse administrators would also meet with financial and personnel officers to work out the details. These are all vital but time-consuming steps.

Value judgments. A value is a clearly defined or implied conception of what an individual or group considers desirable. Values play an important role in the decision-making process. The most important personal variables are individual value systems and individual idiosyncracies and differences. Certain personality types such as individuals who are highly authoritarian and dogmatic and who demonstrate low self-esteem tend to have difficulty valuing others enough to allow them to paticipate in decision making. Conversely, leaders whose values encompass self-respect, honesty, and equality are more likely to invite participation in the decision-making process.[6]

Decision-Making Styles

Newell and Simon[7] studied information-processing theory and concluded that effective problem solving depends on the ability of the problem solvers to adapt to the human limitations of short-term memory. Nurses are required to process a vast quantity of information. Experienced nurses simplify complex situations by clustering or grouping pieces of information; this skill requires time and practice. Benner[8] identified five levels of nursing proficiency: (1) novice, (2) advanced beginniner, (3) competent, (4) proficient, and (5) expert. She describes an expert as one who has an immediate and intuitive grasp of a whole situation, focuses directly on the problem, and takes immediate action. Only after a decision has been made is it likely that an expert will separate and analyze all the components of the whole. Because the nursing staff has a mix of novices and experts, it is necessary for the nurse manager to make effective decisions consistently so that he or she may serve as a role model and teacher.

The scientific approach

Herbert Simon,[9] Nobel prize winner, has described the manager's decision process in three stages: (1) intelligence, (2) design, and (3) choice; this process is called the **scientific approach to decision making,** (Boxes 6-3 and 6-4). The intelligence stage involves searching the environment for conditions requiring a decision; the design stage entails inventing, developing, and analyzing possible courses of action; and the choice stage involves selecting a specific course of action.

The analysis of the decision process by stages emphasizes the difference between management and nonmanagement decisions. Nonmanagement decisions are concentrated on the choice stage only. For example, the nursing assistant needs to decide which patient from the assigned six he or

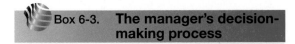

Box 6-3. The manager's decision-making process

Intelligence

Searching the environment for conditions requiring a decision

Design

Inventing, developing, and analyzing possible courses of action

Choice

Actual selection of a particular course of action

she will care for first and what in-stock supplies he or she needs. Management decisions place greater emphasis on the intelligence and design stages, such as making the overall assignments and ordering all supplies. Managers who rely predominantly on the scientific approach tend to be logical, precise, and objective.

The intuitive approach

The **intuitive approach to decision making** involves scanning a situation, anticipating changes, and taking risks without the benefit of rational

Box 6-4. The scientific approach to decision making, applied

PROBLEM (INTELLIGENCE STAGE)	DESIGN STAGE
1. One nurse has failed to report for work.	a. Increase the workload for the existing staff. b. Ask supervisor for staff coverage. c. Ask a nurse to return from another unit. d. Seek help from the registry.
2. A patient requires crash-cart services; as a result, the nurse's other patients are left unattended.	a. Take the nurse's place. b. Ask other nursing staff on the unit to cover the patients during the emergency. c. Ask for coverage from another unit.
3. A nurse-doctor conflict is in progress in the nursing unit.	a. Order the two to stop the conflict immediately. b. Report them to your immediate superior. c. Ask them to step into your office, and stay with them until they do.

The final step in Simon's decision-making process is choice and refers to the actual selection of a particular course of action.

PROBLEM	CHOICE
1. One nurse has failed to report for work.	Call a nurse from the registry to avoid overtaxing the remaining staff on duty and to avoid interfering with a nurse's regularly scheduled day off, which may perpetuate the problem.
2. A patient requires crash-cart services; as a result, the nurse's other patients are left unattended.	Immediately request other nurses on duty to cover for the nurse immediately. If the situation becomes prolonged, seek help from another unit. The manager needs to be free to circulate.
3. There is a nurse-doctor conflict in progress in the nursing unit.	Ask the two to step into your office and guide the way; this prevents a public scene and allows for resolution in private.

processes. Intuition is instinctive knowledge and involves going well beyond current information. It is the capacity for guessing accurately and with sharp insight, and it is usually a result of years of experience. Theorist Piaget proposes that intuitive thinking occurs predominantly between the ages of 4 and 7. After this, the normal child progresses to adulthood, where the main thought patterns become cognitive.[10] The intuitive style is needed in organizational problem solving. Instead of separating a problem into parts and approaching it sequentially and logically, intuitive individuals see things subjectively and prefer to view problems as a whole. However, it is dangerous for managers to depend exclusively on intuition. Unless decisions are also guided by scientific knowledge, factual information, observation, and practical experience, they are likely to be flawed.

The emotional approach

The sharing of feelings is a crucial part of the decision-making process. If emotional responses are not expressed, one inhibits his or her own thoughts about an issue. Allowing people to express their feelings without any judgment can significantly help a group or team open up to each other, which leads to much freer and more productive solutions.[11]

Unfortunately, some nurse managers become so emotionally attached to certain decisions that almost nothing will change their minds. Consider June, a nurse manager who has selected John, a personal friend, to take charge in her absence. Despite John's numerous mistakes and many complaints by nursing staff regarding his poor performance as an administrator of services, June continues to believe that adverse conditions and lack of staff support are the causes of John's problems.

Under such circumstances, managers develop an attitude that says, "Don't bother me with the facts, my mind is made up." Such emotional attachments can have serious consequences for an organization. One solution is for the nurse manager to be made aware of personal biases, which can be accomplished through a group meeting that presents the facts. However, this method can be successful only if the manager is willing to lis-

ten with an open mind and to make necessary changes. Another solution requires the nurse manager to seek out independent opinions. For example, June might ask her nursing supervisor to assess John's performance on several consecutive days. Seeking the opinion of a qualified person who has no vested interest in the situation is good practice.

The nursing process approach

The **nursing process** approach can be applied in all circumstances, and the scientific and intuitive approaches are integral parts of the process.[12] The nursing process involves five steps: (1) **assessment,** (2) analysis and nursing diagnosis, (3) planning, (4) implementation, and (5) evaluation (Figure 6-7). The following situation will be used to illustrate the use of the nursing process in decision making:

> A nurse manager of an outpatient clinic has two patients with a diagnosis of acquired immunodeficiency syndrome (AIDS). One patient who is positive for the human immunodeficiency virus (HIV) is confined to a wheelchair with a catheter and total parenteral nutrition (TPN) therapy; the other is ambulatory and drinks from the common water fountain and uses common restroom facilities. Three members of the nursing staff refuse to come in contact with these patients because they do not want to "catch" the disease. The remaining nurses accept the clients but express fear and apprehension. Therefore the HIV patients are generally shunned.

Assessment. The nurse manager explores the etiology of the situation and may gather the staff together, discuss the problem, and obtain firsthand knowledge of reactions. The leader learns that most nurses know something about AIDS and HIV but not enough to overcome their reluctance and fear. One nurse says, "I don't care what scientists say about how AIDS is spread, I'm not taking any chances." Most of the group expresses concern for the HIV/AIDS patients and regret that they believe it necessary to separate themselves from them.

The nurse manager might distribute an anonymous questionnaire to staff members to allow them more freedom to share their real feelings.

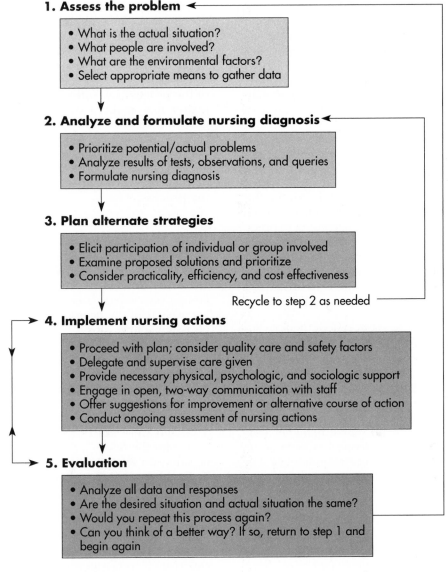

1. Assess the problem

- What is the actual situation?
- What people are involved?
- What are the environmental factors?
- Select appropriate means to gather data

2. Analyze and formulate nursing diagnosis

- Prioritize potential/actual problems
- Analyze results of tests, observations, and queries
- Formulate nursing diagnosis

3. Plan alternate strategies

- Elicit participation of individual or group involved
- Examine proposed solutions and prioritize
- Consider practicality, efficiency, and cost effectiveness

Recycle to step 2 as needed

4. Implement nursing actions

- Proceed with plan; consider quality care and safety factors
- Delegate and supervise care given
- Provide necessary physical, psychologic, and sociologic support
- Engage in open, two-way communication with staff
- Offer suggestions for improvement or alternative course of action
- Conduct ongoing assessment of nursing actions

5. Evaluation

- Analyze all data and responses
- Are the desired situation and actual situation the same?
- Would you repeat this process again?
- Can you think of a better way? If so, return to step 1 and begin again

FIGURE 6-7. The nursing process approach to decision making.

From these questionnaires, the nurse manager can determine how much the staff knows about HIV/AIDS and its transmission and can look for the presence of any judgmental attitudes or biases.

Analysis and nursing diagnosis. After reviewing the responses and observations, the nurse manager arrives at the following nursing diagnosis:

> There is an unfounded fear among nursing staff related to insufficient knowledge about the disease and its transmission, which is demonstrated by a high incidence of refusal to come in contact with HIV-positive patients.

Planning. The nurse manager arranges for a series of seminars on HIV/AIDS. The seminar includes theory and group discussion of the disease process and of feelings and behaviors. Staff members are given assignments to explore various aspects of the problem so that they will become involved in the process. The nurse manager feels she knows the nursing staff well enough to believe that their fear will abate and that they will give the desired care once they are informed and understand the facts concerning the disease.

Implementation. Because it is not feasible for staff members to pick and choose their clients, assign staff members according to procedure. Make it clear to each worker that he or she is expected to carry out responsibilities with concern and attention to quality and that if this is not possible, he or she must seek another workplace.

Evaluation. It is necessary to analyze the results of the solution. In this case the following questions should be asked: Are AIDS patients receiving quality care? Are all staff nurses participating in giving care to AIDS patients? Do these nurses feel "safe" providing this care? After carefully analyzing all the data and staff responses, the nurse manager concludes that although progress has been good, the desired goal has not yet been reached. The nurse manager concludes that the educational plan has been successful but also sees a need to continue group therapy sessions twice a month for support and increased understanding among the nurses. In retrospect, a far better approach would have been to develop a strategy for educating nurses *before* AIDS patients were admitted to the unit. As the arrows in Figure 6-7 indicate, the problem solver is advised to return to any step in the decision-making process when the plan is not working well.

Group Decision Making

Decision making is the central activity of groups.[13] When one thinks of quality decision making, one thinks in terms of *what* decision is made. *How* decisions are made is often just as important and concerns the process a group follows in making a decision.

Various decision-making processes have been discussed, and each decision-making style has pros and cons in terms of the quality of the process and outcome. A knowledgeable leader may make a better decision for the group than less informed members could through discussion and compromise. Group decisions are likely to result in better feelings and ownership of the decision by members, because they have played a more active part in the process.

Process

Like any other organizational activity, decision making does not occur in a vacuum. Groups can aid in the process through committees, study groups, review panels, or task teams. The following aspects of the decision-making process can be assigned to groups:
1. Analyze the problem
2. Identify facts and subjective data that contribute to the problem
3. Determine probabilities, feasibilities, and time and cost estimates
4. Select possible solutions
5. Weigh the risks of each possible solution against the values
6. Choose a solution to the problem
7. Establish an evaluative system to test the solution

Quality

Strongly pressuring group members to be loyal and "team players" can stifle dissent and critique, both of which can be essential to creativity and quality decision making. The following techniques can be used to lessen the likelihood that group members will fit into a mold:
1. Leaders encourage members to think critically.
2. Leaders avoid stating their own preferences and expectations at the outset.
3. Leaders encourage articulate and knowledgeable group members to play devil's advocate and look for alternatives, question the group's

Box 6-5. Advantages and disadvantages of group decision making and problem solving

ADVANTAGES	DISADVANTAGES
Greater pool of information and knowledge	Time consuming
Different perspectives presented	Creativity possibly stifled by social pressures to conform
Positive interpersonal relationships promoted	Responsibilities of members possibly blurred
Increased acceptance and ownership of a solution	Goal displacement occurs if the group loses sight of their primary goal
Training ground for less experienced members	Domination by those who talk the loudest and longest

direction, and ensure that all possible objectives are considered.

The communicative interactions in a group decision can either increase or decrease the quality of a decision (Box 6-5).

Group Cohesiveness

Cohesiveness, or the mutual attraction that holds a group together, is important in the performance, morale, and effective decision making of successful groups. Techniques that foster group cohesiveness include the following:
1. Increasing communication between members
2. Giving the group an identity and emphasizing it; talking about the group as a group
3. Building group traditions such as dates and special occasions
4. Emphasizing teamwork and striving to increase the attractiveness of group participation
5. Encouraging the group to recognize good work
6. Setting clear, attainable group goals
7. Providing rewards for the group
8. Treating group members with respect and dignity, not like parts in a machine.

Group development

A great deal of time is spent in groups of various kinds such as in school, jobs, clubs and associations, community or religious functions, and social activities. The groups in which one partic-

ipates over a lifetime create a wide range of demands and opportunities, and in the process of adjusting to these, one develops, changes, and grows. Everyone has experienced the uneasiness of meeting a new group. Because of uncertainties regarding objectives, roles, and leadership, initially there is little mutual understanding, trust, or commitment between the new group members.

A working knowledge of the characteristics of a mature group can help the manager systematically manage group development. A mature group has the following characteristics:
1. Members are aware of their own and one another's strengths and weaknesses.
2. Individual differences are accepted without being labeled as good or bad.
3. The group develops authority and interpersonal relationships that are recognized and accepted by members.
4. Group decisions are made through rational discussion.
5. Conflict is generated by only important issues such as group goals and the effectiveness and efficiency of the means for achieving them. Conflict produced by emotional issues is at a minimum.
6. Members are aware of the group's process and their own roles within the process.

Power of group decision makers

True group decision making can occur only when the agency agrees to relinquish authority to the group. Decisions made by groups for organizations are usually presented as recommendations. Managers must maintain ultimate accountability for a decision when:

1. The decision has a significant impact on the success or failure of the unit or organization (e.g., purchasing a desk computer for each nurse because budget allocation is out of the group's control).
2. The decision has legal ramifications (e.g., a nurse's refusal to care for AIDS patients).
3. A competitive reward is tied to a successful decision (e.g., one nurse is eligible to receive a promotion).

In less critical areas, the group itself may be responsible for the actual decisions (e.g., designing and developing standardized nursing care plans, deciding the best procedure to follow in a unit emergency).

 **MANAGEMENT BY OBJECTIVES**

Goals and Objectives

The initial step in planning is to determine goals and objectives. Goals are statements of intent that are derived from the purposes of the organization; they are usually stated broadly and in general terms. Objectives are specific aims, purposes, or targets; there should be a harmonious blending of objectives in every enterprise. For example, with the aid of the planning staff, top-level managers establish major or overall goals for the entire organization. They decide what resources the organization will need (e.g., people, facilities, equipment) and how these resources will be allocated among the various divisions or departments. Within the framework of the overall plan, middle-level managers formulate goals and objectives for their divisions or departments. They decide how the resources of their areas will be used to help the organization achieve its overall goals. Lower or first-level managers develop individual and group objectives to achieve the individual and group goals.

Process

The management process begins with goals and objectives and ends with an assessment of how well they have been accomplished. In

1954 Drucker,[14] a noted authority on management, introduced the phrase **management by objectives** (MBO) to emphasize the importance of accomplishment of goals in keeping with objectives. Since that time, MBO has received a great deal of discussion, application, and evaluation. MBO is not a panacea for all management problems, but the system works well in managing nursing activities. Most nurses are familiar with objectives because they have used them during their education and professional practice. This book is an example of the MBO design. Objectives are given, corresponding content is presented, and evaluation is offered. In this cyclic process the learner can move backward or forward at any point during the process of goal achievement.

MBO is based on McGregor's set of assumptions of the Theory Y personality, which states that under the proper conditions people will find satisfaction in work and will accept responsibility for their results (see Chapters 2 and 7). The MBO concept implies that every person or group in a work setting has specific, attainable, and measurable objectives that are in harmony with those of the organization.[14] MBO requires managers and workers to meet to establish specific objectives, develop alternative means of reaching them, and periodically review progress toward those objectives. Nurse managers need to take the lead in using and guiding MBO, because it is the managers themselves who most influence the organizational climate, employee morale, and motivation.

Guidelines

MBO programs can vary enormously. Some objectives are broad and are designed for the organization as a whole (e.g., to provide quality care, to maintain currency in the health field, and to engage in research). Others are more specific and are designed for use in a small subunit of an organization (e.g., to implement primary nursing in the intensive care unit on the fourth floor in 6 weeks or to develop a plan whereby each patient in the medical department on the sixth floor can participate in the management of his or her care in 3 months). Whether broad or narrow in scope, certain elements contribute to the success of MBO systems. Objectives should:

1. Be in harmony with goals of the total organization and committed to the MBO approach at all levels of the orgnization.
2. Consider the technical and human side of planning.
3. Be formulated by those who will participate in their implementation. Vested interest and understanding of their importance lead to increased effort and goal achievement.
4. Answer the questions, What is to be done? Who is responsible? How much is to be accomplished? When and where is the task to be accomplished? What is the cost in time, money, energy, resources, and emotions?
5. Be measurable, stated in observable or behavioral terms, and allow for a realistic evaluation of outcomes.
6. Establish a means of accountability, which is provided through clearly defined responsibilities that are fixed before goals are established. Stating objectives in behavioral terms requires performance criteria, sometimes called job descriptions. These lists of expected activities must relate directly to the stated objectives; otherwise it is difficult to see the relationship between the activities and objectives and therefore to evaluate performance.
7. Be reviewed in regular progress meetings (oral and written) between manager and other participants.
8. Be flexible enough to allow for changes or elimination when they are no longer useful. Once the objectives have been set and agreed on within the normal constraints of organizational policies, managers should have the freedom to develop and implement programs to achieve their goals.

Nursing Management

Top-, middle-, and lower- or first-level managers have different goals and behavioral objectives. Box 6-6 discusses each level's effectiveness in the planning process. See Chapter 4 for other examples of behavioral objectives for team leader activities.

Successful goal achievement requires that everyone commit their time and energy. Each member of the nursing staff must become involved in the overall planning. Note that the objectives presented in Box 6-6 begin with broad, overall goals that can lead to MBO. Each set of objectives is broken down to allow for guidelines every step of the way. Thus objectives become the basis for management of all nursing activity. Methods for implementation of objectives flow easily out of the plan and result in improved performance and higher morale. The nurse manager works toward a successful blending of goals and objectives in patient care management, physical environment operations, and human resources management.

PLAN IMPLEMENTATION

Developing Alternative Courses of Action

Objectives should include a plan of action for accomplishing needs or desired results. Planning involves developing alternative courses of action and choosing the most satisfactory alternative. For example, assume that part of the nursing team's plan is to increase its knowledge of quality nursing care. The objective may be for every team member to satisfactorily pass a test in cardiopulmonary resuscitation every 6 months. Alternative plans for consideration might include (1) each team member assuming responsibility for content and testing at a local Red Cross center, (2) providing education and testing through inservice education at a centralized level in the organization, or (3) each team member being taught and tested on the job by arrangement with the nurse manager or similar person. After the alternatives have been drawn up, they are evaluated with respect to costs and benefits to the organization and personnel and to the probability of 100% success. In this example, total compliance is necessary because lack of knowledge in a single team member becomes life threatening to the patients/clients.

Nursing Care Planning

An excellent way to plan for nursing care is through written care plans. The nursing care plan lists nursing needs for a particular patient and the expected outcomes and nursing interventions necessary to help the patient reach his or her desired goals. Nursing care plans provide for

Box 6-6.   **Goals and objectives of top-, middle-, and lower- or first-level managers**

OBJECTIVES	IMPLICATIONS

Top level

1. To provide quality nursing care to all patients/clients by professional nurses and ancillary personnel
2. To manage patient/client services efficiently and effectively

1. These overall goals are stated in broad terms and tell the nurse manager that the agency is intent on meeting standards beyond the minimal or legal requirements. The nurse manager needs to define "quality nursing" (ANA standards, agency-determined standards, or a combination of both).
2. The nurse manager knows there is to be no discriminatory or preferential treatment of patients/clients and that planning is to occur everywhere nursing is practiced.
3. The nurse manager needs to understand management skills. If he or she lacks such an understanding, he or she will seek help (on-the-job, inservice, advanced education).
4. Performance criteria must be available for all nursing personnel (e.g., job descriptions, procedure manual).
5. The director of nursing services or a designated representative will appoint one middle-level manager (supervisor) to chair a standards committee and another to monitor the management process (in small organizations, it may be the same person).

Middle level

1. To establish a standards committee that is composed of one professional nurse and one ancillary staff member from each subunit (e.g., floors, stations, ICU) and whose purpose is to:
   a. Reach a common understanding of what is meant by "quality nursing"
   b. Compare present standards with an agreed-on definition of quality care
   c. Make necessary additions, changes, or deletions.
2. To devise a plan whereby all nursing personnel have the opportunity to exchange ideas, provide input into the work of the committee, and receive feedback concerning progress
3. To determine if nursing personnel have the opportunity to exchange ideas, provide input into the work of the committee, and receive feedback concerning progress
4. To determine if nursing personnel have the necessary competencies to administer quality nursing care as defined by the committee

1. Actions become more specific. The chairman of the standards committee will contact other middle-level managers for selection of committee members. Before the meeting, available data (e.g., present standards, job descritpions) will be gathered and duplicated so that each person can have a copy. Other resources or persons will be used as needed.
2. Meeting times will be set well in advance to allow lower- or first-level managers to plan schedules. Meetings will start and stop on time.
3. Objectives will be formulated and acted on. For example, a part of the usual definition for quality care is that written nursing care plans are prepared for each patient/client. This specific activity would be one of the first for consideration.
4. The nurse manager will develop a plan for involvement of all members whom he or she represents (input and feedback).
5. A plan for assessing nursing competencies against accepted criteria for evaluation will be developed.

Continued.

Box 6-6.   Goals and objectives of top-, middle-, and lower- or first-level managers—cont'd

OBJECTIVES	IMPLICATIONS

Middle level—cont'd

5. To complete the initial project in 6 months and then establish an ongoing review committee

6. The chairman of the committee(s) will maintain a two-way flow of information between the standards committee and top-level management (director of nursing services or a designated representative).

Lower or first level

1. To appoint representatives from the small work group to the standards committee
2. To meet the standards committee at regularly scheduled times
3. To set up weekly meetings for one-half hour with members of the small work group to keep them informed and to hear their views
4. To make sure that members' opinions are fairly represented at committee meetings
5. To assess each member's understanding of "quality care" as defined by the committee
6. To determine each member's ability to provide "quality care"
7. To devise a plan for helping each member to acquire the necessary knowledge and skills needed to give care

1. At this level the nurse manager works with details that put overall goals and plans into effect.
2. Team leaders and other members appointed to the standards committee will arrange with their immediate supervisor (nurse manager or a substitute) for times to meet with all nursing staff to discuss content and to receive their input (nurse manager will attend).
3. Notes will be taken and referred to at each meeting of the committee.
4. Agreed-on evaluation tools will be used to gain the needed information. The lower- or first-level manager will cooperate in implementing the proper methods (e.g., participate in evaluation procedure, arrange time and place for assessment between nurse and patient/client, use of other facilities).

---

continuity, communication, coordination, individualization, and documentation. Even though optimal nursing care cannot be ensured through the use of patient care plans, it can never be achieved without them.[12]

Each patient is unique; therefore it is necessary to develop a plan for each individual that addresses his or her specific needs. However, preparing an individual care plan for each patient/client is difficult. Time constraints, lack of impetus, and varying abilities of nursing personnel to formulate plans often prevent the use of nursing care plans. The nurse manager can lead the way in preparing and using plans. A list of common diagnoses or nursing problems such as coronary insufficiency, cardiovascular accident, anemia, anxiety, and pneumonia can be compiled, and standard care plans can be developed for each. The prepared standard care plans can be du-

plicated and made available to the nurses on their respective units, or they can be stored in the computer and pulled up when needed. When a patient is admitted, the nurse can take the nursing history and pull the standard care plan that most closely relates to the patient, activate it with the date, circle or check the problems that pertain to the patient, and add any other unique patient needs. An example of one form of standard care plan is given in Box 6-7. Note that only the problems present at the time of admission are activated; if other problems occur, they may be checked and dated.

Nurses on all shifts use the nursing care plan as a basis for practice. Those who are unfamiliar with the patient find far more continuity and comprehensiveness of care with a written plan. Care planning may list all significant persons, including the patient, family, physician, dietician,

Box 6-7. Patient care plan*

diagnosis: colitis

Discharge criteria: 1. Verbalize understanding of and willingness to follow MD's outpatient regimen. 2. Verbalizes understanding of and willingness to follow diet at home and make correct selection from a food list. 3. Demonstrates understanding of medication regimen. 4. Relates realistic plans for coping with stressful situations after discharge (e.g., job, family, recreation).

DATE	NURSING DIAGNOSIS	EXPECTED OUTCOMES	NURSING INTERVENTIONS
	① Abdominal distress: Diarrhea and abd. cramps due to colitis	① Decrease in no. of stools to 1-2 daily; stools of normal consistency	① Document color, consistency, and time of all stools; notify MD of gross change in stools
	② Weight loss due to anorexia, nausea, and/or vomiting	② Maintain admission weight; takes meals without n. or v.; verbalizes understanding of diet	② Weigh daily at _____ AM ✓ Contact dietitian for a patient conference ✓ Reinforce teaching ✓ Give antiemetics as needed ✓ Check 1 hour before each meal, and p.r.n.
	③ Dehydration due to electrolyte imbalance	③ Intake at least 2000 ml per day; most mucous membranes; good skin turgor	③ Record I&O q8h; force fluids to 2000 ml; 1800 ml day and PM shifts; 200 ml noc
	④ Possible perianal discomfort, skin breakdown, or rectal bleeding due to diarrhea	④ Healthy skin around anus; no rectal bleeding	④ If needed, get order for Sitz bath; medication for excoriation ✓ Instruct in cleansing procedure after each b.m.
	5 Weakness due to gastrointestinal malabsorption	5 Ambulates without assistance; does own activities of daily living	5 Establish plan for daily care with patient; encourage self-help as much as possible; allow for frequent rest periods; increase ambulation gradually; record plan and indicate progress on each shift
	6 Frustration and anxiety due to diarrhea and interruption of lifestyle	6 Tolerance for situation; verbalizes realistic plans for coping	6 Spend at least 15 min/day with pt.; listen, guide, and support in therapeutic plans
	7 Potential development of complications: hemorrhage and/or perforation	7 Stable vital signs; normal temperature; no severe pain or sudden increase in pain	7 Check at least every _____ hours for ↑ temperature, pulse, and respirations; listen for hyperactive bowel sounds; check for blood in stool and excessive pain

*Adapted from a Standard Care Plan used at The Good Samaritan Hospital of Santa Clara Valley, San Jose, California.

physical therapist, and clergyman. The plan is kept current and used as a basis for documentation and for transfer or discharge summary and planning. Nursing care plans provide evidence that standards of care have been maintained and that nurses have assumed responsibility and accountability.

EVALUATION OR CONTROL OF THE PLAN

Planning has been described as a process that requires cognitive skills (thinking and decision making). However, the process does not end with a plan because there is a direct link between plans and the evaluation or control of outcomes. To have practical effects, plans must be implemented and monitored. Evaluation or control ensures that performance meets specific goals and objectives. Planning and evaluating are closely interrelated. Evaluation and control cannot occur unless a plan exists, and the success of the plan is uncertain at best unless some effort is made to monitor its progress.

Although planning always leads to evaluation or controlling, the reverse is often true. A nurse manager who is evaluating an activity often sees the need to alter the original plan to meet changing or unforeseen conditions.

Again, if there is employee participation in the evaluation process, members will be more likely to control their own activities to ensure that objectives are met. For example, if all team members agree to satisfactorily pass a cardiopulmonary resuscitation class every 6 months, they might voluntarily spend extra time and effort to complete the task well and on time. Evaluation or control of activities is discussed in greater detail in Chapter 10.

Summary

1. Planning is an intellectual and continuous process of assessing, establishing, implementing, and evaluating goals and objectives.
2. The organizational planning process is applied to people, resources, and the environment for the present and the future.
3. According to need, the manager can enter and exit the planning process at any point.

4. Some managers may not want to engage in the planning process because of lack of knowledge regarding the organization and the value of planning, time and work factors, the desire to deal with immediate instead of future situations, fear of failure, and resistance to change.
5. Reasons for planning include successful achievement of goals and objectives; meaningful work; effective use of personnel, resources, and environment; cost control; preparation for crises; readiness for change; and continuous evaluation of the management process.
6. Scope of planning is defined as how far one can go in developing plans for self and others.
7. The widest scope of responsibility for planning lies with top managers, who are responsible for the overall policies and goals of the organization. Responsibility decreases in proportion to the size of the territory and the tasks assigned, such as with middle and lower or first levels of management.
8. Top managers are the highest managers and are typically called presidents or directors. A nursing manager at this level is commonly called vice president, director, or administrator of nursing services. Planning is broad and general.
9. An example of a middle manager is the nursing supervisor who is responsible for several other nurse managers, usually unit managers, nurse managers, or case managers. Nursing supervisors are concerned with the formation of policies, procedures, and objectives that will realize organizational purposes.
10. Lower- or first-level managers are at the lowest level of the managerial structure. They put overall organizational goals and supervisors' plans into effect at the front line. Unit managers, team leaders, and primary nurses are examples of lower- or first-level managers.
11. Strategic planning is a systematic process of determining how to pursue an organization's long-term goals with available resources. Strategic goals support the organization's mission statement.
12. A trend is a movement or idea that has sound foundation. An example of a trend is the establishment of outlier facilities, which provide services outside the hospital.

13. Traditional healthcare institutions must become part of an integrated network that incorporates diverse outpatient facilities, alternate and nontraditional therapies, and the use of advanced technology.

14. Leah Curtin, editor of *Nursing Management,* believes that hospitals must make strategic plans for the future by having small, flexible, and highly productive work forces; control of outlier patients; and satisfied customers. She believes that the 1990s are an opportune time to implement differentiated nursing practice.

15. Middle managers (usually supervisors, coordinators, case managers, or clinical specialists) direct the activities of other managers. They direct the activities that will implement the broad operating policies of the organization.

16. Lower- or first-level managers are responsible for the work of others, and often participate in the work. Lower-level managers accomplish the objectives designed by strategic planners.

17. Decision making involves developing a commitment to a course of action, and it pervades all basic management functions.

18. Variables in decision making include complexity, uncertainty, and the need to use different information-processing styles.

19. Complexity in management is a self-perpetuating cycle that consists of criteria, intangibles, risk and uncertainty, long-term implications, interdisciplinary input, and value judgments.

20. Nurse managers who are able to assess the degree of uncertainty in a situation are more capable of making effective decisions than are those who cannot.

21. Experienced nurses learn to cluster pieces of information for processing complex situations.

22. The scientific approach to decision making includes using one's intelligence, considering the design and possible courses of action, and making an educated choice.

23. Intuitive decision making relies on personal perceptions, hunches, biases, and personal values.

24. The nursing process approach to decision making includes (1) assessment, (2) analysis and nursing diagnosis, (3) planning, (4) implementation, and (5) evaluation. The scientific and intuitive approaches are an integral part of the process.

25. Groups can aid in the decision-making process through committees, study groups, review panels, or task teams.

26. Given a mix of people who are knowledgeable and interested, a group can frequently perform better than a single person can.

27. Group participation increases acceptance of decisions.

28. Negative aspects of group decision making may be (1) dominance by one individual over the group, (2) social pressure to conform, and (3) competition.

29. Advantages of group decision making include a greater pool of knowledge, presentation of different perspectives, promotion of positive interpersonal relationships, increased ownership of solutions, and a training ground for less experienced members.

30. The disadvantages of group decision making are that it may be time consuming and may stifle creativity through social pressures, blur responsibilities of members, displace the primary goal, and lead to domination of the group by one or two persons.

31. Objectives stem from goals and are specific aims or purposes.

32. In MBO, every person or group in a work setting has specific, attainable, and measurable objectives that are in harmony with those of the organization.

33. Objectives should include a plan of action to facilitate the accomplishment of needs or desired results.

34. Alternatives or choices are judged in terms of costs and benefits to the agency and personnel and the probability of success.

35. MBO is easily adaptable to each phase of nursing practice.

36. Objectives should answer the questions who, what, where, when, and why and be flexible enough to allow for changes or elimination when they are no longer useful.

37. MBO requires commitment by the agency and all personnel.

38. To have practical results, plans must be implemented and monitored.

39. Nursing care is best carried out by using a written care plan, which is a record of nursing assessment (nursing diagnosis), expected outcomes, and nursing interventions.
40. Nursing care plans provide continuity, communication, coordination, individualization, and documentation for round-the-clock care.
41. The use of standard care plans helps ensure care planning and provides for a quick review of the usual problems encountered with a particular diagnosis.
42. Evaluation or control is the ongoing process of making sure that performance meets specific goals and objectives.
43. Planning leads to evaluation, and evaluation leads to altering the original plan as needed to meet changing or unforeseen conditions.

❓ Questions for Study and Discussion

1. Why is planning a primary management function, and why is it particularly important for nurse managers today?
2. Write three behavioral objectives for things you intend to accomplish in the next 6 months.
3. Do you think your personal value system would affect the way you would perform as a department manager? Explain.
4. Explain the differences between first-level, middle-level, and top-level managers.
5. Assume you are the supervisor in a home healthcare agency. You have 6 RNs and 12 home health aides under your jurisdiction. You believe all staff have maximum assignments. The director of the home healthcare agency announces that, as a result of government cutbacks, each nurse and assistant will have to add two clients per day to his or her caseloads. Identify the problem and use the complexity chart in Figure 6-6 to itemize your reactions to each of the sources of complexity.
6. As a new staff nurse, you have a problem. At the time of employment, you were promised verbally by a personnel administrator that you could continue advanced studies in nursing at the local university. You are entering your third month of employment and already have had to miss five classes because of schedule conflicts. Your department manager says that no promises were made because the first priority is to cover the needs of the nursing unit. Use the scientific approach (see Box 6-4) to identify the problem, design possible courses of action, and select a course of action.
7. Explain why it is not a good idea to use only intuition to make a decision.
8. Review the pragmatic assessment and decision-making process presented in Figure 6-7, and work through the following situation: You are the department manager of a labor and delivery area where family members are allowed to attend to the mother from the time of admission until dismissal. The only exclusion is during delivery, when only two adults are allowed at the mother's side. Requests by family members for frequent information and special privileges (e.g., food, drink, extra chairs, sleeping cots) create continual noise and disruption around the nurses' station. Small children create confusion, and you are not sure that they are always safe within the environment. You believe that families should be together but that there should be some control. Work with items 1 to 3 of Figure 6-7 to solve the situation.
9. Are there any instances in which a group of nursing staff could not make a decision for their nursing department? Explain.

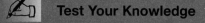 **Test Your Knowledge**

BEHAVIORAL OBJECTIVE

Define the overall planning process and apply it to organizational planning.

Roy aspires to beome a hospital administrator. He is completing an internship at Valley Medical Center.

_____ 1. Roy learns that in organizations the primary management function is to:
   a. Assess and establish goals.
   b. Establish a framework in which to function.
   c. Plan for results.
   d. Control all operations.

_____ 2. Roy found that a primary task in the management process is planning, which is a process best defined as:
   a. A fixed plan.
   b. Short-term goal setting.
   c. A continuous process.
   d. Long-range assessment.

_____ 3. Roy found that one of the following responses is incompatible with the planning process in organizations:
   a. Establishing goals and objectives
   b. Formulating nursing personnel goals first
   c. Evaluating goal implementation
   d. Revising and updating plans

BEHAVIORAL OBJECTIVE

Compare and contrast the scope of planning for top-, middle-, and lower- or first-level managers.

Roy was given the opportunity to work side-by-side with managers at all levels. He learned some important concepts.

_____ 4. Roy was informed that scope of planning in management is defined as all except:
   a. The range of the manager's thoughts or actions.
   b. Breadth or opportunity to function.
   c. How far the manager can go in planning.
   d. The designated area to manage.

_____ 5. Roy recognized which of the following statements to be incompatible with middle management?
   a. It encompasses many levels in an organization.
   b. It directs the activities of other nurse managers.
   c. It helps implement broad operating policies of the organization.
   d. It is identified with one level of management.

_____ 6. Roy was given several examples of lower- or first-level managers in nursing. Which of the following is the exception?
   a. Primary care nurse
   b. Supervisor
   c. Team leader
   d. Department manager

_____ 7. Environmental factors were reviewed in a strategic planning meeting. What was the relevance to the institution?
   a. To help them see how to clean up the grounds
   b. To understand implications for the future
   c. To make decisions concerning light and power
   d. To determine the best sources of information

BEHAVIORAL OBJECTIVE
Discuss the scientific, intuitive, and emotional approaches to decision making.

Roy now enters into a series of decision-making activities. As an intern, he has time to compare and contrast the various approaches.

_____ 8. Roy can see that decision makers face three difficult challenges in today's healthcare industry. Which of the following is the exception?
a. The use of different automated information systems
b. Complexity of organizations
c. Retrospective payment systems
d. Uncertainty regarding the future

_____ 9. Roy was assigned to work with a manager who had difficulty in valuing others and who therefore had a problem with allowing participation in decision making. This problem was probably a result of:
a. High self-esteem.
b. Time pressures.
c. Low self-esteem.
d. The feeling that he could do the job better.

_____ 10. Roy noted that the nurse manager seemed to treat one of the nurses more kindly than the other; the manager spoke sharply to one and softly to the other while offering the decision. What was the decision-making style?
a. Intuitive
b. Scientific
c. Emotional
d. Authoritarian

BEHAVIORAL OBJECTIVE
Demonstrate how the nursing process can be used in decision making.

Roy observed that nurse managers rely on the nursing process for decision making and that the scientific and intuitive approach is used as an integral part of the process.

_____ 11. Nancy, a critical care specialist, is called to the bedside of Mrs. Lowe, who is scheduled to have a laproscopic cholecystectomy. Her pulse is slightly irregular, so Nancy attaches her to a cardiac monitor; the strip shows premature ventricular contractions. She confers with the primary nurse regarding the patient's history. Which step of the nursing process is Nancy using?
a. Planning
b. Evaluation
c. Assessment
d. Analysis and nursing diagnosis

_____ 12. Nancy calls a conference with staff members who are attending Mrs. Lowe. They decide to obtain a 12-lead ECG for a more definitive picture. They conclude that Mrs. Lowe has no serious cardiac or pulmonary problems. Which step of the nursing process is in effect here?
a. Nursing diagnosis
b. Evaluation
c. Planning
d. Assessment

_____ 13. Nancy consults with the attending physician and the anesthesiologist. She advises the primary nurse to procede with the preoperative preparations and to remain alert for any adverse symptoms. Which step of the nursing process is this?
a. Assessment
b. Planning
c. Evaluation
d. Nursing diagnosis

_____ 14. The next morning Nancy confers with Mrs. Lowe's primary nurse. Together they determine that she is ready for surgery. This step of nursing process is:
a. Assessment.
b. Evaluation.
c. Nursing diagnosis.
d. Planning.

BEHAVIORAL OBJECTIVE

State the functions of group decision making, compare the advantages with the disadvantages, and discuss the power of group decision makers.

Victoria has joined a nursing task force to determine how the Visiting Nurse Association can reduce costs yet preserve quality care.

_____ 15. Victoria knows that three of the following statements are true concerning group interaction. Which of the following is the exception?
   a. Groups tend to do quantitatively and qualitatively better than the average individual.
   b. Group participation increases acceptance of the decisions by group members.
   c. A negative aspect of group decision making is that groups may accept the first potentially successful solution.
   d. Group decision makers in most organizations have the power to make major decisions.

_____ 16. Victoria recognizes there are many advantages to group decision making. Which of the following is the exception?
   a. Greater pool of information
   b. Goal displacement
   c. Promotion of positive interpersonal relationships
   d. Training ground for group members

_____ 17. To function well, Victoria must have an accurate concept of power. Which of the following is the best definition of group power.?
   a. The right to tell the group what to do
   b. The right to be addressed as leader
   c. Ultimate authority
   d. Ability to exert influence over the group

BEHAVIORAL OBJECTIVE

Explain the purpose and procedure of management by objectives.

Monique is spearheading a committee to improve the agency's standard care plans. She has studied MBO and is ready to put them into operation.

_____ 18. Monique learns that one of the following statements is false. Which one is it?
   a. The MBO process begins with goals and objectives and ends with assessment.
   b. Goals and objectives are synonymous.
   c. MBO is a cyclic process.
   d. MBO is concerned with time, energy, money, resources, and emotions.

BEHAVIORAL OBJECTIVE

Indicate how plans are implemented to achieve objectives.

Monique's committee for the revision of standard nursing care plans has formulated objectives. Now the committee must place its plan into action.

_____ 19. The success of the committee's work depends on the fact that they have done all except:
   a. Plan for contingencies.
   b. Adhere to one plan of implementation.
   c. Have group consensus.
   d. Have a plan for evaluation.

BEHAVIORAL OBJECTIVE

Explain the evaluation or controlling process as part of the planning process.

Monique realizes that her work as committee chairperson is not over until evaluation has been completed.

_____ 20. Monique knows that evaluation or control is best defined as:
  a. A review of activities after they have occurred.
  b. A continuous process of seeing that performance meets goals and objectives.
  c. Making changes.
  d. Telling people how well or how poorly they have done.

REFERENCES

1. Barney J, Griffin R: *The management of organizations,* Boston, 1992, Houghton Mifflin.
2. Curtin L: Learning from the future, *Nurs Manage* 25(1):7-9, 1994.
3. Health One Corporation: *Environmental assessment tool,* Minneapolis, 1994, The Corporation.
4. Iaoccoa L: *An autobiography,* New York, 1984, Bantam.
5. Kreitner R: *Management,* ed 5, Boston, 1993, Houghton Mifflin.
6. Robbins S: *Essentials in organizational behavior,* ed 4, Englewood Cliffs, 1994, Prentice Hall.
7. Newell A, Simon H: *Human problem solving,* Englewood Cliffs, NJ, 1972, Prentice Hall.
8. Benner P: *From novice to expert,* Menlo Park, Calif, 1984, Addison-Wesley Publishing.
9. Simon H: *The new science of management decision,* New York, 1960, Harper & Row.
10. Lefrancois G: *Psychology for teaching,* Belmont, Calif, 1982, Wadsworth.
11. Henry J, Walker D: *Managing innovation,* Newbury Park, 1991, Sage Publications.
12. Wilkinson J: *Nursing process in action: a critical thinking approach,* Redwood City, Calif, 1992, Addison-Wesley.
13. Mathis R, Jackson J: *Human resource management,* ed 7, Minneapolis/St Paul, 1994, West Publishing.
14. Drucker P: *The practice of management,* New York, 1954, Harper & Row.

SUGGESTED READINGS

Bachand P, Bobis K: Prototyping a bedside documentation system, *Comput Nurs* 1(6):291-295, 1993.

Brookfield S: On impostorship, cultural suicide, and other dangers: how nurses learn critical thinking, *Nurs Manage* 24(5):197-205, 1993.

Case B: Walking around the elephant: a critical-thinking strategy for decision making, *J Contin Educ Nurs* 25(3):101-109, 1994.

Clouten K, Weber R: Patient-focused care...playing to win, *Nurs Manage* 25(2):34-36, 1994.

Cordell B, Smith-Blair N: Streamlined charting for patient education, *Nurs 94* 24(1):57-59, 1994.

Dodaro-Surrusco D: Caring and...curing, comforting, *RN* 57(5):39-41, 1994.

Fleeger M: Assessing organizational culture: a planning strategy, *Nurs Manage* 24(2):39-41, 1993.

Goodwin D: Nursing case management activities: how they differ between employment settings, *J Nurs Adm* 24(2):29-34, 1994.

Luqauire M and others: Focusing on outcomes, *RN* 57(5):57-60, 1994.

Martin L, Hughes S: Using the mission statement to craft a least-restraint policy, *Nurs Manage,* 24(3):65-66, 1993.

O'Brien K, Landstrom G: Using system integration to revise documentation, *Nurs Manage* 25(2):56-58, 1994.

Tennant D: Designing nurses make the ideal real, *RN* 57(6):21-23, 1994.

Smeltzer G, Hinshaw S: Integrating research in a strategic plan, *Nurs Manage* 24(2):42-44, 1993.

Snyder M: Critical thinking: a foundation for consumer-focused care, *J Contin Educ Nurs* 24(5):206-209, 1993.

Wegner W: Support services: contributing to patient care, *Nurs Manage* 25(2):64-66;80, 1994.

West E: The cultural bridge model (plan of care), *Nurs Outlook* 41(5):229-234, 1993.

Wheeler K, Barrett E: Review and synthesis of selected nursing studies on teaching empathy and implications for nursing research and education (to create a caring environment), *Nurs Outlook* 42(5):230-236, 1994.

GIVING DIRECTIONS

BEHAVIORAL OBJECTIVES

On completion of this chapter, the student will be prepared to:

- Define direction giving and explain the implications for nursing at the lower or first level of management.

- State two preconditions for achieving success in direction giving and explain how these preconditions are acquired.

- Using Chapter 7 guidelines, prepare a "to do" list for one upcoming student clinical experience.

- Identify factors that determine the size of a work group, span of control, and the physical support system.

- Explain the guidelines necessary to effectively delegate activities to nursing personnel who are providing care to a group of patients.

- Demonstrate ability to identify priorities in assignment making.

- Identify criteria important to giving directions for a nursing assignment.

In previous chapters, organization has been described as a system in which all personnel relate to each other through specific channels. This chapter discusses directing at the lower or decentralized level. At this level the nurse manager works with a small group of nursing personnel and coordinates persons, equipment, and supplies in a designated environment. Directing is the connecting link between organizing for work and getting the job done. It involves issuing assignments, orders, and instructions that permit the worker to understand what is expected of him or her and guiding and over-

seeing the worker so that he or she can contribute effectively and efficiently to organizational objectives.

It is assumed that the nurse manager knows the organizational structure, policies, standards, and job descriptions of the agency. For the purpose of clarity, the concept of direction is divided into three sections. This chapter discusses the preconditions for achieving success in direction giving. It also discusses the technical aspects of direction giving and the methods and materials used by the nurse manager at the lower or first level of management. Chapter 8 focuses on the interpersonal aspect of management. In reality, technical activities cannot and should not be separated from human considerations; therefore there is some overlap between chapters.

Other chapters have described many important determinants in the organizational process, including people and their values, resources, and the environment. They have emphasized that there is no one best way to design an organization; this will vary from one organization to the next. The same concepts hold true for the direction-giving process.

This chapter presents information that can be applied to any healthcare delivery system. Illustrations show how the major concepts of direction giving can be accomplished at the lower or first level of management.

PRECONDITIONS FOR SUCCESS IN DIRECTION GIVING

It is impossible to offer a sure-fire formula for getting others to do a job. However, it is possible to isolate general preconditions for successful direction giving.

Acquire the Ability to Direct

The ability to direct is the demonstrated capacity to achieve organizational goals both effectively and efficiently through the work of others. Today's manager needs conceptual, technical, and interpersonal abilities. Students of leadership and management are left with one overriding question: "Do I acquire the necessary abilities through theory or practice?" Theory helps one systematically analyze and draw conclusions about the significance of the management and directing process, and work experiences put the newly acquired theories into practice. Therefore what is really important is the personally meaningful integration of theory and practice (Figure 7-1). The manager, especially a new one, must recognize that learning is a process and takes time.

Acquire the Art of Time Management

New nurse managers assume their roles with excitement about future possibilities. However, if they are not careful, their "high" can be quickly

decimated by the everyday stresses of the job.[1] Poor time management is one type of **stressor** that can diminish enthusiasm. Managers frequently state that time is their scarcest and most valuable commodity. Time always moves quickly and this very often leads to a short-circuiting of important issues or activities.

List overall responsibilities

Many daily pressures can be reduced or eliminated through effective time management. One way to achieve this is to list the overall responsibilities for the next day. At the end of a work day, I find it helpful to list the activities for the next day (Figure 7-2). This plan has been helpful, because a barrage of interruptions often greet the manager when he or she first enters the unit:

"Got a minute? I have something I need to talk with you about."

"Oh, there you are! The night nurse must speak with you before she leaves."

"I'm not feeling well. I don't think I can stay."

Such interruptions rob the nurse manager of planning time, and the demands of the day are on the manager before there is time to assess what needs to be done. By completing a plan the day before, the nurse manager can avoid such a problem. At the close of a work day, he or she can review what has been done and what has been neglected. He or she can reassess the unaccomplished things "to do" in order of priority and incorporate them into the plan for the following day; by doing so, the activities are not lost.

Reduce overall tasks to specifics

For those items on the "to do" list that require skill teaching or written direction, more detailed plans are necessary. Note the item on the "to do" list in Figure 7-2 that says, "Orient the new PM manager." This activity requires the time and expertise of the nurse manager, and the new unit manager must know the expectations. Figure 7-3 provides a sample of a detailed plan. If the orientation is interrupted, the nurse manager need only check off where they were in the process and begin there at the next training session. If classes and training manuals have been provided for orientation, the nurse manager functions as a role model and explains items that the new man-

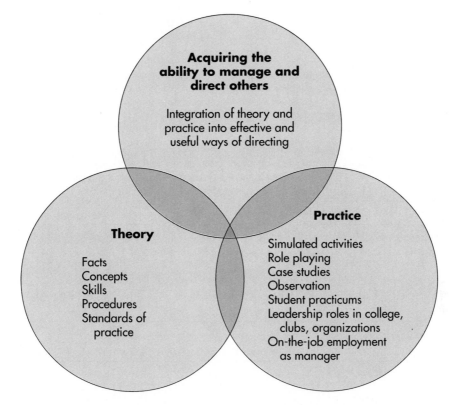

FIGURE 7-1. Acquiring the ability to manage and direct others by merging theory and practice.

Time Management

	Must do	Important to do	Nice to do but not vitally important
	Plan or oversee daily schedules for staff	Oversee daily activities	Greet new personnel director
	Determine needed changes in staffing	Visit patients/clients/families	Meet with representative of volunteer services
	Orient new PM unit manager	Conduct two performance evaluations	Call a staff member who is home on leave
	Attend unit manager's meeting	Investigate excessive disappearance of supplies	Have lunch break with staff

FIGURE 7-2. Example of a "to do" list for the nurse manager of a unit or department.

Day	Time	Activity
Monday	7-9:45AM	Observe unit manager
	10AM-12PM	Review job description; clarify issues; provide practice sheets for assignment making; do simulated exercise; review with unit manager; attend unit managers' meeting
Tuesday	7-9:45AM	Assist unit manager with assignment making; work at desk with manager; learn routines; protocol
	10AM-12PM	Provide practice sheets for making work schedule; review practices for when and how to send staff to other units and how to acquire additional staff
	1-3:30PM	Follow unit manager
Wednesday	7-9:45AM	Fill out daily assignment sheet; assess plan with unit manager; evaluate effects of plan
	10AM-12PM	Work with unit manager in learning manager's procedures
	12:30-2PM	Fill out work schedule for a 2-week period; review with unit manager
Thursday	3-11:30PM	Serve as unit manager; consult evening supervisor as necessary, or if not available, unit manager of another unit
Friday	1-3:30PM	Meet with unit manager who served as mentor; discuss events of previous evening; clarify any issues that need attention; serve as unit manager
	3-11:30PM	Function as nurse manager

FIGURE 7-3. Sample of a specific time plan for orienting a new PM unit manager.

ager does not understand. Note the irregularity of hours in this plan. The novice needs time to assimilate the material, and time is included for coming in early on the day following the initial unit manager activity.

Written plans are particularly useful for a new graduate or for an experienced nurse who is new to the job. Without preplanning, a nurse can feel overwhelmed. A written list can provide the necessary guidelines for the tasks of the day, and the nurse can work in an organized fashion (Figure 7-4). As the staff nurse becomes acclimated to routine, he or she no longer needs specific, detailed plans. He or she may make a shorter, more concise "to do" list at the top of the current worksheet and check off items as they are accomplished.

TECHNICAL ASPECTS OF DIRECTION GIVING

Size and Mix of the Work Group: Span of Control

A nurse manager has many possible combinations of tasks. The nurse is expected to plan, organize, direct, and control quality nursing care that is given by a group of nursing personnel with diversified abilities and personalities. In addition, that nurse is to have the technical knowledge and expertise to handle any situation. He or she is a teacher, counselor, and role model.

At lower- or first-level management, the number of people who report directly to a manager represents the managerial span of control. Man-

Time Management

Must do	Important to do	Nice to do but not vitally important
Receive assignment	Supervise team members	Assist physicians on routine rounds
Count narcotics	Make self available for assistance as possible	Teach staff about new medications/procedures
Obtain worksheet		
Review patients' records	Take breaks when scheduled/report to nurse who is covering	Restock shelves with supplies
Listen to noc report		
Make patient rounds	Cover for other team leaders as scheduled	Clean the medication room
Conduct team conference		
Set up meds and IVs	Talk with family members/significant others	
Order necessary meds/supplies		
Administer meds/IVs on time		
Note med/IV schedule on worksheet		
Give treatments		
Maintain patient records		
Give off-duty report		

FIGURE 7-4. Example of a "to do" list for a staff nurse team leader.

agers with a narrow span of control oversee the work of a few people, such as a three-bed dialysis unit, whereas managers with a wide span of control have more people reporting to them (e.g., supervisors, department or unit managers, case managers, and functional or team leaders) (Figure 7-5). With a larger span of control, fewer managers are necessary; a larger span of control also results in a greater hierarchy. A narrow span of control has greater decentralization.[2]

Unlicensed assistive personnel

The pace of healthcare delivery settings has greatly accelerated. Nurse managers are faced with problems of high patient acuity, shortened hospital stays, and cost containment. Registered nurses (RNs) are also being asked to supervise more unlicensed nursing personnel, also called nursing assistants, nurse extendors, patient care technicians, and unit attendants.[3,4] The restructuring of the healthcare delivery system has

Narrow span of control

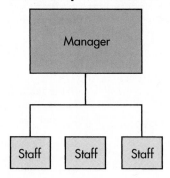

Wide span of control

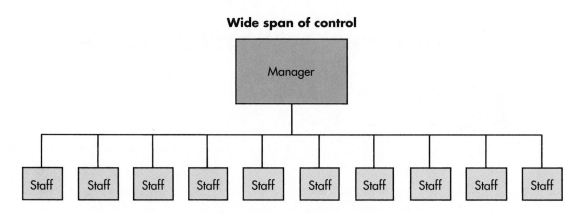

FIGURE 7-5. Spans of control.

changed the role of nursing and has increased the need for professional nurses to manage assistive personnel and to understand their legal responsibilities when delegating nursing care (see Chapter 12).

The new generation of nurses has been taught the concept of primary nursing and total patient care in which the nurse functions independently; past generations of nurses are more familiar with functional or team nursing. With the readmission of assistive nursing personnel, RNs must now practice as a manager of self and a manager of others who are unlicensed and dependent on the RN for supervision and delegation of activities. Such a situation may cause the nurse to feel threatened and insecure.

The American Nurses Association defines delegation as "the transfer of responsibility for the performance of an activity from one person to another while retaining accountability for the outcome." The RN must delegate duties appropriately and adequately supervise them. The RN cannot assign responsibility for total nursing care to an unlicensed person, but he or she can assign certain tasks *that fit an individual's job description, knowledge base, and demonstrated skills.*

The nursing process of assessment, diagnosis, care planning, and evaluation can provide a framework for the RN in supervising unlicensed nursing personnel. For example, a nursing assistant may be assigned to measure vital signs, collect intake and output, gather specimens, administer hygienic care, and assist with activities of daily living; however, the RN assesses these activities and is responsible for patient outcome.

Until the RN is familiar with the assistant's ability to record and follow directions, he or she may want to ask the assistant to repeat the instructions or review the assistant's worksheet for completeness and accuracy. A newly graduated nurse or an experienced nurse who is new to the situation can explain to the assistant that he or she is new at being a leader and therefore wants to be sure that he or she gave the correct instructions.

RNs who practice in public health, community, or home care settings must often give directions in written form or by telephone when delegating patient care duties to assistive personnel. The nurse who does this must have a reasonable knowledge of the assistant's ability to receive the message.

It is important for hospitals and other healthcare agencies to assess the ancillary workers and to orient, train, and supervise them on the job. The RN who is overseeing assistive personnel must very carefully document care given by the assistant to ensure that the assistant has followed instructions satisfactorily.

Factors influencing number of workers and span of control

Ideally the right span of control strikes an efficient balance between too little and too much supervision.

Selecting the span of management and an appropriate number of people for the nurse to lead is important to an efficient operation because sometimes a wider or narrower span can make it more difficult for the nurse manager to integrate the group's activities as a whole or with other personnel. The factors that most affect the numbers of workers and choice of span of control are:

1. The standards for care adopted by the healthcare agency.
2. The number and similarity of clients/patients and functions supervised, or the degree to which the care and support services are alike or different (e.g., long-term care versus immediate postsurgical care).
3. The number and mix of nursing personnel and the degree of supervision that group members require (e.g., nursing assistants, temporary staff, new graduates, or experienced nurses). Downsizing the number of full-time

employees has become the current trend; thus many healthcare agencies use temporary or part-time workers. The part-time employee is acclimated to the agency and usually fits into the schedules and activities with ease. However, the temporary worker may create problems with assignments and direction as a result of unfamiliarity with agency policies.

4. The complexity of supervised functions and the nature of the patients/clients and functions for which the nurse manager is responsible (e.g., multiple diagnoses, technical equipment).
5. The planning required of the nurse manager and the degree to which he or she must program and review the activities of the subunit (e.g., daily, weekly, or monthly schedules; audits of care; evaluation of personnel; budget).
6. The coordination required of the nurse manager or the degree to which he or she must try to integrate functions or tasks within the subunit or between the subunit and other parts of the organization (e.g., dietary, pharmacy, x-ray, occupational therapy, physical therapy, clinics, home healthcare, or skilled facilities).
7. The amount of help that the nurse manager receives from the organization or from assistants and other support personnel (e.g., unit manager, clerk, auxiliary services).

Attempting to assign an exact number and mix of workers for a given level of nursing care ignores the need for adjustments that accommodate specific situations.

Criteria for assurance of quality care

A more dependable procedure for determining staff size and span of control is to consider the criteria used to ensure the provision of quality care to a specific group of patients/clients. Accrediting agencies set the standards and behavioral objectives for care. Whatever the circumstances, enough staff must be employed so that (1) the needs of the patients/clients are met, (2) all time periods are covered adequately, (3) patient care does not suffer seriously if a staff member is absent, and (4) enough latitude is allowed for the growth and development of the nursing staff.

In many cases the location and purpose of care determine staffing size and span of control.

For example, a 6-bed intensive care unit, a 10-bed recovery room, a 15-bed pediatric area, a clinic, a skilled facility, and a community health agency each have specific needs. However, in some general care areas of a hospital the span of management is usually less definitive. For example, a 45-bed medical unit can have a number of possible spans of control. The unit can be treated as one large entity or divided into two, three, or more subunits. One or any combination of care delivery systems can be applied, such as case management or total care, functional, team, or primary nursing. Working with smaller subunits and bringing the directional process as near the point of action as possible usually results in the best nursing care.

Physical Support System

Work organization and direction giving are affected by the space, equipment, and physical environment available for the support of nursing care. Some facilities are barely adequate, whereas others have every possible convenience and innovation. Resources range from cramped quarters with simple necessities—such as beds, other furniture, linens, and wheelchairs—to large, airy, and attractive surroundings filled with modern equipment and automated devices that lift, turn, breathe, move, and monitor almost every bodily function. The installation of complex computerized informational systems is on the increase and supplies almost limitless amounts of information. With the addition of each piece of equipment comes responsibility for knowing how to operate it or how to apply the information supplied.

Unpleasant working conditions can result from factors such as malfunctioning equipment, excessive cold or heat, noise, darkness, poor sanitation, and odors. The more factors present, the less pleasant most workers find the job; this may reduce the probability of workers performing to their potential or even remaining on the staff.

The challenges in direction for a nurse manager of a subunit in a small health facility are different from those faced by a nurse manager in a university center in a large city. Regardless of the setting, the nurse is to perform within the prevailing circumstances while working toward the desired adaptations or changes.

Significance of the Delegation Process

Managers can benefit greatly from adopting the habit of delegating. By passing along well-defined tasks and responsibilities to staff members, managers can devote more of their time to other important activities such as planning and evaluating. **Delegation** is also a helpful tool for management training and development. Staff members who desire greater challenges generally become more committed and satisfied when they are given opportunities to tackle significant tasks or challenges. A lack of delegation can stifle staff initiative.

Barriers to delegation

There are several reasons why managers generally do not delegate as much as they should:
1. The belief that "I can do it better myself"
2. Lack of confidence and trust in workers
3. Low self-confidence; insecurity
4. Time involved in explaining the task
5. Vague job definition
6. Fear of competition
7. Reluctance to take the risks involved in depending on others
8. Lack of controls that provide an early warning of problems with delegated duties
9. Fear of loss of power

Overcoming barriers to delegation

As stated in Chapter 3, the human relations approach to management emphasizes that the behavior of people is the key to productivity. Success depends on motivated and skilled employees who are committed to organizational objectives. Individuals are more committed to activities in which they have a choice. Some employees perform better when given the opportunity to set their own goals, whereas other individuals perform best when they are assigned goals by their leader.[2] Extensive research has determined the relationship between achievement need and job performance. Individuals with a high need to achieve prefer job situations with personal responsibility, feedback, and an intermediate degree of risk.[2] Nurse managers can be more effective in delegation by recognizing what prevents them from delegating as they should and what motivates workers to respond favorably to challenging work.

COMPONENTS OF DIRECTION GIVING

Many variables help determine who gives care to whom. No matter what system of care is in progress, the person giving directions must consider factors such as *who* is best suited for the job, *what* tasks are to be performed, *where* the job is to be done, *when* and *how* the job is to be accomplished, and *why* the task is necessary (Figure 7-6).

Functional, team, primary, and modular nursing and nurse case management are the systems most commonly used when delegating tasks; however, the principles of effective assignment making and direction giving can be applied to all nursing care delivery situations.

Functional Nursing

In functional nursing the nurse manager assigns the work for all nursing personnel in the depart-

ment or subunit. Work organization and personnel assignment are simplified with a specialty or task-oriented approach. Personnel are programmed into specific roles (e.g., medication or treatment nurse) or are assigned to blocks of rooms for production efficiency. The nurse manager first assigns the RNs, licensed practical nurses (LPNs), or licensed vocational nurses (LVNs) to the tasks that require licensure such as providing medication and some treatments. The RN or LPN/LVN may be assigned desk work or to provide major care to critical patients.

The next step is to assign hygienic care. The patient/client load is divided among the remaining staff. For example, if there are 45 patients/clients in a nursing department and seven staff members to provide hygienic care, three workers are assigned six patients/clients, and three workers are assigned seven patients/clients. Usually the division of labor is not exact, and the nurse manager must decide which worker(s) should be assigned more. The nursing staff is assigned to rooms primarily by territory; each assignment covers as little space as possible to avoid a waste of excessive energy and time. Other general areas of responsibility and times

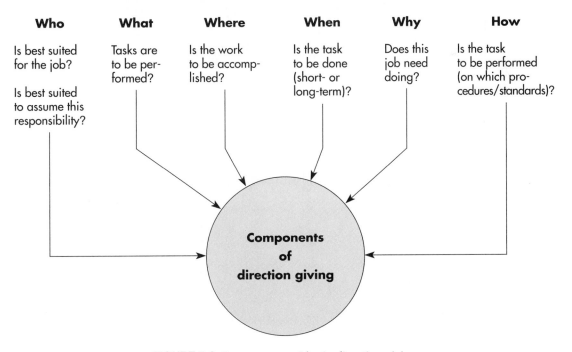

FIGURE 7-6. Factors to consider in direction giving.

for coffee and lunch breaks are posted at the top of the assignment sheet, and specific room assignments are given below. Extra assignments and break times may be posted on a separate sheet. Assignments should be posted in a place that is easily accessible to the staff.

Figure 7-7 shows a fairly rigid plan for assignment making. Note that this task-centered plan considers coverage from the vantage of roles (RNs, LPNs, nursing assistants) and geographic location. It attempts to divide the categories of workers as equally as possible and to provide equal coverage during break times. RN X's activities are confined to administration of medications for 46 patients/clients. The nurse manager has assigned RN Y to the administration of treatments and care of two patients because administering treatment does not require the nurse's full attention. Dividing the number of remaining patients/clients (44) by the number of remaining

nursing personnel to give hygienic care (7), the nurse-patient ratio is 1:6, and one nurse has seven patients. Because circumstances in health-care delivery are not fixed, there will be some deviation from the formula, as with the sample provided in Figure 7-7. The nurse-patient ratio* is as follows:

RN	X	None	NA 1	1:8
RN	Y	1:2	NA2	1:6
LPN	A	1:6	NA3	1:6
LPN	B	1:4	NA4	1:6
			NA5	1:8

The nurse manager begins making assignments with the formula in mind, but he or she needs to use judgment. He or she rationalizes

*Formula: divide number of patients by number of nursing staff.

Nurse	Assignment	Break		Lunch
RN X	Medication nurse	RN X	9:40-10	12-12:30
RN Y	Treatments and rooms 1 and 2	RN Y	10-10:20	12:30-1
		LPN A	9:40-10	11:30-12
Nursing assistant 2	Treatment room	LPN B	10:10-10:30	12-12:30
Nursing assistant 3	Kitchen	NA 1	9:30-9:50	11:30-12
Nursing assistant 4	2 PM TPRs/BPs	NA 2	9:50-10:10	12-12:30
		NA 3	9:30-9:50	11:30-12
		NA 4	9:30-9:50	12-12:30
		NA 5	9:50-10:10	11:30-12

Nurse	Rm. no.	No. pts./rm.	Nurse	Rm. no.	No. pts./rm.
RN Y	1	1	RN Y	2	1
LPN A	3	1	LPN B	4	1
LPN A	5	1	LPN B	6	1
LPN A	7	2	LPN B	8	2
NA 1	9	4	NA 5	10	4
LPN A	11	2	NA 5	12	4
NA 1	13	2	NA 4	14	2
NA 1	15	2	NA 4	16	2
NA 2	17	2	NA 4	18	2
NA 2	19	2	NA 3	20	2
NA 2	21	2	NA 3	22	2
NA 3	23	2			

FIGURE 7-7. Sample assignment made by a nurse manager using functional nursing.

that patients/clients in private rooms generally have critical needs or special problems that require special competencies or more time than normal. Conversely, patients/clients in rooms that accommodate more than one patient/client more often need intermediate care. This factor coupled with easier accessibility to patients/clients and supplies, enables the care provider to complete the assignment more quickly. LPN A and nursing assistant (NA) 1 have their assignments distributed over a wider territory than do other staff members. The nurse manager wants the LPN to care for the more critical patients/clients in rooms 3 and 5. If the assignment ended with room 7, the LPN would have only four patients/clients; if room 9 were added, the load would increase to eight. Not wishing to place two nurses in a four-bed unit and create space problems and confusion regarding who is assigned to whom, the nurse manager chose to extend the parameter of the assignment for LPN A and NA 1. The staff members with lighter patient/client loads are given the support assignments of keeping the kitchen and treatment room in order and of taking afternoon vital signs.

It is possible in the functional system to give attention to the individual needs of the patients/clients and workers, but the task is more difficult than in a more personalized system. The nurse manager has less opportunity and time to become aware of the many ramifications that are significant to a complex nursing situation.

Team Nursing

In team nursing the nurse manager gives each team leader responsibility for that team instead of assigning patients/clients to personnel. Members receive directions from the team leader and are accountable to that leader for their implementation. The major responsibility of a team leader is to provide quality care to a group of patients/clients, primarily through the work of others. This role requires translating the needs of a nursing team into goals and objectives that are realistic, clearly defined, and reflective of nursing and agency purposes. As Chapter 6 states, the nurse manager focuses on two major goals when determining needs: (1) the provision of optimal nursing care for all patients/clients through assessment, problem identification, formulation of plans for nursing action, implementation, and planning for evaluation of care, and (2) the provision of nursing care through an effective management process. The following behavioral objectives can help the team leader provide coordination and efficiency of service:

1. *Determine the number and characteristics of patients/clients assigned to the nursing team.* This is accomplished by reviewing the orders and nursing care plans; consulting with individual patients/clients, significant others, and physicians; reviewing clients' records; and listening to reports from nursing team members as they leave at the end of their shift. At first this procedure can seem overwhelming to a novice leader. The amount of available data can blur into meaningless content until the nurse learns to extract the most relevant information. An experienced nurse soon learns to accomplish this task quickly and well. It is helpful to use a worksheet for sorting information, and color-coding priority activities helps the nurse to see them at a glance when making assignments. Figure 7-8 offers a portion of one such worksheet that may be used by a nurse team leader.

2. *Assess priority of care for all patients/clients,* beginning with those who need the greatest amount of care. Establishing needs in order of priority serves as an indicator for action. The leader uses three criteria when considering the importance of each need to the patient/client and to the nursing work group: (1) preservation of life, dignity, and integrity; (2) avoidance of destructive changes; and (3) continuance of normal growth and development.[5] The team leader can use distinguishing marks such as an "X" or "*" beside the patient's/client's name to indicate immediate or special attention. The team leader quickly scans the worksheet and notes any special tests and procedures and their specific times, reverse isolation or isolation techniques, or intravenous fluids; he or she also plans the routing of patients/clients to other departments for special services, blood transfusions, and other activities. The team leader assesses the number of total care patients, those who require intermediate help, and those who are fairly independent. Attention is given to psychologic, sociologic, and spiritual needs,

Staff member to be assigned	Room no.	Name/ physician	Age	Diagnosis	Diet	Activity	TPR BP	I and O	IVs	Treatments and special meds	Needs and problems
	60	June Kizon Dr Jones	22	Tubal occlusion	Reg	Amb.				Air studies 2pm	Worried
	62	Laura Coff Dr. Fox	48	Sq. cell Ca cx Ra insert	30° Bed Rest		✓	✓ Foley		Personal care p.r.n. Irrig. Foley 10	Force Fl No visitors Psych support
	64	Mrs Heather Dr. Ball	66	Cataract Ⓛ eye	Reg	Bedrest	✓			Eye shield Ⓡ eye	Skin fragile 20% vision Ⓡ eye
	66	Ray Small Dr Tenis	41	Terminal Ca lung	As tol	Bedrest Rails ft. bed	✓	✓		Maintain airway Cough suction db Turn q 2 h	No code Feed Encourage family
	68a	Mrs Fletcher Dr Able	71	Buerger's disease	Salt free 1,000 cal.	Bedrest	✓	✓		Pedal pulse 10-2 Soak feet + dress 10 Buerger exercises 10-2	✓ for pain/med Depressed Obese Needs help to turn
	68b	Laura Vargos Dr. Kast	55	Aortic bypass graft 1-4	Lo fat	Bedrest			5% D.W. ≠ KCl 100 ml q h	Encour. d.b. On valium	
	70a	Elaine Metz Dr. Barton	68	Ca colon	Lo fiber Kosher	amb. help	✓				Colostomy tomorrow Preop teaching ✓ re rabbi
	70b	Lola Smith Dr. Salt	71	Gastric ulcer	Soft force fl.	amb.					Hard of hearing

FIGURE 7-8. Sample of a partially complete worksheet used by a nurse team leader to record pertinent information about patients before making assignments and for guidance of team activities. Additional abbreviations may be used to conserve space.

which may be of highest priority with some patients/clients.

3. *Review available staff and consider their roles, competencies, and preferences.*[6] Delegating tasks is simplified if the nursing staff is composed of all licensed personnel. However, many healthcare agencies use the services of technical or semiskilled workers such as nursing assistants and temporary workers. Ideally team leaders participate in the selection of team members. With time and attention, the team leader becomes well acquainted with the nursing staff. Preparation and experience are weighed against the responsibilities of the assignment. Individual preferences are considered as much as possible. The team leader keeps in mind the need for licensure for certain activities such as distributing medication and providing some treatments.

4. *Assign patients/clients who require the most skilled attention to the most qualified staff member(s).*[6] A major goal in assignment making is to divide the total load into a number of activities that can be performed logically and comfortably by one person. People cannot be assigned tasks for which they are not suited, and they should not carry a workload that is either too heavy or too light. A too-heavy workload can mean that the job will not be completed well or on time, whereas a workload that is too light can lead to idleness and inefficiency. The philosophy of team nursing subscribes to "team" effort, in which each person helps the others achieve common goals. Although it is expected that underassigned personnel will help the overassigned member(s), problems may be created that could be avoided with careful preplanning.

The team leader may need to assume responsibility for administering medications and monitoring intravenous fluids. Assigning the leader to these activities provides him or her with more time to move among the patients/clients and nursing staff. Patients/clients who need treatments that require licensed personnel may be assigned to a licensed member for care, or the team leader can assign the treatment to a licensed person but the hygienic care to another member if the team leader believes that the licensed member is needed more elsewhere. The leader at-

tempts to match the greatest need with the person best prepared to meet that need; this team member is also assigned to nearby patients/clients in consideration of the geographic and physical setting. This system calls for some compromises in matching abilities of staff members to the needs of patients/clients. If the criteria for assignment making were followed exactly, staff assignments might consist of one patient/client at the far end of a hall, two in the middle, and three on a side, with two or more staff members providing care in one room. Fragmented assignments are at odds with criteria for provision of quality care and run the risk of patient/client hostility because of inadequate attention. In turn, the team member becomes fatigued because of confusion and unnecessary activity.

Some delegators advocate that the team leader administer care to the most acutely ill patient/client on the team or that the leader attend to the one who requires the most complex nursing care. The rationale is that the team leader is the most qualified for the task and that the patient would derive the greatest benefit from the leader's services. The leader also serves as a role model to the team members. However, when team functioning is viewed realistically, it becomes apparent that it is impossible for the team leader to fulfill other team commitments if he or she has been assigned to an area that requires undivided attention. Therefore, it is better to assign the patient/client with high priority needs to another qualified member of the team. The team leader can assist with the patient's/client's care at the times when special expertise is required. The nurse leader is available to the patient/client needing special care and to all of the other patients/clients assigned to the team.

5. *Double-assign a patient/client or groups of patients/clients if assistance with care is anticipated.* Sometimes providing care to a patient/client requires more than one person (e.g., lifting, turning, treatments). If possible, a team member who is working in an adjoining room or adjacent area is given a double assignment so that he or she is easily accessible and can provide the necessary help with a minimal loss of time and energy.

6. *Note coverage for breaks.* Coffee breaks, meals, and conferences are scheduled to ensure continued supervision and care by qualified personnel. There must be continuous coverage by a registered nurse, and each team should have equal staff coverage as much as possible. Planning with other team leaders and perhaps with the nurse manager is necessary to see that adequate personnel are continuously available to all teams. Such arrangements take time, especially in a complex setting, but staff time is conserved, team functioning is smoother, and patients/clients receive the necessary constant supervision.

Many health facilities also expect nursing personnel to perform supportive services such as keeping the unit in order (cleaning up kitchen and utility room, straightening linen closets, transporting patients, and preparing vacated rooms for new admissions). The requirements for this kind of ancillary service usually depend on the size of the hospital and the availability and distribution of personnel. The nurses' time need *not* be spent in these activities. Large hospitals and other health facilities usually maintain a separate staff for housekeeping duties and another for distribution of supplies. Many hospitals have auxiliary groups who perform services such as caring for flowers, transporting patients, and running errands.

Figure 7-9 gives an example of a nursing personnel assignment using the team system. In this example the major purposes of assignment making have been completed. At the top of the sheet are the names and roles of each staff member; break times are also listed. Each team has continuous coverage, and alternate teams have RN coverage for coffee, lunch, and conference times. Supportive services are assigned, and teams share these duties. These supportive duties are rotated between teams every week. Because the nurse manager has considered established criteria, the patients are not divided equally among the nursing staff. The RN is responsible for medications and care of patient Kerzan in room 60. The patient is near the nurses' station, needs minimal nursing care, and needs teaching and emotional support. The LPN is responsible for treatments and the care of the most critical patients; assistance is provided for care of patients Snell and Fletcher. NA2 has a greater number of patients, but the total workload is considered equitable.

All workers are kept in as small a geographic area as possible. The team leader circulates during the shift to make observations and adjustments as necessary.

Primary Nursing

In primary nursing it is the nurse manager's responsibility to assign patients to nursing staff. To be effective in this function, he or she needs to consider the following principles:

1. Each RN or LPN/LVN is delegated responsibility and accountability for planning, giving, and communicating all phases of care for one or more patients/clients from the time of admission through discharge.[6] Patients/clients must be assigned a primary nurse at admission or within the first 24 hours. If it is not possible to make a primary nursing assignment at admission, a total care assignment is made in which one nurse is assigned to provide all the nursing care needed during one shift. Total care assignments are continued until a primary nurse is selected. The nurse's responsibilities for one shift include assessment of nursing needs, medications, treatments, hygiene and comfort measures, teaching, providing support, and communicating through charting, reporting, and care planning.

2. There should be an optimum match of patient/client need with staff preference and competency. Some nursing units keep a master board near the nursing station, and the names and diagnoses of new patients/clients are recorded as they are admitted. Staff members are invited to state their preferences by writing their names beside those of the new patients/clients, and the nurse manager complies with the requests as much as possible. The nurse manager can also assign staff to a group of adjacent rooms. As patients/clients are admitted to these rooms, the nurses choose their own patients/clients. This technique allows for decentralization of decisions, autonomy of the primary nurse, and improved efficiency.

3. Geography of the unit must be considered. For conservation of energy and cost-effectiveness, a nurse's patient/client assignments should be consolidated in one general area. Decentralization of nursing services initially gave nurses the option to choose patients/

Team A / **Team B**

Date: _____
Charge nurse: _____

Team A

	AM break	Lunch	Conferences	
RNT ldr: Marge Singer	9:45-10:05	12-12:30	7:30-7:50	Special assignment
LPN: Ruth Telfer	9:30-9:50	11:30-12	2:00-2:30	
NA 1: Jean Rass	9:30-9:50	11:30-12	Kitchen NA 1	
NA 2: Tam Spivey	9:50-10:10	12-12:30	Rx room	

Meds ____ Rxs ____ Other ____

Assignment	Room no.	Patient	Diagnosis
	61		
	63		
	65		
	67		
	69a		
	69b		
	71a		
	71b		
	73a		
	73b		
	75a		
	75b		
	77a		
	77b		
	79a		
	79b		
	79c		
	79d		

Team B

	AM break	Lunch	Conferences	
RNT ldr: Cleo Hastings	10:05-10:25	12:30-1:00	7:50-8:10	2:30-3:00 Special assignment
LPN: Bea Kindall	9:30-9:50	12-12:30		
NA 1: Vici Wilson	9:50-10:10	11:30-12	Kitchen	
NA 2: Linda Grace	10-10:20	12-12:30	Rx room NA 2	

Meds ____ Rxs ____ Other ____

Assignment	Room no.	Patient	Diagnosis
RN	60	June Kerzan	Tube Occu.
LPN	62	Laura Cobb	Ca Cx
LPN	64	Mrs. Heather	Cat. (L)eye
LPN/NA 1	66	Roy Snell	Ca Lung
LPN/NA 1	68a	Mr. Fletcher	Buerger's
LPN	68b	Lem Vargas	Aortic ByPass Graft
NA 1	70a	Elaine Metz	Ca Colon
NA 1	70b	Lela Smith	Pneumonia
NA 1	72a	Reva Farrell	Mastectomy (R)
NA 1	72b	Barb Brink	Cholecystomy
NA 2	74a	Terry Erbb	Prostatectomy
NA 2	74b	John Baker	CHD
NA 2	76a	Angela Castro	Bunionectomy/Diabetes
NA 2	76b	Terry Meltzer	Hysterectomy
NA 2	78a	Bob Perry	Fx (L) Leg
NA 2	78b	Sam Frieson	x-rays BL Studies
NA 2	78c	David Cooper	Laminectomy
NA 2	78d	Larry Berg	Duodenal ulcer

FIGURE 7-9. Sample assignment sheet for a two-team nursing unit that indicates patient assignment for team B and cooperative assignments for breaks and other activities.

clients anywhere in the unit. Consequently a primary nurse could have patients/clients from one end of the unit to the other, which resulted in much travel time and a loss in efficiency.

4. Each nurse should have a caseload that is equitable to those of other nurses, not necessarily in terms of numbers of patients/clients but in time and energy required.

5. The assignment remains throughout the patient's/client's stay on the unit unless (a) his or her condition changes beyond the capability of the primary nurse, (b) there are unresolvable patient-nurse conflicts, (c) the nurse or patient/client requests a change (if the nurse requests the change, the reasons must be reviewed carefully before a decision is made), (d) the nurse rotates to a block of night shifts or goes on vacation or leave, or (e) the patient/client is transferred to a room that is geographically inconvenient for the primary nurse.

6. Nurses should care for a variety of patient/client problems to ensure professional growth.

7. The nurse should be identified and visible to the patient/client, family, physicians, and other healthcare providers. This can be accomplished by simply introducing the patient/client to the nurse and by posting the primary nurse-patient assignments in a prominent place so that everyone can easily and quickly see which nurse is responsible for a particular patient/client.

8. The same associate nurses should be on alternate shifts and on the primary nurse's days off as much as possible, since it is their task to carry out the plan of care initiated by the primary nurse and to suggest or make changes as necessary. The greater the continuity of care, the better the quality of care.

Modular Nursing

Modular nursing is a modification of team and primary nursing and is used most often when there are not enough RNs to cover the scope of care.[7]

1. In each module, patients who would most benefit from 24-hour primary nursing care are identified. Depending on the number of primary nurses available, these patients are assigned to such care in order of priority.

2. The remaining patients are assigned in clusters of RNs/nursing assistants or LPNs/LVNs/nursing assistants in which the RN or LPN/LVN delivers direct care to the patients with the help of ancillary personnel.

Case Management

Weil[8, p.127] describes delegation in case management as a "set of logical steps and a process of interaction with service networks, which assures that a patient receives needed services in a supportive, efficient, and cost effective manner."

One of the three components of the case management model is the development of monitoring systems that help the case manager evaluate patient progress against preestablished expectations. This monitoring system is commonly referred to as a "critical pathway" or case management plan.[9] One proven system is used at Hillcrest Medical Center in Tulsa, Oklahoma.[11] This facility aims to achieve a purposeful and controlled connection between the quality and cost of care by having the case manager delegate and monitor all care that the client receives. Delegation of responsibilities extends beyond the traditional nursing unit (in which client needs are met only during hospitalization) by focusing on the patient's entire episode of illness from preadmission to postdischarge care. The hospital is likely to benefit the most from case managing patients who fit into Diagnosis Related Groups (DRGs) or who have specific diseases or problems because this constant surveillance prevents duplication of services and keeps the patient's stay at a minimum. Examples of DRGs are Diseases of the Circulatory System and Coronary Artery Bypass Graft with Catheterization. Patients who fit into these categories are covered by Medicare with specific governmental restrictions. A predetermined number of days and a fixed rate of reimbursement is allotted for each DRG. If a patient exceeds the allotted number of days or accrues bills beyond the prescribed limit and does not have additional insurance to cover the costs, the hospital is responsible for the excess amount. Under the guidelines of Prospective Payment Systems, reimbursement for readmissions may not be provided unless a patient remains out of the hospital for a specified period of time. Therefore healthcare agencies are pressed to achieve a purposeful and controlled connection between quality of care and cost.

Case managers must keep abreast of all current agency guidelines that have a significant impact on the patients they manage.[10]

The case manager is assigned or selects patients and is expected to exercise full professional accountability for clinical practice. The first step in the delegation process is to meet with the patient and family before or at least on the day of admission, either in person or by telephone. After the case manager has assessed the patient and identified needs, he or she collaborates with individuals (e.g., primary care nurse) or groups (e.g., respiratory therapist, physician) to prepare a case management plan. To facilitate the process, case management plans should be preprepared for the targeted DRGs on the basis of historical clinical and financial data; these preprepared plans can be adapted to the needs of the individual patient (Figure 7-10). The plan includes the anticipated length of stay (LOS); all tests, procedures, and medications; and target dates for accomplishment, completion, and date of dismissal. The case manager can note the line of progress and follow up on any deviations from the norm. For example, if a patient's laboratory or pharmacy charges exceed the hospital average, the case manager can evaluate the number and types of tests and medications to determine if there is test duplication or if generic drugs can be substituted for brand sources. The case manager also monitors the LOS using historical care data for the patient's DRG. He or she also monitors patient care and satisfaction through the caregiver and the patient and family.

EXAMPLE: Thelma, nurse case manager, meets Mr. and Mrs. Amber at preadmission screening. Mrs. Amber is to have a knee replacement. Thelma explains the nurse case management concept and tells them what Mrs. Amber can expect while she is in the hospital. She explains that for a knee replacement, Mrs. Amber can anticipate approximately a 7-day stay in the hospital and that, although Thelma will not give direct care, she will coordinate and monitor Mrs. Amber's care during and after her hospital stay. At this point Thelma plans for Mrs. Amber's discharge requirements and ensures that home needs are properly met. A home health aide will be needed, so Thelma contacts the Visiting Nurse Association; a bedside commode and walker will be necessary, so she arranges for these commodities to be delivered on the day Mrs. Amber returns home.

On her admission to the hospital, Thelma plans Mrs. Amber's care with the primary nurse who will give the nursing care. Thelma uses a predeveloped care plan for a knee replacement patient, and she fills in target dates for completion of tests, procedures, medications, and discharge. She meets with the respiratory and occupational therapists to plan for hospital and follow-up treatment. Thelma reviews Mrs. Amber's progress daily and confers with any person or group when necessary. Thelma also ensures that the supplies and services used for Mrs. Amber's care are within normal guidelines. If guidelines are exceeded, she records a justification or attempts to correct the situation.

After Mrs. Amber's dismissal, Thelma maintains contact with her and the home health aide by telephone. If a home visit is required, she arranges for the services of a visiting nurse. Because Mr. Amber is unable to manage cleaning and meals, Thelma arranges for homemaker services and Meals on Wheels. When nursing care and other assistance is no longer required, Thelma contacts the Public Health Nursing Department for continued surveillance and follow-up visits in the home.

Developing a critical path plan that is reviewed for efficiency and necessity and is tailored to each patient's needs leads to cost-effectiveness and patient and nurse satisfaction.

RESPONSIBILITIES OF DIRECTION GIVING

The central task of direction giving is to demonstrate that the goals of the health service organization and those of staff members are compatible. Certain managerial responsibilities are common to all healthcare agencies: (1) preserving the regulatory, day-by-day activities that make the system productive, which is by far the major share of a nurse manager's activity (regulatory), (2) correcting any dysfunction in the system after it has occurred, (corrective), (3) preventing problems and difficulties by anticipation (preventive), and (4) promoting ways and means for improvement of personnel and the system (promotive).

Guidelines for Implementation of Responsibility

The regulatory, corrective, preventive, and promotive types of managerial direction are applied by nurse managers according to the individual situation. The following objectives incorporate

Continued on p. 173

Case-Managed Care

Harper-Grace Hospitals
Detroit, Michigan

☐ Harper Hospital Division (48201)   BPH with TURP
☐ Grace Hospital Division (48235)

NURSING CARE PLAN

DISCHARGE PLAN

Discharge to ☐ Home ☐ Nursing Home ☐ Other _____ ☐

Expected Patient Behaviors on Discharge __ Pt. will void clear urine per urethra after Foley catheter is removed. PT. will state

intention to drink 2 liters fluid/day at home. Pt. will state S&S to report to physician e.g. acute pain, hematuria.

Patient Teaching Needs _____

Referrals Made (Date/Name)

Dietary _____   Pastoral Care _____   Social Service _____

Home Care _____   Patient Education _____   Other _____

Nurse Consultant _____   Pharmacy _____

	NURSING DIAGNOSIS/ CLINICAL PROBLEM	Date	Initials	NURSING DIAGNOSIS/ CLINICAL PROBLEM	Date	Initials
NURSING DIAGNOSIS/ CLINICAL PROBLEM	Knowledge deficit: pre & post-op regimen			PC: Hematuria/retained clots		
EXPECTED OUTCOMES	Verbalize pre & post-op regimen for TURP			Has clear straw-color urine 30 cc/hr.		
PLAN/INTERVENTIONS	1. Teach pt/family about TURP surgical experience & document response 2. Give prostate book 3. Show prostate film strip 4. Discuss Foley cath care/fluid intake 5. Ask pt. perceptions of pre/post-op care 6. Answer questions/clarify misperceptions			1. Maintain Foley cath tension for tamponade— release on: _____ 2. Force oral fluids to 2000 cc/day 3. Strict intake & output 4. Run NS bladder irrigation fast enough to keep urine clear 5. Monitor color of urine/clot formation 6. Monitor Hbg & Hct & lytes		

	REVISIONS	Date	Initials	REVISIONS	Date	Initials
EXPECTED OUTCOMES	7. Teach S&S to report to physician			7. Notify physician of bleeding		
PLAN/ INTERVENTIONS						
	RESOLVED	Date	Initials	RESOLVED	Date	Initials

INITIAL	SIGNATURE & PROFESSIONAL DESIGNATION	INITIAL	SIGNATURE & PROFESSIONAL DESIGNATION	INITIAL	SIGNATURE & PROFESSIONAL DESIGNATION	INITIAL	SIGNATURE & PROFESSIONAL DESIGNATION

FIGURE 7-10. Sample of a case-managed standardized care plan. (From Cronin C, Maklebust J: Case managed care: capitalizing on the CNS, *Nurs Manage* 20[3]:44-46, 1989.)

NURSING DIAGNOSIS/ CLINICAL PROBLEM	Date	Initials	NURSING DIAGNOSIS/ CLINICAL PROBLEM	Date	Initials

NURSING DIAGNOSIS/ CLINICAL PROBLEM

PC: Acute pain/bladder spasms

EXPECTED OUTCOMES

Displays no signs/symptoms of acute pain/ bladder spasms

PLAN/INTERVENTIONS

1. Monitor for S&S of bladder spasm
   a. acute pain
   b. need to defecate
   c. leakage around catheter
   d. GU irrigant won't run on wide open
   e. can't manually irrigate bladder
      because of increased pressure

REVISIONS	Date	Initials	REVISIONS	Date	Initials

EXPECTED OUTCOMES

2. Administer B + O suppository q 6 h prn
3. Administer pain med prn
4. Manually extract retained clots

PLAN/INTERVENTIONS

   a. instill 100 cc normal saline
   b. withdraw same
   c. repeat until urine clear or until
      patient verbalizes relief of pain/
      spasm
5. Notify physician if unable to extract clots

RESOLVED	Date	Initials	RESOLVED	Date	Initials

INITIAL	SIGNATURE & PROFESSIONAL DESIGNATION	INITIAL	SIGNATURE & PROFESSIONAL DESIGNATION	INITIAL	SIGNATURE & PROFESSIONAL DESIGNATION	INITIAL	SIGNATURE & PROFESSIONAL DESIGNATION

DISCHARGE SUMMARY Date _____ Signature _____

Summary of unresolved problems and follow-up _____

_____

Patient/family understanding of discharge instruction _____

Diet Instruction Given ☐ No ☐ Yes Type _____ Activity Reviewed ☐ No ☐ Yes

Prescriptions Reviewed ☐ No ☐ Yes Type(s) _____ Type _____

_____ Home Care Arranged ☐ No ☐ Yes

_____ Type _____

_____ Supplies Arranged ☐ No ☐ Yes

_____ Type _____

Follow-Up Appointment ☐ No ☐ Yes Type _____ Type _____

Discharge Via ☐ Walking ☐ Wheelchair ☐ Ambulance ☐ Accompanied By _____

Belongings Sent _____ Discharged To _____

FIGURE 7-10, cont'd.

Continued

Date					
Day of Adm.	**1**	**2**	**3**	**4**	**5**
Discharge planning/ Teaching	Prostate booklet pre-op Prostate film pre-op Foley catheter care --▷ Fluid requirements ---▷ Signs/symptoms to report --▷				Discharge
Functional level/ Activity	Up ad lib	Flat for 6 hours post spinal	Up ---▷		
Nutrition/ Diet	Reg as tolerated NPO at midnight	NPO pre-op Reg as tol. post-op Force fluids ---▷	Regular --▷		
Consults	Medical clearance if indicated				
Noninvasive tests	CXR ECG				
Invasive tests/OR		OR-TURP Spinal anesthesia			
Labs	CBC, Lytes, PT, PTT SMA₁₈, Acid Phos. U/A	CBC & Lytes in PAR	CBC & Lytes		
Treatments	Fleet enema hs	Compression stockings Foley →Tension GU irrigation --▷	DC stockings Release Foley Tension	Foley DD	D.C. Foley
Meds		IV for 24° --------------- B&O suppository prn --▷ Analgesic IM Stool softener	DC IV Analgesia p.o.		

Expected Patient Outcome: Patient will void clear urine per urethra after Foley is removed. Patient will verbalize intention to drink 2000 cc/day at home, and identify signs & symptoms to report to physician.

Critical Pathway for: TRANSURETHRAL RESECTION OF PROSTATE

Case Manager: _____

12/03/87, 12/20/87

FIGURE 7-10, cont'd.

these four components and can serve as guidelines for the lower- or first-level nurse manager when delegating day-to-day activities:[11]

1. Formulate objectives for care that are realistic for the health agency, patient/client, and nursing personnel.
2. Give first priority to the needs of the patients/clients assigned to the nursing staff.
3. Provide for coordination and efficiency among departments that provide support services.
4. Identify all activities for which the nursing staff is responsible.
5. Provide for safe, continuous care.
6. Consider the need for variety in task assignments and for development of personnel.
7. Ensure the leader's availability to staff members for assistance, teaching, counsel, and evaluation.
8. Trust members to follow through with their assignments.

EXAMPLE: Carolyn is a staff nurse who is enrolled in a managerial program at the local university and who aspires to become a nurse manager. The unit manager offers to allow Carolyn to put some of the theory she is learning into practice in the clinical area. She assigns Carolyn the preparation of the time schedule for a 2-week period and the making of clinical assignments for a 1-week period. Carolyn is delighted. However, the unit manager hovers over her and is critical of her every move: "You should do it this way," "That will never work," "Oh, don't assign Mary to that patient—it's not a good match." Initially Carolyn tries harder to please the unit manager, but to no avail. Before the 2 weeks are over, she asks the unit manager to take back the given authority. During evaluation, the unit manager records that Carolyn lacks initiative and gives up before she has ample opportunity to prove herself. One observer said, "Carolyn won't be here long, you can be sure. She'll get her education and be long gone."

9. Interpret protocol for responding to incidental requests.
10. Explain the proper procedure for emergencies.
11. Give clear and concise formal and informal directions.
12. Use a management control process that assesses the quality of care given by nursing personnel and evaluates individual and group performance.

Adhering to these guidelines allows goals to be accomplished with order and precision, within the bounds of safety, and in an environment that promotes individual and group initiative and creativity. A brief discussion of each guideline follows.

Formulating objectives for care that are realistic for the healthcare agency, patient/client, and nursing personnel

This book has emphasized that it is important for the agency, subunits, and nursing personnel to manage by objectives on the basis of mutually acceptable standards. The following guidelines for formulating objectives for care may apply to a nursing group at the lower or first level:

1. Provide a comprehensive and continuous holistic approach to care. (The patient/client is the central focus for assessing, planning, implementing, and evaluating care.)
2. Initiate and keep current a written nursing care plan that includes physical, emotional, psychosocial, and religious needs and problems; the assignment of priorities of care; and the alternatives for meeting needs.
3. Assign staff to patients/clients according to accepted criteria.
4. Ensure safety of the patient/client.
5. Assign staff members according to their legal and professional ability to perform.

Giving first priority to the needs of the patients/clients assigned to the nursing staff

Assignment making considers two general categories: provision of patient/client care and support services. The nurse manager works with a number of patients/clients and therefore needs to determine what should be done and the order of importance. To achieve the primary goal of nursing, the providers of nursing must decide what constitutes quality care. After nursing standards are accepted by the agency, each nursing department and/or subunit determines how to implement these standards. Nursing care plans offer the best assurance of quality care. Assessing needs and problems, deciding how they are to be met, controlling the process, and evaluating the results provide the mechanism for adherence to priority.

Nursing care plans provide the nurse manager with input from everyone who helped form the plans since the patient's/client's admission. The nursing care plan provides a way to centralize information and offers a definite advantage to the nurse manager whose time for direction giving is often limited. Nursing care plans constitute the basis for work assignments. The nurse can check through the nursing care plans quickly for needs and priorities that are pertinent to direction giving. The nurse delegator then ranks them in order of priority, from life-threatening problems to those of lesser importance and from short-term, immediate needs to long-term needs. Priority setting through assessment of problems and formulation of nursing care plans helps the nurse manager to organize and direct care with a rational and realistic approach.

Providing for coordination and efficiency among departments that provide support services

An enterprise is said to exist in a complex environment if the number of factors it deals with is large. Most healthcare facilities are complex because there is great dependence on and interdependence between forces that meet the many needs of the consumer. Essential support services include departments such as personnel, admitting, records, dietary, pharmacy, x-ray, laboratory, laundry, housekeeping, maintenance, and business or budget control. Unlike the common market, where competition is high, healthcare agencies have only one source for each major service; therefore departments and subunits depend on each other.

There are two major supply systems used in healthcare agencies; those that meet requests on a one-to-one basis (e.g., dietary, pharmacy, treatment) and those that respond to requests according to estimations of need (e.g., linens, stock supplies of drugs, equipment for treatments, paper products).[12] When the work is divided or decentralized into departments and subunits, it becomes important to coordinate these services. For example, the pharmacy has no way of knowing when the daily medications are needed in each area unless the activities of the various departments and subunits are coordinated. Unless alerted, the laboratory is not aware of the need to draw blood samples and provide results at specific times throughout the hospital.

Tools and methods are devised by each support service to facilitate its work. Nurses deal with a myriad of forms and computerized information and messages. For example, a primary nurse contacts the pharmacist about a specific drug needed for a patient, whereas a problem of repeated delay in service is given to the nurse manager for resolution.

The overall communication structure is constructed in organizational charts from top levels of administration to the lower or first level. Managers at all levels must work within the system. Because of the high degree of dependence on others for services in large organizations, the nurse needs to develop the habit of frequently referring to agency policy and to acquire and use skills of coordination and negotiation. The nurse manager is responsible for the overall management of the individual nursing department and therefore communicates with departments that provide service regarding major matters of control. Lower- or first-level managers oversee the activities of their assignment and inform the nurse manager about significant matters according to policy.

Clerical assistance lessens the demands on the nurse to accommodate each support service. Computers also greatly reduce the workload. Sufficient physical and technical help in coordinating services allows the nurse manager to spend time and energy meeting the goals of quality care.

Identifying all activities for which the nursing staff is responsible

Delegation is the foundation of organization. The leader/manager must know the patients/clients assigned for care and the workers available to provide that care, grasp the nursing situation as a whole, determine what needs to be done, and subdivide the whole into manageable parts. The leader assigns tasks in such a way that cooperation is reciprocal, high standards of performance and conduct are possible, and sound decisions are made.

Effective direction is best carried out by one person for one group. When nursing service is provided by a group of personnel with varied preparations and backgrounds, such as a nursing team or functional group, the leader is the centralizing force. This leader receives directions from the nurse manager regarding patient/client load, staff appropriation, group responsibilities, and special assignments; the leader routes these directions to the team or group members for implementation. It is important that the team leader maintain control of activities of the assigned group. Nurse leaders are the closest professional link between patients/clients and caregivers and should be able to determine the ideal patient-staff relationships. Group members should receive instructions from their leader and be accountable to that leader.

Good direction is not dictatorship. Caregivers expect to be given needed information on quantity, quality, and time limits of work. Nurses expect the information to include what is to be done, who is to do it, when and where the activity will occur, and, when necessary, how and why. Nurses expect their assignments to be within the limits of their skills and abilities, and they expect the materials necessary to complete the task to be provided.

To be an effective delegator, the nurse leader must have authority to act. Authority is having the power to achieve an end; sanction is given to the nurse leader by a higher authority in the organization. With this power the nurse has the right and obligation to define limits within which others must function to achieve goals. The nurse leader accepts responsibility and accountability for individual performance and for the performance of those who are led.[13]

Providing for safe, continuous care

Each healthcare facility must meet the minimal safety regulations established by law and those adopted by the agency to meet its unique needs. As do all staff members, the nurse leader learns these regulations during orientation, and he or she assumes responsibility for learning new changes. The leader is responsible for regularly assessing each member's understanding of safety regulations for a fire, earthquake, tornado, or other disaster. Unused knowledge and skills are quickly forgotten, so the nurse manager must reinforce instructions in handling equipment, using proper procedures, and working with dangerous drugs.

Considering need for variety in assignments and for development of personnel

Primary consideration is given to assigning staff members to patients/clients so that the most effective use is made of each member's knowledge and abilities. The nurse leader is also concerned with expanding the knowledge and improving the skills of each member. Variation in assignments provides nurses the opportunity to expand their capabilities, enrich their day-to-day work experience, increase their self-esteem, and enhance their career potential. Employees who perform multiple assignments demonstrate increased motivation and productivity and an increased interest in the organization. The leader may also arrange for each member to spend some time in advanced preparation through on-the-job instruction, inservice classes, or workshops. Assignments that are limited to a narrow span of care inhibit growth of staff members and are costly to the institution because the employee's potential is not being used.

Ensure the leader's availability to staff members for assistance, teaching, counsel, and evaluation

Overseeing nursing activities requires the nurse to be present in the area of action. For a nurse leader, being available means being accessible and of some value to others. The leader must be ready and willing to provide or delegate assistance whenever necessary to teach a procedure, relay knowledge, supervise a nursing function about which a member feels insecure, offer advice with patient/client or staff problems, and evaluate a member's performance. Therefore the leader's personal assignment should be restricted to activities that will allow him or her to be in the mainstream of activity, such as administering medications or giving treatments.

Trusting members to follow through with their assignments

It is possible for a nurse manager to feel secure that directions will be carried out to the best of the members' abilities. However, success in directing others depends greatly on the attitude of the nurse manager because his or her attitude will dictate the approach taken. As McGregor's

Theories X and Y[14] suggest, one manager may be convinced that most human beings have an inherent dislike of work and will seek to avoid it. Another may believe that the nursing staff enjoy their work and want to work as a part of their basic nature. As a result, one manager uses coercion to get work done, whereas the other relies on the staff's own initiative.

The attitudes of most nurse managers probably lie somewhere between these extremes. An atmosphere of trust allows team members to function somewhat independently. After the assignment is given, the staff member has some liberty in deciding such things as task order and can use his or her judgment about matters that are not already programmed. However, the nurse leader still controls the management of the work group and is available for help and guidance.

Interpreting protocol for responding to incidental requests

All time-consuming tasks that have not already been delegated such as incidental requests from physicians, special technicians, and other staff members should be channeled through the nurse manager or team leader as appropriate. Such centralized control (1) identifies a single channel of command for staff members, (2) keeps the nurse leader informed of all activities, (3) allows for allocation of tasks to the most capable and/or available person, and (4) protects staff members from excessive time and energy demands. A physician who asks a favorite nurse to assist with an extensive treatment for a patient not assigned to her disrupts assignment completion if he or she complies without consulting with the nurse manager or team leader.

Explaining procedure for emergencies

There are always some uncertainties in nursing. This is particularly true in acute treatment areas, but no unit is exempt from crises. Anything can happen, including an accident, a hemorrhage, an extreme reaction to a medication or treatment, or a cardiac arrest. It is extremely important for nursing staff members to know that in times of emergency, autocratic rule prevails. The nurse in charge (nurse manager, team leader, or other) as-

sumes command of the situation and directs activities until the crisis is past. If this person is not available, the next best qualified person takes over. Other staff members are to remain in their assigned areas, ready to respond for service as needed. Excited personnel do little to alleviate already tense situations.

Nursing personnel need to know in advance what their responsibilities are in the event of an emergency. Specific instructions are given regularly in conferences and in special sessions such as fire and disaster drills. With a patient/client emergency, the staff member present calls for help on the intercommunication system. If there is no other way to get assistance, another person can be sent for aid, or the staff member can simply call out for help. In the meantime, that staff member begins appropriate emergency measures according to protocol and capability, especially when inaction can threaten a life.

Giving clear and concise formal and informal directions

Individual and group effort requires direction for success in attaining individual and group ends. Each member of the nursing group must have the information required to complete his or her assignment. Staff members are provided with information needed for good performance through official instructions. Some instructions are given through formal procedures such as the assignment sheet, one-to-one instructions, records, and the direction-giving conference. Other instructions are informal, such as orders given to members by the leader as incidental needs arise. Whether written or verbal, formal or informal, all orders are to elicit a response.

Complete and undistorted communication between two or more people is more of an ideal than a reality; however, many concepts and techniques can be used to improve communication when giving instructions (see Chapter 8).

Oral shift report. A report from nursing staff going off duty usually involves staff members listening to the report from the off-duty staff, jotting down notes about individual assignments, and recording information pertaining to all other patients assigned to the nursing team. Ideally staff members of the team going off duty provide coverage for the incoming staff so that they can listen to the report without interruption. A conference room where all members can sit facing each other increases the probability of note taking and encourages free exchange of information. The report usually takes approximately 20 minutes for a team caring for approximately 15 patients, depending on the complexity of the cases and the characteristics of the nurses giving and receiving the report. The procedure is helped by following a routine format for giving information (e.g., room number, patient's/client's name, diagnosis, physician, treatments, medications, and nursing care problems). Clarification of details can occur as each patient is discussed. It is important to allow time for adequate coverage of priority items. A more detailed account of the conference technique is discussed later in this chapter.

Taped shift report. Taping shift reports is an inexpensive and simple mechanism that can provide information and direction about patients/clients and alert the incoming shift to needs. These tapes can be prepared at a time convenient to the staff and can be listened to by the incoming staff without the usual distractions that often occur during report time (e.g., telephone, last-minute medications). Taping shift reports saves time because nurses tend to organize their reports more concisely when they know their voices will be recorded and because irrelevant chatter is absent. In total, primary, and functional nursing systems, each incoming staff member listens to the taped report and takes notes on the assigned patients/clients. In team nursing only the team leaders listen because relevant information is relayed by the leader to the team members during the direction-giving conferences. Questions, answers, and clarification with the staff going off duty occur after the report.

There are further advantages to taping a shift report. If a staff member needs clarification, he or she can replay the tape, and if a staff member's tour of duty begins after the report he or she can listen to it individually. The recorder should follow these guidelines when taping reports:
1. Organize the report well before beginning.
2. Introduce self at the beginning of the tape.

3. Speak slowly and clearly so that accurate notes can be taken.
4. Give patient's/client's room number, name, age (if appropriate), diagnosis, and physician's name.
5. Provide a brief systematic account of each patient's/client's condition, including new or changed orders.
6. Refer to vital signs, temperature elevations, intravenous fluids, and intake and output as relevant.
7. Indicate the names of all pain medications, the number of times they should be given, and the last time they were given.
8. Cover necessary information about preoperative patients/clients (e.g., whether the chart is in order, if preoperative teaching has been completed, time of preoperative medications).
9. Give information about postoperative patients/clients such as time of arrival from operating or recovery room; general condition; vital signs; IVs (kind, rate of flow, fluids to follow); dressings; voiding; diet; tolerance; nature of breathing; coughing; and number, position, and patency of tubes.
10. Sign off, noting any issues that may have been overlooked or that need to be discussed with incoming staff members after they have heard the recording.

After giving his or her report, a nurse who is learning how to record properly should take a worksheet, listen to the report, and record the necessary information as if he or she were the nurse receiving the information for the incoming shift. This exercise helps improve report giving by identifying strengths and weaknesses.[15]

These same guidelines for presenting comprehensive coverage for a group of patients/clients can be used by a nurse leader in giving information face-to-face. This method presents information clearly and matter-of-factly and enables the incoming leader and staff to apply the information to individual and group plans.

Walking rounds. Nurse-to-nurse communication can be upgraded significantly by reporting and discussing patient care at the bedside during *walking rounds* rather than by reporting from nurse to nurse in an isolated patient's room. This method is more easily accomplished in primary nursing because fewer people are involved, but it is possible to manage with modifications with larger groups (e.g., the team leader could have walking rounds with an LPN or nursing assistant).

Direction-giving conferences. In the direction-giving conference the nurse leader meets with the entire nursing group for 15 to 20 minutes in a quiet, undisturbed environment and apprises the members more fully of their assignments. Assignments are posted as quickly as possible after staff members come on duty to allow them to begin the rudiments of their work while waiting for more specific instructions. Members of an alternate nursing team or group cover for these members during their conference as designated on the assignment sheet. The direction-giving conference is primarily for the leader to give instructions regarding individual and group assignments. Time is limited; therefore the leader must impart the necessary information quickly and well. To ensure a successful direction-giving conference, a nurse leader should:

1. Prepare thoroughly before meeting with the nursing personnel.
   a. Prepare a detailed worksheet that (1) contains all known pertinent information; (2) indicates areas of priority, special concerns, and needs for additional information; and (3) allows space for updating data as necessary (see sample worksheet provided in Figure 7-8).
   b. Receive reports from those who have had prior responsibility for patient/client services; update worksheet.
   c. Check pertinent data such as tests, preoperative orders, and special treatments, or confer with nurse manager or physician as needed; update worksheet.
   d. Visit all patients/clients briefly for individual assessment; make necessary notations on worksheet.
   e. Make patient/client care assignments according to criteria for effective assignment making.
2. Organize conference activity for efficiency and conservation of time.
   a. To provide for continuity of work and give all members an opportunity to develop a routine, keep to the same time schedule for at least a week at a time if possible, and begin and end the meeting according to schedule.
   b. Seat all members for comfort and to encourage the recording of information on individual worksheets.
   c. Introduce self and group members to one another as needed. The composition of nursing groups changes frequently in some settings, and giving names and role identification in a warm, friendly atmosphere promotes group morale and facilitates comprehension.
   d. Ask that each member record relevant information pertaining not only to his or her individual assignment but also to *all* patients/clients assigned to the team. This technique provides for informed coverage for all other members. It is very helpful to have worksheets containing basic information (name, age, diagnosis, physician, diet, and activity) ready for the nursing personnel when they report for duty. These sheets may be prepared by computer services or by clerical staff from the previous shift. Having basic information available reduces the amount of time spent in recording, enables the members to listen better and to clarify directions, and reduces the high possibility of error that occurs when many people transcribe directions at one time.
   e. Use the procedure and pace that is appropriate for the purpose and the nurses. Use direct and simple language. The more accurately words and phrases are tailored to the level of the receivers, the more effective the communication is likely to be. A certain amount of redundancy may be necessary in direction giving. If a message is very important or complicated, it is probably necessary to repeat it in a different way and add the reason for the procedure. However, unnecessary repetition should be avoided because it dulls the receiver's attention. Speak clearly and adjust the speaking pace to the receivers' preference and need to allow for accurate recording of necessary information. Directions should proceed systematically. For example, it is most effective to offer information accord-

ing to the format of the worksheet (e.g., name, age, physician, diagnosis, diet, activity, intake and output IVs) and to give instructions and explanations after each item as needed. Irregularity in presentation increases the time spent in recording and also increases the probability of incorrectly transcribing information.

f. Include all necessary information. The direction giver does not need to repeat all information that is already known or provided on the worksheet because time is better spent in reviewing items that require reinforcement or elaboration. Documented, well-written nursing care plans provide detailed information on who, what, when, where, and how. However, enough information should be included in the meeting to help the group understand what is needed to function together with purpose and harmony.

g. Use feedback and look for verbal and nonverbal cues from receivers. The more complex the information, the more essential it is to encourage receivers to ask questions and indicate areas of confusion. For example, the direction-giving process breaks down when the team leader instructs the caregiver to "Give Buerger's exercises to Mr. Fletcher for 15 minutes at 10 and 2," and the caregiver duly records the order on the worksheet without understanding it. If time is limited or certain items are not relevant to the total group, the leader may note items needing clarification and attend to these matters later with individual staff members.

h. Leave group members with the belief that he or she is available to them for assistance. This allows members to address uncertainties about their assignments with assurance that support and help will be forthcoming if needed.

Information direction giving by the nurse leader is occasionally necessary. As the delivery of nursing care proceeds, matters arise that may not have been anticipated in time for the direction-giving conference or that simply may have been overlooked. Therefore nursing staff members should expect some interruptions in assignment completion. Give additional tasks to the staff member assigned to the area in which the action is to occur. For example, if a new treatment is ordered, the nurse assigned to care for that patient/client is asked to administer it, or if a patient needs more assistance than one nurse can provide and there is no double coverage for that patient, the leader asks the nurse nearest to that locale to provide assistance. When assigning such tasks, the leader considers other factors of assignment making such as overassignment versus underassignment.

Using a management control process that assesses the quality of care given by nursing personnel and evaluates individual and group performance

Management control is the continuous process by which nurse managers ensure that actual activities conform to planned activities. This definition illustrates the close link between planning and controlling individual and group activities. The fundamental standards and objectives of the overall organization and separate nursing units and the method for obtaining them are established during the planning process. Such standards and objectives can be in the form of quality measures, quantity, time, cost, and performance. They identify and assess specific conditions, behaviors, the environment in which nursing activities occur, and the criteria of acceptable conditions and behavior. The management control process measures progress toward those standards and objectives and enables managers to detect deviations from the plan so that they can take whatever remedial action is necessary, including changing the plan (see Chapter 10).

Summary

1. Direction is the connecting link between organizing for work and work accomplishment.
2. Directing is issuing assignments, orders, and instructions that permit the worker to know what is expected of him or her. Directing also involves guiding and overseeing the work.
3. Achieving success in direction giving requires acquiring the ability to direct and to manage time efficiently.

4. Integrating theory and practice leads to effective and useful direction giving.

5. The nurse manager who makes a "to do" list of upcoming activities and reduces these activities to specifics saves time and accomplishes goals effectively.

6. Registered nurses are being asked to supervise an increasing number of unlicensed nursing personnel, also known as nursing assistants, nurse extendors, patient care technicians, and unit attendants.

7. The American Nurses Association defines delegation as transferring responsibility of an activity to another person while retaining accountability for the outcome.

8. Responsibility for total nursing care cannot be assigned to unlicensed nursing personnel, but the nurse professional can assign certain tasks that fit the job description, knowledge base, and demonstrated skills of the individual.

9. Agencies who employ ancillary workers have the responsibility to orient, train, and adequately supervise them on the job.

10. The registered nurse who is overseeing assistive personnel must very carefully document care given by the assistant to ensure that what was delegated was carried out satisfactorily.

11. Work flow, equipment, techniques, and procedures used to complete work assignments are the technical aspects of directing.

12. At the lower- or first-level of management, the number of people who report directly to a manager represents the managerial span of control. The larger the span of control, the greater the hierarchy; with a lesser span of control, there is greater decentralization.

13. The span of control depends on standards of care, kinds of patients/clients, numbers and kinds of nursing staff needed, capabilities of the nurse leader, and the leader's responsibilities.

14. The physical support system includes space, equipment, and physical environment. There is great variation among healthcare facilities. A nurse manager must work with prevailing circumstances toward desired adaptations and changes.

15. Delegating responsibilities includes regulating activities, preventing and correcting problems, and promoting quality care through growth and development of nursing personnel.

16. Delegating well-defined tasks and responsibilities to staff members frees managers to do other important activities and also serves as a helpful management training and developmental tool. Lack of delegation can stifle initiative.

17. Barriers to delegation include a lack of trust in others; low self-confidence; vague job descriptions; and fear of competition, risk taking, and relinquishing control.

18. Nurse managers can overcome barriers to delegation by recognizing what keeps them from delegating properly and what motivates workers to respond favorably to challenging work.

19. No matter what system of care is in progress, the direction giver must consider such factors as *who* is best suited for the job, *what* tasks are to be performed, *where* the job is to be done, *when* the job is to be accomplished, *why* the task is necessary, and *how* the task is to be accomplished.

20. Direction giving is best handled by one person for one group, with the leader having authority to act.

21. In the functional nursing system the nurse manager makes assignments and gives direction to all nursing personnel on the nursing unit. The primary purpose is to accomplish tasks with the greatest efficiency, which makes giving personal attention to patient/client needs difficult.

22. Team nursing provides a mechanism in which the nurse manager relinquishes responsibility for assignment making and direction giving to team leaders whose primary purpose is to match staff members to patients/clients according to their needs and problems.

23. In primary nursing an RN or LPN/LVN is delegated responsibility and accountability for planning, giving, and communicating all phases of care for a patient or

group of patients from admission through discharge.

24. Modular nursing is a modification of team and primary nursing. The system differs from team nursing in that the RN provides direct care to assigned patients with the help of nursing assistants.

25. In case management, delegation of responsibilities extends beyond the traditional nursing unit or shift-specific boundaries and focuses on the patient's entire episode of illness from before admission, to care after dismissal.

26. Case managers develop a critical path, review step-by-step the quality and cost of care the patient receives, and compare this with predetermined standards for that treatment.

27. Effective delegation of activities considers goals of the agency, gives first priority to needs and problems of the patients/clients, and provides for coordination and efficiency among departments that provide support services.

28. Determining patient/client needs and problems is accomplished through current nursing care plans, the patient/client, significant others, the physician, records, reports, and caregivers.

29. Preparation of a comprehensive worksheet provides data for assignment making and guidelines for activities of the nursing team.

30. Effective assignments ensure continuous coverage for all nursing staff (RNs, LPNs/LVNs, nurse assistants) and provide specific guidelines for all absences from work (coffee and lunch breaks, conferences).

31. Nursing personnel should not be required to engage in nonnursing activities such as cleaning the kitchen and utility rooms; however, the supportive systems that *are* required should be assigned on a rotational basis. Protocol for responding to incidental requests is established.

32. All nursing assignments consider safety standards, regulations, mechanisms for handling emergency situations and the need for patients/clients to have continuous care given by the same nursing staff as much as possible.

33. Variety in assignments enables nurse members to identify needs and interests and develop their potential, therefore becoming versatile and valuable staff members.

34. Directions for work accomplishment by nursing personnel for a group of patients/clients are managed through the mechanisms of one-to-one instructions, tape-recorded reports, in-person reports, and formal conferences.

35. When giving directions, the leader should present information in a clear, concise manner; be well prepared, organized, and friendly; elicit feedback; and leave the receivers feeling confident in themselves and in the leader's availability to provide necessary assistance.

36. Control of nursing care and work performance is a continuous process through which nurse managers ensure that actual activities conform to planned activities. Activities and behaviors are measured against predetermined criteria.

❓ Questions for Study and Discussion

1. If you were a nurse manager, would a small or large scope of responsibility appeal to you? Why?

2. If you were asked the question, "What is the right span of control?" how would you respond?

3. All nursing positions require some management skill. How do you plan to acquire this necessary ability?

4. Because many healthcare agencies are downsizing their nursing staff, RNs must be responsible for an increasing number of unli-

censed assistive personnel. What is your reaction to this situation? How will you cope if you are faced with this problem?

5. Explain the differences between regulatory, corrective, and preventive managerial responsibilities.

6. The department manager feels insecure in preparing the departmental budget and therefore delegates the procedure to the assistant manager, who understands the hospital system and enjoys working with figures. Do you agree with the department manager's decision? Explain your response.

7. Of the reasons given by managers for not delegating as much responsibility as they should, with which of them do you identify? What procedure might you follow to overcome the difficulty?

8. Select one of the systems used for delivery of nursing care. Explain its basic structure and use of nursing personnel.

9. Which nursing care delivery system appeals to you? Why?

10. Which of the nursing care delivery systems is least attractive to you? Why?

11. As team leader for 12 patients, you arrive to work one-half hour late. You decide to catch up by giving only the absolutely necessary information to your team members for work accomplishment. Your rationale is that they are all experienced workers and will know what to do. Do you think this is an appropriate choice of action? Why?

Test Your Knowledge

BEHAVIORAL OBJECTIVE

Define direction giving and explain the implications for nursing at the lower or first level of management.

After 3 years of experience as a staff nurse and after completing a master's degree program in nursing, Amy has been given her first post as nurse manager of a medical unit. She learned many things in her program but now must put them into practice.

_____ 1. Amy learned that direction at the lower or first level of management in nursing means all except:
   a. Issuing assignments and instructions to a small group of workers.
   b. Overseeing a small group of workers.
   c. Coordinating the hospital's safety committee.
   d. Attaining organizational objectives.

BEHAVIORAL OBJECTIVE

State two preconditions for achieving success in direction giving and explain how these preconditions are acquired.

Amy learned that there is no sure way of getting others to do a job but that there are general preconditions for success in direction giving.

_____ 2. Amy knows that the ability to direct depends on:
   a. Being officially appointed to the position.
   b. Applying theory to practice.
   c. Having followers who are willing to be led.
   d. Having confidence in self to do the job.

BEHAVIORAL OBJECTIVE

Using Chapter 7 guidelines, prepare a "to do" list for one upcoming student clinical experience.

Carlos is a second-year student who is assigned to a home healthcare agency. He knows he will be making a home visit to Mr. Peterson, who has suffered a stroke and requires physical care and range-of-motion (ROM) exercises on his left side.

_____ 3. Carlos prepares a "to do" list for the experience. He decides that before the visit it is vital that he:
   a. Learn all that he can about Mr. Peterson.
   b. Bone up on ROM exercises.
   c. Review the physiologic facts concerning strokes.
   d. Practice speaking with patients with aphasia.

BEHAVIORAL OBJECTIVE

Identify factors that determine the size of a work group, span of control, and the physical support system.

Amy is grateful that she took classes on directing the work of others because she sees how important good delegation can be. Some of the facts and concepts that she learned follow.

_____ 4. Several factors determine the size of a work group at the lower level. Which is of least importance?
   a. Standards for care
   b. Complexity of patient care
   c. Precise number of nursing personnel
   d. Competencies of nursing personnel

_____ 5. The span of management for a 45-bed medical nursing unit is:
   a. Best determined on the basis of patients and work conditions.
   b. Best determined by nursing staff assigned to a nursing unit.
   c. Best divided into two subunits.
   d. Best determined by those who provide care.

_____ 6. Whatever the size of a work group or span of control at the lower level, enough staff must be available to accomplish certain purposes. Which of these purposes is the exception?
   a. Meet the needs of the patient
   b. Provide help to other units as needed
   c. Cover all time periods adequately
   d. Allow for growth and development of nursing staff

BEHAVIORAL OBJECTIVE

Explain the guidelines necessary to effectively delegate activities to nursing personnel who are providing care to a group of patients.

In light of the restructuring of some rules of the healthcare system, Amy is concerned about her responsibility for supervising assistive personnel and about her responsibilities for all the staff under her control.

_____ 7. Which of the following systems of care is not appropriate for a nursing assistant?
   a. Functional
   b. Case management
   c. Primary care
   d. Total care

_____ 8. In the human relations approach to management, the key to productivity is:
   a. The behavior of people under direction.
   b. The degree of independence allowed.
   c. Firm control of the work situation.
   d. Organizational objectives.

_____ 9. Amy wants to revise the scheduling process by instituting a self-scheduling plan. She holds a series of conferences in which the plan is discussed. Which managerial system is she using?
   a. Corrective
   b. Regulatory
   c. Preventive
   d. Promotive

_____ 10. Guidelines for formulating objectives for nursing care at the lower level should consider all of the following except:
   a. The holistic approach.
   b. Written nursing care plans.
   c. Staff preferences.
   d. Accepted standards.

_____ 11. Assignment of patient care responsibility to the nursing staff requires the nurse manager at the lower level to know all of the following information except:

    a. Patients' needs and nursing staffs' capabilities.

    b. The number of nursing staff available.

    c. How to divide work into manageable parts.

    d. Which staff member is feeling tired.

BEHAVIORAL OBJECTIVE

Demonstrate ability to identify priorities in assignment making.

Amy wants to make appropriate assignments. She considers all the principles she was taught regarding the process. Some of them follow.

_____ 12. Which of the following responses offers the best way to give priority to patient needs?

    a. Assessing nursing needs and problems

    b. Deciding how nursing care needs are to be met

    c. Controlling and evaluating administration of nursing care

    d. Using the top-level assignment process

_____ 13. The best way to assure the patient that priority needs are met is to:

    a. Use the nursing process and care plans.

    b. Check with the patient.

    c. Consult with the physician.

    d. Consult with nursing personnel assigned to care for the patient.

_____ 14. A member of Amy's staff oversees care before, during, and after hospitalization. The system of care in effect is:

    a. Managed care.

    b. Case management.

    c. Primary care.

    d. Modular.

_____ 15. On another day, group leaders make nursing assignments for staff members under their control. What system is this?

    a. Primary care

    b. Managed care

    c. Team nursing

    d. Functional nursing

BEHAVIORAL OBJECTIVE

Identify criteria important to giving directions for a nursing assignment.

Amy makes certain that her staff understands the rudiments of direction giving. She evaluates her staff carefully.

_____ 16. Amy has instituted reporting by tape and recognizes that there are some disadvantages to the system. Which of the following can be considered a disadvantage?

    a. Saves time

    b. Report tends to be more organized

    c. Anticipates questions and indicates need for clarification

    d. Can be replayed as needed

_____ 17. Amy is responsible for assigning nonnursing activities. They are best assigned as follows:

    a. Tasks are matched with staff members' proficiency.

    b. Tasks are assigned according to individual preference.

    c. Nonnursing tasks are reserved for control of personnel.

    d. Tasks are assigned on a rotational basis.

REFERENCES

1. Silber M: Handling hemorrhages and hassles of leadership, *Nurs Manage,* 25(2):80D-80H, 1994.
2. Robbins S: *Essentials of organizational behavior,* ed 4, Englewood Cliffs, NJ, 1994, Prentice Hall.
3. Barter M, Furmidge M: Unlicensed assistive personnel: issues relating to delegation and supervision, *JONA* 24(4):36-40, 1994.
4. Herrick K and others: My license is not on the line: the art of delegation, *Nurs Manage* 25(2):48-50, 1994.
5. Christensen P, Kenney J: *The nursing process: application of theories, frameworks and models,* ed 3, St Louis, 1990, Mosby.
6. Swansburg R: *Introductory management and leadership for clinical nurses,* Boston, 1993, Jones and Bartlett.
7. Bennett M, Hylton J: Modular nursing: partners in professional practice, *Nurs Manage* 21(3):20-24, 1990.
8. Weil M: *Historical origins and recent developments: case management in human services practice,* San Francisco, 1985, Jossey-Bass.
9. Salmond S: In-hospital case management, *Orthop Nurs* 9(1):39, 1990.
10. McKenzie C, Torkelson N, Holt M: Care and cost: nursing case management improves both, *Nurs Manage* 20(19):30-34, 1989.
11. Hellriegel D, Slocum J: *Management,* ed 5, Reading, Mass, 1989, Addison-Wesley.
12. Longest B: *Management practices for the health professional,* ed 4, Norwalk, Conn, 1990, Appleton & Lange.
13. Robbins S: *Organization theory: structure, design, and applications,* Englewood Cliffs, NJ, 1990, Prentice Hall.
14. McGregor D: *The human side of enterprise,* New York, 1960, McGraw-Hill.
15. Cox S: Taping report: tips to record by, *Nurs 94* 24(3):64, 1994.

SELECTED READINGS

Ameduri P: Directing others is a demanding role, *RN* 57(10):21-24, 1994.

Bassler S, Goedde L: Clinical activities and the nurse manager, *Nurs Manage* 24(1):63-64, 1993.

Dangot-Simpkin G: Becoming a better manager: avoiding team busters, *Nurs 94* 24(2):320-320V, 1994.

Davis B: Effective utilization of a scarce resource—RNs, *Nurs Manage* 25(2):78-80, 1994.

Edwards G and others: Unit-based shared governance can work, *Nurs Manage* 25(4):74-77, 1994.

Gallard L, Soo Hoo W: Maximizing limited resources through TEAMCARE, *Nurs Manage* 24(1):36-43, 1994.

McVey C, Moore L: Managing mediocrity, *Nurs Manage* 24(6):68I-68N, 1993.

NURSING NEWS: Job functions: waste not, want not, *Nurs 94* 24(4):10, 1994.

Pesce L: Evaluating nursing intensity: it's time to transfer the patient, *Nurs Manage* 26(2):36-39, 1995.

Pierson D: Advance directives: implementing a program that works, *Nurs Manage* 25(10):54-56, 1994.

Professional Notes: Supreme Court rules on nurses as supervisors, (those who direct work of others are not protected by federal labor law), *Nurs Outlook* 42(5):248, 1994.

COMMUNICATION PROCESS

BEHAVIORAL OBJECTIVES

On completion of this chapter, the student will be prepared to:

- Differentiate between interpersonal and organizational communication and indicate the importance of the communication process.

- Name and define the steps in an effective communication model.

- Offer guidelines that promote effective feedback.

- Identify barriers to effective communication in nursing service and describe ways to overcome them.

- Define the informal or "grapevine" channel of communication and recognize positive and negative features of the system.

- Review the health communication model and describe how relationships, transactions, and contexts offer a systems perspective on communication in healthcare.

- Describe the channels of communication in management.

- Define a team and indicate how polarity management can promote and build effective working teams.

- Explain how a nurse manager effectively engages in cross-cultural communication.

- Define "nursing informatics" and indicate the steps nurse managers take to purchase, develop, and implement an information system.

Communication is a cyclic process whereby a message is passed from sender to receiver and back again with the hope that the exchanged information is correctly understood. One difficulty in communication is that people are seldom totally effective in transmitting their intended meanings to others and frequently send unintended messages. Medication and treatment errors and policy infractions often result from ineffective communication. Unfortunately, the action taken to resolve these errors usually centers on the error itself, and no attempt is made to study the faulty communication process that exists in the clinical setting. The goal of communication is to narrow the gap between the intended message and the received message. Nurse managers can accomplish this goal by understanding the communication process, which will enable them to identify, define, and resolve communication problems.

This chapter considers the history and the importance of the communication process in organizations and in the nurse manager's role. Models of interpersonal communication, barriers to effective communication, and suggested ways to overcome these barriers are presented. The positive and negative features of the informal channel of communication in organizations are discussed. A health communications model is presented, which stresses the importance of relationships, transactions, and contexts in which health communication takes place. Management functions and communications are explored from the downward, upward, horizontal/lateral, and diagonal perspectives. Teams and teamwork are defined and discussed, using polarity management as an example of how communication within healthcare settings can be facilitated and enhanced. The process of cross-cultural communication is outlined, especially in terms of intercultural relations, cultural influences, and cultural blindness. Information and computer technology and an introduction to the specialty of nursing informatics are included. Examples of how community health nurses and home healthcare nurses use the informatics system are given. Help is offered to the nurse manager for the purchase, development, and implementation of an informatics system.

HISTORY OF THE STUDY OF COMMUNICATION

Communication has a rich and lengthy history that can be traced to Babylonian and Egyptian writings before the fifth century B.C.[1] Scholars viewed communication as the practical art of persuasion. Aristotle and Plato saw communication as not only an art but also as a legitimate area of study. During the early twentieth century, the advance of radio and the development of

television led to wider applications of communication and the development of more theories. The 1940s and the 1950s were decades of interdisciplinary growth. In the 1960s the study of communication went beyond the source; the content, treatment, and code of the message; and the channel and receiver to the implications of the message as well as the skills, attitudes, knowledge, culture, and social systems of the communication.

In the early 1970s, interpersonal communication and the study of nonverbal interaction became increasingly popular. Group, organizational, political, international, and intercultural communication emerged as distinct areas of study. In the 1980s and 1990s there has been an increasing interest in telecommunication and computer industries, which has had a significant impact on the healthcare industry.

IMPORTANCE OF THE COMMUNICATION PROCESS

The communication process is the foundation on which nursing management achieves interpersonal and organizational objectives. *Interpersonal communication* is the process of exchanging information and meaning either between two people or in small groups of people. *Organizational communication* is the process whereby managers use the established communication system to receive and relay information to people within the organization and to relevant individuals and groups outside the organization.

Communication is the key process that enables the middle-management nurse to serve as a role model of exemplary patient care, to direct staff, to challenge peers to produce, and to support higher management. In its broadest sense the purpose of communication is to effect change and influence action toward the welfare of the clinical setting.

Nurse Managers Spend Most of Their Time Communicating

Managers spend most of their work time communicating, giving information, and implementing decisions.[2] Nurse managers are rarely alone when thinking, planning, or contemplating action. In fact, a large amount of time is spent in face-to-face communication with nursing personnel, physicians, supervisors, people in supportive services, or patients/clients. When not conferring with others, nurse managers may be recording information; monitoring the development of nursing care plans; preparing schedules and reports; or reading orders, memorandums, and reports. Even in those few periods when nurse managers are alone, they are frequently interrupted.

Good Communication Motivates Staff Members

Staff participation and interest is positively influenced by good communication. Sharing information that is of mutual interest and benefit to the group gives vital support to an employee's sense of belonging. Nurse managers can enhance motivation by explaining plans and reasons for their actions and by asking for feedback in the form of questions, clarification, or suggestions.

> EXAMPLE: A nurse manager says to a nurse on her staff, "Jennifer, I have been asked to select someone from our department to serve on the case manager committee. This would be a new system in delivery of nursing care for many patients. The role would be broader in scope than the primary care system we currently use. The case manager would not replace primary nurses but would work with them to conserve costs and improve the quality of care. Would you be interested in serving on this committee?"

In this example, Jennifer is given information regarding the case manager position and the opportunity to accept a challenging role on the committee responsible for developing the position. This timely communication may motivate Jennifer to respond affirmatively.

Communication Leads to Influence and Power

When nurse managers effectively communicate information to individuals and groups, they are more likely to be viewed as influential individuals. Nursing has great potential to effect changes in healthcare, yet because it is primarily a women's profession, attempts to use such potential can lead to power struggles. The tradi-

tional nursing role has been one of subservience and service to others. Nurses must develop effective communication skills so that they can articulate their ideas, control their environment, and achieve results. These accomplishments will increase their self-esteem and, consequently, the esteem of the profession.

Because nurse managers are in the center of the communication network, they can acquire vast amounts of information, use that information to achieve organizational goals and objectives, and provide workers with the opportunity to grow personally and professionally. There is a direct relationship between position and power; persons in a central position with high status in the communication system can receive and give more messages and exert greater influence than can people with lower status. For example, the vice president of nursing services can influence the board of directors to open a new wing of the hospital or to grant an across-the-board increase in nurses' salaries. The lower- or first-level nurse manager can exert influence to institute a treatment or to change the direction of the nursing care plan. Through effective communication the nurse manager can influence nursing supervisors to adopt a different care delivery system or to add another member to the nursing staff.

Communication of power can result in a chain reaction. The nurse manager who feels secure in personal skills and abilities is likely to release power to others through work delegation, which creates an atmosphere in which staff members feel secure and capable of assuming responsibility for their work. As a result, productivity increases, and more goals are achieved.

GUIDELINES FOR EFFECTIVE COMMUNICATION

Communication Model

It is easy to tell people that they should be good communicators; it is much more difficult to tell them *how* to be good communicators. Figure 8-1 reflects the basic elements of the communication process: sender, receiver, message, encoding, transmitting, decoding, action, and feedback.[3]

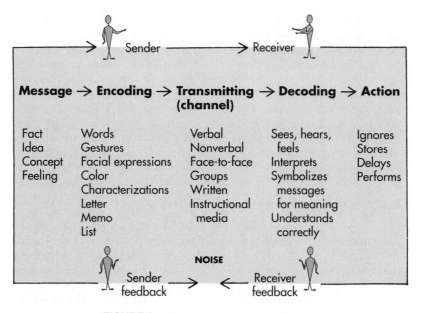

FIGURE 8-1. The communication process.

Sender and receiver

The sender is the source of information and the initiator of the communication process. The sender tries to choose the type of message and channel (e.g., computer, telephone, written memo) that will most effectively meet the needs of the receiver, who receives the sender's message and translates it into a meaningful form.

Message

The first step for the sender is to choose a fact, concept, idea, or feeling and to organize the thought(s) into a coherent package. This is the content of communication; it is the basis of a **message.** In an organization, the nurse manager is a person with needs, feelings, information, and a purpose for communicating them. A nurse manager motivates other members of the nursing team and informs them about patients/clients or organizational matters.

> EXAMPLE: During a staff meeting, the nurse manager presents a new concept: "As you may know, our agency is investigating the pros and cons of using case managers throughout the hospital." (The manager knows that information travels quickly. She wants the staff to receive the correct message that a final decision has not yet been made.) "I have asked Jennifer to serve on the planning committee;

she will serve as the liaison between you and the planning committee."

Encoding

Encoding is the second step and involves translating the message into words, gestures, facial expressions, and other symbols that communicate the intended meaning to the receivers. Words have many meanings. Each of the 500 most often used words in the English language has approximately 28 different meanings. The meanings of words are determined not only by dictionary definitions but also by the way they are used in a sentence and by the context and setting in which they are used.

All methods of communication use symbols to represent persons or things. It must be kept in mind that only the symbols are transmitted. The meaning received depends on the receiver's interpretation of the symbols. For example, the cross has special meaning to Christian people, just as the Star of David has special meaning to Jewish people. To some, the color red symbolizes happiness; to others, it is a color linked with prostitution. Black is a symbol of conservatism to many; to others it is equated with death. Words, gestures, facial expressions, and all other symbols are learned through the influence of parents, culture, school, religion, friends, and employment. Communication is never perfect because none of the symbols used in communication has universal meaning.

Encoding the message requires decisions regarding not only what will be said but also how, when, and where it will be said. Encoding may also involve decisions about expressing or concealing emotion. Effective communication depends on the appropriate degree of intensity of the message. For example, while working in an emergency or crisis situation, the nurse manager may decide not to show fear or frustration and to communicate in a matter-of-fact, unemotional manner. He or she may decide to talk with patients/clients and nursing personnel later, tailoring the message to the circumstances and communicating with them informally or formally as appropriate.

The following concepts should be understood by nurses who want to encode messages well: (1) words mean different things to different people, (2) the message should be encoded in the simplest terms, (3) if complex, the message should be expressed in several ways, and (4) the language used should reflect the personality, culture, and values of the receiver.[4] Effective encoding depends on a clear message that is delivered at the right pace and phrased in such a way as to attract the receiver's attention. Encoding may occur within a few seconds, as when one person greets another with a "Hi" rather than with a more formal greeting. Regardless of the time required and the degree of conscious planning, the transmission of a message depends on proper encoding.

EXAMPLE: A nurse manager presents information regarding case management in a positive tone of voice: "Case management, if used in this hospital, will mean that nurses who have at least a bachelor's degree and who receive the necessary training will be responsible for managing care of patients in selected diagnosis-related group categories from the time of their admission through at least 2 weeks of care. The case manager will work closely with the primary nurses. Some primary nurses will become associate case managers, which is a role very similar to that of the associate primary nurse but somewhat expanded. I believe that the hospital would benefit from this system as a result of more carefully controlled costs and more efficient nursing care."

Transmitting

As shown in Figure 8-1, **transmitting** is the channel used to communicate a message, or what form the message takes. A manager uses different language in a phone call than in a formal report. The number of receivers to be addressed is also important. Usually the greater the number of receivers, the more formal the language should be. The message may be in any form that can be experienced and understood by one or more of the receiver's senses; for example speech may be heard, written words may be read, and gestures or facial expressions may be seen or felt. A touch of the hand may communicate messages ranging from love and comfort to anger and hate. A wave of the hand can communicate widely diverse messages depending on the position (e.g., "Come here!" or "Get lost!"). Nonverbal messages are often more honest or meaningful than verbal or written exchanges. For instance, the patient or client who smiles and laughs while saying, "I have an unbearable headache" and the staff member who frowns and is uncooperative while saying "Everything is fine" are transmitting nonverbal messages that are different from their verbal ones.

In addition to verbal and nonverbal messages, instructional media can be used effectively to transmit information. Client records, charts, computer printouts, articles, books, slides, overhead transparencies, videocassette tapes, and films are frequently used resources.

EXAMPLE: For staff meetings the nurse manager prepares visual materials and says, "I have brought an organizational chart to show how case managers might function throughout our hospital and community and what our roles would be in the new system. I have also brought copies of articles that explain how the case manager system works in similar hospitals. I'll leave them in this room for you to read. After you have read and talked about case management with one another, bring your reactions and questions to Jennifer or to me, and come to our next meeting prepared to talk about it further. Be thinking about whether or not you would be interested in becoming a case manager or an associate case manager."

Decoding

In the **decoding** step of the communication process, the initiative transfers from the sender to the receiver, who perceives and interprets (de-

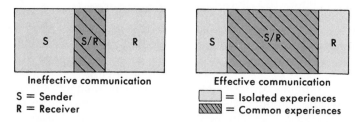

FIGURE 8-2. Effectiveness of communication depends on commonality of experiences.

codes) the sender's message into meaningful information. Ideally the information consists of what the sender believes the receiver *should* know and *wants* to know. Understanding is the key to the decoding process. Words and symbols have multiple meanings, and there is no assurance that what the sender encodes will be what the receiver decodes.

The decoding process is affected by the receiver's experiences, personal interpretations of the symbols used, expectations, and mutuality of meaning with the sender. Normally receivers make a genuine attempt to understand the intended message. However, a receiver may not understand the intended message because the sender and receiver have different perceptions. The more experiences the sender and receiver have in common, the more likely it is that the intended meaning will be communicated (Figure 8-2). People with different experiences must have a shared language to be able to communicate. Before a nurse manager can communicate with personnel who have various fields of preparation and experience, he or she must learn how they think, feel, and respond in a variety of nursing situations. With this knowledge, nurse managers are usually able to predict with acceptable accuracy how a given message will be decoded.

EXAMPLE: Following the group meeting and before the nursing staff has read the articles, several nurses express fear: "Those of us who don't have bachelor's degrees are going to lose our jobs"; "I don't see why we need to change; we are getting along fine with primary nursing"; "They must not think we are doing a good job." Jennifer helps to allay fears and says, "The way I see it, we will all have a chance to do more for our patients. We'll know more about them and will be able to contribute to cost efficiency by identifying duplication of services and instances when the patient might benefit from other

services or by dismissing the patient sooner to the care of other professionals and/or family members. We could learn a lot from case managers since they will be clinical specialists in our area of care. I realize that this potential change may be frightening. Reading the articles may help reduce your concerns. After you've read them, we'll talk more."

Action

Action is the next step in the communication process and is the behavior taken by198 the receiver as a result of the message sent, received, and perceived. Action is the process of doing or performing something; it is behaving or functioning in a certain way. The sender has no guarantee that what has been heard and decoded will be carried out as intended. The receiver may or may not choose to act on the message. Many nurse managers overlook this important fact when giving instructions or explanations. They assume that merely giving a staff member a message ensures that the intended action will occur. Communication is not successful until the message is understood and acted on appropriately.

Several options are available to the receiver once a message is received: (1) ignore the information and fail to act, (2) store it as reference material until choosing to respond, (3) respond by saying one thing and doing another (credibility gap), or (4) respond to the message according to the receiver's interpretation.

EXAMPLE: Five of the six staff nurses heed Jennifer's suggestion to read the articles. The sixth goes about her work disconsolately and expresses negative feelings about the proposed change of delivery system.

Feedback

The communication process is not complete until the last step, **feedback,** occurs. Feedback is an integral part of the communication process whereby senders and receivers exchange information and clarify the meanings of the message. Two-way rather than one-way communication allows both the sender and the receiver to search for verbal and nonverbal cues. Effective two-way communication occurs when a receiver acknowledges a message and sends meaningful feedback to the sender. The more complex the message, the more essential it is to encourage receivers to ask questions and indicate areas of confusion throughout the entire communication process.

Feedback may be direct and indirect, verbal and nonverbal. Behaviors such as recording information in a direction-giving conference, nodding in acknowledgment, smiling, and moving to accomplish the given task offer one kind of feedback. Actions such as a blank stare, lack of motion to respond, or a frown provide quite different feedback. For nurse managers, feedback serves as a control measure. In most organizational communications, the greater the feedback, the more effective the communication is likely to be. For example, early feedback enables a nurse team leader to know whether the instructions given to team members have been understood and accepted. Without such feedback the nurse manager might not know whether the instructions given were accurately received and carried out until it is too late.

EXAMPLE: After reviewing the articles on case management in other hospitals and discussing their reactions with Jennifer, the unit managers, and one another, most nurses become convinced that case management is worth trying. They ask Jennifer to find out just how the primary nurse will relate with the case manager and whether the primary nurse will be stripped of his or her authority. The sixth nurse is drawn reluctantly into the discussion.

The following guidelines can ensure that feedback between managers and staff is effective:[5]
1. *Feedback should be well timed.* Feedback is most effective when it closely follows the behavior on which it is focused. Giving feedback to a nurse at a departmental party is altogether different from giving feedback in a private setting.
    Poor timing. At a party, the nurse manager laughs in the presence of others and says, "Mary, you sure goofed up today when you went off to lunch at the wrong time. We had no coverage for you—we had to scramble."
    Good timing. After Mary returns from lunch, the nurse manager takes her aside and asks, "Mary, did you misunderstand the schedule?" Together they explore the situation and identify ways to prevent it from recurring.
2. *Feedback should be targeted to specific behaviors.* A description of what was noted that carries no overtones of personal judgment may help an individual to respond without anger or resentment. Feedback should always be related to performance goals, not personality traits.
    Inappropriate targeting. "Mary, the staff members are angry with you because of your thoughtlessness, and I agree with them."
    Appropriate targeting. "Mary, you took your lunch hour at a time that was not scheduled. Was there a misunderstanding?"
3. *Feedback should be tactful.* Messages that consider the feelings of another are more likely to be heard than those that are abrasive and accusing.
    Tactless feedback. "Mary, how could you have put us in such a spot? You were thinking only of yourself when you went off to lunch at the wrong time."
    Tactful feedback. "Mary, it is not like you to leave us in a jam. Was there a mixup in the schedule?"

BARRIERS TO EFFECTIVE COMMUNICATION

Communication in an organization is difficult because many organizational and interpersonal aspects must be considered. By comprehending barriers common to communicating in healthcare facilities and taking steps to minimize them, the nurse manager can improve his or her ability to communicate effectively. Three broad types of barriers occur in nursing services: (1) physical, (2) social-psychologic, and (3) semantic (interpretation of meanings).[6]

Physical Barriers

Physical barriers are environmental factors that prevent or reduce opportunities for the communication process to occur. Some examples of barriers include physical space or distance, temperature and ventilation, structural or equipment problems, and distracting noise. As mentioned previously, face-to-face communication is the best way to confirm that the intended message has been received. A greater space or distance between the sender and receiver offers more opportunity for misunderstanding. Face-to-face conversation with the persons involved increases the probability that the message will be received correctly. Extreme cold or heat may be distracting and affect communication. The presence or absence of walls and equipment also influences the kind of communication possible. Correcting or adapting to most of these barriers is relatively easy.

Noise

Noise is an integral part of the communication process and may influence it at any or all points (See Figure 8-1). Noise is any disturbance, especially a random and personal disturbance, that obscures or reduces the clarity or quality of a message. Examples include static on a telephone line, commotion in the halls, unusual noises from maintenance or construction, screams or moans from patients, angry exchanges, many people moving about and talking or asking questions at the same time, and the loud ringing of telephones. Noise can be minimized by foreseeing and neutralizing potential sources of interference (e.g., limiting the nursing unit system or central area to strictly business, requesting that repair work or refurbishing be done in the nursing unit during nonpeak hours, reducing the volume of the telephone ring, and attending to patient needs quickly).

System overload

Members of a health team are limited in their capacity to send and receive messages; a **system overload** can occur unless communication is controlled. Overload can also occur when an individual is confronted with messages and expectations from a number of sources that cannot be heard well or completed within the given time and according to established standards of quality. Such dilemmas are a constant part of the nurse manager's position.

A nurse manager can never expect to respond to every sound or gesture, even if it is possible to be aware of all of them. Lower- or first-level managers who receive more messages than they can handle can reduce system overload by isolating and attending to the most important messages. The nurse manager uses the problem-solving process as it relates to priority setting to differentiate between relevant and irrelevant messages. Often the process is rapid and is based on accumulated information, experience, and judgment. For example, life-threatening situations such as respiratory and cardiac failure or natural disasters demand an immediate response, whereas a request for a walker can be attended to when convenient. Similarly, a staff member's request for help in computing a drug dosage takes precedence over another member's request to discuss special privileges regarding vacation time.

Managers can learn a variety of time-saving techniques such as recording and combining messages rather than interrupting other individuals with a number of details. Again, judgment enters into each decision. Although skills commonly improve with practice, the ability to cope well with all noises and sensory overload may not be physically possible. Critically important information may be lost in the volume of input. Options need to be considered such as increasing delegation, adding staff support or technical equipment, or changing or modifying the nurse care delivery system to reduce the number and kinds of noises and communication contacts. For example, changing from functional nursing to team or primary care nursing or case management can automatically reduce these problems.

Social-Psychologic Barriers

Social-psychologic barriers are blocks or inhibitors in communication that arise from the judgments, emotions, and social values of people. Just as physical interferences may create barriers between people, psychologic and social distance can develop and prevent communication or cause a misinterpretation. Life experiences and emotions act as filters in nearly all communication. Individuals see and hear what they are emotionally tuned in to see and hear; therefore communication cannot be separated from personality and social implications. For example, messages may not be given or received accurately if the communicators are experiencing stress.

Barriers can confront both the sender and the receiver. The dominating emotion (e.g., eagerness, anticipation, trust, lethargy, fear, defensiveness) affects the communication process. Positive emotions indicate that the process is open and receptive, whereas negative emotions indicate the presence of a barrier.

Lack of trust in the nurse leader/manager is a major barrier to communication. Trust is a firm reliance and confidence in the integrity and ability of another. Team members, for example, commit guidance of their activities into the care of a nurse manager and believe that the manager will maintain their trust. Relying on a person also implies a decision to accept the positive or negative consequences of the actions taken. Open communication is important to a free flow of information. The relationship between openness and trust has been emphasized since the 1930s when human relations advocates recognized that authoritarian practices created secretiveness and fear.

An open climate rests on a foundation of mutual trust. A study of employees in four organizations showed that the higher the trust in their manager, the more they believed that information received from the manager was accurate.[7]

There are three major barriers to the development of trust: (1) insincerity, when managers ask for feedback and do not value their members' opinions; (2) time, when the demands of task accomplishment preclude devoting time to hearing what the workers want to say; and (3) defensiveness, when the manager's ego is threatened by an open climate as a result of inadequate knowledge and skill or low self-image.[8]

Defensiveness can be aroused early in the sender or receiver if certain characteristics are present: evaluation (judgment), control (rules and regulations), strategy (manipulation), neutrality (noncaring), superiority, or certainty (dogmatic). Communication can be enhanced if these defenses are reduced. A supportive climate helps individuals concentrate more on the content and cognitive meaning of the message than on spending time searching for hidden meanings and innuendos. Supportive behaviors include description (presentation of message that gives facts without value judgment), problem orientation (a

desire to collaborate), spontaneity (freedom from deception), empathy (caring), equality (mutual trust and respect), and provisionalism (willingness to experiment and investigate).[7]

Communication between nurses and doctors can be positive or negative. I once worked with a patient who had multiple and serious problems. The attending physician bounded into the room, noted that I was new to the case, and began barking orders and criticizing the treatment. My first reaction was to retaliate angrily; however, I waited until we were alone in the chart room and said, "Doctor Lee, when you spoke to me as you did in Mrs. Fine's room, I felt very angry. I am a competent nurse, fully capable of meeting Mrs. Fine's needs. I felt you criticized me because you don't know me and because I perhaps have different ways of doing things. Am I correct is my assessment?" I used a nondefensive tone and attitude and simply stated facts and feelings. This strategy caught the usually abrasive doctor off guard. He looked at me as if for the first time, then responded, "I didn't realize that I came across that way. Please accept my apology." The use of defusing tactics helped. Using open, forthright communication in an area away from patients and distractions helped resolve the situation.

Semantic Barriers

The interpretation of messages through signs and symbols is often referred to as semantics. The importance of accurately encoding and decoding messages has been emphasized because information that is not clearly comprehended *(misinterpretation of meaning)* becomes a barrier in the communication process. Barriers in interpretation include defects in verbalizing, listening, telephoning, writing, and reading.

The ability to speak effectively *(verbal communication)* is a requisite for nurse managers. Oral communication requires one-to-one or face-to-face exchanges, fosters a cooperative spirit, and encourages feedback. The lower- or first-level nurse manager must develop verbal skill in one-to-one relationships and in leading small groups. Such skill supports the high value placed on group or participatory decision making.

A barrier in the communication process occurs when the manager has difficulties with his or her verbal skills. A constant challenge in communication is to develop a delivery that is inviting to hear and that avoids talking too much or too little. Some members may "tune out" unpleasant, confusing, or extreme numbers of messages (sensory overload). Others may not have enough information to perform well.

The following suggestions may improve a nurse manager's verbal communication skills: (1) clarify ideas before speaking; (2) consider the physical and human setting (time, place, and emotions); (3) use a tone of voice and choice of language that makes the desired impact; (4) speak clearly and to the point, using as little time as necessary for the communication to be effective; (5) repeat the key concepts of the message; (6) restate difficult messages; (7) recycle ideas wherever feedback indicates they are weak or misunderstood; and (8) use synonyms for the key words in an attempt to clarify.

Listening is "tuning in" or giving heed to something. It involves hearing but also includes thought processes. Eugene Raudsepp, Ph.D.,[6] believes that most people develop poor listening habits. Instead of listening, people allow their minds to wander and think of what to say next before the other person finishes talking. Such poor listening habits can cause misunderstandings on a busy nursing unit.

> EXAMPLE: April, a staff nurse, approaches the busy nurse manager and says, "Will you tell Dr. Fox when he comes that Mrs. Frazier needs a change of pain medication? I'll be busy in Room 402." "Uh-huh," the department manager replies, returning to his work. Dr. Fox comes and goes without receiving the message. April is angry, the patient's need is not served, and the nurse manager is upset with himself for not following through. Communication broke down because the nurse manager did not hear what was said. Had he really listened, he would have realized that he, too, might be busy when Dr. Fox arrived and would have requested April to leave a note for Dr. Fox in the patient's record.

Raudsepp[6] offers seven fundamental listening skills:

1. *Take time to listen.* Many people have difficulty expressing what they want to say, which makes careful listening essential for the receiver. If possible, set work aside and establish eye contact with the communicator. Provide cues of understanding by nodding or by asking questions as needed for clarification.

2. *Teach self to concentrate.* It is often easy to fix a gaze on someone who is speaking yet think about other things at the same time. One reason for this is that the thinking process is three to four times faster than a person's rate of talking. Pace the thinking process with the speaker's rate of speech; keep analyzing what he or she is saying.

3. *Do not interrupt.* The point of anticipating and summarizing the speaker's message is to help one concentrate on what he or she is saying, not to jump to a conclusion. Do not finish sentences for another person; this is a most effective way to break down communication. Apologize every time this happens, which will help to break the habit.

4. *Listen to what a person is saying, not how he or she is saying it.* Poor grammar, disorganized thought patterns, and slow speech can inhibit the listener from understanding the message. Instead of concentrating on delivery problems, think, "What is he saying that I need to know?"

5. *Suspend judgment.* Most people are convinced that they are correct in their thinking. Therefore, when ideas are presented that do not match one's own ideas and beliefs, the ideas tend to be tuned out. By not listening very carefully, one tends to hear only what one wants or expects to hear.

> EXAMPLE: Staff nurse Carol says, "Patients in this unit should be able to monitor their own oral medications. We should leave the medications in their rooms with instructions and simply record each day what they say they have taken." Carol also speaks of establishing standards of safety with dangerous drugs, educating patients before the use of the system, and documenting information on a medication flow chart. Fern does not agree with Carol's idea. With such a system she envisions danger and loss of control and as a result does not hear the latter part of Carol's idea.

6. *Listen between the lines.* People often speak of other things to hide the real message.

> EXAMPLE: Before each of the last three consecutive staff nurse meetings, Darrel told the department manager that he could not attend. He had a headache, an emergency came up, or he was tied up in traffic. The department manager observed that Darrel was rarely late or absent from work or

any other required function. She discussed the issue with the staff nurse and discovered that Darrel is afraid of being asked to serve on a committee or to contribute his views because he feels uncomfortable speaking in a formal setting. Understanding the underlying cause helped the department manager handle the problem.

7. *Listen with the eyes.* Facial expressions often communicate more than words. The department manager may say, "I'm glad you will be working with us," but averted eyes and a fixed expression belie his or her words. Look directly at the person who is speaking, which indicates a readiness and willingness to hear what is being said.

INFORMAL COMMUNICATION— THE GRAPEVINE

Informal or casual groups emerge whenever people come together and interact regularly. This type of communication is commonly called the **grapevine,** a term that was coined during the Civil War when intelligence telegraph lines were strung loosely from tree to tree in the manner of a grapevine. The messages were often garbled.[7]

Emergence

Rumors or grapevines emerge as a response to *important situations, ambiguity,* and other conditions that cause *anxiety.* Work situations frequently contain these three elements, which explains why rumors flourish in organizations. A rumor persists until the desires and expectations creating the uncertainty are fulfilled or until the anxiety is reduced.[7]

Process

Davis and Newstrom,[8] two of the foremost authorities on informal communication, have written some pertinent information about the grapevine process:

1. The grapevine is a social interaction that fulfills people's needs for communication and recognition. It is as varied as the people who communicate within it.
2. The grapevine is based on a natural motiva-

tion to exchange information. If members of a work team do not talk informally about their work and the people involved, they are probably disinterested.
3. The grapevine occurs at all levels in an organization in horizontal, vertical, and diagonal patterns.
4. The grapevine is extremely influential, shapes people's attitudes, and has the capacity to carry helpful and harmful information to the organization.
5. The grapevine has an unusual ability to discover even the most tightly guarded organizational secrets.
6. Employees become active in the grapevine when they have news that is fresh and "hot."
7. The grapevine can become active when information is of high interest to the individual and when messages regarding that interest are vague or unclear. If a subject has no interest to a person, then that person has no cause to rumor about it. If the individual knows enough facts to be satisfied there is no need to set rumor in motion.
8. The source and believability of information directly affects the strength and duration of the grapevine. The greater the believability, the more legitimate the grapevine becomes.
9. In organizations the grapevine is more a product of situation than personality. The grapevine flourishes wherever anticipation or fear becomes dominant within an organization, such as when a major change in the agency's management causes fear of transfer or dismissal or uncertainty regarding wages and benefits. The grapevine can also thrive when an individual member becomes known for some achievement, either good or bad.

Use

According to Davis and Newstrom,[8] the accuracy of the grapevine in normal situations tends to be approximately 75%. Inaccurate information may lead to serious problems. Often only part of the story is shared. Managers sometimes hope the grapevine will go away, but it will not. Informal communication channels emerge whether or not managers encourage them. If suppressed, the grapevine emerges in another place or in another form. The best approach for managers is to offset a negative impact by using the grapevine to help the organization as much as possible. The nurse manager can use the following methods:

1. Keep staff as well informed as possible concerning relevant work-related issues.
2. Maintain an open communication system that encourages feedback.
3. Listen and learn from the grapevine. Learn who the leaders are, how the grapevine operates, and what information it carries. The object is to determine what is important to nursing staff members. Once omissions in information or false messages are identified, strategies can be developed to heighten areas of satisfaction and to reduce anxiety, conflict, and misunderstanding.
4. Try to influence the grapevine by giving relevant information to liaison or key people. This strategy is especially necessary when the grapevine has been spreading incomplete or inaccurate information such as possible layoffs, transfers, or mandatory rotation of shifts.

In management the nurse leader must discourage the development and use of grapevines for work-related matters and promote the use of formal communication channels. The effective nurse manager recognizes the need for informal communication and uses the grapevine to enhance organizational goals.

HEALTH COMMUNICATION MODEL

Peter Northouse and Laurel Northouse[9] have constructed a **health communication model** that illustrates the transactions between healthcare workers regarding health-related issues (Figure 8-3). This model takes a broader systems view of communication and shows how a series of factors can affect interactions within healthcare settings. Three important variables of the health communication process are highlighted: (1) relationships, (2) transactions, and (3) contexts.

Relationships

Four major types of relationships exist in healthcare settings: professional-professional, professional-client, professional-significant other, and client-significant other. In this model the health professional is any person who has the education, training, and experience to provide services to others. Health professionals include nurses, social workers, administrators, physicians, and therapists.

Transactions

Transactions refer to the health-related verbal and nonverbal interactions that occur between

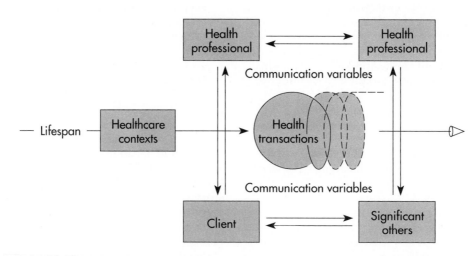

FIGURE 8-3. Health communication model. (Northouse P, Northouse L: Health communication: strategies for health professionals, ed 2, Norwalk, Conn, 1992, Appleton & Lange. Used with permission.)

participants in the health communication process. In the center of the model, health transactions are illustrated by a circle from which an unending spiral emerges. This spiral indicates the ongoing, transactional nature of health communication, which can occur at different times and at different points in the life of a person or organization. The feedback loop of communication is implied and allows for assimilation of messages and appropriate changes as new understandings are acquired. Communication variables are referred to at the top and bottom of the model and include factors such as empathy, control, trust, self-disclosure, and confirmation.

Contexts

Context refers to the settings in which health communication takes place such as intensive care units, homes, hospices, clinics, hospitals, skilled facilities, and schools. Context also refers to the number and nature of individuals or groups involved in communication. Communication can be one-to-one, in small groups or teams, or in large groups of people; each type of communication has a mission. A third contextual factor is the delivery system in effect such as primary care, team nursing, functional plan, or case management. In the healthcare communication model, relationships, transactions, and contexts

offer a systems perspective on communication in healthcare. The model illustrates a way to integrate the basic communication process illustrated in Figure 8-1 with the complexities of the current healthcare system. As nurse managers move through the systems in their various settings, they can use these models to improve or use more effectively their communication techniques and strategies.

MANAGEMENT FUNCTIONS AND COMMUNICATIONS

Formal channels of communication are very important in organizations. Leaders and managers determine the work climate and influence the attitudes of staff members. Figure 8-4 illustrates the roles of communication in the managerial process. There are four forms of necessary managerial communication: downward, upward, horizontal, and diagonal.[3]

Downward Communication

As noted in Chapter 2, downward communication is a significant type of communication and is recognized by managers of the classical school. There are several important reasons for downward communication: (1) to provide information

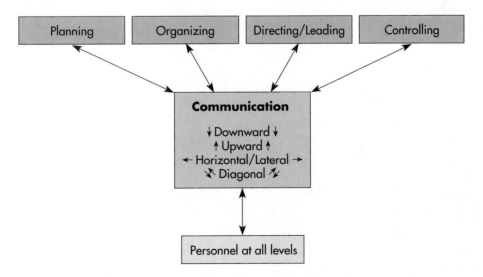

FIGURE 8-4. Management functions and types of communication channels.

about the mission and goals of the organization, (2) to state what is expected of the individual or group, (3) to explain the extent of the worker's authority and responsibility, (4) to define the role of the manager and how his or her job relates to others, (5) to outline the procedures, policies, and practices in effect, and (6) to provide performance feedback (Figure 8-5).

Two basic methods of downward communication within the healthcare organization are oral and written. Oral communication is provided quickly and in a direct, face-to-face manner. Listeners often believe that the information must be important and correct if they are spoken to directly. The major problem with oral communication is that one cannot remember everything that is said and that what is remembered can be distorted, such as in the grapevine. Written methods of communication are more formal and perma-

nent. However, if there are too many things to read, employees tend to skim through them or not read them at all. Written words can also be impersonal and lack immediacy. To ensure effective downward communication, it is best to combine these two methods by first communicating orally if possible and then following up in writing. Be sure the content is accurate, specific, forceful, meaningful, easy to understand, and without hidden meanings.

Upward Communication

With the advent of the human relations movement, management began to turn its attention to the social needs of employees. This focus led to the introduction of formal upward communication channels, which allow information to flow from worker to those in authority. This two-way

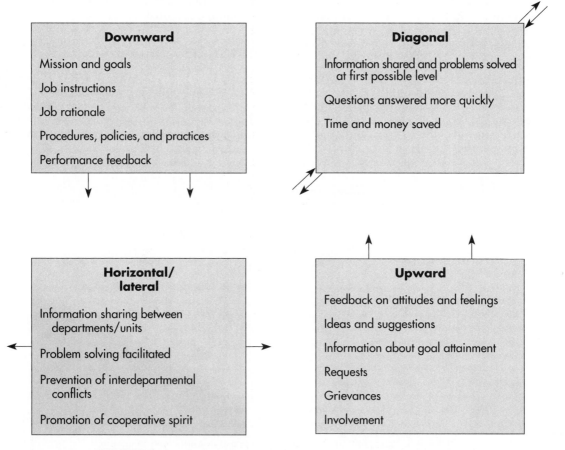

FIGURE 8-5. Outcomes of four organizational communication channels.

system greatly helps the nurse manager learn what is happening in the healthcare system.

The main benefits of upward communication include (1) feedback regarding employee attitudes and feelings, (2) suggestions for improvement and new ideas, (3) information about goal attainment, (4) requests for supplies, assistance, and support, (5) the sharing of employee grievances before small problems erupt into major ones, and (6) stronger employee involvement in their organization and in their roles (Figure 8-5). Problems may arise if employees fear reprisal, if they believe that ideas may be filtered until the meaning is changed, or if the manager gives the impression that he or she does not have time to listen to what employees need to say.

Horizontal/Lateral Communication

Horizontal or lateral communication occurs between people who are at the same level of the formal structure. Horizontal communication is very important to the nurse supervisor, nurse manager, and nurse case manager for several reasons:

1. It is the primary method of coordinating efforts between interdependent units and departments. Without effective horizontal channels a case manager cannot arrange to move the client easily through the healthcare system.
2. Socialization of people occurs in the horizontal communication process, which gives staff a sense of camaraderie and belonging.
3. Horizontal communication is the primary method of information sharing. It allows peers to share communication regularly and therefore prevents hoarding of information.
4. Horizontal communication facilitates problem solving. It allows people and units to learn from one another.
5. Horizontal communication prevents the interdepartmental conflict that can result from misconceptions, communication distortions, and misunderstandings (Figure 8-5). It promotes a cooperative spirit across the organization and lessens the "we-they" attitude that can develop among interdependent units.

Diagonal Communication

Diagonal communication occurs between people who are at different levels of the organizational hierarchy and in different departments or units. For example, a quality assurance nurse may communicate regularly with the directors, supervisors, managers, and staff of any department within the healthcare system in an effort to resolve a problem. Diagonal communication (1) strengthens open communication and participative management, and (2) facilitates the operation of interdepartmental coordination. Diagonal communication nurtures an organizational culture in which cooperation is valued and internal competition is discouraged. It also saves the agency time and money. As Figure 8-5 indicates, by moving up, down, and horizontally through the organizational hierarchy, questions are answered, information is shared, and problems are solved at the first possible level. However, an employee who skips a level risks offending supervisors and others who may believe they should have been involved in the communication. Employees should always inform all people involved in the process so that communication gaps do not occur.

TEAMS AND TEAMWORK

For quite some time, healthcare organizations have used **teams** to solve problems, coordinate activities, and accomplish tasks. Recently there has been an increased interest in team and teamwork as a result of competitive and technologic forces. The quality movement has identified "continuous improvement" as a must.[10] This is often accomplished through the use of teams, which are viewed by organizations as an effective and efficient way to get work done.

A nurse manager is expected to build an efficient and enthusiastic team. To accomplish this task, the manager must know what a team is and how it functions. Sovie[11] provides a working definition: "A team is a distinguishable set of two or more individuals who interact interdependently and adaptively to achieve specified, shared and valued objectives."[p.278] In Chapter 5, team nursing was defined as a system of care in which a professional nurse leads a group of healthcare personnel in providing for the health needs of an individual or group of people through collaborative and cooperative effort. Teamwork is rapidly expanding to include groups of people who do not work together but come together from different departments or units to perform a specific task or project. The groups may be problem-solving teams created to answer a specific question (e.g., Why is the ageny's newborn number decreasing when the general population is on the increase?) or cross-functional teams created to perform a specific project such as determining how quality can be maintained or increased in the pharmacy while reducing costs. These kinds of teams are usually mandated by administration and are authorized to be self-managing within boundaries. Another type of cross-functional team is that of case management, in which the manager moves freely throughout the system to achieve client-care goals; this type of teamwork functions on an ongoing basis. Effective communication is vital to the success of all teams.

Polarity Management
Individuality versus teamwork

In the standards of the Joint Commission of Accreditation of Healthcare Organizations, administrators are instructed to maintain organizational responsibility for standard setting and overall goal achievement, yet they are also instructed to collaborate and share specific areas of decision making, accountability, and responsibility with nurse managers and staff members. Keenan,

Hurst, and Olnhausen[12] see this statement as contradictory in that the nursing staff is to be empowered to make decisions but the administrators are to control the results. They see this situation as a polarity, or separation, that exists between managerial control and self-direction of the nursing staff. They believe that **polarity management,** or bringing the groups together, can help with decision making, promote collaboration, and build effective work teams. Collaboration between management and staff is a commitment to identify and acknowledge areas of interdependence and to recognize that all have a part in achieving ongoing and changing goals of quality care. These authors see polarity management as a teeter-totter with ups and downs and back-and-forth movement (Figure 8-6).

In polarity management, the problems are viewed as active, dynamic, and ever-changing. Polarities shift back and forth between the two poles like the teeter-totter. Polarities do not offer an "either-or" choice but instead require "both-and" choices that consider the two opinions. A problem-solver may select one or two solutions, implement them, and be finished, whereas the polarity manager analyzes and weighs the potential outcomes for both poles, implements the activities that tend to support a balance between both poles, and returns to determine if a long-term balance is being maintained.

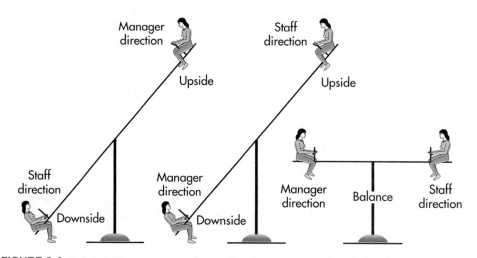

FIGURE 8-6. Polarity management: individuality versus teamwork. (Modified from Keenan M, Hurst J, Olnhausen K: Polarity management for quality care: self-direction and manager direction, *Nurs Adm Q* 18[1]:23-29, 1993.)

Achieving balance through polarity management

In polarity management the first step for the team of managers and staff is to identify the task or problem and then identify the two opposing sides of the dilemma. For example, in Figure 8-7 the team is presented with the issue of reducing the number of professional nursing staff while increasing the number of assistive personnel in a skilled nursing facility. The next step is to list the positive (upside) and negative (downside) implications of the proposal. It is much easier to list what one believes in rather than an unpreferred position or opposing view.

The next step in the polarity management process is to engage in team building. Using effective communication strategies, the group looks for similarities in their opinions. In Figure 8-7 both management and staff believe that a reduction in professional nursing staff and an increase in assistive personnel will give more power to the professional nurse, allow more opportunities to teach and mentor assistive staff, and reduce costs. Both management and staff are concerned about quality of care and a possible inability to collaborate with other nurse professionals. During the process of reaching a balance, the team gives each person an equal opportunity

Issue: Reduction of the number of professional nursing staff, with an increase in the number of assistive personnel in a skilled facility.

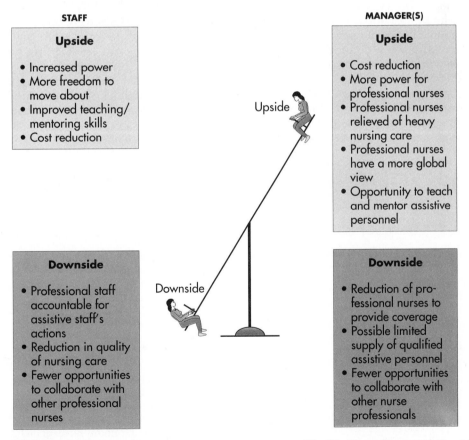

STAFF

Upside
- Increased power
- More freedom to move about
- Improved teaching/ mentoring skills
- Cost reduction

Downside
- Professional staff accountable for assistive staff's actions
- Reduction in quality of nursing care
- Fewer opportunities to collaborate with other professional nurses

MANAGER(S)

Upside
- Cost reduction
- More power for professional nurses
- Professional nurses relieved of heavy nursing care
- Professional nurses have a more global view
- Opportunity to teach and mentor assistive personnel

Downside
- Reduction of professional nurses to provide coverage
- Possible limited supply of qualified assistive personnel
- Fewer opportunities to collaborate with other nurse professionals

FIGURE 8-7. Example of the polarity management process. (Modified from Keenan M, Hurst J, Olnhausen K: Polarity management for quality care: self-direction and manager direction, *Nurs Adm Q,* 18(1):23-29, 1993.

to participate in influencing the agenda and in making decisions. The team also recognizes that conflict is a factor that can strengthen team relationships if handled appropriately (see Chapter 9). As a result, outcomes can be determined together, and the team knows that the balance achieved is subject to ups and downs.

Team Building with Registered Nurses and Nursing Assistants

Another approach to polarity management is demonstrated in the following example. One general hospital decided to use **team building** to improve work relationships between registered nurses (RNs) and nursing assistants (NAs).[13] The RNs and NAs who were to participate in the sessions worked closely together for a period of time. This association alone helped achieve a climate of cooperation and clearer communication. A series of team-building meetings followed and were conducted on three units where work-related relationships needs were identified (Box 8-1).

Notice that there are some commonalities in the team building process. Both RNs and NAs want to feel secure and give and receive feedback. However, there is a decided polarity in perceptions regarding whether or not the NAs feel wanted, needed, and valued. Views were clarified through discussion and relationships were improved through purposeful effort and practice. Both RNs and NAs need clear expectations when working together, and RNs must have legitimate authority over the NAs. Recommendations from the team-building sessions included clarifying expectations and conflicting perceptions, as well as teaching RNs how to better supervise and mentor NAs and confront inappropriate behaviors (see Chapters 9 and 11).

CROSS-CULTURAL COMMUNICATION

Cultural Diversity

The 1970s and 1980s were times of dynamic social change that profoundly affected the health-care delivery system. The Vietnam War ended in the 1970s and thousands of refugees from Vietnam, Cambodia, and Laos fled to the United States. Along with their social and personal problems came a system of traditional health and illness beliefs and practices. People are presently flocking to the United States from Mexico, Cen-

---

Box 8-1.   Results of team-building session for registered nurses and nursing assistants

WORK-RELATED RELATIONSHIPS

Needs that assistive personnel have from registered nurses

A feeling of belonging
Recognition
Self-worth
Control, suggestions and impressions listened to and acted on

Needs that registered nurses have from nursing assistants

To feel secure that assigned activities will be completed as requested
Feedback from assignments

Perceptions

Not welcome as team members
Not recognized as individuals
RNs would prefer to work alone
Contribution to patient care and the nursing unit not valued
Want to be team members and contribute meaningfully

Perceptions

Could not run the unit without NAs
What NAs do makes a difference in patient comfort and feelings
What NAs do makes a difference to the RN
NAs are critical of RN's work
NAs prefer not to be team members

Modified from Hayes P: Team building: bringing RNs and NAs together, Nurs Manage, 25(5):52-54, 1994.

tral and South America, and Eastern Europe. Healthcare delivery agencies are struggling to meet the needs of the tremendous numbers of clients from these countries.

Among this influx of people are many nurses and assistive nursing personnel who have become registered in the United States. Coupled with this situation are the many diverse groups of people born in this country who comprise a significant number of nursing personnel. The nurse manager must take into consideration people of differing ages, cultural and geographic origins, abilities, and genders. Other factors, including varied lifestyles, personalities, and family arrangements affect each individual's performance.[4]

Most nurse managers in the United States are white and middle class. Almost all of them are naive in their knowledge about and awareness of the racial and ethnic differences among their staff and how these variables can become problem areas. To be effective leaders, managers must provide an environment that encourages the performance of all individual leaders, and management practices must be flexible enough to accommodate diverse individuals.

Intercultural Relations

Each relationship, group, organization, and society has a culture that is somewhat unique. Culture is defined as "that complex whole which includes knowledge, belief, art, law, morals, customs, and any capabilities and habits acquired by an individual as a member of society; it is a way of life of a group of people, the configuration of all the more or less stereotyped patterns of learned behavior, which are handed down from one generation to the next through the means of language and imitation."[14,pp.14-15]

As people engage in communication, they are contributing to the creation or maintenance of cultural mores. Each time people behave in a culturally consistent manner by adhering to customs, following conventional modes of dress or speech, or using a traditional greeting or gesture, they are helping to reinforce and perpetuate that culture. People tend to assume that their cultural practices are *correct*, whereas contrasting cultures are often regarded as *wrong* rather than

simply *different*. When people move to a new country, locale, relationship, or job, they go through a process of adaptation as they learn to fit themselves within the new culture. They may experience culture shock, depending on their own expectations and adaptability and on the degree of difference between the previous and new circumstances.

Cross-cultural communication occurs when a person from one culture correctly understands a message sent by a person from another culture. Cross-cultural miscommunication occurs when the person from the second culture receives but misinterprets the sender's intended message. Every communication situation is somewhat intercultural because no two people have precisely the same cultural backgrounds. The greater the difference in cultural backgrounds, the greater the communication challenges and the less likely that the message sent will be the message received.[14]

Influence of Culture on Communication

J.D. England defines culture as something that is shared by all or most members of some group, something that the older members try to pass on to the younger members, and something (as in the case of rules, morals, values, customs, and attitudes) that is imposed on the group members, shapes their behavior, and structures their perception of the world.[15] Individuals express culture and its normative qualities through the values they hold about life and the world around them. These values affect their attitudes regarding which behaviors are appropriate and effective in a given situation. As behaviors, attitudes, and values are shared, people change, and the cyclic process begins again (Figure 8-8).

Cultural Blindness

Cultural diversity affects the way people function within an organization. Nancy Adler,[14] a professor and student of cultural diversity, states that cultural norms, especially in North America, encourage members to blind themselves to gender, race, and ethnicity; to see people only as individuals; and to judge them according to their pro-

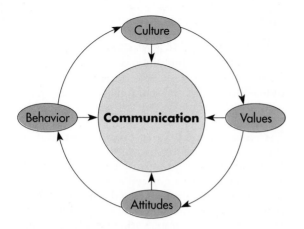

FIGURE 8-8. Influence of culture on communication. (Modified from Adler N: *International dimensions of organizational behavior,* ed 2, Belmont, Calif, 1991, Wadsworth Publishing.)

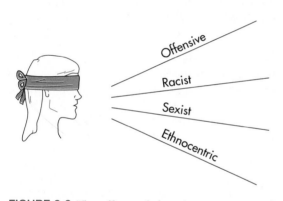

FIGURE 8-9. The effects of choosing not to see cultural differences and judging cultural diversity as good or bad. (Modified from Adler N: International dimensions of organizational behavior, ed 2, Belmont, Calif, 1991, Wadsworth Publishing.)

fessional skills. Although this is believed to be a democratic attitude, Adler is convinced that this approach causes problems because it confuses recognition with judgment. *Recognition* occurs when a manager recognizes differences in behavior, values, and attitudes. However, *judging* cultural differences as good or bad can lead to offensive, racist, sexist, and ethnocentric attitudes and behaviors (Figure 8-9). With any form of cultural diversity, management must make an effort to recognize cultural diversity without judging it

and to see difference where difference exists. Adler believes that choosing not to recognize cultural diversity limits the manager's ability to minimize the problems it causes and maximize the advantages it allows.

Effective Cross-Cultural Communication

Effective communication is difficult under the best of conditions. Adapting to the culture of another person or group requires the development of personal theories, representations, maps, and images of the cultures. As the nurse manager meets and works with new people, he or she enters into new relationships and new relational cultures. Efforts to improve the manager's individual communication skills can help bridge the culture gap. The first steps in the cross-cultural communication process involve:

- Having respect, empathy, tolerance, and nonjudgmental attitudes for people with different behaviors, values, and attitudes.
- Obtaining knowledge of the cultures of the people or group involved in communication.
- Being sensitive to cultural differences in language, conversation, and nonverbal rules.
- Developing a capacity to balance the task-oriented managerial role with the support-oriented managerial role.[1]

The following actions can help reduce misconceptions, misinterpretations, and misevaluations of people and groups from different cultures:

- Assume differences until similarity is proven.
- Emphasize description rather than interpretation or evaluation. Nurses are mandated to record client progress in descriptive and nonjudgmental terms, and they are to be nonjudgmental when assessing people and groups of other cultures and backgrounds. As a result, judgment can be delayed until there is sufficient time to observe and interpret the situation from the perspective of the culture involved.
- Treat interpretations as a working hypothesis. Test assumptions for validity and encourage feedback from people of differing

cultures to see if it confirms these interpretations.[7]

⧉ THE GENDER FACTOR IN NURSING

A Profession Traditionally Held by Women

Most RNs are women and function in a healthcare society in which physicians and top administrators are predominantly men.[16] Although in the past few years the proportion of male RNs has increased sharply from approximately 3% to 11% of all RNs, male RNs remain a distinct minority. These men experience many kinds of discrimination in their roles as professional nurses and are sometimes labeled as effeminate or as a usurper of women's territory. A higher percentage of male nurses are advanced to managerial roles, which tends to create friction among female nurses. Male nurses have proven themselves to be highly capable in caregiving and in nursing administration. Female RNs need to increase their understanding and acceptance of male nurses. However, they must also make sure that gender discrimination is not allowed.

Gender Differences in Verbal Communication

Researchers have identified differences between men and women in their use of language in conversation.[16] The areas of differences include (1) initiation, (2) verbosity (amount of talking) and interruptions, (3) conversational maintenance and question asking, and (4) vocabulary.

Initiation

Women generally spend more time initiating support or meeting expectations for turn taking.

Verbosity and interruptions

Women tend to be more talkative than men when giving instructions or engaging in conversation. Women also exhibit more impatience than men as evidenced by their frequent interruptions of others' comments.

Conversational maintenance and question asking

Women generally spend more time and effort facilitating the continuation of conversation. When researchers analyzed tapes of actual conversations, they found that women asked 70% of the questions.

Vocabulary

Studies show that women use a larger vocabulary to discuss topics about which they have greater interest and experience. In areas where men have greater expertise, their vocabularies are broader. An example is the male physician and female nurse talking about the intricacies of a medical condition.

⧉ INFORMATION AND COMPUTER TECHNOLOGY IN NURSING

Estimates show that nurses generate over 50% of patient care information. Data collection and information management are time-consuming; time management studies show that such activities consume over 30% of a nurse's time. Most systems in use are based in technology from the 1960s, which focuses primarily on basic tracking systems and financial charges.[17] However, imagine a single device that can list patient intake data; record vital signs; help make a nursing diagnosis and assess acuity level; organize the work lists for each shift; notify dietary, laboratory, and other departments of a client's need; track outcomes, and search literature for answers to clinical dilemmas. The technology for all this and much more exists now, yet only a few healthcare agencies nationwide have systems that feature many of these advanced functions. Cost is a major factor, but so is the lack of availabilty of computers and software. Many manufacturers are just beginning to design computers with nurses and other providers in mind.[18]

Nursing Informatics

In 1989 nursing informatics defined the field in the *Journal of Nursing Scholarship:* "Nursing informatics is a combination of computer science, information science, and nursing science, designed to assist in the management and processing of nursing data, information, and knowledge to support the practice of nursing and the delivery of nursing care."[18,p.18]

Many kinds of messages are sent and received within healthcare environments. From the clinical perspective, nurses follow standards of care that are developed by professional organizations. These standards facilitate clear communication among nurses, consumers, and members of other disciplines. The electronic transmission and exchange of clinical information must also have a standard to ensure that messages arrive and are decoded correctly.[19]

The 14th Annual Nursing Management Congress was held in 1993. At this Congress the first Nursing Informatics Conference had approximately 250 participants, who discussed ethical issues, national certification of nursing informatics, the Nursing Minimum Data Set, case studies, software development, and computer technology. Heavy emphasis was placed on supporting the nurse manager with applied technology. Mary McHugh, chair of the American Nurses Association Council on Computer Applications in Nursing (CCAN), addressed the assembly regarding the status of national certification in nursing informatics by saying that the first certification examination was to begin in 1995.[20]

Nursing informatics programs

The University of Maryland in Baltimore and the University of Utah in Salt Lake City offer graduate programs in nursing informatics. The University of California San Francisco and the University of Virginia in Charlottesville offer informatics subspecialties within doctoral programs in nursing administration. The University of Texas at Austin offers a specialty in informatics within its nursing master's degree.[18]

Potential job market for informaticians

The University of Maryland surveyed the potential job market for nurse informatics specialists, or nurse informaticians. Of the 128 healthcare facilities surveyed, almost half already employed nurses in computer/information management positions, and two thirds of the remaining facilities anticipated a need for nurses in these positions within 5 years.[18]

Use of informatics systems in community and home healthcare

Almost any community nurse or home health nurse will describe documentation as the most frustrating part of clinic or home healthcare. Because of the prominent position held by Medicare and numerous preferred provider groups, forms ranging from one to several pages must be completed for each client visit. Correct and accurate completion of these forms is the key to reimbursement. Also important for reimbursement is documentation of the quality of care provided and the ability of the patient and family to manage the care at home.[21] Community health nurses were among the first to have good information systems in the 1960s. They now use computer systems, depending on available funds and informatics systems knowledge and expertise.

Handheld patient documentation and support system

An Atlanta-based patient care technology company is marketing a handheld point-of-care computer that is specifically designed for clinical documentation while the work is being done. It weighs only 14 ounces and can be programmed with only one hand. Each computer can hold a day's schedule of patient charts, including each patient's care history to date. Information is loaded from a DOS PC-based server using provided software. Nurses can use compact modems to retrieve charts from any location that has an available standard phone jack. Updated and current information is sent back to the server during or after the day's activity. The system produces progress notes, care plans, physician's orders, clinical referrals, patient medication profiles, and a variety of administrative and scheduling reports. Patient charges and administrative information such as payroll hours and mileage are also collected on the handheld computer.[22]

PURCHASE, DEVELOPMENT, AND IMPLEMENTATION OF AN INFORMATION SYSTEM

Technology in various levels of development and use are all available today. Most healthcare agency information systems are not current or are virtually nonexistent. Therefore nurse administrators must be prepared to develop their own systems or to contract others to do it for or with them. In all cases the nurse manager who is submitting a proposal for the purchase and implementation of an information system should seek help from those who have the ability and knowledge to meet departmental needs. Experts who are already on staff throughout the agency can be tapped for assistance, consultants can be hired, or salesmen representing information systems can provide help. Roy Simpson,[23] an information systems specialist, advises nurses to look at their own nursing department and how it interacts with other departments in the organization. Thoroughly understanding the mission, long-range financial and product plans, building and technology plans, and overall vision of the hospital or healthcare agency is necessary. He cautions the nurse manager to be certain that the desired proposal for a system is consistent with the overall strategic plan of the organization. The assessment must include a review of what is already in place and how it fits the manager's plans for another system.

Operational and Implementation Plan

Simpson[24] outlines the following plan, which he compares to a roadmap; it helps the nurse manager reach his or her goal without running into unnecessary detours:

- Review short- and long-term objectives and establish timelines for implementation. Include how staffing and facility resources would be affected.
- Name the departments that would be involved. Will there be a test site?
- Itemize every piece of major equipment that is needed, including hardware, software, and additional telephones and lines.
- Project how staffing will be affected during each stage of the implementation. List the staff who play key roles in the process.
- List costs for everything. Include additional phone bills, office furniture, staff, and training costs.
- Formulate a plan for evaluation and control. Explain how quality will be maintained during the implementation time.
- Develop a financial plan and schedule (staffing, expenses, capital expenditures, and miscellaneous items). Have no hidden costs or agenda; they must be faced sooner or later.

Introducing Nurses to Computers

Kathleen Herrick and Sandra McCullough,[25] information systems analysts at Sharp Health Care in San Diego, California, say that educating nurses in the use of computers does not sound difficult until one considers a multihospital environment with varying nursing structures and a mandatory implementation period. Acceptance and proper use of computers and coordination between nursing and all concerned in the provision of healthcare are vital to successful implementation of the system. Most large health agencies begin to orient their nursing staffs at least 1 year before activating a computer system. Because many nurses do not have computer skills, most educational departments use commercially available programs to teach the basics and rely on experienced staff for hands-on training. Time is needed to learn new systems. Computers are strange and threatening to some people. Without adequate preparation, the computer system may fail and result in great expense and lost potential. For example, in a large hospital where nurses are expected to be on-line with a new computer system in approximately 6 months, nurse managers meet regularly and learn the system. The next step is to orient the nursing staff through the nursing education department and to introduce the system one nursing unit at a time.

Whatever the future brings, nurse managers will play a key role in designing computer systems and programs to better meet their needs and the needs of their staff and patients during the 1990s. This is an exciting and challenging opportunity.

Summary

1. Communication has been described as the practical art of persuasion, including rhetoric and public speaking. In the 1970s group, organizational, political, international, and intercultural communication emerged as distinct areas of study.

2. Interpersonal communication involves passing a message from one person to another or within a small group of people with the intention that the message will be received and understood as intended.

3. Effective communication is accomplished when clarity and accuracy are sufficient to influence desired actions toward the welfare of the enterprise.

4. The communication process serves as the foundation that the nurse manager uses to achieve organizational objectives. Effective communication between nurse-nurse, nurse-physician, and all others leads to influence and power.

5. An effective communication model consists of sender, receiver, message, encoding, transmitting, decoding, action, and continuous feedback.

6. The nurse manager's message should have a reason or goal that consists of a fact, idea, or feeling.

7. Encoding means translating a message into verbal and nonverbal symbols that will communicate the intended meaning to the receiver(s).

8. Transmitting involves the channel used to communicate the message and includes speech, written word, electronic media, and action.

9. Decoding is the process whereby the receiver perceives and interprets the sender's message into meaningful information. The effectiveness of the communication process depends greatly on commonality of experiences.

10. Action is the behavior taken by the receiver as a result of the message sent, received, and perceived. Communication is not successful until the message received has been understood and acted on appropriately.

11. Feedback is a continuous two-way process wherein sender(s) and receiver(s) exchange information and clarify meanings of messages. The greater the complexity of information, the greater the need for feedback.

12. Accurate feedback is best achieved with face-to-face communication; simple and direct language; and sensitivity to the individual's values, needs, attitudes, and expectations.

13. Effective feedback between managers and staff is characterized by proper timing, a focus on specific behaviors, and tact.

14. Three types of barriers to effective communication occur in nursing services: physical, social-psychologic, and semantics (interpretation of meanings).

15. Physical barriers consist of environmental factors such as space or distance, temperature and ventilation, structure and equipment, and distracting noises.

16. Noise that obscures or reduces the clarity or quality of a message interferes with the communication process and must be corrected.

17. Social-psychologic barriers are those blocks that arise from judgments, emotions, and social values. Communication cannot be separated from personality and social implications because whatever emotion dominates a person at the time affects the communication process.

18. A major barrier to communication in the nursing management process is lack of trust in the leader/manager. Distrust results when the manager is insincere, fails to devote enough time to the members, and is defensive.

19. Establishing supportive climates with behaviors such as description, problem orientation, spontaneity, empathy, equality, and provisionalism motivates members to participate in the work assignments.

20. Semantics occurs in the encoding and decoding process. Barriers arise when there are defects in verbalizing and listening.

21. Fundamental listening skills include taking time to listen, concentrating on the messenger and not interrupting; listening to *what* is being said, not *how* it is said; suspending judgment; listening be-

tween the lines; and listening with one's eyes.

22. Informal or casual communication, commonly called the grapevine, is a social interaction that occurs outside established organizational channels.

23. Rumors or grapevines emerge in response to important situations, ambiguity, and anxiety.

24. The source and believability of information directly affects the strength and duration of the grapevine. Grapevine information is usually about 75% accurate.

25. The effective nurse manager can use the grapevine advantageously by maintaining an open and trusting relationship by using formal communication channels and by giving pertinent information to liaison or key people.

26. In management, four forms of communication occur: downward (from top management down), upward (from staff and lower- and middle-management up), horizontal/lateral (between people at the same level), and diagonal (between people at different levels and in different departments or units).

27. The healthcare communication process includes a study of relationships, transactions, and contexts in which health communication occurs.

28. A team is a distinguishable set of two or more individuals who interact interdependently and adaptively to achieve specified, shared, and valued objectives. Effective communication is vital to the success of all teams.

29. Polarity management resolves the differences between managerial control and self-direction and can be used as a tool for decision making and as a means for promoting collaboration and building effective work teams.

30. Polarity management involves identifying the task or problem and giving each person an equal opportunity to participate in influencing the agenda and in making decisions.

31. Since the 1970s dynamic social changes have occurred in the United States and have significantly affected the healthcare system. Refugees from war-torn countries have come in droves and have brought with them a multitude of social, personal, and health problems.

32. Effective nurse managers must be aware of cultural diversity in accommodating all individuals and groups within the healthcare scene.

33. Each relationship, group, organization, and society has a culture that is somewhat unique. Culture is defined as that complex whole that includes knowledge, beliefs, art, laws, morals, customs, and any capabilities and habits acquired by a member of society. Culture is a way of life of a group of people, and it is the configuration of all the more or less stereotyped patterns of learned behavior that are handed down from one generation to the next through language and imitation.

34. People tend to assume that their cultural practices are correct and right, whereas contrasting cultures are often regarded as wrong rather than simply different.

35. Cross-cultural communication occurs when a person from one culture understands a message that is sent from a person of another culture.

36. Individuals express culture and its normative qualities through the values they hold about life and the world around them. These values affect their attitudes regarding appropriate and effective behaviors in a given situation. As these values are shared, people change, and the cyclic process begins again.

37. Recognition occurs when a manager recognizes differences in behavior, values, and attitudes. Judging cultural differences as good or bad can lead to offensive, racist, sexist, and ethnocentric attitudes and behaviors.

38. Adapting to a culture of another person or group involves the development of personal theories, representations, maps, and images of the culture.

39. The cross-cultural communication process includes having respect, empathy, and tolerance for and nonjudgmental attitudes toward people with different behaviors, values, and attitudes.

40. Problems with people and groups from different cultures can be reduced if one assumes differences until similarities are proven, emphasizes description rather than interpretation or evaluation, and treats interpretations as a working hypothesis until they are confirmed.

41. Nurses generate over 50% of patient care information, which consumes over 30% of their nursing time.

42. Nursing informatics is a combination of computer science, information science, and nursing science and is designed to support the practice of nursing care by helping to manage and process nursing data, information, and knowledge.

43. National certification of nurse informaticians began in 1995. The job market for this group is promising.

44. Nurse managers must be prepared to develop their own information systems or to seek assistance from others to do it for or with them.

45. An operational and implementation plan for an information system reviews short- and long-term objectives, establishes timelines for implementation, names all departments involved, itemizes every piece of necessary equipment, projects how staffing will be affected, lists costs for everything, formulates a plan for evaluation and control, and develops a financial plan and schedule. The plan must have no hidden agenda.

46. Time is needed to learn new systems. Most large healthcare agencies begin to orient their nursing staffs at least 1 year before activating a computer system.

? Questions for Study and Discussion

1. Describe in your own words what comprises an effective interpersonal communication system.

2. Diagram an effective communication model from memory.

3. You have just attended a morning team conference and are mulling over one of the instructions for care. Which part of the communication process is in effect? If you do not understand what to do, which part of the communication model should you use?

4. In your daily face-to-face contact with others, which link in the communication process tends to be weakest? Why? What corrective action could you take?

5. Think of a situation that could be a serious communication problem for a nurse manager.

6. What kinds of communication barriers can block the transfer of understanding in the classroom? Can any of your responses apply to a nursing unit? Explain.

7. You feel hurried, yet you need to hear what your supervisor is saying. What can you do to help yourself understand the message?

8. How can a nurse manager best use the grapevine?

9. Refer to the healthcare model in the text on p. 198. Discuss how the model might be used by the nurse in a large hospital to effectively communicate with a social worker.

10. You are a case manager and want to plan care for a client from admission through discharge. Which communication channel would be most appropriate for this effort? Explain.

11. Building teams is important to you as a nurse manager. However, you recognize that some of your staff prefer to exercise their individuality rather than take direction from a manager. How could you achieve an acceptable balance?

12. At work you are assigned to participate in a culturally and racially diverse group. As much as you hate to admit it, you find yourself uneasy in this situation. Although you cannot put your finger on any specifics, you feel uncomfortable. What is going on here? What, if anything, can you do to put yourself at ease?

13. What experience have you had with computers in the workplace? Summarize the positive and negative aspects of your experience.

14. Does the idea of bedside and handheld computers appeal to you? As a nurse manager, how could you sell the idea to higher management?

Test Your Knowledge

BEHAVIORAL OBJECTIVE

Differentiate between interpersonal and organizational communication and indicate the importance of the communication process.

Kay is working to improve her communication skills as a nurse manager. There are specific principles and practices that she can apply to achieve her goal.

_____ 1. Kay recognizes that the goal of communication is to:
  a. Understand the communication process.
  b. Inform others what you want to say in clear and concise terms.
  c. Narrow the gap between the intended message and the received message.
  d. Get the person to whom you are communicating to listen to what you have to say.

_____ 2. Kay sends a memorandum to her supervisor requesting a 2-week leave. She receives a written reply granting approval of the request. This procedure describes:
  a. A health communication model.
  b. An example of using position to gain favor.
  c. An organizational model.
  d. Lateral communication.

_____ 3. Kay's power base as nurse manager:
  a. Depends on her level of preparation.
  b. Is vested solely in top administration.
  c. Depends on the salary scale.
  d. Is directly related to position in the organizational system.

BEHAVIORAL OBJECTIVE

Name and define the steps in an effective communication model.

_____ 4. One of Kay's nursing assistants asks the team leader to repeat the instructions. Which communication step is in progress?
  a. Decoding
  b. Transmitting
  c. Encoding
  d. Message

BEHAVIORAL OBJECTIVE

Offer guidelines that promote effective feedback.

_____ 5. Kay observes one of her staff speaking harshly to a team member and saying, "I've told you two times to send that specimen to the lab! Nevermind, I'll do it myself!" This type of feedback is best described as:
  a. Targeted and specific.
  b. Well-timed.
  c. Tactless.
  d. Goal producing.

BEHAVIORAL OBJECTIVE

Identify barriers to effective communication in nursing service and describe ways to overcome them.

_____ 6. Factors that indicate an organization is interested in the physical communication system include all of the following except:
  a. Constancy of temperature in the rooms.
  b. Decentralization of services.
  c. Proximity of showers to patients.
  d. Availability of maintenance personnel.

_____ 7. When Kay is confronted with more messages than she can handle, the condition is called:
   a. System overload.
   b. Burnout.
   c. Overextension.
   d. Inefficiency.

_____ 8. Nurses have much patient/client information to record. They have responsibility to give priority to all factors except:
   a. Clarity.
   b. Impressions.
   c. Natural flow of words.
   d. Conciseness.

BEHAVIORAL OBJECTIVE

Define the informal or "grapevine" channel of communication and recognize positive and negative features of the system.

Kay understands that the grapevine is a common phenomenon among task forces. She knows also that erroneous information can be passed along, which can have serious ramifications. She makes an effort to understand the process.

_____ 9. Kay knows that rumors or grapevines emerge as a response to all of the following except:
   a. Situations that are important to the group.
   b. A news bulletin.
   c. Ambiguity.
   d. Anxiety.

_____ 10. On Kay's nursing unit, a false rumor is spread among one nursing team that a popular team member is to be transferred to another unit because of a predicted reduction in patient number. The best approach for Kay to take is to:
   a. Ignore the rumor, knowing it will pass.
   b. Wait until individual team members request feedback.
   c. Find out who started the rumor and reprimand that person.
   d. Call the team members together and tell them the rumor is false.

BEHAVIORAL OBJECTIVE

Review the health communication model and describe how relationships, transactions, and contexts offer a systems perspective on communication in healthcare.

Kay has transferred to a community healthcare setting. She recognizes that the health communication model takes a broader systems view of communication and shows how a series of factors can affect the interactions in healthcare settings. She is eager to implement this knowledge.

_____ 11. In the health communication model, the best definition for a health professional is:
   a. An RN with a community health certificate.
   b. Any person who has the education, training, and experience to provide the necessary service.
   c. All RNs, physicians, and social workers.
   d. An RN or a significant other.

BEHAVIORAL OBJECTIVE

Describe the channels of communication in management.

Because Kay is nurse manager of a community health unit, she wants to understand the essentials of communication in management. She reviews several concepts and principles.

_____ 12. The classical form of communications in management is:
   a. Downward.
   b. Upward.
   c. Horizontal.
   d. Diagonal.

_____ 13. Kay is communicating with the hospital to coordinate clinical activities. What level of communication is she using?
   a. Downward
   b. Lateral
   c. Diagonal
   d. Horizontal

BEHAVIORAL OBJECTIVE

Define a team and indicate how polarity management can promote and build effective working teams.

Kay is a novice in working with teams. Her goal is to develop her staff into a team that works efficiently and enthusiastically. To accomplish this task, Kay must know what a team is and how it functions.

_____ 14. Kay settled on the following definition of a team:
   a. Two or more individuals who share a goal
   b. Two or more people who act interdependently to achieve goals
   c. Two or more people who exercise a system of care
   d. Two or more individuals who perform a specific task or project

_____ 15. Kay learns that polarity management involves:
   a. Individuality.
   b. Teamwork.
   c. Self-direction.
   d. Manager direction.

BEHAVIORAL OBJECTIVE

Explain how a nurse manager effectively engages in cross-cultural communication.

Both Kay's staff and clientele comprise a mixture of races, values, behaviors, and attitudes. Kay must interact effectively with each person and group.

_____ 16. At one point there was much discussion among the staff about adhering to schedules. To some this was very important, and to others it was not. A nurse from India who was being maligned for failing to comply with schedules remarked, "Americans seem to be in a perpetual hurry. They never allow themselves the leisure to enjoy what they are doing." Kay's role as nurse manager is to:
   a. Agree with the nurse from India.
   b. Ask staff to study Indian culture.
   c. Attempt to balance the cultural differences with the task requirements.
   d. Make it clear that schedules in the clinic must be kept.

BEHAVIORAL OBJECTIVE

Define nursing informatics and indicate the steps nurse managers take to purchase, develop, and implement an information system.

The clinic Kay manages is large, and the information system is not commensurate with progress. Kay is interested in having a nurse informatician on the staff because she believes this person could add a new dimension to the provision of care and assist with cost containment.

_____ 17. Kay understands that a nurse informatician would provide advanced skill in:
   a. Information systems.
   b. Computer science, information science, and nursing science.
   c. The delivery of nursing care.
   d. Software development and computer technology.

REFERENCES

1. Ruben B: *Communication and human behavior,* ed 3, Englewood Cliffs, NJ, 1992, Prentice Hall.
2. Kreitner R: *Management,* ed 5, Boston, 1993, Addison-Wesley Publishing.
3. Gibson J, Hodgetts R: *Organizational communication: a managerial perspective,* ed 2, 1991, Harper Collins.
4. Spector R: *Cultural diversity in health and illness,* ed 3, Norwalk, Conn, 1991, Appleton & Lange.
5. Blankenship P, Woodward-Smith M: Feedback...to a "T," *Nurs 90*(4):32Q, 1990.
6. Raudsepp E: 7 ways to cure communications breakdown, *Nursing 90* 20(4):132-142, 1990.
7. Robbins S: *Essentials of organizational behavior,* ed 4, Englewood Cliffs, NJ, 1992, Prentice Hall.
8. Davis K, Newstrom K: *Human behavior at work: organizational behavior,* ed 7, New York, 1985, McGraw-Hill.
9. Northouse P, Northouse L: *Health communication: strategies for health professionals,* ed 2, Norwalk, Conn, 1992, Appleton & Lange.
10. Sovie M: Nurse manager: a key role in clinical outcomes, *Nurs Manage* 25(3):30-34, 1994.
11. Morgan B, Salas E, Glickman A: An analysis of team evolution and maturation, *J Gen Psychol* 120(3): 277-291, 1993.
12. Keenan M, Hurst J, Olnhausen K: Polarity management for quality care: self direction and manager direction, *Nurs Adm Q* 18(1):23-29, 1993.
13. Hayes P: Team building: bringing RNs and NAs together, *Nurs Manage* 25(5):52-54, 1994.
14. Adler N: *International dimensions of organizational behavior,* ed 2, Belmont, Calif, 1991, Wadsworth Publishing.
15. Mathis R, Jackson J: Human resource management, ed 7, Minneapolis/St Paul, 1994, West Publishing.
16. Rubin B: *Communication and human behavior,* ed 3, Englewood Cliffs, NJ, 1992, Prentice Hall.
17. Hammond J and others: Clinical evaluation of a computer-based patient monitoring and data management system, *Health-Lange* 20(2):123, 1991.
18. Wann M: Software design with RNs' input streamlines care, *Nurseweek* 7(8):18-19, 1994.
19. Simpson R: Managed care software: the next generation, *Nurs Manage* 25(3):28-29, 1994.
20. Shaffer F: Nursing informatics: moving into the 21st century, *Comput Nurs* 12(1):9, 1994.
21. Sanson J, Albrecht M: *Community health nursing: promoting the health of aggregates,* Philadelphia, 1993, WB Saunders.
22. PICT introduces home healthcare documentation and support system, *Comput Nurs* 12(1):9-10, 1994.
23. Simpson R: Why an IS (Information System) business plan, *Nurs Manage* 24(3):26-27, 1993.
24. Simpson R: The role of technology in a managed care environment, *Nurs Manage* 25(2):26-28, 1994.
25. Herrick F, McCullough S: Introducing nurses to computers in a multi-hospital environment, *Nurs Manage* 20(7):31, 1989.

SUGGESTED READINGS

AONE update: Influencing healthcare informatics, *Nurs Manage* 25(7):31, 1994.

Ballantyne M, Westra R: PACE: An innovative approach to fostering teamwork, *Nurs Manage* 25(3):81-83, 1994.

Chu S: Clinical information systems: the nursing interface, *Nurs Manage* 24(11):58-60, 1993.

Cornell D: Say the words: communication techniques, *Nurs Manage* 24(3):42-44, 1994.

Curtin L: "I know you think you heard," *Nurs Manage* 24(3):7-8, 1993.

Fiesta J: Communication: the value of an apology, *Nurs Manage* 25(8):14-16, 1994.

Hettinger B, Brazile R: Health level seven (HL7): standard for healthcare electronic data transmissions, *Comput Nurs* 12(1):13-16, 1994.

Hezekiah J: Creating bicultural experiences in nursing, *J Contin Educ Nurs* 24(5):249-254, 1993.

Jader G: Ten steps to effective persuasive speaking, *Nurs Manage* 24(3):46-48, 1993.

Nauright L, Simpson R: Benefits of hospital information systems as seen by front-line nurses and general hospital staff, *J Nurs Adm* 24(45):26-32, 1994.

Puetz B, Thomas D: Don't let difficult people catch you off guard, *RN* 58(2):24, 1995.

Rasmussen N, Gengler T: Clinical pathways of care: the route to better communication, *Nurs 94* 24(2):47-49, 1994.

Raygor A: A study of the paper chart and its potential for computerizarton, *Comput Nurs* 12(1):25-28, 1994.

Rich J: Communicating your expectations, *Nurs 94* 24(2):322, 1994.

Simpson R: Software application and function for managed care, *Nurs Manage* 25(4):14-16, 1994.

Simpson R: How to manage in the wired hospital, *Nurs Manage* 26(2):18-19, 1995.

Sonnenberg F: The age of intangibles, *Manage Rev* 83(1):48-52, 1994.

Spicer J and others: Supporting ethnic and cultural diversity in nursing staff, *Nurs Manage* 24(1):38-40, 1994.

Talton C: Touch of all kinds is therapeutic, *RN* 58(2):61-64, 1995.

CHANGE, STRESS, and CONFLICT RESOLUTION

BEHAVIORAL OBJECTIVES

On completion of this chapter, the student will be prepared to:

- Define change and identify forces that influence change.

- Explain a planned change process.

- Name four organizational stressors, outline Selye's three-phase stress responses, and state one way to reduce or buffer burnout.

- Define conflict as applied to organizations.

- Differentiate conflict between health organizations from conflict within health organizations (interpersonal and intergroup).

- Identify underlying factors that may lead to conflict in multicultural environments, and state how these conflicts may be resolved.

- Propose an effective procedure to use when experiencing sexual harassment.

- Discuss the positive and negative consequences of conflict.

- State five responses used in resolving conflict, and identify which response is most appropriate for a given situation.

- Differentiate between assertive and aggressive behavior.

This chapter speaks of change, stress, and conflict; one often leads to the other. Change, stress, and conflict are inevitable, but this does not mean that people always are willing to confront the issues. Many reasons exist for resistance, which can take numerous forms. This chapter examines the meaning of change, forces that impinge on change, and steps in the change process. Causes of stress in organizations are introduced, including role, physical, and interpersonal demands. The nurse manager is given ways to reduce burnout when these feelings are experienced. A study of conflict is presented, including attitudes toward conflict; the kinds of conflict that occur in and among individuals, groups, organizations; the consequences of conflict; and a model for conflict resolution. Passive, aggressive, and assertive behaviors are highlighted as ways to cope with change, stress, and conflict.

 ## CHANGE

Change is any alteration in the status quo. *Change* means substituting one thing for another, experiencing a shift in circumstances that cause differences, or becoming different than before.[1] During the last 20 years lifestyles, organizations, and values have changed rapidly and dramatically. Examples of change include attitudes of "Be what you want to be" and "If it feels good, do it!"; the information revolution and a more computerized society; structural reorganizations such as mergers of healthcare agencies and new healthcare delivery systems; the general questioning of social structures such as hierarchy versus teamwork; and a focus on cultural diversity. These changes and many others have confronted nurse managers and their organizations with a host of new challenges. Some people view change as a positive influence, whereas others see it as being disruptive. Whether change is good or bad, it is inevitable.

Forces That Influence Change

Forces can be external or internal. *External forces* on an institution generally influence the organization as a whole or its top administrators. Examples of external forces include the following:
1. Changes may occur such as hospital resizing, employee buyouts, early retirements and termination, continued substitution of RNs by lesser-trained and lower-paid healthcare workers, increasing economic pressure on hospitals and physicians to discharge patients early, and possible limits on the numbers and types of treatments given to certain patients.[2]
2. Some proposals for healthcare reform provide for nursing within the parameters of the work force and nurse education but do not address such issues as fair opportunities for advanced nursing practice.[3]

3. Acquired immunodeficiency syndrome (AIDS) confronts nurses with epidemic proportions. Nurses who have an aversion to working with human immunodeficiency virus (HIV) or AIDS or caring for clients with this disease are warned to change their attitude.[4]
4. Major structural changes in the healthcare delivery system are occurring in the 1990s. Nurses have a vested interest in the outcomes of these significant and profound changes. They need to become fully engaged in designing new ways of organizing and structuring nursing care delivery.[5]

Internal forces originate primarily from inside operations or result from external changes. A number of internal factors are involved in anticipated changes in an organizational work force:
1. The composition of staffing patterns can change such as a reduction in the number of registered nurses (RNs) and an increase in the number of licensed practical nurses/licensed vocational nurses (LPN/LVNs) and nursing assistants. There will be a need to phase out some RNs, orient new workers, and plan for additional roles and responsibilities of RNs and cope with their reactions. There may also be a need to develop strategies to combat the change in staffing pattern.
2. Productivity may need to be increased such as when top administration decides the nurse-patient ratio is to be changed from 1:4 to 1:6. There will be a need to acquaint staff with the dictum and train them in establishing different priorities of care.
3. The quality of working life may need to be improved. There is a growing popularity of the concept that the time spent at work should be satisfying, fulfill basic needs, and provide for self-actualization, which will lead to a feeling of challenge and excitement about the job. People spend a lot of time in work-related activities, and they want and expect pleasant and productive conditions. Because "quality of working life" is a broad concept, nurses have focused on certain issues that include the following:
   a. Provision of quality nursing care
   b. The need for sufficient numbers of qualified nurses to provide care
   c. Staff development programs
   d. Budget limitations that do not provide for realistic personnel requirements (e.g.,

salaries, fringe benefits, equipment and supplies, promotions)

e. Absenteeism among staff

f. Time spent by nursing personnel in performing nonnursing duties

g. Improper use of personnel

h. Instability and inflexibility of staff

i. Work schedule problems (e.g., too many weekends and holidays worked, time schedules not posted far enough in advance; little leeway for change; no provision for options other than the 8-hour day, 5 days a week)

j. Lack of communication among either the nursing unit staff or among different levels of personnel

k. The need for formal nurse-employee representation in negotiating work contracts (a professional organization versus a union)

The Change Process: A Planned Procedure

The process of change is change with a purpose and is devised to solve problems that affect nurses and their work. The process of planned change concerns making alterations by choice and deliberation rather than by indoctrination, coercion, natural growth, or accident.

Many changes in organizations just happen. For example, the nurse manager may receive a complaint from a physician such as, "Nurses don't pay attention to me. I want one to go along every time I visit my patients in case I need something." The nurse manager ignores the fact that there has been a reduction in RN staff and therefore no time for a nurse to drop what he or she is doing and routinely accompany doctors. The nurse manager announces, "Hereafter all RNs will go with physicians to the bedside." This is an example of change that has been devised to solve a problem. However, this decision was not based on planned change; it was an accidental occurrence. Change is a natural state, and managing change is a continual process. This chapter concerns change activities that are proactive and purposeful and respond appropriately to the environment. Because an organization's success or failure is essentially a result of the things that staff do or fail to do, planned change is also concerned with altering the behavior of individuals and groups within an organization.[6]

The process of planned change involves a number of distinct steps or subprocesses. Applying the problem-solving process is central to successful change, and step-by-step procedures and analysis provide an orderly way to proceed.[7] Figure 9-1 illustrates how the process operates while effecting change.

The following is a situation that requires change. A step-by-step analysis of the application of the change process also follows:

> In a decentralized organizational system, the staff nurses on the sixth-floor oncology unit are disgruntled because they believe there is inequity in nursing assignments. Their particular concern lies with assignments for weekends and holidays. Some of the nurses' friends, fiancé(e)s, spouses, and families are pressuring the nurses to rebel.

Step 1. *Perceive a need for change.* The nurse manager of the oncology unit senses unrest among nurses, which is demonstrated by angry comments about the time schedule such as "I have weekend duty again, and you guessed it! Jane has the time off; this makes three weekends in a row for her. Man, is that unfair. You'll see! When Thanksgiving and Christmas come around, Jane will be off and I'll be right here! I hear it's like that all over the hospital." Several other staff nurses nod their heads in agreement. Passive-aggressive actions are occurring: staff nurses arrive for work late, there is an excess of absences, and it is difficult to get a nurse to volunteer for helping services.

Step 2. *Initiate group interaction.* Two or more nurses may gather together for discussion of any perceived work-related problem. A variety of techniques can be used, such as an informal discussion group, a committee or task-force group, or a general meeting to explore a situation. The method used depends on the power or status of the nurse (administrative or staff person) and the availability of resources for meeting and action. In this situation the nurse manager posts an invitation to all nursing staff of the oncology unit to attend one or two meetings that have been scheduled so that all shifts can attend. The nurse manager posts the subject for the meeting and time schedules, asks members who attend to select a recorder

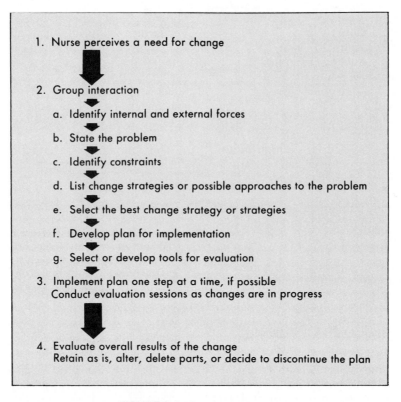

1. Nurse perceives a need for change

2. Group interaction

   a. Identify internal and external forces

   b. State the problem

   c. Identify constraints

   d. List change strategies or possible approaches to the problem

   e. Select the best change strategy or strategies

   f. Develop plan for implementation

   g. Select or develop tools for evaluation

3. Implement plan one step at a time, if possible
   Conduct evaluation sessions as changes are in progress

4. Evaluate overall results of the change
   Retain as is, alter, delete parts, or decide to discontinue the plan

FIGURE 9-1. The change process.

to transcribe the remarks, and encourages each member to participate in the discussion. During the meeting the following events occur:

a. *Identify external and internal forces for change.* The group gathers, and the nurse manager presents the perception of dissatisfaction among some staff members that has been resulting from work schedules. The nurse manager defines external and internal forces and asks the recorder to use a chart pad to log responses *without judgment or comment.* Using a chart allows for a written record of the actual proceedings (Figure 9-2). The nurse manager may or may not leave, depending on the mix of the group. If the members can express their feelings freely with the nurse manager present, he or she stays; if they are hesitant, he or she leaves and receives the records of the meeting.

b. *State the problem.* This is a critical step in the change process. The external and in-

ternal forces are examined; the basic questions of who, what, when, where, and why are addressed; and a clear statement of the problem is formulated. In this example the problem is the dissatisfaction among staff nurses on the sixth-floor oncology unit regarding the time schedule for weekends and holidays and the belief that this problem exists on all other nursing units in the hospital.

c. *Identify constraints.* A constraint is something that restricts, limits, or regulates people and activities. Constraints present in leadership may be leadership climate or style (authoritarian versus participative); organizational climate (centralized versus decentralized); individual characteristics (attitudes such as an unwillingness to change); or a general fear of repercussions to change. Given the situation, the group lists on the chart pad their perception of constraints that might affect a change. A staff member

External forces	**Internal forces**
Negative reaction from: Boyfriends / girlfriends Fiancés / fiancés Spouses Families	Unfairness in scheduling Nurse Manager plays favorites with one person (Joan works very few weekends or holidays) The same thing happens in other nursing units in the hospital It makes me feel like not reporting to work on time I stay home on a holiday I'm scheduled whenever I think I can get away with it

FIGURE 9-2. Chart pad.

takes notes to allow for freedom of expression (Figure 9-3).

d. *List change strategies or possible approaches to solving the problem.* Allow sufficient time for dialogue to occur. Again, the nurse manager may or may not be present. Remember that two sessions of staff members are being held to address the same issues. The process of planning for change may cover several meetings over time in consideration of time constraints and to allow assimilation and reflection. Continue to use a group-designated staff member to transcribe feedback from the participants. Promote a free, open, and receptive climate; make no comments about responses (Figure 9-4). Continue the discussion until all possible solutions have been exhausted. Invite the members to include other alternatives for consideration at the next meeting.

e. *Select the best change strategy or strategies.* In this example the nurse manager is the focal point of the problem and therefore should not be the group leader. The nurse manager may be asked to withdraw from the group at any stage of the change process to allow complete freedom of ex-

Constraints
My family doesn't want me to work on holidays and weekends. (Jane)
I find it hard to talk to our Nurse Manager.
𝍸 // (Six others concur)
I feel that our nurse manager has the power to do whatever she wants with the time schedule and we have to take it.
// (One other member agreed)

FIGURE 9-3. Constraints.

pression. Group members may wish to invite an outside person, such as a staff development educator, who has the oncology unit as part of his or her responsibilities. Care must be taken not to invite people who are not skilled in the art of facilitating;

Possible approaches to solving the problem

1. Talk to the Director of Nursing.
2. Let's join a union.
3. Seek help from the Professional association who bargains for our Contracts.
4. Let's stage a sick-out; all stay home for one Saturday, Sunday or Holiday.
5. See if we can talk this out with our nurse Manager.
6. Conduct a survey of all staff nurses to see if the problem is Hospital-wide.
7. Ask nurse Manager to insist that Jane take her fair share of weekends and holidays; if she refuses, Transfer or dismiss her.
8. Report the problem to Supervisor or Coordinator.

FIGURE 9-4. Possible approaches to solving the problem.

otherwise they may take matters into their own hands or tell the group what to do.

In this example the group decided on the following priorities:

Priority	Number of alternative	Rationale
1	Item 5: Talk with nurse manager	Perhaps the nurse manager is unaware of extent of the problem and will be amenable to change without any further action.
2	Item 7: Problem with Jane	Resolution of priority 1 might also resolve this problem, but make the priority known.
3	Item 8: Report to supervisor or coordinator	It is wise to follow the lines of authority in an agency. In the decentralized system the supervisor is the next person in authority.
4	Item 6: Conduct a survey	If a satisfactory resolution has not occurred, poll other nurses in the hospital.
5	Item 3: Seek help from a professional association	This step may occur before or after the survey, depending on the group's ability.
6	Item 1: See director of nurses	By this time data will have been collected and professional advice about procedure will have been given.
7	Item 2: Join a union	Give the professional association a chance first.
8	Item 4: Sick-out	This action is unprofessional and may be harmful to clients.

Add alternatives and engage in the priority exercise. In so doing, another answer might be selected as the clue to success.

f. *Formulate a plan for implementation.* Priority 1 is to talk with the nurse manager. Before the meeting the group decides on the following strategy:
(1) Select representatives of the group who are to meet with the nurse manager. Choose members with the best interpersonal skills.
(2) Make an outline of the group's position and request.
(3) Conduct a simulated setting in which one person plays the part of the nurse manager and those selected to represent the group make the presentation.
(4) Ask for feedback and suggestions from the remaining group members.
(5) Make changes as decided.
(6) Contact the nurse manager and arrange for a meeting. Tell the nurse manager what it is about.
(7) Arrive on time, make the presentation. Depending on the outcome, either consider the change process complete or still in process.
(8) If it is necessary to carry the problem further, follow similar strategies of be-

ing prepared with data and using effective communication techniques.

g. *Develop or select tools for evaluation.* In this situation the criterion can be that the step taken was successful or unsuccessful. However, if there is a need to conduct a survey, then tools that have already been developed may be used, or one may be designed by the group or by an associate. Situations that involve standards of care or other protocol would use those standards as the basis for the evaluation and check each factor item by item.

Step 3. *Implement the change one step at a time, if possible.* In this example the change would probably occur at once; however, if major changes are to be made, implementation by stages would be better. *Hold evaluation sessions with persons involved as changes are in progress.* In the work-schedule situation it would be advisable for the nurse manager to periodically meet with the staff to hear their reactions. If the change process was taken further than the first step, then each phase would be evaluated in the same careful manner. It is much easier to handle problems in the formative stages rather than to wait until the problem seems insurmountable.

Step 4. *Evaluate the overall results of the change and make adjustments as necessary: retain, alter, delete parts, or discontinue the process.* In this example the nurse manager assesses the general satisfaction level of the group through group meetings or anonymous comments in a suggestion box. Group discussion is preferable because unsigned comments may reinforce passive-aggressive behavior.

Other situations are presented below. Use the change process to find optimal answers to the problems listed:

1. A nursing assistant on a surgical unit is creating conflict among the other nurses by pitting one against the other.
2. To comply with standards of the Joint Commission on Accreditation of Health Care Organizations (JCAHO) the quality control committee of a community hospital recognizes the need for more consistent documentation of nursing care on patients' records.
3. The turnover of nurses is high on a neurology unit. Exit interviews reveal that new employ-

ees are treated coolly by the staff and are expected to prove themselves with little help from the stable staff.
4. You are one of the nurses in a clinical area who wants to change the pattern of nursing care from team nursing to primary nursing.
5. A preceptor assesses himself or herself as one who enjoys the beginning of precepting when the novice is very dependent on a mentor for learning. However, the preceptor does not like relinquishing the dominant role to the new person, even when the two agree that the novice is ready to manage the assignment. The preceptor wants to continue precepting.

Change Agents

Change agents can be any member of an organization. The nurse manager institutes official change in a unit or department, often as a result of suggestions made by a staff member or other interested person. For major change efforts such as changing from manual to computerized information systems, internal management may hire the services of a nurse informatician or use internal or outside consultants to provide teaching, advice, and assistance. Outside consultants may have an inadequate understanding of the agency's operating procedures and personnel and need support and assistance from managers.

STRESS

According to Hans Selye,[8] who developed the modern concept of stress, "Complete freedom from stress is death." Selye labeled all things that create "wear and tear" on the body as stressors, and he labeled all responses to that wear and tear as stress. Stressors are any perceived pressure, strain, distress, hardship, burden, or oppression on an individual, group, or organization. Selye maintains that stress responses have three phases: (1) the excitement phase (the "fight-or-flight" response), (2) the resistance phase, and (3) the exhaustion phase.

In the excitement phase an alarm is activated and the person experiencing stress prepares for fighting or running with an increase in epinephrine, faster breathing to increase the oxygen supply to the brain, and a quickened heartbeat to pump more blood through the system. A moderate amount of stress from excitement may improve performance. For example, the nervous tension that a nurse manager experiences while in conflict about what to do in a crisis situation may have a helpful, energizing effect.

The resistance phase is that period when the body mobilizes its resources to fight stressors while trying to do the job. This stage is often the one in which diseases are manifested. The physiologic overactivity that accompanies constant strain or the use of maladaptive ways to cope with strain, such as smoothing and avoidance, can cause the body to develop headaches, lower back pain, nervous tension, sleeplessness, hypertension, ulcers, heart disease, and other manifestations.

The exhaustion phase occurs after stress has accumulated over a long period of time, which depletes the individual's physical and emotional resources. For example, the manager literally gives up, walks away, and never finishes the task; or the staff member quits the job and feels helpless and hopeless.

It is important to recognize that stress is not all good or bad. An optimal level of stress can result in motivation, excitement, and innovation. Good events such as gaining recognition, receiving a promotion, getting married, and receiving an inheritance can create stress, but each is accompanied by appealing challenges. Some of the most common causes of stress are organizational characteristics or stressors. Other events affect people outside of organizations and are called life stressors.[9]

Stress in Organizations

Organizational stressors consist of four categories: (1) task demands, (2) role demands, (3) physical demands, and (4) interpersonal demands (Figure 9-5).[9]

Task demands

Task demands are associated with the specific task or job that the person is performing. Some tasks in nursing are inherently more stressful than others. Making fast, life-threatening decisions with less than complete information (e.g., a triage nurse in the emergency department, a labor and delivery nurse, a nurse called to the scene of a patient in cardiac arrest) is one example of a stressful task. Nursing tasks that are more routine are less stressful. Although all nurses make important decisions, those who function in a stable environment are likely to have more time to make decisions. However, work overload in any setting can cause an individual to feel stress.

Role demands

A role is a set of expected behaviors that is appropriate for an individual with a specific position in an organization. Stress can result from role ambiguity. For example, a nurse who is oriented properly but is told by team members to "forget all that stuff they told you in orientation; we do it this way; it saves time, but don't get caught!" experiences stress because he or she wants to be liked by his or her peers yet also wants to comply with standards.

Physical demands

Physical demands are associated with the job setting. Nurses caring for patients may suffer from such things as back strain or feet problems. Nurses may become allergic to some solution or medication used in the course of treatment. They also face the danger of infection from any number of viruses or diseases. Protective gear

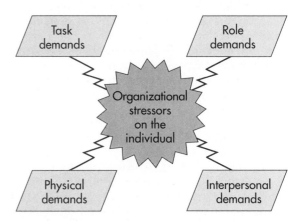

FIGURE 9-5. Organizational stressors. (Modified from Barney J, Griffin R: *The management of organizations: strategy, structure, behavior,* Boston, 1992, Houghton Mifflin.)

may add to the nurses' stress level by making the health threat more apparent.

Interpersonal demands

Interpersonal demands are associated with relationships within organizations. Individuals with conflicting personalities may experience stress if they are required to work too closely together. A nurse manager's leadership style may cause stress if the manager's style is autocratic and a team member feels a strong need to participate in decision making but is not allowed to. A nurse with a dominant personality who takes advantage of a passive co-worker can also cause unwanted stress:

Shelia: Terry, you wouldn't mind taking over for me for an extra half hour at lunch, would you? I know I impose on you a lot but this great guy I am seeing is only free for lunch today. I know you are the kind of person who does not mind helping out now and then.

Terry: Well, I suppose so. I really have a heavy workload today and will probably have to stay overtime to catch up. If you could make it another day . . .

Shelia: Thanks a lot, Terry. You are a gem. I'll never forget what you're doing for me!

BURNOUT

Burnout is defined as physical and emotional exhaustion that involves a negative job attitude and a poor professional concept. It is characterized by apathy, alienation, job dissatisfaction, and a depersonalization of others (e.g., patients, peers, staff members), which leaves the stressed individual feeling alone in the world.[10] Burnout and severe stress do not just happen but involve a complex interplay of personal, job, and organizational culture characteristics (see Figure 9-5). Burnout is not shameful. It is a common phenomenon and is most likely to occur in highly stressful occupations such as nursing.

Kathryn Tarolli-Jager[10] wrote her master's thesis on managing stress in the nursing profession. She discovered that researchers are beginning to measure the variables that reduce or buffer burnout. One important buffer is personal hardiness.[11] Researchers have found that the higher one's level of personal hardiness, the less likely one is to experience burnout. Characteristics of hardiness are *commitment* (e.g., feeling committed to a job of managing others), *control* (e.g., being in control of one's life), and *challenge* (e.g., feeling challenged instead of threatened when asked to do something new). Tarolli-Jager suggests that if one is beginning to lose interest in a job, one can become more involved in what is happening by joining a task-force or committee or by saying to oneself several times a day, "I like nursing and want to make a difference" until confirmation of the statement "kicks in." Each person has the ability and the control to make choices and to choose feelings for every situation. For example, an already overworked nurse manager who is told to assume responsibility for the care of two patients each shift in addition to managerial activities has several options. The nurse manager can choose to become resentful and verbalize anger while giving care, to hold feelings in while complying with the order, or to be assertive and document the reasons why this is not a good plan. Challenges can be approached as positive or threatening. An effective nurse manager accepts that change is inevitable. The manager eagerly embraces the challenge to improve individual leadership, and improved quality of nursing care ultimately results. Burnout and stress lead some nurses to drop out of nursing; these factors also cause some to feel miserable in their jobs. Developing personal hardiness is one way to prevent the onset of burnout and stress.

CONFLICT

Conflict is a disagreement among two or more individuals, groups, or organizations. The disagreement may be relatively superficial, or it can be very strong. Conflict may be short-lived or exist for months or even years, and it may be work related or personal. Conflict may manifest itself in a variety of ways. People may compete with one another, glare at one another, exchange angry words, or withdraw. Groups may band together to protect their members, or organizations may seek legal remedy.[9]

Most healthcare organizations experience a substantial amount of conflict because a complex organizational structure requires its members to engage in numerous and varied interdependent relationships. For example, more and more patients/clients are becoming aware of their rights, and nurses are learning how to serve as their advocates. Nurses and other health agency personnel are also learning ways to promote their work-related interests through means such as negotiation, strikes, or integrative decision making. Administrators, physicians, and nurses are experiencing conflict as they attempt to understand and meet the expectations of others.

Depending on how it is managed, conflict can threaten the harmony and balance of an organization or can be desirable and useful in improving organizational performance. The task of the nurse manager is to identify the source of conflict and understand the points of friction. The nurse manager can proceed with the process of conflict resolution and strive to see that all participants are left with a feeling of self-worth because their views, feelings, and behaviors have been treated with respect and value.

Attitudes Toward Conflict

Most people assume that conflict should be avoided because it connotes antagonism, hostility, unpleasantness, and dissension. Before 1940, manager and management theorists viewed conflict as a problem to be avoided at all costs. Most nurses favor this traditional view of conflict and confrontation: to maintain stability and keep the peace. Therefore nurses and many managers tend to equate confrontation with aggression and often do not act at all rather than confront the issue directly. In reality confrontation can be a valuable method of solving issues. It can help nurses reconcile perceptions, correct behavior as needed, and ultimately grow professionally. Nurse managers are advised to develop confrontation skills to enhance personal development and to improve the staff and department.[12]

Types of Conflict

Change, stress, and conflict have similar origins. There are three types of conflict: (1) within the

individual, (2) between organizations, and (3) within organizations (interpersonal and intergroup) (Figure 9-6).

Conflict within an individual

Intrapersonal conflict in a nurse manager occurs when he or she is confronted with two or more incompatible demands. Inner conflicts that are fairly common in health organizations occur (1) when there is uncertainty about the work expectations as a result of insufficient or unclear information, (2) when the nurse is confronted with an ethical issue and is torn between loyalty to personal convictions and loyalty to the organization, (3) when there is a role conflict such as trying to meet job demands in addition to the demands of being a spouse and parent, (4) when the nurse believes there is work overload and when expectations from a number of sources cannot be completed within given time and quality limits, (5) when the nurse feels divided between a desire for personal independence and a commitment to conform to the demands of the organization, or (6) when expectations exceed capabilities and the nurse is confronted with deciding whether to "bluff" the situation through while learning the job or to risk the consequences of admitting incompetence for the role.

Conflict between health organizations

Conflict between health organizations is usually restricted to issues that pertain to competition for buildings, types of facilities, funding, and business. Today an increasing number of satellite health centers are springing up. Each competes for the same healthcare dollar, which causes tensions to rise and conflicts to emerge among providers. This form of conflict is considered desirable in American society because it can lead to the development of new and better services.[13] Lower- or first-level nurse managers may become involved in interagency conflict when information is needed to justify new or expanded services or when data are needed regarding the use of methods, time, or resources. They may also offer their views on organizational issues at public and professional gatherings.

Within the individual

Within Organizations
Interpersonal

Within Organizations
Between individual and group

Between agencies

FIGURE 9-6. Types of conflict.

Conflict within health organizations— interpersonal and intergroup

The major sources of organizational conflict within health agencies include (1) differences between management and staff, (2) the need to share resources, (3) the interdependence of work activities in the organization, and (4) differences in values and goals among departments and personnel regarding the delivery of nursing care.

Differences between management and staff. One of the most common forms of organizational conflict occurs between staff members and management. The root of the conflict lies in the fact that staff members (e.g., nursing assistants, LPNs/LVNs, and staff nurses) view one another and their roles from a perspective that is different from that of supervisory or management personnel (e.g., nurse manager, supervisor, and vice president of nursing). Staff members' orientations are usually geared to the present and focus on accomplishing their respective tasks effectively, whereas managers share this concern but also attend to broader horizons in terms of time and accomplishments. Issues that concern staff members center on complaints about staffing, blocks or barriers in communication, wages, benefits, and other concerns. Conflicts between management and staff may arise when staff members go beyond their lines of authority, fail to meet job expectations, and demonstrate a lack of dedication to the job or a lack of understanding of the managers' process and position regarding issues.

Shared resources. An effective nurse manager works through the established system to obtain what is needed. The manager needs to know the supply source, method of allocation, and procedure for requests of resources. Sharing resources in a health organization frequently leads to conflict because vital resources may be limited. If every department has access to unlimited amounts of manpower, space, supplies, and equipment, problems with sharing these resources would rarely arise. However, resources must be allocated, and inevitably some groups get less than they want or need. Lack of cooperation or even direct conflict can result when people seek to satisfy only their own wants and needs. The lower- or first-level nurse manager in a hospital is often confronted with the problem of acquiring enough linen, wheelchairs, lifts, scales, hardware, software, and other equipment. The leader may also be asked to cooperate by sharing a staff member with another department for a few hours or for a day. A conflict may occur when the team leader determines that the needs of the team are so great that the member cannot be spared. These types of problems require the nurse manager to have sufficient knowledge and understanding about available resources so that the conflict may be resolved on the basis of facts.

Work interdependence. Work interdependence exists when two or more departments, subunits, or individuals depend on each other to complete their respective tasks. For example, nursing departments must relate with many

other groups such as admitting, discharge, x-ray, laboratory, pharmacy, and dietary. The potential for a high degree of conflict or cooperation exists and depends on how the situation is managed. Sometimes conflict occurs when groups have too much to do. Conflict may flare if one individual or group is perceived by another to be shirking responsibilities. Potential for conflict is greatest when one department or individual is unable to begin work until the other unit or individual completes a job (e.g., "How can we serve breakfast if the lab doesn't take the fasting specimens?" or "How can I complete my assignment on time if I have to wait until X is ready to help me?").

Differences in goals and values. Differences in goals and values among departments and personnel regarding the delivery of nursing care frequently lead to conflicts of interest or priorities. Such conflicts can occur even when everyone agrees on the overall goals of the organization. As an agency becomes departmentalized and specialized, each subunit develops its own goals, tasks, and problems that may not be in harmony with the goals of all other departments. For example, the maternity department might want to discharge infants and mothers at times most convenient for the family members, whereas the business office insists on adhering to a specified time of discharge. Both departments may express concern for the family but may be in conflict regarding how best to serve their respective interests.

The differences in goals among members of various departments are influenced by differences in attitudes, values, and perceptions and may be another soure of conflict. Lower- or first-level nurse managers may be stressed as a result of pressure to accomplish a workload that is too large. The manager is told to "just do the best you can—we'll talk about it later." Issues of safety and poor quality care plague the leader until conflict erupts. Conflicts among personnel and between nursing personnel and patients/clients are also common. Attitudes, values, and perceptions play a major role in these relationships. Because each individual is unique, it is often difficult to resolve conflict amicably without exercising strong communication skills.

Conflict in a multicultural environment

As discussed in Chapter 8, nurse managers must not assume that everyone has similar behaviors, beliefs, and values. Cultural conflict may be a significant underlying factor in staff disputes. Therefore "areas such as handling conflict, decision-making, language differences, motivational factors, and role expectations must be explored in a multicultural context."[14,p.49]

Three nurse administrators of a 608-bed teaching facility in midtown New Jersey offer an example of conflict in which both staff and patients are from diverse ethnic backgrounds.[1] In this facility, blacks and Hispanics comprise the majority of the patient population. Nurses are employed from various ethnic backgrounds; 60% are Philippino, 25% are American, and 15% are Middle Eastern, Indian, and Korean. This cultural mix resulted in several areas of conflict: (1) different interpretations of role expectation among foreign nurse graduates, patients, families, and nursing administration; (2) multidisciplinary team conflicts; (3) lack of a caring attitude in foreign nurses, as perceived by patients; (4) American nurses feeling isolated because of their minority status; (5) lack of attention to conflicts by nurse management; (6) misunderstanding as a result of language differences; (7) foreign nurses demonstrating a paternalistic relationship with physicians; (8) a more functional approach to care delivery; (9) differing values in the areas of grief, death, and dying; and (10) differing views concerning documentation practices.

In an attempt to resolve the hidden conflicts, the nursing department formulated several goals: (1) to improve communication and to promote harmony among culturally diverse staff, families, and patients; (2) to increase awareness of diverse cultures and their impact on the healthcare setting; (3) to clarify values that affect attitudes toward workplace behavior and healthcare delivery; and (4) to identify common concepts held by the healthcare professionals. A program was devised to achieve these goals, which centered around team building (see Chapter 8). Although not all staff members attended all of the sessions, some inroads were made. A follow-up study revealed that some improvement had occurred in multicultural communication and that much had been learned about the differences in culture, values, and beliefs. The administrative staff has planned similar programs to ensure a more harmonious future and recommends that nurse administrators who are experiencing such conflicts consider these programs.

Conflict as the result of sexual harassment

Sexual harassment refers to "actions that are sexually directed, unwanted, and subject the worker to adverse employment conditions or that create a hostile work environment."[15,p.141] The Equal Opportunity Commission guidelines define sexual harassment as unwelcome verbal or physical conduct of a sexual nature that interferes with an individual's work performance by creating an intimidating, hostile, or offensive working environment.[15] The problem of sexual harassment exploded on the nation's conscience in 1991 during the Senate confirmation hearing for Judge Clarence Thomas' appointment to the United States Supreme Court. The Thomas hearings heightened awareness of sexual harassment in the workplace. More than 7400 sexual harassment complaints are filed annually in the United States. The most frequent complaints made by victims include the following:[16]

- Sexual teasing or sexually explicit jokes
- Sexually suggestive looks or gestures
- Repeated requests for dates or meetings outside work
- Actual touching, fondling, or pinching
- Physical cornering, "trapping," or leaning over a worker

One researcher noted a high prevalence of sexual harassment in the hospital workplace.[17] Staff nurses reported being harassed by patients, physicians, and co-workers. Others have noted that women are much more likely to be sexually harassed than men and that the majority of sexual harassment stems from male co-workers, including physicians. The essential criteria for identifying sexual harassment is that it is one-sided, unsolicited, unwelcome, repetitive, and clearly not under the victim's control.[18]

Sexual harassment is an important issue for nurse managers because it can lower staff morale and efficiency and reduce productivity. Nurses who have experienced sexual harassment report becoming so distracted that they were unable to think clearly or make rational decisions. When asked to describe their emotional responses to the harassment, nurses stated "anger," "embarrassment," and "disgust." As a result, both the quantity and quality of nursing care was impaired.[19]

The common response to sexual harassment is to do nothing and to avoid the harasser. The victim may fear that he or she is being overly sensitive, fear some type of retaliation, or believe the myth that sexual harassment is brought on oneself. Unfortunately not responding to the situation does not stop sexual harassment. In fact ignoring sexual harassment or avoiding the harasser may encourage the perpetrator to continue the behavior.

Sexual harassment is a legal issue, and harassers must be confronted when it occurs. Institutions must have policies, methods, and strategies to deal with sexual harassment in the

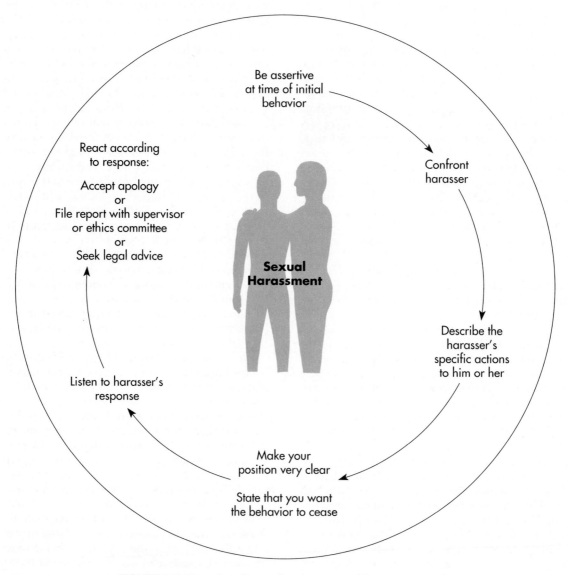

Be assertive
at time of initial
behavior

Confront
harasser

React according
to response:

Accept apology
or
File report with supervisor
or ethics committee
or
Seek legal advice

**Sexual
Harassment**

Describe the
harasser's
specific actions
to him or her

Listen to harasser's
response

Make your
position very clear

State that you want
the behavior to cease

FIGURE 9-7. Procedure for confronting a sexual harasser at work.

workplace. Nursing staff members should be involved in the formulation of these procedures. An atmosphere of openness and honesty is imperative. The following situation suggests approaches to use when confronting a sexual harasser (Figure 9-7):

> SITUATION: Mr. B, head of a large department in the healthcare agency, is making sexual advances to Nurse L. Examples of his behavior include brushing his hand across Nurse L's breast, showing her a pornographic picture, relaying an off-color joke, and commenting on her beautiful curves. Nurse L has tried to ignore the overtures. Today he slipped his arm around her waist, drew her to him, and whispered, "You really turn me on. Let's go to my place after work."

1. *Be very assertive and confront the issue.*

> EXAMPLE: Nurse L looks Mr. B in the eyes and says, "I want to make something very clear to you. Your actions toward me are not acceptable. I am talking about touching my breast, showing me pornographic pictures, telling me dirty jokes, and just now suggesting that I sleep with you. I will not tolerate any more of these kinds of behaviors!"

2. *Listen to the sexual harasser's response.*

> EXAMPLE: Mr. B replies, "Well, what do you know? I didn't know we had little Miss Prissy among us. Hey, I'm sorry. I guess I didn't read the signs right. Let's forget it, OK?"

3. *Make your position clear.*

> EXAMPLE: Nurse L says, "I hear your apology and will accept it, but I want you to know that I will not hesitate to report your behavior to the ethics committee if it occurs again. I am preparing a report that I will file with my supervisor, just in case this happens again."

Suppose the harasser makes an alternate response:

2. *Listen to the sexual harasser's response.*

> EXAMPLE: Mr. B replies, "Do you realize who you're talking to? I could have you out of here in nothing flat. Who would believe you over me?"

3. *Make your position clear and imply legal action.*

> EXAMPLE: Nurse L says, "We both know that it is illegal to sexually harass an employee. You have sexu-

ally harassed me. I have witnesses and will file a report itemizing each of your actions."

4. *File a written report of the incidents with your immediate supervisor.* Indicate in the report the dates and names of the people who saw the proceedings or heard the exchanges. Keep a copy of the report for future reference should it become necessary to file charges.

5. *If such a situation occurs again, confront the behavior immediately.*

No matter what form the harassment takes, it is essential to present a direct and positive objection and tell the perpetrator in no uncertain terms that he or she will be reported to the appropriate authority in the healthcare agency or to a legal advisor if the behavior does not stop. Educational programs that are attended by nurses, physicians, and allied health staff members help with the recognition, labeling, and control of the various manifestations of sexual harassment.

Consequences of Conflict

Conflict can lead to positive or negative results. Two or more people are involved in a relationship, and the outcome of their social exchange depends on the communication process used. Consequences of conflict include the following:

1. *Issues are recognized and brought out in the open.* Suppressing feelings within an organization leads to trouble. When conflict arises, it should be identified and handled. Recognition of conflict by management encourages open communication between the individuals or group members and is the first step in conflict resolution.

2. *There is a rise in group cohesion and performance.* Group members in an intergroup conflict situation close ranks and put aside former disagreements. For example, during a conflict the group follows its chosen leader, who may or may not be the leader appointed by management. The heightened closeness of the group can be positive (the staff can choose to pull together to accomplish the workload while negotiating with management) or negative (the team may choose to accomplish only what they believe is feasible,

or they may engage in a work slowdown to emphasize the problem).

3. *Poor performance.* Extremely low levels of conflict may result in poor performance. Passive people who are afraid to "rock the boat" to find new and better ways of getting things done repress their feelings of conflict and accept things the way they are. Individuals and group members drift along and tolerate each other's weaknesses and lack of performance, which builds up tension and stress.

4. *Constructive or destructive results.* Although moderate conflict may produce a constructive resolution of problems, high levels of conflict almost always produce results that are destructive to the organization. High levels of conflict may also lead to distorted perceptions. In situations of conflict there is a tendency to regard individual and group ideas irrationally (e.g., "Management thinks we are machines" or "Those staff members just do not want to work"). Negative stereotypes are likely to be developed as each side belittles the other's views and ideas. Competitive struggles adversely affect the rivals' ability to grasp and think accurately about their respective positions. Strong group identification, heightened by a fear of defeat, blinds both sides to the similarities in their views that could make conflict resolution possible.

5. *There may be a rise of leaders.* When conflict occurs, individuals whose talents might not otherwise have been recognized may emerge as leaders.

Conflict Resolution

Organizational structure and climate influence how beneficial conflict resolution is likely to be. Conflict can call attention to the problem areas of an organization and can lead to better ways of getting things done. However, if an organization, individual, or group rigidly resists change, the conflict may never be resolved. Tensions will continue to mount, and each new conflict will split the parties involved farther apart. Unresolved conflict can adversely affect subgroups (e.g., nursing teams) in which there is a great deal of dependence on one another to accomplish goals.

Poorly managed conflict can tear apart an individual or group. Many nurses have developed ineffective responses to conflict, which leads to frustration, helplessness, and low self-esteem. Five responses are used in resolving conflict: (1) competition and power, (2) smoothing, (3) avoidance, (4) compromise, and (5) collaboration. Figure 9-8 demonstrates how Collyer[20] applies nurse leadership styles to Blake and Mouton's Managerial Grid in resolving conflicts.

The conflict resolution style used to solve each conflict depends on the nurse manager's values regarding work production and human relationships. The following situation serves as the basis for discussing the five approaches to conflict resolution:

Nurse manager Don is faced with a serious and persistent staffing shortage and economic pressures to keep costs within budget. Employing registry nurses is more costly than employing regular staff. Consequently there are fewer registry nurses than are needed. Don has felt it necessary to assign the more complicated patients to nurses who are familiar with the unit and to give them heavier assignments to accommodate the new personnel's need for orientation. He is sitting in his office one afternoon grappling with a budget problem when his concentration is suddenly interrupted by a loud knock on the door. Without waiting for an invitation to enter, three of the hospital nursing staff burst into the office. They are obviously upset and angry. They slam the door, and one nurse says, "We've just about had it! If you're trying to get us to quit, you're doing all the right things!" Taken aback, Don asks the reason for their anger, and they reply, "You should know—you take advantage of us every day by overloading us without a break. We never get a chance to relax. You'd better do something about this situation or we'll quit!"

Competition/power

As Figure 9-8 indicates, when the nurse manager is primarily concerned with work accomplishment and has minimal regard for staff relationships, he or she exercises power, restriction, and coercion. There is an all-out effort to win, regardless of the cost.

Don responds to the three nurses, "I'm in charge here and I'm doing what I think best for all con-

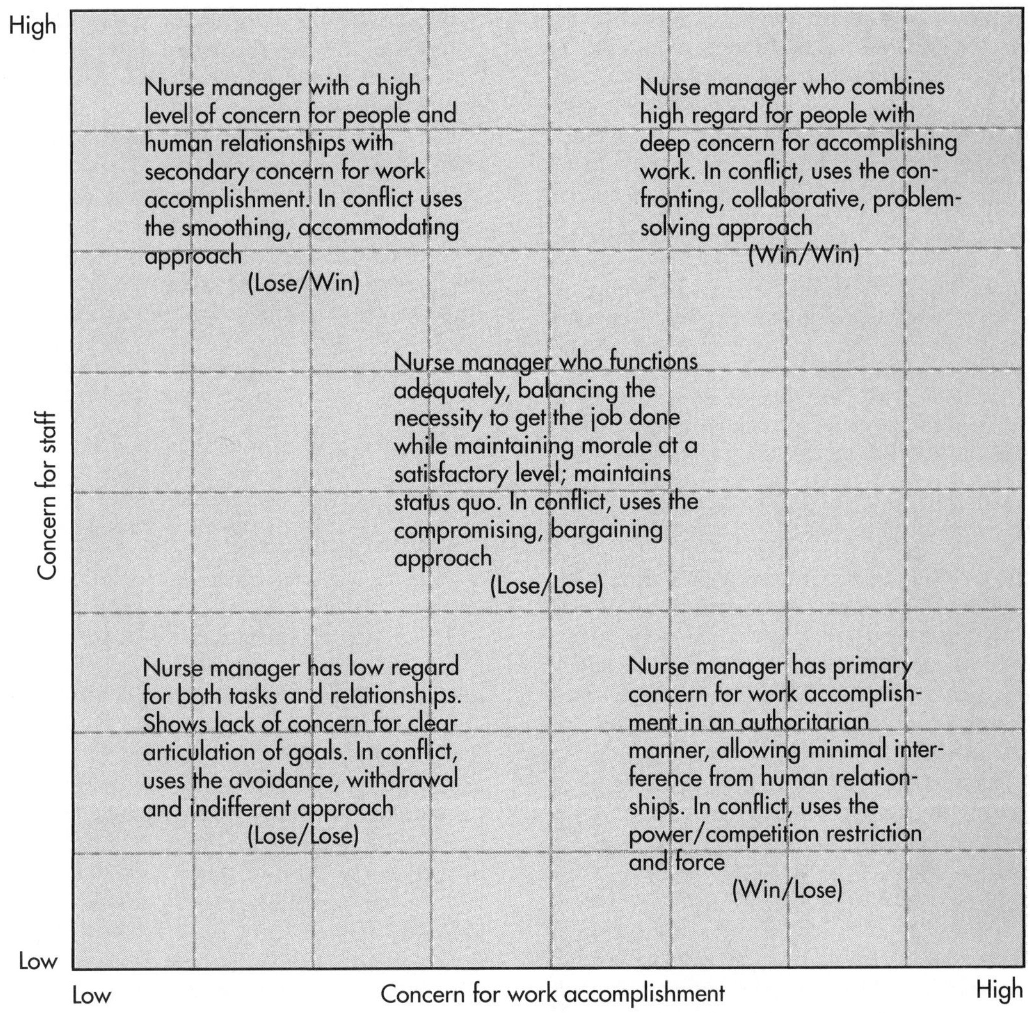

High

Nurse manager with a high level of concern for people and human relationships with secondary concern for work accomplishment. In conflict uses the smoothing, accommodating approach
(Lose/Win)

Nurse manager who combines high regard for people with deep concern for accomplishing work. In conflict, uses the confronting, collaborative, problem-solving approach
(Win/Win)

Nurse manager who functions adequately, balancing the necessity to get the job done while maintaining morale at a satisfactory level; maintains status quo. In conflict, uses the compromising, bargaining approach
(Lose/Lose)

Nurse manager has low regard for both tasks and relationships. Shows lack of concern for clear articulation of goals. In conflict, uses the avoidance, withdrawal and indifferent approach
(Lose/Lose)

Nurse manager has primary concern for work accomplishment in an authoritarian manner, allowing minimal interference from human relationships. In conflict, uses the power/competition restriction and force
(Win/Lose)

Concern for staff

Low

Low   Concern for work accomplishment   High

FIGURE 9-8. Leadership styles and conflict resolution. (Modified from Blake R, Mouton J: *The managerial grid: the key to leadership excellence,* Houston, 1985, Gulf Publishing; modified from Collyer M: Resolving conflicts: leadership style sets the strategy, *Nurs Manage* 20[9]:77-80, 1989.)

cerned *(power)*. Surely you can hang in there until this crisis is over *(coercion)*. If you choose to quit, I'll see to it that your lack of cooperation goes on your record" *(restriction)*.

The nurse manager "wins" because the nurses do not wish to transfer or resign under negative circumstances and therefore return to work. The staff nurses "lose"; and their resentment, hostility, anger, and frustration increase. Later these feelings

may be actualized in other ways, such as poor performance, absenteeism, undermining the nurse manager in his relationship with his peers, or taking their problem to a grievance committee.

Smoothing

Smoothing behavior is a more diplomatic way to suppress conflict. The nurse manager who has a high concern for relationships and a secondary concern for work accomplishment might use the smoothing, accommodating approach (Figure 9-8). Smoothing is accomplished by complimenting, downplaying differences, and focusing on minor areas of agreement as if little disagreement exists.

> Don jumps up from his chair and asks the nurses to join him for a Coke, "on me" *(accommodating)*. He tells them, "I know just how you feel—I would feel the same way if I were in your shoes *(agreement)*. I've given you the complicated assignments because you are the best nurses I have and I know you're concerned with giving high quality care *(complimentary)*. This situation is rough, but it won't last long. We'll be getting new nurses soon and won't need to use as many people from the registry *(downplaying the issue)*. I will get an additional nurse from the registry to ease your load" *(accommodating)*.

Approaching conflict this way sets up a lose-win situation. Don is accommodating the nurses at his own expense. He will exceed his budget, be forced to cut back, and will demonstrate a lack of competency to his superiors and a lack of trust to his staff. The nurses win in that they were listened to and are promised a more equitable number of nursing staff. Smoothing tactics are never satisfactory because they are only surface measures and another eruption is likely to occur.

Avoidance

The nurse manager who uses **avoidance** strategies has low regard for both the workers' output and their relationships. Shunning or avoiding a problem means not taking a position regarding the conflict. The nurse manager reasons, "If we don't talk about the problem, it will go away."

> Don responds to the irate nurses, "I'm sorry, but I don't have time to discuss this now—later perhaps." This is a lose-lose situation. The avoidance response does nothing but create a higher degree of frustration and anger on the part of the staff nurses. The problem will accelerate and eventually force the nurse manager to address the ever-increasing conflict.

Compromise

Compromise is a means of settling differences in which each side makes concessions. Concession-making behavior is moderately assertive and co-operative; however, it produces a lose-lose situation because each party gives up something to gain something and neither gets what he or she wants. Compromise is sometimes the only choice, such as when a decision must be made immediately or when the two parties in conflict have equal power. From a management point of view, compromise is a weak resolution method because the process usually fails to reach a solution that best helps the organization to reach its goals.

> After hearing the angry nurses' complaints, Don responds, "I see we have a bigger problem here than I imagined. Sit down and we'll see what can be worked out." He explains that a staff increase is out of the question but agrees to assign patients equitably among the regular staff and registry personnel. He states, "The registry people will need to understand how it is and dig in a bit harder. Will you promise to help them get oriented as much as you can?"

In an effort to balance the necessity for adequate nurse coverage with the importance of maintaining regularly employed nurses' morale at a satisfactory level, the nurse manager agrees to a situation in which both parties lose. The nurse manager compromises his commitment to provide quality nursing care by lowering his standards in making assignments. The regularly employed nurses lose because they will not be satisfied to see patients receive less than the best care and will feel put upon if they have to frequently interrupt their caregiving to assist the registry nurses. The registry nurses will feel equal dissatisfaction because they may be given assignments beyond their ability. This solution will soon fail, and the organization is not helped to reach its goals.

Collaboration

Collaboration is a constructive process in which the parties involved recognize that a conflict exists, confront the issue, and openly try to solve the problem that has arisen between them. Instead of using dominating, suppressing, or compromising behaviors, the individuals look for a resolution that they all want to accept. The outcome is integrative problem solving in which all members and groups involved work together toward a common goal in an atmosphere of open

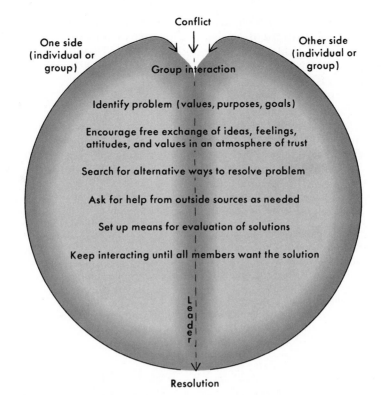

FIGURE 9-9. Model for conflict resolution.

and free exchange of ideas and stress the benefits of finding the best solution.

The collaborative approach to conflict resolution requires (1) problem identification; (2) clear definition of values, purpose, and goals; (3) open and honest communication of facts and feelings; (4) a sense of responsibility in all who participate; and (5) an environment of trust and commitment to the success of the process. A constructive plan is to designate a specific time for meeting all persons who are involved in the disagreement, allow enough time to discuss the issue, and provide coverage for the group while it is in session.

Figure 9-9 presents a model for effective conflict resolution. Leadership through the conflict resolution procedure is important. First the persons in conflict must be helped to state their values, purposes, and goals and be guided toward a solution that is acceptable to all parties. It is impossible to meet goals that are absolutely incom-

patible, but many established ideas can be changed if all parties are committed to the process.

All members should be encouraged to share both positive and negative thoughts in an atmosphere of acceptance. The leader should discourage behaviors that are destructive to the process. One destructive behavior is apologizing prematurely: "OK, you're right, I'm sorry." This kind of comment stops the process. Another unhelpful behavior is refusing to take the conflict seriously: "Oh, you shouldn't feel that way. Ha, ha, ha. . . ." These responses are repressive and dehumanizing. The silent treatment of withdrawal is another dead-end behavior. Distracting others or addressing unrelated issues is a tool used by some and makes it difficult for members to focus on the problem.

The leader should encourage constructive behaviors such as full expression of positive and negative feelings. As the positive comments increase, the negative will decrease. In conflict resolution the leader does not stop the disagreement. The effort is to hear what individuals are thinking and feeling.

A paraphrasing ground rule should be established, whereby one person cannot respond to another until the first person is satisfied that his or her feelings have been heard and understood. Phrases such as "Are you saying . . .?" and "Tell me in another way" promote clarification. After two or three exchanges it is frequently discovered that there really was no conflict of goals; the problem was a matter of semantics, or how to reach the goal.

> Nurse manager Don recognizes that he is confronted with a problem: the conflict has reached a state of crisis, and some immediate action must be taken. He allows the nurses to confront him and then responds, "I can see this is a serious matter *(respect for the nurses' opinions)*. We do not have time to work it out now, but I will give the matter serious thought and we will discuss the problem at staff meeting this afternoon" *(accommodation)*. When the group convenes, Don has a chart pad set up, ready to record the proceedings. He begins the discussion by saying, "I value your opinions, and I want to hear what you have to say, whether positive or negative *(open, honest, and trusting)*. We must get at the problem." He asks for a volunteer to record the messages *(participation)*.
>
> "We're overworked."
> "We never have time to be together."
> "I resent always having the heavy assignments."
> "Registry nurses do less and get paid more."
> "The hospital should have more nurses."
> "You play favorites."
> "I'm afraid I'm going to make a mistake."
> "My family life is going to pot."
> "I hate to come to work and I used to love to."
>
> After making certain all have had their say, Don asks group members to identify what it is they want:
>
> "We want an equitable patient assignment that we can comfortably manage."
> "We want to believe that our patients are being cared for."
> "We want registry nurses to be able to carry their load."
> "We want to believe that you (nurse manager) care enough about us to meet our needs."
>
> Don asks, "From the discussion thus far, how would you identify the problems?" After discussion the group agrees on the following problem:

> "Continuous pressure as a result of overassignments and a feeling of lack of support from the department manager."
>
> From this point, Don moves to a search for alternate ways to solve the problem. Again, the responses are recorded:
>
> "Department manager fights for our rights."
> "Hire more nurses."
> "Stage a few 'sick-outs' to show administration we are serious."
> "Take the problem to the grievance committee."
> "Train the registry nurses better."
>
> Don concludes, "You have helped to clarify the issues. I ask that you give me a week to see what can be done. I realize the problem is real and serious, and I will do what I can to resolve the matter." From here, Don meets with his supervisor and plans strategies that address the problem. The department manager and supervisor go through the decision-making process of weighing actions against risks and come to a decision.

Use the problem-solving process to develop possible answers to the problem.

PASSIVE, AGGRESSIVE, AND ASSERTIVE BEHAVIORS

Deciding which style of behavior to exhibit while communicating in the role of manager is often difficult for nurses. Even when a decision is made as to the best approach, the nurse may hesitate to act. There is no one right way to respond all of the time; the nurse behaves in a specific manner according to circumstances. Imposing one style of behavior on others indicates a desire for the members to respond in a similar manner, and all participants in the communication process become victims every time circumstances change and alternate behaviors are warranted. Three common styles of behavior are used by leaders/managers: passive, aggressive, and assertive. The effective nurse manager learns the process used in each and the advantages and disadvantages of each.

Passive Behavior

Passive behavior is submissively accepting whatever circumstances are in force without resistance or complaint. The passive individual has low self-esteem and is unable to initiate contact with others and stand up for individual rights or the rights of patients/clients and staff. Passive nurses often see themselves as second-class employees who are unable to exert influence and power in strategic circumstances rather than as peers or equals with the right to act on their own convictions. Behaviors characteristic of the passive person are apologetic speech (e.g., "You're right. I'm wrong. I'm sorry.""I don't really know, but . . ."), avoidance or withdrawal, hedging when asked to make a decision, and giving of oneself willingly. The passive nurse manager avoids direct confrontation, which allows people and circumstances to dominate the situation. This type of leader is unable to assertively articulate thoughts or feelings and therefore feels powerless. These feelings prevent the manager from accomplishing the managerial role.

A usual behavioral pattern of the passive nurse is to engage in self-pity, self-righteousness, and superiority by telling others (usually those outside the work scene) of the oppressive conditions caused by the bureaucracy, the nurse manager, or any other scapegoat. Periodically the typical passive person reaches a breaking point and has an emotional outburst of aggressive behavior (e.g., shouting, crying, blaming). Immediately afterward the nurse feels guilty and ashamed and quietly returns to the passive routine. Passive individuals have not learned that each individual is responsible for his or her reactions to circumstances, and they continue to allow others to manipulate them.

Aggressive Behavior

An aggressive individual acts in a bold, attacking, and hostile manner and often accomplishes his or her purposes at the expense of others and with injurious and destructive results. Aggression is disagreeing by being unpleasant and cantankerous. Aggressive behaviors include blaming, shaming, refusing to take no for an answer, making belittling remarks, humiliating or embarrassing another in the presence of others, stomping feet, banging doors, cursing, slamming the receiver down, and crying.

Assertive Behavior

In a "win-win" conflict resolution, the nurse manager uses the confronting, collaborative, and problem-solving approach, each of which requires assertiveness.

Assertive behavior requires maintaining a balance between passive and aggressive behavior. As Table 9-1 illustrates, assertiveness requires openly expressing one's positive and negative beliefs and reactions without infringing on the rights of others. The assertive person makes choices regarding how, when, where, and why actions are taken and who will take them. Assertiveness means controlling what happens to oneself, making requests and having needs met, and refusing to comply with unrealistic demands or requests. Assertiveness helps the individual initiate and terminate conversations with confidence. Assertive behavior allows the nurse manager to act in the best interests of self, patients/

Table 9-1. Comparison of behaviors exhibited by passive, assertive, and aggressive nurses		
PASSIVE	**ASSERTIVE**	**AGGRESSIVE**
Low self-esteem	High self-esteem	High-low self-esteem
Feels self-pity	Feels self-worth	Mixed feelings of worth
Shy, withdrawn	Forthright	Forward and attacking
Apologetic	Open and honest	Hostile, manipulative
Denies rights and needs of self and patients/clients	Acts in best interest of self and patients/clients	Demands needs be gratified for self and others
Feels victimized	Feels self to be on peer level	Feels must fight for rights
Allows situation to control self rather than controlling situation	Controls situation	Attacks situation

clients, and members of the healthcare team by expressing honest feelings comfortably and without undue anxiety.

Marie Manthey[22] urges nurses to develop a professional mindset that allows clients, co-workers, and the public to view nurses as responsible individuals who can care for their own needs. In this way nurses become more capable of caring for the needs of others. She lists nine ways to be assertive:

1. Learn to say what one thinks. People can have different opinions without drawing sides of "right" or "wrong."
2. Admit that there is a possibility of being wrong.
3. Do not accept persuasion, coercion, manipulation, or guilt if this is not desired.
4. Set limits as to how far to go and learn to say, "This is what I will do; I expect this much from you."
5. Expect healthy interpersonal relationships within all work groups and promote whatever is necessary to achieve them (e.g., support groups; free, open, and honest communication).
6. Show concern and compassion without trying to rescue the person in trouble. "What do you need from me?" is an appropriate question.
7. Discuss feelings and problems but expect others only to listen, not to rescue.
8. View talking as a tool and a pleasure because talking helps in understanding oneself and others.
9. Take responsibility for communication and be honest, direct, and open. Be firm, or gentle and loving when appropriate. Give first priority to being oneself and saying what needs to be said.

Summary

1. Change is substituting one thing for another, experiencing a shift in circumstances that cause differences, or becoming different than before. Change is inevitable and can be positive or negative.
2. Forces that influence change can be external or internal.
3. The process of change is change with a purpose and is directed toward solving problems that affect nurses and their work. The process of planned change makes alterations by choice and deliberation rather than by indoctrination, coercion, natural growth, or accident.
4. Change agents can be any member of an organization. The nurse manager is the one to institute official changes in a unit or department, which are often a result of suggestions made by staff members.
5. The change process involves several steps: (1) perceiving a need for change, (2) having group interaction, (3) implementing the plan for change one step at a time, and (4) making a cyclic evaluation of the overall results of the change and making necessary adjustments.
6. Stressors are any perceived pressure, strain, distress, hardship, burden, or oppression on the individual, group, or organization.
7. Organizational stressors consist of task demands, role demands, physical demands, and life stressors.
8. Burnout is physical and emotional exhaustion that involves a negative job attitude and a poor professional concept. Burnout is manifested by apathy, alienation, job dissatisfaction, and a depersonalization of others.
9. An important buffer for burnout is personal hardiness, which consists of commitment, control, and challenge.
10. Conflict is present when an inner or outer struggle occurs regarding ideas, feelings, or actions.
11. Before 1940 managers and management theorists viewed conflict as something to be avoided. However, confrontation can be a valuable way to solve issues.
12. Human relations theorists take a liberal attitude toward conflict and contend that it is a normal, frequent occurrence that is sometimes desirable because the resolution may lead to greater effectiveness.
13. Intrapersonal (inner) conflict within a nurse manager occurs when the leader is confronted with two or more demands such as an uncertainty about expectations, an ethical dilemma, a role conflict, or a work overload. All of these conflicts cause the body to respond in helpful or harmful ways.
14. Selye's theory offers three phases of the stress response: excitement (the individual

goes into a "fight or flight" stance), resistance (the body mobilizes its resources to combat stress, which is often manifested by illness), and the exhaustion stage (the individual gives up).

15. Conflict between organizations is usually restricted to broad issues such as competition for buildings, grounds, and facilities. Lower- or first-level nurse managers usually play a secondary role in this type of conflict.

16. Conflict within health organizations occurs between people (interpersonal) and groups (intergroup). The major sources of conflict include differences between management and staff, shared resources, interdependence among departments, and values and goals regarding delivery of nursing care.

17. Cultural conflict may be a significant underlying factor in staff disputes.

18. One major hospital with a multicultural environment attempted to resolve hidden conflicts among nursing management, nursing staff, and patients by using the team-building approach. The goals of the hospital were to improve communication, increase awareness of diverse cultures and their impact on the healthcare setting, clarify values and attitudes, and identify common concepts. This approach is recommended in multicultural healthcare agencies that are experiencing conflict.

19. Sexual harassment refers to actions that are sexually directed and unwanted and that subject the worker to adverse employment conditions or create a hostile work environment.

20. Direct action is the first line of defense against sexual harassment. One must present a positive objection and let the perpetrator know that action will be taken (legal if necessary) if the behavior does not stop.

21. There are several possible consequences of organizational conflict: (1) issues may be recognized, (2) there may be a rise in group cohesion and performance, (3) constructive problem solving may be used in moderate levels of conflict, (4) incorrect information or distortion of perception may lead to destructive or dysfunctional actions, and (5) leaders may emerge who might not otherwise have been recognized.

22. Competition and power, smoothing, avoidance, compromise, and collaboration are the methods used to resolve conflict. All methods may be used at some time by managers, but the collaborative approach offers the most constructive way to resolve conflict.

23. The collaborative approach to conflict resolution requires a clear definition of values, purposes, and goals; open and honest communication; responsibility; and trust.

24. A model for conflict resolution consists of an effective leader who brings together the individuals or groups in conflict and facilitates identification of the problem; free exchange of ideas, feelings, attitudes, and values; and a search for alternate ways to solve the problem. This strategy also involves getting help from outside sources when necessary and establishing a plan to evaluate the proposed solutions and the chosen solution.

25. Assertive behavior requires maintaining a balance between passive and aggressive behavior. The assertive person chooses which behavior to use and expresses positive and negative beliefs and reactions without infringing on the rights of others. Assertive behavior allows the nurse manager to act in the best interests of self, patients/clients, and members of the healthcare team by expressing honest feelings comfortably and without undue anxiety.

26. Nurses need to develop a professional mindset that allows clients, co-workers, and the public to view nurses as responsible individuals who can care for their own needs. In this way they can care for the needs of others more effectively.

27. Assertive behaviors include learning to say what one thinks, admitting that it is possible to be wrong, not accepting pressure from others unless by choice, setting limits as to how far to go, and expecting and promoting healthy interpersonal relationships within all work groups. Assertiveness also means showing concern and compassion without trying to rescue the person in trouble, discussing feelings and problems with others and expecting them to listen, viewing talking as a pleasure and a tool, taking responsibility for communication, and giving first priority to being oneself and saying what one needs to say.

❓ Questions for Study and Discussion

1. Imagine yourself as the department manager of the nursing unit where you have student practiced or are currently employed. What one change would you like to see? Outline how you would go about effecting the change.
2. Have you ever experienced burnout as a student? What measures did you take to overcome the situation? Could you have done anything differently?
3. Pick one multicultural healthcare agency in which you have had a clinical rotation or been employed. On the basis of the content of this chapter and other information you have gleaned, would you say there were any identifiable cultural conflicts? Explain. To your knowledge is anything being done to resolve the problems? What could be done?
4. You work in a center for severely disabled children. You love the job because you believe you are making a significant contribution. You also need the money. However, the personnel manager is obviously attracted to you. He makes a point of joining you for breaks and meals and sits so close that he often touches you. He calls you "Darlin'" and makes suggestive remarks about your figure. One day he tells you a dirty joke and states that he has free time after work and would like to take you to his place for a drink. You like everything about the job except this man. He holds power because he employs and dismisses all personnel. What can you do?
5. Are there any positive outcomes of conflict? Explain.
6. Why is it naive to think that dysfunctional on-the-job conflict can be completely avoided?
7. A staff member approaches you, her manager, with the complaint that "You always give me the most disagreeable assignments, and I'm not going to take it anymore!" How would you respond to the staff member? Which of the five interpersonal conflict-management styles have you used?
8. Think of your most recent (or present) employer. How would you describe that person's use of the five interpersonal conflict-management styles? Give an example.

✍️ Test Your Knowledge

BEHAVIORAL OBJECTIVE
Define change and identify forces that influence change.

Jasmine is appointed as the nurse manager of an operating room (OR). After 6 months, she knows there are many changes she would like to effect. Internal forces are impinging on the unit and bringing unwanted change.

_____ 1. Jasmine knows that in a healthcare agency, a change agent:
   a. Can be any member of an agency.
   b. Is the one appointed by top management.
   c. Is the nurse executive or manager.
   d. Is the one best prepared to make change.

_____ 2. Other factors of change are important for Jasmine to know, such as examples of internal forces, which include:
   a. Staffing patterns and a population explosion.
   b. An economic setback and work productivity.
   c. An increase in the number of RNs and a new nurse manager.
   d. Federal legislation and a pay cut.

_____ 3. Jasmine senses an increasing unrest among the staff because some RNs are being replaced by surgical technicians. The best action to take is to:

a. Ignore the problem because the staff will eventually accept the change.
b. Bring the group together and discuss the issue.
c. Report the unrest to her supervisor.
d. Discuss her perceptions with a peer.

BEHAVIORAL OBJECTIVE
Explain a planned change process.

_____ 4. Jasmine notes increasing conflict among RNs, nursing assistants, and surgical technicians, which is affecting work productivity. She should:
a. Evaluate the overall results of the unrest.
b. Develop a plan and implement it.
c. Identify internal and external forces.
d. Initiate group action.

BEHAVIORAL OBJECTIVE
Name four organizational stressors, outline Selye's three-phase stress responses, and state one way to reduce or buffer burnout.

With all the pressures accompanying these changes, Jasmine is aware that stress and burnout among the staff may occur.

_____ 5. Three RN staff members accuse Jasmine of not doing enough to protect their jobs. Selye describes this action as:
a. A confrontation.
b. A stressor.
c. A stress.
d. Wear and tear.

_____ 6. One nurse worked double shift, and one of her patients died on the operating table. The RN broke into uncontrollable sobbing. According to Selye, this phase of stress is called:
a. Overreaction.
b. Beneficial.
c. Resistance.
d. Exhaustion.

_____ 7. It is time for Jasmine to inform an RN that she is being terminated. Jasmine's pulse rate increases. Selye describes this reaction as which phase of stress?
a. Excitement
b. Fear
c. Resistance
d. Conflict

_____ 8. It becomes necessary to use the paddles in the OR in an attempt to resuscitate a young boy. However, there is something wrong with the current. In organizations, this type of stress is known as:
a. A role demand.
b. An interpersonal demand.
c. A physical demand.
d. A task demand.

_____ 9. Because of the stress and conflict among the OR personnel, signs of burnout are showing. Jasmine conducts a conference on the subject and outlines ways to reduce or buffer burnout. One important buffer she presents is to:
a. Quit if one does not like the job.
b. Keep feelings to oneself.
c. Maintain commitment to the job.
d. Reach out and help someone.

BEHAVIORAL OBJECTIVE
Define conflict as applied to organizations.

_____ 10. Jasmine is feeling uncomfortable lately because she believes that she is frequently made the scapegoat for everything that goes wrong in the OR. Her best recourse is to:
a. Identify the source of the conflict and understand the points of friction.
b. Convince herself that she is feeling paranoid and continue with her responsibilities.
c. Get an opinion from an outside observer.
d. Begin to look for other opportunities where she is more likely to be appreciated.

BEHAVIORAL OBJECTIVE

Differentiate conflict between health organizations from conflict within health organizations (interpersonal and intergroup).

Jasmine increases her understanding of conflict to become a more effective leader. She is interested in an outlying facility for paraplegics. Jasmine must investigate procedure before she can develop plans.

_____ 11. Jasmine is informed that she needs to negotiate with an agency that is now owned by the hospital in which she is employed. When she calls to set up an appointment, she is treated with hostility by the outlying facility's business manager. This action is called:
   a. Conflict between management and staff.
   b. Interpersonal conflict within health organizations.
   c. Multidisciplinary conflict.
   d. Conflict between health organizations.

BEHAVIORAL OBJECTIVE

Identify underlying factors that may lead to conflict in multicultural environments, and state how these conflicts may be resolved.

Jasmine has a Middle Eastern heritage. For 7 years she has worked hard to understand American culture and to become acclimated to working conditions in the United States. She makes a point of employing staff from diverse ethnic backgrounds.

_____ 12. Jasmine employed Hieu, a surgical technician from Thailand who is very skilled in technique and understands OR terminology. However, he knows very little about American culture, which leads to interpersonal problems. Jasmine's best approach is to:
   a. Reinforce Hieu as a worthy employee.
   b. Ask the OR staff to do their best to help him.
   c. Establish team-building conferences.
   d. Evaluate Hieu's ability to relate with team members.

BEHAVIORAL OBJECTIVE

Propose an effective procedure to use when experiencing sexual harassment.

Jasmine believes that she promotes an atmosphere of openness and two-way communication. To her surprise Sonya, a workroom employee, comes to her with a complaint of sexual harassment that she claims has been occurring for 6 months. Jasmine is appalled and intends to do something about the situation.

_____ 13. Jasmine invites Sonya into her office where they can be alone. She asks Sonya to describe graphically what has occurred between her and the alleged harasser. What is Jasmine doing?
   a. She is making an assessment.
   b. She is attempting to see if Sonya is telling the truth.
   c. She is trying to calm Sonya down.
   d. She is getting facts for legal action.

BEHAVIORAL OBJECTIVE

Discuss the positive and negative consequences of conflict.

_____ 14. Which of the following statements concerning conflict is not true?
   a. Can be destructive if the level is too high
   b. May create leaders
   c. Is better avoided
   d. May result in poor performance

BEHAVIORAL OBJECTIVE

State five responses used in resolving conflict, and identify which response is most appropriate for a given situation.

Jasmine has used the following expressions at one time or another. The more she studies, the more she recognizes the value of an educated approach to conflict resolution.

_____ 15. "I will discuss the matter later" is an example of:
   a. Collaboration.
   b. Smoothing.
   c. Compromise.
   d. Avoidance.

_____ 16. "Let's not do anything until we determine what the group is thinking" is an example of:
   a. Avoidance.
   b. Smoothing.
   c. Compromise.
   d. Power.

_____ 17. "First we will identify the problem" is an example of:
   a. Smoothing.
   b. Collaboration.
   c. Compromise.
   d. Power.

BEHAVIORAL OBJECTIVE

Differentiate between assertive and aggressive behavior.

Jasmine tends to be more passive aggressive than assertive but is attempting to learn new skills.

_____ 18. When Jasmine speaks to Teresa about her break in technique, Teresa replies, "The scrub nurse bumped into me." Identify the behavior.
   a. Passive
   b. Assertive
   c. Aggressive

_____ 19. One staff member declares, "I have decided to get a degree." Which behavior is he expressing?
   a. Passive
   b. Aggressive
   c. Assertive

REFERENCES

1. Mathis R, Jackson J: *Human resource management,* ed 7, Minneapolis/St Paul, 1994, West Publishing.
2. Buerhaus P: Economics of managed competition and consequences to nurses: Part I, *Nurs Econ* 12(1):10-17, 1994.
3. Sharp N: Healthcare reform: where are we now? *Nurse Manage* 25(1):17-18, 1994.
4. Blouin A, Brent N: Legal concerns related to workers with HIV or AIDS, *JONA* 25(1):17-18, 1995.
5. Anderson C: Restructured organizations: traversing hills and valleys, *Nurs Outlook* 41(5):198-199, 1993.
6. Robbins S: *Essentials of organizational behavior,* ed 4, Englewood Cliffs, NJ, 1994, Prentice Hall.
7. Sullivan E, Decker P: *Effective management in nursing,* ed 2, Menlo Park, Calif, 1988, Addison-Wesley Publishing.
8. Selye H: *The stress of life,* ed 2, New York, 1976, McGraw-Hill (Historical).
9. Barney J, Griffin R: *The management of organizations: strategy, structure, behavior,* Boston, 1992, Houghton Mifflin.
10. Tarolli-Jager K: Personal hardiness; your buffer against burnout, *Am J Nurs* 94(2):71-72, 1994.
11. Kobasa S: Stressful life events, personality, and health: an inquiry into hardiness, *J Pers Soc Psychol* 37(1):1-11, 1979.
12. Jones K: Confrontation: methods and skills, *Nurs Manage* 24(5):68-70, 1994.
13. Kreitner R: *Management,* ed 5, Boston, 1992, Houghton Mifflin.
14. Martin K, Wimberly D, O'Keefe K: Resolving conflict in a multicultural nursing department, *Nurs Manage* 25(1):49-51, 1994.
15. Equal Employment Opportunity Commission: Guidelines on discrimination because of sex. In *EEOC Rules and Regulations,* vol 45, no 72, Chicago, 1980, Commerce Clearing House, pp 25024-25025.
16. Pollan M, Levine M: Confronting a sexual harasser, *Working Woman,* March, 1994.
17. Grueci A: Scope and nature of sexual harassment in nursing, *J Sex Res* 23(2):161-165, 1987.
18. Julias D, DiGiovanni N: Sexual harassment: legal issues, implications for nurses, *AORN J* 52(1):5-104, 1990.
19. Libbus M, Bowman K: Sexual harassment of female registered nurses in hospitals, *JONA* 24(6):26-31, 1994.
20. Manthey M: Vulnerable no more, *Nurs Manage* 20(4):26, 1989.

SUGGESTED READINGS

Beyers M: Nurses responding to change, *Nurse Manage* 25(11):37-38, 1994.

Beyers M: The consequences of change, *Nurs Manage* 26(5):22, 1995.

Bushy A, Kamphuis J: Response to innovation: behavioral patterns, *Nurs Manage* 24(3):62-64, 1993.

Giovinco G: When nurses strike: ethical conflicts, *Nurs Manage* 24(5):86-90, 1993.

Hance J: Drive change or be driven by it, *Bank Manage* 32(1):18-19, 1994.

Hargerman Z, Tiffany C: Evaluation of two planned change theories, *Nurs Manage* 25(4):57-60;62, 1994.

Lamb G, Stempel J: Nurse case management from the client's view: growing an insider expert, *Nurs Outlook* 42(1):7-13, 1994.

Lewis-Ford B: Management techniques: coping with difficult people, *Nurs Manage* 24(3):36-38, 1993.

Peyton J: Dealing with resentment effectively, *Nurs 94* 24(2):32X, 1994.

Narasi B: A tool for living through stress, *Nurs Manage* 25(9):73-75, 1994.

Schwartz K, Tiffany C: Evaluating Bhola's configuration theory of planned change, *Nurs Manage* 25(6):56-61, 1994.

Songer N: Mediation as a management tool, *Bus Econ Rev* 40(1):1721, 1993.

Tetlock P, Boettger R: Accountability amplifies the status quo effect when change creates victims, *J Behav Decis Making* 7(1):1-23, 1994.

CONTROL

BEHAVIORAL OBJECTIVES

On completion of this chapter, the student will be prepared to:

- Define the control process and the steps necessary for successful implementation.

- Distinguish among anticipatory, concurrent, and feedback control.

- Explain the impact of managed competition and third-party control on nursing.

- Discuss how the decentralized budget process for middle-level nurse managers is used.

- Differentiate among operating, capital expenditure, and personnel budgets.

- Define the process used to prepare a budget in a decentralized system.

- Identify the basic steps used in a nursing services control system.

- Differentiate between task analysis and quality control of nursing care.

- Explain the philosophy of quality assessment and quality improvement.

- Define performance appraisal and its inception.

- Describe the components of an effective nursing appraisal system and recognize problems and pitfalls associated with personnel appraisal.

- Relate methods of performance measurement to their usefulness in nursing.

- Give the purpose of a nursing performance review session and list guidelines for an effective session.

- Review the process for managing the problem employee.

 **CONTROL PROCESS**

The Nature of Control

Control is the regulation of organizational activities so that some targeted element of performance remains within acceptable limits. Without this regulation, organizations have no indication of how well they perform in relation to their goals. It is like the old axiom, "If you do not know where you are going, you aren't going to get there." Control provides an organization with a way to adjust its course if performance falls outside acceptable boundaries (Figure 10-1). Without effective control procedures, an organization is not likely to reach its goals, or, if it does reach them, to know that it has.

The Purpose of Control

The word *control* suggests the functions of checking, testing, regulating, verifying, and adjusting. Control involves taking the necessary preventive or corrective actions to ensure that the organization's missions and objectives are accomplished as effectively and efficiently as possible. If actual performance is consistent with the appropriate objective, things proceed as planned. If performance is inconsistent with objectives, changes are made. Successful nurse managers detect deviations from desirable standards and make appropriate adjustments. When used effectively, control is a normal, positive, and pervasive process. It can guide behavior and set into motion plans for the future.

Types of Control

There are three types of control: (1) anticipatory, (2) concurrent, and (3) feedback[1] (Box 10-1). A successful nurse manager exercises the three types of control in today's healthcare organizations. **Anticipatory control** involves seeing problems coming in time to do something about

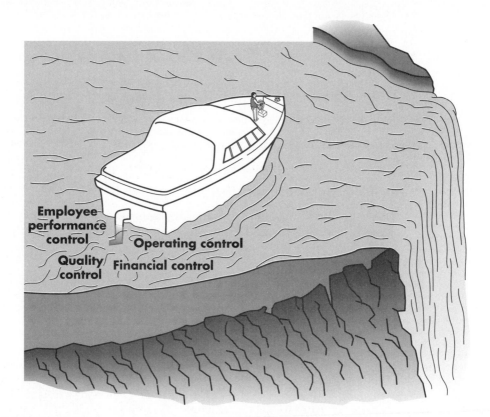

FIGURE 10-1. Control, like a ship's rudder, keeps an organization moving in the desired direction.

Box 10-1. Three types of organizational control

ANTICIPATORY	CONCURRENT	FEEDBACK
Review mission and goals	Monitor ongoing activities	Gather information of ongoing or completed activities
Review past successes and failures	Make adjustments	
Assess needs		Learn from mistakes
Project for the future		Take steps to improve situation

them, rather than reacting after the fact. It is the only way managers can exercise control effectively. The nurse manager must review what has gone on before, know the organization's mission and goals, anticipate needs, and project for the future. Planning addresses the question of "What can we do ahead of time to help our plan succeed?" Planned and preventive measures can save time, money, errors, and many headaches. Concurrent control deals with the present rather than with the future or past. **Concurrent control** involves monitoring and adjusting ongoing activities and processes to ensure compliance with standards. This type of control occupies much of the nurse manager's time, for he or she is most concerned with the day-by-day activities of the unit. **Feedback control** involves gathering information about an ongoing or completed activity, evaluating that information, and taking steps to improve that activity or similar activities in the future. For example, by monitoring the comments from discharged patients regarding their nursing care, a nurse manager learns that personal attention to hospital stay activities needs improvement.

A well-designed nursing control system (1) uses an effective communication method to establish trust and commitment to the system by all personnel concerned; (2) clarifies organizational and individual objectives; (3) prepares a well-planned budget; (4) presents uniform and fair standards and precise definitions of each standard, goal, and objective; (5) compares expectancy with performance; (6) improves organizational development by providing information for decision making regarding staffing, care delivery systems, and quality of care; and (7) promotes growth and development of personnel. A combination of standards, well-planned objec-

tives, strong organizational support, and capable direction has a high probability for success when an adequate system of control is in effect.

FINANCIAL CONTROL TRENDS

The Impact of Managed Competition and Third-Party Control

The healthcare industry is under tremendous pressure from all sources to control costs and improve productivity. Just a few years ago most hospitals were reimbursed on the basis of itemized charges or the full cost of services by the vast majority of third-party payers such as Blue Cross, Blue Shield, Medicare, and Medicaid. Because of changes in Medicare reimbursement and the increasing number of health maintenance organization (HMO) and preferred provider organization (PPO) contracts, most hospitals must now assume some financial risk when providing care to 50% to 70% of their patients.[2] The former system encouraged hospitals to promote extended hospital stays. Long hospital stays resulted in high reimbursement from third-party payers and increased hospital profits. The costs of these long stays were passed on to the consumer in the form of increased insurance rates. The purpose of prospective reimbursement was to establish in advance the amount that would be paid for inpatient hospital care in each diagnosis related group (DRG) category. Hospitals now have an incentive to control costs because if their costs are below the amount set by prospective payment guidelines, they may keep the "difference"; if their costs are higher, hospitals could lose money.

Managed Competition

Managed competition is designed to create a domino effect that results in competition among prepaid, fee-for-service providers such as HMOs and PPOs on the basis of price and quality. Under the pure form of managed competition the public sponsor would be a Health Insurance Purchasing Cooperative (HIPC), whereas in the current administration's proposed Health Security Act, health alliance organizations would be created by individual states for the purpose of performing sponsor activities. This proposed plan would allow far greater regulatory powers than what was planned for the HIPC.[3]

As price competition among HMOs intensifies under the managed competition strategy, nurses will feel the effects. Several outcomes are predicted[3]:

- More pressure on the healthcare organizations to discharge patients as rapidly as possible
- Lower annual rates of wage growth
- Eliminated or narrowed wage differentials linked to nursing education (e.g., BSN versus APN preparation)
- Buyout or early retirement of nurses who are paid more or who are nearing their time to become vested in security and benefits
- Substitution of registered nurses (RNs) by lesser-trained and lower-paid workers
- Increased use of advanced practice nurses (APNs)
- Increased use of registered nurses (RNs) as utilization reviewers
- Resized hospitals or mergers

Although it seems likely that healthcare reform will occur, questions remain as to how soon, how much it will cost, who will finance it, and exactly how the system will change. Further documentation of the impact of these changes on the cost and quality of care by nurse providers is necessary.[4] Both threats and opportunities exist for nurses. Nursing organizations, nursing leaders, and all members of the profession must be educated on the economics and political nature of the healthcare system and make their voices heard. Staff nurses and nurse managers must actively participate in committees that address changes in healthcare policies in their organizations.

Advanced Practice Nurses: Cost Effectiveness

Direct access to a full range of qualified APNs offers more efficient use of healthcare resources. Studies have proven that APNs such as clinical nurse specialists (CNSs) provide care at a lower cost than physicians and psychologists with equivalent or better patient outcomes.[5] Legal barriers are slowly and consistently being removed. APNs now receive direct reimbursement in more than half of the states. Insurance companies have been the nurse specialist's strongest opponent.

Patient Care Redesign
Managed care and case management

Nursing departments are experiencing organizational, structural, and process change as a result of patient care redesign. Case management is a classic example. Case management is used to integrate and coordinate services and advocate for people who require extensive services. The goal of case management is to make healthcare less fragmented and more holistic for individuals with complex healthcare needs. A variety of healthcare professionals provide both direct care and negotiate with systems on behalf of their clients. Both managed care (the delivery system) and case management (the provider) are designed to effect public accountability through decreased costs and improved outcome or quality of care.[6] Nurse managers can and should lead the way in developing creative budgeting approaches to support these new models of nursing care.

Case managers and economic control

Insurers typically view case management as a utilization review or a link to various patient activities. However, it is more than this. Case management involves the development of integrated care pathways, sometimes known as critical paths, that connect not only inpatient care but an entire episode of illness (see Chapter 5). Phyllis Ethridge, vice president of patient care services at St. Mary's Hospital in Tucson, reports that this hospital has an extensive case management program. St. Mary's employs 22 nurse case managers who track and make 7000 to 8000 home visits each year. Case managers serve as the primary link between patients and their physicians and provide care, education, and assessment.[7]

St. Mary's obtained contracts with Medicaid and HMOs that paid per patient served. Under the case management system costs have decreased and quality of care has increased. Plans are underway to study 10,000 patients who will receive care under the integrated case management model, with a control group receiving current Medicare-approved services. One goal is to determine how to cost out nursing care services in the case management system.[7] The phrase *costing out nursing services* simply means determining the cost of services provided by nurses.

Any cost-containment effort must begin with an understanding of interacting components (e.g., patient age, primary diagnosis, medical treatment, nursing diagnosis, means necessary to meet all patient needs), a way to measure productivity, and a way to measure changes in output against resource consumption. The nurse manager's role is to seek ways to learn the budgeting and control process to establish harmony between cost and provision of care.

FINANCIAL CONTROL SYSTEMS

The first healthcare information systems actually began as financial accounting systems more than 20 years ago and helped institutions manage costs, income, and expenditures. Today these systems do a great deal more. They have moved from being tools used merely for reporting financial status to being strategic assets used to set and manage the institution's goals, directions, and strategies.[8] The ultimate survival of an organization is dictated largely by how proficiently funds are acquired and managed. Financial control is vital because it monitors the organization's financial health.

A **financial control system** is implemented by a **budget,** which is defined as a tool for planning, monitoring, and controlling cost. It is also defined as a systematic plan for meeting expenses. A statement of estimated future expenditures is prepared each year on the basis of previous records and educated predictions of future needs. The purpose of the budget is allow the organization to stay on top of changes in the

healthcare system and to maintain quality care while containing costs.[9] The budget can be a powerful instrument because it guides nursing performance and allocation of personnel, supplies, support services, and facilities.

An effective budget system (1) has enough sources to supply sufficient funds, (2) allocates financial resources to specific units or departments on the basis of certain criteria, and (3) conducts a controlling system that shows how effectively financial resources are being used. Budgets form the link in the management process that began with goals and strategies; they are the most detailed management practice used to ensure that an organization's goals are achieved.

Centralized Budgeting

Some organizational budgets are centralized. They are developed and imposed by the comptroller, hospital administrator, and director of nursing services. There is little or no consultation with lower-level managers. Nurse managers are expected to use all hospital information systems but have relatively little input into the selection, implementation, and evaluation of those systems, including budget development. Therefore this top-down approach leaves the implementors of the budget (e.g., nurse managers) without autonomy or the right to appropriate or control expenses.

Decentralized Budgeting

More and more health agencies are recognizing the value of having budgets prepared by those who must implement them. With **decentralized budgeting** the middle-level manager (nurse manager or department manager) becomes actively involved in the planning and budgeting process; autonomy, accountability, and authority are placed at the practitioner level.[9] Top-level managers still attend to overall forecasting needs for the new fiscal year and look at past experiences and records, considering changes such as closing or opening facilities or services, study anticipated population changes, and consider any regulating changes that might result in policy change or legislation. Middle-level nurses are given the authority to develop and monitor the annual budget for their respective units. This decentralized approach, or bottom-up budgeting, has five distinct advantages:

1. Unit managers have a more intimate view of their needs than do those at the top.
2. Middle-level managers can provide a more realistic breakdown to support their requests.
3. Vital needs are less likely to be overlooked.
4. Morale and satisfaction are usually higher when individuals actively participate in making the decisions that affect them.
5. There is room for more flexibility and quicker action.

I believe that decentralized budgeting is the most effective approach.

Types of Budgets

The budget types most commonly managed by nurses in institutions are operating budgets, capital expenditure budgets, and personnel budgets (Box 10-2).

Operating budget

An **operating budget** includes services to be provided and goods that the unit expects to consume or use during the budget period. The operating budget relies on the patient-day forecast. Most health institutions provide managers with a medical supplies stock list, a linen supplies list, and a stationary stock list from which to order. In some institutions the movement of supplies throughout the organization is so closely monitored that decreases in any item to a preestablished critical level triggers a computerized order for that item from outside vendors who are tied into the system.[10]

What is included in the nursing department's operating budget varies among institutions. The cost of supplies, small equipment, and other miscellaneous items is included in the operating budget. However, utilities, housekeeping, and engineering services are usually considered indirect expenses and are not direct budget items. For these services a portion of the total cost is assigned to the unit by top-level management after hospital cost studies have been made.

Capital expenditure budget

A **capital expenditure budget** consists of an itemized list of current capital assets (usually items over $500) and enumerates each piece of capital equipment together with its serial number, current value, and physical location. If a new item is intended to replace an outmoded piece of equipment, the older piece of equipment and its serial number should be removed from the capital equipment inventory to prevent later confusion.[10] Capital items are usually requested on a special form that requires a statement of justification. Capital costs consider long-term goals and must complement the agency's objectives.

Personnel budget

The **personnel budget** consists of the numbers and types of nursing and support personnel required to operate a nursing unit and the money allocated for that personnel. The personnel budget is an especially important part of the budgeting process because it can account for as much as 90% of the total nursing service budget. Factors that influence staff projection include the following[10]:

1. The delivery system in effect (e.g., case management or total care, modular, team, or primary nursing)

Box 10-2.	Example of items usually included in a nursing operating, capital, and personnel budget		
OPERATIONAL BUDGET	**CAPITAL BUDGET**		**PERSONNEL BUDGET**
Supplies	Large equipment (usually in excess of $500)		Number and types of personnel
Services	Physical changes		Salaries
Small equipment	Physical additions to the unit		Working days
Miscellaneous items			Time off
			Fringe benefits

2. The mix of nursing personnel (e.g., RNs, including clinical specialists, licensed practical nurses/licensed vocational nurses [LPNs/LVNs], nursing assistants)
3. The acuity level of nursing service given
4. The healthcare facility's occupancy rate

Classification system. Patient census and patient acuity are used in a patient classification system (PCS) to determine the number and mix of nursing personnel needed (see Chapter 5).

Full-time equivalent positions. A position is allotted to each person employed by the healthcare agency. For example, a nurse who works 80 hours during a 2-week pay period is assigned a 1.0 **full time equivalent** (FTE), and a second nurse who works 40 hours in a 2-week pay period is assigned a 0.5 FTE. The nurse manager cannot exceed the number of FTEs approved by nursing administration for the fiscal year but can use ingenuity in filling the positions. For example, one FTE position could be shared by three nurses, two working 2 days each and one working a single day. When nurses are on paid leave, sick time, or vacation, their FTE positions are not available for full-time replacement because their salaries are being paid. For these occasions "on call" nurses are used as needed. In the budgeting process the department manager determines the number of FTEs needed for a year on the basis of past records. The department manager uses an electronic spreadsheet to track positions shift by shift, which can provide a summary of the filled and vacant positions budgeted for each job category, as well as an itemized account of times when census or patient acuity was low and the full complement of anticipated staff was not needed.[11]

Preparation of the Budget

Almost every manager in nursing is involved in budgeting. At the sound of the word *budget* one can almost hear the silent groans. Few management words conjure up such negative emotions. The much-maligned budget is commonly neglected, but it should be a power management tool. By not considering the budget as a necessary evil but instead considering it as a potential force for better performance, nurse managers create for themselves a positive attitude, which is useful in planning the important document.[12]

Preparation of the budget begins several months before the end of each fiscal year to allow time for careful preparation. The budgetary process in a decentralized system has several steps: (1) participants review agency policies, standards, and objectives; (2) top-level administrators project for the future and prepare guidelines; (3) middle-level nurse managers prepare the annual budget; (4) the administrator of nursing services and the comptroller review the budget; (5) the budget is accepted or modified; and (6) the budget is implemented and regularly evaluated (Figure 10-2).

Review of agency policies, standards, and objectives

Because all types of budgets are projections or plans of future events, they provide managers with standards for control. Before preparing a budget it is important to review *policies,* which are broad guidelines for making all decisions. Policies made at the top level are interpreted and implemented through each division's own standards and objectives. For example, one agency's policy might be to provide care for all people regardless of their ability to pay. Another policy might be to include education and research as an integral part of all organizational operations. A more common policy is that enough income must be generated to offset all expenditures.[13]

Standards are established levels of quality or quantity used to guide performance. They constitute the norm of activity that is acceptable in an institution (e.g., standards for admission and dismissal of patients, standards of nursing practice). *Objectives* state how the policies and standards will be carried out. A review of policies, standards, and objectives at the top level focuses on the broad picture. Then from the top level down all budget deliberations consider the agency's broad policies, standards, and objectives, which are then reflected in budgeting appropriations.

Top-level projections and guidelines

Those who prepare budgets must exercise judgment when using historical data and forecasts of

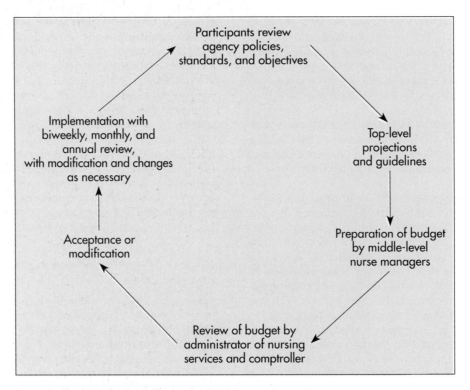

FIGURE 10-2. Model of a budget process in a decentralized system.

changing conditions and costs. The principal focus when making projections and establishing guidelines is to maximize efficiency and productivity. Top-level administrators project and guide in broad terms, and these projections are used as guides by all administrators. Examples of broad *projections* include increasing patient census by one tenth in the next fiscal year and adding a new wing to the hospital in the next 2 years. Examples of broad *guidelines* might be exploring ways to use labor more productively, upgrading existing facilities, maintaining a work environment that nourishes people and rewards their accomplishments, and giving first priority to the needs of patients.

Preparation of budget by middle-level managers

The key to controlling a budget begins with preparation of the annual budget. Middle-level managers (nurse managers or department managers) prepare the budget for their units on the basis of past expenditures and predictions for the coming year,

which are provided by the chief fiscal officer within the framework formulated by top-level management. Department managers communicate with other department managers and their supervisors, whose operations are related and interdependent. In decentralized budgeting, coordination is important; otherwise each department might operate without regard to what other departments are doing or without consideration of the organization's overall goals. Computer printouts of the master operating budget and related departments' past budgets are shared and used in projecting budgets for the upcoming year.[14]

Costing out nursing services

Hospitals. Attempts by hospitals to separate nursing costs from room rates have been underway for at least 10 years. Concern has increased with the development of DRGs and the increased use of APNs and the case management system. The goal is to identify the cost of nursing for a specific patient so that nursing costs can be reflected as a separate charge on the patient's

bill. There are several reasons to support these efforts (Box 10-3). To evaluate nursing costs, the following issues must be explored:[15]

1. The cost of nursing time for each DRG and acuity level in a particular institution
2. Direct (hands-on) versus indirect (other) costs of nursing
3. Comparison of nursing costs with total hospital cost
4. Comparison of nursing costs with other departments
5. Comparison of nursing costs at one institution with nursing costs at other institutions

Identifying costs for specific nursing interventions or services allows for cost evaluation of nursing care such as which nursing diagnoses are associated with which medical diagnoses (DRGs) and which nursing interventions provide the best outcome for specific nursing diagnoses.[15]

Community health agencies and nursing homes. Community health agencies have kept cost records based on nursing cost per visit for many years. However, this cost analysis has included all costs of the agency (operative and capital expenditure budgets); there has been no attempt to identify only nursing costs. What is needed is the cost per diagnosis or nursing treatment.

With nursing homes, some states have prepared a list of nursing services based on an assumed provider (usually an LPN/LVN or nursing assistant) along with the average amount of time needed to deliver those services depending on time-and-motion studies and expert opinion. Costs for nursing are treated the same as hospital costs and little effort is given to determining the costs of specific nursing services. Until this is done nurses cannot justify the numbers or levels of nurses needed to provide care for a specific unit or agency.[16]

Skilled- and intermediate-care facilities. Before the passing of the Omnibus Budget Reconciliation Act, skilled-nursing facilities were required to provide adequate, state-regulated nursing services. As of October 1, 1990, a skilled-nursing facility or an intermediate-care facility must have sufficient nursing staff to provide nursing and related services so that the facility can "attain or maintain the highest practical physical, mental, and psycho-social well-being of each resident, as determined by [its] assessments of individual plans of care."[17,p.539] Compliance will be

---

Box 10-3. **Reasons why hospital directors would support efforts to determine the costs of nursing services**

1. Efforts lead to knowledge about nursing care cost, which is presently hidden in room cost.
2. Nursing care is the largest product of any hospital. Although the costs of other products are known, nursing costs remain obscure.
3. Knowing the cost of nursing allows for accurate billing of nursing services, contracts with HMOs and PPOs for nursing services, and better determination of the cost of a new service.
4. Knowledge of nursing cost does *not* mean higher healthcare costs. It opens the door to cost reduction in nursing through design of more effective delivery methods.
5. If costing out nursing services leads to the conclusion that nursing is being unfairly compensated or that nursing is subsidizing other services, the hospital administrator should be the first to have this information so that he or she can promote a more equitable allocation of reimbursement among providers.
6. Knowing the type, quality, and cost of services of all healthcare providers allows consumers and managers a safe substitution of cheaper alternatives. Increased competition in the healthcare arena reduces costs for the consumer.
7. Efforts to cost out nursing services are consistent with the values of hospital directors to promote quality care in a cost-effective manner.
8. Local efforts to cost out nursing services are in line with the national trend. Hospital and nurse directors can take a proactive role in defining and collecting their own data or can wait passively until it is done by others, who may not collect or use the data appropriately.

Modified from McCloskey J: Implications of costing out nursing services for reimbursement, *Nurs Manage* 20(1):49, 1989.

costly, with intermediate-care facilities without skilled nursing beds tending to bear the largest cost increases.

To satisfy the sufficient nurse staff requirement, skilled and intermediate care facilities must have an RN on duty at least 8 consecutive hours a day, 7 days a week, and a full-time RN must serve as director of nursing. Nurse managers are in a position to estimate new costs that stem from the new rules. This is important because Medicare and Medicaid are directed in the new law to pay their share of reasonable costs of the new requirements. Full justification must be included when preparing a budget for staff members, especially for new categories such as occupational therapist or psychologist.

Review of budget by administrator of nursing services and comptroller

Budgets from each unit are received by the administrator of nursing services and the comptroller or chief financial officer, who reviews and compares them with past budgets, budgets from all other nursing departments, and the amount of revenue that can reasonably be expected in the coming year. Some administrators require written justification for budget requests.

Acceptance or modification

Budgets must often be reduced or modified to balance expected costs and revenues. Items of lowest priority are generally cut first. However, when revenue is very limited even high-priority items must be eliminated. Once the budget is accepted, it is approved by the administrator and governing board and sent to each department or unit to serve as the financial guide for the coming year.

Implementation with review and modification and changes as necessary

Ongoing surveillance of the budget is vital to its success. The most effective system uses a two-way flow of information between middle and top management, with a utilization report issued every 2 weeks or every month. Figure 10-3 illustrates how budgetary responsibilities can be analyzed. The nurse manager is regularly provided with a computerized statement from the comptroller that indicates the items for which he or she is responsible, the current period of budget, and how much has been spent. The statement also indicates *variance* (the amount spent over or under the budget). By comparing what is actually spent with what was budgeted, the nurse manager is able to monitor unit operation. Variations from the projected budget show excess supply costs, too many or too few of the wrong types of personnel, and overuse or underuse of the nursing unit.[17] The manager is also given the year-end data analysis and a comparison of the previous year's budget.

In addition to the utilization reports there is a quarterly evaluation. Projections and actual occurrences are compared, and minor modifications can be made. No major changes are made without going through the entire budgetary process. With sufficient information the nurse manager can see what is working satisfactorily and identify problem areas and unfavorable trends to initiate corrective action when necessary.

NURSING SERVICES CONTROL SYSTEM

The definition of control provides for the intention of control; it does not tell the manager how to establish and implement a process that will lead to desired results. The control process may be divided into the following basic components: (1) establishing standards, objectives, and methods for measuring performance; (2) measuring actual performance; (3) comparing results of performance with standards and objectives and identifying strengths and areas for correction; and (4) acting to reinforce strengths or successes and taking corrective action as necessary (Figure 10-4).

Establishing Standards for Measuring Performance

Standards can be a way to measure and evaluate quality and quantity of performance. They are formulated at all levels and are stated in terms of desired levels of attainment. Standards are a mutual level of excellence, or an established norm. Standards have several distinguishing characteristics:[18]

Monthly responsibility summary
(computer printout)

Items budgeted	Current period			Year-to-date			Prior year		
Area of service / Month / Year / Nurse manager	Actual	Budget	Variance	Actual	Budget	Variance	Actual	Budget	Variance
Salaries									
Management									
R.N.									
L.V.N.									
Nursing assistants									
Orderlies									
Clerical									
Total wages									
F.I.C.A. taxes									
Vacation pay									
Group health insurance									
Group life insurance									
Pension and retirement									
Worker's comp. insur.									
Holiday pay									
Sick leave									
Surgical packs; CSS sterilizer									
Surgical supplies, general									
IV solutions									
Pharmaceuticals									
Other medical care supplies									
Office/administration supplies									
Instruments/minor equipment									
Repairs and maintenance									
Depreciation/equipment									
Equipment rental									
Telephone									
Training sessions; books									
Travel									
Dues and subscriptions									
Other expense									
TOTAL EXPENSE									

FIGURE 10-3. Example of a form in which monthly expenditures for an area of responsibility can be logged.

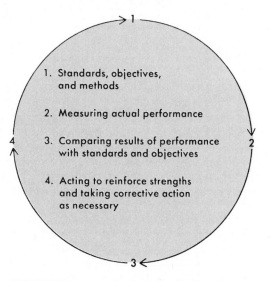

1. Standards, objectives, and methods

2. Measuring actual performance

3. Comparing results of performance with standards and objectives

4. Acting to reinforce strengths and taking corrective action as necessary

FIGURE 10-4. Basic steps in the control process.

- They are predetermined.
- They are established by an authority, often with staff input, and they are accepted by those affected by the standards.
- They are used as measurement tools and therefore must be measurable and achievable.

The development of standards often leads to increased pay for staff members because higher levels of achievement are reached and can be validated. A universal standard to which healthcare agencies must adhere is the requirement for licensure, accreditation, and certification for employees and the agency. Healthcare agencies may want to develop standards that exceed the requirements of outside interests, or they may wish to develop standards that are not vested in regulations but uniquely apply to them.

There are three types of standards: structure, process, and outcome. **Structure standards** focus on the setting or management system used by an agency to organize and deliver care; the equipment, policies, procedures, medical records; and the number and categories of personnel who provide that care. When evaluating structure, the conditions under which nursing care will be given are assessed; the quality or inner workings of those conditions is not assessed. For example, a structure sample might be that "A team leader is responsible for no more than 20 patients/clients with no fewer than three team members to provide

care," or "A case manager has access to all records, staff, and services that pertain to the care of his or her clients." **Process standards** refer to actual nursing procedures, or those activities nurses perform when giving care. The nursing process is individualized and occurs between the nurse and the patient/client. Process standards are task oriented and are used in nursing as audits to see if standards of practice are being met. **Outcome standards** are designed to measure the results of nursing care. Responses or changes in the patients/clients are compared with patient/client criteria. Outcome standards can be either concurrent or retrospective. Over the years emphasis has moved from structure and process standards to outcome standards, or how the care has helped the patient/client. The emphasis is now on accountability.[19] According to Luquire and colleagues,[20] "Outcomes management asks staff nurses to take on several new responsibilities, to consider cost containment, to assert themselves in order to ensure that efficient care is delivered and to evaluate care constantly to find ways of improving it."[p.60]

The outcomes management department of St. Luke's Episcopal Hospital in Houston uses critical pathways, which are a mainstay of case management. The department also emphasizes a more multidisciplinary approach that includes nurses and other healthcare providers. Statistical analysis is used to monitor patients and track complications, or variances. Outcomes management looks not only at the frequency of complications, but also at how they affect the length of the patient's stay or his or her outcome.[20] Outcomes management fits in with recent healthcare proposals for practice guidelines.[21] Outcomes management also influences changes in the way that staff nurses and other caregivers function. St. Luke's has used outcomes management since 1991 and has found the following to be true: (1) it provides staff nurses with more autonomy, (2) it increases collaboration among health professionals, (3) it improves the quality of patient care, (4) it results in shorter hospital stays, and (5) it reduces agency costs for care.[20]

Establishing Methods for Measuring Performance

Before process and outcome can be evaluated within a structure, measurable criteria or objectives specific to giving nursing care must be developed. Developing criteria is difficult because nursing care is delivered within a framework of interdependent relationships with physicians and other healthcare personnel. Until more progress is made the best approach is to select tools for measurement that are easy to use and provide a valid assessment and to select appropriate evaluators. The most commonly used methods for measurement of nursing care are task analysis and quality control. The ANA Congress for Nursing Practice has developed and published standards of practice for nurses in many areas, which can be used in the development of standards for performance evaluation.

Measuring Actual Performance

Like all aspects of control, measurement of performance is an ongoing, repetitive process; the actual frequency of measurement depends on the type of activity being measured. For example, safety factors must be continuously monitored, whereas a formal appraisal of performance may occur only once or twice a year. Measurements may be scheduled in advance, may be done at periodic but unannounced intervals, or may occur at random. The use of all methods provides a more comprehensive assessment. One should not confuse measurement of tasks with quality nor allow too long a time to pass between measurements. It is much better to clarify the purpose of the measurement and to measure performance on a continuous basis. In this way the manager and staff can be alerted to those tasks and levels of care that need attention. This strategy prevents waiting until remedial action is necessary; impossible; or costly in time, money, and emotional involvement.

Comparing Results of Performance with Standards and Objectives

A comparison of nursing tasks and quality of nursing practice is made in the organization and can serve as a basis for comparison of nursing from one institution to another. The pivotal question addressed is: "Does the performance match the standards and objectives?" In some ways comparison is the easiest step in the control process. The standards, objectives, and methods of measurement have been set; it is

now a matter of comparing these standards with measured results. If performance matches standards and objectives, managers may assume that things are under control; if performance is contrary to standards and objectives, action is necessary.

Reinforcing Strengths or Successes and Taking Corrective Action as Necessary

One part of the control process that is often overlooked is the identification of those areas that have contributed to successful accomplishment of goals. Positive aspects need to be identified so that they may be translated into encouragement and motivation for the nursing members involved. Corrective action may need only minor changes because of temporary circumstances, but there may be a real flaw in the plan that necessitates changes in standards or objectives. Unless managers see the control process through to its conclusion, they are merely monitoring performance and not exercising control. The emphasis should always be on finding constructive ways to improve performance rather than on placing blame or looking for areas to criticize.

TASK ANALYSIS AND QUALITY CONTROL OF NURSING CARE

Goal achievement in nursing is assessed by measuring task performance and quality of care. In **task analysis**, actions and procedures such as written guides, schedules, rules, records, and budgets are inspected. In *quality control* the level of nursing care provided and its effects on the patient/client are assessed. Task analysis and quality control indicate both process and outcome of nursing activity. The lower- or first-level nursing manager has an important role in each.

Task Analysis

Task-oriented measurements use such tools as time studies and checklists and consider the actual process of giving nursing care. Task analysis studies determine issues such as how long it takes a nurse to give a bath or perform a procedure or how many staff members are needed to care for a specific number of patients/clients.

One problem in evaluating nursing tasks is that there are few tangible, identifiable, and fixed "returns on investment" to study; the physical, psychologic, social, and spiritual factors are closely interrelated. Task analyses have serious drawbacks because they fail to measure needs other than physical support and always deal with the present situation rather than with the ideal. In addition the delivery of nursing care and the effects of that care fluctuate greatly according to the patient/client, caregivers, type of agency, and type of service. Resistance is another deterrent to task analysis. Like all workers nurses may become comfortable in their niches and routines and may be hesitant about or even resistant to inspection and change.

Quality Control

Quality control is the responsibility of all employees within an organization. It is achieved through a variety of preventive and corrective methods that are intended to ensure compliance with established standards. Quality control generally focuses on measuring inputs, organizational functions, and outputs. The results of these measurements enable management to make decisions about products or services.

The evolution of quality assurance (assessment and improvement) in the nursing profession has been greatly affected by several fundamental sources: (1) the Nurse Practice Act and Medical Practice Act of each state and (2) the development of standards by which to evaluate the delivery of healthcare. The Social Security Amendments of 1972 that mandated Professional Standards Review Organizations (PRSOs) provided the impetus to the Joint Commission on Accreditation of Health Care Organizations (JCAHO) to stipulate that "there shall be evidence of a well-defined, organized program designed to enhance patient care through ongoing objective assessment of important aspects of patient care and correction of identified problems."[22,p.85]

Quality assurance versus quality assessment and improvement

The term *quality assurance* (QA) is gradually being replaced with terms that better define the process, such as **total quality improvement**

(TQI), *quality improvement* (QI), and *total quality assessment and improvement* (TQAI).[23,24,25] Professional associations, accreditation agencies, federal and state regulatory bodies, and third-party payers are all pressing for TQI. The JCAHO has developed standards for the review of quality assessment and improvement (QAI).[22] The JCAHO has an "Agenda for Change" that includes three initiatives for QAI: (1) revision of the standards, (2) redesign of the survey process, and (3) development of performance measures or indicators. QAI involves participation at both centralized and decentralized levels by all members.[26]

One 566-bed hospital in New York has a three-pronged approach to QAI: (1) to monitor and evaluate the important aspects of nursing care, (2) to identify opportunities and plans for improving nursing care, and (3) to resolve patient care and clinical performance problems as they occur.[27] Nurse managers are responsible for establishing QAI activities in their units and managing their progress. They document the nature and outcomes of their units' QAI activities, follow up QAI projects to correct problems, and submit written reports of QAI findings and related actions to the appropriate individuals and committees.

The American Nurses Association model for quality control of nursing care

The American Nurses Association (ANA) suggests that Standards of Nursing Practice set forth by the ANA Divisions on Practice can be applied to nursing practice in any clinical situation and therefore can serve well as a model for quality assurance (Figure 10-5).[28] This model is a more explicit adaptation of the basic functions of control (standards, measurement, correction) and is geared directly toward control of nursing care.

In this model value identification examines such issues as patient/client philosophy; needs and rights from an economic, social, psychologic, and spiritual perspective; and values of the healthcare organization and providers of nursing services.

The identification of the type of structure, process, and standards in an institution that provides health services offers a framework for the review process. Examples of structure include the institution's status in relation to requirements

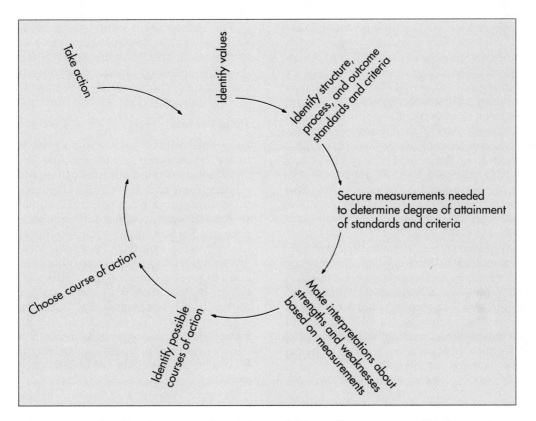

FIGURE 10-5. The American Nurses Association model for quality assurance and implementation of standards.

of licensing boards, the JCAHO, and medical and nursing groups.

Process describes the nature and sequence of nursing activities (what nurses do, how they do it, and in what order). Standards refer to the level of nursing care that is to be provided. Criteria are the characteristics or behaviors used to measure the level of care (e.g., "A nursing team provides care from nursing care plans that are updated at least once every 8 hours," or "The patients/clients are protected from accident and injury"). Outcome standards and criteria reveal the end results of nursing care. Outcome measures may focus on what the patient/client has learned as a result of nurse contact on the basis of items chosen to measure end results.

Measurements are those tools used to gather information or data as determined by the selection of standards and criteria. Audits and appraisals of cost, quality, and accountability are mandated by the JCAHO and are accomplished by individuals, physicians, nursing staff, patients/clients, community, and other health disciplines. A standard rating scale is an example of a method used for quality control. Standards are listed and checked off by an evaluator according to the level of accomplishment. Other methods used are questionnaires, observations, peer review, and tabulations of patient/client records or patient care audit.

The nursing audit provides nurses with an opportunity to have a voice in the control of nursing practice. The director of nursing services or an appointed representative (e.g., a patient care coordinator) is responsible for initiating and maintaining a nursing audit program by using methods decided on within nursing, including established standards and criteria, measurement of actual practice against standards and criteria, and evaluation of results. The auditor is also responsible for taking actions to reinforce strengths and correct deficiencies in nursing service. Nursing audits consider the past or the present and document compliance with standards established by the agency; the nursing department; and professional, governmental, and accrediting groups.[29]

A retrospective or closed chart audit is an inspection of a patient's/client's chart after he or she has been discharged. Retrospective audits provide an objective way of assessing accountability for care.[29] A current or open chart audit is an evaluation of the record of a patient/client who is still receiving care in the hospital or agency. Measuring quality of care through inspection of the nursing process in a variety of ways prevents relevant information from being overlooked.

Interpretation of conclusions about strengths and weaknesses in nursing care delivery are made after the information has been analyzed. Possible courses of action are identified, and a course of action is chosen by using the problem-solving method, weighing the options, and following through with a carefully considered plan. Finally a course of action is taken and the assessment procedure is completed.

The management control process and the ANA's model are similar (Figure 10-6). The ANA model can be helpful to nurse managers because the steps proposed directly apply to evaluation and control of the Standards of Nursing Practice.

Peer review

Peer review involves the examination and evaluation by associates, of another nurse's practice. Preestablished standards, objectives, and methods are used as a basis for judgment. A new nurse manager of a diabetes unit at the University of Michigan Hospital in Ann Arbor discovered that her staff did not fully understand documentation standards.[29] Peer review of closed charts was initiated to improve documentation and to develop peer review skills within the group. A chart audit worksheet was developed for use by all staff (Figure 10-7). Staff members were oriented to the system and taught how to audit the chart. The Ann Arbor staff audited charts of recently dismissed patients in small groups because the nurse manager believed that

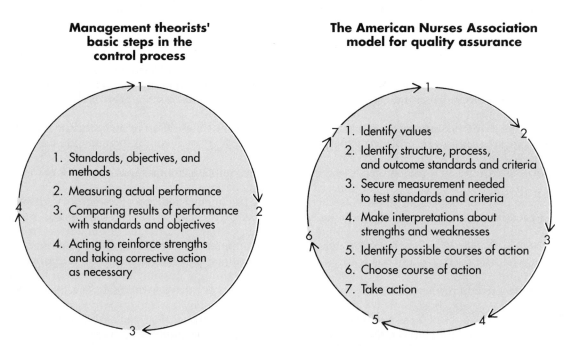

FIGURE 10-6. Comparison of management theorists' basic steps in the control process and the American Nurses Association model for quality assurance.

1. Mechanisms for coping with stress
   How does the patient react to stress?
   What does the patient do to cope with stress?
   e.g., Eats more or stops eating when under stress
   Nursing assessment_____
   Nursing progress note_____
   Other_____
   Absent_____
2. Literacy
   Can the patient read and write?
   What level of education has the patient reached?
   Nursing assessment_____
   Top of database form_____
   Other_____
   Absent_____
3. Foot condition
   Is there a description of the patient's foot
   condition?
   Nursing assessment_____
   Nursing progress note_____
   Other_____
   Absent_____

FIGURE 10-7. Sample of a chart audit worksheet used in peer auditing. (From Christensen M: Peer auditing, *Nurs Manage* 21[1]:50, 1990.)

Audit results—first 6 months % of criteria achieved			
Criteria	April	July	Sept
Mechanisms used to cope with stress	25	75	83
Literacy	87	100	100
Foot condition	75	75	90

FIGURE 10-8. Audit results of the first 6 months, which shows the percentage of selected criteria achieved in peer auditing. (From Christensen M: Peer auditing, *Nurs Manage* 21[1]:52, 1990.)

small group interaction encouraged constructive communication. Through this process nurses gained increased insight into areas that needed improvement, began making constructive changes in their nursing practice, and began helping their peers to grow. Documentation has markedly improved over a period of several months (Figure 10-8). Staff nurses have also become more comfortable with other types of peer review and with each other. When they see the need for additions on a current or open chart, they feel free to leave a note on the chart or to communicate with the nurse. The overall improvement in documentation has more than met the nurse manager's objectives.[29]

Problem-focused quality assurance program

The JCAHO mandates a written plan and a comprehensive approach to QA.[22] In planning for their next visit from the JCAHO, the Veterans Administration Medical Center in San Diego renovated their existing QA program to "provide an ongoing objective assessment and correction of those problematic aspects of nursing care which have the greatest impact on patients."[30,p.55] Each major nursing service, every clinical unit, and all special care units participated, and shifted the focus of QA activities to problem-focused patient care evaluation studies. Such a program is more in line with QAI. Box 10-4 provides guidelines for writing a problem-focused patient care evaluation summary. Note that after problems have been identified, a correction plan is developed along with a reassessment plan and time frame. The San Diego VA reports positive results from its QA program and invites all nursing services to use these guidelines if they wish.[30]

PERFORMANCE APPRAISAL

Performance appraisal is a method of acquiring and processing the information needed to improve an individual employee's performance and accomplishments. Performance appraisal consists of setting standards and objectives; reviewing progress; having ongoing feedback between the appraiser and the employee; and planning for reinforcement, deletion, or correction of identified behaviors as necessary. Performance appraisal of staff nurses and assistants is one of the most important tasks a nurse manager must accomplish, because an organization depends on its nursing personnel to provide the prescribed level of nursing care at a reasonable cost and in a

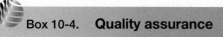

Box 10-4.   Quality assurance

Nursing service quality assurance program, San Diego VAMC
Guidelines: writing the problem-focused patient care evaluation summary

The purpose of the *problem-focused patient care evaluation summary* is to provide a written account of specific elements, which are derived from the evaluative QA studies that nurses on your unit have conducted.

The specific elements on the *problem-focused patient care evaluation summary* are: (1) topic, (2) sample and time of review, (3) basis for problem selection, (4) preestablished clinically valid criteria, (5) objectives, (6) data collection, (7) results, (8) corrective action plan and time frame and (9) reassessment plan and time frame.

In the section to follow each of the nine topics above is discussed separately and an example(s) is provided to assist you in writing each section.

Topic	*Topic* refers to what you wrote on your initial QA topic statement form that was submitted to the QA Committee. All you need do is repeat what you said on that form. For example, your topic may have been *Patient Anxiety,* or *Patient Falls* or *Heparin Lock Use.* Do not write your topic as a complete sentence. As you can see in the example, a few words or word will identify your topic.

Sample	*Sample* refers to (1) the number of elements in your QA Study (e.g., 15, 25 patient records) or procedures (e.g., code blues, arterial catheterizations) or personnel (e.g., nurses, doctors or patients or staff interviewed or surveyed), and (2) when these elements were measured. For example, *retrospectively* (in the past), *concurrently* (in the present), or *prospectively* (in the future [e.g., forecast of patient care needs at a future point in time]). Hence, your entry in this section may appear as:
	
	    25 Patient Records; reviewed retrospectively
	    46 I&O Slips; reviewed retrospectively
	Another example might be:
	    10 SICU patients; interviewed concurrently
	    12 RNs; surveyed concurrently
	    100 code blues; reviewed concurrently

Basis for problem selection	*Basis for problem selection* refers to those factors which indicated that the topic you selected for QA Review was problematic. This statement has been written on your topic sheet that you submitted several months ago to the QA Committee. For example: 1. Nurses on the Oncology ward do not have current information on the potential complications of chemotherapeutic agents. This has negative consequences for oncology patient care. 2. Nurses in the Mental health clinic have observed low follow-through from the Psychiatric inpatient service and are concerned about problems in exchange of pertinent, timely patient information.
Preestablished clinically valid criteria	*Preestablished clinically valid criteria* refers to specific elements against which you may measure your problem. The source of these specific elements may be: (1) standards of practice, (2) published nursing research, (3) policies and procedures, (4) experts in the field, and/or (5) VA guides. For example, the following are critical criteria elements derived from a VAMC Blood Transfusion Protocol:

From Harris S, Kreger S, and Davis M: A problem-focused quality assurance program, *Nurs Man* 20(2):57-58, 1989.

Box 10-4.   Quality assurance—cont'd

	CRITICAL CRITERIA ELEMENT	STANDARD	EXCEPTION
Preestablished clinically valid criteria—cont'd	1. Baseline vital signs obtained prior to administration	1. 100%	1. None
	2. Blood initiated within 30 minutes from time of arrival on ward	2. 100%	2. None
	3. Line clamped immediately with reaction	3. 100%	3. None
	4. Blood absorbed within 2 hours	4. 100%	4. MD specifies otherwise

One criterion may suffice, or you may need to cite several criteria. There is no requirement that a specific number be used.

Objectives

Objectives refers to what you want to find out about the problems you selected for your QA Study. Your objectives have already been written on the topic sheet you submitted to the QA Committee, so all you need to do is rewrite in this section what you had written. Examples:
1. To determine the incidence of patient falls occurring on 3 North
2. To identify patterns about when patients falls occur most frequently on 3 North
3. To find out what factors may be causing or contributing to patient falls on 3 North

You will probably have more than one objective. There is no specified number. Remember, statements of your objectives should always begin with the word "to" . . . to find out, to determine, to assess, etc.

Data collection

Data collection refers to the tool(s) and/or method(s) which you have used to collect information about the problem you studied. If a tool was used, simply say "see attached tool." Again this should be an easy task since you have already indicated on your topic sheet your method and/or tool for collecting your data. All you need do is repeat in this section what you have written. For example:

Random audit of patient records

Patient questionnaire and interviews (See attached tool)

Observation of team conferences (See attached tool)

Review of incident reports, patient records and tabulation of incidence patterns of medication errors

Random audit of patient records and tabulation of no show appointment in MHC

A copy of the tool should be attached to the Summary Sheet

Results

Results refers to what you found out (e.g., the findings) from your data collection.

In this section, write about your results first. Then if you have any table(s) which summarize that data, refer the reader to them. The table(s) should be attached to the Summary Sheet.

The Results section should be limited to one brief, factual paragraph which can be confined to the space provided on the Summary Sheet.

To begin the Results section, simply complete the following sentence or a variation of it. "Analysis of the data revealed that. . . ."

Analysis of the data revealed that eight (8) medication errors occurred during the period of review. Four (4) errors were made by RNs and four (4) errors were made by LVNs. Six (6) errors were made during the night tour.

These errors consisted of:
a. Medication given to the wrong person (3)
b. Medication not given (2)
c. Incorrect dosage administered (1)
d. Topical medication applied to wrong site (1)
e. Medication given at wrong time (1)

Continued

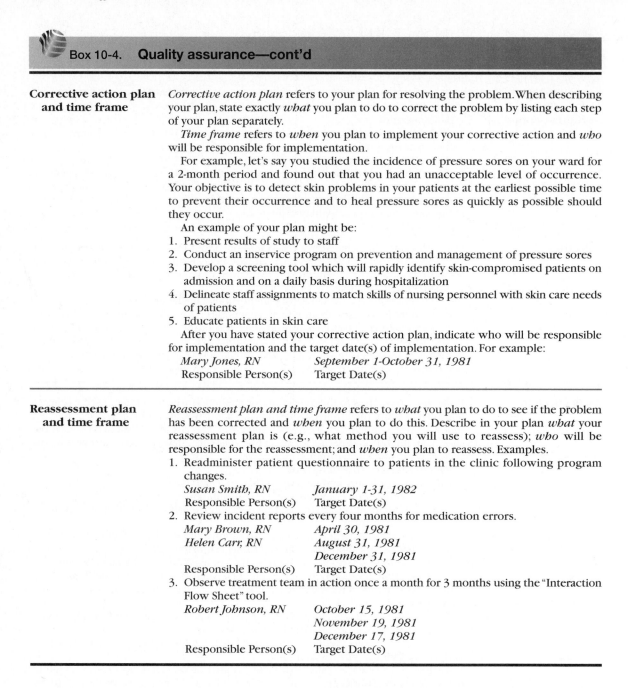

Box 10-4.   Quality assurance—cont'd

Corrective action plan and time frame

Corrective action plan refers to your plan for resolving the problem. When describing your plan, state exactly *what* you plan to do to correct the problem by listing each step of your plan separately.

Time frame refers to *when* you plan to implement your corrective action and *who* will be responsible for implementation.

For example, let's say you studied the incidence of pressure sores on your ward for a 2-month period and found out that you had an unacceptable level of occurrence. Your objective is to detect skin problems in your patients at the earliest possible time to prevent their occurrence and to heal pressure sores as quickly as possible should they occur.

An example of your plan might be:

1. Present results of study to staff
2. Conduct an inservice program on prevention and management of pressure sores
3. Develop a screening tool which will rapidly identify skin-compromised patients on admission and on a daily basis during hospitalization
4. Delineate staff assignments to match skills of nursing personnel with skin care needs of patients
5. Educate patients in skin care

After you have stated your corrective action plan, indicate who will be responsible for implementation and the target date(s) of implementation. For example:

Mary Jones, RN   *September 1-October 31, 1981*
Responsible Person(s)   Target Date(s)

Reassessment plan and time frame

Reassessment plan and time frame refers to *what* you plan to do to see if the problem has been corrected and *when* you plan to do this. Describe in your plan *what* your reassessment plan is (e.g., what method you will use to reassess); *who* will be responsible for the reassessment; and *when* you plan to reassess. Examples.

1. Readminister patient questionnaire to patients in the clinic following program changes.
   Susan Smith, RN   *January 1-31, 1982*
   Responsible Person(s)   Target Date(s)
2. Review incident reports every four months for medication errors.
   Mary Brown, RN   *April 30, 1981*
   Helen Carr, RN   *August 31, 1981*
                              December 31, 1981
   Responsible Person(s)   Target Date(s)
3. Observe treatment team in action once a month for 3 months using the "Interaction Flow Sheet" tool.
   Robert Johnson, RN   *October 15, 1981*
                              November 19, 1981
                              December 17, 1981
   Responsible Person(s)   Target Date(s)

satisfactory environment. However, most nurse managers have difficulty handling the assessment procedure adequately. It is not easy to judge a nurse's performance accurately, and it is often harder to convey that judgment to the employee in a comfortable or helpful manner.

Nurse Manager's Responsibility

In hospitals and other healthcare agencies supervisors usually review the performance of nurse managers. Nurse managers in turn are responsible for preparing appraisal forms and interviewing nursing personnel assigned to their respective departments or subunits. Lower- or first-level nurse managers participate in the procedure by preparing the initial evaluation of each nursing staff member assigned to them because they are best equipped to assess activities of the team members on a day-to-day basis. Assessments made by the team leader or primary nurse are reviewed with each worker and are followed by a conference between the team leader and immediate supervisor. This process ensures a clear, complete, and fair report.

Historical Events in the Development of Performance Appraisal

The first recording of a performance appraisal system was made around 1800 by Owens of Scotland, who devised a plan using different-colored blocks to represent various levels of performance. Each day workers would find a colored block of wood at their place that best corresponded with Owens' assessment of their work from the previous day.[28] Other time-and-motion studies were developed until World War I highlighted the need for a tool to identify and evaluate military leaders. Business and industry began studying appraisal of managers. Many forms that still focused primarily on time and motion became available.

Rating scales were introduced during this period. Individual performance was graphed on a scale from "poor" or "unsatisfactory" to "good" or "excellent." Because of the surge of interest in human relations, appraisal forms in the 1930s and 1940s concentrated on personality and behavioral characteristics. By 1950 the tools included both work-related activities and human elements. During this decade management by objectives (MBO) was introduced. Emphasis was on the determination of objectives for both the organization and its managers and on the measurement of performance against these objectives.

After the U.S. Supreme Court decision in 1970 *(Griggs vs Duke Power Company)*, performance appraisal has become a legal matter and therefore has increased significance for the nurse manager. The Supreme Court decision mandated that any type of testing procedure for a particular job must relate directly to the job duties to be performed. Soon after this ultimatum the Equal Employment Opportunity Commission (EEOC) developed guidelines that reinforced the Supreme Court decision and stated that "when used as

tools for selection, promotion or transfer, performance appraisals are considered tests and the Supreme Court decision applies."[31,p.12333] The effective nurse manager is aware of governmental controls when developing and working with performance appraisal. These controls are made known to nursing management personnel through the designated channels of communication. For example, under centralized control the personnel office would advise the director of nursing services, who in turn would pass the information along to supervisors, nurse managers, and lower- or first-level managers.

Components of an Effective Nursing Performance Appraisal System

The effective nurse manager knows that the controlling process is used to promote positive and favorable activity. Nurse managers are responsible for securing the common purposes of the total enterprise, but they also are responsible for maintaining a climate in which nursing personnel can obtain job satisfaction. One way to assess progress toward these purposes is through performance appraisal.

A number of factors contribute to a successful nursing performance appraisal system[27]:

1. *There is compatibility between criteria for individual evaluation and organizational goals.* To be realistic and workable, the appraisal procedure must be agreed on at each level of management. Elements in the appraisal process reflect the combined aspirations of all individuals and groups under consideration. Involvement of personnel in all phases of the evaluatory process increases belief in the fairness and accuracy of the evaluation, establishes a commitment to the evaluation, and increases motivation to use the results.

2. *The appraisal applies directly to the performance standards and objectives expected of the worker.* When nursing roles and job descriptions are stated in terms of relevance to nursing practice, there is an objective way to determine whether goals have been reached. If the job description is vague or ends with "and such other duties as may be required," the staff member does not know what direction to take or what goals and objectives are con-

sidered most significant when outcomes are surveyed. Therefore the roles for each member of the health team and goals in the form of behavioral objectives and success criteria (e.g., job descriptions and procedure manuals) are clearly established before appraisal.

3. *Behavioral expectations have been developed or mutually agreed on by the nurse appraiser and the individual being evaluated.* The MBO system provides an excellent example of how behaviors are formulated and tested. Employees who participate in formulating goals for delivery of nursing care are more zealous in seeing them accomplished than are those who are merely given goals for fulfillment.

4. *The nurse appraiser understands the appraisal process and uses the procedure effectively.* All nurses who hold positions of leadership are expected to evaluate themselves and others competently as part of the management process. Not all nurses are prepared to assess the competencies of nursing staff members, but they must assume responsibility for acquiring evaluative skills. Provisions can be made by the employing agency for adequate training in the appraisal process through on-the-job activity or inservice education. The nurse manager may wish to complete one of the many appraisal courses sponsored by professional organizations and groups.

5. *Each individual is rated by his or her immediate supervisor.* This system is by far the most commonly used in management. Although nurse managers partly rely on the views of a number of people such as patients/clients, other nursing personnel, and contacts, appraisals are most accurate when the data are gathered and processed by one supervisor who is knowledgeable about the individual being evaluated.

6. *The performance appraisal concentrates on strengths and notes weaknesses in the individual to improve performance.* Reinforcing strong performance breeds more strong performance.[31] Placing a premium on what an individual does well pays off for management. No one is strong in every area; all are subject to shortcomings. Weaknesses should be noted only if they are perceived as a threat to safety or if they provide a significant deterrent to goal accomplishment.

7. *The appraisal process encourages feedback from nursing members regarding their performance, needs, and interests.* Through daily contact, observation, questioning, and listening, the nurse manager attempts to gain understanding of each staff member. When it is time to prepare a formal appraisal, the nurse manager is better equipped to accurately reflect the profile of the worker. After appraisal staff members are given the opportunity to verify or discredit anything that is written about them.

8. *Provision is made for initiating preventive and corrective actions and for making adjustments to improve the worker's performance.* Performance appraisal can become a positive vehicle when approached from a self-improvement point of view and when given agency assistance through such means as orientation, ongoing coaching, and staff development programs. Emphasis is placed on assuming responsibility for one's own growth with help from management or other nursing staff as needed.[31]

Performance appraisal is a difficult task at best but can be made easier by following these guidelines, which contribute to a successful procedure.

Methods of Measuring Performance

Informing nurses of their performance occurs both informally and formally. **Informal performance appraisal** occurs on a routine basis and may consist of (1) observation of work performance while engaged in individual or group functions; (2) incidental face-to-face confrontation and collaboration with the worker; (3) responses offered by the worker during a conference; (4) noting the worker's reaction to a patient/client, family member, or staff person; or (5) noting the effects of a worker's actions on patients/clients, families, personnel, or the environment. During informal appraisal the nurse manager may spontaneously mention to the worker that a particular activity was performed well or poorly, or the staff member may ask what effect his or her action had on the patient/client. Because of the close association between the behavior and the feedback, informal appraisal quickly encourages desirable performance and discourages undesirable action before it becomes habitual. A further benefit of the informal appraisal method is that if

Staff member	Room no.	Patient's name	Information pertaining to administration of care	Needs and problems
Bea Kindall	66	Roy Snell	Ca Lung	*11 A.M. Bea completed her assignment early and helped Vici.*
Vici Wilson	70a	Elaine Metz	Ca Colon	*12:30 P.M. Vici changed her lunch hr. 3 sanction-no coverage for pt.*

FIGURE 10-9. Sample of personnel appraisal notations made on a nurse manager's worksheet.

the behaviors are recorded with some regularity, the data can provide valid information for compilation of a formal report. The nurse manager can note significant behavior on the daily worksheet (Figure 10-9) or on separate paper or cards and keep these notes for reference.

Formal performance appraisal is best accomplished by regularly and methodically collecting objective facts that can distinguish between what was expected and what actually occurred. Once suitable standards and objectives have been set, a method for formal performance appraisal is selected. There is no one approach that applies to every work setting, but each method should be (1) accurate, (2) timely, (3) objective, (4) focused on the level of performance in every worker category (e.g., nursing assistant, LPN/LVN, other staff nurses), (5) addressed to major roles expected of the worker (job description), (6) economically realistic, (7) appropriate for the organizational structure, and (8) acceptable to the members involved. If the method meets these criteria, there will be positive cooperation in the collection of data.

A number of methods are used to record and report formal evaluations. The checklist and the criterion rating scale are the most commonly used methods in nursing.

Checklist

A checklist contains a compilation of all nursing performances that are expected of the worker. The appraiser's task is to place a mark in the "yes" or "no" column in accordance with the worker's behavior. The checklist is a simple way to assess important items and is an efficient way to assess technical procedures and handle a large number of employees. The checklist may or may not have space provided for comments. The checklist fails to address the degree or frequency of behavior.

Criterion rating scale

A criterion rating scale is the single most commonly used method in nursing appraisal. It is one way to measure present practice and plan for professional growth that is directly related to job description. A criterion is one way of describing success. For example, the criterion in a college course might be the grade. A criterion for a salesperson might be the dollar volume of sales in a 1-month period.

A criterion rating scale for nursing performance appraisal generally includes categories that pertain to patient/client care delivery. It also includes an assessment of how well the steps in the nursing process (assessing, goal setting, implementing, and evaluating) are used. Behaviors relating to communication and interpersonal relations, supervision, and teaching are usually included as appropriate.

There is often a problem for the appraiser in determining the level of performance, particularly for those behaviors that are considered above or below the satisfactory level. It is suggested that space be provided next to each category of performance to allow for notations that illustrate or explain the rationale behind the decision.

When personnel appraisal is weighed against criteria that have been agreed on by the nurse manager and the staff member, all that must be done is to determine whether the worker met the criteria. The rationale for this approach is that "satisfactory" performance in nursing is demanding and consistent with personnel departments' standards and/or unions' specifications. Maslow's and Drucker's theories are applied with the belief that only individuals themselves can make themselves give more to a job than they must. For achievements to reach beyond the satisfactory level, the nurse manager must create a climate that motivates staff members to reach their highest potential. Clues for accomplishing this goal are provided in this discussion and throughout this book.

Performance Review Session

Purpose

The final step in the formal appraisal process is the review session between the nurse manager and the individual being appraised. The review session is a crucial aspect of evaluation and must be treated accordingly. The primary purposes of a performance review are to increase the effectiveness of the nursing staff member in the healthcare setting and to promote worker satisfaction. The formal performance appraisal provides a "physical conversation piece" because there is tangible evidence for the evaluator and staff member to see and discuss. During the interview the immediate supervisor and worker discuss the progress of the worker through (1) clarification of goals and objectives of the agency and area to which the worker is assigned, (2) identification of job-related strengths and weaknesses, (3) promotion of a feeling of satisfaction about the work and the individual's part in work accomplishment, and (4) establishment of new goals.

Process

A key element in the review session is maintaining an open, two-way communication system. The principles of effective communication apply to the review process, but there is a uniqueness about this process. An individual meets with a supervisor to review work progress with a certain amount of nervousness and apprehension. This is particularly true if the individual feels that his or her job performance is questionable or inadequate and that the job is in jeopardy. The situation can be eased by adhering to the following guidelines:

1. Provide a comfortable, private environment. Arrange seating side by side so the written forms can be reviewed by both parties.
2. Ensure freedom from work assignments. Arrange for coverage during the meeting; begin and end the session on time.
3. Establish rapport. Indicate to the staff member concern for sharing the evaluation. A few brief exchanges of chitchat are advisable, but move right on to the business at hand.
4. Indicate that the appraisal is tentative, pending feedback from the individual. Without a response from the worker, one does not know what the worker has heard or his or her reaction to the information.
5. Begin the session on positive terms. Establish as positive a relationship as possible. One must be sincere; if the message is untrue, trust will be destroyed.
6. Include all important issues. The degree of attention that is given to individual items or issues during the appraisal session depends on the time factor and the significance of the matter to the job situation. Preplan the session to allow for appropriate emphasis. Ensure that the worker understands the rules of the conference: standards and objectives for the particular worker are used to assess the worker and feedback is encouraged. Broad categories can be covered with a single statement such as "You function well in these areas." Give a few examples to confirm the assessment. Persons under appraisal need to know that their entire performance is considered, not just a few isolated incidents. Remember that most people respond readily to positive feedback and thereby are motivated to improve their performance.

7. Present criticism sparingly and carefully. The purpose of criticism is to effect constructive behavioral change, not to reduce the individual to tears or to cause anger and hostility. Negative reactions to criticism cannot be avoided but can be made mild enough so that the worker seriously considers the criticism instead of withdrawing or attacking the appraiser. Before recording and offering criticism during an appraisal conference consider whether the behavior is critical and affects job performance.

8. The nurse manager and worker sign the formal appraisal form. After the review session has been completed and necessary adjustments have been made, the signatures of both parties should be affixed to the form. This act simply indicates that the appraiser and employee have met and reviewed the assessment. A space should always be reserved for comments from both parties, which provides an opportunity to react to the content or process of the review session. Unresolved differences can be mentioned, which provides the next supervisor to receive the report with as much input as possible.

9. Establish new goals for modifying or improving behavior. If one accepts the concept that human resources are the greatest asset to goal accomplishment, that each individual is unique, and that each person has the potential for improvement, then one will try to understand and help individuals meet their needs. A nurse manager can greatly affect the quality of work performance by using the review session as a way to plan for change. Simply stating that new goals are needed does not make them materialize. However, too much structure can lead to undesirable outcomes. The effective nurse manager maintains a balance between too much and too little control. Nurse managers need to develop a managerial style that considers people, resources, and environment. This is true with the degree of control exercised. In detecting important deviations and in guiding behavior in the desired direction, some structure and limits are necessary. As illustrated in Figure 10-10, too much control causes workers to feel over-controlled, and the environmental climate becomes stifling, inhibiting, and unsatisfying. With too little control the environment becomes chaotic and people become disorganized and ineffective in achieving goals. The nurse manager works to balance control by allowing enough freedom to exercise individual judgment and initiative and by providing structure and having enough check points to ensure goal-oriented activity.

Before the review session with the staff member, the nurse manager has planned methods to help the worker grow and develop professionally. At the close of the conference the manager and worker agree on a plan that best suits the individual's needs and the interests of the organization.

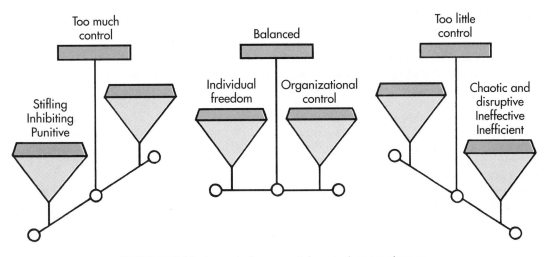

FIGURE 10-10. Impact of managerial control on employees.

CONTROLLING THE PROBLEM EMPLOYEE

A problem employee is one who exhibits chronic disruptive behavior. This person can wreak havoc on a unit's productivity and cause peers to feel anger and resentment toward the troublesome worker. The behavior of the problem employee is characterized by absenteeism; tardiness; personality conflicts; excessive griping; and displays of dissatisfaction, resentment, pessimism, or indifference.

An even more serious problem employee is the substance abuser. People with alcohol or other drug addictions often have personality changes and gradually move from being productive, cooperative workers to workers whose efficiency level drops. They become erratic in attendance and adherence to schedule and have an increasing number of accidents.

The chronically disruptive employee is far more common than the substance abuser, but all behaviors that create problems with effective control must be managed.

Progressive Discipline Policy and Procedure

It is customary for agencies to have a progressive discipline policy prepared from broad representation of the work force.[32] Such a policy specifies that certain steps will be taken if an employee's behavior becomes chronically disruptive. Disruptive behavior is documented, and the documentation is witnessed by the nurse manager (or a designee) and the disruptive employee. If the employee refuses to witness the documentation, another person such as the assistant nurse manager or team leader is asked to witness the fact that the conference was held and the employee refused to sign. The nurse conducting the conference is not to act as a therapist; instead dialogue occurs, observations are made, and recommendations are given. An example of disciplinary procedure follows:

1. *Gather the facts.* Meet the problem employee in a private area, such as the nurse manager's office, and state the reason for the conference:
   Nurse manager: Mary, I am concerned about your behaviors this month. I have noted several of them for us to discuss. (Note that dates and times are included.)

   11/1   Added 20 minutes to morning break (10:30 AM to 11:00 AM)
   11/2   Left unit without notice for 30 minutes (1:30 PM to 2:00 PM)
   11/3   Forty minutes late for work (arrived at 7:40 AM)
   11/4   Called in sick; told peer (JL) she was too tired to come to work
   11/5   Talked on phone to friend for 25 minutes (11:00 AM to 11:25 AM)

   Mary: I didn't realize I'd broken the rules so many times. Since my husband left I've been sort of crazy. I can't sleep, and when I do I don't hear the alarm. I go out at night to get out of the house, and then I'm too tired to go to work. I need to talk with someone. I won't do these things again.

2. *Develop a written plan with the employee for a change in behavior.* Record what behaviors are expected. If the employee will not participate, document that fact.
   Nurse manager: Mary, I'm sorry that you're upset about your home life. My responsibility is to the unit here in the hospital. We have standards and policies to follow for the benefit of the patients. You are breaking some of them and creating serious problems. Let's review each behavior and decide on necessary changes.
   - Will abide by time allotment for breaks
   - Will ask for coverage if there is a valid reason for leaving the unit
   - Will arrive for work on time
   - Will not be absent unless ill or there is an emergency
   - Will restrict personal phone calls to no more than one per day, not to exceed 3 minutes

   Mary, I suggest that you seek counseling from hospital services or a therapist of your choice. Whatever you do, please know that these changes in behavior are mandatory. We'll meet in 2 weeks. In the meantime, I'll be observing your behavior.

3. *Obtain signatures and schedule a meeting for 2 weeks later.* The signature means only that the employee was present, not that he or she agreed with the statements. The employee is free to record comments about the content or process of the conference.

4. *Document significant positive and negative behaviors during the next 2 weeks.*

5. *Hold a second meeting.* If only positive behaviors are recorded give positive reinforcement to the employee and do not meet again to discuss the disciplinary matters. Record the change in behavior on the disciplinary form. If conditions were not met or were only partially met, review the accounts.

Nurse manager: Mary, in the past 2 weeks you have improved. However, you were late to work two times (stipulate when and by how much), and you left work 1 hour early last Tuesday without letting me know.

Mary: Well, I did do better. It's hard to change all at once. Something came up last Tuesday that I didn't want to talk about. I just had to leave.

Nurse manager: You are choosing to let your private affairs interfere with your professional responsibility. According to our policy, you have one more period of 2 weeks to change your behavior. If you fail this time, you will be dismissed.

Mary: You can count on me.

6. *Repeat step 3.*

7. *Meet with the employee again.* Refer to documented activity.

Nurse manager: Mary, your behaviors are such that I am forced to dismiss you. (Itemize the absences, tardiness, and leaving the unit without coverage). Please get your things and leave the department.

Note that the nurse manager made no specific reference to peer relationships or to the impact Mary had on others, nor did the nurse manager resort to recriminating statements such as "How could you do this to us or to yourself?" Conversations are to be as objective as possible and focused on facts. The key to the entire process is good documentation. When disciplinary procedure is followed, the nurse manager and the healthcare agency are protected against legal action should the nurse decide to challenge the decision.[33]

Summary

1. Control is a normal, positive, and pervasive process. It is the regulation of activities so that some targeted element of performance remains within acceptable limits. Control involves taking the necessary preventive steps or corrective actions to ensure that the mission and goals of the organization are accomplished as efficiently and effectively as possible.

2. There are three types of control: (1) anticipatory (seeing problems in time to do something about them), (2) concurrent control (dealing with ongoing activities), and (3) feedback control (dealing with ongoing or completed activities).

3. A well-designed nursing control system establishes trust and commitment of all personnel, clarifies objectives, operates fairly, prepares a well-planned budget, compares expectancy to performance, provides the organization with necessary information on staffing and quality of care, and promotes growth and development of personnel.

4. Because of the impact of third-party control on nursing, healthcare agencies have an incentive to control costs.

5. Managed competition is designed to create a domino effect that results in competition between prepaid, fee-for-service providers such as HMOs and PPOs on the basis of price and quality.

6. Managed competition is predicted to affect nurses by (1) bringing pressure on healthcare organizations to discharge patients early, (2) lowering annual rates of wage growth, (3) eliminating wage differentials linked to nursing education, (4) buying out or retiring early those nurses who are higher paid or who are nearing vesting, (5) substituting lesser-trained personnel for RNs, (6) increasing the use of APNs, (7) increasing the use of RNs as utilization reviewers, and (8) resizing or merging hospitals.

7. Studies show that APNs provide quality care at a lower cost than physicians or psychologists.

8. Both managed care (the delivery system) and case management (the provider) are designed to effect public accountability through improved outcome or quality of care and decreased costs.

9. Financial control systems have moved from being tools used merely to report financial status to being strategic assets used to set and manage the goals, directions, and strategies of an institution.

10. An effective budget system has enough resources to supply sufficient funds, allocates funds on the basis of criteria, and conducts a controlling system that shows how resources are being used.

11. Top-down budgeting is centralized; bottom-up budgeting is decentralized.

12. Decentralized budgeting allows those most familiar with circumstances to plan for their needs and promotes greater satisfaction among the managers.

13. The budget types most commonly managed by nurses are operational (supplies and services) and capital (large equipment, physical changes, or additions to the facilities), and personnel (number, salaries, working days, time off, and fringe benefits).

14. The budgetary process consists of the review of policies, standards, and goals; top-level projections and guidelines; preparation of the budget by middle-level managers; review of budget by top-level managers; acceptance or modification; implementation; and evaluation with changes as necessary.

15. *Costing out* nursing services means determining costs of services provided by nurses.

16. The control process involves establishing standards, objectives, and methods for measuring performance; measuring actual performance; comparing results of performance with standards and objectives (expectations); and acting to reinforce strengths and taking corrective action as necessary.

17. There are three types of standards: (1) structure (the management system used by an agency to organize and deliver care), (2) process (actual nursing procedures), and (3) outcome (standards designed to measure concurrent or retrospective standards).

18. The current trend is to focus on outcome standards because they are believed to (1) provide the nurse with more autonomy, (2) increase collaboration among health professionals, (3) improve quality of patient care, (4) result in shorter hospital stays, and (5) reduce costs for care.

19. Goal achievement in nursing is measured by analyzing task performance and determining quality of care.

20. Motions, actions, and procedures used in the actual process of giving nursing care are inspected in task analysis. Such methods as time studies and checklists are used. Although this method provides worthwhile information, it fails to consider many important intangible aspects of nursing.

21. Quality control is the responsibility of all employees and is concerned with assessing the level of nursing care provided and its effects on the patient/client through process (studying the nature and sequence of activities undertaken by nurses in the care of patients/clients) and outcome (studying the end results of nursing care). Methods used to gather information include rating scales, questionnaires, observations, peer reviews, and audits of open and closed records.

22. The term *quality assurance* is gradually being replaced with terms such as *total quality improvement* (TQI), *quality improvement* (QI), and *total quality assessment and improvement* (TQAI). Professional associations, accreditation agencies, federal and state regulatory bodies, and third-party payers are all pressing for TQI.

23. The ANA offers a model for quality assurance, which uses standards of nursing care that can be applied to nursing practice in any clinical setting. The model is compatible with processes of control proposed by management theorists.

24. Peer review is the examination and evaluation by associates of another nurse's practice.

25. The JCAHO mandates a written plan and comprehensive approach to quality assurance.

26. Performance appraisal is a way to acquire and process the information needed to improve the individual worker's performance and accomplishments.

27. Performance appraisal consists of setting standards and objectives; reviewing progress; maintaining ongoing feedback between the appraiser and subject; and planning for reinforcement, deletion, or correction of identified behaviors.

28. Lower- or first-level nurse managers participate in performance appraisal by preparing the initial evaluation of each nursing staff member assigned to them, reviewing the appraisal with the worker, and giving it to the next immediate supervisor.

29. The first formal performance appraisal was recorded in approximately 1800. Emphasis

was placed on time and motion studies until the 1930s and 1940s, when personality and behavioral characteristics were added. By 1950 task analysis was combined with human elements. In the 1950s MBO was introduced as a way to measure performance against specific objectives at all levels in the organization.

30. In 1970 appraisal of performance became a legal matter. Any testing procedure for a particular job is required to relate directly to the job duties to be performed.

31. An effective nursing performance appraisal system applies directly to standards and objectives of the worker; is compatible with organizational and individual goals; contains expectations that have been mutually agreed on by the appraiser and the subject of evaluation; is conducted by an appraiser who understands and uses the appraisal process effectively; ensures that each individual rating is performed by the worker's immediate supervisor; encourages feedback; and gives nurturing, preventive, or corrective actions as appropriate.

32. There are two kinds of methods for measuring performance: (1) informal appraisal, which occurs on a day-to-day basis through observation, incidental face-to-face confrontation and collaboration, responses of workers during conferences, and reactions noted in contacts with involved persons such as patients/clients or other staff members; and (2) formal appraisal, which consists of regular and methodical collection of objective data.

33. Methods used to acquire information on a worker's performance must be accurate, timely, objective, and focused on the worker's role and performance. It must also be economically realistic, fit within the organizational structure, and be acceptable to the members involved in the appraisal process.

34. The methods most commonly used to appraise nursing performance are the checklist and the criterion rating scale. The criterion rating scale is the most commonly used.

35. Performance review sessions are conducted to increase the effectiveness of the nursing staff member in the healthcare setting and to promote worker satisfaction.

36. A key element in the performance review session is maintaining an open, two-way communication system by providing a comfortable environment and freedom from work responsibilities, supplying ground rules for the conference, beginning the session on positive terms, including all important issues, accentuating the positive, and offering criticism sparingly.

37. New goals for the worker are established after the personnel review session. Successful implementation of goals requires a reciprocal relationship of trust and security between the worker and manager, the individual's motivation to change, realistic goals using principles of learning, handling only one or two problems at a time, and planning for feedback and reinforcement.

38. A problem employee is one who exhibits chronic disruptive behavior. Behavioral change is facilitated through progressive disciplinary policy.

❓ Questions for Study and Discussion

1. Control has been defined by some as a negative force that dominates the work life of staff members. Discuss this statement in light of what you know about the control function.

2. How do the planning and control functions work together?

3. Describe the impact of government control on healthcare agencies.

4. In observing a nursing unit, what symptoms of inadequate control might you detect in services and personnel?

5. As nurse manager, it is your job to stay within the designated number of FTEs. Several of your RN staff want more flexibility in their schedules (e.g., long weekends, extra days off). What are some options within the allotted FTEs for meeting staff wishes?

6. What has been your experience with performance appraisals (including student evaluations of teacher effectiveness)? Would the instrument(s) you have used constitute a defensible criterion reference tool?

Test Your Knowledge

BEHAVIORAL OBJECTIVE

Define the control process and the steps necessary for successful implementation.

Lavonna is nurse manager of an intensive care unit (ICU). Recently hospital executives decided that budget control is to become more decentralized. As a result Lavonna has been in training for the role.

_____ 1. As baseline information, Lavonna learns that the best definition for control is:
  a. Moving in the right direction.
  b. Checking, testing, and regulating.
  c. Regulating activities so that targeted elements remain within acceptable limits.
  d. Preventive or corrective actions.

BEHAVIORAL OBJECTIVE

Distinguish among anticipatory, concurrent, and feedback control.

Lavonna has previously been concerned with ongoing activities. However, she must now expand her role to include past practice and future projections. She considers a number of factors.

_____ 2. Lavonna establishes a task force to study the present plan for tracking supplies. This action is called:
  a. Feedback control.
  b. Anticipatory control.
  c. Concurrent control.

_____ 3. Lavonna realizes that she has ordered too many IV tubings. She determines how many she will actually need and adjusts the order. What is this called?
  a. Feedback control
  b. Anticipatory control
  c. Concurrent control

BEHAVIORAL OBJECTIVE

Explain the impact of managed competition and third-party control on nursing.

Even in ICU, where patients' lives hang in the balance, Lavonna must be concerned with costs for service, which requires becoming familiar with terminology.

_____ 4. Because of changes in reimbursement systems, Lavonna must give priority to all of the following except:
  a. Diagnostic related groups.
  b. Length of stay.
  c. Retrospective payment.
  d. Preferred provider organizations.

_____ 5. Lavonna understands that case management best fits the following category:
  a. The delivery system
  b. The budgetary system
  c. The provider system
  d. The diagnostic system

BEHAVIORAL OBJECTIVE

Discuss how the decentralized budget process for middle-level nurse managers is used.

As a middle-level manager Lavonna is beginning to appreciate the value of preparing the budget for the ICU. She has much to learn before she becomes proficient.

_____ 6. A budget is best defined as:
  a. A statement of future expenditures.
  b. A list of current expenditures.
  c. A plan for meeting expenses.
  d. A recording of past expenditures.

_____ 7. Lavonna recognizes that one of the following statements is false. Which one is it?
   a. Department managers know their units better than do those at the top.
   b. There is room for more flexibility and quicker action.
   c. Middle-level managers have a broader perspective of problem areas.
   d. Morale is usually higher when managers can develop their own budgets.

BEHAVIORAL OBJECTIVE

Differentiate among operating, capital expenditure, and personnel budgets.

_____ 8. Capital budgets include items such as:
   a. Supplies.
   b. Physical additions to the unit.
   c. Services.
   d. Fringe benefits.

_____ 9. Lavonna budgets for a suction machine priced at $475. Which is the category of budget?
   a. Operational
   b. Personnel
   c. Miscellaneous
   d. Capital

BEHAVIORAL OBJECTIVE

Define the process used to prepare a budget in a decentralized system.

Lavonna uses the budget process to prepare the ICU fiscal needs.

_____ 10. Which of the following does Lavonna do?
   a. Studies top-level projections and guidelines
   b. Prepares the actual budgetary plan
   c. Reviews agency policies, standards, and goals
   d. Gains acceptance from her supervisor

_____ 11. After approval of the ICU budget, Lavonna decides to add two more RNs to her staff. To effect the change she needs to:
   a. Send a memo to her supervisor.
   b. Alter the budget and send a copy to administration.
   c. Justify the added staff in writing.
   d. Begin the budgetary process all over again.

BEHAVIORAL OBJECTIVE

Identify the basic steps used in a nursing services control system.

_____ 12. The basic steps in a nursing services control system include all of the following except:
   a. Measuring actual performances.
   b. Comparing salaries with performance.
   c. Standards, objectives, and methods.
   d. Reinforcing strengths and taking corrective action.

_____ 13. The best evidence of a successful completion of the control process for nursing activities is that:
   a. Employees are happy.
   b. All activities are completed on time.
   c. Patients are content.
   d. Actual activities conform to planned activities.

BEHAVIORAL OBJECTIVE

Differentiate between task analysis and quality control of nursing care.

_____ 14. When responses of patients are compared with nursing care plans, the type of standard used is:
   a. Structure.
   b. Outcome.
   c. Process.

_____ 15. When nursing procedures are decided, the type of standard used is:
   a. Outcome.
   b. Structure.
   c. Process.

BEHAVIORAL OBJECTIVE

Explain the philosophy of quality assessment and quality improvement.

_____ 16. The JCAHO Quality Assessment and Improvement plan is based on all of the following except:
   a. Revision of standards.
   b. Naming ways to improve patient care.
   c. Published studies and research.
   d. Development of performance measures.

BEHAVIORAL OBJECTIVE

Define performance appraisal and its inception.

Lavonna states that evaluating personnel is the most difficult part of her role as nurse manager. Nevertheless she has prepared herself for this aspect of the job.

_____ 17. Lavonna learns that performance appraisal consists of all the following activities except:
   a. Setting specific standards and activities for individual performance.
   b. Using agency standards as a guide.
   c. Determining areas of strength and weakness.
   d. Focusing activity on the correction of identified behaviors.

BEHAVIORAL OBJECTIVE

Describe the components of an effective nursing appraisal system and recognize problems and pitfalls associated with personnel appraisal.

_____ 18. Lavonna recognizes that three of the following statements are false. Which one is true?
   a. Informing members of the nursing staff regarding specific impressions of their work helps members to improve their job performance.
   b. If a nurse manager is pressed for time a verbal appraisal is an acceptable substitute for a written report.
   c. The patient/client is the best source of information regarding personnel appraisal.
   d. Responsibility for the outcome of performance appraisal rests primarily with the evaluator.

BEHAVIORAL OBJECTIVE

Relate methods of performance measurement to their usefulness in nursing.

_____ 19. Informal appraisal has many benefits. Which is the exception?
   a. The staff member is observed in natural surroundings.
   b. Incidental confrontation and collaboration is allowed.
   c. The evaluation focuses on objective data systematically.
   d. The evaluation may provide valid information for compilation of a formal report.

BEHAVIORAL OBJECTIVE

Give the purpose of a nursing performance review session and list the guidelines for an effective session.

_____ 20. Lavonna is conducting a 6-month performance review session with a staff member. Which of the following actions is appropriate?

a. She chooses another nurse to attend the session as a witness.

b. She informs the staff member that she may ask a peer to read the appraisal before the session is over.

c. She tells the staff member that this session is manager-centered.

d. The session is private between the two members.

_____ 21. In the above situation Lavonna:

a. Avoids all conversation except that which pertains to the formal review.

b. Engages in a brief exchange of chitchat and moves on to the performance review.

c. Encourages the staff member to vent feelings before beginning the session.

BEHAVIORAL OBJECTIVE

Review the process for managing the problem employee.

Janet has been coming to work in the ICU with a flushed face and hand tremors. She is increasingly irritable with her peers and patients. She is failing to follow through with nursing orders. Her usual response is, "Oh, I forgot." Lavonna suspects that Janet is engaging in substance abuse.

_____ 22. Lavonna's first responsibility is to:

a. Ask Janet if she is taking illegal drugs or abusing alcohol.

b. Hold a conference with Janet.

c. Document the behaviors.

d. Report her assumptions to her supervisor.

REFERENCES

1. Kreitner R: *Management,* ed 5, Boston, 1992, Houghton Mifflin.

2. Pointer J, Pointer R: Case-based prospective reimbursement, *Nurs Manage* 20(4):30-34, 1989.

3. Buerhaus P: Economics of managed competition and consequences to nurses: Part II, *Nurs Econ* 12(2):75-81, 1994.

4. Baradell J: Cost-effectiveness and quality of care provided by clinical nurse specialists, *J Psychol Nurs* 32(3):21-24, 1994.

5. Baradell J: Fee survey for clinical specialists, *Pacesetter* 18(2):4, 1991.

6. Harrington C, Estea C: *Health policy and nursing: crisis and reform in the U.S. health care delivery system,* Boston, 1994, Jones & Bartlett Publishers.

7. Lumsdon K: Beyond four walls: case management evolves into management of a continuum of care, *Hosp Health Network* 68(5):44-45, 1994.

8. Simpson R: Nursing informatics: the evolution of financial systems, from accounting to EISs (Executive Information Systems) *Nurs Adm Q* 17(4):80-82, 1993.

9. Barney J, Griffin R: *The management of organizations: strategy, structure, behavior,* Dallas, 1992, Houghton Mifflin.

10. Longest B: *Management practices for the health professional,* ed 4, Norwalk, Conn, 1990, Appleton & Lange.

11. McCabe J, Hartnack J: FTE reports and fiscal management, *Nurs Manage* 20(11):46-48, 1989.

12. Finney R: Budgeting: from pain to power, *Manage Rev* 82(9):27-31, 1993.

13. Robbins S: *Organization theory: structure, design and applications,* Englewood Cliffs, NJ, 1990, Prentice Hall.

14. Francisco P: Flexible budgeting and variance analysis, *Nurs Manage* 20(11):40-43, 1989.

15. McCloskey J: Implications of costing out nursing services for reimbursement, *Nurs Manage* 20(1):44-49, 1989.

16. Swanson J, Albrecht M: *Community health nursing: promoting the health of aggregates,* Philadelphia, 1993, WB Saunders.

17. Kreitner R: *Management,* ed 5, Boston, 1992, Houghton Mifflin.

18. Western P: QA/QI and nursing competence: a combined model, *Nurs Manage* 25(3):44-46, 1994.

19. Mitchell P: Perspectives and outcome-oriented care systems, *Nurs Adm Q* 17(3):1-7, 1993, Aspen Publishers.

20. Luquire R and others: Focusing on outcomes, *RN* 57(5):57-60, 1994.

21. *The White House Domestic Policy Council: the president's health security plan,* New York, 1993, Times Books.

22. Joint Commission on Accreditation of Health Care Organizations: *Accreditation Manual for Hospitals,* Oak Terrace, Ill, 1992, The Commission.

23. Lopresti J, Whetstone W: Total quality management: doing things right, *Nurs Manage* 24(1):34-36, 1993.

24. Ventura M, Rizzo J, Lenz S: Quality indicators: control maintains—propriety improves, *Nurs Manage* 24(1):46-50, 1993.

25. Schroeder P: *Improving quality and performance: concepts, programs, and techniques,* St Louis, 1994, Mosby.

26. The Joint Commission of Accreditation of Healthcare Organizations: *Accreditation manual for hospitals,* Chicago, 1990, The Commission.

27. Seigel H, Bileschi C: The mock survey: preparing for JCAHO visit, *Nurs Manage* 25(3):48-53, 1994.

28. American Nurses' Association: *ANA Standards,* Kansas City, Mo, 1986, The Association.

29. Christensen M: Peer auditing, *Nurs Manage* 21(1):50-52, 1990.

30. Harris S, Kreger S, Davis M: A problem-focused quality assurance program, *Nurs Manage* 20(2): 55, 1989.

31. Equal Employment Opportunity Commission: Guidelines of employment and selection procedure. *Fed Regis* 35(149):12333-12336, 1970.

32. Mathis R, Jackson J: *Human resource management,* ed 7, Minneapolis/St Paul, 1994, West Publishing.

SUGGESTED READINGS

Baker K and others: Costing services, *Nurs Manage* 24(3):56-60, 1993.

Chu S, Thom J: Information technologies: a productive strategic weapon in healthcare, *J Nurs Adm* 24(4): 5-7, 1994.

Corpaz L, Conforti C: Organizing and documenting clinical standards, *Nurs Manage* 25(5):70-72;74-76, 1994.

DePew C: Open vs closed-system endotracheal suctioning: a cost comparison, *Crit Care Nurse* 14(1): 94-100, 1994.

Finkler S and others: Innovation in nursing: a benefit/cost analysis, *Nurs Econ* 12(1):18-27, 1994.

Glotz N, Johnsen G, Johnson R: Advancing clinical excellence: competency-based patient care, *Nurs Manage* 25(3):42-43, 1994.

Grimaldi P: Capitation savvy a must, *Nurs Manage* 26(2):33-34, 1995.

Houghton B: Discharge planners and cost containment, *Nurs Manage* 25(4):78-80, 1994.

Jorgenson C: Cost awareness in emergency department nurses, *Nurs Manage* 25(6):65-66, 1994.

Kleinman L: Quality in nursing home care, *J Gerontol Nurs* 20(3):5, 1994.

Leimtzer M, Ryan D, Nieman V: The hospital-visiting nurse association partnership: a continuous quality improvement program, *J Nurs Adm* 23(1):20-23, 1993.

Maher M and others: Theory M: a restructuring process, *Nurs Manage* 26(1):49-52, 1995.

Press I: The last word: patient satisfaction, *Hosp Health Network* 68(5):60, 1994.

Mitchell P: Perspectives on outcome-oriented care systems, *Nurs Adm Q* 17(3):1-7, 1993.

Peterson B, Springer P, Farnsworth J: Analyzing job demands and coping techniques, *Nurs Manage* 26(2):51-53, 1995.

Sherman J, Malkmus M: Integrating quality assurance and total quality management/quality improvement, *J Nurs Adm* 24(3):37-41, 1994.

Western P: QA/QI and nursing competence: a combined model, *Nurs Manage* 25(3):44-46, 1994.

STAFF TRAINING and DEVELOPMENT

BEHAVIORAL OBJECTIVES

On completion of this chapter, the student will be prepared to:

- Differentiate among technical, human, conceptual, diagnostic, and mentor skills.

- Discuss the expected outcomes of nurse preceptor relationships for the preceptor and the protégé.

- Outline a sound program and content for the development of nurse middle managers.

- Identify staff nurses who need training and development, and give a rationale for their need.

- Define role clarification and differentiate among role expectation, role conception, and role congruence.

- Define the adult learner and describe the teaching-learning process as applied to nurses.

- Define a work group and identify factors that influence work productivity.

- Identify the key factors of programs designed for preceptor training and for orientation of new employees and the new graduate.

- Describe on-the-job development through self-learning.

IMPORTANCE OF TRAINING AND DEVELOPMENT

In today's complex and dynamic environment, it is no longer necessary to debate whether training and development activities are luxuries in which only the largest organizations can indulge during prosperous times. Most organizations, large and small, have come to realize that the development of an effective work force is no more a luxury than having a housekeeping or accounting department. It is an accepted fact that training and development are necessary for the spirit, survival, and performance of an organization and that workers must be trained to manage the organization effectively now and in the future. This is particularly important in agencies that undergo technologic changes. For example, changes such as the implementation of computerized care planning and the use of intricate machines are better received when nurses feel capable of handling the new systems.

Another challenge facing nurse educators is understanding how healthcare reform interacts within the framework of staff training and development. There is a need for real innovation in the healthcare delivery system. Staff developers must participate in each change and be ready to prepare healthcare workers to meet the complex and expanding roles.

Effective managers recognize that training and development are ongoing and continuous processes, not one-time activities. Changes in the system, new procedures and equipment, new discoveries, job losses, and new jobs are constantly creating the need for employee instruction.

IMPLICATION OF HEALTHCARE REFORM FOR STAFF TRAINING AND DEVELOPMENT

Until Medicare and Medicaid were developed in 1965, staff development was called "inservice education." This on-the-job training was usually performed by one person who was responsible for new employee orientation; refresher programs; and mandatory programs in fire, safety, and resuscitation techniques. Orientation and inservice education assumed greater importance when the majority of diploma schools in nursing closed and hospitals were no longer able to employ their own graduates. Orientation and some staff development programs gradually became hospital- or system-wide and used nurse educators and other health professionals to teach nurses, patients, families and even consumers.[1]

Staff Training and Development

Most healthcare reform plans are based on the principles of security, simplicity, savings, quality, choice, and responsibility.[1] These principles have implications for **staff training** and **staff development.** Under the current administration's

healthcare reform proposals, funding for healthcare institutions will be rated on their ability to meet specific criteria.

Staff development will play a significant role in the quality rating of an agency because ongoing education is an essential part of maintaining the competency of a staff. For example, nurses must now practice a higher level of assessment skills, regardless of work setting. They must also be able to function efficiently within a variety of care delivery systems such as case management specialty areas, primary care, and team nursing. Nurse educators need to be aware of ways to make the nursing environment more cost effective. Educators can participate in the development or testing of new product lines and make recommendations to the purchasing agent.

Business and Professional Opportunities

Innovative staff developers can look for opportunities to share their expertise with other professionals and the public. Some business and professional entrepreneurs recognize that staff developers from healthcare agencies can offer a variety of programs to improve the skills and increase the knowledge of employees or the public. Many institutions join forces with other local health agencies or neighboring colleges and universities to present management and educational programs. Staff developers can design seminars, workshops, and self-paced learning tools, or they can serve as consultants. These measures have the potential to generate new clients and increase revenue.

TRAINING AND DEVELOPMENT FUNCTION

For the individual learner, the function of training and development needs to be one of providing an environment and resources that facilitate a learning and maturing process in each person.[2] The goal of staff education is to enable the staff member to learn under conditions that foster changing behavior, attitudes, or opinions. As learning occurs, personal experiences are translated into new and different ways of behaving.[3]

The training and development function in an organization involves a multifaceted purpose and definition.[3] *Training* is an activity that is primarily directed at improving an employee's current job performance. It generally involves both nonmanagerial and managerial personnel acquiring technical and some human skills, such as learning procedures or how to conduct a performance evaluation.

Individual *development* refers to any action or program that provides opportunities for employees to learn and develop skills. Development involves two equally important components: (1) management and leadership, and (2) structure of the organization. Management and leadership development is concerned with the question, "What types of leaders and managers does the organization need now, and what type will be needed tomorrow to achieve its goals in a changing environment?" The age, skills, and role of the managerial staff are considered, as well as the types of managers and leaders required to function in the organizational structure.

A successful program needs *administrative support.* Training and development programs must evolve from a planned, purposeful approach by top nursing administration to the preparation of competent managers and leaders. A supportive climate allows for the performance of functions that fulfill the philosophy and goals of patient care for nursing and the health agency.[4]

This chapter discusses the skills needed by the nurse to lead and to manage, how these skills are acquired, the nurse population in need of training and development, and the knowledge important to the success of training and development programs. It concludes with examples of training and development programs at staff nurse levels.

Management Skills Needed by Staff Nurses

Employees at lower levels of management need technical and human skills. At higher levels, the administrator's effectiveness depends largely on human and conceptual skills. At the top, conceptual skill becomes most important for successful administration.[5]

Most successful nurses have acquired a certain set of skills during their working lives that has had a strong impact on their levels of achievement. Four specific managerial skills are needed by all nurses: (1) technical, (2) human, (3) conceptual, (4) diagnostic, and (5) coaching and mentoring (Figure 11-1).

Technical skill

Technical skill pertains to *what* is done, working with *things,* and one's ability to use technology to perform an organizational task.

The ability to use tools, techniques, procedures, or approaches in a specialized manner is referred to as *technical skill.* Nurses are ex-

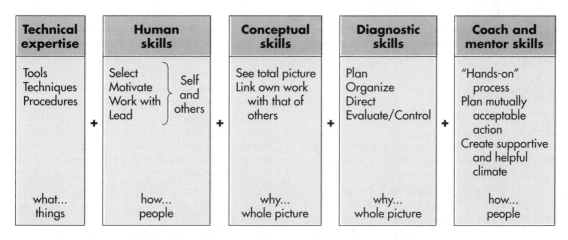

Technical expertise	Human skills	Conceptual skills	Diagnostic skills	Coach and mentor skills
Tools Techniques Procedures	Select Motivate Work with Lead } Self and others	See total picture Link own work with that of others	Plan Organize Direct Evaluate/Control	"Hands-on" process Plan mutually acceptable action Create supportive and helpful climate
what... things	how... people	why... whole picture	why... whole picture	how... people

FIGURE 11-1. Leadership and management skills necessary for nursing practice at any level.

pected to have or to acquire proficiency in a broad variety of skills that relate to every part of the human being. Nurses with technical skills are recognized as **experts** at what they do. Nurse managers are expected to have developed expertise in their areas of professional practice. Technical skills are usually the easiest to acquire because they can be taught through educational and training activities.

Human skill

Human skill pertains to *how* something is done, working with people, and one's ability to work with others to achieve goals.

Nurse managers need the ability to select, motivate, work with, and lead employees, either individually or in groups. Human skills are much more difficult to acquire because interpersonal relations involve attitudes, emotions, and the cultural characteristics of many individuals and groups, including nurse leaders, workers and supervisors. These characteristics vary with different employees, and their impact on performance is difficult to predict.

Conceptual skill

Conceptual skill pertains to *why* something is done, one's view of the organization as a *whole* picture, and one's ability to understand the complexities of the organization as it affects and is affected by its environment.

The nurse manager must be able to link the work of the group with the work of other people (e.g., physicians, clergy, social workers) and other departments (e.g., radiology, laboratory, dietary, therapy).

Diagnostic skill

Diagnostic skill includes the ability to determine, by analysis and examination, the nature and the circumstances of a particular condition or situation. It is the ability to specify *why* something occurred, cut through unimportant aspects, and quickly get to the heart of a problem. For example, many nurse managers have a problem with workers' poor use of time. This inefficiently results in overtime and increased costs. Frustration and anger are also generated because nurses cannot get home to their families or attend to other

obligations on time, and incoming workers experience a delay in beginning their work. The nurse manager who can quickly assess the problem and solve it to the satisfaction of both administration and employees has used diagnostic skill effectively. Conversely, the nurse who is unable to choose a plan of action is on the road to failure. All too often nurses fall into a state of paralysis because they are not able to resolve the doubts in their own minds. President Truman used to lament that when he asked his economists for recommendations, they would answer, "On the one hand...and on the other hand..." Exasperated, President Truman said, "Oh, for a one-armed economist!"[6]

Because they involve time and a certain level of intellectual ability, conceptual and diagnostic skills are interchangeable and the most difficult to acquire. Conceptual and diagnostic skill development depends somewhat on the degree to which technical and human skills have been acquired and mastered. Conceptual and diagnostic skills are mature skills that require a capacity to learn and a level of experience in observing and practicing acceptable behaviors.

Coaching and mentoring skills

Staff members are fortunate when they have a manager who knows how to coach, guide, and teach them. This is especially true early in a career. Coaching is a day-by-day, hands-on process that helps employees recognize opportunities and ways to improve their performance and capabilities. Coaching resembles on-the-job training but requires managers to have skills beyond those of trainer, such as planning mutually acceptable action, creating a supportive and helping climate, and influencing employees to change their behavior. By helping staff members expand their capabilities and improve their performance, managers can gain more time for self-improvement. Managers who are most effective at developing employees have incorporated **coaching skills** into their management style.[7]

Acquisition of Management Skills

At least three mechanisms facilitate the acquisition of managerial skills: (1) education and training, (2) experience, and (3) a preceptor/mentor relationship with a higher-level person (Figure 11-2).

Education

Training in and development of managerial skills are carried out in nursing schools according to their mission and goals (see Chapter 4). Licensed practical nurses/licensed vocational nurses (LPNs/LVNs) are trained to manage their own workload under the supervision of a registered nurse (RN) and to be effective team members. Diploma and associate degree nurses are taught to serve as managers of nursing care for a group of patients/clients with common, well-defined health problems and within structured settings. Baccalaureate degree graduates are accountable for their own nursing practice, qualified to provide nursing care through others, serve as advocates for patients/clients, and apply interpersonal and leadership skills when working with other health professionals. Many other formal and informal programs in leadership and management development are available through on-the-job training, workshops, seminars, and independent and graduate study.

Experience

"Experience is the best teacher" is an old saying that contains much truth for managerial success.

Three factors are necessary to gain experience in management. First, experience is the *exposure* to a variety of situations, problems, and demands. For example, a nurse may have had different roles in several hospitals or other health agencies, which necessitated the use of different managerial and leadership skills in each setting. Exposure involves "learning the ropes" by being an integral part of various organizational activities. The nurse manager may allow the staff nurse with leadership and management potential to make work assignments, take shift report for the entire unit, prepare a time schedule for the month, or attend a midlevel planning meeting. In these situations, learning involves *doing.* Second, gaining experience involves *time,* which is necessary to allow enough exposure to various managerial situations. Finally, with experience it is expected that a level of *maturity* will emerge. Maturity involves the philosophical attitude or belief of the individual and the ability to resist panic in crises by using rational and analytic reasoning. The prepared and experienced nurse can look beyond trivial matters to the cause of a problem. This crucial managerial quality comes from exposure to a variety of situations over time.

Mentor and preceptor relationships

The terms *mentor* and *preceptor* may be used interchangeably. A **mentoring relationship** is de-

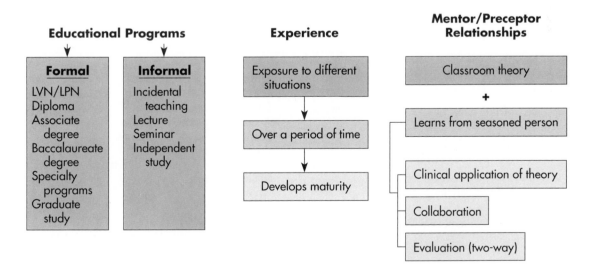

FIGURE 11-2. How management skills are acquired.

scribed as a dynamic and noncompetitive nurturing process that promotes independence, autonomy, and self-actualization in the protégé while fostering a sense of pride, fulfillment, support, and continuity.[8]

A **preceptor** is an instructor, teacher, tutor, trainer, monitor, and director. Because of the similarity in definitions and because most nursing professionals use this term in the literature, the term *preceptor* will be used throughout this chapter. Precepting occurs when an inexperienced person learns a set of skills by observing, working with, and relating to a more experienced person. Precepting can be a formal or informal activity. The novice can be taught through a formal preceptor training program with didactic and practical training, or a more experienced nurse can share knowledge and expertise with a protégé on an incidental basis.

Much may be gained from a preceptor relationship. It provides the protégé not only with an opportunity to learn technical skills from an experienced clinician but also teaches him or her how to relate to people (human skills) and how to approach various problems faced by the nurse in the managerial role (conceptual and diagnostic skills.) A preceptor relationship also gives the protégé an opportunity to acquire some career direction, a mechanism to develop a personal philosophy of management, and the invaluable quality of self-confidence in managerial ability (Figure 11-3).

Four variables appear to affect preceptor relationships: (1) past experiences (e.g., if past life has been dominated by authority figures, one tends to bond with authority figures), (2) mode of learning (e.g., some need almost constant supervision, whereas others need only see or hear something to be fully capable of performing), (3) stage of professional development (e.g., if a person is in the early stages of a career, almost everything about the job needs to be learned), and (4) compatibility.[9] Matching the learner with the right preceptor is crucial to optimal professional development. The problem of cultural diversity illustrates this point. Preceptors are trained as role models, communicators, and teachers. Often they are poorly prepared or unprepared to deal with the cultural diversity of the preceptor and trainee. Consequently the preceptor fails in the mission at hand.

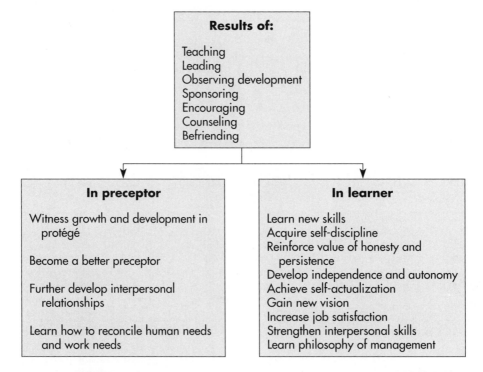

FIGURE 11-3. Expected outcomes from the preceptor relationship.

EXAMPLE: A frustrated preceptor of a Philippine nurse complains, "She listens to me and nods her head as though she understands, but then I find her doing exactly the opposite!"

If the preceptor had studied the Philippine culture, she would understand that Philippines do not think it polite to question authority figures, even if they do not completely understand. Therefore they tend to listen and do the best they can to follow through. An understanding preceptor would have given the directions and asked for feedback to ensure understanding.

MIDDLE MANAGERS

Recruitment and Retention

The Nursing Spectrum and The American Organization of Nurse Executives (AONE) recently sponsored a demographic assessment of 467 RNs.[10,11] Participants completed questionnaires, and five focus groups were held in various locations in which participating nurses elaborated on their responses. Nurses were separated into three categories: new graduates, staff nurses eligible for middle manager positions, and nurses working in middle manager positions. New graduates described their first experience as an employed nurse as staggering as a result of the following factors:

- Numbers of patients requiring their attention
- Acuity levels
- Amount of paperwork

New graduates consistently mentioned the following factors as important:

- A good preceptorship program that is individually tailored, one-on-one, and uses a prepared preceptor who wants to serve
- Friendliness and teamwork of the people in the organization
- Recognition and positive feedback
- Having their opinions sought and valued
- Autonomy
- Salary, benefits, flexibility, and opportunity

RNs who were eligible for promotion to middle manager were unanimous in their disillusions concerning the position. Their reasons for the disillusionment included the following:

- Staff nurses often making more money than managers
- An illusion of autonomy rather than the real thing
- Insufficient "hands-on" experience
- Accountability without authority
- Too much paperwork
- Too few resources
- Lack of support from others (e.g., administration, physicians, and even peers)

Despite the negative reaction to the management role, manager-eligible nurses and all other nurse participants agreed that unit managers should definitely be nurses. They made such comments as, "Professionals should be supervised by members of their own profession," and "Nursing's unique body of knowledge is completely known only to a nurse."

Nurses actually employed as middle managers provided responses that were in direct contrast to manager-eligible nurses. They expressed their enthusiasm for the role in the following ways:

- Having the power to effect change
- Having a sense of personal accomplishment that is derived from the ability to influence and develop staff to provide consistent and quality nursing care
- Recognition from patients, staff, physicians, and upper management
- Being given the dignity that a good manager receives

Although middle managers expressed general satisfaction with their jobs, four areas of discontent emerged:

- Fiscal constraints
- Insufficient time to do everything
- Uncompensated time
- Accountability without authority

All groups were asked to describe what constitutes the middle-management role (Figure 11-4). All groups agreed that the traditional roles of planning, directing, and controlling are important. They also added the concepts of motivating, facilitating, mentoring, problem solving, advocating for staff and patients, and communicating in all directions. The groups agreed further that both strong fiscal skills and clinical competence are necessary and that a charismatic visionary leader is a definite plus. Acquisition of all these characteristics by one nurse is a Herculean task. As with balloons, there is a gap if one character-

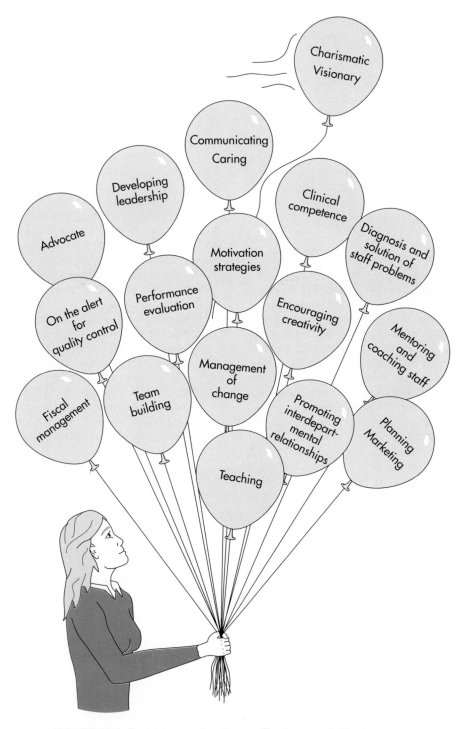

FIGURE 11-4. Content necessary for an effective management program.

istic slips away and is not developed and nurtured along with the others.

Preparation of Middle Managers

Johns Hopkins Health Center, a 1000-bed facility, conducted a study concerning nurse manager activities and found that nurse managers spend only one fourth of their time in direct patient activity and the remainder of their time in administrative and managerial functions. There was unanimous agreement that nurse managers need further development in specific areas, including motivating staff, managing change, creating a unit culture, managing performance, developing leadership, creating a vision, mentoring and coaching staff, and creating development plans with staff members. On the basis of this information, Johns Hopkins appointed a task force to design a program that would prepare nurses who are new to the manager role and further develop nurses who were already serving in the role.[12]

The Manager Development Program is sound and can serve as a guide in any healthcare setting. It covers a 2-year cycle and links learning opportunities for new and existing nurse managers to the mission and goals of the organization and the department of nursing. The management philosophy and the nurse manager performance standards contributed to the design and content of the program. Three groups of learning experiences were designed for nurse managers: (1) orientation guidelines, a fiscal self-learning packet, and optional structured learning activities for the new nurse manager that relate directly to the performance standards; (2) a group development cycle; and (3) a wide spectrum of individualized learning opportunities for nurse managers at all levels.

Orientation guidelines and fiscal self-learning packet

The orientation guidelines provide strategies and resources that help the nurse manager achieve the behaviors identified in the nurse manager performance standards. The nurse can work at his or her own pace. The fiscal self-learning packet introduces the new nurse manager to the budget process that the employing agency uses.

The packet includes the financial reporting system, budget planning, resource allocation, and evaluation and response to financial data. Exercises for practice are provided. The self-learning packet provides the nurse manager with a source of long-term reference.

Nurse manager group development cycle

The group development cycle begins with a 2-day program that is held away from the workplace. The introduction to concepts occurs at this program. Emphasis is placed on team building and networking, which can continue long after this brief workshop.

Peer teams are formed around a common theme, issue, or problem. These teams meet periodically and are the primary mechanism through which action learning is integrated into the program. Members support one another while the nurse manager works on the project or issue.

To keep nurse managers aware of current events in healthcare, a seminar series is held each month for the entire manager group. Lectures are given by qualified people in the agency and by experts from a local university.

Program evaluation is an integral part of the learning cycle and ensures that the program is meeting the needs of the group.

Individualized management learning opportunities

Nurse managers are given the opportunity to learn skills in six different areas. Courses are provided in the areas of quality assessment and improvement, communication, team building, supervision, decision making (a systems or whole approach), and diversity. Nurse managers attend these sessions with other nonnursing managers and may gain a different perspective.

Mentoring of nurse managers is voluntary. The mentor assists the protégé with role development. Selected nurse managers are given the opportunity for continuing education and graduate study, as well as sabbaticals and fellowships. Institution-wide forums on management provide a link between nursing and other departments within the agency.

NURSE POPULATIONS IN NEED OF TRAINING AND DEVELOPMENT

Irrespective of their positions in the agency, all nurses are in need of training and development. Without training and development the worker becomes stagnant and functions far below capability. This section discusses three categories of nurses in need of leadership and managerial training and development: (1) the new graduate, (2) the experienced nurse who is new to a health agency, and (3) the staff nurse who needs additional preparation to fulfill the leadership/management role of preceptor.

New Graduates

Studies have shown that new graduates feel anxious when they first enter an organization. They report feeling overwhelmed and unprepared for the realities of the workplace. They also report difficulties in making decisions, setting priorities, performing psychomotor skills, and identifying their weaknesses. The gap between the "ivory tower ideology" and "the real world" is important in light of the cost of recruiting new graduates and the high resignation rates reported during the first year of employment.[10]

New Employees

Early job experiences play a very critical role in a nurse's career in an organization. During these experiences the expectations of the individual and the organization confront each other. If the expectations are not compatible, dissatisfaction occurs. Therefore effective orientation programs are aimed at reducing the anxiety of new employees.

Orientation programs are designed to provide a new employee with the information that he or she needs to function comfortably and effectively within an organization. Orientation explains the who, what, when, where, and why of an agency. Induction and orientation typically conveys to the new employee three types of information: (1) the physical facilities, history, mission, and goals of the organization and how the employee's job contributes to the needs of the organization; (2) policies, work rules, and employee benefits; and (3) general and specific information regarding role expectations and the daily work routine. Co-workers are introduced and questions by new employees are encouraged.

Staff Nurses

Staff training and development programs are designed for nurses who need additional preparation to fulfill job requirements and to advance to positions in leadership and management. The American Nurses Association (ANA) states that, "Continuing education in nursing consists of planned learning experiences beyond a basic nursing education program. Those experiences are designed to promote the development of knowledge, skills, and attitudes for the enhancement of nursing practice, thus improving health care to the public."[13,p.32]

Continuing education for staff development should give personnel the opportunity to acquire new knowledge and skills on the basis of changes in healthcare practices and investigative new approaches to healthcare delivery; to strengthen their clinical competencies; and to become self-directed in their own learning.

Regardless of level, each component of nursing practice requires leadership and management to some degree. Assessment, gathering data, planning nursing interventions, and evaluating the effects of nursing care are integral parts of the leadership/management process. Every individual needs **motivation** to increase knowledge and skills. Sometimes the desire is internal, and other times the person is motivated by external forces. For example, a nurse manager may see something in a staff member that demonstrates a special ability. The nurse manager may offer the nurse the opportunity to take on added responsibility, such as precepting a new graduate or becoming an assistant. With this offer comes the responsibility of the agency to prepare the staff member adequately for the new role.

There is increasing recognition of the fact that people differ in ability, experience, and personality, and there is a need for creativity in preparing learning experiences.[14] Therefore training and development programs are becoming more tailored to fit the unique requirements of those attending.

CONCEPTS IMPORTANT TO THE SUCCESS OF ALL TRAINING AND DEVELOPMENT PROGRAMS

Training and development involve changing behavior patterns, which is always a difficult task. An individual's personality is partly reflected by his or her method of doing a job, using skills, applying energy and thought, and checking and coordinating with other people. Because new work methods or a change in work structure may be a threat to the nurse, the psychologic needs for security and a sense of accomplishment must be emphasized. Educators and trainers of staff nurses have a particular need to understand the basic concepts of role clarification, teaching and learning, group dynamics, and change.

Role Clarification

Shakespeare said, "All the world's a stage, and all the men and women are merely players." Roles in organizations are like this. They are positions that have sets of expected behaviors. Roles represent "packages" of norms that apply to particular persons within a group.

Assuming the role of nurse involves the process of integrating role expectations and role conception. Role integration proceeds most smoothly when the nurse is clear about the expected behaviors and the new or added responsibilities for which he or she is being trained.[2]

Role Expectation

Role expectation is defined as how others believe one should act in a given situation. Role expectation originates from two sources: the provider of services and the recipient of services. The employing agency establishes a formal set of behaviors that is expected of the employee and in turn agrees to certain employee rights and privileges. For each category of worker the employer has job descriptions that require specific preparation and skills and stipulated protocol for performance. For example, first-level staff nurses must have proper certification if they want to work in an intensive care unit, and the nurse who wants to be a nurse manager or department manager must have at least a bachelor of science degree and management training. The agency may also specify behaviors expected of the nurse, such as those that relate to communications, punctuality, flexibility in time schedules, or ethics.

The administration in turn agrees to certain rights and privileges. Nurses may be given the right to negotiate work contracts with the agency through their professional representative, they may have the right to earn advancement in the organization and to earn fringe benefits, or they may have the privilege of a stipulated amount of paid educational leave per year.

The patient brings a different set of expectations. These expectations are less formal and binding, but their fulfillment forms the very crux of nursing. The patient's role concept for the nurse focuses primarily on himself or herself and his or her significant others. The patient wants individual and family needs approached from a physical, psychologic, social, and spiritual approach. The patient also wants quality care provided in an environment that is safe, supportive, nurturing, and cost effective.

In 1972 the American Hospital Association issued a Patient's Bill of Rights that incorporates the components of quality care in the expectation that they will be supported by the hospital on behalf of its patients as an integral part of the healing process. The ANA adopted a Code for Nurses in 1950 and revised it in 1976. It is consistent with ethical principles and is intended to guide the nurse in the practice of nursing. These documents in themselves are not legally binding but can be persuasive in court proceedings that arise from breakdowns in patient/client care.[15]

Role Conception

Pressures from the employer, the patient/client, and self directly influence the nurse's conception or analysis of his or her role. Another influencing stimulus is the nursing profession itself. Both as a group and as individuals, nursing professionals influence each other in many ways as they develop their role conception. Another important factor in role conception is self-identification, or becoming clear about who one is. People cannot escape the common heritage of their culture; the self places limits on how one perceives and acts in any given role. Individuals think or act in unique ways because of their personalities, abilities, and attitudes; as well as the motives, needs, and ambitions that govern their lives. People cannot escape their heritage, but as they mature they can modify and use that inheritance through their personal perceptions.

Role Congruence and Performance

The role the nurse adopts depends on his or her knowledge of who he or she is in relation to others (Figure 11-5). A person who has moved through the normal developmental process can differentiate between primary and secondary roles in life. The nurse may fulfill roles such as friend, spouse, parent, student, and activist. However, professional attention is given to the role that brings the nurse into contact with the healthcare system in which knowledge and skills are used to maintain or restore health and prevent illness.

Role ambiguity and role conflict occurs when there has been a failure to communicate role ex-

pectations or there is contradiction between expectations and compliance.

EXAMPLE: Jennifer was recently employed as a staff nurse in gynecology. She loves the job, except for one area. When she accepted employment in this area she did not realize that the dilation and curretage (D&C) unit performed abortions. She believes abortion is wrong and has asked not to be assigned there when one is scheduled. However, the nurse manager states that Jennifer must take her turn because special requests complicate scheduling. Jennifer wants to stay on the unit but does not know what to do.

Jennifer is experiencing role conflict and must decide if the positive aspects of the job outweigh the negative. Had she inquired before employment she would have known about the requirement. If she cannot reconcile role congruence with performance, she must resolve the conflict by resigning.

Working continuously toward a common understanding of roles helps reduce the distance that may lie between any of the principles involved. Training and development programs help serve this purpose.

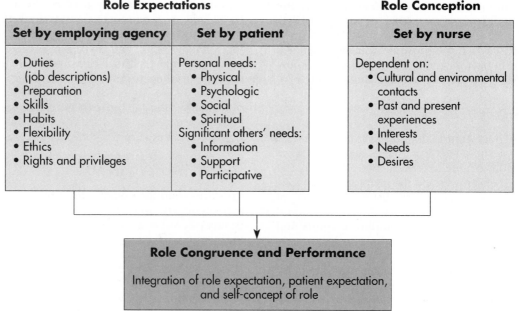

Role Expectations

Set by employing agency	Set by patient
• Duties (job descriptions) • Preparation • Skills • Habits • Flexibility • Ethics • Rights and privileges	Personal needs: • Physical • Psychologic • Social • Spiritual Significant others' needs: • Information • Support • Participative

Role Conception

Set by nurse
Dependent on: • Cultural and environmental contacts • Past and present experiences • Interests • Needs • Desires

Role Congruence and Performance

Integration of role expectation, patient expectation, and self-concept of role

FIGURE 11-5. Factors that determine role performance.

TEACHING AND LEARNING PROCESS

The role of the nurse as a teacher and trainer is basic to professional practice. Not only must nurses learn how to teach and train others, they must learn to do it well.

Nurses as Effective Teachers

By teaching health to people, nurses prevent disease, maintain health, facilitate coping, and enable individuals to learn how to reestablish healthful living patterns. All nurses lead in one way or another and teach others indirectly or directly. Effective teaching strategies can help members to grow and develop and can improve the quality of patient care. A teacher is a catalyst who brings knowledge and the learner together and stimulates a reaction that can either be positive or negative depending on the teacher's skill and the learner's receptiveness.

$$\text{Knowledge} \dashrightarrow \leftarrow - - - \text{Learner}$$
$$\downarrow$$
$$- - - \text{Reaction} + + +$$

All Nurses as Teachers

Nurses teach patients, families, ancillary personnel, and one another. Teaching is inherent in the nursing role whether or not the nurse consciously cultivates and exhibits teaching behaviors. Effective teaching is a learned process. Mastery of teaching requires knowledgeable, careful planning and continuous practice, for it is the teaching *process,* not the teacher, that is the key to learning. It is not what teachers are *like* but what they *do* that determines the outcome of the instruction and how the learners feel about themselves. The nurse serves as teacher in a wide variety of everyday activities:

1. In one-to-one activities for solving nursing problems and learning procedure or policies
2. In preplanning and teaching small or large groups in an informal or formal structure
3. In role modeling directly as a preceptor or indirectly through example

Factors That Influence Learning Capacities

Human beings can develop their **aptitudes** into abilities needed for the job. Individuals generally have different learning capacities, learn at different rates, and learn in different ways at various stages in life. Learning begins at birth and can continue until death. Psychologists such as William James, Abraham Maslow, and Carl Rogers believe that human beings use only 5% to 10% of their capacity. All persons are not equally motivated to learn, but it is possible, with proper motivation, to transform latent talents into tangible skills and competencies.

Intent to Learn

Learning occurs all the time. Learning takes place only when information is received, understood, and internalized in such a way that some change in behavior occurs, or some conscious effort is made to use the information. Working in organizations is a continual learning process. Learning is the ultimate goal of all training activities.[16]

Learning is a complex psychologic process that is not fully understood. It requires an intent to learn, or a specific motivation. The nurse asks, "How important is this job to me?" "How important is it that I learn that information?" "Will learning this help me in any way?" and "What's in it for me?" Nurses are more willing to learn when the material presented is viewed as relevant to what they want or need to do (Figure 11-6).

The Learning Process

Learning is any relatively permanent change in behavior as a result of experience. Figure 11-7 summarizes the learning process. Learning helps one adapt to the environment. An individual enters a job situation with certain attitudes and an established personality. By making adaptations to accommodate the new job environment, the employee can become a responsible and productive employee.[2,17] For example, a nurse may be accustomed to working 5 days a week, Monday through Friday. Now he or she is required to work the night shift and alternate weekends. Unless the new employee's attitude is one of willing compliance, negative attitudes will impair learning.

Goal	Intention or Motivation
Achievement	→ → → → "I want to master this task so that I can feel good about it."
Advancement	→ → → → "If I learn the principles of management, I may be promoted."
Authority	→ → → → "Mastering the role of team captain for Code Blue Team will allow me to take charge of emergencies."
Co-workers' influence	→ → "By advancing a step above my teammates, I will be looked up to."
Comprehension	→ → → → "I want the feeling of knowing I can master the computer."
Curiosity	→ → → → "There never seems to be enough time to learn all that I need or want to know."
Fear of failure	→ → → → "What if I can't learn how to function as case manager; what will people think of me?"
Recognition	→ → → → "I love the thought of being a preceptor. The new grads and new employees will treat me with respect and listen to my advice."
Responsibility	→ → → → "Becoming a unit manager seems a heavy responsibility. So many people depend on the manager to do a good job. Even so, I want the job!"
Status	→ → → → "I will have arrived! It will be worth all the effort to learn this job! Then I will have a new title on my lapel pin and on the door for all to see."
Variety	→ → → → "I want to learn enough to be allowed to float from one unit to another. One day will never be like another. It is so exciting to think about."

FIGURE 11-6. Goals and intentions/motivations that may encourage nurses to learn.

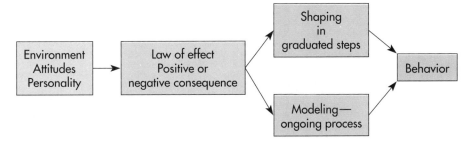

FIGURE 11-7. The learning process.

Learning is built on the Law of Effect, which states that behavior is a function of its consequences. Behavior followed by a favorable consequence **(positive reinforcement)** tends to be repeated. For example, a patient may state, "Oh, you performed that procedure so well, I hardly felt a thing." Behavior followed by an unfavorable consequence **(negative reinforcement)** tends not to be repeated. A nurse manager may say to an employee, "You will need to fill out an incident report. A copy of it will go on your record."

When learning occurs in graduated steps, it is shaped. Nurse managers shape employee behavior by reinforcing each desired behavior. The learner tries, fails, and tries again until the procedure is mastered. In addition to shaping, much of what one learns is the result of observing others and modeling behavior after them. For example, a nurse who is having difficulty mastering a procedure looks around to find someone who has mastered the procedure. The nurse asks for assistance and observes that person to see how the two approaches differ. The nurse then models the skilled person's behavior. The same approach is made when one aspires for a nurse manager role. The employee who wants to be successful looks for someone who is well respected and successful and tries to imitate that person's behavior.

The issue is not whether employees continually learn. They do. The issue is whether trainers and developers allow learning to occur randomly or whether they manage learning.

Learning curves

Nurse teachers need to understand the pattern in which new skills are learned. People learn in different patterns and time frames in different training situations.[17,14] These patterns are called **learning curves** (Figure 11-8). When a person first begins to learn a new skill, he or she is likely to be usually clumsy or inept, or "all thumbs." This syndrome is sometimes referred to as "decreased returns." This can be very discouraging, especially to persons who pride themselves on their ability to catch on quickly. The situation requires the teacher to offer sufficient training, provide for enough return demonstrations, and give support throughout the learning process. After this period the typical learning rate is rapid. This is the stage of increasing returns in which small additional amounts of practice by the trainee produce substantial increases in task proficiency. During this second period the learner's confidence and satisfaction rise.

A plateau develops after more practice time has elapsed. During this time additional training or monitoring results in the same level of performance. Both the teacher and the learner may be deceived into thinking that maximal proficiency has been attained. However, the plateau in learning may occur because of a lack of further motivation or the need to devote time and energy to the development of other new skills. The next step is peak proficiency, or doing the best one can do.

For continued skill proficiency, overlearning needs to occur. Even after reaching top performance, the reflex sequences relating to muscular responses and sensory stimuli become more deeply ingrained when the individual continues to practice. This is demonstrated by the swimmer or a typist who has not swum or typed for years; when the person resumes the skill, proficiency returns after minimal practice. I have con-

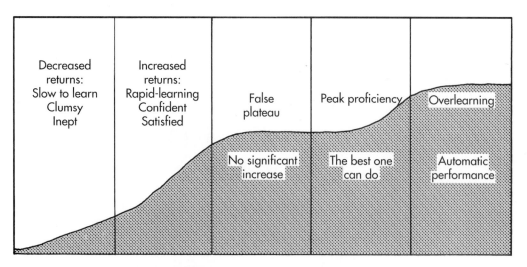

FIGURE 11-8. A typical learning curve.

ducted RN refresher courses and have found that students quickly regain skills that they have not used in years.

Implications for the nurse teacher are important. First, the learning curve is not the same for all people; there are profound differences in the ability to synchronize muscular movement, effect eye-hand coordinations, and sense subtle differences in tactile and muscular responses. When these differences are added to differences in motivation, morale, and knowledge base, they lead to wide disparities in learning rates. The teacher must assess the person's readiness for learning, the areas of knowledge and skill deficit, and the best training for the person.

Adult learners

Teachers of adults should be concerned with philosophical inquiry into the nature, value, and meaning of adult education, as well as the practical aspects of learning.[2,18] The adult learner wants and expects the following from the teacher (Figure 11-9):

1. *The learner is valued as a person and viewed as knowledgeable and worthy of teacher time, effort, and commitment.* Learning involves feelings and intellect. Facilitation of significant learning rests on a positive, trusting relationship between the teacher and the learner. The nurse teacher is committed to

teaching the student, and the student in turn is committed to focusing on the task at hand.

2. *The learner is presented with material and strategies that are practical and meaningful for the learner.* Significant learning occurs when the learner perceives the subject as relevant to his or her own purposes. Learning with understanding is more permanent and transferable than rote learning. For example, a nurse is far more likely to concentrate on learning or refining neurologic assessment skills if they will need to be performed on the unit to which he or she is assigned.

Strategies used for teaching and learning will be selected with the adult learner in mind. Small group participation and problem-solving exercises work very well. Opportunities for independent study and activity are also effective. The important point to remember is that whatever strategy is used, the learning process of *input* (subject and content), *operations* (activities to facilitate learning the subject and content), and *feedback* (verification of progress, feelings, and learning between the teacher and the learner) occurs.

3. *The learner participates in his or her own learning experience.* Significant learning is acquired when the adult learner participates responsibly and actively in the learning process. When adult students are free to determine what they will learn according to

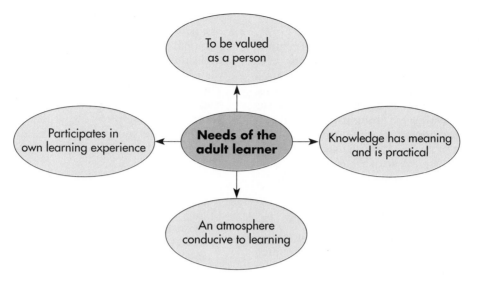

FIGURE 11-9. Four things an adult learner wants from a teacher.

their prevalent life needs, most invest more of themselves, work harder, and retain and use more of what they have learned. In the RN refresher programs that I taught, the students (nurses in their 30s and 40s) were given the opportunity to identify their needs and participate in planning their curriculum. The results were gratifying: motivation was high, and learning occurred rapidly.

Goal-setting is a concept that is central to adult learning. Adults tend to focus on immediate problems and on activities that they can use now. The teacher serves as a provider of necessary knowledge and experiences, a resource person, a facilitator, a validator, a conferee, and a consultant within a structure that promotes security and trust. The learner has the opportunity for an ongoing two-way evaluation of learning experiences. The fact that the teacher has taught something does not mean that learning has occurred. When progress is assessed in relation to established goals, both persons involved in the learning experience know where they stand. Tools such as interviews, job descriptions, a list of skills for assessment, and problem-solving exercises can help the learner determine where needs lie.

The pace of learning is also a very important factor. Increasing the difficulty of learning material in small increments promotes learning success. For example, the learner should not attempt to master how all fluids and electrolytes affect the body, as well as the acid-base balance system, in one sitting. Instead, if given the opportunity, the learner should study one increment at a time. He or she will be more successful if the subject is divided into subcategories, if each concept learned is applied to clinical practice, and if knowledge and activity are validated before proceeding to the next step.

4. *An atmosphere conducive to learning is established and nurtured.* Little attention has been given to the exciting aspects of nursing. However, a basic concern of nurse managers is to arrange a motivating atmosphere for learning. This is an endeavor that not only requires an understanding of people, their roles, and the adult as a learner, but also requires knowledge of how to design, organize, and arrange the work environment to provide channels for learning. A motivating environment provides opportunities for personnel to express and satisfy their own motives in a way that allows them to contribute to the achievement of orgnizational goals. Planned learning helps individuals to participate more, become skilled and competent, and feel good about themselves.

 GROUP DYNAMICS

The study of groups is important to the nurse manager for a number of reasons: (1) groups serve as the focal point of social life and provide a means for understanding social values and norms; (2) individuals may satisfy needs for belonging, status, and security through group participation, and (3) groups provide a major mechanism for the achievement of organizational goals.[19,20] Groups organized for the purpose of achieving work goals are the focus of this discussion.

Definition of a Work Group

In this chapter a **work group** is considered a collection of two or more people who are interdependent and who interact with one another to achieve a common goal.

Two or more → Interaction   → Common goal
people   among members

The main characteristics of this definition—that goals lead to interactions, which lead to performance—are critical to management effectiveness. These characteristics distinguish a work group from a collection of people who congregate together to see a play or a sporting event. Groups of existing healthcare workers in an agency may include such combinations as nurse-physician, nurse-immediate supervisor, nurse-nursing team, and nurse-patient/client/family.

Purpose of an Organized Work Group

Formal groups exist in organizations to achieve the purposes and goals of the organization. In healthcare this means providing quality care according to clearly defined standards. Nursing work groups have different reasons for forming: to hear shift reports, impart assignments, conduct direction-giving sessions, solve institutional or patient/client problems, engage in committee or task-force activities, or simply to hold a one-to-one session.

Group Development

Imagine the differences between a group of people who have just formed and a group of people who have worked together for years. Members of a new group are unfamiliar with one another's personalities and intentions and are tentative in their interactions. They need time to go through the process of becoming a group (Figure 11-10). The first stage is *mutual acceptance.* During this stage the members become aquainted with one another and begin to test which interpersonal behaviors are acceptable and which are unacceptable to the group.

> EXAMPLE: A nurse manager joins the members of a new work group to review the day's goals and activities. All members behave formally, except for John, who banters about his "terrific night out" and shows little interest in becoming serious about the task at hand. Fellow group members do not respond to his attempt at levity, so John alters his demeanor and assumes the role of a responsible group member.

The first stage often occurs quickly. Group members depend on each other to provide cues about acceptable behaviors and attitudes. The basic group rules for the group are established, and a tentative group structure may emerge.

The group moves on to *communication among members and decision-making.* Initially there may be a general lack of unity and uneven patterns of interaction between group members. With time some group members may begin to assert themselves to gain recognition and participate in shaping the group's personality.

> EXAMPLE: June is a member of a nursing team. She is uncomfortable with the fact that her team is always late in completing their work. There are many days when staff members stay overtime. She addresses this issue in group and says, "I think working overtime is becoming a habit with us. I think that we can do something to stop this practice. When any one of us notices that we are falling behind, let's tell the team leader so that she can do something about it before the situation gets out of hand."

This assertive group member encourages the group to assess its situation and to work to alleviate the problem through communication and decision making.

Motivation and productivity occur when members understand and accept what the group is trying to accomplish. Each person begins to recognize and accept his or her role and to un-

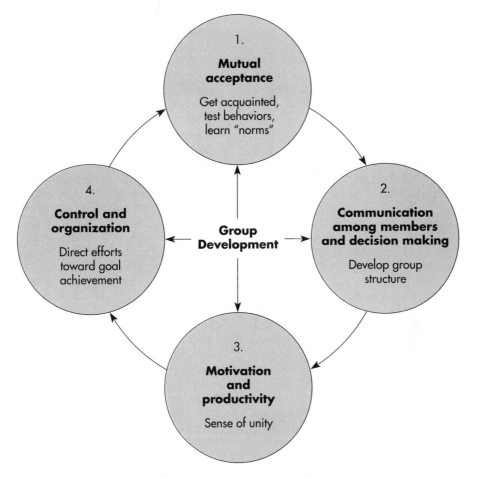

FIGURE 11-10. Stages in group development.

derstand the roles of others. As members become more comfortable with each other, they develop a sense of group identity and unity.

In the final stage, *control and organization,* the structure of the group is no longer an issue but has become a mechanism for accomplishing the purpose of the group. Group members control their behaviors and direct their group efforts toward goal attainment.

As with the learning process, developmental sequence varies from group to group. For example, time, personal characteristics and values of group members, and frequency of interaction can all effect how the group matures. There may also be a slow evolution or a burst of activity from one stage to another.

Group Norms and Conformity

A *norm* is a measure or standard of behavior or performance. Norms for a member of a nursing team might be to check for coverage with another team member before leaving the unit, to assist other group members when his or her assignment is completed, or to check the procedure manual before beginning a special task. Group *conformity* involves following and adhering to the established norms. For example, a new nursing team member might decide that he or she wants to spend his or her "free" time sitting at the desk observing others. In all probability group members attempt to enforce adherence to group norms on the nonadhering member. In such a case a three-phase reaction generally occurs. The new member is first reminded of the norm by another group member, who suggests that it be followed. If the comment is ignored by the new worker, the group becomes less friendly. More members may attempt to persuade the new person. If their efforts fail, the new person is ostracized; no one will eat at the same table, provide help with heavy duties unless forced to do so, or talk to him or her unless absolutely necessary. It is incumbent on the nurse leader to recognize when such a situation is occurring and to decide whether the enforced group norm is actually beneficial to the organization.

Group Status

Status is a social ranking in a group that is given to persons because of their position in the organization. The director of nursing services holds greater status than a nursing assistant. Another important factor is seniority and/or expertise. For example, the oldest nurse in a medical unit might enjoy high status in the group because of age, tenure, or expertise. Like norms, status symbols have positive and negative aspects. The positive aspect is the clarification of relationships, authority, and responsibility. However, overemphasizing status can reduce both the frequency and the level of communication among group members. The team leader who never lets the members forget who is boss or the team member who reminds the group frequently, "I have been here the longest and I should have first preference," creates conflict, and group activity is diverted toward resolving the conflict.

Group Member Roles

The main managerial roles of a nurse are interpersonal (to relate well with others), informational (to provide clear directions), and decisional (to make sound decisions on the basis of the nursing process). Membership roles are also multiple and depend on each person's rank and assignment. They too must maintain a system that leads to *group cohesiveness,* in which the factors acting on group members to remain and participate in the group are greater than those acting on the members to leave it.

Team Building for Special Tasks

Team building is a process for developing work group maturity and effectiveness.[21] It is the most widely used human resource development technique in the business world. Team building emphasizes interactive group processes, or the "how" of effective group behavior. Team builders (1) set goals and/or priorities; (2) analyze or allocate how work is performed; (3) examine the way a group is working and consider such factors as norms, decision making, and communication; and (4) examine relationships among the people doing the work. It is important for the group itself to achieve these purposes by relying on its own leadership to solve real-life problems. A consultant or group facilitator may help get the group headed in the right direction and may coach as necessary along the way.

In nursing, team building is used to prepare groups of people to accomplish particular tasks. A team may be formed to design a new nursing care delivery system or to introduce the use of computerized equipment throughout the healthcare agency. Often these teams consist of individuals who have specific areas of expertise (e.g., nurse specialists, social workers, or business managers) but no allegiance to or even familiarity with each other. Team-building techniques are geared toward developing an appreciation among team members for what the task is, what roles must be filled, and who will fill them. In the process, individual strengths are highlighted as they pertain to the tasks, and mutual trust and group cohesion are developed.

The final ingredient of an effective team is a supportive climate. The team should be internally strong. This strength includes proper training, time and task management, and an evaluative tool by which members can systematically measure progress and outcome. Management must provide the team with the resources it needs to accomplish the special task, as well as positive reinforcement for a job well done.

ORIENTATION AND STAFF DEVELOPMENT PROGRAMS

In this section a description of several staff nurse programs is offered for review: a general orientation program, a nurse internship for the new graduate, a preceptor training workshop, and self-directed learning. The staff developer may adapt the programs to meet the needs of a specific work environment. Information specific to each organization is available through agency documents. The suggested readings at the end of each chapter supply other references that may be used as resources.

General Orientation Program

Overall purpose To provide experienced nurses and others new to the organization with orientation to practice nursing in keeping with the mission and goals of the hospital and to meet Medicare criteria and the standards of the Joint Commission on Accreditation of Health Care Organizations (JCAHO).

Length of program Three months (15 days followed by a probationary period)

Instructors Members of the staff development department (inservice) and representatives from administration (hospital and nursing), personnel, quality assurance, infection control, and other departments as appropriate

Objectives On completion of the program each participant is expected to be able to do the following regarding the hospital in general and nursing service in particular:

Hospital

1. Recognize the overall physical setting of the hospital and specify the work area to which he or she is assigned.
2. Review the mission, goals, and policies of the hospital.
3. Describe the organizational structure of the hospital.
4. Describe the interdepartmental and intradepartmental communication process in effect (e.g., computer, intercommunication systems, forms, notices).
5. Identify the functions of departments other than nursing and the nurse's relationship with them.

Nursing service

1. Read the overall philosophy, goals, and standard of nursing care adopted by nursing service as the criteria for determining quality care.
2. Review nursing organizational structure and focus on staff nurse levels (e.g., levels 1, 2, 3, 4) and conditions for advancement.
3. State the purpose of the hospital staff development department (or inservice department) and ways in which the staff nurse can be served by its offerings.
4. Identify hospital committees on which staff nurses can become members; recognize the conditions for membership.
5. Complete nursing skills inventory by the end of the 15-day orientation period or make arrangements with the staff development instructor for a time extension.
6. Demonstrate a baseline level of understanding and skill in content and procedures that are common to the specified area of practice. (This objective may be accomplished by classroom instruction, demonstration, and/or use of modules for independent study.) Many of the components of orientation are often prepared by the staff development department and transcribed on videotape. Examples of content and procedures include the following:
   a. Nursing process adopted for hospital-wide use
   b. Documentation system (charting)
   c. Discharge planning
   d. Team and/or primary nursing
   e. Pharmacology (drugs used most commonly in the specified area of practice and computation of dosages; these tests need to be developed according to areas of service such as intensive care, cardiovascular, medical, surgical, pediatrics, maternal-neonatal, and oncology)
   f. Intravenous therapy, blood therapy, central lines, monitoring of equipment
   g. Infection control
   h. Quality assurance program
   i. Life support systems (cardiopulmonary resuscitation, advanced life support systems)

Up to this point, all nurse orientees may be oriented and tested together. For induction into the clinical area to which he or she is assigned, the experienced nurse who is new to the hospital is assigned to the care of a trained preceptor. The goal of this plan is for the new employee to ease into the job with as much help as needed.

The experienced nurse is expected to be able to function in the role assigned fairly independently by the end of the 15-day orientation period. The new employee is encouraged to return to the staff development department to review any part of the orientation offerings that remains unclear.

Nurse Internship for the New Graduate

The example presented here is the result of a nurse intern study group charged by the nursing administrators of the Association Hospitals and the California Nurses' Association, Region 10, to develop goals and objectives for an internship program for the new graduate. The group was further charged to develop levels of practice within the internship program and to recommend a time frame for the program.

Good Samaritan Hospital of Santa Clara Valley, California, was one of five participating hospitals selected to conduct a pilot group. I developed the program, which was implemented with 23 new graduates from five different educational programs and was evaluated as successful. The major highlights are given.

Overall purpose To supplement the clinical and leadership skills of the new graduate nurse to facilitate professional and social integration into the healthcare team

Length of program Three months; however, a second program, 9 weeks long, was conducted, and a comparative analysis revealed that 9 weeks was sufficient for an internship program

Instructors Staff development personnel, nurse managers

Other participants Preceptors, nursing staff, and members from other departments, as appropriate

Objectives Four levels outline overall goals and ultimate expectations of its graduates

Level I. Basic nursing skills. The intern functions as a team member or associate nurse to the preceptor and delivers nursing care to patients with a variety of uncomplicated health problems.

Level II. The intern functions as a team member or associate nurse and delivers nursing care to patients with a variety of moderate-to-complicated health problems.

Level III. The intern functions as a team leader or primary nurse with dependence on the preceptor and directs and/or delivers nursing care to patients with a variety of learning needs. The intern recognizes, develops, and uses teaching and learning strategies to meet patient/client, family, and staff learning needs.

Level IV. The intern functions as team leader or primary nurse fairly independently, uses resource persons appropriately, demontrates a consistent pattern of leadership skills needed for problem solving and priority setting, and meets frequently with preceptor to discuss progress in the following areas:

a. Uses data obtained from other disciplines and own assessment to establish priorities of patient care and nursing activities (examples are provided by the intern)

b. Demonstrates ability to reorganize priorities on the basis of changing patient care needs

c. Makes rounds with physician as necessary and collaborates in plan of care to meet patient needs

d. Regularly provides direction, consultation, and, when appropriate (as team leader), supervision of the nursing team

e. Evaluates information from appropriate sources and incorporates into patient care plan

f. Evaluates own and others' documentation or charting when appropriate for evidence of care given and patient progress

g. Evaluates activities of self and others for adherence to hospital policy and procedures; takes appropriate action

Interns were assigned a combination of classroom and clinical activities. Interns were also given the opportunity to come to the nursing education department (staff development) for review or instruction when necessary.

Each intern was assigned to a trained preceptor. The intern and preceptor conferred formally and informally throughout each level of the program. Other conference participants included the nurse manager, the clinical instructor, and others as appropriate.

An evaluation form was prepared for each level of the program. Competency at each level was indicated by successful completion of skills (Figure 11-11). Documentation of competency was required by the preceptor or instructor at least once as determined by the critical nature of the skill.

Among other assessment tools was a six-dimension scale for evaluation of nursing behaviors (Box 11-1). The list contains only a sample of nursing activities. The actual tool lists the usual behaviors exhibited by the nurse under each category (e.g., leadership, critical care, teaching, collaboration). The intern, preceptor, and nurse manager separately and collaboratively evaluate the performance of these behaviors.

Box 11-1. Performance of nursing behaviors

Instructions: This tool contains a list of activities in which nurses engage with varying degrees of frequency and skill. Please indicate how well you believe you perform or how well you believe the intern can perform the activities by using numbers from the following key:

KEY TO SUBSCALES

1—Not very well	L —Leadership
2—Satisfactory	CC —Critical care
3—Well	TC —Teaching and collaboration
4—Very well	PE —Planning and evaluation
	IPR—Interpersonal relationships
	PD —Professional development

TC —Teach a patient's/client's family members about the patient's/client's needs
PE —Coordinate the plan of nursing care with the medical plan of care
L —Give praise and recognition for achievement to those under his or her direction
TC —Teach preventive health measures to patients/clients and families
IPR—Promote the inclusion of the patient's/client's decisions and desires concerning care
CC —Perform technical procedures (e.g., oral suctioning, tracheostomy care)
PD —Attend quality assurance committee meeting
The intern, preceptor, and the nurse manager evaluate the intern's performance toward the end of the program to validate successful achievement and to identify areas that need further attention.

Skill performed by nurse intern	Supervised/ assisted by	Validation of successful completion No. 1	Validation of successful completion No. 2
A. Uses data obtained from other disciplines and own assessment to establish priorities of patient care and nursing activities	Remarks: *Followed procedure - weak on responses. Suggest review.* Date: 4/8/94 Sig.: *L. Douglas Anst.*	Remarks: *Has reviewed theory and skills in skills lab. Demonstrated ability to recognize rales and rhonchi* Date: 4/12/94 Sig.: *D. Gamberg, Preceptor*	Remarks: *Completed admittance of new patient thoroughly and well. Excellent rapport with Pt./family* Date: 4/20/94 Sig.: *D. Gamberg Preceptor*
B. Continue on with objectives for level IV	Remarks: Date: Sig.:	Remarks: Date: Sig.:	Remarks: Date: Sig.:

FIGURE 11-11. Sample of a tool used to assess competencies on the basis of predetermined criteria. (Courtesy The Good Samaritan Hospital, Santa Clara Valley, San Jose, Calif.)

Preceptor Workshop

Overall purpose To prepare qualified nurses to serve as a preceptor, role model, and resource person to new graduates or new employees and to create a supportive, unstressful orientation period
Objectives On completion of the 2-day workshop, each participant is expected to perform the following activities:

1. Serve as a mentor, role model, and resource person for a trainee
2. Use effective communication skills with a trainee
3. Keep within the designated time frame for preparation of a trainee
4. Complete the necessary reports regarding trainee progress
5. Consult with educational staff regarding concerns or problems that relate to the trainee.

Length of program Two days
Qualifications of preceptor candidate The interested nurse should demonstrate the following characteristics:

1. Be permanent and full-time (nurses with exceptional ability and interest may be considered if their status is three-fifths or four-fifths time)
2. Demonstrate proficiency in technical, intellectual, and interpersonal skills
3. Exhibit an interest in teaching new graduates and new employees
4. Desire to work in a close one-to-one relationship with a new employee
5. Agree to attend preceptor training workshops and acquire as much knowledge and skill from the sessions as possible

Suggested content Suggested content for a preceptor training workshop includes the following:

1. Review of orientation program and assessment tools
2. Roles of nurse manager, preceptor, instructor, new graduate, and new employee
3. The adult learner, the teaching-learning process, the development and use of behavioral objectives, coaching the learner
4. The communication process in a one-to-one relationship
5. The group process in working with small groups
6. The change process as applied to the preceptor role

7. The evaluation process as it applies to the preceptor role

The preceptor and intern are provided a day-by-day activity manual with tools to assess accomplishment. The content relates specifically to the objectives listed for the particular program (e.g., new employee, 15-day program; new graduate, 3-month or less program). The key to the success of the preceptor program lies in the application of the principles of effective leadership and management.

Self-Learning Programs

Overall purpose To meet self-learning needs of nursing personnel in health agencies
Objectives Program objectives include the following:

1. To provide programs that address the identified development needs of the nursing staff
2. To have 15- to 20-minute learning programs readily accessible in the workplace available whenever the nurse's workload permits
3. To provide a learning resource center that is available to all nursing staff and contains resources that address the developmental needs of the nursing agency's entire staff
4. To allow the staff nurse to be in control of scheduling his or her own learning programs
5. To identify nurses in the agency who are specialists in their fields and can serve as resource persons when inquiries are made

Length of programs From 15 to 20 minutes in the workplace and from 30 minutes to 1 hour or more in a learning resource center
Suggested format for self-learning in the workplace
Modules

For each subject the staff development department or designated person(s) prepares a module that is contained in a folder. Extracts from available literature and other media information are included. The following is a suggested format and examples:

Format	Example
Subject	Protective measures needed by a nurse caring for a patient with AIDS
Objective	To protect the nurse from contracting AIDS
Content	Facts on how AIDS is transmitted, research, conclusions

Summary	Meaning for the nurse (no need for isolation procedures, except for transmission of blood or body fluids)
Quiz	True or false statements about the main points

The information is capsulized and customized for the learner. The content is approved by an inservice educator, nurse manager, or designated person. The advantages of the modular system are that the modules are economical to prepare, do not require hardware, are portable, and are easily produced. A nurse can review the module anytime the workload allows or during coffee or lunch breaks. However, it is time consuming to prepare the modules, and they do not lend themselves well to procedures that require demonstration and practice.

Bulletin boards

Large fixed or portable bulletin boards can become learning centers. They provide a graphic or pictorial account of a subject that is pertinent to the nursing staff. Bulletin boards can be placed in the chart room, rest areas, or any other place where nurses gather. Brief narrations can be printed or typed on 5 x 8 file cards and mounted on attractive colored paper. Items appropriate for this format include anatomic diagrams; graphs; and pictures of rashes, wounds, and positions.

Bulletin boards need to be changed frequently; once the information is absorbed, staff members tend to ignore the board. Staff members may wish to prepare or assist in the preparation of a display.

Resource material in the nursing unit or department

Information can be acquired quickly from resources that are available in a work area. Each department should have on hand a current *Physician's Desk Reference,* a text or texts covering the areas that the department services (e.g., pediatrics, medical/surgical, cardiovascular, psychiatric), and policy and procedure manuals. Providing nursing periodicals in the nurses' lounge is another excellent means of assisting the staff in self-directed learning.

Portable media

Health agencies are wise to provide each nursing unit with a slide/filmstrip projector and teaching media selected by the staff. Slides and filmstrips are commonly used to illustrate real-life situations, such as "Communication with a Sexually Abused Child," and nursing procedures. Commercially prepared filmstrips on many subjects are readily available at minimal cost. Slides and filmstrips can be changed with ease and can be viewed almost anywhere; a wall or other blank surface reflects the pictures adequately.

The videocassette recorder (VCR) allows any agency, large or small, to benefit from the finest presentations at minimal cost. Staff members can view the videocassettes at their own time and pace. The VCR is probably the most cost-effective media available for staff development considering the quality of content and the number of people who can be served collectively and individually. Two types of presentations are common: those discussing interpersonal relations and psychosocial-religious issues and those demonstrating and explaining procedures. Each presentation should include statements of overall and specific purpose (e.g., "to gain an understanding of arterial bypass surgery," "implications for the nurse in the first 24 hours after the procedure"). Each presentation should be followed by a written quiz to help the nurse assess whether the objectives have been met and to verify completion of the program if continuing education units or some other type of credits are being earned. Because most VCR programs are 30 minutes to 1 hour or more long the nurse usually goes to the agency's resource center to view them. Some agencies, particularly during the afternoon and night shifts, roll a VCR to the nursing department, where nurses can view the program as time permits. Another method is to allow the nurse to sign out the videocassettes from the resource center to view at home. A marked disadvantage of VCR use is the lack of opportunity to communicate with the presenter(s). When possible, a staff development person should be present to respond to inquiries and to conduct follow-up discussion.

Computers

Terminals are becoming increasingly common in healthcare agencies. Videodiscs are incorporating all types of media—slides, motion, audio, and print, in black and white and color. Holographic techniques make it possible to produce 3-dimensional images at different magnifications. However, there is a delay in the preparation of quality instructional materials. Given time and expertise, a nurse will be able to obtain immediate data on any subject that is relevant to nursing practice and will be able to tap quickly into previously unavailable resources through a computer. The computer used for staff development usually presents cases, medication computation problems, or conversion tables for consideration. The nurse requests information, responds, interviews, and receives feedback about the consequences of decisions.

Resource persons

The use of existing personnel is an efficient way to improve and upgrade employee performance. The self-directed nurse can contact the hospital-wide staff development department (or the appropriate person) to identify expert staff members who are willing to share their skill and knowledge with another. Arrangements can be made for responding to individual needs. The response may be a simple telephone call or a meeting for demonstration, practice, or dialogue.

Summary

1. Staff development plays a significant role in the quality rating of an agency. Ongoing education is an essential strategy for maintaining the competency of an agency's staff.
2. Training and development provide an environment and resources that faciliate a learning and maturing process in each person.
3. The managerial skills needed by all nurses are technical, human, conceptual, diagnostic, and those of coach and mentor.
4. Management skills are acquired through education and training, experience, and preceptor relationships.
5. The mentoring relationship is dynamic, noncompetitive, and nurturing. It promotes independence, autonomy, and self-actualization in the protégé while fostering a sense of pride, fulfillment, support, and continuity.
6. Many new graduates feel overwhelmed by their first experience as an employed nurse, partly because of the numbers of patients, acuity levels, and the amount of paperwork.
7. New graduates consider a good preceptor program, friendliness and teamwork, positive feedback, recognition, autonomy, salary and benefits, flexibility, and opportunity to be important in a new work experience.
8. Many middle-manager–eligible nurses are not interested in advancing to that position.
9. Many practicing middle managers express an overall enthusiasm for the role but express some discontent regarding fiscal restraints, overload, uncompensated time, and accountability without authority.
10. Middle managers spend approximately one fourth of their time working directly with patients and three fourths of their time in administrative activities.
11. An effective managing development program includes general orientation, fiscal learning, group development skills, and a wide spectrum of individualized learning opportunities for nurse managers at all levels.
12. All nurses need training and development, regardless of their position in the agency.
13. Knowledge important to the success of training and development programs includes concepts of role clarification: role expectations, role conception, and role congruence and performance.
14. Role clarification is a "package" of norms (measures of standards of behaviors or performance) that applies to particular persons within a group.
15. Role expectations are defined as how others believe one should act in a given situation.
16. Role conception is how the nurse perceives the role. Pressure from the employer, patients, and self directly influence the nurse's analysis of the role.
17. Role congruence and performance concern who the nurse is in relation to others; it is the integration of role expectation, patient expectation, and self-concept of the role.
18. Every nurse has the responsibility to be an effective teacher. Teaching and learning always stimulate a positive or negative reaction. It is the teaching process, not the teacher, that is the key to learning.
19. Learning is an ongoing process. Learning occurs when information is received, understood, and internalized in such a way that a change in behavior has occurred or a conscious effort to use the information has been made.
20. Learning requires the intent or the motivation to learn. The nurse asks, "What's in it for me?" when considering whether to pursue

a goal such as advancement, recognition, status, or responsibility.

21. The nurse enters a job environment with an established attitude and personality. Learning occurs according to the Law of Effect (behavior is a function of its consequences). Positive feedback tends to precipitate repetition of that behavior, whereas negative feedback tends to discourage repetition. Trial and error and modeling by key figures help shape the learner. New behaviors are acquired as a result of the learning process.

22. Learning curve patterns include (1) slow learning (decreased returns), (2) rapid learning (increased returns), (3) false plateau (no significant increase in learning), (4) peak proficiency (the best one can do), and (5) overlearning (automatic performance). Learning patterns vary with each individual.

23. Human beings are affected by their stage in life and by their learning patterns. Adult learners expect to be valued as knowledgeable persons, to have practical and meaningful learning experiences, to participate in the learning experience, and to learn in an atmosphere that is conducive to learning.

24. Work groups fulfill the purposes and goals of the organization through goal establishment, interaction, and performance. Group norms, conformity, status, and roles influence group productivity.

25. Group development is a process of mutual acceptance, communication among members, decision making, motivation and productivity (a sense of unity), and control and organization (direct efforts toward goal achievement).

26. Group status is a social ranking in the group. For example, a team leader has greater status than a nursing assistant.

27. Team building is a process for developing group maturity and effectiveness with an emphasis on goals and group process.

28. Three staff development programs are offered by many hospitals: (1) organization programs for all personnel new to the hospital, (2) nurse internships for new graduates, and (3) preceptor training programs for qualified nursing staff. These and other training and development programs, including provisions for meeting continuing education requirements, are commonly offered by the staff development or inservice department of the institution.

29. A nurse interested in on-the-job, self-directed learning has many avenues to pursue: modules, bulletin boards, resource materials in the department, slide/filmstrips, videocassettes, computers, the resource learning center, and resource persons.

❓ Questions for Study and Discussion

1. Your job is to establish a staff development center for nursing staff. What is your major function?

2. Give an example of a conceptual or diagnostic skill required of a nurse manager.

3. Describe the characteristics of a preceptor you would like to have on your first job. List them in order of priority and explain your rationale.

4. Explain why role analysis and team building are useful to nurse managers.

5. Assume you must learn a nursing procedure that is new to you. What is the best approach to learning for you? What would you do first, second, and so on? Does your plan relate to the "norm" for teaching and learning? If it is unusual, why do you think you learn differently?

6. You have been a staff nurse for 4 years and believe strongly that the authoritarian structure of the unit needs to be changed to allow for more staff input and participation. What could you do to bring about the desired change?

7. After gaining work experience, do you aspire to become a middle manager? What is the rationale for your decision? If you are negative about the idea, what do you propose to make the role of middle manager more desirable?

Test Your Knowledge

BEHAVIORAL OBJECTIVE

Differentiate among technical, human, conceptual, diagnostic and mentor skills.

Janessa is a team leader assigned to an oncology unit. As she interacts with team members, she recognizes the importance of identifying and helping to develop team member skills and abilities. Some of the concepts that she has assimilated follow.

_____ 1. Because she has two Mexican team members, Janessa is attempting to understand the Mexican culture. What type of skill is she acquiring?
a. Technical
b. Human
c. Conceptual
d. Mentor

_____ 2. Janessa is evaluating the work of a nursing assistant. Which skill is in progress?
a. Mentor
b. Conceptual
c. Diagnostic
d. Human

BEHAVIORAL OBJECTIVE

Discuss the expected outcomes of nurse preceptor relationships for the preceptor and the protégé.

_____ 3. Janessa is precepting Carol, who aspires to become a nurse manager. Janessa's first priority is to:
a. Determine if nurse manager and learner are compatible.
b. Assess Carol's past experiences.
c. Ask if there are any cultural differences.
d. Let Carol know that she is prepared to precept.

BEHAVIORAL OBJECTIVE

Outline a sound program and content for the development of nurse middle managers.

Janessa attended a training program for middle managers, where she gained new insights into the role. Some of the things she learned follow.

_____ 4. The most important element of any nurse manager development program is that:
a. It contains a group development cycle.
b. It is conducted within a health-care setting.
c. It is linked to the mission and goals of the organization.
d. It covers a period of 2 years to allow for maturation.

BEHAVIORAL OBJECTIVE

Identify staff nurses who need training and development, and give a rationale for their need.

_____ 5. The best definition of continuing education is that the program consists of:
a. A review of basic knowledge and skills.
b. Recommendations for improvement.
c. Planned learning experiences beyond a basic nursing education program.
d. Classes offered outside the workplace.

BEHAVIORAL OBJECTIVE

Define role clarification and differentiate among role expectation, role conception, and role congruence.

_____ 6. Which of the following is closest in meaning to the term *role?*
  a. Registered nurse
  b. Prescriptions for expected behavior of an individual
  c. A person trained to accomplish a task
  d. When the individual has expectations

_____ 7. Role expectation in a nursing job originates from which source(s)?
  a. The patient and employer
  b. The employer and employee
  c. The employer
  d. The patient

BEHAVIORAL OBJECTIVE

Define the adult learner and describe the teaching-learning process as applied to nurses.

Janessa wants to further develop her skills as a teacher. She adheres to the following principles and concepts.

_____ 8. Which of the following concepts is false?
  a. When knowledge is presented to the learner and the reaction is negative, learning has not occurred.
  b. It is the teaching process, not the teacher, that is the key to learning.
  c. Learning involves feelings as well as intellect.
  d. The adult learner prefers material and strategies that have personal application.

_____ 9. Wanting the satisfaction of knowing that one can master the hemodialysis equipment illustrates which goal?
  a. Curiosity
  b. Comprehension
  c. Variety
  d. Status

BEHAVIORAL OBJECTIVE

Define a work group and identify factors that influence work productivity.

Group activity is an important part of the oncology unit. Janessa encourages each staff member to work interdependently with staff members. She does this on the basis of a body of knowledge.

_____ 10. The main characteristics of a work group in sequence are:
  a. Goals, performance, interaction
  b. Goals, evaluation, interaction
  c. Goals, interaction, performance
  d. Performance, interaction, evaluation

_____ 11. A group norm is defined as:
  a. A standard of performance.
  b. A measure of success.
  c. The 70th percentile.
  d. Average performance.

_____ 12. All of the following elements are stages in group development except for one. Which element does not belong?
  a. Direct efforts toward goal achievement
  b. Mutual acceptance
  c. Aggressiveness
  d. Motivation

BEHAVIORAL OBJECTIVE

Identify the key factors of programs designed for preceptor training and for orientation of new employees and new graduates.

_____ 13. Orientation to the job programs are generally conducted:
  a. Through self-study.
  b. In the classroom.
  c. On the clinical unit.
  d. Before formal employment.

BEHAVIORAL OBJECTIVE

Describe on-the-job development through self-learning.

_____ 14. Which one of the following statements about on-the-job self-learning is false?
   a. Modules designed for on-the-job learning should not exceed 15 to 20 minutes.
   b. The VCR is a cost-effective device for individual learning.
   c. One disadvantage of media presentations is the lack of two-way communication.
   d. Nurses who are specialists in their fields should automatically be assigned to develop self-learning modules.

REFERENCES

1. Donley R: Healthcare reform: implications for staff development, *Nurs Econ* 12(2):71-74, 1994.
2. Robbins S: *Essentials of organizational behavior,* ed 4, Englewood Cliffs, NJ, 1994, Prentice Hall.
3. Barney J, Griffin R: *The management of organizations,* Boston, 1992, Houghton Mifflin.
4. Marquis B, Huston C: *Leadership roles and management functions in nursing: theory and application,* Philadelphia, 1992, JB Lippincott.
5. Wheelen T, Hunger J: *Strategic management,* ed 3, Reading, Mass, 1990, Addison-Wesley Publishing.
6. Levenstein A: Avoiding responsibility, *Nurs Manage* 14(2):28-30, 1983.
7. Orth C, Wilkinson H, Benfari R: The manager's role as coach and mentor, *JONA* 20(9):11-15, 1990.
8. Valadez A, Land C: Mentorship and me, *J Contin Educ Nurs* 24(6):259-263, 1993.
9. Williams J, Rogers S: The multicultural workplace: preparing preceptors, *J Contin Educ Nurs* 24(3): 101-104, 1993.
10. Boston C, Forman H: A time to listen: staff manager views on education, practice, and management *JONA* 24(2):16-18, 1994.
11. Weber J: Collaborative teaching: preparing for the reality of nursing, *Nurs Manage* 24(1):47-52, 1993.
12. Sullivan P and others: Management development: preparing nurses for the future, *JONA* 24(6):32-38, 1994.
13. American Nurses' Association: *ANA nursing standards,* Kansas City, Mo, 1986, The Association.
14. Henry J, Walker D: *Managing innovation,* London, 1991, Sage Publications.
15. Potter D, editor: *Nurse's reference library,* Springhouse, Pa, 1984, Springhouse.
16. Mathis R, Jackson J: *Human resource management,* ed 7, Minneapolis/St Paul, 1994, West Publishing.
17. Lickman P, Simms L, Greene C: Learning environment: the catalyst for work excitement, *J Contin Educ Nurs* 24(5):211-216, 1993.
18. Kreitner R: *Management,* ed 5, Dallas, 1992, Houghton Mifflin.
19. Ruben B: *Communication and human behavior,* Englewood Cliffs, NJ, 1992, Prentice Hall.
20. Rothwell J: *In mixed company: small group communication,* Fort Worth, 1992, Harcourt Brace Jovanovich.
21. Schroeder P: *Improving quality and performance concepts, programs, and techniques,* St Louis, 1994, Mosby.

SUGGESTED READINGS

Carey S, Campbell S: Preceptor, mentor, and sponsor roles: creative strategies for nurse retention, *J Nurs Adm* 24(12):39-47, 1994.

Chapman M: Assimilating new staff in an intensive care nursery, *Nurs Manage* 44(4):96B-96H, 1993.

Cohen P: A meta-analysis of computer-based instruction in nursing education, *Comput Nurs* 12(2):89-97, 1994.

Corley M and others: The clinical ladder: impact on nurse satisfaction and turnover (mentors), *J Nurs Adm* 24(2):42-48, 1994.

Duff M, Kirsivali-Farmer K: The challenge: developing a preceptorship program in the midst of organizational change, *J Contin Educ Nurs* 25(3):115-119, 1994.

Grant P: Formative evaluation of a nursing orientation program: self-paced vs lecture-discussion, *J Contin Educ Nurs* 24(6):245-248, 1993.

Gundlack A: Adapting to change: reconsidering staff development organization, design, and purpose, *J Contin Educ Nurs* 25(3):120-122, 1994.

Jackson K and others: Mock surgery: methodology for measuring compliance and facilitating change, *J Nurs Adm* 24(1):34-39, 1994.

Keys M: Recognition and reward: a unit-based program, *Nurs Manage* 25(2):52-54, 1994.

Kramer N: Preceptorship policy: a tool for success, *J Contin Educ Nurs* 24(6):274-276, 1993.

Kreider M, Barry M: Clinical ladder development: implementing contract learning, *J Contin Educ Nurs* 24(4):166-169, 1993.

Kuhn M: Gaming: a technique that adds spice to learning, *J Contin Educ Nurs* 26(1):35-39, 1995.

Lachat M, Cowen E: Developing a community wide HIV/AIDS nurse education series: a strategy for success, *J Contin Educ Nurs* 24(6):255-257, 1993.

Mark B: The emerging role of the nurse manager: implications for educational preparation, *J Nurs Adm* 24(1):48-55, 1994.

McGoldrick, Hensler-Cullen J: Getting oriented to orientation, *Am J Nurs Career Guide* pp 13-14, Jan 1994.

Neidig J and others: Competency-based orientation in pediatric critical care, *Nurs Manage* 24(5):960-964, 1993.

Percival E, Anderson M, Lawson D: Assessing beginning level competencies: the first step in continuing education, *J Contin Educ Nurs* 25(3):139-142, 1994.

Saleem N, Moses B: Expert systems as computer assisted instruction systems for nursing education and training, *Comput Nurs* 12(1):35-45, 1994.

Thoma G: Evolution of a patient education program in a rural hospital, *Nurs Manage* 25(1):46-48, 1994.

LEGAL and ETHICAL ISSUES

BEHAVIORAL OBJECTIVES

On completion of this chapter, the student will be prepared to:

- Define legal terms important to nursing practice.

- Identify common control areas of the nurse practice act.

- Indicate the significance of risk management to nurses. Name four common reasons for malpractice suits against nurses and identify measures to avoid them.

- Explain the difference between employer and personal malpractice insurance.

- Differentiate among technical, judgmental, and normative errors.

- State two roles of the nurse as a witness in court and describe the nurse's responsibilities.

- Define formal, express, written express, and implied contracts.

- Define ethics, state the purposes of an ethics committee, and explain how an ethical approach applies to nursing.

- Explain the meaning of transcultural nursing and compare ethnocentric and ethnorelative attitudes.

- Indicate the nurse's responsibility for implementing the Patient Self-Determination Act.

LEGAL ISSUES

Importance of Law to the Nurse

Times are changing; contemporary nurses have much more responsibility than before. Over the years nurses have moved from subsidiary roles into roles of leadership and management. Nurses no longer depend on the employing agency and physicians for protection. The expanded roles of the nurse require a higher level of education, knowledge, skill, and decision-making capabilities. Professional nurses also assume accountability for their own acts. But nurses do not function alone; they have guidance and protection from legal forces. Nurses must recognize the law as an essential component of nursing practice that is there to assist in the decision-making process and to protect in times of need. There are often gray areas in which the nurse is uncertain of the grounds for practice. The risk of liability is ever present. The nurse should become aware of the laws and regulations of the profession so that professional responsibility can be defined and appropriate resources can be used in times of need. The many ethical and professional problems that may emerge are solved with greater confidence if the nurse has a sound basis of theory and facts regarding legal and ethical issues.

Legal Terms

A **law** is a rule or standard of human conduct that is established and enforced by authority, society, or custom. It is a set of rules or customs that govern a discrete field or activity. A law is a socially oriented discipline and is committed to the welfare of society. Laws tell us what one can and cannot do. However, laws are not static; they move with the times. What was once law may now be extinct, such as the law of prohibition.

Nursing law is not a separate entity. Instead it draws from general laws and rules and regulations of federal and state as a basis for defining and governing nursing practice. Law and nursing share many societal similarities. Each considers a state of wellness as an optimal condition and seeks it for both the individual and social group. Each intervenes when there is an interruption in the state of wellness that is manifested by altered conduct and takes steps to restore individual or social equilibrium. Each turns to the social and behavioral sciences to understand conduct and to guide remedial action.

Certain types of laws create rights and responsibilities for nurses[1]:

Statutory law is a law passed by federal or state legislature and declares, commands, or prohibits something.

Public law determines an individual's relationship to the federal government and the states. It consists of constitutional law, administrative law, and criminal law. **Private law** or **civil law** determines one's relationship to other individuals, such as the nurse to the patient/client.

Tort law is a private law that concerns any wrongful act, damage, or injury done willfully, negli-

gently, or in circumstances that involve strict liability but not breach of contract, for which a civil suit can be brought. Nurses are most closely associated with this type of law because actions of malpractice fall into this category.

Criminal law refers to action that is harmful to the public and the individual and stipulates punishment for offenders. Examples of criminal acts are gross negligence (e.g., not attending to the vital needs of a patient/client), improper use of narcotics, or illegal practice of medicine. Nurses can be witnesses in criminal cases if they provide care to victims of such acts as child abuse, rape, or assault.

Liability is legal responsibility for acts or a failure to act according to standards that result in another person's harm.

Malpractice is improper or unethical conduct by a professional that results in harm to another person.

Scope of practice is the range of activities a nurse may perform as stipulated in each state's nurse practice act.

Law in the Practice of Nursing

Common law is the cumulative result of many court decisions over the years. **Common practice** is that which falls within both the legal scope and the profession's definition of nursing practice. It is determined by statutes, regulations, basic nursing curricula, specialty nursing curricula, standards of practice, court cases, attorney generals' opinions, and professional associations' policy positions.[1] Just because a nursing function is legal or even common practice does not mean that every nurse should engage in it.

EXAMPLE: All staff nurses employed in the hospital have had some basic nursing education and training in working with infants and children. A nurse from pediatrics was asked by his nurse manager to cover for her in the neonatal ICU during her lunch breaks. Although he had not worked with newborns for 10 years he agreed to cover because the nurse manager believed he was able. The critically ill newborn "went sour" and died in spite of the desperate efforts of the pediatric nurse.

A review of common law and common practice would support the precept that a nurse can work with gravely ill neonatals, but only if that nurse has acquired the technical skill and knowledge necessary to safely administer that care. The staff nurse can be held liable, as well as the nurse manager who sent him to cover for her lunch break. The neonatal nurse must bear responsibility for her actions in leaving the critically ill infant in the care of an inexperienced nurse.

 **NURSE LICENSURE**

Permissive licensure implies that one can practice without a license as long as he or she does not use the title registered nurse (RN) or claim to be licensed.[1] The danger of permissive licensing is that anyone who is not licensed can practice nursing in any form without threat of malpractice. The American Nurses Association (ANA) became concerned with this problem at the turn of the century and was instrumental in seeing that governmental control was placed on nursing practice. By 1917 45 states and the District of Columbia had nurse practice acts; in 1952 all states and territories had such laws. The original law was permissive in all states; the mechanism for licensure was in place, but no one was required to follow the plan. The nurse practice acts confined their content to stating minimal education standards; little reference was made to the practice of nursing. Nursing titles, such as graduate, trained, or licensed, were assigned. The danger of this type of permissive licensing was that schools of nursing could produce nurses without adherence to state regulations, which made it impossible to determine whether a nurse seeking licensure had met even minimal standards for education set by the state board.

Mandatory licensure means that everyone who practices nursing as a professional and for compensation must be licensed. As the years passed it became apparent that to better regulate nursing there had to be a definition of nursing. In 1958 the ANA published a model nurse practice act (see Chapter 4), which defined the scope of nursing practice. This model facilitated progress by providing a basis for setting basic practices.

Requirements for Licensure

To obtain licensure the applicant must meet the following requirements:

1. Complete the content necessary for nursing in a state board-approved school of nursing
2. Pay a fee, determined by the state
3. Pass an examination; the National Council of State Boards of Nursing has sponsored the development of licensure examinations for nursing (NCLEX) (see Chapter 4)

Good physical and mental health and moral character are optional requirements because they are difficult to document. A certain age, citizenship, and residence are no longer required.

Renewal of License

A nurse's license is renewed every 2 years. In almost all states renewal requires a fee and completion of a designed number of hours of board-approved continuing education. The new graduate is exempt from continuing education requirements for the first 2 years after graduation and initial licensure.

 THE NURSE PRACTICE ACT

Composition and Control

Nurse practice acts are designed for each state according to their needs. The nursing profession and the state share responsibility for development of a nurse practice act. Concern is for the health, safety, and welfare of the public. Laws are developed that are realistic, control nursing practice, and provide for flexibility as changes occur. Separate boards are established for the RN and the licensed practical nurse/licensed vocational nurse (LPN/LVN). State nurse practice acts generally follow the ANA code and contain (1) a definition of nursing, (2) requirements for licensure, (3) exemption from licensure, (4) conditions for revocation of license, (5) provisions for endorsement or reciprocity for persons licensed in other states, (6) description of how a board of nurse examiners is created, (7) board responsibilities, and (8) penalties for practicing without a license.[3]

Control Under One Board

In 1976 the ANA recommended that there be only one nursing practice law for each state, with provisions for licensing all practitioners of nursing under one board. The recommendation differentiated between RN and LPN/LVN roles and clearly identified independent functions of the RN and dependent functions of the LPN/LVN. Nursing process (assessment, diagnosis, planning, intervention, and evaluation) is most commonly used to define nursing functions.

Advanced or Expanded Nursing Practice

State legislatures deal with advanced or expanded nursing practice in three general ways:[4,5,6]

1. *Nonamended statutes.* A few states have made no changes from the 1958 ANA model and allow for liberal interpretation of the law by its board members.
2. *Administrative statutes.* These regulations are most widely used by nursing boards and are drawn up by nurses and members of other overlapping professions (e.g., medicine, pharmacy, and physical therapy) under the direction of the board of nursing examiners. In some cases, such as with nurse practitioners or nurse midwives, joint agreements are drawn up between members of more than one discipline.
3. *Authorization.* Authorization permits the performance of basic healthcare procedures according to *standardized procedures,* later defined as policies and protocols.

With the sharp change in economic conditions, which has resulted in competition among healthcare agencies for patients/clients, nurses are being viewed in a new light. Their knowledge, skill, and expertise are being considered an economic advantage to the agency. Concomitantly, physicians, administrators of healthcare facilities, and other involved professionals meet with nurses to develop policies and protocols for nursing actions that exceed the state's nurse practice act.

EXAMPLE: Joan is a nurse practitioner (NP) working in a family practice health maintenance organization (HMO) in Indiana. Recently one of her colleagues told her that NPs are held to the same standard of care as the physicians she works with. That concerned her. She asked for legal advice and was told that she *is* held to a higher standard of care

than an RN, even if the nursing board has not established separate regulations for NPs. The court of appeals in her state has ruled that an NP is a specialist who should meet a standard of care appropriate to her level of knowledge and skill, even if she is working under a physician's standing orders. In fact, the court says that the standard could be the same as that applied to the physician, depending on what the NP does.

 ## BOARD OF NURSE EXAMINERS

Membership

The name of the state administrative agency and the number and composition of members varies from state to state. Until recently the board consisted entirely of nurses. In most states the governor appoints the members from a list of names that is submitted by the state professional nursing association. The number of members ranges from 5 to 20. In recent years membership has changed to include people from a variety of nursing disciplines (e.g., nursing education, nursing administration, and nursing practice), physicians, and consumers or laypersons. Having diverse interests represented on a nursing board can be an advantage to nursing. Danger exists when nonnurse membership exceeds nurse membership.

Responsibilities

The major responsibility of the board is to ensure that the nurse practice act is carried out. Members of the board generally engage in the following activities:

1. Review the nurse practice act regularly and refine or amend as necessary
2. Establish rules and regulations to implement the broad terms of the law
3. Set minimal standards of practice
4. Establish standards for nurses who are engaged in an expanded role
5. Approve nursing education programs and develop criteria for approval of such things as curriculum, faculty, and facilities
6. Evaluate applicants seeking licensure
7. Issue licenses to qualified applicants
8. Discipline those who violate the law or are found to be unfit to practice nursing

As deemed appropriate, the board may conduct or sponsor workshops or hold hearings throughout the state on a given subject to provide information and elicit input. The board may also conduct research (e.g., effectiveness of preceptor programs). Board members are provided with a staff of professional and support personnel to conduct routine business.

Disciplinary Procedures

Most nurses practice their profession year in and year out within the scope of practice that has been designated by their respective state boards of nurse examiners. However, there are a few nurses who endanger a patient's health, safety, and welfare. In the United States 67% of all disciplinary actions are drug related. The ANA has estimated that 6% to 8% of all nurses "use alcohol or other drugs to an extent sufficient to impair their professional performance."[7,p.31] Professionals are not immune to alcoholism, drug addiction, or depression. Many of these problems may be related to the pressures of today's society.

Diversion Program

Before 1985 employers discharged impaired nurses with drug, alcohol, or emotional problems or filed criminal charges for stealing drugs or for causing harm to patients. Some states, such as California, have instituted a **diversion program** in an effort to help the nurse overcome the problem and return to professional practice. Diversion programs usually provide hope, help, and alternatives for RNs who are experiencing problems with chemical dependency or mental illness. Many boards of registered nursing provide intervention services, treatment referrals, and rehabilitation plans.[8]

 NURSE RISK MANAGEMENT

Risk is the possibility of suffering harm, loss, or danger. **Risk management** entails defining the probability that certain incidents will occur if conditions are not corrected and taking the steps necessary to prevent them.

Today the healthcare system and health workers are faced with a burgeoning number of mal-

practice suits. Nurses are considered fair game for such lawsuits. By promoting themselves through increased expertise, specialization, accountability, and autonomy in their professional practice, nurses have opened the door to liability for their actions. The increase in nursing malpractice suits can be attributed to such factors as (1) increased and often unrealistic consumer expectations of nursing services, (2) lack of client understanding of treatments and technology, (3) impersonal delivery of care, and (4) more exposure among the general population to healthcare today than in the past.[9]

For self-protection nurses should become aware of the standards of care that courts expect from nursing and the most common causes of lawsuits. This knowledge can give healthcare agencies the tools to begin a risk-management program to minimize the occurrence of lawsuits. In malpractice suits against nurses courts commonly refer to the ANA Standards of Care, nursing care standards of the Joint Commission for Accreditation of Health Care Organizations (JCAHO), standards of the American Association of Critical Care Nurses, and the standards established by the agency being sued.[9]

A nurse's failure to assess and to communicate continues to lead the list of negligent claims. Other common causes of lawsuits against nurses have been identified as (1) failure to perform treatments correctly, (2) patient falls, (3) medication errors, (4) failure to remove foreign objects (as in surgery), (5) burns, (6) failure to observe and report changes, (7) mistaken patient identification, (8) errors by certified RN anesthetists, (9) use of defective equipment, (10) failure to assess patients and take adequate histories, (11) failure to document pertinent information, and (12) failure to report known or suspected deviations from accepted practice.[10]

Risk-management teams or committees can promote educational programs that provide nursing staff with the knowledge required to ensure quality patient care and to practice preventive nursing. This is especially important because nurses form the first line of defense in preventing malpractice suits.

Risk Management and Incident Reports

Healthcare providers are on the alert for any possibility of risk to patients, service personnel, or building and grounds. Before a risk management process can be established, risks must be identified. The **incident report** is used most often. Until recently an incident report was viewed with fear and trepidation because it was used not only as a tool to identify incidents such as a patient injury or a medication error but also as a punitive measure to be used during performance review.

The current concept of incident reports is much broader and includes, "any unusual event or occurrence in which potential liability may occur."[11,p.17] The rationale for expanding the purpose of the document is to prevent injuries from occurring as much as possible. For example, a nurse should complete an incident report if he or she often cuts his or her finger when opening a sterile container from a particular supplier. Two patients with the same name who are assigned to one room require a warning signal via an incident report. The present situation could be handled on the nursing unit by simply arranging for a change in bed assignments, but the situation may occur again.

Incident Reports and Litigation

The issue of whether incident reports should be protected from discovery and not be admissible in malpractice cases has not been resolved. Healthcare providers argue that incident reports have **peer review,** attorney-client, and attorney–work product privilege, which includes preparation in anticipation of litigation. In some cases the court has ruled that the privilege may be overcome if the party seeking the information shows a substantial need for it and cannot get the information any other way. In other cases incident reports were judged to be privileged communications of a peer review committee and therefore were not subject to discovery.

Although it is true that such information is necessary for an individual plaintiff to prove his case, the reality is that healthcare givers may be reluctant to complete incident reports if they fear ending up in court. Attorney Janine Fiesta states, "While the interest of disclosure versus confidentiality must be carefully weighed and evaluated, the public policy should weigh more heavily toward nondisclosure in favor of encour-

aging the processes of peer review and risk management to continue and flourish."[11,p.18]

MALPRACTICE INSURANCE FOR NURSES

Malpractice suits are on the increase. Most suits are settled out of court between the **plaintiff's** lawyer and the agency. However, many nurses have found themselves in court because a plaintiff dreams of huge monetary awards or believes that he or she has been wronged by the nurse and demands public recourse. Being named in a lawsuit can destroy a nurse financially; therefore insurance protection is imperative.

Employer Coverage

A nurse's employer is obligated to carry malpractice insurance on its employees. The nurse must know what is covered by that employer's policy. An employer is liable for the nurse's actions while on duty because of the principle of **respondeat superior.** Each professional liability has a maximal dollar coverage limit. Most hospitals have a deductible provision that makes the employer responsible for damages under a certain figure. The nurse employee should know this limit because the employer can settle a claim against the nurse's name without the benefit of defense, which could harm the nurse's reputation. The nurse who is named in a suit should keep abreast of the proceedings and know what decisions are being considered.

Nurse Coverage

Every RN should carry personal malpractice insurance. Policies are available through the professional nurses' association, the Nurses' Services Organization, and independent insurance agents. The usual malpractice policy covers the nurse with (1) 1 million dollars for each occurrence or 2 million dollars annually, if a malpractice suit is lost; (2) legal defense; and (3) lost wages. Some policies cover incidents that occur in or around the home. The cost of these policies is relatively inexpensive—under $100 per year.

LAWSUITS AGAINST NURSES

Statute of Limitations

A **statute of limitations** is a law that specifies a limited number of years when one person can seek damages from another. The statute of limitations is specified in each state's medical malpractice law (usually 1 to 3 years), depending on the statute set. However, a nurse can be sued for malpractice many years after providing the nursing care because the court sometimes extends the limitation in favor of the plaintiff.[1] When the statute of limitations begins is an important issue also. Some begin on the date of the plaintiff's injury; others begin when that injury is discovered. For example, a patient/client may fall and think he is uninjured, only to discover 6 months later that he has back trouble and difficulty walking. Accurate and complete documentation of all nursing care can provide invaluable assistance in this case. Recall becomes dim as the years pass. Patient records are official and therefore admissible in a court of law; they become the first line of defense.

Avoiding Lawsuits

Nurses who function within the standards of care identified by the nurse practice act of their state, the ANA Code of Ethics, and the standards of care adopted by the employing agency reduce the risk of being named defendant in a lawsuit. However, the risk is ever present, and precautions should be taken at every turn.

Accountability

Nurses are autonomous in that they are qualified to make decisions and act responsibly in their own interest and in the interest of others. *Nurses accept responsibility for their own actions in all situations.* With the right of independent practice comes **accountability.** The independent NP has direct liability to the patient/client, which increases the risk factor considerably and calls for strict adherence to legal and ethical codes. The employing agency is accountable for a nurse's actions and the nurse is responsible for his or her own. A nurse who works with others enjoys the benefits of interdependent activity, which includes collaboration about nursing problems and their solutions. The nurse defendant stands alone in a lawsuit, but having colleagues testify that they had a part in determining the nurse's actions lowers the potential for legal liability.

Proper Documentation

In court, a nurse's notes are evidence of the quality of nursing care provided. The completeness and consistency of **documentation** may determine a lawsuit's outcome.

Charting by exception/selective documentation

The court assumes that if something is not written down, it did not happen. The general principle of charting by exception is to chart only when something unusual or out of the ordinary happens. **Charting by exception** is used by some hospitals in an effort to save the nurse's time. However, this policy may be perilous to the nurse and the hospital. When it is not clear what has transpired between the time of each recording, attorneys are given license to try to fill in the blanks. If a nurse believes that the agency's documentation policy is ambiguous or unsafe in some way, he or she can assume a leadership role and collaborate with other nurses and nursing supervisors and approach administrators with a plan that meets acceptable standards.[13]

The following example describes a nurse who acted responsibly with the patient/client but did not document her actions carefully:

EXAMPLE: When Mr. Snare fell out of bed, Joan, the nurse, put on the call bell for help and stayed with the patient until assistance arrived. She made a physical assessment; immobilized the hip; transferred the patient back to bed with help; and notified the nurse manager, physician, and family. It was near the end of her shift, and in her hurry Joan jotted down only the bare essentials: "Discovered on floor; returned to bed; called physician; good condition." Later the patient's family served Joan with a summons, citing that she failed to properly position Mr. Snare's hip before returning him to bed. The family claimed that because of Joan's failure to immobilize the hip before moving the patient, his hip did not mend properly and left him with a limp. Verbal testimony stating that Joan did immobilize Mr. Snare's hip before moving him proved invalid because there was no documentation to prove the point.

If a nursing action is not recorded on the chart, then legally it was not performed. Box 12-1 suggests how to document correctly and what to avoid.[13]

One might ask, "How can a nurse do all these things and meet all job expectations?" An observation of efficient nurses who consistently provide quality care in routine times and times of stress shows that they frequently make pertinent notations on their worksheets, noting time, activity, and reactions. When the nurse takes time to document in the patients'/clients' records, he or she has quick access to accurate details and does not need to backtrack for information or rely on memory.

Transcribing Orders

Contemporary procedure in most health agencies is to have a unit secretary transcribe physicians' orders. All orders are reviewed for correctness of transcription by an RN. The nurse's responsibility includes a review of the orders on the basis of knowledge and clinical expertise.

The nurse looks for such details as proper sequence of diagnostic tests, medications, dosages, and diet. If any order seems inappropriate for a patient/client, the nurse has a responsibility to question that order. Nurses may be liable for failing to challenge incorrect orders.

EXAMPLE: A physician wrote an order for "colchicine 1.0 mg IV" for a patient with a flare-up of gout. The nurse did not see the decimal point, interpreted the order as "10 mg," and used 10 1 mg ampules of the medication to administer the drug to the patient. Within hours the patient suffered diarrhea, stomach pain, nausea and vomiting, which indicated colchicine toxicity. There is no known antidote for colchicine overdose. Despite supportive care, the patient died. During the investigation, it was acknowledged that the order was poorly written. There was no need for a zero in the order. But the nurse did not use common sense or follow routine steps to correct the medication order. The nurse did not have anyone check the order, even though the preparation (as the order was perceived) required 10 vials, which should have been cause for concern. Had the nurse referred to the information about the medication, she would have known that the total dose of colchicine should not exceed 4 mg per day. Clearly this was cause for liability.[14]

With the advent of computers, the percentage of transcribing mistakes has vastly decreased. Or-

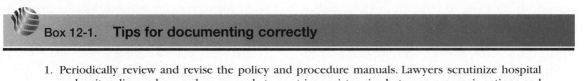

Box 12-1.   Tips for documenting correctly

1. Periodically review and revise the policy and procedure manuals. Lawyers scrutinize hospital and unit policy and procedure manuals to spot inconsistencies between a nurse's actions and written policy.
2. Chart everything that other nurses and physicians need to know to assess the patient's/client's needs (who, what, when, where, and why).
3. Document any nursing action taken in response to the problem (e.g., called Code Blue, administered CPR, notified physician and family, gave medication).
4. Describe the patient's/client's responses (e.g., stated, "I feel better," unable to state his name or where he is).
5. Document all safeguards used (e.g., siderail, Posey belt, soft arm restraints, splints).
6. Document procedures *after* they are completed, not before. It is illegal to document something that has not happened.
7. Record on every line. Do not leave empty spaces. Sign every entry.
8. Chart an omission as a new entry. Never backdate or add to previous entries, which negates the authenticity of the recording.
9. Never erase or cover an error; follow the prescribed procedure for corrections.
10. Never document for someone else. A nurse who documents for someone else will be held liable in a court of law.

ders are placed on the menu and routed to the various departments for processing. Photocopies also help detect errors. For example, a copy of the original order can be sent directly to the diet center, pharmacy, or laboratory. If the nurse fails to catch an error when it is first transcribed, others can note mistakes and make corrections.

Questioning Physician's Orders

Physician's orders are often a source of conflict between the nurse and the physician. This is particularly true when the order is given verbally in person or over the phone. The message may be vague, ambiguous, or inappropriate. The physician knows what treatment or medications he or she has in mind, but sometimes the message is not conveyed clearly. As an employee the nurse has a legal responsibility to carry out the physician's orders, but as a liaison and patient/client advocate the nurse has a responsibility to take appropriate action when the orders raise serious questions.

> EXAMPLE: Bill, a nurse, works on a med-surg unit. He has been caring for an 80-year-old woman with colon cancer who has developed acute renal failure. Bill receives an order from a physician to administer 8 mg of bumetanide (Bumex), a diuretic, by slow IV push. Having administered this medication many times before but not at this dose, Bill consults the *Physicians' Desk Reference,* which reports that the usual initial IV dose is 0.5 to 1 mg. Bill telephones the physician about the high dose. The physician replies, "Just follow the order. I don't have time to justify my treatment decisions to everyone who asks." Bill gives the patient the drug, and the patient is not harmed. However, Bill later consults a nurse lawyer for an opinion.
>
> The lawyer's opinion is as follows: (1) If the physician does not offer a good explanation, refer the matter to an immediate supervisor, who can then pursue it through established procedures; (2) document actions and any other facts relevant to the situation on an incident report by writing "Referred to PDR which stated that the normal initial dosage is . . . Called physician to discuss order of Bumex 8 mg slow IV push. Dr. X responded by stating . . . Notified supervisor who advised . . ."; and (3) Record the procedure and patient's response on the patient's chart; do not record that an incident report was filed because this would alert anyone reviewing the case to problems. The lawyer suggests that before giving the medication in the fu-

ture, Bill should consult a pharmacist regarding the dose. If still uneasy about giving the medication, Bill should ask the house physician, if one is available, to administer the drug. In this way Bill would be relieved of liability.[15]

Nurses must know the agency's policy on verbal orders, in person or by telephone. If no policy exists, the nurse must not accept nonwritten orders because he or she could legally be held liable for the consequences.

The usual policy for the nurse taking orders over the phone is to (1) have a nurse listen on the phone as a witness, who then initials the order for verification of accuracy; (2) repeat the order aloud to the physician and ask, "Is that correct?" (3) document the order on the appropriate forms, including date, time, and what prompted the call; and (4) get the physician's signature on the order when he or she returns to the hospital.

Falsifying Records

Accountability rests on the integrity, competence, and reliability of the healthcare agency and personnel. Deliberately falsifying records to serve one's own purposes compromises patient safety and the nurse's integrity.

> EXAMPLE: At the end of shift, Ruth, a nurse manager, checks the narcotics count with Stephanie, a newly hired BSN. They discover that 50 mg of Demerol is unaccounted for. The hour is late and both are tired. Stephanie says, "Just a minute, I think I know where the mistake is." She pulls the chart of a patient who has an order for the drug but who did not require it and records a dosage that was not given. She then adjusts the narcotics record sheet so that it is consistent with the count. Ruth has no reason to doubt Stephanie until the next day when the patient declares, "I've gone 48 hours without pain medication. Isn't that great?"

The ANA Code for nurses requires RNs to take definite action to safeguard both patient and public against incompetent, illegal, or unethical practices.[3] In this case neither the institution nor the patient incurred negligible risks. The nurse manager reported the incident to the Board of Nurse Examiners, suspended the nurse for 2 weeks without pay, and placed her on probation for 1 year with the promise of dismissal should any other legal infraction occur.

THE LAW AND NURSING ERROR

Nurses do not like to make mistakes because mistakes violate the nurses' ethic of "do no harm." But try as one may, mistakes do happen. Nurses often practice in a chaotic environment in which almost everyone seems to be vying for the nurse's time. The patient assignment may reach the maximum. It is not uncommon for nurses to be responsible for 12 patients on a shift that has such demands as time-sensitive medication schedules and complicated treatments and procedures. There is documentation, medication checks, narcotics counts, and admissions and dismissals. Visitors, physicians, peers, and people from supportive services each attempt to draw the nurse's attention away from the task at hand. Given all these interruptions it is inevitable that sometime, somewhere, the nurse will make an error.

Categories of Errors

Error is categorized into three major and progressively intense categories: technical, judgmental, and normative.[16]

Technical

Technical error is the honest error of technique. For example, a nurse might err in the management of a patient lift and cause the patient to experience bruises and fright, might break sterile technique when acting as scrub nurse, or might push the wrong button and cause a parenteral infusion to be completed in half the prescribed time. When a nurse acts in good faith and discloses the error promptly to the immediate supervisor and by incident report, the honest technical mistake can be taken care of and would most probably be excused if the matter were litigated.

Judgmental

Judgmental error is an honest error in which the nurse chooses the wrong action by commission or omission. Errors involving poor judgment may be caused by such things as *stress,* as with an emergency or personal problems; *work overload* in which the nurse must handle too many decisions at once; *insufficient knowledge;* or *lack of concentration.* One nurse's technical error could be another's judgmental error. Good nursing judgment depends not only on technical skills and on an ability to provide nursing care but also on the ability to make sound decisions in professional circumstances.

Nurses are human and make mistakes, even in judgment. In reviewing a judgmental error, the usual patterns of the nurse must be considered. What is the nurse's safety record? Have there been other incidences in which judgment was a factor? Nurses who care about their patients or clients do not allow unsafe situations to be repeated. Were there extenuating circumstances that if avoided may have prevented the error? If the mistake caused by poor judgment is litigated, blame could be affixed to the nurse, to the employer for lack of a safe and supportive environment, or to both.

Normative

Normative error is the most serious of all errors. It is a breach of honesty, trust, and good faith. When a nurse decides to cover the error by (1) failing to disclose the incident, (2) altering circumstances to make the error appear right, or (3) lying to protect oneself, he or she is invalidating the right to practice nursing. Consider the following incident:

EXAMPLE: Barbara, an RN refresher student, had almost completed a 1-year program after which she was to be employed in the hospital where she was doing her practicum. One night she was assigned to practice independently, with the evening nurse manager available to her. Barbara was anxious to do well but very nervous. In her anxiety she hung an IV containing heparin to another patient's line, which was a "keep open" of 5% dextrose and water. Barbara did not discover her mistake until 2 hours later when she went to add the IV containing heparin.

Barbara was desperately afraid that if she disclosed her error, she would be dismissed from the program and lose her job. She quickly checked the patient who was receiving the heparin, and there seemed to be no adverse effects. She switched the bags as they were meant to be, which was simple to do because the patients were in the same room. At this point her instructor walked by, saw what

Barbara was doing, and investigated her course of action. Barbara stated that she planned to document that the IVs were given as ordered with no untoward effects. Barbara reasoned, "Sure, the patient for whom the heparin was ordered did not receive the prescribed amount and might have hemorrhaged, but he didn't. The patient with the "keep vein open" line received a dangerous drug, but there was no harm done, so what's the big deal?" Barbara was dismissed from the program and an incident report was submitted to the hospital. A copy of the report was sent to the state board of registered nursing. Had Barbara disclosed her technical error immediately, demonstrating that her first priority was to do no harm to the patients, her case would have been reviewed in light of her record and the circumstances. Instead she committed a normative error and could not be trusted to "do no harm" to her patients.

Dealing With Human Error

Every healthcare institution needs a system that ensures a never-ending process of quality improvement and that identifies possible or likely situations that might result in error. Such a system takes the blame from the individual and directs attention toward the system that might have allowed the error. For example, with a medication error, the analysis asks what will happen if a person mistakes one drug for another; administers an incorrect dose; gives the medication to the wrong patient, by the wrong route, or at the wrong rate; omits a dose; makes an error in drug calculation; transcribes the order incorrectly; or fails to recognize signs of drug toxicity.[17]

The system should set up procedures for prevention, or change conditions where mistakes are waiting to happen. For example, follow procedures for safe administration, do not have two drugs with similar names and dosages side by side on a crash cart, label dangerous drugs with bright colors and post warnings, consult with pharmaceutical companies for "error-proof" devices, and make conversion charts readily available. Continuing education must occur at the workplace and in the classroom.

Even if all of these measures are in effect, the occasional error and the resultant litigation will occur. However, with standards of practice and prescribed measures of control, the number of incidences will be markedly reduced and lawyers can more easily make a case for the defendant.

PROTECTION OF CIVIL RIGHTS: DEFAMATION OF CHARACTER

Nurses are responsible for guarding the reputation of patients/clients, physicians, and colleagues as closely as they do their own. A casual negative remark such as "I wouldn't go to that doctor for any amount of money—he's a butcher," or "If that nurse were assigned to me, I would jump out the window," supply the ingredients for a lawsuit for defamation of character. A nurse also has the civil right to protect his or her own good name.

> EXAMPLE: One nurse in Texas filed suit against a physician for making false statements about her.[18] The physician declared that the nurse had rearranged laboratory slips to cover up a mistake. The nurse had to prove that the physician was well aware that his statements were probably false. The nurse was awarded $250,000 because the wrong seemed decidedly intentional.
>
> Fortunately a suit is not filed each time a defaming remark is made. However, it is wise to be careful about what one says and to refrain from making negative statements about another.

LEGAL ASPECTS OF ASSIGNING, DELEGATING, AND STAFFING

Healthcare systems demand cost-effective measures and balanced budgets and also expect that quality care be provided. However, the two expectations are not always compatible. Downsizing the number and types of personnel and merging nursing services leads to problems in assigning, delegating, and staffing. The Nursing Congress of 1992 focused on these issues and their relationship to the employment law area.[19]

The Relationship of Assigning, Delegating, and Staffing to Law

Each nurse has an obligation to be aware of policies and pertinent litigations that affect what nurses may or may not do. One current issue for hospitals and other healthcare agencies is that of assigning, delegating, and staffing. Nurse managers hire staff expecting them to fulfill their professional roles according to agency policy. In turn, staff nurses expect sufficient support people and services. A nurse should inquire about staffing procedures before accepting employment. Because the ultimate decisions regarding the quality and quantity of staff are made at the highest levels of management, staffing issues are generally considered to rest at the corporate level.[20]

Two recent cases illustrate staffing issues. In one case a hospital was found negligent in the care of a patient that resulted in injury. This damage was a result of inadequate staffing. Another hospital was found negligent in retaining, supervising, and assigning a nurse in the care of an ob-

stetric patient. This negligence resulted in a brain-damaged newborn and a settlement in excess of 1 million dollars. In another case an RN walked off the job 1 hour into her shift which left 29 patients in the care of nursing assistants and orderlies. In this case the agency was not held liable because it covered the situation as rapidly as possible. However, the RN lost her license for 1 year.[21]

If staff nurses are uncomfortable in accepting an assignment, they must alert the nurse manager. Figure 12-1 presents one such situation and indicates the liability of the staff nurse, nurse

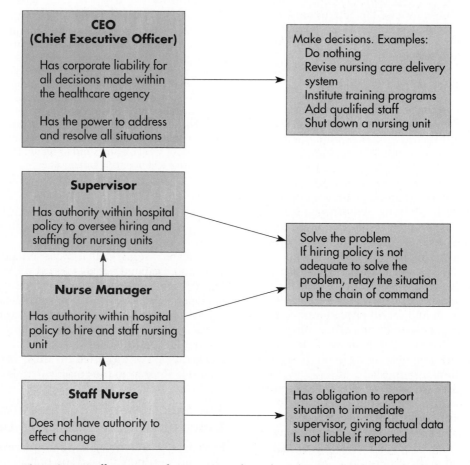

CEO (Chief Executive Officer)

Has corporate liability for all decisions made within the healthcare agency

Has the power to address and resolve all situations

Make decisions. Examples:
  Do nothing
  Revise nursing care delivery system
  Institute training programs
  Add qualified staff
  Shut down a nursing unit

Supervisor

Has authority within hospital policy to oversee hiring and staffing for nursing units

Solve the problem
If hiring policy is not adequate to solve the problem, relay the situation up the chain of command

Nurse Manager

Has authority within hospital policy to hire and staff nursing unit

Staff Nurse

Does not have authority to effect change

Has obligation to report situation to immediate supervisor, giving factual data
Is not liable if reported

Situation: Staff nurse Jennifer states, "Lately we have been so busy in postcardiac surgery. Nurses on other units where the census is low are being asked to help us. Floating is an unwritten policy in our hospital. I'm very upset about this because some nurses are grossly inadequate to care for heart patients. I try very hard to teach and supervise them, but I do not have enough time to carry my load and theirs too."

FIGURE 12-1. Liability and procedure for a staffing situation that jeopardizes patient welfare.

manager, supervisor, nurse vice president and CEO at the corporate level.

Supervising Assistive Nursing Personnel

A fundamental premise of nursing practice is that a professional nurse is personally responsible for all acts or omissions undertaken within the scope of practice. Delegation of nursing care falls directly within the scope of nursing practice and is categorized as a service that indirectly benefits the patient. Supervision is also considered an indirect patient service and constitutes usual nursing functions. Therefore a nurse manager may be disciplined or held liable for any nurse who performs these duties in an incompetent or grossly negligent manner. Although the RN is not held directly liable for the subordinate's negligent act, he or she can be held liable if she or he knew that the assistant was unqualified for a job but assigned the assistant to that job anyway.[22]

Improper Delegation of Tasks/ Inadequate Supervision

If a patient suffers injury and the nurse responsible for that patient was assigned improperly or was not supervised adequately, the nurse who made the assignment or failed to supervise adequately is not held liable for the negligent act. However, he or she can be held liable for his or her lack of competence in performing the independent duties of delegation and supervision. Very few cases have involved nursing delegation and supervision. Two such cases address the issue of understaffing and poor judgment[22]:

EXAMPLE: A nurse manager did not assign coverage for a weak, confused, and uncoordinated patient and allowed the nursing assistant who was attending him to go on break. While alone, the patient fell off a balcony and injured himself. The nurse manager was held liable for the injury. In a second case a nurse manager left some infants alone for 1½ hours but intended to move the babies into one room so the available staff could better care for them. While unattended, one infant suffered brain damage from asphyxia. In spite of the nurse's good intention and the fact that she was diverted from accomplishing her plan to move the infants on schedule, she was held liable for her negligence in not assigning a nurse to be with the infant.

LITIGATION AND THE NURSE

Litigation, or any legal action or process, is on the rise in all fields, including nursing. Although nurses win more than 75% of their cases, every nurse being tried must experience the trauma of a courtroom, and 25% of the time the nurse (or the hospital as the nurse's employer) loses in favor of the plaintiff. Most cases involve lack of communication and perceived errors in assessment, planning, intervention, and omission.

Assessment

Assessment errors are involved in most malpractice cases against nurses. Medication errors fall into this category. The nurse is accused of making a poor judgment, failing to monitor a patient, or failing to follow through a procedure correctly.

Poor Planning

A nurse's poor planning can result in serious consequences.

EXAMPLE: Several nurses were asked to move a patient with end-stage chronic obstructive pulmonary disease to a private room. The patient was receiving continuous oxygen, and although the patient was a "no-code," the family asked that he be given a portable oxygen unit during the move to make his breathing easier. The nurses decided not to apply portable oxygen because the move was such a short distance. However, after pushing the bed 15 feet, the patient suffered respiratory distress and died. The family sued and the court awarded damages.[23]

Incomplete Intervention

Failure to complete a procedure accurately may result in litigation.

EXAMPLE: A surgical nurse removed a wound drain from a patient's back, and it was later discovered that a 3½ inch strip of the drain had not been removed. Another surgery was required to remove it, and the patient experienced infection and pain. Both the nurse and the hospital as the nurse's employer were held liable. The patient received considerable damages. The reasoning behind the litigation was that the nurse did not check the operating room report or the packaging to determine the length of the drain before removing it. She also did not observe the drain for irregular edges after removing it.[23]

The best protection for the nurse against litigation is to use assessment skills, planning procedures, and interventions appropriately so that a court of law will not have to be faced.

Omission

Sometimes the failure to do or see something results in a malpractice claim. This includes failing to notify the physician of important events.

> EXAMPLE: Arterial blood was drawn for a preoperative patient, and the report revealed that the patient was hypoxic. The doctor was not notified. Demerol and Vistaril were ordered and given by the nurse. The patient vomited, but still the physician was not notified. After the shift change the patient was found with unequal pupils. It took 2 hours for the physician to return the nurse's call. Another hour passed before the patient was put on oxygen. He suffered severe damage.
>
> A settlement in excess of one million dollars was reached. Poor judgment was exercised by the nurse, perhaps because of a lack of knowledge, but there was no evidence of intent to do harm to the patient. The issues at hand were (1) the failure to observe significant signs, and (2) the failure to communicate relevant information to the proper source.[24]

🕸 THE NURSE AS A WITNESS

A nurse called as a **witness** in court serves one of two capacities: (1) as a witness to the conditions or circumstances present in the issue in question or (2) as an expert witness to give an opinion from the facts presented. Nurses who are summoned to serve as witnesses may or may not be the persons charged. They report what they saw, what they were told, or what they overheard. Witnesses must give only facts that are based on direct knowledge.[25]

Before the early 1970s physicians often served as expert witnesses for nursing care. This practice continues today, but there is a gradual shift toward having nurses serve as expert witnesses. Nurses demonstrate professional self-regulation and professional accountability when representing other nurses.

Qualifications of an Expert Witness

For a nurse to give expert testimony, certain criteria must be met. The nurse must have:
1. Familiarity with nurse standards (ANA Code of Ethics, state nurse practice act, ANA Standards of Practice, specific overall standards of the agency employing the defendant, and specialty standards applicable to the clinical area in question).
2. Clinical expertise and past experience, usually a minimum of 5 years.
3. Effective communication skills and the ability to offer clear, decisive responses to questions while on the stand.
4. General knowledge of the components of malpractice liability.
5. Ability to represent nursing well and demonstrate professional commitment and ethical standards (e.g., membership in a professional association, participation in continuing education and professional activities).[26]

Responsibilities of an Expert Witness

Much is required of the expert witness. The nurse (1) meets with the attorney to get a general idea of the types of reports wanted; (2) reviews documents (medical records, depositions, interrogatories, and other expert reports); (3) decides whether the defendant's action or inaction was the cause of the injury and compares the situation with the standards of behavior expected of a "reasonably prudent nurse" in a similar situation; and (4) gives a verbal expert opinion to the attorney on the basis of the analysis of the case. If asked, the nurse also writes an opinion; attends depositions (testimony under oath) before the trial; and testifies in court, remembering not to volunteer additional information.

A case in Missouri provides a valuable nurse-expert opinion.[27]

> EXAMPLE: A 1-year-old child developed tachycardia following heart surgery and was given 0.1 mg of

digitalis with two follow-up doses of 0.55 mg. The child died after receiving the overdose. A suit was brought against the physician, the intensive care unit (ICU) nurses, and the hospital pharmacist. The plaintiff used a nurse expert to review the case and offer an opinion on the ICU nurses' actions. The nurse expert proved that (1) nursing curricula teaches the calculation of infant dosages, (2) digitalis is commonly given by ICU nurses, and (3) children are weighed specifically to determine drug dosages. With this knowledge, the attorney proved that any nurse should have caught the error at the transcription stage. The suit was settled before it went to court.

GOOD SAMARITAN LAWS

The enactment of **Good Samaritan laws** in many states exempts physicians and nurses from civil liability when they give emergency care "in good faith" with "due care" and without **"gross negligence"** outside the workplace. California was the first state to pass such a law in 1959. By 1979 all states and the District of Columbia had Good Samaritan laws. However, not all Good Samaritan laws include nursing.[2] Victims do not often sue Good Samaritans, because the common law serves as a deterrent.

Nurse Responsibility in an Emergency

A nurse who encounters an emergency such as someone drowning, bleeding profusely, clutching his or her chest and moaning, thrown from a car, or trapped in a vehicle has three choices of action: (1) the nurse can stop and assist the victim(s), (2) the nurse can pass the scene and call from the nearest phone for authorized assistance, or (3) the nurse can pass the scene and do nothing. The victim of an accident or injury is not the nurse's patient; he or she is a stranger and therefore has no right to make any claims on the nurse *unless* the nurse stops at the scene and makes an appearance. Once the nurse makes an appearance, a nurse-patient relationship is established. The nurse must care for the victim(s) with treatment that meets the standard of care of a reasonably prudent nurse who exercises good judgment and common sense. The nurse

must stay with the victim(s) until skilled personnel arrive to assume care.[28]

Breach of Duty

The nurse is at minimal risk when he or she acts according to standard as much as is possible in a given situation. If the victim's condition was worsened as a result of the nurse's action, the court considers the degree of harm. Measurable harm must be proved for the nurse to be considered negligent. The victim must also prove that the probability is better than 50% that the nurse who stopped to help caused his or her injuries.[25]

GUIDELINES FOR NURSES WHO ARE SUED

A nurse can never know if he or she will be sued or even what circumstances provide the highest risk. Receiving a summons that names a nurse as defendant can shock the nurse into actions that might be regretted later. Knowing what actions to take in the event of being named in a suit can save the nurse much pain and loss. The nurse is advised to take action immediately by following a specific plan. The nurse should[25]:

1. Contact legal services administrators at work and follow their directions.
2. Telephone the representative of his or her own professional liability insurance; document the date, time, representative's name, and instructions given; hand deliver or send by certified mail the lawsuit papers; get a receipt because the insurance company can refuse coverage unless the company representative is contacted within a specific time period.
3. Never try to defend himself or herself. The odds are definitely against the nurse who is inexperienced in legal matters or closely involved with the suit.

   The insurance company will:
1. Appoint an attorney of record, which means that the attorney's name appears on the legal records.
2. Obtain copies of all relevant documents.
3. Quiz the plaintiff in the presence of a court reporter.

4. Hire a physician not involved with the case to examine the plaintiff.
5. Prepare the nurse to testify.

Marc Mandell,[29] a lawyer and an editor of a legal newsletter for physicians, has prepared a list of commandments for nurses who are sued:

I. *Don't discuss the case at the hospital with anyone other than the risk manager.* Talking with others in the workplace is harmful. Others may even construe any comments as admissions of guilt.

II. *Don't discuss the case with the plaintiff.* Talking with the plaintiff does not work. His or her mind is set, and he or she might even consider what is said as more incriminating evidence.

III. *Don't discuss the case with the plaintiff's lawyer.* Don't give in to the urge to talk to the plaintiff's lawyer. The lawyer's code of ethics forbids it, unless the defendant's lawyer gives consent. However, an unscrupulous lawyer might listen, hoping to hear something to help the plaintiff's case.

IV. *Don't discuss the case with anyone testifying for the plaintiff.* These people have already decided that the defendant is guilty or they would not be testifying. The case is harmed if the judge or jury suspects the defendant of trying to convince somebody to change his or her testimony.

V. *Don't discuss the case with reporters.* Say, "I choose not to speak about this." Any remark can be distorted, misquoted, or taken out of context.

VI. *Don't alter the patient's/client's records.* This is illegal. Tampering with a chart is the worst mistake a nurse can make. The defense is gone. The jurors will never forget that a patient's/client's record was altered.

VII. *Don't hide any information from the defense lawyer.* The lawyer needs to know every detail, no matter how unimportant or self-incriminating it seems. He or she needs to know the weak aspects of the case as well as the strong ones.

VIII. *Don't go on the witness stand unprepared.* Years can pass between the occurrence of the alleged malpractice and the resulting trial. All records need to be reviewed carefully, especially those involving self.

IX. *Don't be discourteous on the witness stand.* Remain polite and composed, even if the plaintiff's lawyer is rude and abrasive. Jurors generally respond favorably to nurses because they come across as honest and sincere. Good manners count.

X. *Don't volunteer any information.* Answer only the questions asked and keep answers short. Whenever possible, answer with a simple "yes" or "no." Long, thoughtful answers only provide ammunition for the plaintiff's laywer.

DOCTRINE OF SOVEREIGN IMMUNITY

The statute of **sovereign immunity** provides government employees with special legal protection. Unless the sovereign (government employer) agrees, a government employee cannot be sued for on-the-job mistakes. Some states believe that this law is unfair to the patient/client, who has no recourse if injury occurs, and have passed laws that allow patients/clients to sue public hospitals and other government agencies. Some states have set dollar limits on the amount a patient/client can receive if he or she wins the suit.

CONTRACTS FOR NURSES

Fewer problems occur when the nurse and employer understand each other's rights and responsibilities. Understandably the nurse is nervous when going for an interview. The position desired may be a "plum"; the nurse may feel like doing almost anything to get the job. The nurse may already be employed and seeking a promotion or expanded role. In these stressful situations, a cool head is needed. Papers signed or verbal agreements made without careful consideration may cause trouble later.

Types of Contracts

A *formal contract* is an agreement between two or more parties that is written and enforceable by law. A **contract** is valid when the nurse (1) meets specifications for the job, such as having current licensure and being of age and sound mind; (2) agrees to perform specified services; (3) agrees to abide by the employer's terms; and (4) receives remuneration for services. The formal contract may be an individual contract between the employer and nurse or may be a collective contract with a labor organization, such as a union that has negotiated with the employer for the employees.

An *express contract* may be written or oral. For example, a nurse may talk with his or her nurse manager about his or her need to grow professionally. The nurse manager may offer the new position of patient advocate that is being created in 2 months. If the nurse agrees to take the position, he or she has entered into an **oral express contract.** When he or she signs papers indicating that he or she has the position, he or she has participated in a **written express contract.**

An *implied contract* is an agreement between two or more persons that involves matters that are understood but not clearly or openly expressed. Many contracts contain implied conditions. For example, the employer assumes that the nurse will maintain proper decorum and will practice nursing safely; conversely, the nurse assumes the employer will maintain an environment and provide facilities that are conducive to performing nursing duties effectively.

Breach of Contract

A **breach** is any failure to keep the law or fulfill one's duties without justification. A nurse breaches a contract when all or any part of the contract is not kept. Employers are loathe to seek an **injunction** against a nurse for failing to live up to the agreement because such a procedure is very costly. An injunction keeps the nurse from working for another employer. Instead the employer may reprimand the nurse and demand compliance, or the employer may discharge the nurse. In either case the nurse's reputation is damaged. The nurse should understand the terms of the contract before agreeing to employment and hold to that agreement or resign in good stead.

 **ETHICS**

Ethical Issues

Ethics is a discipline in which one applies certain principles to determine the correct thing to do in a given situation.[30] Ethics in nursing is an ethical moral reasoning that is applied to nursing practice. Ethics concerns how one treats people and the choices one makes about self and others. One ethicist states that ethics is rooted in integrity, which means that a person integrates experience, virtues, and moral rules throughout his or her career. A person of integrity is one who has integrated life experiences with existing rules (or principles) and available theories to make rational, justified choices.[31]

An **ethical problem** occurs when an individual does not know the right thing to do. However, it is not enough to know what is right; the nurse must also *do* what is right. There is a difference between a moral and an ethical issue. If the conflict concerns what one *wants* to do, the nurse is probably grappling with a moral issue rather than an ethical problem. The conflict also becomes a moral issue if the nurse struggles with what he or she thinks is right and acts to the contrary.[30]

In the past few years, ethical nursing research has focused on responsiveness to others, or the ethics of caring. Recent studies have focused not only on the ethics of care and caring but also on the incorporation of principles or the application of rules or standards of good behavior.[31]

ANA Code of Ethics

The ANA first suggested a code of ethics in 1926 and adopted an official code in 1950. After a series of revisions, a Code of Ethics for Nurses was published in 1985 (Box 12-2).[3,28] For example, if a nurse wishes to relieve a patient's pain by administering medication but is uncomfortable with the possibility that his or her actions may hasten death, he or she could support the action by referring to the Code of Ethics, which states that:

1. The action itself cannot be inherently evil. Like pain management, it must be good or at least morally neutral.

Box 12-2. American Nurses Association Code of Ethics for Nurses

Preamble

The Code of Ethics for Nurses is based on belief about the nature of individuals, nursing, health, and society. Recipients and providers of nursing services are viewed as individuals and groups who possess basic rights and responsibilities and whose values and circumstances command respect at all times. Nursing encompasses the promotion and restoration of health, the prevention of illness, and the alleviation of suffering. The statements of the Code and their interpretations provide guidance for conduct and relationships in carrying out nursing responsibilities consistent with the ethical obligations of the profession and quality in nursing care.

Code for nurses

1. The nurse provides services with respect for human dignity and the uniqueness of the client unrestricted by considerations of social or economic status, personal attributes, or the nature of health problems.
2. The nurse safeguards the client's right to privacy by judiciously protecting information of a confidential nature.
3. The nurse acts to safeguard the client and the public when health care and safety are affected by the incompetent, unethical, or illegal practice of any person.
4. The nurse assumes the responsibility and accountability for individual nursing judgments and actions.
5. The nurse maintains competence in nursing.
6. The nurse exercises informed judgment and uses individual competence and qualifications as criteria in seeking consultation, accepting responsibilities, and delegating nursing activities to others.
7. The nurse participates in activities that contribute to the ongoing development of the profession's efforts to implement and improve standards of nursing.
8. The nurse participates in the profession's efforts to improve standards of nursing.
9. The nurse participates in the profession's efforts to establish and maintain conditions of employment conducive to high quality nursing care.
10. The nurse participates in the profession's effort to protect the public from misinformation and misrepresentation and to maintain the integrity of nursing.
11. The nurse collaborates with members of the health professions and other citizens in promoting community and national efforts to meet the health needs of the public.

Reprinted with permission from the American Hospital Association.

---

2. The nurse's intent must be good rather than evil. In this case the intent is pain relief, not death.
3. The evil effect cannot be a means to the good effect. In this case death is not a means to pain management.
4. The benefit of the administration of medication or treatment must clearly outweigh potential harm.

The ANA code addresses human dignity, nondiscrimination, and protection of the patient/client. The Code emphasizes the independent role of the nurse and participation in activities that promote high standards and quality of nursing care. Like other professional codes, the ANA code of Ethics does not have legal power as state nurse practice acts do, but it can be used as a guideline for professional conduct in a malpractice lawsuit. The Code of Ethics exceeds the minimal standards set by a state board and therefore provides a more realistic guide to expected practice.

Patient Rights

Most patient rights are established in common law. However, many healthcare organizations feel the need to identify patient rights more specifically. President John F. Kennedy summarized four basic consumer rights in his 1962 message to Congress: (1) the right to safety, (2) the right to be informed, (3) the right to choose, and (4) the right to be heard.

The American Hospital Association (AHA) prepared a Patient's Bill of Rights in 1972, recognizing that legal precedent has established that the institution itself also has a responsibility to the patient/client (Box 12-3). Most communities and hospitals and other healthcare agencies subscribe to the practices in the AHA Bill of Rights. However, some healthcare agencies develop their own bills, using the AHA bill as a guideline. Patients' bills of rights, either adopted or developed by major healthcare providers and consumer groups across the country, have made today's patients very much aware of what is being done to and for them.

Advocacy

An effective leader/manager is always an advocate for his or her group. An **advocate** supports or defends someone or something and recommends or pleads on another's behalf. The leader/advocate works to change the power structure so that a situation is improved. For example, a nurse manager might work for an increase in the number of nursing staff so that the quality of nursing care can be improved. A primary care nurse might discuss communication with an employee whom a patient/client perceived as rude. A team leader might recognize that team members are avoiding a "difficult" patient/client and hold a team conference on behalf of that patient/client.

Nurses have long been concerned with acting on behalf of their patients/clients. The AHA's Patient's Bill of Rights and the ANA's Code for Nurses have given credence to patient/client advocacy and have accentuated the need for nurses to assume the role of patient/client rights advocate. Nurses should carefully review their employing agency's policies on employee handling of patients' rights so that they can identify the parameters for action.

As healthcare reform comes into existence nationwide, it is crucial that nurses retain their ethical responsibilities as patient advocates. To do this the nurse must (1) develop awareness of the issues (e.g., whether to close a dialysis unit or eliminate evening clinics in the ghetto), (2) determine the means to identify the problems (e.g., questionnaires, interviews, open meetings), (3) identify the values of the community or group in-

volved (e.g., nurses, physicians, patients/clients), and (4) find the best possible solution to the situation (e.g., close the dialysis unit and refer patients to a nearby facility, open clinic in ghetto 2 evenings a week).[31]

Ethics Committees

A growing number of healthcare agencies have established ethics committees to process ethical problems. Some are more effective than others, probably as a result of the composition and purpose of each committee. Most members of ethics committees are drawn from the healthcare professions, and a few represent the community that the committee is serving. Ethics committees perform consultations, engage in conflict resolution, and offer educational programs. Ethics committees must be knowledgeable if they are to perform well. Therefore a new committee must spend time developing expertise before it can effectively serve the healthcare community.[32]

The need for self-education is obvious. Members must become familiar with the major types of ethical theory and understand the major principles of bioethics (autonomy, beneficence, and justice). It is helpful if the basic core of knowledge is supplemented with information regarding the moral views of the major religious traditions and the differences in various cultures, particularly those groups that frequent the healthcare center. The education of the committee is not complete until it develops an ability to work together to apply ethical theory. Normal techniques of the university classroom can be used (inviting guest speakers and discussing central writings), as well as workshops and seminars.

Ethics committee members must also have available to them copies of applicable federal, state, and local regulations and laws; organizational standards of ethical behavior; and professional standards of ethical behavior. The initial question to be addressed is: "Does the behavior or anticipated result comply with the mandated action?" If the situation under scrutiny meets this criteria, the ethics committee is free to move on to consideration of the moral or ethical issue.

Ideally an ethics committee discusses actual situations as they happen and is concerned with issues that directly relate to the institution. For example, if the hospital is in a community with

Box 12-3.   American Hospital Association's Patient's Bill of Rights

1. The patient has the right to considerate and respectful care.
2. The patient has the right to obtain from his physician complete current information about his diagnosis, treatment, and prognosis in terms the patient can be reasonably expected to understand. When it is not medically advisable to give such information to the patient, it should be made available to an appropriate person in his behalf. He has the right to know, by name, the physician responsible for coordinating his care.
3. The patient has the right to receive from his physician information necessary to give informed consent prior to the start of any procedure and/or treatment. Except in emergencies, such information for informed consent should include but not necessarily be limited to the specific procedure and/or treatment, the medically significant risks involved, and the probable duration of incapacitation. Where medically significant alternatives for care or treatment exist, or when the patient requests information concerning medical alternatives, the patient has the right to such information. The patient has the right to know the name of the person responsible for the procedures and/or treatment.
4. The patient has the right to refuse treatment to the extent permitted by law and to be informed of the medical consequences of his action.
5. The patient has the right to every consideration of his privacy concerning his own medical care program. Case discussion, consultation, examination, and treatment are confidential and should be conducted discreetly. Those not directly involved in his care must have the permission of the patient to be present.
6. The patient has the right to expect that all communications and records pertaining to his care should be treated as confidential.
7. The patient has the right to expect that within its capacity a hospital must make reasonable response to the request of a patient for services. The hospital must provide evaluation, service, and/or referral as indicated by the urgency of the case. When medically permissible, a patient may be transferred to another facility only after he has received complete information and explanation concerning the needs for and alternatives to such a transfer. The institution to which the patient is to be transferred must first have accepted the patient for transfer.
8. The patient has the right to obtain information as to any relationship of his hospital to other health-care and educational institutions insofar as his care is concerned. The patient has the right to obtain information as to the existence of any professional relationships among individuals, by means, who are treating him.
9. The patient has the right to be advised if the hospital proposes to engage in or perform human experimentation affecting his care or treatment. The patient has the right to refuse to participate in such research projects.
10. The patient has the right to expect reasonable continuity of care. He has the right to know in advance what appointment times and physicians are available and where. The patient has the right to expect that the hospital will provide a mechanism whereby he is informed by his physician or a delegate of the physician of the patient's continuing health-care requirements following discharge.
11. The patient has the right to examine and receive an explanation of his bill, regardless of source of payment.
12. The patient has the right to know what hospital rules and regulations apply to his conduct as a patient.

a high concentration of elderly people, the ethics committee should spend more time considering problems that arise when treating the elderly.

Common ethical problems include the question of removing life support systems, informing a patient/client that he or she is dying, performing abortions, performing transfusions, restraining an unwilling patient, performing needed cosmetic surgery on patients/clients who are unable to pay, and determining in times of shortage who will get the best care. An ethics committee can listen, teach, and make suggestions on the basis of a multidisciplinary approach.

Confidentiality of Patient Records

The provision of high quality patient care depends on obtaining precise and accurate information and keeping that information confidential. Privacy has been defined as the right of individuals to determine the degree to which they share information about themselves with others. Healthcare administrators and managers, as well as the quality assurance activities of the JCAHO, subscribe to these premises.[33]

Computerized patient records and confidentiality

With the increase in healthcare costs, automation of patient records is considered to be a cost-containment approach for effective and efficient processing of patient care information. With the disclosure of patient information by automation comes the danger of disclosure to unwanted sources. Availability of information and secrecy are not compatible.[34]

Ethics regarding accessing information

Confidentiality of personal information is key to patient dignity. Patients entrust healthcare personnel with very personal and private information about themselves and their lives and expect health professionals not to violate that trust. A study of confidentiality was conducted in a 1000-bed acute hospital and included RNs, LPNs, unit secretaries, nurse managers, and nursing assistants.[33] The study addressed the matter of using the computerized patient care system to access

information about neighbors, friends, or patients not on their assigned units. Two questions were asked: (1) "Have you ever used the computer to obtain information (other than room number) about persons who are not patients on your assigned clinical areas?" and, if the answer is yes, (2) "How many times a month do you access information in this manner?"

Of the 214 respondents, 72% acknowledged that they had obtained information about patients who were not in their assigned area. Of this 72%, 76% were RNs. Respondents reported frequency of access to be one to two times a month. Some hospital employees have expressed concerns about becoming a patient in the hospital in which they work because employees who know them can have access to their financial and medical records. It seems that no matter what high standards of recruitment are used, in any large organization some people (and in this study, a majority) will inevitably violate the principles of right and wrong.

Computerized information and litigation

Discovery of patient information via automation presents a real problem.[34] As computerized information becomes accessible to more and more people, patients have little protection of their privacy. The most intimate details about their lives become an open book to the public. Physicians also worry about the system because competitors can gain access to their patients, which could hurt their practice and leave them open to intense scrutiny in a court of law. The problem is complex. If restrictions are built into the system, the flow of information is decreased. This decrease could directly affect high-quality care and the usefulness of the system.

Transcultural care

Transcultural nursing refers to nursing care across cultures. It is the shared patterns, knowledge, meanings, and behaviors of a social group.[35] *Nursing practice cannot be ethical unless the culture and beliefs of a patient are taken into consideration.* Judging cultural differences as good or bad can lead to inappropriate, offensive, racist, and sexist attitudes and behaviors. Simply recognizing the differences does not. Choosing not to see cultural diversity limits a nurse's ability to manage it.[36] Transcultural nursing is ethical because moral guidelines are used to select or justify nursing practices.

Western philosophy proposes that all human beings have individual rights and deserve the same rights. Medicine and nursing share the belief that every patient should be treated equally. A basic premise in nursing is to base care on individual needs. This belief assumes that a nurse recognizes culturally different needs and addresses them effectively.

Ethnocentrism. An individual who is labeled as "ethnocentric" believes that his or her own race is superior to all others and that the beliefs of his or her own culture are the best or the only acceptable beliefs. **Ethnocentrism** involves an inability to understand the views or beliefs of another culture. Ethnocentrism may originate from a cloistered life or from a lack of knowledge about other cultures. One should examine one's culture and beliefs very carefully and become aware that alternative viewpoints are possible.[37]

Ethnorelativity. **Ethnorelativity** is the ability to conceive of alternative viewpoints and to respect the beliefs of another culture, even though they differ from one's own. Nurses have their own culture; they have been socialized into the values, customs, and practices of the healthcare system. The healthcare system primarily comprises white, middle-class people who have white, middle-class values. Therefore ethnorelativity should be a primary goal in nursing education.[37] Geissler[38] found that many nurses put the emphasis on the client being wrong and the health provider being right (an ethnocentric approach) when making a nursing diagnosis. Such an emphasis presents a danger of perpetuating stereotypes and mislabeling problems. Geissler uses the example of diagnosing a patient who was not fluent in the English language as having "altered communication." An ethnorelative diagnosis would have been "altered deficiency in the English language." By simply diagnosing the patient as having altered communication, caregivers could interpret that the patient is mentally or physically impaired.

EXAMPLE: Casandra is a Mexican immigrant who believes in the practice of voodoo. The public health nurse diagnoses the woman's infant as having pneumonia as evidenced by high fever, rales, and respiratory distress. Casandra refuses treatment for the infant because she believes that the voodoo doctor will place a curse on the baby if she attends the clinic.

Ethnocentric response:
1. "There is absolutely no truth in voodooism. The witch doctor is just fooling you" (lack of respect for Casandra's beliefs).
2. "You are doing the wrong thing by not taking your baby to the doctor" (judgmental). "The baby could die and it will be your fault" (blame).

Ethnorelative response:
1. "I believe that the witch doctor wants to see your baby get well, don't you?" (affirmation of the witch doctor's integrity).
2. "Will you allow me to talk with the doctor at the clinic and see if I can bring the medicine to you here at home?" (respecting the client's right to choose).

Although an ethical and transcultural nursing approach may not always result in a desired response, the nurse will have applied a caring spirit and moral and ethical principles in an effort to resolve the problem. The most important fact that nurses need to remember is to respect and listen to their clients.

THE PATIENT SELF-DETERMINATION ACT

Intent of the Law

The federal **Patient Self-Determination Act** (PSDA) went into effect December 1, 1991 and pertains to all healthcare institutions that receive Medicare or Medicaid funds. The PSDA has done much to stimulate activity that focuses on giving patients legitimate choices about their own end-of-life decisions. The PSDA recognizes:
1. The right to consent to or refuse treatment. The right to refuse treatment is considered a fundamental right that is guaranteed by the United States constitution. This right has been declared by most state

courts to be protected by the right to privacy. It acknowledges that patients are in the best position to determine where their best interests lie. The patient is not required to give a "good" reason for refusing treatment.

2. The right to know the provisions of the local state's law regarding advance directives. Most states prepare advance directives and documents that they recommend be used for a patient's refusal of treatment.

3. The right to have cultural diversity and various cultural values protected.[39]

Nurse Responsibility

A legal hierarchical order of people are responsible for informing patients of their right to make a self-determination regarding their end stages of life. Nurses are included as a part of this directive. Studies indicate that nurses are the predominant healthcare professionals to facilitate informed decision making. The ANA's Position Statement on Nursing and the PSDA recommend that questions regarding advance directives be part of the nursing admission assessment. If a patient (or proxy or surrogate) wishes to complete an advance directive, the nurse is responsible for ensuring that patients (1) have access to the knowledge on which to base a treatment decision, (2) have clearly expressed their decision and desires, and (3) receive treatment in accordance with their expressed preferences. When clearly expressed in writing or verbally, a patient's wishes take precedence over any other decision.

Healthcare Agency Responsibility

The PSDA provides healthcare facilities with an opportunity to develop clear policies regarding the expectation that healthcare professionals will come forward when they suspect that care is in violation of patient directives. Healthcare facilities also have the opportunity to develop guidelines for their protection should they develop such policies. In hospitals, nursing homes, and home care agencies, responsibility for implementation of the PSDA often rests with nurses. Collaboration among healthcare professionals offers the best assurance that the PSDA will achieve its intended aim: to inform patients of their right to express a treatment preference in advance to protect their autonomy should they lose the capacity to make decisions.[40]

WILLS: THE NURSE'S RESPONSIBILITY

A **will** is a declaration of how a person wishes his or her possessions to be disposed of after death. A will becomes legal when the testator, or person making the will (1) is mentally competent (testamentary capacity), (2) is of legal age for making a will (varies with the state), (3) makes a written declaration that the instrument is a will, and (4) has the proper number of witnesses present (usually two). The witnesses, who cannot be beneficiaries, sign the will in the presence of each other and the testator.[1]

A nurse who is asked to serve as a witness should attempt to find another person to do so, such as the agency's legal advisor or legal representative. If none is available, the nurse, before signing, (1) notifies his or her immediate supervisor and (2) notifies the patient's/client's physician. If sanction is received from both parties, the nurse may serve as a witness without comment on the content of the will. The procedure is thoroughly documented in the nurse's notes.

POLICY CONSIDERATIONS RELATED TO AIDS/HIV POSITIVE PATIENTS

Acquired immunodeficiency syndrome (AIDS) is a life-threatening disease and a major public health issue. Therefore nurse managers have a responsibility to prepare and guide nursing staff to care for patients with AIDS diligently.[33]

The foremost legal obligation of nurse managers is to ensure that staff members do not abandon patients. Nurses may be held liable for abandonment if they make a decision to sever the nurse-patient relationship with an AIDS patient. There is no fault if the nurse and the AIDS patient mutually agree to terminate the relationship. Prejudicial attitudes and discriminatory behaviors are also subject to disciplinary action. Nurses who refuse to care for patients out of fear or moral indignation fall into this category. AIDS patients are considered victims of discrimination if any healthcare facility (including skilled facilities and rest homes) refuses to admit clients with the excuse that it is not prepared to take AIDS patients for whatever reason.

Screening for HIV-positive Employees

AIDS is caused by a human immunodeficiency virus (HIV). HIV is a retrovirus that depends on a DNA host for replication. Contrary to earlier opinion that the lymphocytes are the major cells for infection, any cell can be infected. Once a person becomes infected with the virus, the code for multiplication of the virus becomes a permanent part of his or her DNA.

An individual can acquire HIV by having unprotected sex with someone who is infected with HIV, by sharing drug needles and syringes with an infected person, or through infected blood. Organ transplants can also be a source of infection.

Screening for HIV should be performed by a healthcare professional who obtains a written consent and discusses the purpose of the test. Results should be interpreted by an occupational health nurse or other healthcare professional and should be shared *only* with the tested individual. Confidentiality cannot be ensured over the telephone, and the reaction of the employee cannot be appropriately monitored.[41]

Legislation to Protect HIV-positive Workers

Each state may have specific legislation to protect workers with HIV.[37] However, the Americans With Disabilities Act (ADA) significantly affects both federal and private employers. The ADA states that no employer can discriminate against a person who is HIV positive or has AIDS. Such discrimination applies to hiring, firing, and potential promotions. An employer cannot discriminate against hiring a person who is HIV positive or has AIDS even though the health insurance costs might rise or the person may become too ill to work in the future. If an HIV test is necessary, the employer must prove that the test is necessary for the particular job under consideration.

When an employee with AIDS can no longer perform the essential functions of the job, and reasonable accommodations by the employer still do not allow the employee to perform the job adequately, a consultation between the employee, occupational health nurse (or substitute), and the primary caregiver is necessary to initiate a medical leave or total disability.

Summary

1. Laws are rules or standards of human conduct that are established and enforced by authority for the benefit of society.
2. Tort law is law concerning any wrongful act, damage, or injury done willfully or negligently but not involving breach of contract, for which a civil suit can be brought. Most malpractice suits against nurses are treated under tort law.
3. Common law is the culmination of many court decisions over the years. Common practice is that which falls within the definition of nursing and the legal scope of nursing practice.
4. Permissive licensure implies that one can practice nursing without a license, provided that the RN title is not claimed or used. Mandatory licensure means that all who practice nursing for compensation must be licensed.
5. Nurse practice acts are designed for each state. Most nurse practice acts contain a definition of nursing requirements for licensure or exemption from licensure, conditions for revocation of license, provisions for endorsements or reciprocity for persons licensed in other states, a description of how a board of nurse examiners is created, board responsibilities, and penalties for practicing without a license.
6. The major responsibility of a board of nurse examiners is to see that the nurse practice act is carried out, to set minimal standards of practice, to establish standards for nurses in the expanded role, to approve and monitor nursing education programs, to manage nurse licensure, and to discipline nurses who violate the law or are found to be unfit to practice nursing.

7. The most common reasons for nurse review by a board of nurse examiners is the practice of nursing while under the influence of alcohol or drugs, addiction to or dependency on alcohol or other habit-forming drugs, incompetent or negligent practice, or the practice of nursing beyond the state-prescribed scope of nursing practice.

8. Risk is the possibility of suffering harm, loss, or danger. Risk management entails defining the probability that certain incidents will occur if conditions are not corrected and taking the steps necessary to prevent them.

9. Increased expertise, specialization, accountability, and autonomy in professional practice places nurses in high-risk situations. Failure to assess and to communicate are the negligent claims most commonly filed against nurses. Some common causes of lawsuits against nurses include medication errors; failure to perform treatments correctly; patient falls; and failure to observe and report changes, take adequate histories, or document pertinent information.

10. The current concept of incident reports includes any unusual event or occurrence in which potential liability may occur. The issue of whether incident reports should be protected from discovery and not admissible in malpractice cases is still not resolved.

11. Most agencies are obligated to carry malpractice insurance on their employees. An employer is liable for the nurse's actions while on duty because of the principle of respondeat superior. The nurse should know the extent of this coverage and be apprised of any lawsuits or claims against him or her. Every nurse should carry personal malpractice insurance because the agency's policy does not cover the nurse in all situations, particularly those away from the job.

12. A statute of limitations specifies a limited number of years when one person can seek damages from another. The usual limit is 1 to 3 years.

13. The best way to avoid a lawsuit is to practice nursing within established nursing standards and the ANA Code of Ethics and to be accountable for one's actions. Proper documentation, care in transcribing orders, and

caution in accepting oral or telephone orders are examples of precautionary behavior.

14. Accountability rests on the integrity, competence, and reliability of the healthcare agency and personnel.

15. Errors are categorized into three major categories: technical, judgmental, and normative. A normative error is a breach of honesty, trust, and good faith.

16. Every healthcare institution needs a system that ensures a never-ending process of quality improvement and identifies possible or likely situations that might result in error.

17. Nurses are responsible for guarding the reputation of patients/clients, physicians, and colleagues as closely as they would their own.

18. A nurse should inquire about staffing procedures before accepting employment.

19. Ultimate decisions regarding the quality and quantity of staff are made at the highest levels of management.

20. A nurse may be held liable for another nurse who is practicing under his or her direction. However, the nurse is not held directly liable for any nurse who carries out the duties in an incompetent or grossly negligent manner.

21. Most cases litigated against nurses involve perceived errors in assessment, planning, intervention, omission, and lack of communication.

22. Nurses are called to court as eyewitnesses or expert witnesses to give an opinion from the facts presented. Expert witnesses should be familiar with ANA nursing standards, the ANA Code of Ethics, the state nurse practice act, and the employer's standards, particularly for the clinical area in question. The nurse is also expected to have clinical expertise, effective communication skills, general knowledge of the components of malpractice liability, and an ability to represent the nursing profession well.

23. Good Samaritan laws in most states protect physicians and nurses from civil liability when they give emergency care in good faith, with due care, and without gross negligence. Once a nurse stops and makes an appearance at the scene of an emergency, a nurse-patient relationship is established and the nurse cannot leave the scene until

skilled personnel arrive to assume care. Measurable harm has to be proven for the nurse to be charged with breach of duty.

24. If a nurse is sued, the employer's legal representative and the nurse's personal malpractice representative are consulted and all facts are gathered, including copies of relevant documents. Conversations about the case should be limited to the nurse's legal representative and a trusted friend. No record should be altered, and all testimony should be honest, respectful, and limited to the questions posed.

25. The doctrine of sovereign immunity provides federal employees with special legal protection. Unless the sovereign agrees, a government employee cannot be sued for on-the-job mistakes. In recent years some states have altered this law to some degree and have placed a limit on the amount of money the government would pay if an employee is found guilty.

26. Contracts can be formal, express, or implied. A formal contract is an agreement between two or more parties that is written and enforceable by law. A contract is valid when the nurse meets specifications for the job, agrees to perform specified services, agrees to abide by the employer's terms, and receives remuneration for services. An express contract may be written or oral. It is an agreement between two or more people but does not become a written express contract until placed in documented form. Implied contracts occur between two or more people when terms are understood but not stated verbally or in writing.

27. Ethics is a discipline in which one applies certain principles to determine the right thing to do in a given situation. A person integrates experience, virtues, and moral rules throughout his or her career. An ethical problem occurs when an individual does not know the right thing to do.

28. Published in 1985, the ANA Code of Ethics states that: (1) the action itself cannot be inherently evil; it must be good or morally neutral, (2) the nurse's intent must be good rather than evil, (3) the evil effect cannot be a means to the good effect, and (4) the benefit of the administration of a medication or treatment must clearly outweigh potential harm.

29. Most hospitals and other healthcare agencies subscribe to the practices in the AHA Bill of Rights. Some agencies develop their own bills, using the Bill of Rights as a guideline.

30. An advocate supports or defends someone or something and recommends or pleads on another's behalf. An effective leader and manager is always an advocate for his or her group. Advocacy often requires assertiveness and noncompliance with orders.

31. To retain ethical responsibility as a patient advocate, the nurse must (1) develop awareness of the issues, (2) determine the means to identify the problems within a given situation, (3) identify the values of the community or group of people involved, and (4) find the best possible solution to the situation.

32. A growing number of healthcare agencies have established ethics committees to process ethical problems. The functions of an ethical committee include such activities as consultations, conflict resolution, and educational programs. To function effectively, the committee members need to be educated individually and as a group.

33. The provision of high quality patient care depends on obtaining precise and accurate information and keeping that information confidential. Privacy has been defined as the right of individuals to determine the degree to which they are willing to share information about themselves.

34. Automation (e.g., computers) presents a danger of disclosure of patient information to unwanted sources. Availability of information and secrecy are not compatible. Obtaining patient information for litigation purposes via automation is currently receiving intense scrutiny.

35. Transcultural nursing refers to nursing care across cultures. It is the shared patterns, knowledge, meanings, and behaviors of a social group. Nursing practices cannot be ethical unless the culture and beliefs of the patient are taken into consideration.

36. An ethnocentric person believes that his or her own race is superior to all others and that the beliefs and values of his or her own culture are the best or the only acceptable

beliefs. Nurses have a culture of their own because they have been socialized into the values, customs, and practices of the health-care system.

37. An ethnorelative individual is one who has the ability to respect the beliefs of another culture, even though they may be different from his or her beliefs. Nurses are encouraged to make ethnorelative diagnoses of their patients or clients and to make ethnorelative responses.

38. The Patient Self-Determination Act (PSDA) of 1911 has specific goals. The PSDA ensures that patients (1) have access to the knowledge on which to base a treatment decision, (2) have clearly expressed their decision and desires, and (3) receive treatment in accord with their expressed preferences. The PSDA intends that a patient should have his or her autonomy protected should he or she lose the capacity to make decisions.

39. A will becomes legal when the person making the will is mentally competent, is of legal age for making a will, makes written declaration that the instrument is a will, and has the proper number of witnesses present.

It is not advisable for a nurse to prepare wills for patients/clients or to serve as a witness if legal representatives from the agency are available. If the nurse does serve as a witness, he or she must contact his or her immediate supervisor and the patient's/client's physician for sanction before signing.

40. The foremost obligation of nurse managers regarding AIDS patients is to ensure that staff members do not abandon these patients. Nurses may be held liable for abandonment if they sever the nurse-patient relationship without the patient's consent. There is no fault if the nurse and the AIDS patient mutually agree to terminate the relationship. No health provider receiving federal or state funds can refuse to accept an AIDS patient on the grounds that it is not prepared to treat or care for such an individual.

41. The Americans With Disabilities Act (ADA) affects both federal and private employers. The ADA states that no employer can discriminate against a person who is HIV positive or who has AIDS. Such discrimination applies to hiring, firing, and potential promotions.

❓ Questions for Study and Discussion

1. What are the similarities between the rules or customs of public law and the rules or customs of nursing?

2. With which type of law is the nurse most closely associated? Give two examples.

3. Outline the steps required to obtain nurse licensure.

4. Assume that you are about to become an NP in a rural area. Beyond RN licensure, what measures do you need to take to protect yourself from legal liability?

5. What is your attitude toward legal accountability and risk management in terms of your career aspirations and expectations? How does this compare with your concept of nursing when you first entered the nursing education program?

6. What insurance protection can a nurse expect from his or her employer? Is additional insurance by the nurse advisable? Explain.

7. You, an RN, witnessed the resuscitation procedure of a patient who subsequently died. You believe that the attending nurse went through the proper procedure but that her heart was not in it because she later shared with you her belief that the patient would have been a "vegetable" had he lived. The family is suing the attending nurse for liability. You have been summoned to give testimony as a witness. What would you say?

8. As the nurse assigned to a patient who fell out of bed during your term of duty, you are being sued for malpractice. A family member telephones you and asks you to fill her in on the details so she will be better able to understand the situation. How will you respond?

9. If you were asked about your transcultural attitudes, would they lean toward ethnocentrism or ethnorelativity? Explain your response.

10. You are to discharge a client from a short-procedure unit after teaching her about the dangers of lifting any heavy object. The client replies that she has to lift her 20-pound child. How should you respond?

11. You are one of the nurses to care for a profoundly retarded, blind, and deaf infant who has multiple physiologic problems, including lack of temperature control, diabetes mellitus, and an inability to swallow or digest food well. The infant is not expected to live beyond a few weeks or months. She is a ward of the court, and you have been in-structed to act in the infant's best interest. Decide how aggressive you should be in caring for the infant, particularly in feeding.

12. You are assigned to a patient who is told by her physician that she is dying of leukemia and that chemotherapy is her only hope of survival. The procedure is life threatening and has undesirable side effects. You believe that alternative treatments may benefit the patient, including the use of Laetrile, and that a particular clinic accessible to the patient could help her.[26,27] What should you do?

Test Your Knowledge

BEHAVIORAL OBJECTIVE

Define legal terms important to nursing practice.

Pat is the nurse executive of a skilled facility. She is aware that there is a high risk for falls or injuries with geriatric patients and others who are disabled. Many members of the staff are nursing assistants, who require constant surveillance and guidance.

_____ 1. Pat understands that tort law is:
   a. A rule or standard of human conduct established by authority.
   b. Private law concerning wrongful acts done willfully.
   c. Action harmful to the public and individual, with stipulated punishment.
   d. A law passed by federal or state legislature declaring, commanding, or prohibiting something.

_____ 2. Another term familiar to Pat is *malpractice,* which means:
   a. Legal responsibility for failing to act according to standards and causing harm to another person.
   b. Action harmful to the public. Punishment is stipulated for offenders.
   c. Improper or unethical conduct by a professional that results in harm to another person.
   d. Private law concerning wrongful acts done willfully.

_____ 3. It is particularly important in a skilled facility for Pat to understand the term *permissive licensure,* which means that:
   a. The RN choses when to declare his or her licensure.
   b. A nurse can practice without a license as long as RN status is not declared.
   c. A nurse receives permission from the state to practice.
   d. A nurse is exempt from liability.

BEHAVIORAL OBJECTIVE

Identify common control areas of the nurse practice act.

_____ 4. An RN is controlled by the nurse practice act in all of the following areas except:
   a. Requirements for licensure.
   b. Penalties for practicing without a license.
   c. Conditions for revocation of license.
   d. Good physical and mental health.

BEHAVIORAL OBJECTIVE

Indicate the significance of risk management to nurses. Name four common reasons for malpractice suits against nurses and identify measures to avoid them.

_____ 5. Pat needs to have an understanding of legal risk as it relates to any health-care facility. Select the most appropriate response:
   a. Risk is the possibility of suffering harm, loss, or danger.
   b. Risk is deciding whether or not to practice in a particular setting.
   c. Risk is exposure of the general population to healthcare.
   d. Risk is the increasing number of malpractice suits.

_____ 6. Which of the following is the most common cause of negligent claims filed against nurses?
   a. Failure to perform treatments properly
   b. Failure to assess and communicate
   c. Medication errors
   d. Patient falls

_____ 7. While making rounds Pat notices loose tiles in several bathroom floors. After the maintenance department has failed to respond to two requests for repair, Pat's first responsibility is to:
   a. Send a report to top administration.
   b. Warn the staff to be careful.
   c. Complete an incident report.
   d. Warn patients and their families of the danger.

_____ 8. The skilled facility allows physicians to give orders by phone. Which of the following actions fails to protect the nurse from liability?
   a. Listen to the order, record, and transcribe.
   b. Repeat the order aloud and ask for confirmation.
   c. Ask another nurse to witness the order.
   d. Document the order.

BEHAVIORAL OBJECTIVE
Explain the difference between employer and personal malpractice insurance.

_____ 9. Pat is interested in the concept of charting by exception. She learns that the term means:
   a. Placing emphasis on that which is exceptional.
   b. Recording the things that happen most often.
   c. Charting only when something unusual happens.
   d. Charting at regular intervals.

BEHAVIORAL OBJECTIVE
Differentiate among technical, judgmental, and normative error.

As the nurse executive of the skilled facility, Pat holds ultimate responsibility for all nursing errors. She wants to hold errors to a minimum. Therefore she must be aware of the significance of each breach of conduct.

_____ 10. The night nurse failed to recognize signs of kidney failure in Mrs. Ferrera until it was too late. What kind of error was this?
   a. Normative
   b. Technical
   c. Judgmental

_____ 11. A nursing assistant failed to walk Mr. Brown during her shift but reported that she had. What type of error was this?
   a. Technical
   b. Normative
   c. Judgmental

BEHAVIORAL OBJECTIVE

State two roles of the nurse as a witness in court and describe the nurse's responsibilities.

_____ 12. Which of the following statements is true?
  a. Pat testifies that she was administering care to Mrs. Johnson at the time of injury. She is an expert witness.
  b. Nurse Peters comes to the skilled facility as a specialist in oncology. She testifies on behalf of a patient who died of complications from uncontrolled bleeding during surgery. She is an expert witness.
  c. Nurse Rogers was present when Mr. Jacob's injury occurred. He is an eyewitness.
  d. An expert witness should be prepared to testify at a moment's notice because of his or her expertise.

BEHAVIORAL OBJECTIVE

Define formal, express, written express, and implied contracts.

_____ 13. Pat signs a contract with the skilled facility to advance one step. She is nervous about the new position. Pat's employer tells her, "You will catch on to your new role very easily." This type of contract is called:
  a. Formal.
  b. Express.
  c. Written express.
  d. Implied.

BEHAVIORAL OBJECTIVE

Define ethics, state the purposes of an ethics committee, and explain how an ethical approach applies to nursing.

Since assuming her new role in the skilled care facility, Kay has become more aware of ethics and the nurse's responsibility to do the right thing in a given situation.

_____ 14. Ethics in nursing is:
  a. An ethical, moral reasoning applied to nursing practice.
  b. A person of individual value.
  c. Integrated life experiences.
  d. Responsiveness to others.

Pat reviewed the AHA's Patient's Bill of Rights with the staff of the skilled facility. She presented the following two vignettes and asked for discussion.

_____ 15. Ms. Carlson uses abusive and foul language to all who enter the room to care for her. Which statement is the most appropriate?
  a. Ms. Carlson has the right to receive like treatment from caregivers.
  b. Ms. Carlson has the right to considerate and respectful treatment and care.
  c. Mrs. Carlson has the right to expect confrontation and punishment.
  d. Mrs. Carlson has the right to act, say, and do anything she wishes.

_____ 16. The physician depends on Pat to have a consent form signed for a breast biopsy. He does not want the patient informed of the possibility of a radical mastectomy because he does not want to upset her. However, this possibility is listed on the consent form. The patient is alert and responsive. Which of the following responses is the most appropriate?
  a. The patient has the right to receive from her physician the information necessary to give informed consent before a procedure.
  b. The physician has the right to make such a decision.
  c. As an employee, Pat is obligated to carry out the physician's order.
  d. After obtaining the signature Pat should say, "Consult your physician if you have questions."

_____ 17. Pat has now become a member of the ethics committee at the facility. Pat learned that ethics committees engage in all of the following activities except:
a. Performing consultations.
b. Offering educational programs.
c. Providing legal services.
d. Engaging in conflict resolution.

BEHAVIORAL OBJECTIVE

Explain the meaning of transcultural nursing and compare ethnocentric and ethnorelative attitudes.

_____ 18. Which of the following is the best definition of transcultural nursing:
a. Nurses recognize different needs of different people.
b. Nursing practice is shared patterns of behavior.
c. Nursing practices are based on an honest belief system.
d. Nurses span the globe in providing necessary services.

_____ 19. Pat has a patient whose belief system does not permit surgery. Pat asks her to ask her minister to come in for a conference. This approach is:
a. Ethnocentric.
b. Ethnorelative.

_____ 20. Pat notes impatience in one of her team leaders because she cannot convince a patient to receive much needed IVs. The patient will not explain his reasons for refusal. The team leader is exhibiting which kind of attitude?
a. Ethnocentric.
b. Ethnorelative.

BEHAVIORAL OBJECTIVE

Indicate the nurse's responsibility for implementing the Patient Self-Determination Act.

_____ 21. Which of the following is not accurate information about the Patient Self-Determination Act of 1991?
a. The patient is not required to give a reason for refusing treatment.
b. The patient has a right to know the provisions of the advance directive.
c. The PSDA is for people of all ages, regardless of creed or circumstance.
d. The patient is in the best position to determine where his or her best interests lie.

REFERENCES

1. Gifis S: *Dictionary of legal terms,* ed 2, New York, 1993, Barron's Educational Series.
2. National Council of State Boards of Nursing: *Candidate information for NCLEX,* Chicago, Ill, 1994-1995, The Council.
3. American Nurses' Association: *Enforcement of the Nursing Practice Act,* publication no D-89, Kansas City, Mo, 1986, The Association.
4. Pearson L: Annual update of how each state stands on legislative issues affecting advanced nurse practice, *Nurs Pract* 19(1):11-13;17, 1994.
5. Birkholz G, Walker D: Strategies for state statutory language changes granting fully independent nurse practitioner role, *Nurs Pract* 19(1):54-58, 1994.
6. Chow M: Nurses as primary care providers: an old idea whose time has come, *Calif Hosp* 8(4):10;12-14, 1994.
7. Hughes T, Smith L: Is your colleague chemically dependent? *Am J Nurs* 94(9):31-35, 1994.
8. California Board of Registered Nursing: *Nursing diversion program,* Sacramento, p1, State of California—State and Consumer Service Agency.
9. Fiesta J: Duty to communicate—"Doctor notified," *Nurs Manage* 25(1):24-25, 1994.
10. Luquire R: Nursing risk management, *Nurs Manage* 20(10):56-58, 1989.
11. Fiesta J: Incident reports—confidential or not? *Nurs Manage* 25(10):17-18, 1994.
12. Tammelleo A: Charting by exception: there are perils, *RN* 57(10):71-72, 1994.
13. Martin F: Documentation tips to help you stay out of court, *Nurs 94* 24(6):63-64, 1994.
14. Davis N: Beware of trailing zeros, *Am J Nurs* 94(1):17, 1994.
15. Brown L and others: Questionable dose, *Am J Nurs* 94(6):48, 1994.
16. Biordi D: Nursing error and caring in the workplace, *Nurs Adm Q* 17(2):38-45, 1993.
17. Cohen M, Senders J, Davis N: Failure mode and effects analysis: dealing with human error, *Nurs 94* 24(2):40, 1994.
18. Fiesta J: Nursing torts: from plaintiff to defendant, *Nurs Manage* 25(2):17-18, 1994.
19. American Nurses' Association: *Suggested state legislation nursing practice act, nursing disciplinary act, prescriptive authority act,* publication no NP-78, Kansas City, Mo, 1990, The Association.
20. Fiesta J: Legal update for nurses, Part II: assigning, delegating and staffing, *Nurs Manage* 24(2):14-16, 1993.
21. Fiesta J: Staffing implications: a legal update, *Nurs Manage* 25(6):34-35, 1994.
22. Barter M, Furmidge M: Unlicensed assistive personnel, *JONA* 24(4):36-40, 1994.
23. Calfee B: Litigation: steering clear of trouble: a look at three malpractice cases involving nurses and ways you can sidestep, *Nurs 94* 24(1):46-47, 1994.
24. Fiesta J: Nursing torts: from plaintiff to defendant, *Nurs Manage* 25(2):17-18, 1994.
25. Siegel M: *How to survive a deposition,* New York, 1994, John Wiley & Sons.
26. Salmond S: Serving as an expert witness, *Nurs Econ* 4(5):236-239, 1986.
27. Cushing M: Brosseau vs Children's Mercy Hospital, *Am J Nurs* 86(10):1107, 1986.
28. Nurses' Reference Library: Practices: legal risks, ethics human relations, career management, *Nursing 84,* Springhouse, Pa, 1984, Springhouse.
29. Mandell M: Ten legal commandments for nurses who get sued, *Life* 6(3):18-21, 1986.
30. Curtin L: DNR in the OR: ethical concerns and hospital policies, *Nurs Manage* 25(2):29-31, 1994.
31. Hadley J: Nurse advocacy, ethics, and healthcare reform, *J Post Anesth Nurs* 9(1):55-56, 1994.
32. Griener G, Storch J: The educational needs of ethics committees, *Camb Q Healthc Ethics,* 3(3):467-476, 1994.
33. Curran M, Curran K: The ethics of information, *J Nurs Adm* 21(1):47-48, 1994.
34. Fishman D: Confidentiality, *Comput Nurs* 12(2):73-77, 1994.
35. Mathis R, Jackson J: *Human resource management,* ed 7, Minneapolis/St Paul, 1994, West Publishing.
36. Olson T: Transcultural care, *Nurs Outlook* 42(5):243, 1994.
37. Eliason M: Ethics and transcultural nursing care, *Nurs Outlook* 41(5):225-228, 1993.
38. Geissler E: Transcultural nursing and nursing diagnosis, *Nurs Health Care* 12(4):190-192; 203, 1991.
39. Loewy E: Furthering the dialogue on advance directives and the patient self-determination act, *Camb Q Healthc Ethics* 3(3):405-421, 1994.
40. Mezey M and others: The patient self-determination act: sources of concern for nurses, *Nurs Outlook* 42(1):30-38, 1994.
41. De Margo C, Goodgame J: When an employee is HIV positive, *AAOHN J* 42(5):241-246, 1994.

SUGGESTED READINGS

Blouin A, Brent N: Legal insights: managing a culturally diverse staff: legal considerations, *J Nurs Adm* 24(11):13-14, 1994.

Blouin A, Brent N: Legal concerns related to workers with HIV or AIDS, *J Nurs Adm* 25(1):17-18, 1995.

Calfe B: Things you should never chart, *Nurs 94* 24(3):43, 1994.

Calliari D: The relationship between a calculation test given in nursing orientation test and medication errors, *J Contin Ed Nurs* 26(1):11-14, 1995.

Cohen M, Senders J: 12 ways to prevent medication errors, *Nurs 94,* 24(2):34-41, 1994.

Coston B: Fighting through an appeals process, *RN* 58(2):57-59, 1995.

Curtin L: Of confidentiality, co-workers and adoption: ethics in management, *Nurs Manage* 25(4):22;24-25;28, 1994.

Curtin L: Ethics for, in, and about nursing administration, *Nurs Manage* 25(12):25-28, 1994.

Davis N: Med errors, *Am J Nurs* 94(10):9, 1994.

Dean H: Service and education: forging a partnership, *Nurs Outlook* 43(3):119-123, 1995.

Fiesta J: Duty to communicate-"Doctor notified," *Nurs Manage* 25(1):24-25, 1994.

Fiesta J: Incident reports—confidential or not? *Nurs Manage* 25(10):17-18, 1994.

Fox A: Confronting the use of placebos for pain, *Am J Nurs* 94(9):42-45, 1994.

Haddad A: Ethics in action: acute care decisions, *RN* 58(1):21-23, 1995.

Maija P: Ethical dilemmas: botched circumstances: fear of floating, *Am J Nurs* 94(3):56, 1994.

Murphy E: OR nursing law: legal ramifications of RN staffing policies, *Oper Room Nurs J* 59(5):1064-1070, 1994.

Neubs H: Sexual harassment: a concern for nursing administration, *J Nurs Adm* 24(5):47-56, 1994.

Olsen D: The ethical considerations of managed care in mental health treatment, *J Psychosoc Nurs* 32(3):25-28, 1994.

Starch M: Social accountability: an ongoing commitment to community health, *Calif Hosp* 8(40):23-24, 1994.

Stephany T: Speak up! Needlestick—one year later, *RN* 25(2):80, 1994.

Sullivan G: Home care: more autonomy, more legal risks, *RN* 25(5):63-64;67-68, 1994.

Tarrant C: Liability for employer purchasers of healthcare benefits, *Am Assoc Hosp Nurs J* 42(5):250-254, 1994.

Zink M, Titus L: Nursing ethics committees—where are they? *Nurs Manage* 25(6):70-71;75-76, 1994.

Glossary

ability Possession of skills, proficiency, or expertness; can accomplish a purpose

accountability Liability for one's actions; willing to be judged against performance expectations; willing to live with the results of one's actions and be able to determine whether those results were successful and how they need change or modification

accreditation To supply with credentials or authority to function as a supplier of health services, occurring at municipal, state, and national levels

acquisitions A larger organization takes over a lesser-sized organization that is linked by common technologies and common clients

action The process of performing in a certain way; the behavior adopted by an individual as a result of a message sent, received, and perceived; putting thoughts into observable behaviors

Acute Care Nurse Practitioner (ACNP) Certified by ANA in physiology, advanced assessment, advanced pathophysiology, pharmacology, diagnostic reasoning, clinical decision making, and advanced therapeutics

advanced practice nurse (APN) An RN who is prepared by certification or by an advanced degree to deliver competent, quality care

advocate One who supports or defends someone or something and recommends or pleads on another's behalf

alternate path to a BSN A nurse who has earned a diploma or associate degree may attend NLN-accredited programs that offer the nurse an opportunity to earn a BSN degree outside the physical boundaries of a college or university

American Hospital Association (AHA) Professional association made up of U.S. hospitals

American Nurses Association (ANA) National professional association of RNs in the United States; founded in 1896

ancillary nursing personnel Individuals who provide supportive nursing services to the RN; may be orderlies, nursing assistants, attendants, or practical/vocational nurses who provide such services as comfort, personal hygiene, and protection of patients

anthropology (cultural) Study of effects of culture on human behavior

aptitude A natural or acquired talent or the degree of quickness in learning and understanding

assessment Data collected from tangible and intangible elements that is classified, analyzed, placed in order of priority, and translated into a diagnosis or need

assistive nursing personnel Can be nurse assistants, orderlies, and attendants; perform designated nursing and support services for patients that do not require RN/LPN licensure

authority (formal) Official or positional sanction to take actions to carry out managerial functions of the position held

authority (functional) The right to act derived from personal qualifications of the leader in professional competency, experience, technical expertise, and knowledge of managerial functions and human relations

authority (general) The power and right to take action; sanction to act

autonomy Independence or freedom to make choices

avoidance Shunning or avoiding a problem

behavior The actions or manner in which one responds to stimuli under specified circumstances

behavior (aggressive) Acting in a bold, attacking, and hostile manner, often accomplishing purposes at the expense of others with injurious and destructive results

behavior (assertive) Maintaining a balance between passive and aggressive behavior; expressing positive and negative beliefs and reactions and needs openly without infringing on the rights of others

behavior (passive) Submissively accepting any circumstance without resistance or complaint

behavior modification Changes in the behavior of an individual that result from certain conditions or behavior control techniques

behavioral science approach Incorporation of the sciences of psychology, sociology, and cultural anthropology

breach of contract Failure to perform all or part of the contract without justification

budget   A tool for planning, monitoring, and controlling cost; a systematic plan for meeting expenses

budget (capital expenditure)   An itemized list of current capital assets over $500

budget (decentralized)   Middle-level managers are actively involved in developing and monitoring the budgets for their respective units

budget (operating)   Includes services to be provided and goods the unit expects to consume or use during the budget period

budget (personnel)   The numbers and types of various nursing and support personnel that are required to operate a unit

bureaucratic   A technical and scientific hierarchical structure based on legalized, formal authority that is guided by rules and regulation, work specialization, appointment by merit, and an impersonal climate

burnout   Emotional exhaustion, depersonalization, and a diminished sense of personal accomplishment

caring   Recognizing that people are human and need emotional support, physical safeguards, recognition, dignity, and respect

case management   Involves the development of integrated care pathways from the time of entrance into the healthcare delivery system through discharge

centralization   A hierarchical system with control emanating from the top down

certification   A credential issued by a professional body that helps protect the consumer by affirming a person's excellence in a particular specialty area

change   Any alteration in the status quo; substituting one thing for another; experiencing a shift in circumstances that cause differences; becoming different than before

change agent   Any individual or group that serves as a catalyst to effect change

characteristics (leader)   Personality traits or distinguishing features about a person

charting by exception   Charting only when something unusual happens

Chris Argyris structure   A matrix organizational structure in which workers are allowed a high degree of independence and decision-making power within an informal and flexible organizational climate; encourages teamwork and special projects

classification system (patient)   A method of grouping patients according to the amount and complexity of their nursing care requirements

client   An individual, family, group, community, or agency who receives nursing services in any setting; person(s) dependent on the services of another or others; synonymous with patient

climate (emotional)   Concerns behavior, attitudes, and feelings of personnel

clinical nurse specialist (CNS)   Registered nurse with education and clinical practice beyond licensure in a specialty area; expands the scope of nursing practice by providing patient care with greater comprehensiveness, continuity, and coordination of patient services

cognitive   The mental process of thinking, reasoning, feeling, and perceiving

collaboration   Recognition that a problem exists; confronting the issue and openly trying to solve the problem through integration of ideas

common law   The cumulative result of many court decisions over the years

common practice   That which falls within both the definition of nursing and the legal scope of nursing practice

communication (cross-cultural)   Occurs when a person from one culture sends a message to a person from another culture and that message is understood

communication (grapevine)   An informal communication system of social interaction that focuses on personal and group interests

communication (grapevine, cluster chain)   Information communicated selectively according to interest in the subject

communication (grapevine, gossip chain)   One person seeks out and gives everyone information indiscriminately

communication (grapevine, probability chain)   Information imparted to individuals at random

communication (grapevine, single chain)   A system in which one person transmits a message to another, that person tells another, and so on

communication (interpersonal)   The process of exchanging information and meaning from sender to receiver with the hope that the message sent will be received and understood as the sender intended

communication (organizational)   The formal process by which managers use the established organizational channels to receive and relay information to people within the organization and to relevant individuals and groups outside it

community health/public health nurse (PHN)   Delivers care to the community as a whole, to populations within the community, to families, and to individuals

competition/power   When the nurse manager is primarily concerned with work accomplishment and has minimal regard for staff relationships, he or she will exercise power, restriction, and coercion regardless of the cost

Computer Adaptive Testing (CAT) A computerized process that calculates the level of competence shown by an applicant on the examination for nurse licensure

conflict (general) An inner or outer struggle regarding ideas, feelings, or actions

conflict (organizational) Struggles relating to differences between management and staff, sharing of resources, interdependence of work activities in the organization, and values and goals among department and personnel regarding delivery of nursing care

consideration The extent to which a person is likely to have job relationships characterized by mutual trust, respect for co-workers' comfort, well-being, status, and satisfaction

contract An agreement between two or more parties that is written and enforceable by law

control The ongoing and continuous process by which managers ensure that actual individual or group activities conform to plan; a check to make sure that what is done is what is intended

control (anticipatory) Seeing problems in time to do something about them; reviewing what has happened before; knowing the organization's mission and goals and anticipating needs; projecting for the future

control (concurrent) Deals with the present rather than the future or past; involves monitoring and adjusting ongoing activities and processes to ensure compliance with standards

control (feedback) Gathering information about an ongoing or completed activity, evaluating that information, and taking steps to improve the ongoing activity or similar activities in the future

control process A system of establishing standards, objectives, and methods; measuring actual performance; comparing results of performance with standards and objectives; acting to reinforce strengths; taking corrective action as necessary

criminal law Punishment stipulated for those who commit acts harmful to the public and individual

critical care nurse (CCN) A nurse specialist who is backed with a solid body of scientific knowledge and intricate skills; preferably has a BSN degree and advanced preparation

cross-functional, multidisciplinary teams Integration of nursing care with other units and other people requiring frequent communication; networking; planning creative patient care; and seeing in and beyond the care unit to achieve a goal

cultural blindness Choosing not to see cultural differences and judging cultural diversity as good or bad

cultural diversity/intercultural relations People of differing ages, cultural and geographic origins, abilities, genders, lifestyles, personalities, and family arrangements that impact each individual's performance

culture Deep-rooted assumptions, beliefs, and values; socially inherited characteristics that are handed down from one generation to another

data processing Assembles, sorts, stores, correlates, or otherwise processes and/or prints information derived from predetermined sources

decentralization A top-down management system in which each department is on a par with all other departments

decision making The process of developing a commitment to some course of action

decision making (emotional) Expression of feelings in a group without judgment, which results in freer and more productive solutions

decision making (group) Communicative interaction toward resolution of group goals

decision making (intuitive) Involves scanning a situation, anticipating changes, and taking risks without benefit of rational processes; using instinctive knowledge or going well beyond the information currently possessed

decoding Interpreting messages for meaning

delegation The transfer of responsibility for the performance of an activity from one person to another while retaining accountability for the outcome

democratic A style of leadership in which the participative or consultive methods are used; people oriented; focuses attention on human aspects and building effective work groups

Diagnosis-related group (DRG) A prospective reimbursement system whereby the most common diseases are placed in groups and a set fee is established for services rendered during hospitalization

direction Issuance of assignments, orders, and instructions that permit individuals or group(s) to understand what is expected of them; the guidance and overseeing of workers so they can contribute effectively and efficiently to the attainment of organizational objectives

diversion program A means to rehabilitate registered nurses whose competency has been impaired by the use of drugs or alcohol or by mental illness

documentation Preparation or assembly of written records

encoding Translating a message into words, gestures, facial expressions, and other symbols that communicate the intended meaning to the receiver(s)

entrepreneur   An individual who organizes, operates, and assumes the risk for business ventures

ethical problem   Occurs when the individual does not know the right thing to do

ethics   Beliefs about moral principles and standards that govern the conduct of workers in a profession

ethnocentrism   A belief that one's own race is superior to all others and that his or her own cultural group's beliefs and values are the best or the only acceptable beliefs

ethnorelativity   The ability to conceive of alternative viewpoints and to respect the beliefs of another culture, even though they are different from one's own

error (judgmental)   An honest error in which the nurse chooses the wrong actions by commission or omission

error (normative)   A breach of honesty, trust, and good faith

error (technical)   An honest error of technique

expanded role   Expansion of the nurse role beyond the traditional limits of nurse practice acts; common roles are primary nurse and nurse practitioner; necessitating legal coverage through establishment of standardized procedures or amendments or changes in nurse practice acts

experience   Exposure to a variety of situations, problems, and demands

expert   A person with a high degree of skill in or knowledge about a certain subject

express contract (written or oral)   Agreement between two or more people to do or not to do something

family   Persons who are related by blood or marriage; members of a household; a group of people with like interests

feedback   A process whereby senders and receivers exchange information to clarify the meanings of the message sent

financial control system   Strategy used to set and manage institutional goals, directions, and strategies

follower   An individual or group who is willing to be led

full-time equivalent position (FTE)   The number of hours per week considered by the employing agency to constitute a full-time position; one worker or a combination of workers may constitute a full-time equivalent position

functional nursing   A centralized pattern or system of nursing care that is task- and activity-oriented

goal   The purpose toward which an endeavor is directed; things an individual, group, or organization wishes or strives to achieve

Good Samaritan law   Protects the professional from liability for damages for alleged injuries or death after the professional has rendered first aid or emergency treatment in an emergency away from proper medical equipment (unless there is proved gross negligence)

government-owned health agencies   Official bodies that provide health services to selected groups of people under the support and direction of local, state, or federal government

grapevine   The informal exchange of information among members of an informal group or work team

gross negligence   Flagrant disregard for duty; failure to act in a reasonable manner; reckless disregard of consequences

group (work)   Two or more people who are interdependent and who interact with one another for the purpose of achieving a common goal

harassment (sexual)   Actions that are sexually directed and unwanted and that subject the worker to adverse employment conditions or create a hostile work environment

health agency (government)   Official bodies that provide health services to the public under the support and direction of the voting public

health agency (proprietary)   An organization that operates for profit; serves people who can pay for services, directly or indirectly

health agency (voluntary)   A nonprofit organization designed to meet religious, ethnic, economic, or special interest health needs of the public

health communications model   Illustrates the transactions between participants in healthcare regarding health-related issues; shows a series of factors that can affect the interactions in healthcare settings (relationships, transactions, and contexts)

health maintenance organization (HMO)   An organized system that provides a comprehensive range of healthcare to a voluntarily enrolled consumer population

healthcare system   The resources (money, people, physical plant, and technology) and the organizational configurations necessary to transform these resources into health services

hierarchy   A body of persons or things organized or classified in pyramidal or vertical fashion according to work, capacity, or authority

home healthcare   A system in which healthcare and social services are provided to homebound or disabled people in their homes rather than in medical facilities

home healthcare nurse/visiting nurse   A nurse who plans, coordinates, and delivers care to homebound or disabled people in their homes

hospice nurse   Licensed RNs with at least 2 years of experience in hospice practice; certification covers end-stage disease process, palliative therapeutics, interdisciplinary collaborative practice, education and advocacy, and issues that pertain to the dying

hospital   An institution designed for the care of the sick and well; depending on agency goals, emphasis is on administering patient care, educating health agency personnel and the public, research, and protection of the health of the public

human relations approach to management   A participative, democratic structure with concern for work effectiveness and human satisfaction

incident report   A report of any unusual event or occurrence on which potential liability may occur

induction   Formal procedures an employee follows immediately after employment, such as getting on the payroll, learning about benefits, and completing records

influence   The ability to affect the perceptions, attitudes, or behaviors of others

influence (managerial)   A host of managerial actions such as motivation, power, leadership, and behavioral modification

initiating structure   The extent to which a leader is likely to define and structure his or her role in the search for goal achievement

injunction   A court order that prohibits a party from a specific course of action

input   Any information fed into a communication system, such as thinking or reasoning, facts, theory, or instruction

intangible elements   Cognitive ability or knowledge to think and to problem solve; feelings, emotions, and attitudes

intern   A recent graduate who undergoes supervised practical training

interpersonal relationships   Verbal or nonverbal communication or actions between two or more persons

intrapersonal   Inner thoughts and feelings

intuitive approach to decision making   Relies on personal perceptions, hunches, biases, and personal values

job descriptions   A written account of roles, activities, and responsibilities expected of a staff member

law   A rule or standard of human conduct established and enforced by authority, society, or custom

leader   One who influences others toward goal achievement, either formally or informally; has power to enforce decisions as long as followers are willing to be led

leadership   The ability to influence others to attain goals

leadership (authoritarian)   A closed system that ranges from rigid to benevolent; a practice that demonstrates a high concern for task accomplishment and a low concern for people

leadership (democratic)   A people-oriented approach to work, with participation and collaboration between manager and personnel

leadership (participative)   An open, democratic environment with mutual responsibility to meet work-related goals

leadership (permissive)   A general climate of ultra-liberalism or laissez-faire management, with workers given free reign to function

leadership style   The way in which an individual uses personal and interpersonal influences to achieve goals

learning curves   Learning in different patterns and time frames and in different training situations

learning process   Information received, internalized, and understood in such a way that some change in behavior occurs or some conscious effort is made to use the information

liability   Legal responsibility for acts or a failure to act according to standards, which results in another person's harm

licensed practical nurse/licensed vocational nurse (LPN/LVN)   A nurse who has completed a certified program, which enables him or her to serve in an ancillary role to the RN

Likert studies   An organizational design that provides for bureaucratic methods in which organizations and managers are held accountable for their group's performance; also provides for a system in which supportive relationships are encouraged; group decision making occurs when appropriate and high performance goals are set, which develops a sense of pride and accomplishment

listening   To give heed to something through hearing and thought processes

litigation   Any legal action or process

magnet hospitals (rural)   Small hospitals with bed capacities that range from 37-96; offer medical-surgical care to adults and children, emphasize geriatric care and usually offer a specialty service

magnet hospitals (urban)   Medium-to-large community hospitals or medical centers that have a reputation for higher rates of retention of nurses and for excellence in nursing practice

malpractice   Improper or negligent treatment of a patient, which results in damage or injury

managed care   An integration of healthcare financing with provision of quality care

managed competition   An economic strategy to reform the healthcare system by stimulating price competition and quality improvement

management by objectives (MBO)   A system of

management in which every person or group in a work setting has specific, attainable, and measurable objectives that are in harmony with those of the organization

management by situation   A process that is composed of a range of possible options in which the manager chooses a leadership style complementary to the situation

management (polarity)   Bringing management and staff together for decision making and as a means to promote collaboration and build effective work teams

management process   Consists of working with human and physical resources and organizations and psychologic processes within a creative and innovative climate and for the realization of goals

manager   One who carries out predetermined policies, rules, and regulations with official sanction to act

manager, nurse (lower or first level)   One who has responsibility for administering direct nursing care to a small group of patients; common titles are team leader and primary care nurse

manager, nurse (middle level)   One who directs the activities of other nurse managers that lead to implementation of the broad operating policies of the organization; common titles are supervisor and head nurse

manager, nurse (top level)   One who has broad and general responsibility for establishing overall policies and goals for the management of the organization; responsibility for all activities of the facility that require nursing services; common title is director of nursing services

mandatory licensure   Stipulates that everyone who practices nursing for compensation must be licensed

Maslow's motivation theory   A study of human needs and their influence on behavior; based on the premise that people have physiologic, security, social, ego, and self-actualization needs, depending on their individuality

matrix system   A system that uses the benefits of both centralized and decentralized control

Mayo-Hawthorne studies (1927-1932)   Encouraged employee participation in decision making

McGregor studies   Believes that organizations can meet their goals more effectively if they attend to the human needs of organization members and use their potential with the aid of formal organizational structure, policies, and goals

mentor   A dynamic, noncompetitive, and nurturing process that promotes independence, autonomy, and self-actualization in the learner while also fostering a sense of pride, fulfillment, support, and continuity

mentoring relationship   A dynamic, noncompetitive, nurturing process that promotes independence, autonomy, and self-actualization in the protege

merger   The incorporation of groups of hospitals, nursing homes, psychiatric facilities, HMOs, and home care agencies into multiunit systems

message   A concept, fact, idea, or feeling that is transmitted by spoken or written words, signals, or other means from one person or group to another

Mind Extension University (ME/U)   A cable network that specializes in long-distance education; is in partnership with California State University and is accredited by the NLN and the Western Association of Schools and Colleges

modular nursing   A modification of team and primary nursing; a geographic assignment that encourages continuity of care by organizing a group of staff to work with a group of patients

motivation   An incentive, inducement, emotion, desire, physiologic need, or similar impulse that provides desire to act

National Council Licensure Examination (NCLEX)   Designed to test knowledge, skills, and abilities that are essential to the safe and effective practice of nursing at the entry level

National Council of State Boards of Nursing (NCSBN)   Comprised of membership from 59 boards of nursing; organized in 1978; chief function is to develop and evaluate licensing examinations for RNs and LPNs/LVNs

nurse (assistant)   See ancillary nursing personnel

nurse (associate degree)   A graduate of a community college nursing program who uses the nursing process to assess, plan, implement, and evaluate individualized nursing care; is prepared to communicate with others, teach clients, manage within structured settings, and assume responsibility for professional activities and development

nurse (baccalaureate degree)   A graduate of a baccalaureate program in a senior college or university; prepared as a generalist and is able to provide, within the healthcare system, comprehensive services that assess, promote, and maintain the health of individuals and groups; accountable for own practice; can serve in leadership and managerial roles in a variety of hospital and community settings

nurse case management   The nurse assesses patient and family needs, establishes nursing diagnoses, develops nursing care plans, delegates nursing care to associates, activates interventions, coordinates and collaborates with the interdisciplinary team, and evaluates outcomes before admission and through at least 2 weeks after discharge

nurse (diploma) A graduate of a diploma program, sometimes affiliated with an associate degree program; skills are equivalent to the associate degree nurse

nurse entrepreneur Organizes, operates and assumes the risk of a nursing business venture

nurse informaticist The combination of computer science, information science, and nursing science to assist in the management and delivery of nursing care

nurse intrapreneur Develops innovative ideas for improving patient care, education and other nursing services or hospital operations; offers nurses the opportunity to harness their ideas and reap the rewards without having to start a business of their own

nurse management process Involves active participation by managers in four basic interrelated, usually simultaneous, and managerial functions: planning, organizing, directing, and controlling to achieve organizational goals

nurse midwife A nurse who follows the birthing process from inception through delivery

nurse (practical, LPN) A nurse who is licensed to practice within the definition and roles specified by the nurse practice acts of the state(s) to which requirements have been met; sometimes called a licensed vocational nurse (LVN); accountable to registered nurses in the employing agency

nurse practitioners (NP) A select group of nurses who have special preparation beyond that required for nurse licensure in medical history taking, physical assessment, and patient management; also known as family nurse practitioner (FNP), obstetric-gynecologic nurse practitioner (OGNP), and psychiatric-mental health nurse practitioner (PNP)

nurse (registered, RN) A nurse who is licensed to practice in one or more states within the definition and roles specified by the nurse practice acts of the state; may be a graduate of a diploma program, community college, or a baccalaureate program

nursing care delivery systems An approach devised to deliver nursing care effectively and efficiently to patient or client populations

nursing process Includes assessment, analysis, nursing diagnosis, planning, implementation, and evaluation

objectives Specific, measurable aims or purposes that address the questions of who, what, where, when, and why

occupational health nurse (OHN) or industrial nurse A nurse who provides consultive services, assesses environmental hazards, conducts

preemployment history and physical examinations, provides health teaching, and is available to employees for their health needs

Omnibus Budget Reconciliation Act (OBRA) An annual process in which healthcare spending that is not controlled through the regular congressional appropriations process is brought into conformity with the annual budget resolution

operating room nurse (ORN)/perioperative registered nurse Monitors client progress from the time of entry into the operating room until the patient is dismissed to the staff nurse in attendance; outpatient ORNs engage in patient assessment, prepare for surgery, set up for and assist the surgeon, and manage the recovery and follow-up of patients by telephone or home visits

organization An institution or functional group, such as a hospital or health department, that arranges and allocates the people and resources so that the goals of that enterprise can be achieved

organizational chart A formal diagram in which each department, position, and function is outlined and the relationships between them shown

organizational climate Behavior, attitudes, and feelings of personnel

organizational structure A mechanism through which work is arranged and distributed among members of the organization so the goals of the organization can logically be achieved; the process by which a group is formed; a group's channels of authority, span of control, and lines of communication

organizing Putting together people and resources in an orderly, systematic manner

orientation The formal process of apprising the new employee of the organization and his or her part in it

orientation program A program that is designed to introduce the novice to the needs of a specific work environment

outcome standards Designed to measure the results of nursing care

outlier services Services that are provided to patients outside the hospital

participative A style of leadership in which group members manage the workload and solve problems for the good of the whole and for individual accomplishments

patient The recipient of nursing care, which includes the prevention of illness or the promotion of care; an individual, group, family, significant other, community, or agency that receives nursing services

Patient Self-Determination Act Gives patients legitimate choices about their end-of-life decisions

pattern of nursing care   That system used for the delivery of nursing care to patients, such as total, primary, functional, team nursing, and case management

peer review   Examining and evaluating, by associates, another nurse's practice

peers   Those in like positions or equal standing

performance appraisal (formal)   The process of regular and methodic collection of objective data by setting standards and objectives; reviewing progress; providing ongoing feedback; and planning for reinforcement, deletion, or correction of identified behaviors as necessary

performance appraisal (informal)   Incidental observation and/or recording of work performance

permissive   A style of leadership which is ultraliberal or laissez-faire and in which the general climate is one of lack of central direction or control

permissive licensure   Nursing can be practiced without a license as long as the title "RN" is not used and licensure is not claimed

philosophy (nursing)   An intentionally chosen set of values or purposes that serve as the basis for choosing the means to accomplish nursing objectives

philosophy (organizational)   The sense of purpose and reasoning behind organizational structure and goals

plaintiff   The party that institutes a suit in a court

planning (general)   A continuous intellectual process of assessing, establishing goals and objectives, implementing, and evaluating; subject to change as new information is known; knowing what should be done and determining how to do it

planning (organizational)   A continuous process of assessing, establishing goals, and implementing and controlling them to ensure that decisions regarding the use of people, resources, and environment help achieve agency goals for the present and future

planning (strategic)   A systematic process of determining how to pursue the organization-wide, long-term goals with the resources expected to be available

polarity management   Bringing management and staff together for decision making to promote collaboration and to build effective work teams

power   The ability to perform effectively, exercise authority, and control through personal, organizational, and social strength

power (coercive)   Founded on fear; depends on the manager's ability to use punishment, harassment, reprimands, isolation, and blaming for noncompliance with orders

power (expert)   Derived from some special ability, skill, or knowledge; demonstrated by the individual

power (referent)   Shown in at least two forms of organization; charisma; based on a person's connection or relationship with another powerful individual

power (reward)   The ability of the manager to control and administer rewards to others for compliance with the leader's orders or requests

pragmatic approach to decision making   Deals with actual facts or occurrences by using the problem-solving approach

preceptor   An instructor, teacher, tutor, trainer, mentor, or director

preferred provider organization (PPO)   A health financing and delivery arrangement in which a group of healthcare providers (e.g., hospitals and physicians) offers its services on a predetermined financial basis to healthcare purchasers (e.g., employers of large numbers of people)

primary nursing   A continuous and coordinated process in which a primary nurse provides the initial patient care assessment and assumes accountability for planning comprehensive, 24-hour care for individual patients for the length of hospitalization or duration of care needed; patient-oriented rather than physician-oriented care

priority   Actions established in order of importance or urgency to the welfare or purposes of the organization, patient, or other person at a given time

private or civil law   Determines one's relationship to other individuals, such as the nurse to the patient

process standards   Designed for those activities that nurses use to administer care

professional nurse case manager   A nurse who assesses the patient and develops care around expected outcomes, both in terms of cost and quality, from the patient's point of entry into the system through discharge

proprietary health agencies   Operate for profit and serve people who can directly or indirectly pay for their services

prospective payment system (PPS)   Payment levels that are set on services before they are provided

public health services   Acts that are intended to maintain or improve health (e.g., communicable disease control, environmental health services, and personal health services)

public law   Determines an individual's relationship to federal government and the states

quality control   Examination of the actual process of providing care and the outcome of care for the protection of the public

recruitment The process of seeking nursing personnel to fill open job positions

rehabilitation nurse Assesses client progress and teaches the client how to perform self-assessment, make decisions about undertaking or continuing various self-care measures, carry out everyday activities, and evaluate his or her own progress and recovery; serves on the rehabilitation team as an educator, consultant, and liaison with the organizations and community

reinforcement (negative) An unpleasant or punishing consequence that discourages repetition of a behavior

reinforcement (positive) A favorable consequence that encourages repetition of a behavior

respondeat superior Stipulates that an employer has legal responsibility for an employee's wrongful acts that result in harm to a patient

responsibility A trustworthy performance in caring for the welfare of patients and in working with others; a feeling of obligation to perform activities and assigned tasks efficiently

retrospective payment system Reimbursement for services already provided

risk management Protecting nursing practice by being aware of the standard of care that is expected from nursing by the state, the employing agency, and the courts

RN-BSN traditional path The registered nurse who wishes to earn a BSN matriculates with a college or university that is NLN-accredited

role An organized set of behaviors that are attributed to a specific office or position

role analysis Systematic clarification of interdependent tasks and job behaviors

role characteristics A person who accepts a role behaves in a certain, prescribed way

scheduling (self) A system in which nurses are given the responsibility for selecting their own work schedules within daily staff requirements, usually for one month periods

school nurse Supports the educational process by helping students maintain health and by teaching students and teachers preventive health practices

scientific approach to decision making Uses one's intelligence to consider the designs and possible courses of action to make an educated choice

scope The breadth or opportunity to function; how far a manager can go in developing plans for self and others

scope of practice The range of activities a nurse can perform as stipulated in each state's nurse practice act

self-scheduling Nurses are given responsibility for selecting their own work schedules within daily staff requirements

sexual harassment Actions that are sexually directed and unwanted and that subject the worker to adverse employment conditions or that create a hostile work environment

skill (coach or mentor) A day-by-day, hands-on process that helps employees recognize opportunities and ways to improve their performance and capabilities

skill (conceptual) Pertains to why something is done, to one's view of the organization as a whole picture, and to one's ability to understand the complexities of the organization as it affects and is affected by its environment

skill (diagnostic) The ability to determine, by analysis and examination, the nature and circumstances of a particular condition or situation

skill (human) Pertains to how something is done, to working with people, and to one's ability to work with others in the achievement of goals

skill (technical) Pertains to what is done, working with things, and one's ability to use technology to perform an organizational task

smoothing An accommodating approach that is accomplished by complimenting, downplaying differences, and focusing on minor areas of agreement as if little disagreement exists

sociology Study of group behavior in modern society

sovereign immunity Provides government employees with special legal protection; the government employee cannot be sued for on-the-job mistakes

span of control The number of persons who report directly to the manager and the territory to be supervised

staffing The process of assigning competent people to fill the nursing roles designed for the organizational structure through recruitment, selection, and placement of personnel

staffing (centralized) A system in which a master plan for staffing for all nursing personnel is developed at the top level

staffing (cyclic) A system in which days for work and time off are regularly repeated for a designated number of week periods, such as 4, 6, and 12 weeks

staff development To expand or realize the potential of an individual to a fuller or greater state

staff training To coach or accustom someone to some mode of behavior or performance; to make someone proficient with specialized instruction and practice

statute of limitations A law that specifies a limit on the number of years a person can seek damages from another

stress (organizational)   Consists of task, role, physical, and interpersonal demands

stressors   Any perceived pressure, strain, distress, hardship, burden, or oppression that is placed on an individual, group, or organization

structure   The framework of jobs, relationships among jobs, and operational systems and processes that an organization uses to carry out its strategy

structure (organizational)   The process or way a group is formed, as well as its channels of authority, span of control, and lines of communication

style   The way in which something is said or done; a particular form of behavior directly associated with the individual

style (leadership)   How a leader uses interpersonal influences to accomplish goals

supplemental staff   Nurses who make themselves available for service on an on-call basis from their homes or through nurse registeries

system overload   Inability to cope with messages and expectations from a number of sources that cannot be heard well, understood, or completed within the given time and according to established standards of quality

tangible elements   Things that can be seen or touched, such as buildings and grounds, equipment, rules, charts, and records

task analysis   Measurements that are used to consider the actual process of giving nursing care; uses such tools as time studies and checklists

team   A distinguishable set of two or more individuals who interact interdependently and adaptively to achieve specified, shared, and valued objectives

team building   A process for developing work group maturity and effectiveness

team nursing   A decentralized system of care in which a qualified RN leads a group of healthcare personnel in providing for the nursing needs of an individual or group of people through participative effort

third party payers   Payment for healthcare services is received from a source such as private insurance, government programs, or charitable organizations rather than directly from the individual who received the care

time management   Arranging activities that need attention in order of priority and sequence of accomplishment

tort law   A legal wrong independent of a contract liability action brought in civil court

total care   The assignment of one nurse to one patient for the provision of total nursing care

total quality improvement (TQI)   A process designed to assess and improve standards and to survey process and development of performance measures at centralized and decentralized levels

trait theory   Focuses on personality traits or distinguishing features of an individual, such as intelligence, shyness, aggressiveness, ambition, or laziness

traits   Personal, psychologic, and physical characteristics that are identified in an individual

transactional analysis (TA)   A method of examining how people relate with others through the study of ego states of parent, child, and adult

transmitting   The channel used to communicate a message, either verbal or nonverbal

travel nurse   An RN who has an adaptable personality, is competent in nursing skills and abilities, is not afraid of challenge, meets specific criteria, and is willing to travel

trust   Confidence in the integrity, ability, or character of a person or thing

values   Principles, standards, and qualities that are considered worthwhile, important, useful, or desirable

voluntary health agencies   Nonprofit, tax exempt organizations that are designed to meet the health needs of the general public

Weber, Taylor, and Fayol approach to management   A scientific, centralized, and hierarchical structure that is based on a bureaucratic approach; focuses on the concept that a rational person is motivated by personal economic needs

will   A declaration of how a person wishes his or her possessions to be disposed after death

witness   One who has seen or heard something; one who furnishes evidence

Answers to Test Your Knowledge

Chapter 1

1. c
2. c
3. a
4. c
5. b
6. a
7. b
8. d
9. c
10. b
11. a
12. c

Chapter 2

1. d
2. d
3. b
4. c
5. c
6. a
7. d
8. a

Chapter 3

1. a
2. c
3. b
4. a
5. a
6. c
7. c
8. b
9. d
10. c
11. d
12. c
13. c
14. a
15. a
16. a
17. c

18. c
19. a
20. d
21. b

Chapter 4

1. a
2. c
3. a
4. b
5. b
6. c
7. c
8. a
9. c
10. b
11. d

Chapter 5

1. a
2. b
3. c
4. d
5. a
6. b
7. c
8. a
9. a
10. b
11. d
12. b
13. b

Chapter 6

1. c
2. c
3. b
4. a
5. d
6. b
7. b
8. c
9. c

10. c
11. c
12. a
13. b
14. b
15. d
16. b
17. c
18. b
19. b
20. b

Chapter 7

1. c
2. b
3. b
4. c
5. a
6. b
7. b
8. a
9. d
10. c
11. d
12. d
13. a
14. b
15. c
16. c
17. a

Chapter 8

1. c
2. c
3. d
4. a
5. c
6. b
7. a
8. b
9. b
10. d
11. b

12. a
13. c
14. b
15. b
16. c
17. b

Chapter 9

1. a
2. c
3. b
4. d
5. b
6. d
7. a
8. d
9. c
10. a
11. d
12. c
13. a
14. c
15. d
16. c
17. b
18. c
19. c

Chapter 10

1. c
2. c
3. a
4. c
5. c
6. c
7. c
8. b
9. a
10. c
11. d
12. b
13. d
14. b

15. c
16. c
17. d
18. a
19. c
20. d
21. b
22. c

Chapter 11

1. b
2. c
3. a
4. c
5. c
6. b
7. d
8. a
9. b
10. c
11. a
12. c
13. b
14. d

Chapter 12

1. b
2. c
3. b
4. d
5. a
6. b
7. c
8. a
9. c
10. c
11. b
12. c
13. d
14. a
15. b
16. a
17. c
18. a
19. b
20. a
21. c

INDEX

f indicates figures; *t* indicates tables.

Critical Thinking Activities

TO THE STUDENT:

The exercises and activities in this section are offered in response to employers' increasing demand for nursing graduates who can exercise sound analytic skills in the performance of their responsibilities. It is becoming increasingly apparent that success in the workplace depends not only on the nurse's ability to perform well technically but also on his or her ability to apply information to the task at hand with forethought. Employers are looking for problem solvers and decision makers.

Thinking is a purposeful, mental activity, and for the most part, it is a conscious activity. Thinking is also two-sided: ideas are produced, then they are evaluated. To produce ideas, the thinker widens the focus. To evaluate them, the thinker narrows the focus. The ideas generated are sorted until the most reasonable ones can be selected. Although thinking is a natural activity for human beings, it is rarely done well without training and conscientious practice.

These activities are designed to help you hone your critical thinking skills. Each chapter in this section begins with an exercise that asks you to define key terms that have been used within the corresponding chapter of the text. The ability to explain a term in your own words is the first step toward understanding and internalizing the concept. When completing this initial exercise, close your book and write the definition in your own words. Then review the sections of the text that correspond to any definitions that presented problems for you. With this solid foundation, you can move through the critical thinking activities with confidence.

CHAPTER 1

Activity 1-1

Define the following terms:

1. Abdicate _____

_____

_____

2. Authoritarian _____

_____

_____

3. Characteristics/traits _____

_____

_____

4. Coercive _____

_____

_____

5. Democratic/participative _____

_____

_____

6. Exploitation _____

_____

_____

7. Initiating _____

_____

_____

8. Laissez-faire _____

_____

_____

9. Permissive _____

_____

_____

10. Power _____

_____

_____

11. Restrictive _____

_____

_____

12. Style _____

_____

_____

13. Surveillance _____

_____

_____

14. Trust _____

_____

_____

15. Ultraliberal _____

_____

_____

Activity 1-2

Select a leader (from any sphere) whom you admire. Respond to the following questions:

1. Who is this person? _____

_____

_____

2. What is his or her position of power? _____

_____

_____

3. List the qualities in this person that you think make him or her a successful leader. _____

_____

_____

4. Refer to the list in Chapter 1, page 5. Which type of influence do you think this person uses primarily to achieve his or her purposes? _____

_____

_____

5. Give one example of how the person uses this type of influence. _____

_____

_____

Activity 1-3

Read the section on climate, culture, and caring of the organization on page 12 of Chapter 1. Respond to the following situation, and offer a rationale for your choice of action.

Situation: You are the nurse manager of a busy pediatric unit. One of your RN staff members is recently divorced and is caring for three small children; one is an infant. She needs to work to help support herself and her children. There is a problem with this nurse, because she often telephones the babysitter to check on her children and is often late getting to work because she has so much to do to get the children ready. This nurse also takes sick time off when you suspect that she is not ill but tired. However, when she is functioning in her role as staff nurse, she is excellent and well liked.

1. Keeping in mind the content on climate, culture, and caring, how would you approach this situation? _____

_____

_____

_____

2. How does the action you propose relate to the discussion on climate, culture, and caring in Chapter 1? _____

_____

_____

CHAPTER 2

Activity 2-1

Definition of terms

Match the definitions given in the right column with the words or phrases given in the left column. Place the letter of choice in the blank space provided to the left of each number.

_____ 1. Follower
_____ 2. Characteristics
_____ 3. Power
_____ 4. Personal power
_____ 5. Leadership style
_____ 6. Initiating structure (Ohio State study)
_____ 7. Consideration (Ohio State study)
_____ 8. Authoritarian style of leadership
_____ 9. Permissive, ultraliberal, or laissez-faire style of leadership
_____ 10. Democratic, participative, or consultive style of leadership
_____ 11. Contingency theory
_____ 12. Management by attention (Warren Bennis)
_____ 13. Management of meaning (Warren Bennis)
_____ 14. Management of trust (Warren Bennis)
_____ 15. Management of self (Warren Bennis)

a. Leader develops own strategies and learns from own mistakes
b. People-oriented with collaborative, joint effort
c. How the manager organizes and defines the work to be done
d. A lack of central direction or control
e. Overcomes feelings of ineptness; classifies events as helpful or harmful to one's personal or organizational goals; makes appropriate changes and is committed to the organization while on the job
f. Behaviors that convey mutual trust, respect, and rapport between manager and staff
g. One who responds to the direction of others
h. Leader possesses unusually effective communication skills
i. A review of the work situation, the manager's leadership style and expectations, and the follower's characteristics and expectations
j. High concern for task accomplishment and low concern for people
k. The ability to impose the will of one person or group to bring about certain behaviors
l. A mix of vision or intelligent foresight and strong personal commitment
m. How the leader actually behaves
n. The leader remains constant, secure, and steady of purpose
o. Qualities or features that distinguish one individual from another

Activity 2-2

1. From your study of Chapter 2 and the supplemental readings, what are the major principles concerning traits?

_____

_____

_____

2. Describe your own individual traits or characteristics. _____

_____

_____

3. Is it possible to eliminate or alter traits? Explain your answer. _____

_____

_____

_____

4. If you could, which of your traits or characteristics would you alter? _____

_____

5. Select one trait you would like to change, and outline a plan for making the change. _____

_____

_____

_____

_____

Activity 2-3

Study the following situations and determine whether the nurse leader's attitude is authoritarian, participative, or permissive. Offer a rationale for your responses.

Situation 1: All nurse managers of a large metropolitan hospital are informed by the hospital Chief Executive Officer that the hospital is to be merged with three other hospitals of similar size to boost purchasing clout and to slash overhead. Nurse manager Sophia experiences feelings of fear for her job because the plan is to increase the span of control and replace some RNs with trained assistive personnel. Sophia decides to bide her time and see what happens.

a. Sophia's attitude is identified as _____.

b. How did you reach this conclusion? _____

_____

_____

_____

Situation 2: Gary, another RN nurse manager at the same hospital, has heard the plans for the merger and decides to take some action. He gets a group of department managers together to discuss their reactions and to consider what options they have to either combat the situation or to cope with it.

a. Gary's attitude is identified as _____.

b. Explain the reasoning process behind your conclusion. _____

_____

_____

_____

Activity 2-4

1. What is your opinion of male versus female leadership? _____

    _____

    _____

2. Support your response with documentation. _____

    _____

    _____

 **CHAPTER 3**

Activity 3-1

Define the following terms:

1. Health maintenance organizations (HMO) _____
   _____
   _____

2. Retrospective payment system _____
   _____
   _____

3. Prospective payment system (PPS) _____
   _____
   _____

4. Diagnosis-related groups (DRGs) _____
   _____
   _____

5. Managed care _____
   _____
   _____

6. Managed competition _____
   _____
   _____

7. Preferred provider organizations (PPO) _____
   _____
   _____

8. The Omnibus Budget Reconciliation Act (OBRA) _____
   _____
   _____

9. Government-owned health agencies _____
   _____
   _____

10. Voluntary health agencies _____

_____

_____

11. Proprietary health agencies _____

_____

_____

12. Mergers _____

_____

_____

13. Magnet hospitals _____

_____

_____

14. Public health services _____

_____

_____

15. Community health nursing _____

_____

_____

16. Home healthcare _____

_____

_____

17. Organization _____

_____

_____

18. Organizational structure _____

_____

_____

19. Centralization _____

_____

_____

20. Decentralization _____

_____

_____

21. Participatory management _____

_____

_____

Activity 3-2

1. How is the college/university you attend owned and organized?
   Owned by: _____

   Organizational structure: (Request a copy from the administrative office of your school and attach it to worksheet.)

2. Compare your school's organizational structure with one type of healthcare agency structure given in this text.

   Agency selected for comparison: _____

   Similarities: _____

   _____

   _____

   Differences: _____

   _____

   _____

3. Why do you think these similarities and differences exist? _____

   _____

   _____

Activity 3-3

1. What is your view concerning healthcare reform? _____

   _____

   _____

   Do you agree that healthcare should be made available by the government to all persons regardless of their ability to pay? _____

   What is the reasoning behind your answer? _____

   _____

   _____

2. In what ways has the healthcare issue affected your perception of nursing? _____

_____

_____

3. What do you think about your role as a future RN in light of the current healthcare scene?

_____

_____

_____

Activity 3-4

Dr. Abraham Maslow submitted the theory that humans are ever-wanting creatures and that as one need is satisfied, another appears to take its place. The individual is motivated to satisfy the new need.

Situation: Robyn has been a department manager for 3 years. She has mastered the basic skills required for the job and is experiencing boredom and a lack of challenge. She discusses her feelings with her supervisor. Using the following styles of management, outline how you would respond to Robyn if you were her supervisor.

Autocratic: _____

_____

_____

Permissive: _____

_____

_____

Participative: _____

_____

_____

Activity 3-5

Of all the styles of management presented in Chapter 4, which style most appeals to you? ____

_____

Explain why you selected this style. _____

_____

_____

CHAPTER 4

Activity 4-1

Define the following terms:

1. Role _____

_____

_____

2. Nurse license _____

_____

_____

3. Computer adaptive testing (CAT) _____

_____

_____

4. Advanced practice nurse _____

_____

_____

5. Certification _____

_____

_____

6. Nurse practitioner (NP) _____

_____

_____

7. Professional nurse case manager (PNCM) _____

_____

_____

8. Nurse informaticist _____

_____

_____

9. Unlicensed assistive personnel _____

_____

_____

Activity 4-2
Interview with a nurse manager

Request a 10-minute interview with a nurse manager in any area of nursing practice. Adhere to the following instructions:

1. Explain that you are a student in a nursing leadership class who is studying the role of nurse manager and would appreciate his or her help.

2. Ask for persmission to take notes or to record the conversation. State that no names will be mentioned in class. Address the following subjects:

    a. What is your official title? _____

    b. What is your area of responsibility? (e.g., entire hospital, several nursing units, one nursing department, clinic) _____

    _____

    c. How long have you been in this position? _____

    d. What are your major responsibilities as (insert the nurse's title)? _____

    _____

    _____

    _____

    _____

    _____

    _____

    _____

    _____

3. Thank the nurse for the time given and leave within the 10-minute time allotted.

Activity 4-3

Study the responses given during your interview with a nurse manager in Activity 4-2. Separate these responses into the following categories:

Planning: _____

_____

Organizing: _____

_____

Staffing: _____

_____

Leading: _____

_____

Communicating: _____

_____

Decision making: _____

_____

Controlling/budgeting: _____

_____

Were all of the areas of management covered? _____

If not, why do you think they were omitted? _____

_____

_____

Was more emphasis placed on one area than another? If so, which one? _____

_____

_____

Why do you think this happened? _____

_____

_____

Activity 4-4

1. Review the roles considered to be the most important in nursing management given on page 74 of Chapter 4. How does the result of your interview correlate with this list? _____

_____

_____

_____

_____

2. Most students enroll in nursing programs because of their desire to care for the health needs of people. How do you react to the pressure placed on nurses to exercise management skills?

_____

_____

_____

_____

3. Do you think that it is feasible for a nurse to expect to move from staff nurse to nurse manager to supervisor and on up the ladder with only on-the-job training? _____

What is the rationale for your answer? _____

_____

_____

_____

Activity 4-5

Reread the section in Chapter 4 entitled "Changes Needed in the Nursing Educational System" (page 79). Complete the chart given below and indicate how you think your nursing program meets these suggested needs.

Suggested needs	How is my nursing program complying?
Studying nursing practice roles and competencies to match the needs of consumers	
Primary care and skills	
Integrating structure and system in organizations	
Economic framework as part of all delivery systems (cost effectiveness with quality)	
Initiating and advancing interdisciplinary collaboration (working well with all care providers)	
Program to prepare primary nursing and APNs	

If your nursing school does not offer some of these programs, consider the reasons (e.g., not within the purposes of the program, insufficient interest, lack of funding) and describe them here: _____

_____

_____

_____

CHAPTER 5

Activity 5-1

Define the following terms:

1. Staffing process _____

_____

_____

2. Supplemental staffing _____

_____

_____

3. Induction _____

_____

_____

4. Orientation _____

_____

_____

5. Burnout _____

_____

_____

6. Patient classification system _____

_____

_____

7. Centralized staffing _____

_____

_____

8. Decentralized staffing _____

_____

_____

9. Cyclic scheduling _____

_____

_____

10. Self-scheduling _____

_____

_____

11. Total care _____

_____

_____

12. Primary nursing _____

_____

_____

13. Functional nursing _____

_____

_____

14. Team nursing _____

_____

_____

15. Modular nursing _____

_____

_____

16. Case management _____

_____

_____

17. Managed care _____

_____

_____

18. Nurse case manager _____

_____

_____

Activity 5-2
The job market

1. In which area of practice are you planning to work after graduation? _____

_____

2. From what you have learned about the job market, can you expect to find the position of your choice fairly easily? _____

3. What obstacles can you expect? _____

   _____

   _____

4. How do you plan to overcome these obstacles? _____

   _____

   _____

5. Are you willing to move to another location if there is the possibility of a job? _____

6. What about second or third choices of a job? Will you take what you can get or wait until you can find the job you want? Why? _____

   _____

   _____

7. What are your feelings concerning advanced preparation at this point in your life? Why?___

   _____

   _____

   _____

Activity 5-3
Burnout

1. Have you ever experienced burnout as a student, on the job, or simply in daily living? _____

2. Describe the situation and what you believe led to your feelings of burnout. _____

   _____

   _____

   _____

3. How did your reactions correlate with or differ from the syndrome of feeling exhausted, overextended, and depersonalized as described in Chapter 5? _____

   _____

   _____

   _____

4. What did you do to overcome burnout? _____

   _____

   _____

5. How does the method you describe correlate with the discussion in Chapter 5? _____

_____

_____

Activity 5-4

From your study of case management, outline briefly what you think a nurse case manager would do in his or her position in (a) a 350-bed community hospital, and (b) in an HMO facility such as Kaiser-Permanente.

Functions in a community hospital: _____

_____

_____

_____

Functions in an HMO: _____

_____

_____

_____

Activity 5-5

Scheduling

1. Visit a nursing unit in your area and ask to see the current work schedule for nurses. If possible, obtain a copy.

2. From what you have learned about scheduling, how would you label the system (e.g., cyclic, traditional, self)? _____

   Explain your conclusion. _____

   _____

   _____

3. If possible, approach a staff person concerning the scheduling process. Explain that you are a nursing student who is studying the scheduling process. Ask if that person is satisfied with how schedules are compiled. If not, does he or she have another preference? What is it? Record the main points of your dialogue with the nurse. _____

   _____

   _____

   _____

   _____

4. If you were a staff member, which scheduling process would you prefer? _____

For what reasons? _____

_____

_____

_____

_____

Activity 5-6

1. Assume that you are an RN staff member of a postsurgery department. Which system of delivery of nursing care appeals most to you? _____

2. Define the system you have chosen. _____

_____

_____

3. What is the reason for your choice? _____

_____

_____

CHAPTER 6

Activity 6-1

Define the following terms:

1. Planning process _____
   _____
   _____

2. Strategic planning _____
   _____
   _____

3. Outlier facilities _____
   _____
   _____

4. Middle managers _____
   _____
   _____

5. Lower- or first-level managers _____
   _____
   _____

6. Nursing process _____
   _____
   _____

7. Objectives _____
   _____
   _____

8. Management by objectives (MBO) _____
   _____
   _____

9. Nursing care plans _____
   _____
   _____

10. Standard care plans _____

    _____

    _____

11. Evaluation _____

    _____

    _____

Activity 6-2

1. Why is planning particularly important for nurse managers today? _____

   _____

   _____

2. Define your personal value system relative to yourself as a nurse: _____

   _____

   _____

   How might these values change if you were to become a nurse manager? _____

   _____

   _____

Activity 6-3

Situation: You are the supervisor in a home healthcare agency. You have 6 RNs and 12 home health nursing assistants under your jurisdiction. You believe that all staff members have maximum assignments. The director of the home healthcare agency announces that, as a result of government cutbacks, each nurse and assistant will need to add two clients per day to their caseloads.

Use the complexity chart provided in Figure 6-6 on page 132 of Chapter 6 to assess the problem. Apply the nursing process to resolve the situation. Because this is a hypothetical situation, you need to imagine the circumstances, using an educated approach.

1. Assess the problem:

Complexity (Figure 6-6 in text)	Your reaction to the complexity What might be happening?
Risk and uncertainty	
Long-term implications	
Interdisciplinary input	
Value judgments	
Multiple criteria	
Intangibles	

2. Apply the nursing process to the problem.

    a. Formulate a nursing diagnosis. _____

       _____

    b. Plan alternate strategies. _____

       _____

       _____

    c. Implement nursing actions. _____

       _____

       _____

    d. Evaluate strategies. _____

       _____

       _____

3. Considering the present times, do you consider your nursing care plan realistic? _____

    What factors could hinder your plan from being realized?_____

    _____

    _____

Activity 6-4
Groups

1. List the types of groups in which you are currently involved (home, work, recreation, social):

    _____

    _____

    _____

    _____

2. Reflect on your experiences in these groups. Consider the section in Chapter 6 (p. 139) on group development and interaction. What is your opinion of group activity? ___ _____

    _____

    _____

    _____

    _____

3. Do you prefer to make decisions independently, or would you rather work in groups? Why?

_____

_____

_____

_____

4. How would your opinion affect your ability to function in a leadership/management role?

_____

_____

_____

_____

Activity 6-5
Management by objectives (MBO)

1. Write two behavioral objectives for improving your skill in a specific procedure or function of nursing.

   a. _____

      _____

   b. _____

      _____

2. How might you implement these objectives? _____

_____

_____

_____

CHAPTER 7

Activity 7-1

Define the following terms:

1. Directing ability _____

_____

_____

2. Span of control _____

_____

_____

3. Delegation _____

_____

_____

4. Supervision _____

_____

_____

5. Responsibility _____

_____

_____

Activity 7-2

1. List four primary preconditions for the achievement of success in direction giving:

    a. _____

    b. _____

    c. _____

    d. _____

2. Explain why you believe these preconditions might be important. _____

_____

_____

_____

Activity 7-3

Time management

Complete a "to-do" list for tomorrow (review Chapter 7 in the text). Focus on an activity for class, a practicum, a work experience, or a group assignment.

Must do	Important to do	Nice to do but not important

Activity 7-4

In Chapter 7, study the sections on span of control and the directive process. Complete the following exercise.

1. *True-false:* Managers with a narrow span of control oversee the work of a few people.   T   F
   Give an example of a narrow span of control.

   _____

   _____

   _____

2. Name three factors that affect the number of employees needed and the choice of span of control.

   _____

   _____

   _____

3. List some of the purposes of managerial direction giving.

   _____

   _____

   _____

4. What are some of the positive outcomes of the delegation process?

_____

_____

_____

5. List reasons why managers may not delegate as much as they should.

_____

_____

_____

_____

6. Define and give examples of guidelines.

_____

_____

_____

_____

7. Define and give an example of a corrective guideline.

_____

_____

_____

8. Define and give examples of preventive guidelines.

_____

_____

_____

_____

9. Explain promotive guidelines.

_____

_____

_____

Activity 7-5
Direction and span of control
Consider the following information regarding each patient. In the lefthand column, indicate which of the staff members (listed at the top of the worksheet) you would assign to the patient. In the righthand column, list your reason(s) for making the assignment. The first one has been completed for you as an example.

Worksheet for assignment making

Staff:
1 RN (1 patient)
1 LVN/LPN
1 NA

Nurse assignment	Patient, age, diagnosis, treatments, needs	Justification for assignment
NA	John Peterson, 65; 3rd day post-op; laminectomy; ambulate	*Uncomplicated assignment*
	Ted Brooks, 48; hemorrhoidectomy; sitz baths	
	Carrie Jackson, 28; colon resection; 1st day post-op; IVs; dressing change; depressed	
	Lila Parks, 32; mastectomy; 2nd day post-op; drains; dressing change; depressed	
	Terry Dixon, 18; chest drainage; isolation	
	Tim Smedley, 22; facial reconstruction; ambulate; feed	
	Carolyn Petrino, 75; leg amputation; 2nd day post-op; diabetic; S&As; wheelchair	
	Ashley Winter, 54; splenectomy; DOS; multiple contusions; IVs; bed rest; TCDB	
	Douglas Intel, 87; prostatectomy; 1st day post-op; IVs; ambulate	
	Sheryl Meltzer, 72; ca large colon; colostomy (closed); 1st day post-op; IVs; ambulate	

CHAPTER 8

Activity 8-1

Define the following terms:

1. Communication process _____

_____

_____

2. Interpersonal communication _____

_____

_____

3. Organizational communication _____

_____

_____

4. Encoding _____

_____

_____

5. Transmitting _____

_____

_____

6. Decoding _____

_____

_____

7. Action _____

_____

_____

8. Feedback _____

_____

_____

9. System overload _____

_____

_____

10. Semantics _____

_____

_____

11. Grapevine _____

_____

_____

12. Polarity management _____

_____

_____

13. Cross-cultural communication _____

_____

_____

14. Intercultural communication _____

_____

_____

15. Cultural blindness _____

_____

_____

16. Nursing informatics _____

_____

_____

Activity 8-2

On the following scale, circle an assessment of your communication skills.

Low				Average				High	
1	2	3	4	5	6	7	8	9	10

1. Why did you give yourself this rating? _____

_____

_____

2. In what areas of the communication process do you need to improve? _____

_____

_____

Activity 8-3

Read the following situation. Describe the communication process in the spaces provided.

Situation: Felicia, an RN immigrant from the Philippines, has completed all the requirements for licensure in the United States. She is employed as a staff nurse on the coronary care unit. Her knowledge of English is limited. Felicia's peers answer her questions but leave her primarily to herself. One day, Margaret, a fellow RN team member, finds Felicia in the utility room wiping tears from her eyes. "Is anything the matter?" Margaret inquires. "No, nothing," is the reply. "I'd like to help if you will share with me," Margaret persists. Felicia bursts into tears. "It's just that I am so lonely. I feel I am not wanted here." The truth is that the staff *does* resent Felicia. They believe that she has been given a position that an American nurse needs.

Analyze the communication process, referring to Figure 8-1 on page 190.

Message: _____

_____

Encoding: _____

Transmitting: _____

Decoding: _____

_____

Action taken: _____

_____

_____

Activity 8-4

1. Having read the reactions of some RNs to working with and supervising nursing assistants, what is your opinion of working with nursing assistants? _____

_____

_____

_____

2. Do you feel threatened about having to direct and supervise nursing assistants? _____

Explain your feelings. _____

_____

_____

_____

Activity 8-5
Cultural blindness

1. Select someone from a different culture whom you know through student experiences, clinical relationships, social activities, family, or friends. Complete the chart and compare this person's similarities and differences with yours.

	You	Individual from a different culture
Culture		
Values		
Behaviors		
Attitudes		

2. Describe a cross-cultural communication process that you have used to bring together two persons or groups with diverse cultures. _____

_____

_____

Activity 8-6

1. Does the subject of nurse informatics appeal to you? _____

   Why or why not? _____

   _____

   _____

   _____

2. If you were to complete an informatics program for nurses, what area would you choose, and what would be your goals in the workplace?

   Area of practice: _____

   Goals: _____

   _____

   _____

3. If you were given the freedom to design and implement an informatics system, what would you like to see accomplished? _____

   _____

   _____

   _____

CHAPTER 9

Activity 9-1

Define the following terms:

1. Change _____

    _____

    _____

2. Change process _____

    _____

    _____

3. Change agents _____

    _____

    _____

4. Stress _____

    _____

    _____

5. Stressors _____

    _____

    _____

6. Roles _____

    _____

    _____

7. Organizational stressors _____

    _____

    _____

8. Burnout _____

    _____

    _____

9. Hardiness _____

    _____

    _____

10. Conflict _____

_____

_____

11. Conflict resolution _____

_____

_____

12. Smoothing _____

_____

_____

13. Avoidance _____

_____

_____

14. Compromise _____

_____

_____

15. Collaboration _____

_____

_____

16. Sexual harassment _____

_____

_____

17. Passive behavior _____

_____

_____

18. Aggressive behavior _____

_____

_____

19. Assertive behavior _____

_____

_____

Activity 9-2
Change process

Imagine yourself as the department manager of a coronary care unit. The delivery of nursing care is primary, and you have been making assignments at the beginning of each day. There has been increasing animosity among members of your staff regarding the assignments. One member thinks that she is being assigned most of the difficult, time-consuming patients; another is complaining that he is not challenged enough; and two nurses express dissatisfaction at having to wait until the last minute to know to which patients they have been assigned. You know that a change in the assignment-making procedure is needed. Describe the steps you would take to effect the change.

_____

_____

_____

_____

_____

_____

_____

_____

_____

_____

_____

_____

_____

Activity 9-3
Stress

1. What type of stressors are you most prone to in the clinical area? _____

_____

_____

_____

2. Select one stressor and discuss how you would reduce the tension.

    Stressor: _____

    Actions to reduce tension: _____

    _____

    _____

    _____

Activity 9-4
Conflict resolution

Read Chapter 9 of text. Place a "T" in the space if the following statement is true, and an "F" if the statement is false. If false, explain why the statement is incorrect. You may refer to the chapter for confirmation or clarification as necessary.

_____ 1. A nurse's leadership style is reflected in his or her strategy for conflict resolution.

_____

_____

_____ 2. Bureaucratic managers believe that conflict is a normal, common occurrence.

_____

_____

_____ 3. Intrapersonal organizational conflict in the department manager is best set aside when handling the problems of others.

_____

_____

_____ 4. Conflict between health organizations in the United States is desirable.

_____

_____

_____ 5. The major sources of organizational conflict in health organizations include interpersonal and intergroup conflict.

_____

_____

_____ 6. An example of organizational conflict in healthcare agencies is a difference between the procedure manual and the nurse's perception of how a procedure should be done.

_____

_____

_____ 7. During a conflict, it is possible for a leader to emerge that might not otherwise have been recognized.

_____

_____

_____ 8. It is possible to experience conflict and to cooperate at the same time.

_____

_____

_____ 9. Power and competition are necessary for successful conflict resolution.

_____

_____

_____ 10. The compromising, bargaining approach is the best approach to conflict resolution.

_____

_____

_____ 11. High concern for work accomplishment and high regard for people are incompatible.

_____

_____

_____ 12. Assertive behavior involves saying what you think, feel, and believe anytime and anywhere.

_____

_____

_____ 13. Examples of assertive behavior include admitting that you might be wrong and setting limits as to how far you will go.

_____

_____

_____ 14. "What are you asking from me?" is an example of aggressive behavior.

_____

_____

Activity 9-5
Sexual harassment

Situation: Cheryl works in a center for severely disabled children. She loves the job and believes that she is making a significant contribution to the lives of needy people. She also needs the money. The personnel manager is obviously attracted to her. He calls her "darlin" and makes suggestive remarks about her figure. One day he tells her a dirty joke and indicates that he is free after work and would like to take her to his place for a drink. Cheryl declines and says that she has an important engagement. She likes everything about the job but this man. He has power in that he hires and dismisses all personnel.

Identify the problem; then indicate what Cheryl's course of action should be.

Problem: _____

Course of action: _____

_____

_____

_____

_____

_____

CHAPTER 10

Activity 10-1

Define the following terms:

1. Control _____

   _____

   _____

2. Anticipatory control _____

   _____

   _____

3. Concurrent control _____

   _____

   _____

4. Feedback control _____

   _____

   _____

5. Managed care _____

   _____

   _____

6. Managed competition _____

   _____

   _____

7. Case management _____

   _____

   _____

8. Third-party control _____

   _____

   _____

9. Economic control _____

   _____

   _____

10. Centralized budgeting _____

_____

_____

11. Operating budget _____

_____

_____

12. Capital expenditure budget _____

_____

_____

13. Policies _____

_____

_____

14. Personnel budget policies _____

_____

_____

15. Full-time equivalents (FTEs) _____

_____

_____

16. Standards _____

_____

_____

17. Objectives _____

_____

_____

18. Comptroller _____

_____

_____

19. Outcomes management _____

_____

_____

20. Task analysis _____

_____

_____

21. Quality control _____

_____

_____

22. Quality assurance _____

_____

_____

23. Quality assessment _____

_____

_____

24. Performance appraisal _____

_____

_____

Activity 10-2

Situation: You are in big trouble. As a student, you have a small but adequate income if you live within your means. The trouble is that you have used your credit card indiscriminantly. You charged some new clothing, a few gifts, groceries, and signed for some cash several times. Now you are making interest-only payments.

Use the three types of control (anticipatory, concurrent, and feedback) to determine what you can do to take control of your financial situation.

Anticipatory control: _____

_____

_____

Concurrent control: _____

_____

_____

Feedback: _____

_____

_____

Activity 10-3
Managed competition

Considering the possible consequences of managed competition to nurses, name two actions you could take to protect yourself in the job market.

1. _____

2. _____

Activity 10-4
Full-time equivalents

Situation: As a nurse manager, it is your responsibility to keep within a designated number of full-time equivalents (FTEs). Several members of your RN staff want more flexible schedules. Some of the options for you to consider include allowing the staff to work 2 or 3 days per week, to work only weekends, to work half days, or to have extra days off for special occasions.

After reviewing the relevant sections of Chapter 8, complete the following items:

1. Name two limitations of the FTE system:

    a. _____
    b. _____

2. Name two options available to the department manager with the FTE system:

    a. _____
    b. _____

3. What are two advantages of sharing an FTE position?

    a. _____
    b. _____

4. Thinking of the cost factor, can you think of any disadvantages of sharing a FTE position?

    _____

    _____

Activity 10-5
Performance appraisal

In your professional life, you will experience many performance appraisals. It is best to be prepared.

1. On the job, how can you know on what you are being evaluated? _____

   _____

   _____

2. At your present stage of development, how would you rate yourself for a staff nurse position in a medical or surgical unit? Consider 1-3 as low, 4-7 as average, and 8-10 as high.

Nursing skills	1	2	3	4	5	6	7	8	9	10
Nursing process	1	2	3	4	5	6	7	8	9	10
Knowledge	1	2	3	4	5	6	7	8	9	10
Communication	1	2	3	4	5	6	7	8	9	10
Adaptability	1	2	3	4	5	6	7	8	9	10
Group/team skill	1	2	3	4	5	6	7	8	9	10
Management skill	1	2	3	4	5	6	7	8	9	10
Attitude	1	2	3	4	5	6	7	8	9	10
Time management	1	2	3	4	5	6	7	8	9	10

3. Were any of the above items difficult for you to evaluate? _____

   _____

   Which of the items caused you difficulty? _____

   _____

   _____

4. Why do you think these items were difficult to evaluate? _____

   _____

   _____

CHAPTER 11

Activity 11-1

Define the following terms:

1. Training _____

_____

_____

2. Development _____

_____

_____

3. Technical skill _____

_____

_____

4. Human skill _____

_____

_____

5. Conceptual skill _____

_____

_____

6. Diagnostic skill _____

_____

_____

7. Mentor _____

_____

_____

8. Preceptor _____

_____

_____

9. Middle manager _____

_____

_____

10. Role _____

_____

_____

11. Role expectation _____

_____

_____

12. Role congruence _____

_____

_____

13. Teaching _____

_____

_____

14. Learning _____

_____

_____

15. Teaching-learning process _____

_____

_____

16. Group dynamics _____

_____

_____

17. Work groups _____

_____

_____

18. Motivation _____

_____

_____

19. Productivity _____

_____

_____

20. Status _____

_____

_____

21. Team building _____

_____

_____

22. Internship _____

_____

_____

23. Self-learning _____

_____

_____

Activity 11-2
Preceptor

1. Assume that you are beginning your first day as a staff nurse. Describe five characteristics you would like your preceptor to have:

    a. _____

    b. _____

    c. _____

    d. _____

    e. _____

2. Renumber your responses in order of priority. What is your reasoning for the order of importance? _____

_____

_____

_____

Activity 11-3
Learning process

1. Reflect on the many times it has been necessary for you to learn new knowledge and skills in your nursing program and be tested on your mastery of the subject matter. What is your general pattern of preparing for an examination?

    Step 1: _____

    Step 2: _____

Step 3: _____

Step 4: _____

Step 5: _____

2. What do you do to retain necessary knowledge and skills? _____

_____

_____

_____

3. You have an idea of how successful you have been by your grades and by your individual assessment. If there is room for improvement, suggest actions that you could take to improve your learning process. _____

_____

_____

Activity 11-4
Middle managers

In this class, you are being asked to learn how to function as middle managers. This role allows very little time for actual patient care activities, but almost all nurses must serve as managers to some degree.

1. What is your attitude regarding practicing as a nurse manager? _____

_____

_____

2. Does your attitude affect your ability to master what you are expected to in this class?

_____

Explain your response. _____

_____

_____

3. If you have no opportunity to serve as nurse manager in a work setting at this time, what can you do to retain the knowledge you have learned? _____

_____

_____

CHAPTER 12

Activity 12-1

Define the following terms:

1. Litigation _____

_____

_____

2. Law _____

_____

_____

3. Statutory law _____

_____

_____

4. Public law _____

_____

_____

5. Private and civil law _____

_____

_____

6. Criminal law _____

_____

_____

7. Liability _____

_____

_____

8. Malpractice _____

_____

_____

9. Scope of practice _____

_____

_____

10. Common law _____

_____

_____

11. Common practice in nursing _____

_____

_____

12. Mandatory licensure _____

_____

_____

13. Permissive licensure _____

_____

_____

14. Respondeat superior _____

_____

_____

15. Statute of limitations _____

_____

_____

16. Tort law _____

_____

_____

17. Diversion program _____

_____

_____

18. Risk management _____

_____

_____

19. Incident reports _____

_____

_____

20. Charting by exception _____

_____

_____

21. Technical evaluation _____

_____

_____

22. Judgmental error _____

_____

_____

23. Normative error _____

_____

_____

24. Defamation of character _____

_____

_____

25. Witness _____

_____

_____

26. Expert witness _____

_____

_____

27. Good Samaritan law _____

_____

_____

28. Sovereign immunity _____

_____

_____

29. Ethics _____

_____

_____

30. Patients' rights _____

    _____

    _____

31. Advocacy _____

    _____

    _____

32. Transcultural nursing _____

    _____

    _____

33. Ethnocentrism _____

    _____

    _____

34. Ethnorelativity _____

    _____

    _____

35. The Patient Self-Determination Act (PSDA) _____

    _____

    _____

36. Will _____

    _____

    _____

Activity 12-2
Nurse Practice Act
Review the Nurse Practice Act for your state.

1. What are the requirements for licensure? _____

    _____

    _____

    _____

2. What are the conditions for revocation of a license? _____

    _____

    _____

    _____

3. Do you believe that a nurse who has been addicted to drugs or alcohol should be given a second chance to practice nursing? _____

Explain your answer. _____

_____

_____

Activity 12-3
Incident reports and litigation

Situation: In your hurry, you administered medication to the wrong patient. You reported the action to your nurse manager and completed an incident report. The patient suffered only temporary consequences.

1. Do you think you would have been hesitant to report the mistake if you knew the incident report you completed might be made known in a court of law? Why or why not? _____

_____

_____

_____

Do you believe your response is representative of most nurses? _____

2. What is your view of the patient's or his or her legal representative's right to review any incident report that concerns the patient? _____

_____

_____

_____

Activity 12-4
Ethics and transcultural care

Situation: Nurse manager George's staff consists of members from diverse cultures. He takes the stance that if cultural diversity is recognized, prejudice and racism will emerge and workers will be judged on who they are rather than what they can do. His philosophy is that people are the same the world over and should be treated that way. What is your reaction to George's philosophy? _____

_____

_____

_____

Activity 12-5

Legal issue

Situation: You are a psychiatric nurse on the PM shift. Mr. Harvey is admitted with a diagnosis of depression. He is quiet and cooperative with all procedures. During your initial assessment interview, Mr. Harvey tells you that he has considered committing suicide many times.

1. What are the appropriate procedures to follow to protect Mr. Harvey from himself and to protect the nurse from a possible lawsuit should he act on his thoughts? _____

   _____

   _____

   _____

   _____

2. What guidelines should you follow if Mr. Harvey succeeds in committing suicide while you are on duty and you are sued by his family for failing to protect him? _____

   _____

   _____

   _____

   _____

Activity 12-6

Ethics

Situation: You have been employed as a nurse manager of the Postpartum unit for 3 years. Because of the effects of managed competition, pressure is now being applied on physicians, case managers, and nurse managers to see that postpartum women are dismissed the day following their delivery. In your opinion, some patients are being dismissed at a risk to their health. One case in point is Rubina, a new mother whose blood pressure is elevated and who is experiencing abnormal discharge. She does not speak English and you do not think she understands the instructions regarding home care and follow-up appointments.

1. What should you as the nurse manager do as your first course of action? _____

   _____

   _____

2. What are the nurse manager's next appropriate actions? _____

   _____

   _____

   _____

Activity 12-7

HIV-positive healthcare employees

You have read about legislation that prevents any employer from refusing to employ an individual on the basis of being HIV positive. What are your feelings regarding this law as it applies to healthcare employees? Why do you feel as you do? _____

_____

_____

_____

_____

_____

_____